The Common Market and Common Law

The Common Market and Common Law

Legal Aspects of Foreign Investment and Economic Integration in the European Community, with Ireland as a Prototype

JOHN TEMPLE LANG

THE UNIVERSITY OF CHICAGO PRESS

CHICAGO & LONDON

Library of Congress Catalog Card Number: 66–26774

The University of Chicago Press, Chicago & London

The University of Toronto Press, Toronto 5, Canada

Printed in the United States of America

THE AMERICAN BAR FOUNDATION

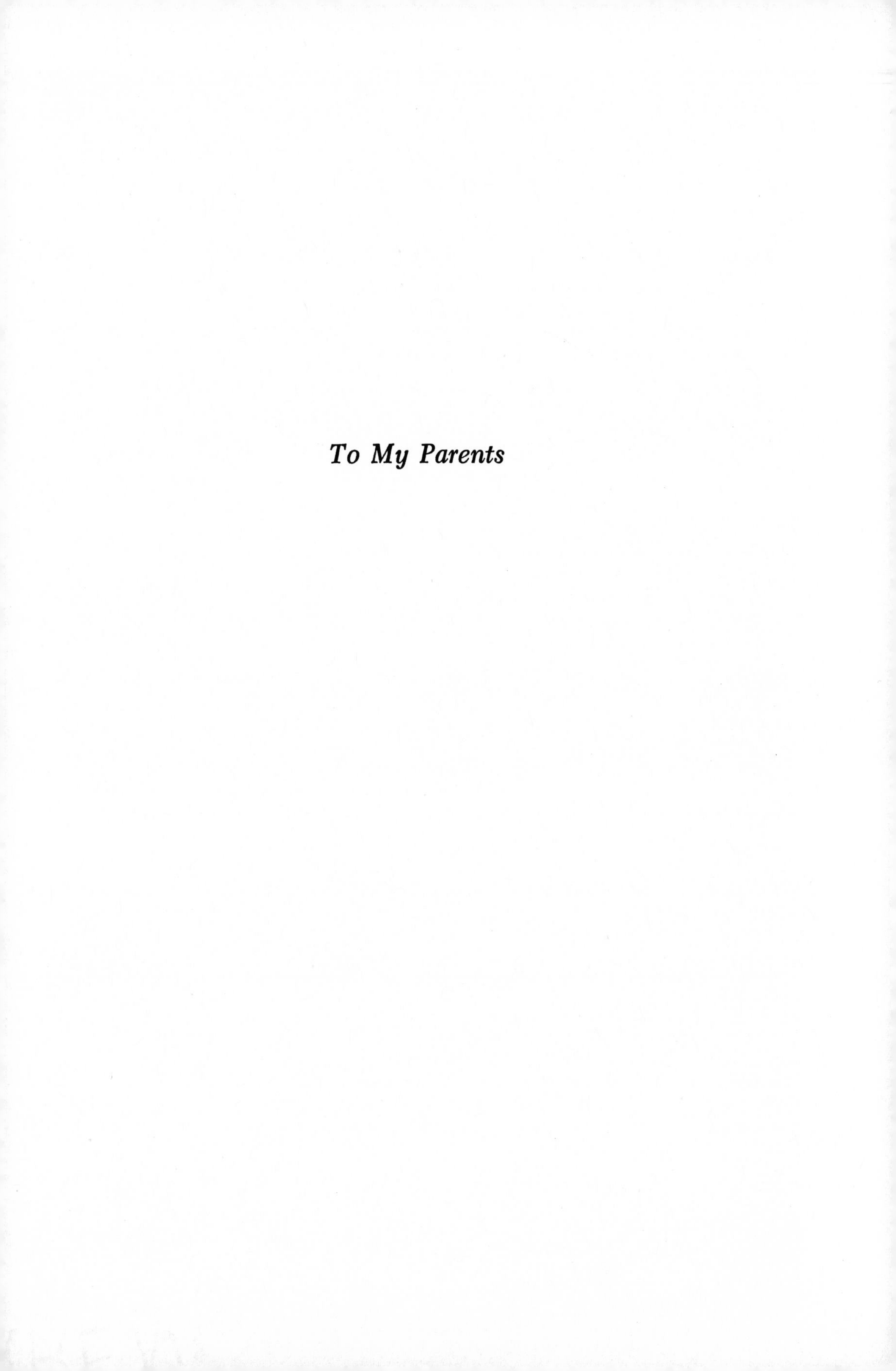

To My Parents

Foreword

The European Economic Community is now in its ninth year. Despite some minor and occasional major difficulties, integration has remained a motive force and its institutions have endured. The immediate objective of the Rome Treaty—creation of a customs union—is almost accomplished, although some areas have proved particularly troublesome and difficult to resolve, notably agriculture and a unified energy policy. The wider objectives of the Treaty, which envision a broadly integrated economic system among the Six, have seen beginning and partial fulfillment in the Community's antitrust and social policy, in the attempts to coordinate national economic policy, and in the initiative which the Community has taken for the introduction of a European patent, for a European bankruptcy law, and for the mutual recognition of judgments.

With its economic program almost assured of success, the Community now approaches important crossroads. Internally, the future role and position of the institutions pose the most important problem. The Council and the Commission, particularly the latter, could continue the economic task, be implementors, guardians, and administrators of more or less well-defined, and limited, economic rules. On the other hand, they could be innovators and contribute to further integration both in the socio-economic field and beyond and, as a natural and necessary byproduct, move closer to the realization of the political aims which underlay European cooperation and integration at its inception in the early 1950's. Recent case law of the Community's Court of Justice displays notable federal-mindedness and could serve as the legal basis for the further federalization of the relations of the Six. And the Convention for the merger of the executives of the three Communities furnishes the institutional basis; it would not be difficult to add to it a revision of the Treaties which would unify their substance and the powers of the single executive. The choice is of course a political question, bound up at once with considerations of the proper role of each constituent, sovereign state in the Community and in the world and with conflicting economic philosophies as to the Community's function in promoting free trade on a regional or wider basis.

The problem of the Community's future direction is also of great concern to the outside world. A broadening of the Community's free trade concepts would permit many states to join with it in trade relations by means of the traditional methods of reciprocal negotiation and concessions. In contrast, internal consolidation of the Community and a more inward-looking policy which might be its result would require review on the part of some states to determine whether the safeguarding of their interests does not indeed require membership in the Community. But membership raises anew for these states the political and legal problems to which approaches are only now beginning to emerge in the Community itself. And additional considerations, such as the potential member's level of industrialization (a measure of its ability to compete) and its cultural and geographic homogeneity with or similarity to present members, may contribute further obstacles.

Uncertainty about the Community's future direction affects perhaps most immediately private enterprise which is outside the Community but looks toward participation in this market of 179 million consumers. Should an enterprise assume for its planning that the present structure of the EEC will be maintained and that winning a share of the market therefore will call for the establishment of operations within the Community? Or should it anticipate a possible geographic expansion of the EEC in Europe in order to secure the best possible location for its establishment, perhaps in a less industrialized potential member where the labor market, material and financial resources, and governmental policy create the most inviting climate? Important questions underlying the problem concern the domestic law and policy of such potential member states and the effect on and changes in their law which membership in the EEC would entail. The Common Market literature so far has given little attention to these problems. Its focus is mainly the Community's own commercial and constitutional law, and its relevance for foreign enterprises is therefore restricted to enterprises already located in or contemplating establishment in the present area of the Six.

John Temple Lang's book approaches the problem of investment and establishment from the viewpoint of a non-Community state which looks toward EEC membership, is less industrialized than the Six and therefore would face special problems of adaptation, but which, for many reasons, might be ideally suited for the establishment of base companies by foreign enterprises. On the realistic assumption that Ireland will participate in the Common Market in some form before long, Mr. Temple Lang uses Ireland as the prototype and offers a study of extraordinary breadth: Irish commercial, antitrust, and tax law, as well as governmental policy, as they apply to foreign investments in Ireland; the substantive law of the Community and its relation to Irish law; and the constitutional law problems which membership in the Community would pose for Ireland.

Mr. Temple Lang's book is a major contribution: as the first exhaustive analysis of Irish law relating to foreign investments, it is an indispensable handbook for investors. For the investor looking to the Community, it offers a comprehensive and up-to-date analysis of the complex Community legal system. And its thorough and detailed scholarship, its extensive use of national legal materials, as well as the interesting treatment of the law of a common law country in relation to the civil law tradition of the Continent, make the book a valuable contribution to comparative law and research.

The study is an admirable undertaking. It is a splendid legal handbook, and its scope and results give insight and suggest answers to the many basic problems of the Community's relationship to the outside world.

University of Illinois PETER HAY

Preface

The European Economic Community is probably more important politically and economically to the United States than any other entity in the world. Politically, the EEC provides the means of pooling and strengthening the resources of six highly industrialized countries so that they can become partners and allies of the United States on equal terms. Economically, the EEC is an increasingly strong competitor of the United States in markets everywhere, and it is a community within which the members benefit from a tariff preference which United States exports do not share. Economic growth and expanding markets in the EEC have caused many United States companies to invest in Europe. Between 1958 and 1964, the total value of United States direct investment in Europe almost trebled, reaching approximately $11.5 billion. By 1964, more than 2,500 United States companies had opened subsidiaries or joint ventures in Europe or had licensed European enterprises to manufacture their products. United States companies in Europe have been estimated to obtain an average return of 12 per cent on investment, as against 9 per cent in the United States. At the same time, United States exports to Europe have been increasing rapidly, and in 1964 they reached about $8.3 billion.

In these circumstances United States lawyers in the international field have taken an increasing interest in the legal aspects of doing business in Europe, in particular in EEC member countries. United States lawyers in government agencies, in international organizations, and in private practice are also concerned with the economic, political, industrial, and commercial developments in Europe because of their importance for the foreign and even the domestic economic policies of the United States government.

On an academic level, the interest in the EEC lies in the fact that it is a new type of international organization with much greater powers over member countries than those traditionally given to international institutions. In the long run, it is intended to be a political union. It can alter national law directly and will carry out a far-reaching program of assimilation of national laws on economic and business affairs. The EEC has therefore introduced two new dimensions into international law and comparative law—a new type of international organization and an economic principle as a basis for uniform laws. It has resulted in the creation of many new international rules of law directly binding on private enterprises, such as the EEC antitrust laws. The EEC is the most far-reaching, most important, and most carefully organized of an increasing number of arrangements for regional economic cooperation and integration in the world, and so is a prototype for such arrangements. The EEC presents, in an acute form, the problems of non-tariff legal and economic factors affecting free and equal conditions of trade which have been faced by the European Free Trade Association and the signatories to the General Agreement on Tariffs and Trade. Harmonization of law will become necessary in EFTA as tariff barriers are abolished.

Behind the common external tariff which the EEC customs union is establishing, trade and investment are to be freed, and laws causing competitive advantages or disadvantages to business interests are to be eliminated. The United States investor in Europe is directly concerned with free trade for his products and those of his competitors. The kinds of law which require amendment are therefore precisely the kinds which the investor is interested in, because he wishes to take advantage of every law which alters competitive conditions in his favor and to know of laws which will prejudice him. In particular, some laws give special advantages to business in order to aid economic development. These laws are particularly important in depressed areas and in capital-importing countries. Investors' lawyers need to know not only the practical effect of the existing laws but also the changes which the EEC is likely to require in them and the rights of the investors if a law on which they relied is repealed.

The main objectives of this book are to provide a comparative analysis of the effect of entry into the EEC on the laws of a particular country presenting legal and economic problems typical of capital-importing countries and to analyze the problems of Community law raised by the accession of a new member state. At present some ten countries have applied for membership in, or association with, the EEC. The legal aspects of the EEC in relation to a particular country have never been made the subject of a full-length study. The legal problems of enacting and interpreting the EEC Treaty in a new member state and the constitutional problems arising from accession to the Treaty have never been adequately dealt with in English. This book is also intended to be a practical guide to lawyers acting for potential investors in the EEC and in Ireland. Only a country-study can give an over-all picture to the potential investor. Some practical difficulties for foreign investors in the existing Irish law are pointed out and suggestions are made for improvements. Such a country-study can never eliminate the need for a local lawyer, but it can give the United States lawyer sufficient detail about the relevant laws to enable him to plan his clients' investments in outline without lengthy inquiries. At present, no real guide to foreign investment in Ireland exists, and the same is true of most of the other less industrialized countries in Europe.

Though problems which arise in industrialized states, such as constitutional issues, are discussed, the less industrialized and capital-importing European regions and countries are the primary subject of this book. This is because they offer advantages to foreign investors, such as tax concessions and an abundance of cheap labor. Any such country in the EEC would face a conflict between the need to equalize legal and economic conditions of competition throughout the EEC to bring about economic integration and the need for special legal measures to encourage economic growth. This conflict is important to United States investors in both capital-importing and industrialized regions. Since certain economic problems are common to every plan for economic integration and others common to less developed economies, the legal problems are similar also. For example, the entry of Ireland into the EEC would raise the question of the need to modify EEC antitrust policy to encourage economic development and to modify the relationship between EEC antitrust rules and national antitrust laws, which are intended to protect and develop the national economy; the question of the compatibility of tax incentives for investors and exporters with the EEC Treaty and the possibility of obtaining compensation for investors if tax incentives are held to be incompatible with the Treaty; the legal implications of introducing freedom of establishment and the effects of the proposed EEC tax measures on economic development and on tax discrimination in favor of local investors and local investment; and the question of how the need for a simple corporation law in Ireland can best be reconciled with the need for a uniform corporation law throughout the EEC. All these problems arise in the underindustrialized areas in the EEC and in countries associated with the EEC and planning full membership in it. The capital-importing countries in Europe are increasingly important for direct United States investment and as markets for United States capital and consumer goods, and it is United States as well as EEC policy to encourage their economic development through private investment. Many of the legal problems discussed, such as company law and tax law, are not peculiar to capital-importing countries but present special problems for them. Too little has been written, particularly in English, about the changes in national laws brought about by economic integration and the economic effect of legal rules on business enterprises. The literature on the legal problems of less developed regions in the EEC and associated countries is less than is required by the theoretical and practical importance of the subjects involved—economic integration, foreign investment, economic development, and liberalization of international trade. Transnational plans for economic integration will be increasingly important among capital-importing countries.

There are various reasons why Ireland, a common law country, is regarded as sufficiently typical of capital-importing countries to be chosen for a comparative study. Irish law is basically the same as English law and is therefore similar to that in many former British colonies. Various Commonwealth countries should reach Ireland's present stage of economic development in a few years, including several countries planning to join common markets. A study of Ireland will facilitate a study of the more complex problems of the EEC for Britain and for the EFTA countries, some of whose laws are more like those of Britain than those of the Six. For reasons of space, detailed references to British law have not been included; but in many fields, such as tax and company law, it is very similar to Irish law, so the same changes would be necessitated by entry into the EEC. A fair amount of material has already been published on the laws of the EEC member states, which are civil law countries. Harmonization of law in the EEC has not progressed very far, and there is no question of new entrants' simply adopting a uniform law already agreed upon in the EEC. New member states will influence the common type of law eventually adopted, and a common law country will have a more significant influence than a civil law country. Comparative studies gain in value if comparisons are made between common law and civil law countries. Though technically different, the rules of civil law and common law which are affected by the EEC are similar in substance, since they deal with similar economic problems and with international business transactions. It is preferable to study a country which has faced the problems of altering its legal and economic system to join the EEC and which is likely to have to do so again.

The constitutional problems arising under Ireland's written constitution are basically similar to those arising under the written constitutions of the present EEC member states and to those arising in Britain; they are not, of course, peculiar to capital-importing countries. They are fundamental to the whole question of accession to the EEC Treaty, and they involve questions, such as the relationship of national law to Community law, which have not yet been solved in the Six. They may affect a foreign investor or any individual subject to Community law.

Ireland's economic problems are typical problems of how to encourage industrialization and economic development and are not complicated by low standards of education or infrastructure. Ireland is a capital-importing country that is economically partly integrated with a highly industrialized country. Its position is therefore similar in various respects to that of the African states of the French Community in relation to France. In common with most underindustrialized regions and countries, Ireland needs to stimulate her industries to greater competitiveness and, if Ireland were in the EEC, she might need to take whatever steps would be compatible with the Treaty to improve their efficiency. Ireland has a unique double taxation arrangement with Britain especially suited to two highly integrated economies and similar to that suggested for use ultimately in the EEC. The Irish program of state aid to industry is an elaborate one using most of the methods used elsewhere to encourage foreign investment, modernization, and capital formation. Legally, Ireland is typical of capital-importing countries and regions in its small capital market, its simple restrictive practices legislation, and its dependence on indirect taxation. The present Irish restrictions on the freedom of establishment of foreigners are typical of capital-importing countries and raise all the questions relating to the rights of nationals of nonmember states under the EEC Treaty and under treaties of friendship, commerce, and navigation which must come up in these countries on accession to the EEC Treaty. Like most capital-importing countries, Ireland has a complex of legal devices which provide protection from competition from abroad, such as "Buy Irish" requirements in state contracts, all of which must be dismantled in the EEC. Considering all these similarities, the conclusions drawn in this book from a comparative analysis of the Irish problems are therefore valid for those of other countries.

Ireland's interest for the United States investor lies partly in its proximity to Europe and the availability of cheap English-speaking labor. Ireland's double taxation arrangements with Britain give special advantages to Irish industries exporting to Britain, and Irish-made goods get tariff preferences there. Ireland is the only politically stable country in Europe offering an adequate infrastructure and the advantages typical of capital-importing countries to foreign investors. Ireland has been receiving attention in legal and business journals in the United States, in Europe, and elsewhere, and has been attracting an increasing volume of foreign investment in new industry. In 1964 Ireland was the subject of the American Management Association's three-day annual conference on United States investment abroad. Between 1958 and 1965, 267 new factories were established. In December 1965, 49 new factories were in the course of construction, 33 with foreign investors; capital investment in these enterprises was approximately $46.2 million. About one-third of the total amount of foreign capital now invested in Ireland is United States–owned, and this is distributed among more than 30 companies. In 1963 for the first time there was more investment in Ireland by United States companies than by companies of any other single country.

This book assumes that Ireland and Britain will join the EEC as full member states at a time when the structure of the EEC and therefore the consequences of membership are not radically different from what they are at present. This assumption cannot be proved at this time, and history may prove it incorrect. However, the Irish government's Second Program for Economic Expansion, published after the breakdown of the negotiations between Britain and the EEC, expressly assumes that Ireland will be in the EEC before 1970. A vice-president of the EEC Commission has described this assumption as realistic. Even since the breakdown of negotiations in 1963 and the British general election in 1964, the British government has stressed that it is anxious to do nothing that would increase the technical or political difficulties of Britain's joining the EEC, and the reasons prompting Britain to apply for membership in 1961 still apply. Discussions of Britain's joining the EEC recently have greatly increased. Countries planning to join the EEC will follow developments in the EEC and alter their laws to facilitate their eventual entry. Investors in these countries therefore will be affected by changes similar to those in the laws of the Six. Some of the legal changes required by membership of the EEC probably will be made in Ireland anyway because of the present law reform and economic development programs and because of the interest of the Irish Department of Justice in civil law.

Considerations of time and space cause this book to be confined to the legal aspects of investment and doing business through companies and to disregard laws—in particular tax laws—affecting only individuals. Even though all aspects of the EEC are interrelated, the topics of agriculture, transport, and state trading are omitted, although they are of special interest to Ireland, to developing regions in the EEC, and to countries associated with it. These topics involve economics more than law; Community policy does not seem ready for study and is of less direct interest to foreign investors than the topics considered. Only direct investment is dealt with; neither portfolio investment, which is becoming important for British investors in Ireland, nor licensing, in which countries such as Ireland have a considerable interest, is covered. Euratom and the European Coal and Steel Community are referred to only incidentally. While the writing of a book such as this involves the use of a considerable amount of economic data and economic theory, an effort has been made to limit the text to legal problems and to leave economic matters, except where discussion of them is necessary to explain the legal problems, to those better qualified. No attempt therefore has been made at quantitative analysis, although some of the legal problems, such as the compatibility of the Irish tax concessions with the provisions of Article 98 of the EEC Treaty, cannot be solved without it. Considerations of time, space, and general interest caused the omission of the laws on tariffs, excise taxes, sales, partnerships, arbitration, bankruptcy, reciprocal enforcement of judgments, public contracts, industrial law, insurance, exchange control, labor law, social security, and patents and other industrial and commercial property, except insofar as they touch on questions of tax and antitrust law. All of these fields of law will be affected by the EEC.

Since this book is intended as a guide to investors' lawyers, it sets out many of the present rules of Irish law. No effort has been made to state systematically the law in force in Britain, in the Six, or elsewhere, since this information is readily available in the standard academic and practitioners' manuals and in the spate of brief descriptions of the national laws of the Six which the EEC has brought about. However, comparisons have been made wherever there are differences between the laws of Ireland and the laws of any of the Six which are believed to be significant from the viewpoint of harmonization of laws or the viewpoint of the foreign investor.

The existence of several excellent bibliographies on the EEC makes the compilation of yet another unnecessary. Since the book has been written primarily for United States lawyers, references have been chosen which are fairly readily available in the United States.

In Summary

Part I describes the institutions of the EEC with particular reference to the changes necessitated by the accession of a new member state to the EEC Treaty, the constitutional and other basic legal questions which arise out of the state's new relationship with the EEC institutions, and the protection of the interests of private enterprises. Part II briefly describes the Irish economy and details its essential similarity to the economies of other underindustrialized regions and countries that are in or are likely to enter or to become associated with the EEC. Part III considers harmonization of company law and the rules on freedom of establishment in the EEC and provides for the investor a comparative analysis of the existing Irish law on these topics and the changes in the law of a new member state necessitated by the EEC. Part IV analyzes the EEC proposals for the harmonization of direct and indirect taxes, outlines the present Irish tax law from the viewpoint of the investor, and mentions the changes likely to result from the EEC proposals. It also deals with the principles on which double taxation can be avoided in the EEC and the extent to which double taxation conventions can help to produce equal tax burdens in member states. The principles for eliminating double taxation proposed by the Neumark Committee are analyzed from the viewpoint of capital-importing countries in conditions of close economic integration, on the basis of the Anglo-Irish double taxation convention, which is based on the same principles. The present Irish double taxation conventions with the United States and Germany, the OECD Fiscal Committee's model double taxation convention, and unilateral relief against double taxation are also analyzed from the point of view of the investor in the EEC. Part V discusses tax concessions for exports and their compatibility with the EEC Treaty, deals with state aids to industry and regional economic policy in the EEC, and analyzes the present state aids given under Irish law. Analyzed also are the legal rights, if any, of an investor who is prevented by the EEC Treaty from obtaining state aid. Part VI sets out the antitrust law of the EEC, discusses its application to less developed regions, and summarizes the existing Irish antitrust law and the changes which would result from EEC membership. As far as clarity of presentation permits, the EEC law is given first, and is followed by the present Irish law and the changes in the laws of capital-importing countries and regions which would result from accession to the EEC Treaty.

JOHN TEMPLE LANG

Acknowledgments

In writing and collecting material for a book such as this, which deals with recent developments, an author inevitably becomes indebted to many people in many ways. In the American Bar Foundation my greatest debt is to S. Houston Lay, Director of the International Legal Program, without whose continual direction and encouragement this book could not have been written, and to Larry Coffey, whose expert revisions and comprehensive editing removed many faults and resulted in a greatly improved manuscript. I am grateful also to E. Blythe Stason, former Administrator of the Foundation, for his support during the project.

To Dr. Ernst Wohlfarth, Legal Adviser to the Council of Ministers of the European Economic Community, Professor Peter Hay of the University of Illinois, and Thomas L. Nicholson, attorney of the law firm of Isham, Lincoln and Beale, Chicago, my thanks are due for reading and commenting on the completed text. My thanks are also due to the following, who, as well as giving me information, read parts of the manuscript at various times: the Honourable Mr. Justice Kenny, Judge of the High Court of Ireland; Professor T. B. Smith and Dr. Victor MacKinnon, of the Department of Civil Law, University of Edinburgh; Professors George A. Duncan and W. J. L. Ryan, of the Faculty of Economics, Trinity College, Dublin; G. Buttanshaw of Craig Gardner and Co., Dublin; Dr. Peggy Richman of the Department of Economics, University of Pennsylvania; P. van Ommeslaghe, avocat près la Cour d'Appel, Brussels; D. Vignes of the Legal Service of the EEC; Dr. Sidney Z. Ehler of the Law School, University College, Dublin; Dr. E. J. Cohn of Lincoln's Inn, London; P. Lalor of the Industrial Development Authority; in the Department of Finance, Denis J. Maher, S. O Cromien, and P. Carty; P. McMahon of the Revenue Commissioners; S. Holloway, Department of Industry and Commerce; in the Irish Civil Service, H. E. Sean Morrissey, Irish Ambassador in Berne and formerly Legal Advisor, Department of External Affairs; and in the Lord Chancellor's Office in London, K. M. Newman.

I must also express thanks to several experts who have read parts of the manuscript but who for professional reasons have asked to remain anonymous. To all those in Europe and the United States who gave me advice, information, and comments while I was gathering material I also owe a debt. It would be impossible for me to name them all, but I would like to mention in particular Gerard Ryder, Solicitor to the U.K. Board of Trade, Michel Gaudet, Legal Adviser to the EEC, and Leon Liddell, Librarian of the University of Chicago Law School, whose help was only exceeded by their friendliness to me.

Finally, my thanks go to: Dr. P. Verloren van Themaat, Director General, P. Nasini, Director, Directorate on Competition, Messrs. Albrecht, A. de Baerdemacker, G. Bebr, Ciancio, Gleske, Norbert Koch, M. Hauschild, LeTallec, Gerrit

Linssen, Richard Mayne, Karl-Heinz Narjes, P. van Praet, H. von Stein, and D. Zillian, all of the EEC Commission; Liam de Barra, Secretary, Irish Commission on Income Taxation; F. V. Buckley and Dr. F. G. Hall, Fair Trade Commission, Dublin; Alan Campbell, Barrister-at-Law of the Temple, London; F. Casey and P. Tracey, Industrial Credit Company, Dublin; Joseph Charleton, A.C.A., Dublin; R. Chevallier, Dr. Hans Wolfram Daig, and Dr. H. Sperl, Librarian, all of the Court of the European Communities; Sidney M. Cone III, Dr. Walter van Gerven, James G. Johnson, Jr., Joseph Morgan, Andrew Newberg, Lyman M. Tondel, Jr., and Richard Webster, all of Cleary, Gottlieb, Steen & Hamilton; François Duchêne, Action Committee for the United States of Europe, Paris; Dr. Klaus Edelman, OECD Secretariat; Senator Garret FitzGerald, Economist Intelligence Unit, Dublin; E. I. Giusseppi, Richard Butler & Co., London; H. J. Glaesner, Legal Service of the EEC; Professors Goldman and Roger Houin, Law Faculty, University of Paris; Roger Hayes, Assistant Secretary, Irish Department of Justice; Sir Edwin Herbert, former President, The Law Society, London; Charles Higginson and Jack Myerson, U.S. Mission to the European Communities; Maître F. C. Jeanet, Paris; Professor Otto Kahn-Freund, University of Oxford; Andrew Kennen, Irish Department of Industry and Commerce; E. H. van Kleffens, ECSC Ambassador to the United Kingdom; Professor Jean Limpens, Director, Centre Interuniversitaire de Droit Comparé, Brussels; Professor François Luchaire, Institut des Etudes d'Outre-Mer, Paris; C. MacFadyean, Slaughter & May, London; Norman Marsh and Denis Thompson, British Institute of International and Comparative Law; John Methven, Imperial Chemical Industries, London; E. Nortcliffe, Unilever, Ltd., London; Seán Réamonn, Chairman, J. M. Gleeson, and W. T. Hamill, Irish Revenue Commissioners; Bernard J. Reverdin, Lovejoy, Morris, Wasson & Happuch, New York; E. Rippingall, Treasury Solicitors Office, London; Maître Raoul A. Sasson and Derek Wise, Theodore Goddard & Co., Paris; J. C. Stebbings, Payne, Hicks, Beach & Co., London; Professor Eric Stein and Mrs. Lily Roberts, Librarian, Law School, University of Michigan; Professor Victor Stone, Law School, University of Illinois; Walter Supp, Cahill, Gordon, Reindel & Ohl, Paris; L. E. M. Taylor, Board of Trade, London; H. Horsfall Turner, The Law Society, London; Michel Waelbroeck, Avocat, Brussels; Professor G. S. A. Wheatcroft, London School of Economics; and Dr. E. Zimmerman, ECSC branch of the Legal Service of the European Communities.

Research on this book was substantially completed before June 1965, and the book therefore does not deal fully with the literature published since that date. Also, it does not discuss in detail the Irish Finance Bill, 1966, which was published while the book was in press; the United Kingdom government's proposals for substituting cash grants for investment allowances, which have not yet been embodied in a published bill (see Investment Incentives, Cmd. No. 2874 [1966]); the abortive British Companies Bill, 1966, which lapsed on the dissolution of Parliament before the recent general election; the recent German corporation law reform act (Aktiengesetz, Sept. 6, 1965); the French company law of November 1965; or the most recent decisions of the EEC Commission on antitrust matters, some of which are subject to appeal to the Community Court.

Financial support for this study was provided by the American Bar Foundation, and for this I am extremely grateful. However, the analyses, conclusions, and opinions in this book are entirely my own and must not be taken to be the views of the Foundation or of any of those who have read the manuscript or helped me with comments.

My thanks and those of the American Bar Foundation are due to Her Majesty's Stationery Office for permission to quote from the Foreign Office translation of the EEC Treaty.

J. T. L.

Summary of Contents

Contents

Part I INSTITUTIONAL AND CONSTITUTIONAL ASPECTS

Part I

INSTITUTIONAL AND CONSTITUTIONAL ASPECTS

Chapter 1

The Institutions of the European Economic Community and Harmonization of Law

THE NEED FOR COMMUNITY INSTITUTIONS

Institutions are required by the European Economic Community[1] (the EEC) to carry out the object of the EEC Treaty,[2] which is to integrate the national markets of the Six member countries[3] into a single market. The common institutions also are intended to be the embryonic organs of a United States of Europe.[4] The customs union which is the basis of the EEC seeks to bring about the free movement of labor and capital, free movement of services, and freedom of establishment which are essential to a unified market. Common institutions are necessary to maintain the unified market by enforcing the common rules on competition, developing common economic policies, and coordinating the exercise of the economic powers of member states, and to protect the interests of the smaller member states. They are needed also, as a step towards political integration, to take the viewpoint of the Community as a whole and so unify the outlook of member states.

The EEC Treaty is wider in scope, more far-reaching in its implications, and less detailed and specific[5] than the treaty establishing the European Coal and Steel Community[6] (the ECSC). The EEC Treaty is the constitution of the EEC—a "framework treaty,"[7] and com-

[1] Uri, "Economics and Politics of the Common Market," in Competition, Cartels and Their Regulation 378, 379 (Miller ed. 1962); OEEC Special Working Party, Report on the Possibility of Creating a Free Trade Area in Europe, pt. III (1957). On the institutions of the EEC, see Lichtheim, The New Europe 58–83 (1963).

[2] Treaty establishing the European Economic Community, March 25, 1957, in the four official languages of the EEC—Dutch, French, German, and Italian. There are unofficial English translations by the British Foreign Office, published by Her Majesty's Stationery Office (1962), and by the Secretariat of the Interim Committee for the Common Market and Euratom (1957), reprinted in 298 U.N.T.S. 14 (1958) and in 51 Am. J. Int'l L. 865 (1957). Throughout this book, the EEC Treaty is referred to as "the Treaty." Unless otherwise noted, the translation used is that published by Her Majesty's Stationery Office.

[3] Belgium, France, the Federal Republic of Germany, Italy, Luxembourg, and the Netherlands.

[4] In the striking phrase of M. Gaudet, speaking of the three Communities, "the Communities constitute in fact a political union of which the activity is up to now limited to the economic and social sphere." "Incidences des Communautés européennes sur le droit interne des Etats membres," 8 Annales de la Faculté de Droit de Liège 5, 11 (1963).

[5] Reuter, "Communautés européennes et techniques d'unification," in Les Problèmes Juridiques et Economiques du Marché Commun [hereinafter cited as Les Problèmes Juridiques] 15 (Colloque des Facultés de Droit, 1960).

[6] Treaty establishing the European Coal and Steel Community, April 18, 1951. English translations have been published by the High Authority of the ECSC and by Her Majesty's Stationery Office (1962).

[7] Cartou, Le Marché Commun et le Droit Public 27–29 (1959).

mon institutions are required to work out in practice the meaning of the principles laid down in the EEC Treaty and to fill in the details omitted from it.

The principal institutions of the EEC are the Council, the Commission, the Court of Justice, the European Parliamentary Assembly,[8] and the Economic and Social Committee.

THE COUNCIL

The Council[9] consists of one representative of each member state, generally the Minister of Economics or the Minister for Foreign Affairs, and meets regularly at Brussels. Subject to the Treaty, the Council exemplifies the traditional method of international cooperation and is the principal executive and legislative organ of the Community.

A unanimous vote is required for decisions of fundamental importance,[10] decisions where the extent of the powers is not limited by the Treaty,[11] and certain other decisions.[12] If a unanimous vote is required, an abstention by a member state which is represented at the meeting does not prevent adoption of a proposal.[13] In other cases decisions can be made by qualified majority or by simple majority. Some decisions which require unanimity during the transitional period, before the complete establishment of the customs union, can be made by a qualified majority at a later stage.[14] This insures that "agreements to agree" are carried out and that the progress of the Common Market is not unduly delayed by a national veto. Many important decisions can be taken by qualified majority. A simple majority vote of any four member states is rarely required.[15] The votes of member states are weighted so that Luxembourg has one vote; Belgium and the Netherlands, two votes each; and Germany, France, and Italy, four votes each.[16] A qualified majority requires twelve votes. The more important resolutions which the Treaty requires to be passed on a proposal of the Commission can be carried by the twelve votes of the three large countries.[17] The interests of the smaller states are safeguarded by the Commission, which formulates its proposals in the interests of the Community as a whole. A resolution which must be proposed by the

[8] Called the "Assembly" in the Treaty, it first adopted the name "European Parliamentary Assembly." 1958 Journal Officiel des Communautés Européennes [hereinafter cited as Journal Officiel] 6/58. Then it changed its name to "European Parliament." 1962 Journal Officiel 1045/62.

[9] Arts. 145–54.

[10] Such as under art. 8, on transition to next stages of the transitional period; art. 212, on conditions of service of Community officials; art. 235, on amendment in detail of the Treaty; and art. 237, on admission of new member states. In other cases unanimity is required to permit a derogation from or waiver of a provision of the Treaty (e.g., art. 93). See Cartou, Le Marché Commun et le Droit Public 87 (1959).

Practically all of the Council's acts dealing with agriculture, transport, and the common commercial policy will be taken by majority vote after the end of the second stage of the transitional period.

A more complete analysis is given by Samkalden et al., "The Effect of the Admission of New Member States on the Institutions of the E.E.C.," 10 Sociaal-Economische Wetgeving 345, 368–73 (1962); Barmann, "Les Communautés européennes et le rapprochement des droits," 12 Rev. Int. de Droit Comp. 9, 34–36, 38–39 (1960).

[11] Arts. 99 and 100, on harmonization of tax and other laws.

[12] E.g., art. 84, on extension of common transport policy to sea and air transport.

[13] Art. 148(3).

[14] Arts. 33(8), 43(2), 54(2), 63(2), 69, 75, 87, 101, 111(3), 112(1).

[15] Art. 148.

[16] Special arrangements exist under arts. 44(6) and 203, art. 4 of the Statute of the European Investment Bank, and art. 7 of the Convention on the Association of Overseas Countries (now expired).

[17] Art. 148(2).

Commission can be amended only by unanimous vote.[18] The proposal of the Commission can be referred back by the Council for amendment and resubmission. Resolutions which need not be proposed by the Commission require twelve votes cast by four member states, so that one of the three small states must support the resolution, even if Germany, France, and Italy are agreed.

The proceedings of the Council are secret, and the result of voting is not made public, but in practice the qualified majority provisions are apparently rarely invoked.[19] However, the possibility of a qualified majority vote to override dissent probably encourages the general community spirit of compromise and discourages hard bargaining.

Accession of a new member state to the EEC Treaty would involve amendment of the rules on qualified majorities.[20] Qualified majority voting would certainly be retained. The present weighting of votes favors the small states relative to their population and gross national product. Voting rights are not based on clear criteria and might be affected by the interests of present member states.[21] If Britain accedes to the Treaty, she will presumably get the same number of votes as France, Germany, and Italy. Ireland, Denmark, and Norway, which also applied for membership in 1961, might get two votes each or one vote each. To avoid treating countries of unequal wealth and population as equals, the whole scale could be altered and Luxembourg given two votes; Ireland, Denmark, and Norway, three votes each; and Belgium and the Netherlands, four votes each.[22]

A qualified majority in an enlarged Council would probably continue to be

[18] Art. 149.

[19] Noel, "How the European Economic Community's Institutions Work," EEC Doc. No. 6126–1/PP/62–E (1962); 6 Revue du Marché Commun 14 (1963). It is understood that, for some years after 1958, a vote by qualified majority has been seriously threatened only once. See also Alting von Geusau, European Organizations and Foreign Relations of States 190, 196 (1962); Lindberg, The Political Dynamics of European Economic Integration, ch. XIII (1963); Lando, "E.E.C. Council and Commission in Their Mutual Relationship: A Survey of Law and Practice," 12 J. Pub. L. 337 (1963).

[20] See generally Ljubisavljevic, Les Problèmes de la Pondération dans les Institutions Européennes (1959); Sidjanski, "Voting Procedures in an Enlarged Community," 1 J. Common Market Studies 173 (1962); Henig, "Voting Procedures–A Reply," 1 J. Common Market Studies 219 (1962).

See also Rapport fait au nom du comité des présidents sur le cinquième rapport général sur l'activité de la Communauté économique européenne, A.P.E. [European Parliamentary Assembly] Doc. No. 74, para. 69 (1962); A.P.E. Compte Rendu No. 17, Oct. 17, 1962, at 729–37.

[21] The Netherlands and Belgium might want the three small new member states to have two votes each (if the present scale were not altered) to increase the total voting power of the small states. France might wish Ireland and Denmark, as agricultural countries with interests similar to hers, to have two votes each but might feel that Ireland, because of its close trade connections with Britain, might vote with Britain against the interests of France. Because of their relative economic strength, Ireland and Norway might be given one vote less than Denmark, which might get the same number of votes as Belgium and the Netherlands even if the scale were altered.

[22] Samkalden et al., "The Effect of Admission of New Member States on the Institutions of the E.E.C.," 10 Sociaal-Economische Wetgeving 345, 353 (1962). This would give France, Germany, Britain, and Italy eight votes each. The total would be fifty-one votes, and a qualified majority of two-thirds would be thirty-four votes. The eighteen votes needed for a veto could come from two large states with the support of any one small one, from the six small states together, or from various other combinations. The total voting power of the small states vis-à-vis the large ones would be slightly reduced; "Qualified Majority Voting in an Enlarged Community," 2 Common Market 188 (1962). Samkalden also calculates the position if Britain were to join and suggests that where the Council may act without a proposal of the Commission, a simple majority should be required (i.e., six states, if Britain, Denmark, Ireland, and Norway all joined).

two-thirds of the total votes—the present proportion. This principle was informally accepted[23] in the abortive negotiations with Britain. The balance of power would shift[24] slightly away from the large member states if the four potential member states all joined.

Administrative problems would arise in the Council if there were ten EEC member states, i.e., the present Six, plus Britain, Denmark, Norway, and Ireland;[25] but ten members are not so many that reorganization would be necessary.

The Council is not responsible to the European Parliamentary Assembly, which has no power to question it or to remove its members. Only national parliaments, through their control over their respective governments, can exercise democratic control over the Council. Whether governments must answer parliamentary questions about the instructions given to their representatives on the Council depends on national law. If parliamentary questions need not be answered, the view of a government on a particular question cannot be ascertained, unless the Council or the government reveals it. This is serious in view of the great powers of the Council.

The enormously important powers of the Council are legislative and executive. The most obviously legislative functions relate to determining the common agricultural policy,[26] freeing movement of workers,[27] putting the antitrust provisions of the Treaty into effect,[28] setting up machinery for the control of state subsidies for industry,[29] and determining the common transport policy.[30] In each of these cases the proposal of the Commission, and in some cases consultation with one of the advisory institutions, is required.[31]

THE COMMISSION

The Commission, which corresponds to the European Coal and Steel Community High Authority with which it is now

[23] Rapport fait au nom de la Commission politique sur les aspects politiques et institutionnels de l'adhésion ou de l'association à la Communauté [hereinafter cited as the Birkelbach Report], A.P.E. Doc. No. 122, para. 80 (1961–62); Report to the European Parliament on the State of the Negotiations with the United Kingdom, A.P.E. Doc. No. 6, at 106 (1963). See also Western European Union Assembly, Consequences of the Accession of the United Kingdom for the Functioning of the Institutions of the European Communities, 8th Sess., Doc. No. 248 (1962).

[24] Unless Norway and Ireland got one vote each and Denmark two, making a total of twenty-five votes, and a qualified majority was sixteen, i.e., slightly less than two-thirds.

[25] Austria, Denmark, Britain, Norway, Portugal, Sweden, and Switzerland are the members of the European Free Trade Association. Sweden and Switzerland do not seek membership in the EEC. Greece and Turkey (which have association treaties with the EEC) and Portugal and Spain will not be economically ready for membership for some years. Portugal and Spain might not be politically acceptable under their present regimes. Austria may seek a special association status.

[26] Arts. 40(1), 43(2). The Assembly must be consulted.

[27] Art. 49. The Economic and Social Committee must be consulted.

[28] Art. 87. The Assembly must be consulted.

[29] Art. 93. There is no requirement for consultation.

[30] Art. 75. Both the Assembly and the Economic and Social Committee must be consulted.

[31] Sawyer & Doeker, "The European Economic Community as a Constitutional System," 4 Inter-Am. L. Rev. 217, 221 (1962), list the following types of binding acts which the Council can take:

1) Council action on the proposal of the Commission after consulting the Assembly: thirteen cases.

2) Council action on the proposal of the Commission: fifty cases.

3) Council action on its own initiative: thirty-three cases.

4) Commission decision on its own initiative: forty-two cases. Most of the cases in which the Commission acts on its own initiative concern the execution of existing legal rules, whether derived from the Treaty or from acts of EEC institutions.

to be merged,[32] consists of nine members, most of whom are lawyers as well as economists. They and their staff of two thousand civil servants, drawn mostly from the national administrations of the Six, act only in the interests of the Community[33] and are completely independent, though the Commission works very closely with the Council. As a civil service they are formally separated from the political organ of the Community executive, the Council. The Commission has power to enforce the Treaty, to initiate Community policy, and to represent the Community. Two members from each of the three large states and one member each from Belgium, the Netherlands, and Luxembourg are appointed by the member states by unanimous vote and can be removed individually only by the Court for misconduct or inability to perform their duties and collectively only by a vote of censure by the Assembly.[34] The Commission is therefore responsible to the European Parliament, not to the Council. After the accession of Britain, Denmark, Ireland, and Norway, the Commission would have fifteen members if the present principles were adhered to.[35] Each member of the Commission is now the head of a Directorate-General with specialized functions. The number of employees of the Commission would

[32] Agreement to merge both the executives of the three Communities—the High Authority of the ECSC and the Commissions of the European Atomic Energy Community (Euratom) and of the EEC—and their Councils was reached on April 8, 1965. See an unofficial translation of the agreement in 4 Int'l Legal Materials 776 (1965); see also Reuter, "Juridical and Institutional Aspects of the European Regional Communities," 26 Law & Contemp. Prob. 381, 383 (1961); A.P.E. Débats, Sess. 1961–62, at 265–84; EEC Commission, First General Report on the Activities of the Community, paras. 31–35 (1958). [Hereinafter the Commission Reports are cited as First General Report, Second General Report, etc.] Integration of the three Communities increases their political importance, but it will be a step toward political integration only if the revision does not reduce their powers. Coordinating the Communities' activities is particularly difficult in the sector of energy, where the ECSC, Euratom, and the EEC are responsible for coal, nuclear energy, and oil and electricity, respectively, because of the conflict of interests among the member states owing to the different extent to which they have access to the sources of energy. See EEC Commission, Action Programme of the Community for the Second Stage [hereinafter cited as Action Programme for the Second Stage], ch. v (1962). The powers of the executive under the ECSC Treaty are different from those under the other two Treaties. The intention is that after a transitional period the number of members of the unified executive will return to nine.

[33] Art. 157. Arts. 155–63 deal with the institutional aspects of the Commission. See Hammarskjöld, The International Civil Servant in Law and in Fact (1961); Munch, "Le système institutionnel des Communautés européennes," lecture at the Université Internationale des Sciences Comparés, Faculté Internationale de Droit Comparé, Luxembourg (1962).

[34] Art. 144.

[35] Reuter, "Juridical and Institutional Aspects of the European Regional Communities," 26 Law & Contemp. Prob. 381, 386 n.5 (1961), says that it is necessary to have one national from each member state on the High Authority, although the members in no way represent their member states, and that the total number should be uneven to prevent the Authority, which acts by simple majority, from being equally divided. The same principles apply to the EEC Commission. Art. 157 provides that no more than two members may be nationals of the same state. Britain, France, Germany, and Italy would expect an equal number of nationals on the Commission and would expect more than the smaller countries. This means a total of eight members from the large countries and six from the small, plus one to make an uneven number. If the number of members is to be kept down, either the larger states would have to accept one national only or not all member states would be represented. The nationality of the members could vary, but changes in membership must be minimized. The Treaty does not require each member to be the head of a Directorate-General, but a member "without portfolio" is unlikely. See de Soto, "Le Problème de l'exécutif dans les Communautés européennes," in Les Problèmes Juridiques 121, 133–35 (1960). Samkalden et al., "The effect of the Admission of New Member States on the Institutions of the E.E.C.," 10 Sociaal-Economische Wetgeving 345, 356 (1962), contemplate fourteen members.

have to be increased to cope with the additional work. There is controversy[36] as to whether fifteen members would be too many for efficiency.[37]

All members are jointly responsible for decisions of the Commission. Formally, the Commission has very limited power to delegate any of its functions;[38] it remains responsible for any action it is empowered to take. As an administrative matter the Commission relies on committees of three members which supervise each Directorate-General, on the member in charge of each Directorate-General, and on its staff.[39]

The Commission insures that member states and enterprises comply with the Treaty[40] and implements the Treaty in matters not reserved to the Council.[41] In consultation with the standing Committee of Permanent Representatives of member states, the Commission formulates proposals for adoption by the Council[42] in most of the economic fields of the EEC, though agriculture is the only major sector in which its policy is effectively in force. The Commission's duty is to reconcile national interests, not to represent them. In practice the Commission has been in favor of more far-reaching measures of economic integration than has the Council. It safeguards the Community interest and the interests of smaller member states. The latter duty will be even more important when the Community is enlarged. The assurance that the Commission's proposals will be made in the general interest makes decisions by qualified majorities in the Council acceptable, even on sensitive issues. Apart from the abolition of tariffs and the freeing of movement of the factors of production, the Treaty requires the Commission to formulate policy[43] on

[36] Ibid. The authors, basing their opinion on the views of government representatives, say that fourteen "is not so large as to prevent efficient functioning."

[37] When the merger of the Community executives was under discussion, the Commission apparently took the view that nine was the maximum number for efficiency. See art. 157(1).

[38] See Meroni v. High Authority, 4 Recueil de la Jurisprudence de la Cour (de Justice des Communautés Européennes) [hereinafter cited as Recueil] 14 (1958) with regard to the power of the High Authority of the ECSC to delegate its functions; Lagrange, "Le rôle de la Cour de Justice des Communautés européennes," in Les Problèmes Juridiques 41, 43 (1960); Dumon, "La formation de la règle de droit dans les Communautés européennes," 12 Rev. Int. de Droit Comp. 75, 78 (1960); EEC Commission, First General Report, para. 18 (1958). For the Rules of Procedure of the Commission on delegation of its functions, see 1963 Journal Officiel 181/63.

[39] Frequent use is made of the "written procedure" by which a file and the draft decision are submitted by the appropriate Directorate-General to all members of the Commission and the proposal is considered, for internal purposes, to have been adopted if no objection is raised within a given time limit; Noel, "How the European Economic Community's Institutions Work," EEC Doc. No. 6126-1/PP/62-E (1962). With regard to the making of regulations, see Alting von Geusau, European Organizations and Foreign Relations of States, 185–97 (1962).

[40] E.g., arts. 155, 169, 170 and 79, 80, 89, 91, 93, 102, respectively.

[41] E.g., arts. 10(2), 13(2), 14(6), 15, 17, 22, 26, 33(2), 33(4), 35, 46, 64, 71, 81, 108, 155, 226.

[42] E.g., arts. 7, 43, 49, 51, 54–57, 63, 69–70, 75, 79, 87, 94, 99, 100, 103, 108, 112. See Gaudet, "The Legal Framework of the Community," in Legal Problems of the European Economic Community and the European Free Trade Association, Int'l & Comp. L.Q. Supp. No. 1, at 8, 12–13 (1961); Cartou, Le Marché Commun et le Droit Public 46 (1959); Pickles, "Political Power in the E.E.C.," 2 J. Common Market Studies 63, 69 (1963); Lindberg, The Political Dynamics of European Integration, ch. IV (1963).

[43] "In the E.E.C. it is a question of arriving at decisions, each of which is the equivalent of what the E.C.S.C. Treaty has stipulated in its economic provisions." Reuter, "Juridical and Institutional Aspects of the European Regional Communities," 26 Law & Contemp. Prob. 381, 389 (1961). See also art. 235.

agriculture, transport, economic trends, commercial and social matters,[44] and regional economic problems[45] for the Community as a whole. This is especially important because of the limited powers of the European Parliament. These policies can be formulated only with the cooperation of member states, which retain jurisdiction over these matters, although these policies need not be referred to the parliaments of member states (except under Articles 220 and 235) but must be adopted by the Council. In deciding questions of policy, the Commission consults governments, private enterprises, labor, and other interested parties and then prepares its proposals without further outside discussion. In this way the Commission manages to be both impartial and well informed. On technical questions, the Commission consults national experts.[46] The Commission is given numerous detailed powers by regulations made by the Council.

The Commission negotiates treaties for the Community with non-member states and with international organizations;[47] these treaties are concluded by the Council by a unanimous decision after any consultation with the Assembly which the Treaty requires. If the agreement is not compatible with the Treaty, the Treaty must be amended, and the Community Court may give an advisory opinion as to whether this is necessary.[48]

Treaty-making powers in connection with the common commercial policy[49] may be exercised by means of a qualified majority after the end of the first two stages.[50] After the second stage, therefore, a member state can be bound by a treaty concluded by the Community without having given its consent.

The Commission also represents the Community in legal proceedings and maintains relations on behalf of the Community with other international organizations.[51] The Community has legal personality in international law and full capacity in national law.[52] The Commission, not the Council,[53] is the organ which exercises the legal powers of the Community as such.

THE COUNCIL AND THE COMMISSION—MEANS OF ACTION AND TYPES OF ACTS

Means of action

The Treaty states various types of action which the Council and the Commis-

[44] Arts. 43, 75, 103, 110–11, and 113 and 118, respectively, and 123–28 (the Social Fund).

[45] Arts. 39(2), 42, 75(3), 80(2), 92(3), 123–28, 129–30.

[46] Noel, "How the European Economic Community's Institutions Work," EEC Doc. No. 6126-1/PP/62-E (1962); see "How Decisions Are Made," 2 Common Market 130 (1962), 6 Revue de Marché Commun 14 (1963).

[47] Art. 228; see arts. 229–31. See also Pescatore, "Les Relations Extérieures des Communautés Européennes," 103(2) Recueil des Cours (Académie de Droit International) [hereinafter cited as Recueil Académie D. Int.] 9 (1960).

[48] Art. 228.

[49] Arts. 111, 113, 114.

[50] Art. 114. It may be difficult to decide if a treaty creates a special relationship with the Community, in which case it is a treaty of association and requires unanimous approval. Since treaties in connection with the common commercial policy will not require unanimity, the distinction may be important.

[51] Art. 211; arts. 229–31.

[52] Arts. 210, 211. Art. 6 of the ECSC Treaty provides that the ECSC has legal personality in international law and in domestic law. Cf. Euratom Treaty, arts. 2(h), 184–85. See Glaesner, "Treaty Making Power and Legislation in the European Communities," 33 Annuaire de l'Association des Auditeurs et des Anciens Auditeurs de l'Académie de Droit International [hereinafter cited as Annuaire de l'A.A.A.] 147, 149 (1961); Megret, "Le Pouvoir de la Communauté économique européenne de conclure des accords internationaux," 7 Revue du Marché Commun 529 (1964).

[53] See, however, arts. 111, 113–14, 228. The Council exercises certain supervisory powers and authorizes negotiations by the Commission.

sion can take when found advisable.[54]

REGULATIONS

Regulations are uniform laws directly applicable in each member state, without confirmation or promulgation by the state. They are binding in every respect on all bodies, both public and private, to which they apply. Regulations may be made under powers conferred by the Treaty or by other regulations. Since regulations are law in each member state, national courts must apply them, subject to the ruling of the Community Court on questions of interpretation. Regulations may be a particular means of action contemplated by the Treaty or may be an alternative to directives or some other means of action. Regulations are appropriate where the legal rule must be the same in each member state, where Community law is a self-sufficient set of rules not interrelated with national law, or where the law in each member state must be under the direct control of Community institutions, such as for agriculture prices. Regulations are also used to govern the procedures of the common institutions.[55] If an EEC organ may choose between regulations and some other means of action,[56] it should choose the means which is most appropriate to the subject matter and to the effective performance of the required function and which will impose the least burden on interested parties and make the smallest inroads on national legal systems. Since regulations have general application, they should not be used when the interested parties are limited in number,[57] unless it is necessary to lay down a rule binding generally for the future.

DIRECTIVES

Directives[58] bind only the member states[59] to which they are addressed, not private enterprises. They bind the states to bring about a specified result, but the choice of form and methods of carrying out directives is left to the national authorities.[60] A Community act setting out the terms of draft legislation and requiring member states to enact it would probably be a decision or a regulation, not a directive.[61] Directives never become part of national law, and the disadvantage of directives is that they do not insure uniform rules in each member state.

Directives are appropriate where no uniform rule is necessary or where a change in a body of national law is required which, if brought about by regu-

[54] Art. 189. In the translations of the EEC and Euratom Treaties by Her Majesty's Stationery Office, art. 161 of the Euratom Treaty is translated more accurately than art. 189 of the EEC Treaty. The official texts are identical. Compare ECSC Treaty, art. 14. Regulations within the meaning of art. 189 are called throughout this book simply "regulations."

[55] E.g., art. 94.

[56] E.g., arts. 49, 87, 43(2).

[57] See art. 173, para. 2.

[58] "Directives shall be binding, as to the result to be achieved, upon each Member State to which they are directed, while leaving to national authorities the choice of form and means." Her Majesty's Stationery Office translation of Euratom Treaty, art. 161. Throughout this book, "directives" means directives within the meaning of art. 189 unless otherwise indicated.

[59] Directives may be addressed by the Council to the Commission; arts. 111(2), 113(3). It seems clear that although art. 189 contemplates that directives should be addressed only to member states, a directive addressed by the Council to the Commission has the same legal characteristics of binding the Commission as to the result but leaving it free as to form and means.

[60] This is of some importance with regard to federal states, where the legislative power may be shared between different member states. Usually, form and means will involve a choice among parliamentary legislation, regulations having the force of law, and a change of administrative practice, and a decision on the exact content of the new rule to replace the old.

[61] For example, the Treaty does not contemplate that the matters set out in art. 220 should be dealt with by directives.

lation, would necessitate much consequential national legislation.

Directives are the normal means of requiring member states to carry out harmonization of laws[62] and to deal with spheres regulated in different ways and in accordance with different concepts, such as the right of establishment. When common law countries such as England and Ireland are in the EEC, directives may be appropriate where it would be difficult to frame a regulation which would fit all the existing national laws.

Decisions

Decisions are made in individual cases and are binding in every respect on the member states or private enterprises to which they are directed. Unlike a directive, a decision addressed to a member state may bind it to use a specified form and means to bring about a certain result. Decisions addressed to private enterprises, if they involve a pecuniary obligation, are enforceable as a judgment of a court.[63] As administrative acts, they are binding in national law since they are made under powers conferred by the Treaty or by regulations, both of which are in force in national law. Questions of interpretation and validity of decisions raised before national courts are referred to the Community Court for a ruling.[64] A private enterprise directly affected can usually challenge the validity of decisions in the Community Court, but the validity of regulations can be challenged only in limited circumstances.[65]

Types of acts

If the type of measures to be taken by the Council is not specified,[66] the Community institution may choose among the different types of Community action. The Treaty lays down the effect of regulations, directives, and decisions and does not give any other indication what acts of these types are.[67] This is important, since the Treaty recognizes that a decision can be "disguised" as a regulation.[68]

Regulations, directives, and decisions of both the Council and the Commission must state the reasons for which they are adopted. They must refer to the relevant proposal of the Commission or the views of the Assembly or the Economic and Social Committee, where these are required.[69] This is because the validity of these acts may have to be considered by the Community Court. Failing to give the reasons in the preamble to the act or giving improper reasons will render the act invalid.

The Treaty provides the framework for an elaborate but flexible hierarchy[70] of legal rules. The Council issues a directive; the directive is carried out by the member states through their legislative

[62] Art. 100.

[63] Art. 192.

[64] Art. 177.

[65] Art. 173; however, see art. 184.

[66] E.g., arts. 20, 51, 75.

[67] Valentine, "The Jurisdiction of the Court of Justice of the European Communities to Annul Executive Action," 36 Brit. Yb. Int'l L. 174, 180, 210 (1960).

[68] Art. 173(2); see Confédération Nationale des Producteurs de Fruits et Légumes v. EEC Council, 8 Recueil 901 (1962), [1963] Common Market Law Reports [hereinafter cited as C.M.L.R.] 160; Fédération Nationale de la Boucherie en Gros v. EEC Council, 8 Recueil 943 (1962), [1963] C.M.L.R. 160; Sangarides, "Nature juridique des actes émis par le Conseil et la Commission de la C.E.E.," 14 Revue Hellénique de Droit International 138 (1961).

[69] Art. 190; see EEC Commission v. Italy, 7 Recueil 633 (1961), [1962] C.M.L.R. 39; Germany v. EEC Commission, 9 Recueil 129, [1963] C.M.L.R. 347 (the "import duties on wine" case); Germany v. EEC Commission, 9 Recueil 269, [1963] C.M.L.R. 369. It is not clear if reasons must be given explaining why the views of the consultative institutions are not being accepted; see Macciorlati Dalmas & Figli v. High Authority, 11 Recueil 227 (1965).

[70] Cartou, Le Marché Commun et le Droit Public 80 (1959).

or administrative authorities; and decisions under the new national law are taken by the courts or tribunals. Or the Council issues a regulation which may authorize the Commission to issue more detailed regulations, and decisions under these regulations will be made by the national courts, the Commission, or the Community Court.

Authorizations[71] are a type of decision permitting what would otherwise be illegal instead of applying a rule of law to a particular situation. Authorizations usually relate to matters which are left by the Treaty to member states and over which the Community institutions have only supervisory power.[72] These matters include monetary measures[73] and regional economic policy.[74]

The Council and the Commission may also address recommendations or opinions, which are not binding, to member states or to enterprises. They may be given either as a preliminary to a binding decision[75] or some other action[76] or without any subsequent measure.[77] Proposals of the Commission for action to be taken by the Council should probably be regarded as recommendations. The Treaty contemplates recommendations by the Commission to speed up economic integration or to adopt common policies.

Some acts are not within any of these categories, such as the general programs on freedom of establishment and services,[78] amendments of the Treaty,[79] and institutional acts, such as budgetary acts and the creation and enactment of rules of committees.[80]

THE ASSEMBLY AND OTHER PRIMARILY CONSULTATIVE INSTITUTIONS

The Assembly[81] is composed of six delegates from Luxembourg, fourteen each from Belgium and the Netherlands, and thirty-six each from Italy, Germany, and France. The delegates sit according to their party affiliation—Christian Democrat, Socialist, Gaullist, or Liberal—and not according to nationality. The present representation is weighted in favor of the smaller states to insure representation of all their principal political parties. It is based on the system used in the Consultative Assembly of the Council of Europe,[82] each state having twice the number of seats allocated to it in the Consultative Assembly. If this system was adhered to, Britain would have thirty-six seats; Denmark, ten; Ireland, eight; and Norway, ten. However, the system would almost certainly be altered if direct elections for the Assembly were instituted.

The political importance of the Assembly would increase if its members were elected by direct universal suffrage. Its most important legal power at present is the power to dismiss the Commission.[83] This power is probably too drastic

[71] Contemplated by arts. 17(4), 33(6), 37(3), 46, 73, 91, 98, 107, 108, 115.

[72] Cartou, Le Marché Commun et le Droit Public 81, 88–89 (1959).

[73] Arts. 104–109, especially art. 108.

[74] Art. 92.

[75] E.g., arts. 169, 170, 37(6), 109.

[76] E.g., arts. 91, 102.

[77] E.g., arts. 14(6), 15(2), 35, 64, 71, 81, 105(1), 108, 111, 113, 118. See art. 155.

[78] Arts. 54, 63.

[79] Arts. 14(7), 33(8), 138(3), 235.

[80] Art. 153.

[81] On proposals to strengthen the powers of the Assembly, see its resolution of June 27, 1963, in 1963 Journal Officiel 1916-18/63. See also Political and Economic Planning, Direct Elections and the European Parliament (1960).

[82] Samkalden et al., "The Effect of Admission of New Member States on the Institutions of the E.E.C.," 10 Sociaal-Economische Wetgeving 345, 348 (1962).

[83] Art. 144; ECSC Treaty, art. 24; Euratom Treaty, art. 114. For the proposals on direct elections, see 1960 Journal Officiel 834/60.

to be used, but it symbolizes the principle of democratic control over the European executives, which are not subject to control or dismissal by the governments of member states. Members of the Assembly may question the Commission,[84] and the Commission's annual general report is made to the Assembly.[85] Private enterprises can therefore obtain information officially by getting a question asked by a member of the Assembly. Apart from the cases in which it is consulted,[86] including cases where consultation is not required by the Treaty, the Assembly has no control over the acts of the Council or Commission,[87] and national parliaments have very little. The Council can be heard by the Assembly.[88] The Commission is supervised by the Assembly in its work, including its work of collaboration with the Council.[89].

The Economic and Social Committee[90] is an institution common to the EEC and Euratom. It is established on the basis of vocational representation. Belgium and the Netherlands have twelve members each and Luxembourg has five; the other three states have twenty-four each. The members are appointed in their personal capacities by the Council, acting unanimously after consultation with the Commission, from lists prepared by each member state. The Treaty requires that the Committee be consulted in connection with certain matters,[91] but it may be consulted at any time. The Committee is a forum in which interested groups can organize themselves on a Community-wide basis to express their points of view, to insure that they can join in the work for economic integration. Like the Assembly, it is Community-minded, and its importance in formulating Community policy and a Community outlook is considerable.

The Committee of Permanent Representatives is important in practice, although it is barely mentioned in the Treaty and has only the legal powers which the Council confers on it. It consists of one representative from each member state. It provides a standing liaison between the Commission, the Council, and the governments of member states and enables them to work together when the Council is not in session; it does much of the preparation of the work done by the Council.[92]

[84] Art. 140.

[85] Art. 143.

[86] These cases are listed by Sawyer & Doeker, "The European Economic Community as a Constitutional System," 4 Inter-Am. L. Rev. 217, 226 (1962). In its First General Report, para. 28 (1958), the EEC Commission announced its intention to consult the Assembly as much as possible. See Rapport . . . sur les compétences et les pouvoirs du Parlement européen, A.P.E. Doc. No. 31 (1963).

[87] See Birkelbach Report, A.P.E. Doc. No. 122, paras. 75, 77 (1961–62).

[88] Art. 137. See, however, Alting von Geusau, European Organizations and Foreign Relations of States 137 (1962).

[89] Cartou, Le Marché Commun et le Droit Public 46–49 (1959). Professor Hallstein, A.P.E. Débats, Sess. 1963–64, Séances du 24 au 28 juin 1963, at 167, stresses the following reasons for the importance of the Assembly: it establishes the Community as an entity separate from the member states; it stresses the political nature of the Community; it is the democratic element in the Community; and it constitutes the most dynamic element in the Community. The whole debate on the powers of the Assembly (id. at 156–86) is of importance.

[90] Arts. 193–98. The Règlement Intérieur of the Economic and Social Committee is at 1959 Journal Officiel 493/59.

[91] Arts. 43, 47, 49, 54, 63, 75, 79, 100, 118, 121, 126, 127, 128.

[92] See art. 151(2); Alting von Geusau, European Organizations and Foreign Relations of States 132–33 (1962). M. Schaus has said that the Permanent Representatives were "not merely the ambassadors of the countries to the Community but also of the Community to the countries." See also Lindberg, The Political Dynamics of European Economic Integration, passim (1963), and art. 16 of the provisional rules of procedure of the Council.

Reference should be made to the Consultative Committee on Cartels and Monopolies,[93] the committees of the Assembly,[94] the Economic Policy Committee, the Monetary Committee,[95] the Transport Committee,[96] and the Committee on the European Social Fund.[97]

THE COURT

Jurisdiction over member states

The Court of Justice is common to all three Communities. Its jurisdiction under the EEC Treaty is considered here.[98] At present, the Court consists of seven judges.[99] The number of judges must be uneven,[100] and there should be at least one judge from each member state to provide detailed knowledge of its laws. If four more states joined the EEC, the Court would therefore probably be increased to eleven judges.[101] Advocate-General Lagrange[102] describes the prin-

[93] Reg. 17, art. 10, 1962 Journal Officiel 204/62, 1962 EEC Bull. No. 2, Supp.

[94] Heidelberg, "Parliamentary Control and Political Groups in the Three European Regional Communities," 26 Law & Contemp. Prob. 430 (1961).

[95] Arts. 105, and 69, 71, 73, 107, 108, 109; 1958 Journal Officiel 390/58; EEC Commission, Premier Rapport d'activité du Comité Monetaire, Annex III (1959).

[96] Art. 83; 1958 Journal Officiel 509/58.

[97] Art. 124; 1960 Journal Officiel 1201/60. The effect on these Committees of the entry of new states is discussed by Samkalden et al., "The Effect of Admission of New Member States on the Institutions of the E.E.C.," 10 Sociaal-Economische Wetgeving 345, 359–67 (1962).

[98] Arts. 164–88. The corresponding provisions in the other treaties are ECSC Treaty, arts. 31–45, and Euratom Treaty, arts. 136–60. The Rules of Procedure of the Court are published at 1960 Journal Officiel 17/60 and have been translated by the European Institute of the University of Leyden. On the Court generally, see Bebr, Judicial Control of the European Communities (1962) [hereinafter cited as Bebr, Judicial Control]; Stein & Hay, "New Legal Remedies of Enterprises: A Survey," in 1 American Enterprise in the European Common Market: A Legal Profile 459 (Stein & Nicholson ed. 1960); Lagrange, "The Role of the Court of Justice of the European Communities as Seen Through Its Case Law," 26 Law & Contemp. Prob. 400 (1961); Valentine, The Court of Justice of the European Coal and Steel Community (1955); van Reepinghen & Orianne, "La Procédure devant la Cour de justice des Communautés européennes," 1961 Journal des Tribunaux 89, 111, 125.

[99] Art. 165.

[100] See art. 165(2); Protocol on the Statute of the Court, art. 15.

[101] Samkalden et al., "The Effect of Admission of New Member States on the Institutions of the E.E.C.," 10 Sociaal-Economische Wetgeving 345, 356–59 (1962), say that the number of judges should be different from the number of member states. Since the volume of work will increase, due to both the progress of the Community and the admission of new states, an increase in the number of judges seems reasonable. The learned authors also suggest that the independence of the judges should be more fully secured by allowing longer terms of appointment (the present term is only six years). They also suggest the appointment of a third Advocate-General, from a common law country (presumably Britain rather than Ireland; a Scots lawyer would seem suitable since he would know both common law and civil law). See Schwarzenberger, "Federalism and Supranationalism in the European Communities," in English Law and the Common Market 17 (Keeton & Schwarzenberger ed. 1963); Lloyd, "The Court of Justice of the European Economic Community," in id. at 34.

Judges of the Court are appointed by the governments of member states acting unanimously; art. 167.

[102] "Le rôle de la Cour de Justice des Communautés européennes," in Les Problèmes Juridiques 41, 42. In their excellent study, Dumon and Rigaux use the classification of van Hecke found in "La structure institutionnelle de la Communauté du charbon et de l'acier," 1951 Journal des Tribunaux 277, 279. The Court has (1) an administrative jurisdiction to control the legality of Community acts; (2) a constitutional jurisdiction to maintain the balance of powers between the Community organs; (3) a civil jurisdiction over actions involving the Community; (4) an international jurisdiction dealing with disputes involving the actions of member states; and, Dumon and Rigaux add, (5) a disciplinary jurisdiction over matters relating to in-

cipal functions of the Court as the protection of the rights of the individual against illegal acts of the administrative authorities and the maintenance of the institutional balance and the limits imposed by the Treaty on the powers delegated by it. The provisions relating to the Court clearly demonstrate the state-like institutional structure of the Community.[103]

The Court has an international jurisdiction to decide if a member state is in breach of its obligations under the Treaty. The Commission can initiate proceedings by asking the state to submit its arguments, after which the Commission issues a reasoned opinion, which is not binding.[104] If the state does not comply with the opinion, the Commission refers the matter to the Court.

A member state can initiate proceedings before the Commission against another state. Both states present their cases and reply to the other's arguments in writing and orally, and the Commission gives a reasoned opinion. If this is not complied with, or if the Commission gives no decision within three months, the plaintiff state may take the case to the Court. To minimize the direct conflict between the states and to clarify the issues for the Court, the Commission is required to give an opinion presenting an impartial point of view. The defendant state is bound by the decision of the Court. A private enterprise cannot bring a member state before the Court directly under the EEC Treaty.[105]

The Court also has jurisdiction to decide any dispute between member states connected with the object of the Treaty and submitted to it under a special agreement[106] and to decide whether treaties to be concluded on behalf of the Community are compatible with the Treaty.[107] Apart from this, the Court has no power to give advisory opinions under the EEC Treaty.[108]

Jurisdiction over Community institutions[109]

Actions to Annul Illegal Acts

The Court has administrative jurisdiction to insure that Community institutions comply with the Treaty. The Court alone can invalidate illegal acts and compel the institutions to take action. Non-binding acts of the Council or Commission are not within the Court's jurisdiction.

Proceedings to have an act of the Commission or the Council declared invalid can be brought by these two institutions themselves or by a member state, even if the state is not affected by the act in question. An enterprise may sue for

---

dividuals whose tenure of office is normally guaranteed; Dumon & Rigaux, "I Tribunali Internazionali e Sopranazionali," in 2 Primo Congresso Internazionale dei Magistrati 621, 651–52, 689–94 (1959) [hereinafter cited as Dumon & Rigaux].

[103] Cartou, Le Marché Commun et le Droit Public 10 (1959); Fédération Charbonnière de Belgique v. High Authority, 2 Recueil 199, 231, 263 (1956) (conclusions of Advocate-General Lagrange); Monaco, Observations sur la juridiction de la Cour de Justice des Communautés européennes (1962).

[104] Art. 189.

[105] See with regard to the ECSC, Buergenthal, "The Private Appeal Against Illegal State Activities in the E.C.S.C.," 11 Am. J. Comp. L. 325 (1962). It was thought preferable to give the plaintiff state the right to bring the case before the Court directly, if the Commission failed to issue an opinion, rather than raise it indirectly by asking the Court to order the Commission under art. 175 to give an opinion. See, however, N.V. Algemene Transport- en Expeditie Onderneming Van Gend & Loos v. Administration Fiscal Néerlandaise [hereinafter cited as the *Van Gend & Loos* case], 9 Recueil 1, [1963] C.M.L.R. 105.

[106] Art. 182.

[107] Art. 228(1).

[108] See, however, ECSC Treaty, art. 95(4).

[109] See Buergenthal, "Appeals for Annulment by Enterprises in the E.C.S.C.," 10 Am. J. Comp. L. 227 (1961).

annulment of a decision directed to it or a decision which "is of direct and individual concern" to it, even if the decision is made in the form of a regulation or a decision addressed to another person.[110] An enterprise cannot sue for annulment of a directive or of a decision addressed to a member state.[111] An act not addressed to an enterprise concerns it directly and individually only if it is in substance a decision and not a legislative act. To apply this provision, the Court has made use of the concept of "interests aggrieved" derived from national administrative laws.[112] Actual injury, or a certain and immediate threat of direct injury, is essential. If an enterprise has only the same interest as all other enterprises within the terms of a regulation, the enterprise cannot sue for annulment of the regulation. The fact that the plaintiff is a group or association of enterprises is not enough to give it standing to sue, since it is not individually affected by regulations affecting its members generally.[113] The enterprise may be able to persuade its member state to sue to annul a regulation or a decision which the enterprise itself cannot challenge. The grounds on which an act can be annulled are the same in all cases.

Article 184: Holding a Community Regulation Invalid Without Annulling It

The Treaty allows an enterprise which cannot directly challenge the validity of a regulation to invoke the grounds of invalidity, so as to have the regulation held "inapplicable." This allows the validity of a decision to be contested in the Community Court on the grounds that the regulation under which the decision was taken was vitiated by one of the faults specified in Article 173.[114] This is necessary, since enterprises cannot normally challenge the validity of regulations directly. Holding a regulation "inapplicable" does not amount to annulment; an act can be annulled only in an action under Article 173 brought for that purpose. A successful plea of "inapplicability" or "exception of illegality"[115] affects only the litigants and operates from the

[110] Art. 173(2). The French text reads: "*décisions . . . prises sous l'apparence d'un règlement . . .*" ECSC Treaty, art. 33; Euratom Treaty, art. 146. See Confédération Nationale des Producteurs des Fruits et Légumes v. EEC Council, 8 Recueil 901 (1962), [1963] C.M.L.R. 160; Fédération Nationale de la Boucherie en Gros v. EEC Council, 8 Recueil 943 (1962), [1963] C.M.L.R. 160; Glucoseries Réunies v. EEC Commission, 10 Recueil 811, [1964] C.M.L.R. 596; Plaumann & Co. v. EEC Commission, 9 Recueil 197 (1963), [1964] C.M.L.R. 29.

[111] Stein & Hay, "Legal Remedies of Enterprises in the European Economic Community," 9 Am. J. Comp. L. 375, 387 (1960).

[112] Bebr, Judicial Control 69–71; Groupement des Industries Sidérurgiques Luxembourgeoises v. High Authority, 2 Recueil 87 (1956), and the conclusions of Advocate-General Roemer at 123–24; Lagrange, "The Role of the Court of Justice of the European Communities as Seen Through Its Case Law," 26 Law & Contemp. Prob. 400, 407–408 (1961); Fédération Charbonnière de Belgique v. High Authority, 2 Recueil 199, 246–47 (1956) (conclusions of Advocate-General Lagrange); Migliazza, "La jurisprudence de la cour de Justice des Communautés européennes et le problème des sources de droit," 31 Annuaire de l'A.A.A. 96, 100 (1961); Lagrange, "Les Actions en Justice dans le Régime des Communautés européennes," 10 Sociaal-Economische Wetgeving 81, 85 (1962).

[113] Bebr, Judicial Control 77–79; Fédération Nationale de la Boucherie en Gros v. EEC Council, 8 Recueil 943 (1962), [1963] C.M.L.R. 160.

[114] This is the purpose of art. 36 of the ECSC Treaty, which is, however, more narrowly phrased. Meroni v. High Authority, 4 Recueil 51, 101 (1958) (conclusions of Advocate-General Roemer); Compagnie des Hauts Fourneaux de Chasse v. High Authority, 4 Recueil 155, 186 (1958).

[115] Bebr, Judicial Control 138–48. In Roman law and in modern civil law an exception is an affirmative defense corresponding to the common law "confession and avoidance" which does not contest the obligation or duty alleged

time of the decision[116] because of the need for certainty in administration, since Article 184, unlike Article 173, is not subject to a time limit. The "exception of illegality" is available in the EEC only in connection with regulations.[117] The provision creating the "exception of illegality" does not apply in the national courts.[118]

An "exception of illegality" may be pleaded by an enterprise, on any ground mentioned in Article 173(1), against any regulation.[119] If an "exception of illegality" is successful, a decision of any Community authority based upon the regulation in question is invalid. The regulation is rendered ineffective, since any decisions based on it will be met by "exceptions of illegality" based on the same grounds. Presumably, therefore, the Commission or the Council will take steps to remedy the defect in the regulation, even though they are not formally required to do so.[120]

The "exception of illegality" is of limited usefulness because it can be used only after a decision addressed to the interested enterprise has been taken pursuant to the regulation. The "exception" is a shield and not a sword, and an enterprise may be prejudiced by being unable to bring proceedings which would clarify its position.

The Grounds for Invalidity and for the "Exception of Illegality"

The grounds for contesting the validity or "applicability" of an act of the Commission or the Council in either the Community Court or the national courts are specified in Article 173. The grounds under Article 173 are *incompétence* (roughly, lack of jurisdiction), *violation des formes substantielles* (roughly, violation of basic procedural rules), *détournement de pouvoir* (roughly, misuse of power), and infringement of the Treaty or of any rule of law relating to its application.[121] The four grounds overlap, and the Court has not yet defined

but introduces a new element relieving the defendant from liability. Art. 184 creates an exception in the Roman law sense not because of the substance of the allegation (which is that the decision is improper and should be treated as ineffective) but because the regulation cannot be annulled under it.

[116] Bebr, Judicial Control 139, 147. Note that a decision of the Court annulling an act has retroactive force and affects everyone. If the act annulled is a regulation, all decisions based on it are automatically invalidated.

[117] Even if a directive was invalid for one of the reasons given in art. 173, its invalidity would not affect the validity of the act the national authority had taken pursuant to it, by which alone an enterprise would be affected. It is difficult to visualize a case in which an enterprise which could not have challenged a decision under art. 173 would be in a position to plead its illegality before the Community Court.

[118] Bebr, Judicial Control 142–43. See Milchwerke Heinz Wöhrmann & Sohn KG v. EEC Commission, 8 Recueil 965 (1962), [1963] C.M.L.R. 152; Hay, "Federal Jurisdiction of the Common Market Court," 12 Am. J. Comp. L. 21, 28 (1963).

[119] Art. 184.

[120] Art. 176. See Bebr, Judicial Control 199–200; LaGrange, "Les actions en Justice dans le Régime des Communautés européennes," 10 Sociaal-Economische Wetgeving 81, 90 (1962).

[121] These are substantially the same as those for appeals for *excès de pouvoir* under the case law of the French Conseil d'Etat, which is similar to the administrative laws of the rest of the Six. The administrative laws of the Six are much more like each other than like English or Irish administrative law. See Stein & Hay, "New Legal Remedies of Enterprises: A Survey," in 1 American Enterprise in the European Common Market: A Legal Profile 459, 468–70 (Stein & Nicholson ed. 1960), and authorities cited therein; Lagrange, "Le rôle de la Cour de Justice des Communautés européennes," in Les Problèmes Juridiques 41, 42; Valentine, "The Jurisdiction of the Court of Justice of the European Communities to Annul Executive Action," 36 Brit. Yb. Int'l L. 174, 185 (1960); Gormley, "The Significant Role of French Administrative Jurisprudence as Presently Applied by the Court of the European Communities," 8 S. Dak. L. Rev. 32 (1963).

any of them nor has it followed the somewhat technical case law of any of the member states very closely. *Incompétence* is in some ways similar to ultra vires in common law; *violation des formes substantielles* includes denial of "natural justice" in English law and "due process of law," as well as other breaches of procedural requirements; and *détournement de pouvoir* is similar to the "use of a discretionary power for an improper purpose."[122] Infringement of any rule of law relating to the application of the Treaty covers infringement of regulations and of unwritten standards of administrative conduct comparable to the French *principes généraux du droit.*[123] If another Community institution must be consulted before an act is adopted,[124] if the parties affected must be given a chance to state their case,[125] or if an act must state the reasons for its adoption,[126] failure to comply with these rules will be a violation of procedural rules, as well as a violation of the Treaty. Failure to comply with procedural rules will be a ground of invalidity only if the rule is one of substantial importance.

Détournement de pouvoir occurs when an act within the powers or jurisdiction of an institution is done for some purpose not intended by the law.[127] An inquiry must be made into the propriety and adequacy of the actual reasons, as distinct from the stated reasons, for an act. Bad faith is not necessary but a legally improper intention or an arbitrary action constitutes *détournement de pouvoir.* Owing to the wide discretionary powers given by the EEC Treaty, *détournement de pouvoir* may become of great practical importance.

It is not clear when the Court will raise *ex officio* a ground of invalidity not argued by the parties, but it appears that it has on occasion done so.[128]

Other aspects of the Court's jurisdiction

The Treaty provides a remedy where the Council or the Commission illegally fails to act.[129] This remedy is open to a private enterprise only if the Council or the Commission fails to address a deci-

---

The corresponding provisions in the other Treaties are Euratom Treaty, art. 146; ECSC Treaty, art. 33. See Valentine, "The Jurisdiction of the Court of Justice of the European Communities to Annul Executive Action," 36 Brit. Yb. Int'l L. at 176 (1960).

[122] De Smith, Judicial Review of Administrative Action 190 (1959); see generally id. at ch. 4. See Hamson, Executive Discretion and Judicial Control (1954).

[123] The Dutch text of the Treaty speaks only of "regulations relating to its application." See Wolf, "The Role of the Court of Justice of the European Communities in the Antitrust Structure of the Common Market," 31 Fordham L. Rev. 621, 628–29 (1963); Donner, "The Court of Justice of the European Communities," 17 Record of N.Y.C.B.A. 232, 237 (1962).

[124] Consultation of the Assembly or the Economic and Social Committee is required in many places in the Treaty. With regard to decisions in the technical sense, see Reg. 17, art. 10.

[125] ECSC Treaty, arts. 36, 66(4).

[126] EEC Treaty, art. 190. See Germany v. EEC Commission, 9 Recueil 129, [1963] C.M.L.R. 347; Germany v. EEC Commission, 9 Recueil 269, [1963] C.M.L.R. 369.

[127] Netherlands v. High Authority, 1 Recueil 203, 226 (1954); Fédération Charbonnière de Belgique v. High Authority, 2 Recueil 193, 310 (1956); see Wirtschaftsvereinigung Eisen- und Stahlindustrie v. High Authority, 4 Recueil 261, 356 (1958) (conclusions of Advocate-General Lagrange).

[128] Valentine, "The Jurisdiction of the Court of Justice of the European Communities to Annul Executive Action," 36 Brit. Yb. Int'l L. 174, 177–80 (1960), and the cases cited there.

[129] Compare the writ of mandamus in British and Irish law; de Smith, Judicial Review of Administrative Action 263–65, 430–55 (1959). The Treaty provisions discussed in the text are arts. 175–76. The corresponding provisions are ECSC Treaty, art. 35, and Euratom Treaty, art. 148.

sion to it and the failure to act is a violation of the Treaty.[130] Proceedings cannot be brought by an enterprise to compel the adoption of a directive, a regulation, or a non-binding act.[131] No proceedings can be brought in the Court until two months after the Community institution has been called on to act. A private enterprise cannot sue a member state in the Court for breach of the Treaty, nor can it sue the Commission for failure to determine that a state is in breach of the treaty.[132]

In most cases, the Court may uphold an act of the Council or the Commission or annul it on one of the grounds specified, but it may not substitute its own decision for that of the other institutions. However, regulations may give the Court full jurisdiction as to the merits of sanctions imposed by the regulations.[133] The Court cannot annul the decision imposing the sanction except on a ground specified in Article 173, but it can increase, reduce, or suspend all penalties imposed by the decision.[134]

The fact that the Community is a party to a case does not deprive the national courts of jurisdiction.[135] In cases arising out of contracts other than contracts with Community officials and contracts containing an arbitration clause that provides for the exclusive jurisdiction of the Court, national courts have jurisdiction.[136] The contractual liability of the Community is governed by the proper law of the contract. In non-contractual actions, the Court has jurisdiction over claims against the Community for compensation "in accordance with the general principles common to the laws of member states"[137] for damage caused by its institutions or by its officials in the performance of their duties.[138] This jurisdiction is probably exclusive, because the law governing liability could hardly be laid down by a national court.

The Court also has jurisdiction in con-

[130] Appeals against illegal failure to act can be brought in a range of cases slightly narrower than that in which an enterprise could appeal to have the act annulled under art. 173; see Lagrange, "Les actions en Justice dans le Régime des Communautés européennes," 10 Sociaal-Economische Wetgeving 81, 91 (1962); Società Industriale Acciaierie San Michele v. High Authority, 8 Recueil 859 (1962), [1963] C.M.L.R. 13.

[131] This can be done by member states and other Community institutions.

[132] Donner, "The Court of Justice of the European Communities," 17 Record of N.Y.C.B.A. 232, 236 (1963); see, however, for the position in the ECSC, Buergenthal, "The Private Appeal Against Illegal State Activities in the E.C.S.C.," 11 Am. J. Comp. L. 325 (1962); ECSC Treaty, art. 65(5)(ii); Schlieker v. High Authority, 9 Recueil 173, [1963] C.M.L.R. 281; cf. the *Van Gend & Loos* case, 9 Recueil 1, [1963] C.M.L.R. 105.

[133] This concept is also derived from French administrative law.

[134] Art. 172; cf. ECSC Treaty, art. 33(1).

[135] Art. 183; see Ropers, "Des conflits entre la Cour de justice des Communautés et les juridictions nationales," 36 Juris Classeur périodique (Semaine juridique) [hereinafter cited as J.C.P.] 1709 (1962). However, art. 173, e.g., gives the Court exclusive jurisdiction.

[136] See arts. 179, 181.

[137] Cf. Statute of the International Court of Justice, art. 38; Fédération Charbonnière de Belgique v. High Authority, 2 Recueil 193, 305 (1956); Migliazza, "La jurisprudence de la Cour de Justice des Communautés européennes et le problème des sources de droit," 31 Annuaire de l'A.A.A. 96, 104–107 (1960).

[138] Arts. 178, 215. See Stein & Hay, "New Legal Remedies of Enterprises: A Survey," in 1 American Enterprise in the European Common Market: A Legal Profile 459, 490–99 (Stein & Nicholson ed. 1960); Dumon, "La Cour de Justice des Communautés européennes et les juridictions des Etats membres," 14 Rev. Int. de Droit Comp. 369, 385–86, 387–89 (1962). Conflicts of jurisdiction can arise from the phrase "in the performance of their duties" (Dumon & Rigaux 621, 659), since it is not clear whether this provision extends to all cases of non-contractual liability of the Community or is limited to liability for acts in the performance of the duties of the institutions and servants.

nection with disputes connected with the European Investment Bank.[139]

ARTICLE 177

The Treaty, decisions, and regulations are in force in the national laws of member states, and national courts must decide the interpretation and validity of acts of Community institutions and the interpretation of the Treaty.[140] Article 177 goes part of the way towards insuring uniform interpretation and a uniform view on the validity of Community acts by requiring national courts of final appeal to refer such questions to the Community Court.[141] A court whose decisions are open to appeal may refer such questions to the Court but is not bound to do so, so uniformity is not assured in all cases. The decisions of the lower courts in civil law countries are not binding precedents in future cases,[142] so that little harm is done by an incorrect decision on Community law. In Ireland and England, decisions, even of inferior courts, are usually binding precedents, and a modification of this rule with regard to decisions on Community law would probably be necessary.[143]

Tribunals within Article 177

Article 177 applies to courts[144] and to administrative tribunals.[145] In England and Ireland, appeals lie on most points of law from administrative tribunals to the ordinary courts. Some administrative bodies have neither judicial nor quasi-judicial[146] functions and may not be courts of law under Article 177.

Since only points of Community law can be referred to the Court, it is submitted that a court whose decisions can be appealed only on points of law is not bound to refer a question of interpretation or validity to the Court. If the leave of the court is necessary for an appeal from its decision, and if it does not give leave to appeal, it is bound to refer questions of Community law to the Court. Usually, however, leave to appeal is given by the court which will hear the appeal;

[139] Art. 180.

[140] See Dumon & Rigaux 678–79. See also Morelli, "La Cour de Justice des Communautés européennes en tant que juge interne," 19 Zeitschrift für Ausländisches öffentliches Recht und Völkerrecht 269 (1958); Donner, "National Law and the Case Law of the Court of Justice of the European Communities," 1 Common Market L. Rev. 8 (1963); Pépy, "L'article 177 du Traité de Rome et les juridictions françaises," 52 Rev. Crit. Droit Int. Privé 475, 695 (1963).

[141] A similar procedure is well known in French administrative law. Lagrange, "Les actions en Justice dans le Régime des Communautés européennes," 10 Sociaal-Economische Wetgeving 81, 100 (1962).

[142] Lloyd, "The Court of Justice of the European Economic Community," in English Law and the Common Market 34, 47–48 (Keeton & Schwarzenberger ed. 1963). Art. 177 is copied from art. 23 of the Italian Law No. 87 of March 11, 1953, on the jurisdiction of the Italian Constitutional Court; Catalano, "Rapports entre le droit Communautaire et le droit des Etats membres," 1964 Journal des Tribunaux 53.

[143] Since the Court is not bound by its own decisions, an Irish court should not hold itself absolutely bound by a decision of a court of equal standing on a point of Community law.

[144] Art. 177 also covers the interpretation of the statutes of any bodies set up by a formal measure of the Council, if the statutes so provide. This seems unlikely to be of much importance in the national courts. Art. 177 corresponds to Euratom Treaty, art. 150; cf. ECSC Treaty, art. 41.

[145] The French text uses the word *juridiction*, although the other official texts seem to mean courts. See Bebr, "The Relationship Between Community Law and the Law of the Member States," in Restrictive Practices, Patents, Trade Marks and Unfair Competition in the Common Market, Int'l & Comp. L.Q. Supp. No. 4, at 1, 9 (1962); see also the *Van Gend & Loos* case, 9 Recueil 1, [1963] C.M.L.R. 105.

[146] See de Smith, Judicial Review of Administrative Action, ch. 2 (1959); see also U.K. Tribunals and Enquiries Act, 1958, 6 & 7 Eliz. 2, c. 66.

this is the position in certain cases in Germany and Britain. In practice, to carry out the object of Article 177 and to insure uniformity throughout the EEC, the court which may refuse leave to appeal should regard itself as bound to refer the question of Community law to the Court, so that the case cannot be finally decided without the question being ruled on by the Court. If the lower court has not referred the question to the Community Court, the highest court should be bound to give leave to appeal, to prevent a breach of Article 177(3).[147]

In practice, a court of first instance normally should not refer questions to the Community Court, or too many litigants would incur the expense of arguing a case before the Court.[148] If the ultimate court of appeal refers a question of Community law to the Court, the application of the Court's interpretation to the facts by the national court is final. An appeal against the way the law stated by the Court has been applied to the facts is probably desirable. These considerations can be reconciled only if a court of first instance, a court of appeal, and a supreme court exist, as in Britain. Cases would be referred to the Community Court by the court of appeal, and the application of the Court's interpretation to the facts by the court of appeal could be reviewed by the Supreme Court. Of the two considerations, the first is probably more important. It follows that if Ireland joins the EEC, the Supreme Court rather than the High Court, a court of first instance in important cases, should refer questions to the Court; in England, it should be the Court of Appeal. Cases involving points of Community law should be heard by judges who have the necessary specialized knowledge.[149] The court intended to refer questions to the Community Court will not require any special expertise, because it will need only to frame the issue for the Community Court and it need not do so formally or precisely.[150]

Conditions for referral to the Community Court under Article 177

Under Article 177, inferior national courts may refer questions of Community law to the Court in certain circumstances and courts of final appeal must do so. In spite of a difference in the wording of the provision dealing with inferior courts[151] and that on courts of final ap-

[147] Bebr, "The Relationship Between Community Law and the Law of Member States," in Restrictive Practices, Patents, Trade Marks and Unfair Competition in the Common Market, Int'l & Comp. L.Q. Supp. No. 4, at 1, 10–11 (1962); Hay, "Federal Jurisdiction of the Common Market Court," 12 Am. J. Comp. L. 21, 30 (1963).

[148] Art. 177(2) permits a lower court to refer cases to the Court. A lower court should be able to refer cases to the Court by agreement with the parties. For the view that a lower national court should be bound to refer questions to the Court when the parties to the case so request, see Dumon, "La Cour de Justice des Communautés européennes et les juridictions des Etats membres," 14 Rev. Int. de Droit Comp. 372 (1962).

[149] In the House of Lords, before the breakdown of the negotiations, the Lord Chancellor said:

> This supervision of the European Court, which is designed to ensure uniformity throughout the member States is imposed ... by Article 177, which empowers all courts of member States, and requires their final courts, to refer such questions of interpretation or validity to the European Court. I . . . do not believe that the occasions for such a reference would be very many, and I do believe that we could take steps, within *our own system, to see to it that there would be consistent and expert interpretation of the Community law so that the need for reference will rarely arise* in courts of first instance.
>
> 243 H.L. Deb. (5th ser.) 422 (1962).
> (Emphasis supplied.)

[150] Société Kledingverkoopbedrijf de Geus en Uitdenbogerd v. Société de Droit Allemand Robert Bosch GmbH [hereinafter cited as Bosch v. de Geus], 8 Recueil 89, [1962] C.M.L.R. 1.

[151] Art. 177(2).

peal, it is submitted that courts of final appeal must refer a question of Community law to the Court only if its decision is "essential" to the resolution of the case.[152] To argue that a court of final appeal is bound to refer a question to the Court even where its decision does not depend on the resolution of the question is to leave the court with no criteria to decide when to refer questions and to ask the Court to give advisory opinions on academic points.

In theory, a decision as to the validity or interpretation of a Community act or the interpretation of the Treaty is "essential" to the judgment of the national court if the decision would affect the outcome of the case. However, a national court is not bound to refer a question to the Court if the answer is completely clear.[153] This means that a national court can avoid referring cases to the Court by holding that a Community act is clearly valid or invalid, or that a particular Treaty provision or Community act is not applicable to the case before it,[154] or that the meaning of a provision or an act which is applicable to the case needs no interpretation to decide the case. However, it is submitted that even if a Community act is obviously invalid, the question should always be referred to the Court. It is curious that inferior national courts should be allowed to hold an act of the Council or the Commission invalid, even if the decision has effect only between parties.

A ruling on a question of interpretation or validity may be "essential . . . to render judgment," even if the result would be the same under national law. It is important that the Court's decree should refer to any Community rule applicable and not base itself only on national law. Further, it is submitted that the phrase "render judgment" includes both the reasons and the result and that a question of Community law must be referred to the Court if consideration of it would be necessary in a fully reasoned judgment or decree.[155] However, this view has not been acted upon in at least one German case.[156]

Since even rulings that particular questions are clear are decisions on matters of Community law, the Court's decision that national courts need not refer questions to which the answers are clear means that national courts can decide questions of Community law, thus making possible the diversity of interpretations which Article 177 was intended to prevent.[157]

[152] Contra, Bebr, "The Relationship Between Community Law and the Law of Member States," in Restrictive Practices, Patents, Trade Marks and Unfair Competition in the Common Market, Int'l & Comp. L.Q. Supp. No. 4, at 1, 12-13 (1962). The Treaty often proceeds from the general to the particular and does not always repeat in subsequent paragraphs the requirements of the first. It is submitted, therefore, that the same provision should be read into art. 177(3). See Dumon & Rigaux 680; Costa v. ENEL, 10 Recueil 1141, 1177, [1964] C.M.L.R. 425, 436 (conclusions of Advocate-General Lagrange); Re Société des Pétroles Shell-Berre, Conseil d'Etat, June 19, 1964, [1964] C.M.L.R. 462.

[153] See Da Costa en Schaake N.V. v. Nederlandse Belastingadministratie, 9 Recueil 59, [1963] C.M.L.R. 224; Dumon & Rigaux 680–81.

[154] Dumon, "La Cour de Justice des Communautés européennes et les juridictions des Etats membres," 14 Rev. Int. de Droit Comp. 369, 374, 375–76 (1962); Da Costa en Schaake N.V. v. Nederlandse Belastingadministratie, 9 Recueil 59, [1963] C.M.L.R. 224.

[155] Parties before the Community Court are entitled to a ruling on each of their main lines of argument; Rules of Procedure of the Court, art. 67.

[156] 24 Europäische Wirtschaftgemeinschaft 493 (1958), translated in part in Stein & Hay, Cases on the Law and Institutions of the Atlantic Area 227–28 (prelim. ed. 1963); Lloyd, "The Court of Justice of the European Economic Community," in English Law and the Common Market 34, 51 (Keeton & Schwarzenberger ed. 1963).

[157] Some national courts have been unwilling to refer cases to the Court and have refused to

The Treaty provides no way in which the parties to the litigation or, probably, the Commission can raise before the Community Court the question whether a national court should have referred a point of Community law to the Court. This is an unfortunate omission from the Treaty.[158]

It is not clear whether national courts should raise questions of interpretation or validity if the litigants do not do so. If Community law renders illegal a transaction which is before the national tribunal, the tribunal should raise the question *ex officio,* at least if the illegality is clear.[159] The Community Court must insure the observance of law in the interpretation and application of the Treaty;[160] the national courts should do likewise and help to develop and enforce Community law. National tribunals must have this power, as litigants might by agreement avoid raising a question of Community law.[161]

Interpretation of non-binding acts of the Council or the Commission is not usually necessary to enable a national tribunal to give its judgment, but in any case in which it is necessary Article 177 will apply. It is not clear whether Article 177 binds the court of final appeal when the case involves interlocutory proceedings only.[162] If the question will not be reconsidered by the court, referral is necessary. It might result in injustice if the court refused to consider such a question in proceedings, for example, for an interlocutory injunction, but such proceedings cannot usually be delayed for the time required for an appeal to the Court. Since a question of Community law can normally be reopened at the full trial, the interlocutory injunction, even if it is confirmed by the court of final appeal, is probably not a decision "with no possibility of appeal under domestic law" under Article 177.[163] In practice, parties often treat the decision on an interlocutory injunction as the hearing of the case, and the injunction is made permanent without a full trial. Article 177 does not prevent even a court of last resort from considering a question which it is bound to refer to the Community Court, so a court of last resort could make an interlocutory order pending the decision of the Court.

Questioning the validity of a Community act on a referral from a national court

If an enterprise cannot sue directly to have an act annulled, it may be able to bring an action in the national courts which will raise the issue of the validity of the act of the Community institution. The question of validity may then be

---

do so on the grounds that the Community law was clear; see, for example, Re Société des Pétroles Shell-Berre, Conseil d'Etat, June 19, 1964, [1964] C.M.L.R. 462; Costa v. ENEL, Corte Costituzionale (Italian Constitutional Court), Feb. 24, 1964, [1964] C.M.L.R. 425, 430.

[158] See, however, note 178 below; Lenhoff, "Jurisdictional Relationship Between the Court of the European Communities and the Courts of the Member States," 12 Buffalo L. Rev. 296, 318, 323–24 (1963).

[159] Art. 164. This is the rule in English and Irish law. North Western Salt Co. v. Electrolytic Alkali Co., [1914] A.C. 461; Edler v. Auerbach, [1950] 1 K.B. 359, 371.

[160] Art. 164. See Dumon, "La Cour de Justice des Communautés européennes et les juridictions des Etats membres," 14 Rev. Int. de Droit Comp. 369, 376–77 (1962).

[161] The Treaty does not deal with the position before a court of final appeal where the parties agree or concede a particular interpretation of the Treaty. This is analogous to the case in which they fail to raise it. In all cases the Community interest requires that a court of final appeal should be bound to refer the case to the Court.

[162] Bebr, Judicial Control 191.

[163] The French text of art. 177(3) uses the word *recours,* which covers both an appeal and a challenge on technical grounds, such as *excès de pouvoir,* which does not permit the whole case to be reconsidered.

placed before the Community Court,[164] though the act itself cannot be annulled under this procedure. Whether a cause of action can be formulated in the national courts depends on the national law, on the subject matter of the decision of the Community institution, and on the surrounding circumstances. In the case of termination of state aid, for example, the enterprise might be able to sue the state for breach of contract. If the national law permits an action for a declaration of invalidity to be brought, the Treaty does not prevent the national courts from giving a declaration as to the validity of an act of the Community institution. This permits any enterprise with standing to sue in the national court to bring the question of the validity of a Community act before the Community Court, even if the enterprise has no standing to sue under Article 173 in the Community Court.[165]

When a national court whose decisions are subject to appeal decides on the validity of an act of a Community institution,[166] the effect of the decision is substantially the same as a successful plea of inapplicability under Article 184. Presumably, a national court would not allow an enterprise to contest the validity of an act which it could have had annulled under Article 173, if it had failed to do so within the time limit. National courts therefore probably must decide on the validity of Community acts where an enterprise challenges the validity of the regulation on which the decision of a national authority is based.

The grounds of invalidity under Article 177 are those specified in Article 173 as grounds for annulment.[167]

[164] Art. 177. See Milchwerke Heinz Wöhrmann & Sohn KG v. EEC Commission, 8 Recueil 965 (1962), [1963] C.M.L.R 152; Wagner v. Fohrman, 10 Recueil 381, [1964] C.M.L.R. 245.

[165] If art. 173 was directly applicable in national law, it could be argued that national courts, in actions for a declaration, should allow plaintiffs standing to sue only where they are allowed it under art. 173(2). The first paragraph of art. 173 is directly applicable, in a sense, because art. 177, which is directly applicable, contemplates that the validity of the acts of the Community institutions may be decided by national courts, on the grounds on which they can be challenged in the Community Court. Art. 173(1) is therefore directly applicable to the extent to which it is referred to in art. 177. This is hardly a strong argument for regarding art. 173(2) as directly applicable. Whether it is directly applicable will be ultimately a question for the Court to decide. If art. 173(2) is directly applicable, it is a question of national law whether it governs standing to sue for a declaration in the national courts. Clearly, an action for a declaration that a Community act is illegal should be governed by the same rules in the Community Court and in national courts, even though the decision of the national court does not annul the act. It is possible that an action for a declaration on the validity of an act of a Community institution can be brought in England (Rules of the Supreme Court, Order 15, Rule 17; Annual Practice 1963, at 281–85) and Ireland, when they are in the EEC. It is, however, unlikely that an enterprise would have standing to sue under the law of England and Ireland in many more cases than under the Treaty itself, especially since the remedy is discretionary; see Grand Junction Waterworks v. Hampton Urban Dist. Council, [1898] 2 Ch. 331; Merrick v. Liverpool Corp., [1910] 2 Ch. 460, 461; Bull v. Attorney General for New South Wales, [1916] 2 A.C. 564. See, however, generally de Smith, Judicial Review of Administrative Action, ch. III (1959). For a review in English of declaratory judgments in the law of various countries, see Borchard, Declaratory Judgments, ch. III (1941). If the enterprise could not sue for a declaration, it would be deprived of a remedy.

[166] National courts cannot annul Community acts; 2 von der Groeben & von Boeckh, Kommentar zum EWG Vertrag 155 (1960). Under ECSC Treaty, art. 41, a national court must refer a question of the validity of an act to the Court. On the effect of a decision of the Court on a question of "validity" referred to it under art. 177, see Dumon, "La Cour de Justice des Communautés européennes et les juridictions des Etats membres," 14 Rev. Int. de Droit Comp. 369, 377–78 (1962).

[167] Id. at 373; Dumon & Rigaux 674. When the question is referred to the Community Court, it must decide if the Community act is illegal under Community law, not national law.

The procedure under Article 177

If the national tribunal is bound or decides to refer a question to the Court, it may state the question in any appropriate way.[168] The Court will decide what questions of Treaty interpretation arise from the reference. It is the tribunal which notifies the Court, not the parties.[169] The Registrar of the Court then notifies the parties, the member states, and the Commission. The Council is notified only if an act of the Council is in question. Written arguments are submitted by all the parties notified who wish to do so.

All member states may submit arguments on the validity or the interpretation of decisions addressed to single enterprises, so that a uniform Community law will be developed. On questions of importance the Court has the benefit of the conclusions of the Advocate-General[170] and of all other interested parties. The full Court must always sit to deal with a question under Article 177 or with a case submittted by a member state or a Community institution; if the validity of a decision is directly challenged by an enterprise under Article 173(2), the Court may sit as a chamber.[171]

The Court rules on the validity or the interpretation of the act or the interpretation of the Treaty;[172] it does not decide the case formally, even if the only issue is the question of Community law.[173] However, it may not be possible

[168] Bosch v. de Geus, 8 Recueil 89, 102, [1962] C.M.L.R. 1, 26–27.

[169] Protocol on the Statute of the Court, art. 20; see Wagner v. Fohrmann, 10 Recueil 381, [1964] C.M.L.R. 245.

[170] The Advocates-General are standing *amici curiae* who submit impartial conclusions to the Court in addition to the arguments of the parties; arts. 166–67. The Advocates-General are, in theory and in fact, entirely independent of the judges of the Court. The institution is copied from the Commissaires du Gouvernement at the French Conseil d'Etat and from the laws of the Netherlands and of Belgium.

[171] That is, it may hear a case with only three or five judges, and not in plenary session; art. 165.

[172] The function of the Court is similar to that of a court hearing an appeal from a demurrer or an appeal by way of case stated. With regard to demurrers, see Order XXV of the Irish Supreme Court Rules, 1905 (No. 409 of 1905); for "cases stated" see, for example, Courts of Justice Act, 1924 Public Statutes of the [Irish] Oireachtas [hereinafter cited as Pub. Stat.] 75, § 83; Courts of Justice Act, 1936 Pub. Stat. 1219; § 38; Courts of Justice Act, 1947 Acts of the Oireachtas [hereinafter cited as Acts] 313, § 16. Compare the *recours en appréciation de validité* in French administrative law, and the duty of German trial judges and the Federal Supreme Court to refer all cases of the compatability of laws with the Constitution to the Federal Constitutional Court (Bundesverfassungsgericht); German Constitution, arts. 95, 100.

A brief note on citation of Irish legislation is appropriate. A citation which included the information expected by both American and Irish readers would be, e.g., Courts of Justice Act, 1947, 1947 Acts 313. Since the year of the act and the volume where it is found are the same, the year of the act has been omitted. Recent acts, which are not bound in a paginated volume, are cited by the number of the act, e.g., Finance Act, 1963 Acts, No. 23.

[173] Bosch v. de Geus, 8 Recueil 89, [1962] C.M.L.R. 1; the *Van Gend & Loos* case, 9 Recueil 1, [1962] C.M.L.R. 105; for a decision of a national court, see Società Biscotti Panettoni Colussi v. Ministero del Commercio, Consiglio di Stato, Nov. 7, 1962, [1963] C.M.L.R. 133. In the *Van Gend & Loos* case the Court held that art. 12 of the EEC Treaty confers directly enforceable rights on private parties. This is a question of the interpretation of the Treaty, and the case does not seem to be authority for the view that the Court can decide the case before the national court, as distinct from the question of Treaty interpretation. Contra, Hay, "Federal Jurisdiction of the Common Market Court," 12 Am. J. Comp. L. 21, 38 n.97 (1963). See Da Costa en Schaake N.V. v. Nederlandse Belastingadministratie, 9 Recueil 59, [1963] C.M.L.R. 224; Bosch v. de Geus, 8 Recueil 89, 126–28, [1963] C.M.L.R. 1, 13–14 (conclusions of Advocate-General Lagrange); Bebr, "The Relationship Between Community Law and the Law of Member States," in Restrictive Practices, Patents, Trade Marks and Unfair Competition in the Common Market, Int'l & Comp. L.Q. Supp. No. 4, at 1, 14 (1962).

to formulate a question of interpretation in the abstract; the Court may have to apply the Treaty to the facts as found by the national tribunal.[174] In general, the application of the Community law as stated by the Court is left to the national tribunal, but the Court must state the Community law precisely enough for the tribunal to apply it. If the referral is made by the national tribunal after it has found the facts, this reduces the number of points which must be argued and reduces the costs of the hearing in the Court. When the Court gives its decision, the tribunal may hear further evidence to apply the ruling of the Court to the facts.

The Court's decision is binding on the tribunal which refers the question to the Court and on all national courts concerned with the same case.[175] Other national tribunals should regard the interpretation laid down as binding on them, to insure a uniform application of Community law; if a national tribunal does not accept the Court's interpretation, it should refer the question to the Court again. It is difficult to insure that national courts do not disregard precedents of the Community Court with which they disagree. The Court itself will not regard its judgments in other cases as absolutely binding on it,[176] and it would be a misinterpretation of Community law for a national court to regard itself as bound by the Community Court's decision in an earlier case.[177]

Again, the problem is created by the absence of any appeal to the Court against a decision of a national tribunal without the latter's consent.[178] A decision by the

[174] Catalano, "Rapports entre le droit Communautaire et le droit des Etats membres," 1964 Journal des Tribunaux 53, 54. "[F]inding a clear-cut division between application and interpretation is indeed one of the most delicate problems posed by Article 177, all the more so because this dividing line corresponds to that between Community and national jurisdictions. . . ." Costa v. ENEL, 10 Recueil 1141, 1172, [1964] C.M.L.R. 425, 437 (conclusions of Advocate-General Lagrange).

[175] Dumon & Rigaux 682.

[176] Donner, "The Court of Justice of the European Communities," in Legal Problems of the European Economic Community and the European Free Trade Association, Int'l & Comp. L.Q. Supp. No. 1, at 66, 68 (1961); Da Costa en Schaake N.V. v. Nederlandse Belastingadministratie, 9 Recueil 59, [1963] C.M.L.R. 224. For the position in Irish and English law, respectively, see Henchy, "Precedent in the Irish Supreme Court," 25 Modern L. Rev. 544 (1962), and Dworkin, "Stare Decisis in the House of Lords," 26 Modern L. Rev. 163 (1962).

[177] See Dumon, "La Cour de Justice des Communautés européennes et les juridictions des Etats membres," 14 Rev. Int. de Droit Comp. 369, 377 (1962). A decision holding an act of the Commission or the Council valid is unlikely to be challenged.

[178] Because of the independence of the judiciary, it seems unlikely that the failure of a national tribunal of final appeal to refer a case to the Court can be regarded as a failure by a member state to fulfill its obligations under arts. 169–70. On the other hand, there is no other method of insuring that national courts respect their obligations under art. 177, and it is a recognized rule of public international law that a state is responsible for "denial of justice" by its judiciary. The Commission may someday take up a suitable case, but it is unlikely to do so merely to vindicate the right of an enterprise to have a question of Community law argued before the Court. It is submitted that arts. 169–71 would in fact apply to such a case. This is the view of Stein and Hay, but no reason is given; "New Legal Remedies of Enterprises: A Survey," in 1 American Enterprise in the European Common Market: A Legal Profile 459, 481 (Stein & Nicholson ed. 1960). See Bebr, Judicial Control 192–93. Dumon and Rigaux say that, other than art. 177, the Treaty contemplates no Court control of the application of Community law by national courts; Dumon & Rigaux 689. See Lagrange, "Les Actions en Justice dans le Régime des Communautés européennes," 10 Sociaal-Economische Wetgeving 81, 104 (1962); The Zamora, [1916] 2 A.C. 77, 93–94 (opinion of British Solicitor General Mansfield, later Lord Mansfield). Lenhoff holds that, because of the independence of national judiciaries, no review is possible; "Jurisdictional Relationship between the Court of the European Communities and the Courts of Member States," 12 Buffalo L. Rev. 296, 324 (1963).

Court under Article 184 that a Community act is inapplicable, although this decision applies only between the parties, is unlikely to be reversed by the Court.[179]

As the EEC develops, Article 177 will assume progressively greater importance, especially for private enterprises. As more cases are brought to the Court, many of the initial difficulties will be removed and Community law will develop more rapidly.

POSSIBLE LEGAL REMEDIES FOR ENTERPRISES INJURED AS A RESULT OF A DIRECTIVE

An enterprise cannot sue in the Community Court for the annulment of an illegal directive[180] or an illegal decision addressed to a member state,[181] even if the enterprise is injured by the action of the member state pursuant to the Community act. Since such a Community act is not directly applicable in national law, an enterprise cannot normally question its validity in a national court and have it referred to the Community Court under Article 177, or argue that the state has misinterpreted the act and taken action not required by the act which has injured the enterprise.

Since a directive does not override inconsistent national law, national courts probably will apply national law, even when to do so is a breach of the obligations of the state under a directive; the breach is the fault of the legislature or other body in a position to comply with the directive.[182] Even if the national courts take notice of the directive and try to interpret the national law to comply with it, the interpretation of the directive normally would not be "essential" for the national court "to render judgment."[183]

Nor is it easy to see how the enterprise could challenge the validity of a directive in a national tribunal. If a member state acts against an enterprise, pursuant to a directive, and the act is legal under national law, the enterprise has no redress, even if the directive is contrary to the Treaty and need not have been acted upon. The act is illegal under national law only if the state has omitted to amend the law before taking action against the enterprise or if the amendment to the national law is unconstitutional. In either case it seems unlikely that the validity of the directive is relevant, even if the directive is relied on by the state as a defense. Even if there is no constitutional provision, such as that in the Netherlands,[184] which permits an act of a Community institution to prevail over the constitution, a directive cannot be challenged as unconstitutional because directives are not directly applicable.

Except as national laws permit, an enterprise cannot sue a member state

[179] See Bebr, Judicial Control 199–200. One difference is that the invalidity of an act which has been annulled need not be pleaded, while the exception of illegality must be expressly pleaded on each occasion and, in theory, the grounds of "inapplicability" fully argued.

[180] Bebr, Judicial Control 56, 187; Stein & Hay, "New Legal Remedies of Enterprises: A Survey," in 1 American Enterprise in the European Common Market: A Legal Profile 459, 471 (Stein & Nicholson ed. 1960); Hay, "Federal Jurisdiction of the Common Market Court," 12 Am. J. Comp. L. 21 (1963).

[181] Art. 173 does not permit an enterprise to bring an action to annul an act addressed to a member state. Art. 184 applies only to regulations. See, however, Getreide-Import Gesellschaft v. EEC Commission, 11 Recueil 263, [1965] C.M.L.R. 276.

[182] Dumon & Rigaux 627.

[183] Art. 177(2).

[184] Netherlands Constitution, arts. 65–67, as amended [1953] Staatsblad, No. 261, translated in van Panhuys, "The Netherlands Constitution and International Law," 47 Am. J. Int'l L. 537, 538–40 (1953), also translated as arts. 60e–60g in 2 Peaslee, Constitutions of Nations 762 (2d ed. 1956). These articles are discussed on pp. 54–55.

for a breach of the member state's obligations under the Treaty, so the enterprise has no protection against a state's failing to carry out a directive or decision addressed to it.

ENFORCEMENT OF COMMUNITY DECISIONS[185]

Under Article 192, decisions of the Court, the Council, and the Commission against private enterprises are enforceable in the same way as orders of national courts. There is no provision for enforcement of decisions of the Court against member states or against Community institutions. Article 192 applies only to decisions imposing a pecuniary obligation, but fines are the only sanctions for breach of Community law. Daily fines are imposed instead of an injunction or interdict to stop a breach of Community law.[186]

National authorities have been appointed to authenticate copies of the decisions of Community institutions. Each authenticated copy is then executed under the ordinary method of execution in domestic law. Unlike the usual procedure for enforcement of foreign decrees,[187] the national authorities may not question on any ground the correctness of the decision to be enforced. Enforcement may be suspended only by the Court, but the method of enforcement and legal questions arising in the course of enforcement may be decided by national courts.[188]

The effectiveness of Community law and Community decisions could be reduced if the national authorities through which fines are collected neglected to levy execution against enterprises which they wished to protect. However, the national authorities would be in breach of the Treaty if they connived to obstruct the collection of Community fines by means of proceedings on collateral matters in national courts or if they neglected to enforce execution.

Legislation is needed to authorize the issue of subpoenas to witnesses to give evidence before the Community Court. The Court has power to deal with defaulting witnesses.[189] Perjury in the

[185] With regard to the general problem of reciprocal enforcement of foreign judgments in the EEC, see Weser, "Les conflits de juridictions dans le cadre du Marché Commun" (pts. 1–6), 48 Rev. Crit. de Droit Int. Privé 613 (1959), 49 Rev. Crit. de Droit Int. Privé 21, 151, 313, 533 (1960), 50 Rev. Crit. de Droit Int. Privé 105 (1961); Rigaux, "L'efficacité des jugements étrangers en Belgique" (pts. 1–2), 1960 Journal des Tribunaux 285, 302.

[186] Art. 187 applies art. 192 to decisions of the Court. See Cartou, Le Marché Commun et le Droit Public 67–70 (1959). The jurisdiction of the Court under the Treaty does not involve the imposition of fines on enterprises, except under art. 172. Art. 172 permits the Court to be given the judicial function with regard to the imposition of pecuniary penalties in the first instance and not by way of appeal. See Reg. 17, art. 17; Dumon, "La Cour de Justice des Communautés européennes et les juridictions des Etats membres," 14 Rev. Int. de Droit Comp. 369, 379–80 (1962).

[187] British Foreign Judgments (Reciprocal Enforcement) Act, 1933, 23 & 24 Geo. 5, c. 13, § 4, allows the national court to review and refuse to enforce the foreign judgment on certain specified grounds.

[188] If Ireland became a member of the EEC, many minor problems would arise. Ireland has no legislation providing for the enforcement of foreign decrees without an action on the decree in an Irish court, and such legislation would be necessary to make it possible to act pursuant to art. 192. Under art. 192 a national court can authenticate the decision to be enforced; the necessary correspondence could be handled through the court office. When authenticated, the decision would be treated as a High Court judgment and enforced in the ordinary way.

The procedure apparently will be that the Commission, probably through the Executive Secretary, or in appropriate cases the Registrar of the Court, will provide a copy of the decree or decision to the party enforcing it. This copy will be signed by the authority providing it and filed with the specified national authority for authentication. Dumon & Rigaux 667–69.

[189] Statute of the Court, art. 24.

Court[190] would have to be made criminal in Ireland, because the Perjury Act of 1911[191] deals only with persons sworn in Ireland for the purposes of a proceeding in a tribunal of a foreign state. It might not even cover the taking of evidence on commission by an Irish court[192] on behalf of the Community Court, since the Court is hardly a "tribunal of a foreign state."[193] Provision must also be made for authentication of warrants for the inspection of the records of an enterprise by a Community official or by anyone appointed by the Court.[194]

MEMBERSHIP AND ASSOCIATION

The unanimous consent of the Council is required for the admission of a new member state[195] and also for the conclusion of a treaty of association.[196] Amendments[197] to the Treaty on the admission of a new member state must be ratified by each state. Amendments due to an association agreement require consultation with the Commission and the Assembly as well as ratification by member states.[198]

The only explicit requirement for full membership, as opposed to associate membership, is that the state be a European state.[199] The principal economic activities of a member state must be efficient enough to withstand competition without excessive reliance on safeguards or special arrangements. Its economy must therefore be either fully competitive with or complementary to that of the EEC. A new member state must accept all the principles of the Treaty. Special arrangements can be made by protocol for specific aspects of the state's economy, but the extent of these concessions depends on their nature and extent and on the political willingness of the member states to make concessions.

Association can involve membership in the EEC in all save the institutional aspects; for example, a customs union (the essence of the association of Greece), a free trade area, a financial aid arrange-

[190] Statute of the Court, art. 27.

[191] 1 & 2 Geo. 5, c. 16, in force both in England and Ireland. The effect of the Adaptation of Enactments Act, 1922 Pub. Stat. 73, in Ireland is to make the rule as stated in the text. See Dumon, "La Cour de Justice des Communautés européennes et les juridictions des Etats membres," 14 Rev. Int. de Droit Comp. 369, 382 (1962); Dumon & Rigaux 663–66.

[192] Statute of the Court, art. 26.

[193] Perjury Act, 1911, 1 & 2 Geo. 5, c. 16, § 1(4). The "quasi-federal" nature of the EEC is relevant here.

[194] Art. 213; Statute of the Court, art. 22; Reg. 17, arts. 11–14. In 243 H.L. Deb. (5th ser.) 423 (1962), the Lord Chancellor said: "I am confident that there would be no obstacle whatever in Community law to our requiring an order of the High Court backing [a Commission] . . . inspector's warrant."

[195] Art. 237. See A.P.E. Débats, Sess. 1961–62, at 284–89.

[196] Art. 238; Poulantzas, "Aspects juridiques de l'association prévue par l'article 238 du Traité de la C.E.E.," 31 Annuaire de l'A.A.A. 31 (1961); Varouxakis, "La nature juridique de l'association entre la C.E.E. et la Grèce," 7 Revue du Marché Commun 537 (1964).

[197] The word used in the French text—*adaptations*—indicates the intent that the Treaty not be altered substantially.

[198] Art. 236.

[199] Art. 237. See generally Birkelbach Report, A.P.E. Doc. No. 122, paras. 84–121 (1961–62); Rapport . . . sur la politique commerciale commune de la C.E.E. à l'égard des pays tiers et sur les demandes d'adhésion ou d'association de pays européennes, A.P.E. Doc. No. 134 (1962–63); Council of Europe, The Position of Certain European Countries Other than the Six in the Event of the United Kingdom Joining the European Economic Community, ch. II (1961); Rapport complémentaire . . . sur la politique commerciale commune de la C.E.E. à l'égard des pays tiers et sur les demandes d'adhésion ou d'association de pays européens, A.P.E. Doc. No. 12 (1963–64).

ment (like the treaty with Turkey),[200] or a non-discriminatory, commercial arrangement may be the basis for associate membership. A customs union and a free trade area are preferential trading groups permitted by the General Agreement on Tariffs and Trade (GATT); a lesser degree of liberalization of trade normally is subject to the most-favored-nation clause. The EEC is reluctant to give to industrialized countries the advantages of any kind of association without the obligations of full membership, but this does not apply to less developed countries or to Austria. If the terms of the treaties of association varied substantially, a large number of associated countries would hinder the operation of the EEC itself, even if a single Council of Association were set up for all of them.

A distinction should be made between treaties of association contemplating full membership and those involving economic aid or a trade relationship, such as those now in force with the African and other associated countries.[201] It has been said[202] that, except where traditional links exist, only countries "geographically connected" to Europe should become associated with the Community within the meaning of Article 238. This does not exclude the possibility of trade agreements which fall short of association.

Treaties of association have not given any associated country a vote in Community decisions. Alternatives are that the Community makes decisions which may vitally affect the associated state or that the associated state is given a voice in Community decisions to which the state's obligations do not entitle it. The difficulty arises when the economy of the associated country competes with that of the EEC irrespective of the content of the treaty of association.

TWO SPECIAL PROBLEMS WITH REGARD TO CERTAIN RULES OF COMMUNITY LAW

A practical question arises in connecnection with regulations and directives adopted by the Council or the Commission after negotiations with a new member state have been concluded but before the Treaty comes into force with respect to the new member state. It is too late to deal with any problem in the negotiations, and the new member state has as yet no voting rights. To insure that the new member is not bound by rules on which it has never had a chance to comment, a solution must be worked out on a case-by-case basis by the Commission and the new member state. At least after the new state has ratified the terms of accession,[203] there is no reason why it should not have a voice in the working of the EEC.

A more difficult problem relates to rules of Community law made not under Treaty powers but by separate treaties among the member states. These eventually will include conventions on European patent, trademark, design, copyright, and bankruptcy laws; a multilateral convention for the elimination of double

[200] Rapport . . . sur l'accord (doc. 91) créant une association entre la Communauté économique européenne et la Turquie et documents annexés, A.P.E. Doc. No. 94 (1963–64). See also the second Convention of Association with the group of French-speaking African states, 1964 Journal Officiel 1430/64.

[201] Rapport . . . sur la convention d'association entre la Communauté économique européenne et les Etats africains et malgache associés à cette Communauté et les documents annexés (Doc. 59-II), A.P.E. Doc. No. 65 (1963–64).

[202] Birkelbach Report, A.P.E. Doc. No. 122, para. 97 (1961–62).

[203] A similar position arises in connection with a state which has concluded a treaty of association which contemplates full membership in due course. The present arrangement with Britain is for regular quarterly meetings at ministerial level between Britain and the Six, under the auspices of the Western European Union, the Commission being represented when economic matters are discussed. This gives Britain no voice in the decisions of the EEC.

taxation;[204] and conventions on reciprocal enforcement of judgments, recognition, change of nationality and merger of companies, and the protection of individuals and of individual rights.[205] These are closely associated with the Treaty. A new member state will be expected to accept any of these conventions which are in force at the time of its accession, as well as the EEC, ECSC, and Euratom Treaties[206] and the regulations and directives made pursuant to them. Since some of these conventions are not even contemplated by the Treaty, a new member state may be required to ratify them on its accession to the EEC Treaty not because it is obliged to do so by law but only because they are part of the legal framework of European integration. (It may be difficult to decide if this is in fact the case.) If non-member states are permitted to accede to any of these conventions, the position will be complicated, but acceptance of the conventions still may be involved in membership of the EEC.

ENACTMENT OF THE TREATY IN A NEW MEMBER STATE

The enactment of the Treaty as part of the national law of any new member state[207] will be scrutinized carefully by the Commission.[208] Regulations made before the date of enactment of the Treaty must be enacted as national law.[209] Regulations adopted after the Treaty has been enacted come into force in the national law of new member states automatically, since enactment of the Treaty gives Community institutions legislative powers in national law. In theory, it probably is permissible to enact only the provisions of the Treaty intended to be directly applicable in national law and not those binding only on member states. Legislation is necessary also to give the regulations of the Council and the Commission the force of national law. However, it is impossible to say if many provisions of the Treaty bind member states only in their international relations or if they are intended to be self-executing[210] and directly applicable in national

[204] See art. 220.

[205] Art. 220(1).

[206] Membership in the ECSC and Euratom is necessary in principle for all member states of the EEC; see in this connection Gaudet, "Incidences des Communautés européennes sur le droit interne des Etats membres," 8 Annales de la Faculté de Droit de Liège 5, 9 (1963).

[207] E.g., Britain and Ireland; see Thompson & Marsh, "The United Kingdom and the Treaty of Rome: Some Preliminary Observations," 11 Int'l & Comp. L.Q. 73 (1962); Marsh, "Le Royaume-Uni devant les problèmes juridiques du Marché Commun," 15 Rev. Int. de Droit Comp. 649, 653 (1963).

[208] "It might have been thought advisable to ensure . . . that the measures contemplated . . . by the British Government really would give the Community law the same force in the United Kingdom as in the member states." Report to the European Parliament on the State of the Negotiations with the U.K., A.P.E. Doc. No. 6, at 104 (1963–64).

[209] If pre-entry regulations are enacted generally by reference, official translations of them for use in courts of the new member states will have to be prepared.

[210] That is, are intended to become part of the municipal law without enactment or implementation other than the ratification of the treaty in question. Under British and Irish law, the ratification of a treaty does not put into force in municipal law even the provisions of the treaty which are intended to be self-executing. See Attorney General for Canada v. Attorney General for Ontario, [1937] A.C. 326, 347–48; Constitution of Ireland of 1937, art. 29(6). In other words, in Britain and Ireland no provision of a treaty can be self-executing. However, even when an entire treaty has been enacted as law in Britain and Ireland, as the EEC Treaty must be, only the provisions of the treaty which are directly applicable, on the proper construction of the treaty, will be in force in national law. The question of which provisions of the EEC Treaty are directly applicable arises whether the Treaty is received into municipal law by

law.[211] Only the Community Court can decide finally what Treaty provisions are directly applicable,[212] and some institutional provisions could have effects on litigation before national courts, so the Treaty will have to be enacted as a whole.[213]

According to principles of statutory interpretation, any rule of law inconsistent with directly applicable provisions of the Treaty is impliedly repealed by enactment of the Treaty.[214] Many existing rules of law must be specifically repealed to avoid uncertainty as to the extent of the implied repeal, to avoid a hiatus if the Treaty provision or regulation did not adequately replace the previous rule, or to integrate the new provisions into the existing law. It may be necessary to give the government power by statutory instrument to repeal previous acts and resolve problems arising out of the reception of a large body of law into the member state's legal system.[215] There is a clear distinction in Community law between national legislation amending national law consequent to the enactment of Community regulations and national legislation purporting to substitute itself for, rephrase, or bring into force Community regulations or Treaty provisions which have the force of national law. The former is permissable; the latter is

---

ratification, as in the Six, or by enactment, as in Ireland and Britain.

See generally Alting von Geusau, European Organizations and Foreign Relations of States (1962); Western European Union Assembly, Legal Implications of the Accession of the United Kingdom to the European Economic Community on the British Constitution, 8th Sess. Doc. No. 249, Explanatory Memorandum 3–5 (1962), set out in Stein & Hay, Cases on the Law and Institutions of the Atlantic Area 34 (prelim. ed. 1963).

[211] Although not so with many Treaty provisions, certain provisions clearly are intended to have force in national law. Notable ones are arts. 85 and 86; this was finally settled by the Court in Bosch v. de Geus, 8 Recueil 89, [1962] C.M.L.R. 1. On the controversy, see the literature cited in Riesenfeld, "The Protection of Competition," in 2 American Enterprise in the European Common Market: A Legal Profile 197, 330 n.634 (Stein & Nicholson ed. 1960). Other provisions are art. 12—see the *Van Gend & Loos* case, 9 Recueil 1, [1963] C.M.L.R. 105, and Da Costa en Schaake N.V. v. Nederlandse Belastingadministratie, 9 Recueil 59, [1963] C.M.L.R. 224—and art. 177, and perhaps arts. 7, 8(7), 13(1), 21, 37(2), 53, 58, 62, 76, 79, 88–89, 90, 91(2), 106(1), 106(3), 119, 173, 184, 189, 192, 211, 215, 221, and certain provisions of the Protocol on the Statute of the Court. There are many directly applicable provisions in the ECSC and Euratom Treaties. See Stein & Hay, "New Legal Remedies of Enterprises: A Survey," in 1 American Enterprise in the European Common Market: A Legal Profile 459, 485–89 (Stein & Nicholson ed. 1960); Gaudet, "Le Marché Commun devant les juges," 21 Annales de Droit et de Sciences Politiques 133 (1961); Dumon & Rigaux 635; Catalano, "Rapports entre le droit Communautaire et le droit des Etats membres," 1964 Journal des Tribunaux 53; Albatros v. Sopéco, 11 Recueil, No. 3, [1965] C.M.L.R. 159. Some tests for identifying directly applicable provisions are laid down in Costa v. ENEL, 10 Recueil 1141, 1162–64, [1964] C.M.L.R. 425, 457.

[212] Art. 177; see the *Van Gend & Loos* case, 9 Recueil 1, [1963] C.M.L.R. 105. Art. 177 clearly is directly applicable in national law.

[213] See De Visscher, "Les Tendances internationales des constitutions modernes," 1952 (1) Recueil Académie D. Int. 556, 558.

[214] On the superiority of Community law over national law, see Bebr, "The Relationship Between Community Law and the Law of the Member States," in Restrictive Practices, Patents, Trade Marks and Unfair Competition in the Common Market, Int'l & Comp. L.Q. Supp. No. 4, at 1–2, (1962). See arts. 5 and 171, and Humblet v. Belgium, 6 Recueil 1127, 1146 (1960); Valentine, "Community Law and English Law," 1 J. Common Market Studies 180 (1962); Costa v. ENEL, 10 Recueil 1141, 1159–60, [1964] C.M.L.R. 425, 455–56.

[215] This was done in France to enable the government to implement directives on freedom of establishment. A clause—known as the "Henry VIII Clause"—giving the government power by statutory instrument to amend an act is unusual in Britain. See Phillips, The Constitutional Law of Great Britain and the Commonwealth 368–69 (1957).

incompatible with the principles of the Treaty.

THE TREATY-ENACTING ACT AND LATER INCONSISTENT NATIONAL LEGISLATION

In Ireland, England, and most other countries, the ordinary rule of statutory interpretation is that where two legislative provisions with the same formal authority[216] conflict, the later prevails and repeals the former to the extent of the inconsistency. This is merely a rule of statutory interpretation derived in England from the principle of parliamentary sovereignty and is not the principle itself.[217] The principle is that "a parliament cannot . . . bind its successors by the terms of any statute so as to limit the discretion of a future Parliament."[218] Because of this principle, a provision in the Treaty-enacting act such as "no subsequent Act may be enacted which is inconsistent with this present Act" would not prevent the subsequent enactment of legislation inconsistent with the act. The question of statutory interpretation, however, concerns the effect of a provision in the Treaty-enacting act to the effect that "where this Act is inconsistent with any subsequent Act, this Act shall prevail except where the subsequent Act expressly (but not merely by implication) provides otherwise." If the later legislation expressly provides that it is to prevail over the Treaty-enacting act, it will do so—subject to the constitutional position discussed in Chapter Two—and no question of statutory interpretation arises. If the later legislation does not expressly amend the Treaty act but is inconsistent with it, there is a conflict between the ordinary rule of statutory interpretation that the later act prevails and the express rule of statutory interpretation suggested above. Since the express rule is part of an act and the ordinary rule is a rule of common law, there is no doubt that the express provision would apply.[219] Thus, the

[216] The phrase "with the same formal authority" is necessary to an accurate statement of the rule to cover the case where the legislature confers on another body the formal authority or power which it has to repeal its own legislation and the case where the Treaty is received into national law by means of an ordinary act of the legislature. The Irish legislation enacting the EEC Treaty must confer on the Council and the Commission the power to repeal, by implication from Community regulations, Irish acts. When this is done, Community regulations will have the same formal authority as Irish acts. See Dicey's principle that "no person or body is recognized by the law of England as having a right to override or set aside the legislation of Parliament." Dicey, The Law of the Constitution 40 (10th ed. 1959).

[217] See Laskin, "Canada's Bill of Rights: A Dilemma for the Courts," 11 Int'l & Comp. L.Q. 519, 527 (1962).

[218] Todd, Parliamentary Government in the British Colonies 192 (1880), cited in Dicey, Law of the Constitution 67 (9th ed. 1939); Phillips, The Constitutional Law of Great Britain and the Commonwealth 48–60 (1957). See Costa v. ENEL, 10 Recueil 1141, [1964] C.M.L.R. 425; Commission's Reply to Question No. 27, 1964 Journal Officiel 2161/64.

[219] There should be a presumption that a later act was not intended to be inconsistent with the Treaty; Dumon & Rigaux 627. Since this presumption is natural, it is difficult to see why the provision suggested in the text should not be given effect; both are rules of statutory interpretation, and neither infringes on the substantive power of Parliament in any way.

The position is analogous to that where the legislature confers power to amend acts by statutory instrument; the express power overrides the normal rule that if an act of Parliament and a statutory instrument are inconsistent, the act prevails. See Phillips, The Constitutional Law of Great Britain and the Commonwealth 368–69 (1957). The act conferring the power delegates, *pro tanto*, the authority of the legislature to repeal acts of previous legislatures.

It is submitted that Parliament would succeed, by adopting the second clause suggested, in tying the hands of its successors to the extent that they may not amend the Treaty-enacting act without either (1) using express words or (2) first repealing the clause suggested in the text. These are merely procedural requirements. Since "Parliament can make or unmake any law whatever" (Dicey, The Law of the Constitution 39–40 [10th ed. 1959]), it would be

method of implementing the Treaty in domestic law could solve the problem of inconsistency between the directly applicable Treaty provisions[220] and later legislation.[221]

The Treaty-enacting act must confer on the Council and the Commission power to repeal prior national acts by implication, since without this provision the legislation would prevail over Community regulations if they were inconsistent.[222]

INTERPRETATION OF THE TREATY IN A NEW MEMBER STATE

The EEC Treaty is a framework or constitution rather than a set of rules. Because it uses constitutional law and ad-

---

remarkable if Parliament could not, by the clause suggested, repeal the rule of statutory interpretation stated in the text, when it can grant power to repeal acts of Parliament (subject in Ireland to art. 15[2] of the Irish Constitution). The rule of statutory interpretation is derived from the constitutional principle, and the principle is not repealed by the repeal of the rule. In any case, Parliament theoretically can repeal them both by using the express words of the clause suggested.

If the later act were inconsistent with the Treaty but contained a rule of interpretation that nothing in it should be interpreted as amending the Treaty-enacting act, the Treaty-enacting act would prevail. In theory, one could argue that the repeal of the second clause suggested in the text could be by necessary implication and need not be by express words—even if the clause applied expressly to its own amendment and not merely to the rest of the Treaty-enacting act; see The State (Ryan) v. Lennon, [1935] Ir. R. 170, especially at 217 (per Kennedy, C.J.). This argument exalts the rule of statutory interpretation into a position superior to that of an act of Parliament and does so on a matter of procedure and not of substance. The constitutional principle deals with the substance; there is no reason why it should be held to deal with the form. In Ellen St. Estates, Ltd. v. Minister of Health, [1934] 1 K.B. 590, 597, Lord Justice Maugham said: "The Legislature cannot according to our Constitution bind itself as to the form of subsequent legislation and it is impossible for Parliament to enact that in a subsequent statute dealing with the same subject-matter there can be no implied repeal." No authority is cited, and the sentence quoted goes further than the judgments of either of the other judges. It is submitted that the substance of the argument which Lord Justice Maugham was refuting was that Parliament had, by implication only, enacted a provision similar to the clause suggested. It is submitted that the sentence quoted is unnecessary to the decision and is wrong insofar as it implies that Parliament cannot alter the form of legislation, for example, by repealing the Interpretation Acts, or alter its procedure, by altering the number of stages through which legislation must go. The conclusion that Parliament would not intend inadvertently to amend the Treaty-enacting act is reasonable since such an amendment would involve a breach of international law; this consideration should be conclusive of the interpretation argued for here (see EEC Treaty, arts. 5, 171). The basis for the rule that Parliament may be presumed to have intended the later legislation to prevail is not applicable in this case, even without such a clause as is suggested in the text. Lord Justice Maugham may perhaps have confused the constitutional principle and the rule of statutory interpretation. See Attorney General for New South Wales v. Trethowan, 44 Commw. L.R. 394 (Austl. 1931), aff'd, [1932] A.C. 526; Cowen, "Legislature and Judiciary: Reflections on the Constitutional Issues in South Africa," 16 Modern L. Rev. 273, 288–90 (1953); Jennings, The Law and the Constitution 162–63 (1959); Friedman & Benjafield, Principles of Australian Administrative Law 2–13 (1962).

The Irish courts generally will not look at the procedure of the Irish Parliament to see if an act has been validly passed; O'Crowley v. Minister for Justice, [1935] Ir. R. 536, 549 (per Johnston, J.).

[220] If the legislation were inconsistent with a Treaty provision which was not directly applicable, arts. 169 and 170 would apply.

[221] The conflict might occur accidentally. If the conflict occurred deliberately, the matter would be a political one, since the Treaty provides no sanction against a member state which refuses to correct a breach of the Treaty which has been so declared by the Court. Member states must insure that in case of conflict between national law and a directly applicable Community rule, the latter will prevail.

[222] Dumon, "La formation de la régle de droit dans les Communautés européennes," 12 Rev. Int. de Droit Comp. 75, 80 (1960). See Costa v. ENEL, 10 Recueil 1141, [1964] C.M.L.R. 425.

ministrative law concepts, national public law is more valuable in interpreting it than is public international law.[223] However, too much time has been spent discussing whether, as a result of the very real transfer of sovereignty by member states to the Community, the EEC has "supranational" characteristics or a "quasi-federal" nature. The Treaty is unique, and its interpretation must take into account its dynamic aspects and the objects which the institutions and the policies are intended to achieve. This teleological approach to interpreting the Treaty requires the use of the economic and political principles on which the Treaty is based as well as legal principles. These are more useful than the comparatively small amount of legislative history, especially since the provisions of the Treaty and of most regulations are usually compromises and may not represent accurately the legislative intent of any particular institution or individual concerned in drafting them. There is much scope for varying Treaty interpretations due to differences in the four official language texts. If an official version of the Treaty in the language of a new member state is drafted carefully, the interpretation of the Treaty may be clarified. Questions of the interpretation of the Treaty are settled ultimately by the Court, and in certain cases[224] the Court must refer specifically to national laws to interpret a phrase or concept used in the Treaty.[225] If Britain and Ireland join, there presumably will be an official English version of the Treaty. If so, in appropriate cases the Court may draw on the common law as well as on the laws of the Six.[226]

Since the Treaty and regulations are drafted in a style entirely different from English and Irish legislative drafting, some changes could be expected in the Community style of drafting if they accede.[227] It would be difficult and probably unnecessary to enact Interpretation Acts requiring English and Irish judges to interpret the Treaty and pre-accession regulations according to civil law principles of interpretation. However, an official government commentary on the Treaty could be made, by the Treaty Act, an aid to judicial interpretation and could

[223] See, for instance, art. 173. Cartou, Le Marché Commun et le Droit Public 10 (1959); Fédération Charbonnière de Belgique v. High Authority, 2 Recueil 199, 263 (1956) (conclusions of Advocate-General Lagrange).

[224] E.g., art. 173, "infringements . . . of any rule of law relating to the effect" of the Treaty and *détournement de pouvoir;* art. 215, noncontractual liability of the Community to be governed by the "general principles common to the laws of member states"; art. 214, professional secrecy; art. 222, systems of ownership; arts. 85–86, antitrust and antimonopoly; and perhaps Protocol on the Statute of the Court, art. 3, immunity from process.

[225] See, for example, Assider v. High Authority, 1 Recueil 143 (1954–55) (conclusions of Advocate-General Lagrange), on the concept of *détournement de pouvoir;* Algera v. EEC Assembly, 3 Recueil 85 (1957), on the concept of *faute de service;* Dumon, "La formation de la règle de droit dans les Communautés européennes," 12 Rev. Int. de Droit Comp. 74, 84–85 (1960). On sources of Community law, see Mathijsen, Le Droit de la Communauté européenne de charbon et de l'acier (1958); Dumon & Rigaux 685–89.

[226] Rey, "Aspects juridiques et politiques de l'élargissement de la Communauté Economique Européenne," in International Law Association, Report of the Fiftieth [1962] Conference 13 (1963). If no new version of the Treaty existed and the Court looked at the national law of the new member state, it would be altering the meaning of the Treaty as signed. It seems improper to hold that accession of a new state can change the meaning of a treaty. However, art. 215, for example, does not seem to admit a distinction between new and original member states, and this distinction is contrary to the idea of a Community.

[227] Although in Britain and Ireland the Treaty will have to be enacted in translation, they will not be allowed to redraft it in accordance with British or Irish legislative styles because then national courts would be interpreting and applying one provision but referring the interpretation of another to the EEC Court under art. 177.

be approved by the Commission. Government reports to the legislatures of the Six on the three Community Treaties are frequently cited before the Court.[228] In cases where a point of Treaty interpretation is unlikely to be referred to the EEC court,[229] provision might be made for the Attorney General to give an opinion on the point as *amicus curiae* to insure that the Community aspects are fully argued and that the judges adopt the interpretation most likely to be accepted by the Court.

HARMONIZATION OF LAW IN THE EEC

The objects of the EEC Treaty are "closer relations between . . . member states"[230] and establishment of "the foundations of an ever closer union"[231] brought about by economic means. In addition, the Commission contemplates ultimately a common currency and common European economic policies.[232] Harmonization of law in the EEC can insure free movement of goods and factors of production and equal conditions of competition—both necessary to an economic union. In addition to eliminating obstacles to economic integration, harmonization of law can promote it positively, for example, by making possible the establishment of a European-type company.

Certain Treaty provisions deal with harmonization of law. As to the extent[233] of harmonization of law, Article

[228] These reports are: Chambre des Députés, Rapport Juridique de la Commission Spéciale, Ministère d'Etat, Service Information et Presse, Le Grande Duché de Luxembourg et la Communauté Economique Européenne [Luxembourg]; (1956–57) Assemblée Nationale, Documents Parlementaires No. 5266, Rapport fait au nom de la Commission des Affaires Etrangères sur les projets de loi (No. 4676) ... par Savary et July [France]; Camera dei Deputati No. 2814 (Legislatura II, 1957) [Italy]; Bijlagen Tweede Kammer, Mémoire van Toelichting No. 3 (Zitting 1956–57, Doc. No. 4725) [The Netherlands]; Chambre des Représentants No. 727, May 9, 1957 (Sess. 1956–57) [Belgium]; Entwurf eines Gesetzes zu den Verträgen von 25 Marz 1957 zur Gründung der Europäischen Wirtschaftsgemeinschaft und der Europäischen Atomgemeinschaft, (1953) Deutscher Bundestag, 2 Wahlperiode, May 4, 1957 (Drucksache No. 3440); Ergänzung zu dem Entwurf des Gesetzes . . . , (1953) Deutscher Bundestag, 2 Wahlperiode, June 13, 1957 (Drucksache No. 3615); Schriftlicher Bericht des 3. Sonderausschusses über den Entwurf . . . , (1953) Deutscher Bundestag, 2 Wahlperiode (Drucksache No. 3660); 2 Schriftlicher Bericht des 3 Sonderausschusses . . . , (1957) Deutscher Bundestag, July 5, 1957, 224 Sitzung at 13.178–13.429 [Germany].

On preparatory materials on the EEC Treaty, see Stein & Hay, "New Legal Remedies of Enterprises: A Survey," in 1 American Enterprise in the European Common Market: A Legal Profile 459, 504 (Stein & Nicholson ed. 1960); McMahon, "The Court of the European Communities—Judicial Interpretation and International Organization," 37 Brit. Yb. Int'l L. 320, 333–34 (1961). For national legislation and other official material, see Bebr, Judicial Control 244–45.

See also Keenan, "Some Legal Consequences of Britain's Entry into the European Common Market," 1962 Public Law 327, 332. On the English rules as to the use of legislative history by the courts in treaty interpretation, see Porter v. Freudenberg, [1915] 1 K.B. 857; Ellerman Lines v. Murray, [1931] A.C. 126. Since treaties are international law and since international law permits the use of legislative history, it would be anomalous if English courts refused to use legislative history when interpreting treaties, and regulations should be regarded as international law for this purpose. See Thompson, "New Laws for Old?" 1 J. Common Market Studies 278–81 (1962).

[229] That is, where the lower court has decided not to refer the point to the Court and where it appears unlikely that the parties will take the case to the court of final appeal.

[230] Art. 2.

[231] EEC Treaty, Preamble.

[232] See generally Action Programme for the Second Stage (1962).

[233] See Monaco, Comparaison et rapprochement des législations dans le Marché Commun européen," 12 Rev. Int. de Droit Comp. 60, 63–65 (1960); Thibièrge, "Le Statut des Sociétés Etrangères," in 1 Le Statut d l'Etranger et le Marché Commun 289, 341–42 (57th Congrès des Notaires de France, 1959); Stein, "An Emergent Legal Community: The Common Market Countries' Plans for Harmonization of

100 contemplates the rapprochement of legislative and administrative provisions and regulations having the force of law which "directly affect the establishment or operation of the Common Market"; it deals with the assimilation of different national laws to a norm. Article 101 speaks of those provisions that falsify conditions of competition and cause distortion. Article 102 deals with prevention of new legislative measures which may cause distortion. "The Commission's right to take preventive action is coupled with the obligation directly incumbent on Member States to consult the Commission before they enact or amend any legislative provisions which might cause a distortion."[234] Article 220 requires negotiations on various matters "insofar as necessary," and Article 3(h) is to the same effect. Other provisions in the Treaty use the concepts of harmonization, coordination, and rapprochement. "The progressive establishment of a common market with the consequent emergence of new requirements will of itself determine the fields in which the approximation of laws is advisable."[235] There is probably no object in trying to see subtle distinctions between the various synonyms for harmonization of law used by the Treaty when the problems will be dealt with on an empirical basis.

It is important that the residual provision on harmonization of law, Article 100, requires a unanimous vote of the Council at all times, while most of the provisions on specific topics relating to change in national laws provide for a qualified majority vote.[236] Under Article 102, after consultation with the member states concerned, a directive may be issued by a qualified majority of the Council.

There are different means of harmonizing national laws. The Treaty provides for regulations[237] and directives,[238] and in many cases requires consultation and a qualified majority vote in the Council. It contemplates certain new treaties,[239] and several treaties will be concluded which were not contemplated by the Treaty at all—for example, on bankruptcy and patents.[240] The directly applicable provisions of the Treaty itself have had a considerable effect on national laws. Uniform laws enacted in each member state have not been suggested, except as

---

Law," 9 Am. J. Comp. L. 351, 353 (1960); Committee on Foreign Law, "Report on the European Economic Community," 14 Record of N.Y.C.B.A. 365, 368 (1959); Gaudet, "Incidences des Communautés européennes sur le droit interne des Etats membres," 8 Annales de la Faculté de Droit de Liège 5 passim (1963).

For an excellent summary of the work of the EEC, see Stein, "Harmonisation of Law in the European Economic Community," in Comparative Aspects of Anti-trust Law in the United States, the United Kingdom and the European Economic Community, Int'l & Comp. L.Q. Supp. No. 6, at 27 (1963).

[234] Third General Report, para. 156 (1960). On arts. 100–102, see Grisoli, "The Impact of the European Economic Community on the Movement for the Unification of Law," 26 Law & Contemp. Prob. 418 (1961); Monaco, "Comparaison et rapprochement des législations dans le Marché Commun européen," 12 Rev. Int. de Droit Comp. 61, 67–72 (1960); Monaco, "Le rapprochement des législations nationales dans le cadre du Marché Commun," 3 Annuaire Français de Droit International 558 (1957).

[235] Fifth General Report, para. 57 (1962).

[236] Stein, "Harmonisation of Law in the European Economic Community," in Comparative Aspects of Anti-trust Law in the United States, the United Kingdom and the European Economic Community, Int'l & Comp. L.Q. Supp. No. 6, at 27, 35–36 (1963).

[237] E.g., art. 87.

[238] E.g., arts. 54(2), 100–102. Curiously, art. 102 provides only for a recommendation; compensatory measures by other member states are expressly permitted.

[239] Art. 220.

[240] Stein, "Harmonisation of Law in the European Economic Community," in Comparative Aspects of Anti-trust Law in the United States, the United Kingdom and the European Economic Community, Int'l & Comp. L.Q. Supp. No. 6, at 27, 36 (1963).

a method of setting up European-type companies, presumably because regulations will be uniform in effect if not in form.

The rest of this book deals with certain aspects of the relationship between Community law and national law and with harmonization of national law in certain fields. In the next chapter, the basic question of the relationship between national and Community institutions is discussed.

Chapter 2

Constitutional Aspects of the EEC in Ireland[1]

Ireland is the first common law country with a written constitution to apply for membership in the EEC. Her application raises certain problems of constitutional law which can be analyzed in the light of the experience of the present member states, in all of which, as is explained below, similar questions have arisen. Problems similar to these arise to some extent in any country contemplating entry into any international institution involving close economic cooperation.[2]

THE RIGHT OF THE PEOPLE TO DECIDE ALL QUESTIONS OF NATIONAL POLICY

The first problem for Ireland, perhaps the most basic legal question for any state joining the EEC, is whether her constitution permits the transfer of some of the rule-making functions of the legislature to the EEC Commission and the EEC Council. Article 6 of the 1937 Constitution of Ireland states:

> 1. All powers of government, legislative, executive and judicial, derive, under God, from the people, whose right it is to designate the rulers of the State and, in final appeal, to decide all questions of national policy, according to the requirements of the common good.
>
> 2. These powers of government are exercisable only by or on the authority of the organs of State established by this Constitution.[3]

If Ireland joined the EEC, the right of the people to decide ultimately *all* questions of national policy would no longer exist. Many decisions could be made by a majority of the Council, which would not necessarily include Ireland, although in practice Ireland's interests[4] would often correspond to those of other countries together having a considerable amount of voting power. Since the Commission and the Council would exercise

[1] The writer is indebted to the editor of the International and Comparative Law Quarterly for permission to reproduce the first section of this chapter, the substance of which was published under the title, "A Constitutional Aspect of Economic Integration: Ireland and the European Common Market," 12 Int'l & Comp. L.Q. 552 (1963).

[2] The English text of the Irish Constitution of 1937 is found in 2 Peaslee, Constitutions of Nations [hereinafter cited as Peaslee] 239 (2d ed. 1956). For constitutional provisions similar to the Irish provisions discussed in this chapter, see Constitution of Greece of 1952, arts. 21–28, 87, in 2 Peaslee 91, 95, 106; Constitution of Liechtenstein of 1921, arts. 63, 65, in 2 Peaslee 622, 630, 631; Constitution of Norway of 1814, as amended on March 8, 1962, to allow Norway to join the EEC, arts. 26, 75, 93; Constitution of Sweden of 1809, art. 87, in 3 Peaslee 301, 316; Constitution of Turkey of 1945, art. 26, in 3 Peaslee 404, 406.

[3] On the phrase "on the authority of," see The State (Killian) v. Minister for Justice, [1954] Ir. R. 207. Officials who are appointed and not elected cannot usually override the wishes of the legislature, except those judges whose powers to do so are given by the Constitution. References in this chapter to arts. 1–50 inclusive are to the Irish Constitution of 1937, unless otherwise indicated, and references to art. 50 and following articles are to the EEC Treaty.

[4] The EEC Treaty recognizes the special needs of less developed regions; see, for example, EEC Treaty, Preamble and arts. 29, 92, 131–36; see also the material on pp. 303–14.

some of the powers of government, to some extent they would be the "rulers" of the state, but they would not have been chosen by the people. The members of the Commission are appointed by the governments of EEC member states acting unanimously. The Irish government could, "in final appeal," veto the appointment of any member of the Commission, and so the appointment of a member would be, very indirectly, controlled by the Irish people. Ireland would have no voice in the appointment of the Council, other than the Irish member. Since the politico-constitutional rights of the Irish people under Article 6 are vague and since measures to provide democratic control over the Council and the Commission are likely in the future, it would be unsatisfactory if the EEC Treaty were held unconstitutional in Ireland on the basis of Article 6.[5] (Nevertheless, the question is important in Ireland, in Germany, and indeed in any state where democracy and sovereignty are taken seriously.)

LEGISLATION BY "SUBORDINATE LEGISLATURES"

The problem is presented more clearly by Article 15(2) of the Constitution, which provides:

1. The sole and exclusive power of making laws for the State is hereby vested in the Oireachtas:[6] no other legislative authority has power to make laws for the State.

2. Provision may however be made by law for the creation or recognition of subordinate legislatures and for the powers and functions of these legislatures.

Thus, legislative power may be exercised "on the authority of"[7] Parliament only by a "subordinate" legislature. Such a legislature may be "recognized" by law, and Parliament may adopt and enact the powers and functions already given to this legislature by international law or Community law.

Under Article 189 of the EEC Treaty, the Council and the Commission[8] may adopt "regulations" which have general application and are binding on companies and individuals without implementing national legislation. These regulations are laws within Article 15. They are of great practical importance and are regarded as legislative by Community lawyers.[9] They are regarded as executive acts only on the ground that the power to make them is delegated and is exercisable only in certain spheres; this argument does not prevent regulations from being legislation under Irish law. They implement the framework of the

[5] It appears that the Commission and the Council were relieved from democratic control partly to give parliamentarians an incentive to add to the "supranational" attributes of the EEC by giving the European Parliamentary Assembly the control of the Commission and the Council. This would probably be done whenever direct elections to the Assembly are instituted.

[6] I.e., Parliament, and hereinafter so called. The national Parliament (art. 15) consists of the President, who is the formal Head of State, and two chambers—the Dáil (lower house), which is directly elected by proportional representation, and the Seanad (Senate), which is largely elected by a complicated system intended to secure vocational representation. See Seanad Electoral (Panel Members) Act, 1947 Acts 729; Seanad Electoral (Panel Members) Act, 1954 Acts 3.

[7] Art. 6(2).

[8] The Commission acts independently of the Council in matters of lesser importance and has more limited legislative power; see Bebr, Judicial Control 52–53 (1962).

[9] See, for example, Birkelbach Report, A.P.E. Doc. No. 122, para. 75 (1961–62); Reuter, "Juridical and Institutional Aspects of the European Regional Communities," 26 Law & Contemp. Prob. 381, 396 (1961); Cartou, Le Marché Commun et le Droit Public 70–74 (1959); Firme I. Nold KG v. High Authority, 5 Recueil 89, 113 (1959). Other authorities are listed in Bebr, Judicial Control 13, 38. See Costa v. ENEL, 10 Recueil 1141, 1177, [1964] C.M.L.R. 425, 436 (conclusions of Advocate-General Lagrange); the remarks of M. Macilhacy in the French Senate on Dec. 2, 1964.

Treaty by general rules. If the same powers were conferred on a body set up solely under Irish municipal law, there would be no doubt that the rules constituted legislation.

The question, then, is whether the Council and Commission would be "subordinate" to the Irish Parliament and thus have powers not limited by Article 15(2).[10] A reasonable interpretation would be that a body exercising lawmaking powers "on the authority of" Parliament[11] would be subordinate if Parliament could withdraw its authority, repeal the legislation enacted by the lawmaking body, set up another body to supervise the lawmaking one, give directions as to how the delegated powers should be exercised, and alter the constitution of the body or the limits of its powers. Subordinate legislation normally must be submitted to Parliament, and it can override parliamentary legislation only when expressly empowered to do so. However, the mere receipt of power from Parliament could not make a body "subordinate." This interpretation would deprive both Article 15(2)(1) and the first part of Article 6(2) of effect. Subordination must be real, and Article 15(2)(2) has always been regarded as authorizing only what is known as delegated legislation.[12] The power of the Commission and the Council to enact regulations does not fulfill any of the tests of subordination suggested above. Their authority to make regulations can be withdrawn only by agreement on the dissolution of the EEC. The duration of the EEC Treaty is unlimited.[13] Parliament could not repeal or alter regulations made by the Community without breaching the Treaty[14] and would be obliged to bring Irish law into line with them. Apart from the right of the Irish government to be represented on the Council and to veto the appointment of any person to the Commission, Parliament would have no control over either body. Parliament would not have even the right to consider changes in the powers conferred, because the Council has power to make decisions that add to or amend the Treaty without having these ratified by the parliaments of the member states.[15] Article 219 prohibits settling disputes that arise under the Treaty except in the ways provided; thus, Parliament could not set up any body purporting to supervise or review the actions of the Commission or Council. To come automatically into force in national law, the regulations must prevail over inconsistent Irish common law or legislation. Parliament could avoid conflict between regulations and subsequent legislation by not enacting legislation inconsistent with the Treaty or the regulations in force. This would hardly be consistent with a "subordinate" position of the Community organs. The powers conferred on the EEC organs are not delegated but

[10] The subordination must be to the Parliament. No other interpretation is possible in view of the position of art. 15(2)(2) and the distribution of powers of government made by the Constitution as a whole. See Pigs Marketing Bd. v. Donnelly, [1939] Ir. R. 413, especially at 421–22; cf. Re O'Farrell & Gorman, [1960] Ir. R. 239, 263. The fact that the Council is "subordinate" to the Treaty can hardly be relevant, and it would not in Community law be subordinate to the Constitution.

[11] Art. 6(2).

[12] Pigs Marketing Bd. v. Donnelly, [1939] Ir. R. 413, 421.

[13] It is suggested below that without agreement there is no right of withdrawal from the EEC in any circumstances.

[14] See Costa v. ENEL, 10 Recueil 1141, [1964] C.M.L.R. 425. The separate question whether Parliament would have power under Irish domestic law to repeal the Treaty once it had enacted it is discussed on pp. 55–64. Even if it had this power, it would not have the right to exercise it, and it is submitted that this is what should be examined.

[15] Art. 235.

irrevocably assigned to them.[16]

It could be argued that the Commission is "subordinate" because it can make regulations only in limited fields of law. The reasons for limiting the delegation of legislative power would favor a body restricted to a limited field. However, this interpretation would permit Parliament to transfer piecemeal the whole of its legislative authority to other bodies.[17] Article 15 speaks of the subordination of the legislature and not of a limitation on the delegated powers (in contrast to Article 37 of the Constitution). This indicates that the lawmaking bodies are to be subordinate in the exercise of their powers within whatever might be their sphere of activity. The word "subordinate" normally does not mean subordinate only in importance.[18] It would be less proper for Parliament to abandon its responsibility for, and its control over, rules on a narrow range of affairs than to delegate its powers over a wide range of subjects but retain supervisory functions and ultimate control. Although the Council and the Commission may enact regulations only on those fields of law specifically mentioned in the Treaty or necessarily affected by it, their economic and political importance is very great.

PARLIAMENT'S EXCLUSIVE POWER TO MAKE "LAWS FOR THE STATE"

Is the EEC Treaty a "law for the State"?

The power of the Parliament relates to making laws "for the State,"[19] i.e., those domestic or municipal laws which are, in principle, binding for all persons within the jurisdiction. The fact that the legislative power of the Parliament is described as exclusive does not affect the powers of the Irish state to make rules of international law by treaty, since at least one other state is required to make a treaty; thus the Parliament does not have this power exclusively. Under Irish law, treaties are binding *on* the state, even without the approval of the Parliament,[20] but not *within* the state. The legislative power of Parliament is thus not "exclusive" in relation to those laws made by the state as a legal entity and binding on it in its capacity under international law, but having a wider territorial application than the jurisdiction of the state. Since Parliament cannot have this power exclusively, it is submitted that treaties cannot be laws "for the State."

The Parliament cannot delegate its exclusive powers because they are its exclusive responsibility. Since the power of Parliament to be associated in the enactment of common rules for Europe is not exclusive and could not be derived solely from the Constitution, it seems reasonable that this power should not be subject to limitations imposed on Parliament's exclusive powers over domestic law, which powers are derived only from the Constitution. Indeed, Article 15 does not deal with the power of Parliament to make laws which are not municipal law, so it does not limit the power of Parlia-

[16] Hayoit de Termicourt, "Le Conflit 'Traité-Loi interne,'" 1963 Journal des Tribunaux 481, 484; cf. Tsangarides, "Nature juridique de actes émis par le Conseil et la Commission de la C.E.E.," 13 Revue Hellénique de Droit International 138 (1961).

[17] Cf. Re O'Farrell & Gorman, [1960] Ir. R. 239, 263–64 (dicta of Kingsmill Moore, J.).

[18] Such an interpretation would be clearly contrary to the Irish word *fo-reachtais*—meaning "subordinate legislature"—in art. 15(2)(2).

[19] Art. 15(2)(1). Cf. the phrase "sole and exclusive power of making laws for the State" with the phrase "the supreme law of the land" in art. VI of the United States Constitution.

[20] Art. 29(4)(1) and 29(5)(1). The assent of the Parliament is required only under art. 29(6) and that of the lower house separately under art. 29(5)(2), subject to art. 29(5)(3). This represents no change from the English practice. See The Zamora, [1916] 2 A.C. 77; Walker v. Baird, [1892] A.C. 491; Western European Union Assembly, Legal Implications of the Accession of the United Kingdom to the European Economic Community on the British Constitution, 8th Sess., Doc. No. 249, Explanatory Memorandum (1962).

ment to delegate its legislative functions in such matters.

The Parliament has only limited powers in external affairs. The executive powers of the state,[21] including its powers in external relations, are exercised primarily by the government and are quite separate from the legislative powers. No limitations on executive powers should be read into the constitutional provisions dealing with legislative powers unless it is clearly necessary to do so. Article 15(2) clearly is not intended to be a limitation on the sovereignty of the state in international affairs, and an international legislative body with wider powers than the Parliament cannot be expected to be subordinate to Article 15(2). Since Parliament need not be consulted before the state is bound, no limitation on the treaty-making power can be drawn from limitations on the power of Parliament in purely domestic matters. Thus, Article 15(2) does not prohibit Ireland's accession to the EEC Treaty.

Are EEC regulations "laws for the State"?

It could be argued that under Article 29(6) international law and domestic law are separate spheres and that legislation implementing the EEC Treaty would be as unconstitutional as any act which purported to confer on a national organ the legislative powers of the Community.[22] Even without joining the EEC, the Parliament could enact legislation in exactly the terms of each regulation adopted by the Council and Commission, to implement the regulation within the state. Apparently the original idea of the Irish government, this scheme would be incompatible with the Treaty.[23] The legislation would in form be domestic legislation and would be subject in every way to the Constitution.

However, if Ireland were in the EEC, the Community law in force in Ireland would be more than merely Irish law. In substance, if not in form, it would be part of a system of uniform law for Europe. Even if it were enacted by the Parliament, it would remain law derived from an international treaty. If Ireland chose to enact the same legislation without having joined the EEC, the situation

[21] Arts. 28–29. Both art. 29(4)(1) and art. 29(4)(2) deal with the "executive power of the State in or in connection with its external relations." Art. 29(4)(1) speaks of "the executive power . . ." and art. 29(4)(2) of "any executive function." The difference in wording, which exists also in the Irish version, does not seem to have any significance for the purposes of this analysis. Art. 29(4)(1) says that executive power shall be exercised "in accordance with Article 28." Art. 28 provides that the executive power of the state shall be exercised by the government "subject to the provisions of this Constitution." The Constitution is, in any case, a part of Irish law within the meaning of art. 29(4)(2). However, the fact that art. 29(4)(2) does not refer to the Constitution is evidence that the power of the government was not intended to be subject to any constitutional restriction, such as art. 15(2).

[22] The question is the validity of Community regulation under Irish constitutional law and not under Community law. If Ireland joined the EEC, it therefore would be a question for the Irish courts, not the Community Court. See arts. 173 and 177. See, however, Costa v. ENEL, 10 Recueil 1141, [1964] C.M.L.R. 425. It would be more difficult if, for example, the Commission adopted a regulation which was retroactive in its operation and thus was contrary to art. 15(5) of the Irish Constitution, but this is only one of a number of questions which may arise unless an effective conflicts-of-law rule is worked out either by the Irish Supreme Court or by an amendment to the Irish Constitution.

The question of the regulations' constitutional validity could be raised in any litigation where the regulations were necessary to the decision. The contention that they were unconstitutional would be made not by the Irish government but probably by an enterprise operating in Ireland and alleged to have contravened a regulation.

[23] There would be no constitutional problem of the kind considered here in enacting the provisions of the EEC Treaty, except those provisions authorizing the Commission and the Council to make regulations. The Parliament could then enact each regulation as it was adopted by the Commission and the Council,

would be radically different. Ireland would not be obliged to enact such laws nor could she insist on their enactment in other countries; the law which she enacted would be purely municipal law, but the Community rules are a self-executing international law. Therefore, regulations in force in Ireland would not be laws "for the State" because they would be international rules governing enterprises in several countries and would be beyond the competence of the Irish Parliament to enact. It is important that Article 177 will require the Irish Supreme Court to recognize that certain rules in force in Irish law are Treaty provisions or Community regulations, not ordinary national law. The Community Court has emphasized that Community law is a legal system separate from national law.[24]

The power of the Community organs to adopt regulations directly applicable in Ireland is constitutional if the regulations are not regarded as "laws for the State." The question is whether this phrase means "rules of Irish municipal law," as is submitted here, or "rules in force in Irish municipal law."[25] However, the primary object of Article 15, like Article 6, is to insure that the Irish people are subject only to laws enacted by their democratically elected representatives. If this object is conclusive as to the meaning of the phrase, the second interpretation would be the correct one. The legislative powers of the Community would be contrary to the Constitution, and Ireland could not effectively join the EEC; if she purported to join it, enterprises in Ireland would not be subject to Community law. To decide the question, however, it is necessary to look at the constitutional provisions dealing with international affairs.

PARLIAMENT'S POWERS IN EXTERNAL AFFAIRS

Article 29 of the Irish Constitution is the only provision which expressly deals with external affairs. It reads:

1. Ireland affirms its devotion to the ideal of peace and friendly cooperation amongst nations founded on international justice and morality.
2. Ireland affirms its adherence to the principle of the pacific settlement of international disputes by international arbitration or judicial determination.
3. Ireland accepts the generally recognized principles of international law as its rule of conduct in its relations with other States.
4. (1) The executive power of the State in or in connection with its external relations shall in accordance with Article 28 of this Constitution be exercised by or on the authority of the Government.

(2) For the purpose of the exercise of any executive function of the State in or

---

The exclusive legislative authority for the state would be the formal source of the regulations in Irish municipal law. Since the Parliament would not be free, under the EEC Treaty, to alter the regulations adopted by the Commission, the implementing legislation could be enacted almost immediately. This arrangement would be contrary to the Treaty, because it would deny to regulations the force of domestic law and would end the difference between regulations and directives. It would be unworkable in practice, because it is essential that a uniform law throughout the Community be under the immediate control of the Commission. Numerous other difficulties would result from these delays; see Lang, "A Constitutional Aspect of Economic Integration: Ireland and the European Common Market," 12 Int'l & Comp. L.Q. 552, 562–64 (1963).

[24] Bosch v. de Geus, 8 Recueil 89, [1962] C.M.L.R. 1. If one takes the view that the EEC is a federation and that Community law is, therefore, the domestic law of the member states rather than international law, the constitutional difficulty is not avoided, though its nature is altered.

[25] Cf. art. 29(6). Before the Irish Constitution was enacted in 1937, the British Parliament had stated that it could legislate no longer for a Dominion without the Dominion's consent; Statute of Westminster, 1931, 22 Geo. 5, c. 4, § 4. Art. 15(2) therefore was not required as denial of the British Parliament's power to legislate for Ireland, although it possibly may have been so intended.

in connection with its external relations, the Government may to such extent and subject to such conditions, if any, as may be determined by law, avail of or adopt any organ, instrument or method or procedure used or adopted for the like purpose by the members of any group or league of nations with which the State is or becomes associated for the purpose of international cooperation in matters of common concern.[26]

5. (1) Every international agreement to which the State becomes a party shall be laid before Dáil Eireann [lower house].

(2) The State shall not be bound by any international agreement involving a charge upon public funds unless the terms of the agreement shall have been approved by Dáil Eireann.

(3) This section shall not apply to agreements or conventions of a technical and administrative character.

6. No international agreement shall be part of the domestic law of the State save as may be determined by the Oireachtas.[27]

Perhaps the question turns on whether, under Article 29(4)(2) and Article 29(6), the Parliament exceeds its normal authority in internal matters if it enacts as domestic law a treaty relating to an international organization. If "part of the domestic law of the State" in Article 29(6) means the same as "laws for the State" in Article 15(2), the freedom of the Parliament to delegate its powers under Article 29(6) is limited by Article 15(2). However, it is submitted that Article 29(6) means "laws in force in domestic law" and Article 15(2) means "laws derived only from the exclusive authority of the Parliament." On this view, Article 29(6) should be read together with Article 29(4)(2), not with Article 15(2), and the Parliament should be regarded as having power to delegate legislative powers to the EEC.

Article 29(6) does not seem to require formal enactment of a treaty as ordinary legislation before it comes into force in Irish domestic law.[28] If a treaty may be determined to be "part of the domestic

[26] Art. 29(4)(2) was drafted to make possible some degree of participation in the British Commonwealth similar to that contemplated by the Executive Authority (External Relations) Act, 1936 Pub. Stat. 1451, and to make possible membership in international organizations of the traditional type, without lawmaking powers, such as the League of Nations. See Chubb, The Constitution of Ireland 17–18 (1963), and compare art. 29(4)(2) with the amendment to art. 51 of the Irish Free State Constitution made by Constitution (Amendment No. 27) Act, 1936 Pub. Stat. 1445.

The writer is indebted to Dr. Ehler of University College, Dublin, for the suggestion that art. 29(4)(2) might have been drafted with the possibility in mind of a federal legislature with powers over what is now the Republic of Ireland and Northern Ireland. See Constitution of Ireland, art. 3. The author has been unable to find any legislative history to confirm this. If it is accepted, it adds weight to the argument that art. 29(4)(2) empowers the government to confer legislative powers on a body outside the jurisdiction of the Irish state as at present constituted. See Constitution of the Irish Free State (Saorstát Eireann) Act, 1922 Pub. Stat. 3, Second Schedule, arts. 11–15.

[27] "Although their constitutional rules and practices in this matter are not identical," the constitutional law of the following countries gives a treaty, when ratified and promulgated, the force of law without legislative action: Austria, Belgium, France, the Netherlands, Germany, Greece, Italy, Luxembourg, and Turkey. A treaty must be implemented by legislation in Denmark, Iceland, Norway, Sweden, the United Kingdom, and Ireland. Council of Europe, European Cooperation in 1961, at 230–31 (1962).

[28] In the English tradition, the ratification and the enactment of a treaty are separated in practice in Ireland. No procedure is provided by which a treaty can become domestic law except enactment in the usual way. In practice, a government may obtain parliamentary approval for a treaty before it is ratified by the government, but this is not legally necessary except under art. 29(5)(2), which requires that any treaty involving a charge on public funds be "approved" by the lower house; however, there is no need for any provision to be inserted in an appropriation act before the state is bound.

The principal purpose of the phrase "as may be determined by the Oireachtas" in art. 29(6) is to make it clear that the Parliament may refuse to enact a treaty in whole or in part or may enact it only with amendments. However, if a treaty is to be implemented in full and received into domestic law as it stands, there is

law of the State" without legislation, it seems different from "laws for the State" under Article 15. This fits perfectly with the interpretation of Article 15 derived from that provision itself. If the Constitution permits the reception of a treaty into domestic law without legislation, it is not easy to see why the Parliament cannot determine the extent to which a treaty is to be received without knowing its exact terms, that is, cannot delegate the power to decide its terms. Even if Article 29(6) is interpreted as requiring formal enactment of a treaty in the same way as any other law, the fact remains that "part of the domestic law of the State" seems to have been deliberately phrased to mean something different from "laws for the State."

DELEGATION BY PARLIAMENT OF THE POWER TO ALTER NATIONAL LAWS BY TREATY

Article 29(6) applies expressly only to international agreements, and the term "international agreements" does not include Community regulations.[29] However, for this purpose, they should probably be regarded as analogous to agreements. If the Parliament could determine in advance that a certain international agreement to be concluded by the government would automatically be part of Irish domestic law, presumably it could "by law" authorize the government to subdelegate its power.[30]

The Parliament can delegate to the government the power to make an international agreement whose content and terms the Parliament has specified and can provide that the agreement, when made, should come into force in Irish law, because this is merely enactment of legislation which will take effect when a specified step is taken by the government. The only power Parliament has delegated is the power to bring the law into force, not to vary the terms laid down by the Parliament.

Article 29(6) may not permit legislation such as the United States Trade Expansion Act of 1962, which authorizes the executive, by treaty, to reduce by specified percentages the tariffs on commodities not directly specified. If so, not only the legislative power of Community institutions but also the Treaty provisions which allow the Council to alter the speed of tariff and quota reduction between member states[31] would be unconstitutional in Ireland. If the object of

---

little point in going through, for example, the committee stage, where detailed amendments are considered in normal Irish parliamentary procedure.

[29] Regulations made by the Commission are not international agreements, although they derive their force from such an agreement, i.e., the Treaty. Regulations made by the Council could be regarded as international agreements. However, they are binding on a minority who have not agreed to them if they are passed by the requisite majority, and they derive their formal force and exact effect from the Treaty which makes them Community acts, not from consensus. To distinguish regulations to which Ireland had agreed from those which were binding on Ireland as legislative acts without her consent would be to draw a distinction which does not exist under the Treaty. It would also have the absurd result that a regulation to which the Irish government had agreed would have to be approved by the Parliament, under art. 29(6), while a regulation to which the government had not agreed would not have to be approved. There is of course a difference between a treaty entered into by Ireland, which must be presented to the lower house at some time, and a regulation which, under the Treaty, would come into force in Irish law without being formally called to the attention of Parliament in any way.

[30] Art. 29(4)(2).

[31] EEC Treaty, arts. 14(7), 33(8). If the Parliament is permitted by art. 15(2) to give the government, by legislation, the power to modify legislation by statutory instrument (the so-called Henry VIII clause), it is hard to see why it may not do so also under art. 29(6), where it does not seem to be limited by art. 15(2).

Article 29(6) is to insure that Irish citizens are subject only to laws enacted by their elected representatives, it is unlikely that such legislation would be constitutional.

If the Parliament can authorize the government to delegate its functions in external affairs, it should be able to delegate to the government some incidental powers over national law. Article 29(6) allows the will of the Parliament to prevail over that of the government in domestic law, but it does not limit the power of the government to bind the state, since the ratification of treaties is entirely a matter for the government. There is no indication that Article 29(6) restricts the power of the Parliament to delegate authority over national law to the government for treaty-making purposes. If the Parliament delegates this authority, the danger of usurpation of the legislative function, which Article 29(6) was intended to prevent, does not arise to a serious extent. An interpretation of Article 29(6) which prevented the Parliament from delegating power over domestic law in advance would involve the Parliament in the ratification of agreements,[32] and this would be contrary to the whole tenor of Article 29, except Article 29(5)(2). When the Constitution authorizes delegation of powers over external affairs to international organizations, it would be odd if the Constitution regarded it as so important to have domestic law made only by an elected body that it prevented the delegation of power over domestic law to the government.

DELEGATION OF POWERS BY THE GOVERNMENT TO INTERNATIONAL INSTITUTIONS

The government may adopt international institutions "for the purpose of the exercise of any executive function of the State in or in connection with its external relations" under Article 29(4)(2). Although the EEC Treaty aims at integrating the economies of signatory states, their relations among themselves are still "external" relations within the meaning of Article 29(4)(2).

Article 29(4)(2) as worded relates to the "executive functions" of the state, not to its legislative powers; but under Article 29 the treaty-making power is an executive function. Under Article 29(4), the government has power to adopt treaties which are not part of Irish domestic law without the consent of the Parliament. Therefore, presumably[33] the government can delegate its power to make international legislation to an international institution.

Article 29(4)(2) contemplates advance determination by the Parliament of the extent to which the government may use international institutions to carry on external affairs. Article 29(4)(2) is couched in the widest terms, and since popular control over the exercise of any powers under this provision necessarily must be remote, there is no obvious reason for interpreting either Article 29(6) or Article 15(2) as a limitation on the powers which may be delegated under it if the Parliament approves. Its language is more technical than the rest of Article

[32] Art. 28 requires a cabinet government system under which the legislature is controlled by the party of the executive, and the approval of the Parliament for a treaty ratified by the government normally can be expected. But even to assume substantial identity of policy between the Parliament and the government does not clarify the interpretation of the constitutional provisions analyzed in the text. Art. 29(5)(1) does not require a treaty to be laid before the lower house before it is ratified by the government; it is intended merely to prevent the government's concealing from the Parliament the existence or the terms of treaties into which it has entered.

[33] The question whether delegation of treaty-making power of the kind contemplated by art. 228 of the EEC Treaty is compatible with the Constitution is discussed on p. 9.

29, and this makes the comprehensiveness of the terms used and the absence of any qualification more significant.

There is no clear constitutional limitation[34] on the power of the government to bind the state,[35] even without the approval of the Parliament. If Parliament approves, strong reasons for limiting the treaty-making power of the state, one of the most important attributes of sovereignty, and for limiting the power of the state to participate in modern international institutions would be necessary. It is suggested that Articles 15(2) and 29(6) preserve the exclusive powers of the Parliament over purely municipal law and prevent unauthorized legislation by way of treaty. They are not intended to limit the power of the government to conclude any type of treaty of which the Parliament approves.

Of course it would be possible to interpret Articles 15(2) and 29(6) together as prescribing an absolute principle that no legislation should be in force in Irish domestic law which had not been enacted by the Parliament or a subordinate legislature. Nationalists might object to having Irish domestic law altered by an international organization. Clearly, neither provision contemplated Irish membership in an organization with power to adopt laws directly applicable in member states. The simplest interpretation is not necessarily correct, however, and has serious practical disadvantages. This chapter points out that a more modern and more sophisticated interpretation is possible and desirable. Considerations of policy are important in applying a constitution to circumstances not contemplated at the time when it was drafted.

LEGISLATION FORMALLY UNCONSTITUTIONAL AND LEGISLATION SUBSTANTIVELY UNCONSTITUTIONAL

If unconstitutional, the delegation of legislative power to the Community institutions would be unconstitutional as contrary to the formal provisions dealing with distribution of powers and not to the substantive provisions of the Constitution.[36] It is submitted that in external

[34] Except art. 29(5)(2).

[35] In this connection, the only item of legislative history which bears on the problem is of peculiar interest. When speaking generally about the draft Constitution at the second stage of the bill, Eamon de Valera, T.D., then President of the Irish Free State and the principal draftsman of the Constitution, said in the lower house:

> [Art. 29 of] the Constitution . . . puts the question of our international relations in their proper place—*and that is outside the Constitution*. . . . The idea of this Constitution is to put this matter of our external relations in its proper position relative to the Constitution, and *that is outside it*. That is what is done here. It is done by giving to the executive authority, namely, the Government, which is the fundamental executive authority, power to use an organ, instrument or method of procedure which may be used for similar purposes by other nations with whom we may be associated, *no matter what it is*. . . . [T]he external relations are kept in a position in which they can be dealt with and handled as a matter of public policy, *without bringing them across the fundamental rights* which govern the working of our institutions.
>
> 67 Dáil Eireann, Parl. Deb., cols. 60–61 (1937). (Emphasis added.) Also quoted in Chubb, A Source Book of Irish Government 18–20 (1964).

Legislative history is, however, without formal authority in the Irish courts, and in fact the interpretation seems inconsistent with art. 28(2), taken together with art. 29(4)(1) and 29(4)(2), as it has been shown must be done. The extract quoted is repetitive, and it seems highly unlikely that it was written by a lawyer. See also The State (Duggan) v. Tapley, [1952] Ir. R. 62, 68. On the personal role of President de Valera in drafting the Constitution, see Chubb, The Constitution of Ireland 15 (1963).

[36] If the Treaty prevailed where it was inconsistent with the substantive provisions of the Constitution, the Constitution would be amended in a way not permitted by art. 46. Neither art. 15(2) nor art. 29(6) limits the substantive powers of the Parliament, except to prevent the Parliament from depriving itself of them. See Re Ó Laighléis, [1960] Ir. R. 93, es-

affairs a distinction should be drawn between Article 15(2), which specifies the bodies to exercise legislative powers, and Articles 40–45, on fundamental rights, which specify legislation which no body may enact. There is no Irish authority for this distinction, but it seems reasonable and has the support of the American decisions mentioned below.[37]

Since Article 15(2) concerns the allocation of legislative power rather than substantive restrictions on the content of legislation, it seem reasonable to compare it with the position in a federal system. In federal systems, powers sometimes are given to the federal authorities to enact legislation which would be exclusively within the legislative powers of the constituent states if external relations were not involved.[38] Of course, not all federations have done this.[39] In the United States, appropriately drafted treaties are self-executing, that is, they come into force without implementing legislation after receiving the consent of the Senate. The Executive and the Senate may conclude treaties, and Congress has the power to enact legislation to implement them,[40] even if the legislation would have been an unconstitutional encroachment on the exclusive legislative powers of the states[41] if it had not been made the subject matter of a treaty. In the leading case, *Missouri v. Holland,*[42] Mr. Justice Holmes made it clear that the Court

---

pecially at 122–25. After stating the rule that treaties are not domestic law until enacted by the Parliament, Mr. President Davitt said, after stating the rule in another form, "If this principle were not observed it would follow that the Executive Government by means of an international agreement might in certain circumstances be able to exercise powers of legislation contrary to the letter and the spirit of the Constitution. The rights of citizens of the State to be bound by no other laws than those enacted by their elected representatives in the Oireachtas assembled is to be carefully preserved and jealously guarded." Id. at 103. It is clear that the learned judge in the first sentence quoted intended to state: "If this principle were not observed, the Executive Government by means of an international agreement might exercise powers of legislation which powers would be contrary to the Constitution," rather than "the Executive Government by means of an international agreement might . . . exercise powers of [enacting] legislation [which legislation would in its content be] contrary to the . . . Constitution." In any case, the second sentence supports the interpretation of arts. 15 and 29 which would make Community legislative powers unconstitutional.

[37] See, however, J. M. Jones, Full Powers and Ratification 151–52 (1946), dealing with the validity in international law of an unconstitutional treaty; Northey, "Constitutional Limitations as Affecting the Validity of Treaties," 11 U. Toronto L.J. 175, 200–201 (1956). United States decisions are frequently quoted on constitutional issues in the Irish courts.

[38] For the position in Switzerland, see Looper, "The Treaty Power in Switzerland," 7 Am. J. Comp. L. 178 (1958).

[39] For instance, art. 69 of the Nigerian Constitution limits the legislative power of the federal legislature in the implementation of treaties on matters over which the regional legislatures would normally have exclusive jurisdiction to the enactment of legislation which will come into force in each Region only by the consent of the Governor of the Region. For the position in Canada, see Attorney General for Canada v. Attorney General for Ontario, [1937] A.C. 326. In the well-known *Concordat* case, the German Constitutional Court upheld a state statute which was directly in conflict with a treaty properly concluded by the German Reich in 1933 on the grounds that the subject it concerned, education, was within the sole competence of the Länder. See 6 Entscheidungen des Bundesverfassungsgericht 309 (1957), discussed in McWhinney, "Federal Constitutional Law and Treaty Making Power," 35 Can. B. Rev. 842 (1957).

[40] Executive agreements may be made without the consent of the Senate, within the limits of the President's powers. It is interesting to consider whether the subject matter of executive agreements in United States constitutional law may be similar to that of "conventions of a technical or administrative character" under art. 29(5)(3) of the Irish Constitution.

[41] Under the Tenth Amendment.

[42] 252 U.S. 416 (1920). The question raised in this case was whether federal legislation carrying out a treaty providing for the protection

was not implying that there were no limitations on the treaty-making power, though he did not say what the limitations were.

In *Reid v. Covert*,[43] the United States Supreme Court held that treaties subjecting the dependents of United States servicemen to the Uniform Code of Military Justice when overseas were unconstitutional because they deprived civilians of their right to trial by jury under the Bill of Rights. Dealing with the contention that the Uniform Code could be sustained as legislation required to carry out the international obligations of the United States under treaties entered into, Mr. Justice Black said:[44]

> The obvious and decisive answer to this is . . . that no agreement with a foreign nation can confer power on Congress or on any other branch of the Government which is free from the restraints of the Constitution. . . . It would be manifestly contrary to the objectives of those who created the Constitution as well as those who were responsible for the Bill of Rights—let alone alien to our entire constitutional history and tradition—to construe [the supremacy clause] . . . as permitting the United States to exercise power under an international agreement without observing constitutional prohibitions. In effect such construction would permit amendment of [the Constitution] . . . in a manner not sanctioned by Article V.[45]

The relevance of this to the problem under the Irish Constitution is clear. Congress may exercise most of the legislative powers of the United States, both federal and state, to fulfill the country's international obligations, but Congress may not enact legislation to implement a treaty which no legislative body in the United States could constitutionally enact.[46] In Ireland, Community legislation certainly could be enacted by the Parliament, and the question is whether the Irish Constitution authorizes the exercise of legislative power by an international body which power would have been unconstitutional if it had been conferred on a domestic body. In the Irish problem, as in *Missouri v. Holland*, the legislation is by hypothesis perfectly legitimate, and the question is whether the constitutional

---

of migratory birds was constitutional. If the subject matter had not been dealt with by a treaty, it would have been exclusively within the jurisdiction of the states.

[43] 354 U.S. 1 (1957). In Geofroy v. Riggs, 133 U.S. 258 (1890), Mr. Justice Field said:

> That the Treaty power of the United States extends to all proper subjects of negotiation between our government and the governments of other nations, is clear. . . . The treaty power, as expressed in the Constitution, is in terms unlimited except by those restraints which are found in that instrument against the action of government or its departments, and those arising from the nature of the government itself and of that of the States. It would not be contended that it extends so far as to authorize what the Constitution forbids, or a change in the character of the government or in that of one of the States, or a cession of any part of the territory of the latter, without its consent. . . .
>
> [W]ith these exceptions, it is not perceived that there is any limit to the questions which can be adjusted touching any matter which is properly the subject of negotiation with a foreign country.
>
> Id. at 226–67.

See also Downes v. Bidwell, 182 U.S. 244 (1901), and United States v. Curtiss-Wright Export Corp., 299 U.S. 304 (1936). Restatement, Foreign Relations Law of the United States § 120 (Proposed Official Draft 1962), contains a brief but authoritative statement of the whole position. See Stein, "When Is an International Agreement 'Self-Executing' in American Law?" in International Academy of Comparative Law, Sixth International Congress of Comparative Law (1962), set out in part in Stein & Hay, Cases on the Law and Institutions of the Atlantic Area 7–13, 158–59 (prelim. ed. 1963).

[44] 354 U.S. at 16.

[45] See also 5 Moore, A Digest of International Law 167 (1906).

[46] Restatement, Foreign Relations Law of the United States § 120 (Proposed Official Draft 1962), says that a treaty may not contravene "any of the limitations of the Constitution applicable to all powers of the United States."

division of legislative powers prevents the lawmaking body in question from enacting it. The objects of the Bill of Rights can only be maintained by prohibiting certain forms of procedure, while the constitutional assurance that the Irish people are governed by laws enacted by a responsible body is adequately carried out by the Treaty of Rome.[47]

POLICY CONSIDERATIONS

Article 29 contemplates the use of any international organization "for the purposes of international cooperation in matters of common concern" and more generally for "friendly cooperation amongst nations"; the EEC is based on both. Economic interdependence is inevitable in the external relations of states, and the EEC is designed to turn it to the common advantage. The EEC was set up to secure "peace and friendly cooperation,"[48] as the Irish Constitution says, and "to establish the foundations of an ever closer union among the European peoples."[49] The ideals set out in the Preamble to the Treaty are similar to the Directive Principles of Social Policy in the Constitution.[50]

Ireland can not join and get the advantages of the Common Market unless EEC regulations are directly applicable in Irish law. Even if the Commission would permit the Parliament to enact each regulation automatically and without alteration, the safeguards for the Irish people would not be improved by this technical adherence to the Constitution. The limitations on the powers of the EEC should not derive from constitutional provisions but from the Treaty itself and from the control of the Community Council, Court, and Assembly. Ireland has chosen to apply for full membership, which, if it involves submission to the Community's legislative powers, also confers a voice in its composition and activities. Since the Constitution does not contemplate self-executing international law rules, or encroachment on the exclusive legislative authority of the Parliament, there are strong technical arguments against the position argued here. As discussed later in this chapter, the Irish government should probably amend the Constitution to allow both entry into the EEC and surrender of sovereignty to a European political union.[51] A constitutional amendment similar to that carried out in the Netherlands will clearly be required for this union, which is politically if not legally involved in accession to the EEC Treaty, since the Irish Constitution gives no power to surrender national sovereignty.[52] It is in the interests

[47] The more doubtful question whether the Commission and the Council could be said to be appointed by and legally and democratically responsible to the Irish people is discussed on p. 39. *Reid v. Covert* has helped to quiet the controversy centered around the Bricker Amendment, S.J. Res. 1, 83d Cong., 1st Sess. (1953), debated by the Senate in Feb. 1954. On the Bricker Amendment and related proposals and for an historical analysis, see the references cited in Bishop, International Law 104–105 (2d ed. 1962). See Hay, Cooley & Moorhead, "Problems of United States Participation in the European Common Market," 23 U. Pitt. L. Rev. 595, 637–58 (1962).

[48] Art. 29(1).

[49] EEC Treaty, Preamble.

[50] Art. 45. This article expressly provides that it shall not be cognizable by any court.

[51] See Proposition de Résolution relative à l'Union politique des Six et à son organisation, A.P.E. Doc. No. 22 (1962–63); Rapport fait au nom de la Commission Politique sur les négociations en vue de la Création d'une Union Politique Européenne, A.P.E. Doc. No. 23 (1962–63); A.P.E. Debats, Sess. 1961–62, Dec. 20, 1961, at 117–37, 140–72; A.P.E. Commission Politique, Le Dossier de l'Union politique (1964).

[52] This amendment should be passed before accession to the EEC Treaty, when withdrawal becomes legally impossible, in order to resolve doubts and to avoid the embarrassment of being compelled to hold a referendum under arts. 5

of Ireland as a small nation to be free to press for greater political integration in the EEC.

THE POSITION IN THE SIX

All of the Six are civil law countries[53] with written constitutions. Only in Germany has the question of whether the EEC is constitutional risen directly, but in the Netherlands and Luxembourg constitutional amendments were enacted. In Germany, a constitutional amendment was enacted to permit the ratification of the abortive European Defense Community Treaty, and no further amendment was adopted for the EEC Treaty. No comparable problem exists in the United Kingdom, which has no written constitution[54] and no judicial review for unconstitutionality.

Germany

The constitutional problem discussed above for Ireland is essentially the same as that in Germany. Article 24(1) of the German Constitution, or Basic Law, authorizes the Federation to transfer "sovereign power" to international institutions by legislation. It is uncertain whether either the EEC Treaty or any regulation would affect a basic right, guaranteed by Part I of the Basic Law.[55] If the powers of the Commission and the Council were not limited powers under the Basic Law, they would not be compatible with the provisions authorizing the exercise of legislative powers by bodies other than the Federal and Länder legislatures, provisions intended to prevent legislation by bodies not democratically elected. However, regulations and decisions of the Commission and the Council or the Community Court are unlikely to be regarded as acts of a German public authority, apparently the only acts within the jurisdiction of the Federal Constitutional Court, in spite of the broad provisions of Articles 93(1) and 100 of the Basic Law which outline its jurisdiction. Under German law, the Constitutional Court may consider a claim based on unconstitutionality only when all other remedies, including presumably that of appeal to the Community Court, have been exhausted. Because of the operation of Article 177 of the EEC Treaty, it has been argued that the Community Court would have two chances to make a ruling which would avoid conflict between the

---

and 171 of the Treaty. It would be undesirable to have a referendum to alter the Constitution after the terms of Ireland's accession were known, since they would be too complex to be the subject of a referendum. The question whether Ireland should equip itself with a constitution which enables it to participate in European integration is precisely the type of question which should be submitted to the people. Norway amended its Constitution in 1962 to allow entry into the EEC; see Norwegian Constitution, art. 93.

[53] Reference to the various parliamentary debates on the ECSC, the prototype of the EEC, are given in Communauté Européenne de Charbon et de l'Acier, Cour de Justice, Service de Documentation, I Etat Actuel des Questions Juridiques et de la Jurisprudence 12–13 (1950–57). For some materials on the constitutional position in the Six, see Stein & Hay, Cases on the Law and Institutions of the Atlantic Area 14–28 (prelim. ed. 1963).

[54] See generally Bebr, "The Relation of the European Coal and Steel Community Law to the Law of Member States," 58 Colum. L. Rev. 767 (1958).

[55] Translated in 2 Peaslee 33; Basic Law, art. 19(2). See Costa v. ENEL, 10 Receuil 1141, 1177, [1964] C.M.L.R. 425, 436 (conclusions of Advocate-General Lagrange); see also Re Import of American Barley, Verwaltungsgericht (Administrative Court), Frankfurt-am-Main, Dec. 17, 1963, [1964] C.M.L.R. 285; cf. Re Tax on Malt Barley, Finanzgericht, Rheinland-Pfalz, Nov. 14, 1963, [1964] C.M.L.R. 130. For a study of the history of the litigation before the Federal Constitutional Court concerning the abortive European Defense Community, see Loewenstein, "The Bonn Constitution and the European Defense Community Treaties," 64 Yale L.J. 804 (1955); see also Constantopoulos, "The Relation of the Law of Nations to Constitutional Law and the New Constitution of Germany," 5 Revue Hellénique de Droit International 42 (1952).

Basic Law and the Treaty or regulation.[56] In Germany, treaties must conform to the Basic Law, and they prevail over prior and possibly over subsequent federal laws[57] and also over the laws of the Länder in matters within the legislative competence of the federal authorities.

Italy

In Italy, "the chambers authorize by law ratification of those international treaties which are of a political nature, which involve arbitration or judicial regulations, or which entail changes in the national territory, financial burdens, or modifications of laws."[58] Articles 70–72 of the Italian Constitution may be inconsistent with the EEC Treaty, and there seems to be no reason why this question should not be raised in the Constitutional Court, under Article 134.[59] However, the Treaty is constitutional in Italy because Article 72 of the Italian Constitution contemplates the delegation of legislative power and Article 11 allows necessary limitations on Italian sovereignty in favor of an international organization set up to insure peace and justice. The EEC is an effort to insure peace and justice, which presumably includes economic justice as contemplated by Articles 35–47 of the Italian Constitution. In Italy, subsequent national legislation and the Constitution prevail over a treaty, and this has given rise to problems.[60]

France

In France, the EEC Treaty was ratified under the Constitution of 1946, which was superseded by the Constitution of the Fifth Republic in 1958. The Conseil Constitutionnel can rule on the constitutionality of a law or a treaty *before* its ratification,[61] but there is no review to insure that treaties which have not been given approval before ratification are consistent with the Constitution. There is thus no chance of a judicial decision as to whether the EEC Treaty is compatible with the constitutional provisions on sovereignty or legislation.[62] *Inter alia*, commercial treaties and treaties relating to international organizations and involving committing state finances or modifying a law require ratification by means of a legislative act of the French legislature.[63] Articles 26 and 28 of the 1946 Constitution provided that treaties when ratified were to take effect without additional formalities and were to prevail over prior and subsequent domestic laws. The 1958 Constitution has similar provisions,[64] with the condition that the other

[56] Stein & Hay, "New Legal Remedies of Enterprises: A Survey," in 1 American Enterprise in the European Common Market: A Legal Profile 459, 483 (Stein & Nicholson ed. 1960).

[57] Basic Law, art. 25. See also Mosler, "L'application du droit international public par les tribunaux nationaux," 91 Recueil Académie D. Int. 625 (1957); Preuss, "On Amending the Treaty-Making Power: A Comparative Study of the Problem of Self-Executing Treaties," 51 Mich. L. Rev. 1117, 1132 (1953).

[58] Constitution of the Italian Republic of 1947, art. 80, translated in 2 Peaslee 482, 492.

[59] On the Constitutional Court, see generally Cassandro, "The Constitutional Court of Italy," 8 Am. J. Comp. L. 1–14 (1959), and Farrelly & Chan, "Italy's Constitutional Court: Procedural Aspects," 6 Am. J. Comp. L. 314 (1957); Telchini, "La Cour Constitutionelle en Italie," 1963 Rev. Int. de Droit Comp. 33.

[60] Costa v. ENEL, Corte Costituzionale (Italian Constitutional Court), Feb. 24, 1964, [1964] C.M.L.R. 425, 430. The rule stated in the text is completely unsatisfactory from the Community point of view; see Costa v. ENEL, 10 Recueil 1141, 1177, [1964] C.M.L.R. 425, 436 (conclusions of Advocate-General Lagrange); statement by Professor Hallstein to European Parliamentary Assembly, June 18, 1964, A.P.E. Débats, Séances du 15 au 19 juin 1964.

[61] Constitution of the Fifth Republic of 1958, arts. 54, 61.

[62] Constitution of 1958, arts. 2, 3, 5, 34–51.

[63] Constitution of 1958, art. 53, substantially enacting Constitution of 1946, art. 27.

[64] Constitution of 1958, art. 55 and Preamble; see Vignes, "L'autorité des traités internationaux en droit interne," Etudes de Droit Contempo-

state implements the treaty. Though there is no judicial review to insure that the treaty does prevail over subsequent domestic laws, in general the courts will not apply a law if a prior inconsistent treaty exists.[65]

Belgium

The Belgian Conseil d'Etat, like the French, follows the strict traditional European interpretation of the doctrine of separation of judicial and legislative powers, and the judges therefore have no power to hold legislation unconstitutional. The Constitution is essentially a political document setting out principles rather than the supreme law of the land.[66] "Treaties of commerce, and treaties which may burden the state or bind Belgians individually" require the approval of both the House of Representatives and the Senate.[67] Other appropriately drafted treaties are self-executing. There is controversy over whether treaties have the same effects in practice as ordinary laws and over whether they may be modified by subsequent legislation.[68] Treaties should be consistent with the Constitution, but without judicial review this cannot be enforced. Articles 25 and 26 of the Belgian Constitution provide:

25. All powers emanate from the people. They shall be exercised in the manner established by the Constitution.

26. The legislative power shall be exercised collectively by the King, the House of Representatives, and the Senate.

The resemblance to Articles 6 and 15 of the Irish Constitution and the conflict with the provisions of the EEC Treaty giving legislative power to Community institutions is clear. It is therefore significant that two declarations under Article 131 have been made by the King and the two houses calling for a revision of the Constitution to allow for the exercise of power by international organizations. This acknowledges that the Treaty is incompatible with the Belgian Constitution; but it would, of course, be dangerous to draw conclusions too readily from a civil law system and apply them in a common law country such as Ireland.

The Netherlands

Both the Netherlands and Luxembourg thought it necessary to amend their constitutions on entry into the ECSC, although in neither country is judicial review for constitutionality possible. The amendments to the Netherlands Constitution[69] are very far-reaching.[70] Both

---

rain, 23 Travaux et Recherches de l'Institut de Droit Comparé de l'Université de Paris 475, 482–84 (1962), translated in part in Stein & Hay, Cases on the Law and Institutions of the Atlantic Area 19–20 (prelim. ed. 1963); Preuss, "The Relation of International Law to Internal Law in the French Constitution," 44 Am. J. Int'l L. 641 (1950); Scelle, "De la prétendue inconstitutionnalité interne des Traités (A propos du Traité sur la 'Communauté européenne de défense')," 68 Revue de Droit Public et de la Science Politique 1012 (1952).

[65] De Visscher, "Les Tendances Internationales des Constitutions Modernes," 80(1) Recueil Académie D. Int. 265–66 (1952). This work of course relates to the Constitution of 1946.

[66] See Lievens, "The Conseil d'Etat in Belgium," 7 Am. J. Comp. L. 572 (1958); Goosens, "La Communauté Européenne du Charbon et de l'Acier et le régime constitutionnel Belgique," 71 Revue de Droit Public et de la Science Politique 98 (1955).

[67] Belgium Constitution, art. 68, translated in 1 Peaslee 162.

[68] See Hayoit de Termicourt, "Le Conflit 'Traité-Loi interne,'" 1963 Journal des Tribunaux 481, who argues strongly that a treaty should prevail over later domestic legislation; Schieble v. Procureur Général près la Cour d'Appel de Bruxelles & Campion, [1926] Pasinomie I. 76; Judgment of June 6, 1960, Comm. Brussels (5th ch.), 1960 Journal des Tribunaux 724; Judgment of Nov. 4, 1960, Brussels (8th ch.), 1961 Journal des Tribunaux 300; Judgment of Nov. 27, 1961, Civ. Brussels (4th ch.), 1962 Journal des Tribunaux 46.

[69] Translated in 2 Peaslee 754.

[70] The relevant amendments read:

Art. 60. Agreements with other Powers

treaties and decisions made by international organizations prevail over domestic laws and over the Constitution itself. There is no possibility of judicial review over treaties. Article 177 of the Treaty of Rome gives the Community Court exclusive ultimate jurisdiction over the validity and interpretation of acts of Community institutions.

Luxembourg

The amendment to the Luxembourg Constitution[71] is not as sweeping.[72] Under the case law of Luxembourg, treaties prevail over both prior and subsequent national legislation. Luxembourg judges may not decide on the constitutionality of a law or of a treaty, so in practice the judges apparently assume the validity of the treaty and apply it rather than the Constitution if the two are irreconcilable. The provisions of the Netherlands and the Luxembourg constitutions prior to the enactment of these amendments are not sufficiently similar to those of the Irish Constitution to require discussion.

The governments of Luxembourg and the Netherlands have been convinced of both the desirability and the imminent necessity of surrendering substantial amounts of legislative power and have passed comprehensive constitutional amendments to allow it. This is more satisfactory than the passage of piecemeal constitutional amendments authorizing the exercise of specific powers by international or "supranational" organizations; the piecemeal practice raises many practical difficulties and probably would be regarded as indicating a country's reluctance to surrender its national sovereignty to a United Europe.

PARLIAMENTARY SOVEREIGNTY[73]

The question is whether an EEC member state has the power under national law to repeal the act enacting the

and with organisations based on international law shall be concluded by or on the authority of the King. If required by such agreements they shall be ratified by the King.

The agreements shall be submitted to the States-General as soon as possible; they shall not be ratified and they shall not enter into force until they have received the approval of the States-General. The judge [i.e., Courts] shall not be competent to judge of the constitutionality of agreements.

60c. If the development of the international legal order [i.e. legal system] requires this, the contents of an agreement may deviate from certain provisions of the Constitution. In such cases the approval of the agreement shall not be given by the States-General but with a two-thirds majority of the votes cast in each of the two Chambers.

60g. By or in virtue of an agreement certain powers with respect to legislation, administration and jurisdiction may be conferred on organisations based on international law.

With regard to decisions made by organisations based on international law the Articles 60e and 60f [which give treaties priority over prior and subsequent domestic law, including the Constitution, so far as the treaties have been published] shall similarly apply.

2 Peaslee 754, 761–62.

Arts. 60c, 60g, 60e, and 60f in the Peaslee translation correspond to arts. 63, 67, 65, and 66, respectively, in the Dutch language version, [1953] Staatsblad, No. 261. On the amendments, see van Panhuys, "The Netherlands Constitution and International Law," 58 Am. J. Int'l L. 88 (1964), and the materials cited therein.

[71] Translated in 2 Peaslee 644.

[72] Art. 49 *bis* reads: "The exercise of powers reserved by the Constitution to the legislature, the executive or the judiciary may be temporarily delegated by treaty to international institutions set up under international law." Translated in 1957, Inter-Parliamentary Union, Constitutional and Parliamentary Information 49–51 (3d ser., no. 30, April 1957). Here, one difference between the ECSC and the EEC is relevant. The ECSC Treaty is to last for fifty years and is therefore "temporary"; the EEC Treaty is of unlimited duration. The Luxembourg constitutional amendment was passed in 1956. The EEC Treaty was not drawn up until the following year, so the amendment does not contemplate permanent delegation of power.

[73] The phrase "parliamentary sovereignty" means both that Parliament has "the right to make or unmake any law whatever; and . . . that no person or body is recognized . . . as having a right to override or set aside the

Treaty.[74] Of course to do so would be a serious breach of international law.

The traditional view

Under the traditional view, a law subsequent to and inconsistent with the Treaty-enacting act prevails over that act.[75] In this case, an enterprise aggrieved by the subsequent act has no remedy in the national courts or in the Community Court. It has no remedy in the latter because it cannot bring an action against a member state for breach of the Treaty; however, it probably could persuade the Commission to take up the matter.

On the other hand, if the Treaty-enacting act prevails over the subsequent act, either because of some constitutional principle or because of a provision in the enacting act that it is to prevail over subsequent inconsistent legislation unless expressly repealed, the aggrieved enterprise can question the validity of the subsequent act in the national courts. The second possibility is controversial and is of limited importance; but the constitutional position requires consideration. From a practical point of view and, in particular, from the point of view of the Community, it is necessary that the Treaty prevail in domestic law over subsequent inconsistent legislation.[76]

The Irish constitutional position at first seems clear. Only the Irish government can conclude treaties binding on the Irish state.[77] However, Article 29(6) provides that an international agreement shall be part of the domestic law of the state only as "may be determined" by the Parliament.[78] From the words quoted it seems clear that the Parliament may accept or reject a treaty or enact it only with modifications or in part. What the Parliament is not bound to enact, it seems free to repeal. The act enacting the treaty therefore would not override later legislation inconsistent with it.

This is the position in Britain, where the principles of the unwritten constitution are similar to those of the Irish Con-

legislation of Parliament." Dicey, The Law of the Constitution 40 (10th ed. 1959). Though drastically modified by the Constitution, both these principles still apply in Ireland. Both are affected by the EEC, but there is no constitutional difficulty in conferring on the EEC institutions the power to override the legislation of the Irish Parliament, other than the question discussed in the first part of this chapter.

[74] This question is of considerable importance; it already has arisen in Germany and in Italy and can arise in any country where the Treaty is enacted as an ordinary law.

[75] Any administrative action inconsistent with the Treaty is invalid under national law; whether the Treaty also is infringed may be decided ultimately by the Community Court, under art. 177. See, for example, the *Van Gend & Loos* case, 9 Recueil 1, [1963] C.M.L.R. 105; Costa v. ENEL, 10 Recueil 1141, [1964] C.M.L.R. 425, especially the conclusions of Advocate-General Lagrange, 10 Recueil at 1177, [1964] C.M.L.R. at 436.

[76] Hayoit de Termicourt, "Le Conflit 'Traité-loi interne,'" 1963 Journal des Tribunaux 481; see Costa v. ENEL, 10 Recueil 1141, [1964] C.M.L.R. 425; statement by Professor Hallstein to the European Parliamentary Assembly, June 18, 1964, A.P.E. Débats, Séances du 15 au 19 juin 1964; Re Customs Duties on Polyethylene, Finanzgericht, Bremen, Sept. 3, 1963, [1964] C.M.L.R. 295; Re Import of Polish Barley Meal, Finanzgericht, Nuremberg, March 23, 1964, [1964] C.M.L.R. 300; Re Import of Siamese Tapioca Meal (No. 1), Finanzgericht, Bremen, April 9, 1963, [1964] C.M.L.R. 304. On the importance of art. 5 of the EEC Treaty in this connection, see Chevalier & Rasquin, "De Quelques Problèmes soulevés par l'application du droit Communautaire en droit interne," 7 Revue du Marché Commun 489 (1964), where the national decisions are discussed; Catalano, "Rapports entre les règles de concurrence établies par le traité CEE et les législations des Etats membres," 15 Rev. Int. de Droit Comp. 269, 279 (1963).

[77] Art. 29(4), subject to 29(5)(2).

[78] In The Zamora, [1916] 2 A.C. 77, 90, Lord Parker of Waddington said:

> The idea that the King in Council, or indeed any branch of the executive, has power to prescribe or alter the law to be administered by the Courts of law in this country [Britain] is out of harmony with the principles of our Constitution. It is true that, under a number of modern statutes, various branches

stitution. In the House of Lords, before the collapse of the negotiations for Britain's entry into the EEC, Lord Dilhorne, the Lord Chancellor, said:

> By agreeing to be bound by a treaty we, of course, commit ourselves to comply with the provisions of that treaty. But making a treaty does not constitutionally involve the surrender of any part of the ultimate sovereignty of Parliament. An Act of Parliament would be required to apply these Treaties . . . and to give effect to present and future legislative acts of the Community institutions. *That Act of Parliament, like any other, could be repealed by a subsequent Act; and if this happened the Treaties would cease to be law in this country, and the power of the European Council to make regulations having effect as law in this country would come to an end.* But while Parliament's power to repeal the Act applying the Treaty remains, and cannot be fettered, I am not implying that it would be right for us to repeal it. The Rome Treaty is not limited in duration, and there is no provision for its termination. Parliament could repeal the Act applying these Treaties; *it cannot be prevented from doing so.* But it must be recognized that, in International Law, such a step could be justified only in exceptional circumstances; and if it were taken without such justification and without the approval of other member countries, it would be a breach of the international obligations assumed on entry into the Common Market.[79]

There is no doubt that the view expressed by Lord Chancellor is, in general, the correct view in English law.[80]

The only Irish precedent is under the previous Constitution of 1922 and is of dubious value and highly controversial. It is the legislation of the Irish Free State Parliament which was contrary to the treaty with Britain which concluded the war of independence. The problems in relation to its validity were complex, and the government of the time treated it as a political and not a legal question. Its weight as a precedent is on the side of the traditional view.[81]

An opposing view

Two arguments against the traditional view are possible. The first derives from the Irish Constitution of 1937; the sec-

---

of the Executive have power to make rules having the force of statutes, but all such rules derive their validity from the statute which creates the power, and not from the executive body by which they are made. No one would contend that the prerogative involves any power to prescribe or alter the law administered in Courts of Common Law or Equity.

See Re Ó Laighléis, [1960] Ir. R. 93, especially at 124–25. If the government has been rash enough to ratify a treaty which the Parliament will not implement, there is no legal way out of the difficulty.

[79] 243 H.L. Deb. (5th ser.) 416, 422 (1962). (Emphasis supplied.) The last sentence in the above passage, which implies that in some circumstances the EEC Treaty could justifiably be broken without the consent of other member states, is controversial.

[80] Dicey, The Law of the Constitution at liii–liv, 62 (10th ed. 1959); Wade & Phillips, Constitutional Law 46 (1960); Phillips, Constitutional and Administrative Law 60–61 (1962). It is probably not true that the Parliament of Britain can alter the terms of the Union between England and Scotland; see T. B. Smith, Scotland: The Development of Its Laws and Constitution 52–60 (1962); T. B. Smith, Studies Critical and Comparative, ch. 1 (1962). On the general English rule, see Vauxhall Estates, Ltd. v. Liverpool Corp., [1932] 1 K.B. 733; Ellen St. Estates, Ltd. v. Minister for Health, [1934] 1 K.B. 590; Jennings, The Law and the Constitution 162–63 (1959); Attorney General for New South Wales v. Trethowan, 44 Commw. L.R. 394 (Austl. 1931), aff'd, [1932] A.C. 526, on form and substance in connection with the power of Parliament to bind its successors. See also Marshall, Parliamentary Sovereignty and the Commonwealth 63–75 and ch. VI (1957); Western European Union Assembly, Legal Implications of the Accession of the United Kingdom on the British Constitution, 8th Sess., Doc. No. 249, Explanatory Memorandum 3–5 (1962).

[81] The controversy concentrated on the Constitution (Removal of Oath) Act, 1933 Pub. Stat. 27, by which the Irish legislature abolished the oath to the British Crown required of its members by Articles of Agreement for a Treaty Between Great Britain and Ireland, 1922 Pub.

ond is from certain principles which, because they are logical as legal principles in any country and because they are inherent in Ireland's constitutional history, might be the law in Ireland in respect of the EEC Treaty, although they are not so in Britain.

Article 29(3) of the Irish Constitution

The first reason for holding that a treaty overrides later inconsistent legislation derives from Article 29(3), which says: "Ireland accepts the generally regognised principles of international law as its rule of conduct in its relations with other States." In *Saorstát & Continental S.S. Co. v. De Las Morenas*,[82] Mr. Justice O'Byrne said: "The immunity of sovereign states . . . has long been recognized as a principle of international law and must now be accepted as part of our municipal law by reason of Article 29(3) of our Constitution." Article 29(3) was merely declaratory insofar as it laid down that rules of customary international law are part of Irish law except where they are inconsistent with common law or statute[83] and insofar as it meant that Ireland was bound by these rules. If a constitution largely re-enacts a previous constitution, there is no presumption of a change in the law. Article 29(3) might have been intended only as a statement of policy.[84] However, the obiter dictum quoted indicates that Article 29(3) made some change in Irish law.

The whole judgment of the Supreme Court in *The State (Duggan) v. Tapley*[85] discusses whether there was a rule of international law inconsistent with certain pre-1937 legislation. The judgment assumes that Article 29(3) repealed legislation inconsistent with customary international law. The judgment of the High Court makes the same assumption.[86]

Stat. 44. These "Articles" were annexed to the Constitution of the Irish Free State (Saorstát Eireann) Act, 1922 Pub. Stat. 3, which was passed by the Third Dáil sitting as a Constituent Assembly. Also annexed to this Act was the Constitution of the newly created Irish Free State, under which the legislature had power to amend the Constitution. However, the 1922 Act provided that no amendment to the Constitution or law passed pursuant to it was valid if it was inconsistent with the Articles. The British government had been unwilling to recognize the insurgents as a government of an independent state and so would not describe the Articles directly as a treaty. Unless it is held that the Free State legislature had power to repeal the 1922 Act as well as the Constitution—unless, in other words, it was the equal of the Constituent Assembly and not a creation of it—the Removal of Oath Act was invalid under Irish constitutional law without reference to the fact that it was also a breach of the treaty. By 1933, the British Parliament had empowered Dominion legislatures to amend and repeal Imperial legislation; Statute of Westminster, 1931, 22 Geo. 4, c. 4, § 2. Thus in British eyes the Free State legislature had the power to abolish the oath, although it had been required by an Imperial act; the Judicial Committee reserved the question of whether it had the right to do so in view of the Articles, which they referred to as "the Treaty," in Moore v. Attorney General of the Irish Free State, [1935] A.C. 484, 499. For an excellent summary of the controversy and for references to the Senate debates where the legal position was discussed, see Donal O'Sullivan, The Irish Free State and Its Senate, ch. XVIII, and 229, 249–55, especially at 253-54 (1940). See note 97 below.

[82] [1945] Ir. R. 291, 298. Since the doctrine of sovereign immunity was part of Irish law before 1937, there was no need to hold that the Constitution had made a change in this respect.

[83] Re Ó Laighléis, [1960] Ir. R. 93; The Parlement Belge, L.R. 5 P.D. 197 (1879); R. v. Keyn, 2 Ex. D. 63 (1876); West Rand Cent. Gold Mining Co. v. The King, [1905] 2 K.B. 391; Chung Chi Cheung v. R., [1939] A.C. 160; Norton v. General Acc. Ins. Co., 74 Ir. L.T.R. 123 (1940); Zarine v. S.S. Ramava, [1942] Ir. R. 148; Fogarty v. O'Donoghue, [1926] Ir. R. 531, 581.

[84] It is doubtful if art. 29(1) and 29(2) have any legal effect.

[85] [1952] Ir. R. 62.

[86] [1952] Ir. R. 62, 67 (per Gavan Duffy, P.). "The first three clauses [of art. 29] affirm general principles, which, as I understand them, are not inconsistent with [the legislation which it was argued had been impliedly repealed].

None of the eight judges gave any indication that he wished to reserve his position with regard to the assumption. If the assumption is not made, the question actually considered does not arise.

The two cases just cited make it clear that Article 29(3) was not a mere statement of policy and that it altered the existing law.[87] The principle that Article 29 altered the previous law is not part of the basis of decision of *The State (Duggan) v. Tapley,* which is much the stronger of the two cases. But it is so bound up in all of the judgments that there is no doubt that, unless the Supreme Court decides to reverse itself, the principle is Irish law. If Article 29(3) has any force in domestic law, it repeals prior inconsistent legislation. Because it is part of the Constitution, any rules of international law which it incorporates into domestic law by reference have the status of constitutional provisions, and legislation which is contrary to these rules is invalid.[88] These rules of customary international law[89] include the principle of *pacta sunt servanda,* so legislation contrary to a treaty which is binding on Ireland, including the EEC Treaty, would be unconstitutional.[90]

. . . There is nothing to offend the recognized principles of international law in continuing a domestic law in force even if it has extra-territorial effect, where the other State or States affected readily acquiesce."

[87] What is the significance of the words "in its relations with other states" in art. 29(3)? If a treaty which Ireland has ratified confers rights on individuals, and it is clear that the EEC Treaty does so, other signatory states have a right to insist that Ireland give those rights to individuals. The individual cannot enforce these rights in Irish courts until the Parliament has enacted the Treaty. But if art. 29(3) repealed previous statutes inconsistent with customary international law, as the cases cited in the text make clear, it may well have altered the rights and duties of individuals. In Re Ó Laighléis, [1960] Ir. R. 93, 124, Mr. Chief Justice Maguire said, "Clauses 1 and 3 of Article 29 of the Constitution clearly refer only to relations between states and confer no rights on individuals." This statement, for which no authority was given, should be read in its context, which was in substance a restatement of art. 29(6), and probably should be taken to mean only that art. 29(3) does not confer any rights on an individual in Irish domestic law as a result of a treaty which has not been implemented by the Parliament, which is undoubtedly the position. It is submitted that the proper interpretation of the phrase in art. 29(3) is that rules of international law are incorporated into Irish law only to the extent to which they apply on their own terms, and not in all cases. They do not apply in Ireland to Irish citizens in the absence of a treaty. For example, the international law rules regarding minimum standards of treatment for aliens would make certain treatment of an alien ipso facto illegal in Irish law, but the same treatment of an Irish citizen would not be illegal unless some other provision of Irish law prohibited it.

[88] This seems to be the position in Austria under art. 145 of the Constitution, and in Germany under arts. 25 and 100(2) of the German Constitution; De Visscher, "Les Tendances Internationales des Constitutions Modernes," 80(1) Recueil Académie D. Int. 515, 568 (1952). Art. 25 of the German Constitution reads: "The general rules of international law shall form part of federal law. They shall take precedence over the laws and create rights and duties directly for the inhabitants of the federal territory." In 2 Peaslee 34. In Germany, the treatment of treaties is complicated by the federal nature of the state. If the principle of the first sentence of the provision of German law just quoted were accepted in Ireland, the result in the second sentence would clearly follow. It would not be possible to hold that, although art. 29(3) repealed previous laws inconsistent with customary international law, it does not invalidate later inconsistent statutes, since this would reduce art. 29(3) to the level of an ordinary statute.

[89] In Re Ó Laighléis, [1960] Ir. R. 93, 124, Mr. Chief Justice Maguire said: "The principle of incorporation [of international law into municipal law] applies to such parts of international law as are based on universally recognized custom and not to such parts as depend on convention."

[90] The legislation would be contrary to the principle *pacta sunt servanda,* not merely contrary to the treaty. Therefore, if customary international law allowed a state to withdraw from the EEC (the Treaty makes no reference to this), the Irish courts would presumably uphold legislation inconsistent with the Treaty if it were enacted after a legal and effective withdrawal.

Historical Legal Principles

DELEGATION AND ASSIGNMENT OF LEGISLATIVE POWER

Subject to the Constitution, the Irish Parliament has the same powers as under previous law to repeal legislation it has enacted, even if this involves a breach of international law. The traditional view was that the joint British and Irish Parliament in 1920 could not bind its successors,[91] although it could regulate its own composition. On this view, an act conferring legislative authority on an ex-colony or on the EEC could legally be repealed like any other act.[92] There are no Irish precedents on conferring legislative power, unless one includes the repeal in 1921 of the Act of Union passed by the Irish Parliament in 1800 by which it had merged itself with the Parliament of the United Kingdom.[93]

Politically, however, the British Parliament, having conferred legislative powers on independent ex-colonies, cannot withdraw those powers or itself legislate for the new independent states. Nor, having conferred legislative powers on the EEC, could it withdraw them without the consent of the other member states. There is some authority for saying that if the British or the Irish Parliament confers some of its own legislative authority on a body which derives its authority also from another source, such as a treaty or the wishes of the people under its jurisdiction, the authority conferred is irrevocably assigned and not merely delegated. The legal position would then be consistent with the political reality. "Freedom once conferred cannot be revoked."[94] The traditional legal view disregards the fact that the constitution of the new legislature derives not only from Imperial legislation but also from a political act of the inhabitants themselves—a fact well established in Irish constitutional law.

[91] Wade & Phillips, Constitutional Law, ch. 4 (1960); Wade, "The Basis of Legal Sovereignty," 1955 Camb. L.J. 172. The previous Irish Constitution of 1922 does not seem to affect the position.

[92] In British Coal Corp. v. R., [1935] A.C. 500, 520, Lord Sankey said, by way of dictum, "The Imperial Parliament could, as a matter of abstract law, repeal or disregard s. 4 of the Statute of Westminster." He went on, understandably, "But that is theory and has no relation to realities." This is the view expressed by the Lord Chancellor in the passage quoted on p. 57. See Cowen, "Legislature and Judiciary: Reflections on the Constitutional Issues in South Africa," 15 Modern L. Rev. 282, 294 n.47 (1952).

[93] In Irish constitutional theory the Constitution in force from 1800 to 1921 was repealed in Ireland by a unilateral act of the Irish people adopting a new Constitution, of which the Constituent Assembly was the manifestation. If the principle argued for in the text is accepted, a difficulty arises. Since separate Irish and British parliaments adopted the Act of Union, action of separate successor parliaments would be necessary to repeal it. It could be argued that this took place, but the adoption of the new Constitution probably would be regarded, from an Irish point of view, as justified by a moral and political, but not a legal, right. See, however, O'Higgins, Book Review, 9 Int'l & Comp. L.Q. 174 (1960). See also Delany, "The Constitution of Ireland: Its Origins and Development," 12 U. Toronto L.J. 1, 3–4, (1957).

[94] Ndlwana v. Hofmeyr, [1937] So. Afr. L.R., App. Div. 229, 237 (per Stratford, A.C.J.). The resolutions of the Imperial Conference in 1926 included a declaration that the Dominions, of which Ireland was then one, and the United Kingdom were "equal in status, in no way subordinate one to another in any respect of their domestic or external affairs." Section 4 of the Statute of Westminster, 1931, 22 Geo. 4, c. 4, was expressed to be declaratory; see the Preamble to the Statute. See the views of Anson and Dicey, quoted by Wade, "The Basis of Legal Sovereignty," 1955 Camb. L.J. 172, 195–96.

Evatt, The King and His Dominion Governors 309 (1936), asks, "Why should not 'abdication' or 'surrender' [of legislative power] be possible upon a functional, as well as a geographical, footing?" See Marsh, "Le Royaume-Uni devant les problèmes juridiques du Marché Commun," 15 Rev. Int. de Droit Comp. 649, 655 (1963).

In a line of Irish cases[95] it has been held that the Irish revolutionary government was a *de facto* government in international law. The government of the Irish Free State, its successor, was established by joint action of the British Parliament and of the revolutionary government. Article 80 of the 1922 Constitution states the dual source of the authority of the Irish Free State:

As respects departmental property, assets, rights, and liabilities, the Government of the Irish Free State . . . shall be regarded as the successors of the Provisional Government, and, to the extent to which functions of any department of the British Government become functions of the Government of the Irish Free State, . . . as the successors of such department of the British Government.

But, in fact, the 1922 Constitution went even further: "Article 2. All powers of government and all authority, legislative, executive and judicial, in Ireland are derived from the people of Ireland." These two provisions stating the dual basis of the legislative authority of the new state were enacted by the British Parliament.[96] Logic demanded that British law should not regard the British Parliament as competent to pass any law amending the 1922 Constitution or legislating for the Irish Free State without the cooperation of the body with which it had joined to enact the Constitution. However, in spite

[95] In an important case, Fogarty v. O'Donoghue, [1926] Ir. R. 531, especially at 565, it was held that funds collected for the pre-independence revolutionary assembly belonged to the government of the Irish Free State as its successor. "[It is] the clear public universal law that any Government which de facto succeeds to any other Government, whether by revolution or restoration, conquest or reconquest, succeeds to all the public property . . . of the displaced power. . . ." United States v. M'Rae, L.R. 8 Eq. 69, 75 (1869), quoted by Fitzgibbon, J., [1926] Ir. R. at 567.

> [T]he Government which succeeded to that of the second Dáil by the express vote of the latter in approving of the Treaty with Great Britain, and by the suffrages of the electorate of [the Irish Free State is] . . . entitled as the lawful successor of the second Dáil. It can scarcely be contended that a Government with whose delegates the delegates of Great Britain entered into Articles of Agreement for a Treaty was not a sufficiently de facto [*sic*] Government to enable it to acquire and hold property.
> [1926] Ir. R. at 568 (per Fitzgibbon, J.).

See also id. at 574 (per Meredith, J.); Irish Free State v. Guaranty Safe Deposit Co., 129 Misc. 551, 559–62, 222 N.Y. Supp. 182, 192–93 (Sup. Ct. 1927); In re Logue, 67 Ir. L.T.R. 253 (1933); In re Reade [1927] Ir. R. 31, 47. "[T]he succeeding Government owes its origin to the Government which it replaces, and owes its recognition to a Treaty negotiated by that Government, which itself handed over the reins of government." [1926] Ir. R. at 576 (per Meredith, J.). For the history of the organizations known as Sinn Fein, see Buckley v. Attorney General, [1950] Ir. R. 67. In The State (Ryan) v. Lennon, [1935] Ir. R. 170, 203–204, Mr. Chief Justice Kennedy said:

> The Constitution . . . is the fundamental structure upon which the State was set up by the Third Dáil Eireann sitting as a Constituent Assembly. The Dáil thereby formulated the system or principles, and created the organs, of government of the State. . . . The Constitution was enacted by the Third Dáil, sitting as a Constituent Assembly, and not by the Oireachtas, which, in fact, it created. . . . That Assembly . . . did not act in combination or association with any other chamber or body or person (Lord Lieutenant or Governor General) and . . . was the Parliament to which the then Executive or administration, including the "Provisional Government" as it was called, was responsible. . . .
> The Constituent Assembly proclaimed the Constitution by virtue of its own supreme legislative authority. . . . [T]he Constitution was proclaimed in the name of the people by Dáil Eireann as an act of supreme authority, which it alone had the right to do, because it was the mouthpiece of the people requiring and receiving no Royal assent.
> [1935] Ir. R. at 225–26.

See Grogan, "Irish Constitutional Development," 40 Studies 385, especially at 387 (1951).

[96] Irish Free State Constitution Act, 1922, 12 & 13 Geo. 5, c. 1 (Sess. 2). The argument in the text disregards the fact that before the act just mentioned the British Parliament had passed the Irish Free State (Agreement) Act, 1922, 12 & 13 Geo. 5, c. 4, which gave the force of law in Britain to the Articles of Agreement for a Treaty.

of the provisions just cited, the British courts regarded the authority of the Irish Free State legislature as derived only from the British statute.[97]

To hold that the British Parliament could legally legislate for, or repeal an act conferring legislative authority on, a former colony is to draw an anomalous distinction between this case and the case of a colony which has won its independence by force, where the British Parliament merely recognizes the new state. It could be argued that in the latter case it is the rules of international law which prohibit the enactment of such legislation by the British Parliament and that such legislation would be valid in the British courts since legislation is valid in Britain even if it is contrary to international law. This argument elevates the incapacity of Parliament to bind its

[97] And therefore as subject to the British law —Colonial Laws Validity Act, 1865, 28 & 29 Vict. c. 63—which denied to the Irish legislature the power to pass a law repugnant to a British statute. The British courts held that it was not until after the Statute of Westminster, 1931, 22 Geo. 5. c. 4, repealed the 1865 Act that the Irish legislature had the power to pass legislation repugnant to a British statute; Moore v. Attorney General of the Irish Free State, [1935] A.C. 484, especially at 497–98. The Attorney General of the Irish Free State did not appear in this case and therefore had no chance to make the point made in the text. The circumstances of the case would have made it extremely difficult for him to do so, although even if the difficulty is regarded as insuperable it does not affect the argument in the text. The case turned on the question whether the right of appeal from the Irish courts to the Judicial Committee of the Privy Council still existed. The Constitution (Amendment No. 22) Act, 1933 Pub. Stat. 1261, had purported to terminate it. This right of appeal had been stated in the proviso to art. 66 of the 1922 Constitution; however, the legislature had power to amend this proviso; The State (Ryan) v. Lennon, [1935] Ir. R. 170. But the Constitution gave the legislature power to amend the Constitution *only* insofar as the amendments were not inconsistent with the terms of the Treaty; art. 50 and § 2 of the Constitution of the Irish Free State (Saorstát Eireann) Act, 1922 Pub. Stat. 3; The State (Ryan) v. Lennon, [1935] Ir. R. 170, 205–206, 210, 218, 226, 230. "[I]t seems that the proviso to Article 66 of the Constitution was inserted to give effect . . . to Article 2 of the Treaty and hence under Article 50 of the Constitution that proviso could not be amended . . . by abolishing the right of appeal because such an amendment would not be within the terms of the . . . Treaty." [1935] A.C. at 494 (per Viscount Sankey, L.C.).

To show that the Constitution (Amendment No. 22) Act, 1933, was valid, the Attorney General of the Irish Free State perhaps could have argued: (1) That it was in fact not inconsistent with art. 2 of the Articles of Agreement for a Treaty, but only with art. 66 of the Constitution; in other words that Viscount Sankey, L.C., was incorrect and that art. 66 was not an explanation of, but an obligation separate from and additional to, art. 2. (If this contention is correct, the following contentions (2) and (3) would not arise.) Contention (1) is necessary not merely to establish that Ireland was not in breach of international law but also to establish that the Constitution (Amendment No. 22) Act, 1933, was valid under Irish constitutional law, since art. 50 of the Constitution prohibited amendments to the Constitution which were repugnant to the Articles of Agreement for a Treaty; see the Constitution (Removal of Oath) Act, 1933 Pub. Stat. 27, § 3. This contention has never been fully argued; see [1935] A.C. at 496–97.

(2) That the act was not, under international law, a breach of the treaty made between the two countries by virtue of the Articles of Agreement for a Treaty (and by virtue of the provisions of Constitution of the Irish Free State (Saorstát Eireann) Act, 1922, and clause 2 of the Schedule to the U.K. Irish Free State Constitution Act, 1922, 12 & 13 Geo. 5, c. 1 (Sess. 2), which are in identical terms) because the Statute of Westminster, 1931, § 2(2), constituted a waiver in international law by Britain of Ireland's obligation not to enact legislation inconsistent with the treaty. As far as the writer is aware, this argument has not previously been suggested. If contention (1) is incorrect, some argument is necessary to show that the Constitution (Amendment No. 22) Act, 1933, was not a breach of Ireland's obligations under international law, although it would not necessarily be invalid in Irish law even if it had been.

(3) That the Constitution (Removal of Oath) Act, 1933, § 2 of which purported to repeal § 2 of the Constitution of the Irish Free State (Saorstát Eireann) Act, 1922, was effective to do so and so validated the Constitution (Amendment No. 22) Act, 1933. This point

successors into an irrational dogma for which there is no judicial authority. The creation of a legislative authority by the joint action of the Imperial Parliament and the people of the colony (or their representatives), as was the case in Ireland, is in substance the transfer of British legislative powers to a new state in the international community.[98] If British law recognizes that the new authority derives its powers in part from the act of the people, the Imperial Parliament has not delegated its legislative powers to a body it has constituted but must be held to have transferred them to a body having an independent existence. If so, the legislative powers cannot in law be exercised by the transferor until the transfer has been effectively revoked; this could not, of course, be done under international law by the unilateral act of the Imperial Parliament.[99]

This argument is applicable to any country. It might be accepted in Scottish law.[100] It is probably contrary to the weight of authority[101] in England, although the position there has been described as "fluid, elusive and obscure."[102]

---

was of great constitutional importance in Irish law. It was not raised at all in Moore v. Attorney General, because the Judicial Committee regarded § 2 as having the same status as any Imperial act and, surprisingly, made no effort to look at the position from the viewpoint of Irish law. In fact, this contention is almost certainly incorrect (unless the legislature under the 1922 Constitution is regarded as the successor of the Constituent Assembly *and as having its powers*), since the Constitution of the Irish Free State (Saorstát Eireann) Act, 1922, was an act of the Third Dáil sitting as a Constituent Assembly and since § 2 was not a part of the Constitution which the legislature would have had power to amend; The State (Ryan) v. Lennon, [1935] Ir. R. 170, 203–206, 210, 218, 226, 230. It follows that unless contention (2) is accepted, the Constitution (Amendment No. 22) Act, 1933, was invalid in Irish constitutional law but not in British constitutional law, an odd result. See Harris v. Minister of the Interior, [1952] 2 So. Afr. L.R. 428, [1952] 1 T.L.R. 1245. On the related questions of the creation of a new Constituent Assembly, see de Valera, 52 Dáil Eireann, Parl. Deb., col. 1219 (1937); Plebiscite (Draft Constitution) Act, 1937 Pub. Stat. 215; Donal O'Sullivan, The Irish Free State and Its Senate 497–500 (1940). On the whole matter, see Ó Dálaigh, "Ireland and the British Commonwealth–A New State's Relationship with Its Former Master," 32 Annuaire de l'A.A.A. 22 (1962); Grogan, "Irish Constitutional Development," 40 Studies 385, especially at 393 (1951); Marshall, Parliamentary Sovereignty and the Commonwealth, ch. VI (1957); Donaldson, Some Comparative Aspects of Irish Law, ch. 3, especially at 85–89 (1957); Delany, "The Constitution of Ireland: Its Origins and Development," 12 U. Toronto L.J. 1 (1957); Phillips, "Ryan's Case," 52 L.Q. Rev. 241 (1936).

Under art. 79 of the Constitution of Germany, which deals with the procedure for the amendment of the Constitution, nothing may affect the federal structure of the republic, the inviolate dignity of man and of human rights (art. 1), and the structure of the state as a democratic and social state under the rule of law (art. 20) *even if it is enacted as an amendment to the Constitution.* The principle that there are some things which even a constitutional amendment cannot do is therefore not peculiar to Ireland.

[98] For a similar problem in Scottish constitutional law, see T. B. Smith, Scotland: The Development of Its Laws and Constitution 52–60 (1962); T. B. Smith, Studies Critical and Comparative, ch. 1 (1962).

[99] See Providence Bank v. Billings, 9 U.S. (4 Pet.) 514, 562 (1830) (per Marshall, C.J.), cited by Mr. Justice Fitzgibbon in The State (Ryan) v. Lennon, [1935] Ir. R. 170, 230. "The proposition is that a power which is in itself capable of being exerted to the total destruction of the grant is inconsistent with the grant, and is therefore impliedly relinquished by the grantor, though the language of the instrument contains no allusion to the subject."

[100] See MacCormick v. Lord Advocate, 1953 Sess. Cas. 396; see also Gray, "The Sovereignty of the Imperial Parliament," 23 Modern L. Rev. 647 (1960).

[101] Moore v. Attorney General, [1935] A.C. 484.

[102] Cowen, "Legislature and Judiciary: Reflections on the Constitutional Issues in South Africa" (pts. 1–2), 15 Modern L. Rev. 282 (1952), 16 Modern L. Rev. 273, 297 (1953). Wade, "The Basis of Legal Sovereignty," 1955 Camb. L.J. 172, points out that the authority of any parliament to legislate must logically be found

Because the argument is similar to Irish constitutional principles, it is more likely to be accepted in Ireland.

ASSIGNMENT OF LEGISLATIVE POWER TO THE JOINTLY ESTABLISHED EEC

Just as with legislative power conferred on ex-colonial legislatures, the power conferred on EEC institutions is derived from the acts of two or more authorities. Because of the EEC's "supranational" characteristics and because of a treaty-created obligation not to revoke the transfer of power, there is clearly a transfer and not a delegation of legislative power.[103] Even apart from the express treaty obligation, what has been jointly constituted cannot be unilaterally dissolved or revoked.[104] If the Irish Parliament repealed the EEC Treaty in Irish law, it would purport to end by a unilateral act the authority of the Community over the state. Although formally like other legislation, the Treaty-enacting act would be different in substance, and it is submitted that the ordinary rule that any act can be repealed should not apply to the Treaty-enacting act.

THE EFFECT IN COMMUNITY LAW OF PURPORTED UNILATERAL WITHDRAWAL

An EEC member state has no right to withdraw unilaterally from the Community, but this does not mean that in international law it has no power to do so. There are two questions: whether a legislature which repealed all Community law in force in its domestic law and denounced the Treaty could terminate its individual obligations under the Treaty and substitute an obligation to make reparation and whether the legislature

---

in some norm more basic than any enactment of that legislature and that a "revolution" takes place in the legal system of an ex-colony when the courts first hold that the authority of the local legislature is based on something other than the act of the Imperial Parliament dealing with it; cf. Kelsen, General Theory of Law and the State, ch. X, pt. C, "The Basic Norm of a Legal Order" (1945); see Wheare, The Statute of Westminster and Dominion Status 276 (5th ed. 1953); see also Cahill v. Attorney General, [1925] Ir. R. 70, 76 (per Meredith, J.); Exham v. Beamish, [1939] Ir. R. 336, 348 (per Gavan Duffy, J.). Wade's analysis is more readily acceptable in a country with a written constitution which is the basis for the authority of the legislature and which derives its authority from the will of the people directly. The position in Ireland between 1922 and 1937 was more complicated. The Constitution of 1922 was a legislative act of the Third Dáil sitting as a Constituent Assembly; The State (Ryan) v. Lennon, [1935] Ir. R. 170, 203, 205–206, 210, 226. The Third Dáil, in turn, derived its authority from the people. Having enacted the 1922 Constitution by the Constitution of the Irish Free State (Saorstát Eireann) Act, 1922, the Third Dáil declared itself dissolved. Because of this, the Irish Free State legislature, a creation of the Third Dáil, almost certainly had no power to amend or repeal § 2 of the Constitution of the Irish Free State (Saorstát Eireann) Act, 1922, under art. 50 of the Constitution. However, the basic norm, which by definition is extra-legal, is not sufficiently specific in its content to solve the questions arising where the Imperial Parliament or the Irish Parliament confers legislative authority on a body which derives its legislative authority also from another source.

[103] It is not clear under international law whether a state which has no right to revoke the appointment of what is, in substance, an agent has power to revoke it so as to invalidate any act of the agent after the revocation, insofar as the act purports to bind the state. If the agency which the state has no right to withdraw cannot effectively be revoked, this would add to the difficulty of regarding the Treaty as compatible with the Constitution.

[104] See the Oscar Chinn Case, P.C.I.J., Ser. A/B, No. 63, at 133–34 (1934) (van Eysinga, J., dissenting). "[T]he General Act of Berlin does not create a number of contractual relations between a number of States . . . which may be replaced as regards some of these States by other contractual relations; . . . it provides . . . a régime, a statute, a constitution. This régime, which forms an indivisible whole, may be modified, but for this the agreement of all contracting Powers is required." In theory, there is a distinction between a transfer of power, which the transferor has no power to revoke, and a delegation of power, even when the transferor is under an obligation not to revoke the delegation.

could make the abrogation of Community regulations within its jurisdiction effective in Community law.

This problem is a purely theoretical one in the sense that nobody contemplates that any member of the EEC, having joined, will withdraw. The problem can arise only in a country where internal parliamentary sovereignty is unfettered by treaties, such as Belgium or Britain. It is, however, a problem of Community law and international law. It is not proposed to analyze it fully, but a few comments may be made. The problem is, for practical purposes, peculiar to a state's membership in international organizations or its adherence to treaties which involve implementation in national law.

The Treaty is concluded for an unlimited period,[105] and there is no right of withdrawal without the consent of all member states.[106] Therefore, the denouncing state remains bound by all the provisions of the Treaty until its denunciation is accepted by other states.

The next question is whether Community regulations repealed in national law are still in force, under Community law, in the denouncing state. There are various ways in which this issue could be raised in the Community Court, although the Court does not apply national law. Since Article 171 requires a state which has enacted legislation contrary to the Treaty to repeal it, it seems that the legislation is not automatically invalid even in Community law, but this probably applies only to legislation contrary to Treaty provisions which are not directly applicable. It seems therefore that the Community Court would regard enterprises in the denouncing state as bound under Community law by Community regulations and by the directly applicable Treaty provisions, even if the state had followed up its denunciation by repealing the Treaty and the regulations in its domestic law.

Practical and comparative aspects

The view that the Irish Parliament cannot constitutionally enact legislation inconsistent with a binding treaty has no direct authority to support it. It is illogical, because the Parliament may constitutionally refuse to enact legislation implementing a treaty binding on

[105] Art. 240.

[106] The Treaty contains safeguards, including power to derogate from the Treaty if necessary—art. 226 gives the Commission and the Council wide discretion on various matters, and arts. 235–36 provide for alterations in the Treaty only by unanimous vote—so it does not seem to contemplate withdrawal. Certainly that was the intention of the individuals responsible for setting up the EEC. Numerous provisions of the Treaty require a state to accept acts of the Commission and the Council to which it has not consented. The matter is academic in that it would be impossible to compel a state to stay within the EEC if it were unwilling to do so. Even if customary international law allows a state to pay damages where it has infringed a treaty, this can hardly apply where the signatories were "determined to establish the foundations of an ever closer union among the European peoples," as stated in the preamble to the EEC Treaty. If withdrawal from the EEC without the consent of the other member states is not possible in Community law, all rules of Community law will continue to apply to the state in question, in the eyes of the Court, though not in the view of the national courts. During the preparation of the EEC Treaty, France asked for the right of withdrawal to be given by the Treaty, but this was rejected by the rest of the Six.

On the right of withdrawal from international organizations, see the authorities collected in Briggs, The Law of Nations 916–17 (2d ed. 1952). For the British view on the application of the *rebus sic stantibus* doctrine to the EEC Treaty, see the speech of the Lord Chancellor, quoted in the text on p. 57. On the question of the extraterritorial effect of a British act disregarding the Statute of Westminster, 1931, 22 Geo. 5, c. 4, see Gray, "The Sovereignty of the Imperial Parliament," 23 Modern L. Rev. 647 (1960). On the problem raised in the text, see Catalano, "Rapport entre le droit communautaire et le droit des Etats membres," 1964 Journal des Tribunaux 53, 54; see also the *Van Gend & Loos* case, 9 Recueil 1, [1963] C.M.L.R. 105.

the state. But the two rules together would protect Irish citizens from legislation by the executive by way of international agreement and would insure that once their elected representatives had implemented a treaty the representatives would not have the power to break it—a reasonable result.

While it is reasonable that a treaty duly incorporated into domestic law should prevail if it conflicts with later legislation, this is by no means the position in all countries. In Belgium a later law may prevail over a prior treaty.[107] However, in Belgium the judges have no power to hold an unconstitutional law invalid. Hence it would be anomalous if they could hold a law invalid because it was inconsistent with a treaty. In France Article 55 of the 1958 Constitution expressly provides that treaties have authority superior to that of ordinary laws; however, it was not clear under the corresponding provision of the 1946 Constitution whether the French courts had power to invalidate a law inconsistent with a prior treaty.[108] In Luxembourg the treaty overrides inconsistent later legislation, and there is judicial control to invalidate such a law.[109] In Germany a treaty probably does not prevail over later inconsistent legislation, but in the Netherlands a treaty prevails over even the Constitution.

EEC INSTITUTIONS AND THE IRISH CONSTITUTION

The EEC Court

CONSTITUTIONALITY OF JURISDICTION

It is doubtful if the jurisdiction of the Community Court would be compatible with the provisions of the Irish Constitution dealing with the Courts.[110] There are specific provisions in both the Constitution and the Treaty with regard to the appointment, tenure, and oaths of judges.[111] Apart from "limited functions and powers of a judicial nature,"[112] under Article 34, "justice shall be administered in courts established by law [only][113] by judges appointed in the manner provided by" the Constitution. The judges of the Community Court have more limited tenure than Irish judges. Judges of the Community Court cannot be regarded as exercising limited functions and powers,[114] and they cannot be appointed or sworn in the manner prescribed by the Constitution. Here again the question is whether a constitutional provision relating to internal affairs applies to an international body. The Constitution can hardly require presidential appointment of the judges of the International Court of Justice if these judges will have to decide a case between Ireland and another state, nor

[107] Dumon & Rigaux 626–29.

[108] De Visscher, "Les Tendances Internationales des Constitutions Modernes," 80(1) Recueil Académie D. Int. 515, 565–66 (1952).

[109] De Visscher, Note, 44 Rev. Crit. de Droit Int. Privé 296 (1955).

[110] Arts. 34–38. The Constitution uses a capital letter where it refers to national courts. For clarity, the practice used elsewhere in this book of capitalizing "Court" only where it refers to the Community Court is adhered to in this section. The Constitution contemplates a court of final appeal (the Supreme Court), a High Court with universal jurisdiction at first instance, and "courts of local and limited jurisdiction," but it does not exclude the possibility of another court of first instance which would not fall into this category.

[111] The judges of all Irish courts "established in pursuance of Article 34" are appointed by the President, art. 35(1), and make a declaration in open court, art. 34(5). The judges of the Community Court are appointed by the governments of member states, art. 167, and take an oath, Protocol on the Statute of the Court of Justice, art. 2. Compare also art. 35(2) and 35(4) with art. 167 of the Treaty.

[112] Art. 37.

[113] The bracketed word is clearly implied by arts. 34(1) and 37 read together.

[114] See Re O'Farrell & Gorman, [1960] Ir. R. 239.

can the Constitution require them to make the declaration required of Irish judges. Therefore, under Article 34, "justice" does not mean justice as between Ireland and another state.[115] Cases under Articles 169–171 of the EEC Treaty that involve Ireland are thus not within Article 34. Clearly, if the Irish courts had jurisdiction in these cases, Article 34 would apply to cases involving aliens, international organizations, or foreign states. Consequently, the problem is more difficult with regard to cases from Irish courts under Article 177, appeals by Irish enterprises for annulment of Community acts under Article 173 or against penalties under Article 172, or tort actions by Irish enterprises against the Community under Article 215.

It can be argued that Article 34 does not require justice to be administered in courts that have been established in accordance with Irish law if Irish law alone could not have established a court with the jurisdiction in question, even if some cases coming before this court could have been heard by the Irish courts. Under this principle, the jurisdiction of the European Court of Human Rights would be compatible with the Irish Constitution even though individuals may be parties before it.[116] Irish law alone cannot confer on any tribunal the powers of the Community Court, under Articles 177, 172, 173, or 215, over cases arising all over Europe, and therefore Irish law should be free to accept the jurisdiction of a court set up by treaty. What the Constitution cannot authorize by itself, it should not be regarded as regulating.

It is doubtful if this principle should be read into the Constitution merely to relieve the judges of a tribunal constituted by Ireland acting jointly with another state from taking an oath in the Irish form and to allow their appointment by some authority other than the President.[117] The principle is not necessary to avoid a limitation on the substantive treaty-making power of the state, and there is no reason to think that the constitutional safeguards provided by Articles 34–37 (in particular, those as to the judges' tenure of office) are less necessary or that they should be disregarded in the national interest when Ireland acts jointly with another state.

Extraterritorial Tribunals

Irish legislation conferring on military tribunals wide judicial powers over Irish armed forces abroad[118] would probably be unconstitutional, even though both the tribunals and the accused persons

[115] This view could hardly be disputed, although there is nothing in the Constitution to indicate that art. 34 does not apply in such a case. It is submitted that art. 29(4)(2) should be regarded as including the power to submit Ireland to an international jurisdiction, but there is no express clause saying that art. 29 takes precedence over art. 34.

[116] The writer accepts that the jurisdiction of the European Court of Human Rights is compatible with the Irish Constitution. The principle suggested above is not necessary to support this view; it could equally be based on the principle, suggested on p. 68, that only a tribunal exercising judicial functions "on the authority of" (art. 6) Irish law must comply with arts. 34 and 37. Ireland has never enacted legislation to implement the European Convention on Human Rights in national law, although she has accepted the jurisdiction of the European Court of Human Rights. That court therefore exercises no powers under Irish municipal law, but only under a treaty by which Ireland is bound. This involves a distinction between judicial powers exercised pursuant to laws enacted by the Irish Parliament, which would be subject to arts. 34, 35, and 37, and judicial powers exercised pursuant to laws (i.e., treaties) derived from the executive powers of the government. This distinction may well be valid, although it would apparently authorize the Irish government to conclude a treaty establishing an international tribunal for the trial of war crimes committed by Irish citizens without the safeguards of arts. 34, 35, and 37.

[117] There is nothing in the Constitution to prevent judges from being appointed by some authority in addition to the Irish President.

[118] That is, judicial powers not within art. 37.

were outside the jurisdiction. There is no reason why the location of a tribunal should be relevant if the tribunal is established by Irish law.

Under ordinary conflict-of-laws principles, the Irish courts will recognize the validity of decrees of foreign courts even if the Irish courts would have had jurisdiction. Presumably, in the absence of any contrary rule of Irish law, the Irish courts would accept a decision of an international court that affected private rights within their jurisdiction. These cases can be explained on the principle that a court which does not derive its jurisdiction from Irish law is not subject to Articles 34 and 37, at least if its jurisdiction is derived from public or private international law. Under this narrow principle, the jurisdiction of the Community Court would be unconstitutional. This is much closer to the traditional view than the wider principle suggested above.[119] The Community Court would be more than a mere foreign court, and its jurisdiction in Ireland would result from Irish legislation. The Court would be deciding points of Irish law that are also points of Community law or international law in cases where the Irish courts normally would have jurisdiction, perhaps exclusive jurisdiction. This is constitutional only if Article 34 permits the exercise of jurisdiction by a tribunal with international, as well as national, characteristics over law having international, as well as Irish municipal law, characteristics.[120] This is in essence the wider principle. Although it is unfortunate that the question should be essentially a technical

[119] On p. 68. Irish law has always regarded all questions of the exercise of judicial functions in Ireland as subject to the jurisdiction of the ordinary courts. The British courts took the view that the common law writs of prohibition and certiorari could issue to authorities under a duty to act judicially where Parliament had made no express provision for a challenge; de Smith, Judicial Review of Administrative Action 273 (1959). The two writs would issue to any authority exercising legal authority, but not to a body exercising powers derived from non-statutory sources; id. at 275–76; The State (Colquhoun) v. D'Arcy, [1936] Ir. R. 641; The State (O'Duffy) v. Bennett, [1935] Ir. R. 70. They would not normally issue extraterritorially. It is suggested that arts. 34, 35, and 37 were intended to govern the powers of all bodies exercising judicial functions in Ireland, the same bodies to which the two writs could issue.

[120] Since the Constitution does not contemplate any third category, once again the problem arises whether self-executing Community laws should be regarded as international law or municipal law.

The principles of natural justice in English law apply to a tribunal whose jurisdiction is based on consent and not on law; Dawkins v. Antrobus, 17 Ch. D. 615 (1881); Fisher v. Keane, 11 Ch. D. 353 (1878); Gray v. Allison, 25 T.L.R. 531 (1909); Lapointe v. L'Association de Bienfaisance et de Retraite de la Police de Montréal, [1906] A.C. 535; Abbott v. Sullivan, [1952] 1 K.B. 189, 199. Art. 37 requires that bodies exercising even limited functions must be "duly authorized by law." It has never been decided whether art. 37 prohibits the exercise of judicial functions by bodies whose authority is derived not from municipal law but from consent or from ecclesiastical law. If it does not (and it would be surprising and unreasonable in practice, if not in theory, if it does), then by analogy the jurisdiction of the Community Court, which is not derived from Irish law by its own force but from agreement between member states, should also be permitted. The argument is not, however, a very strong one. Art. 6 of the Constitution provides that "all powers of government, legislative, executive and judicial . . . are exercisable only by or on the authority of the organs of State established by this Constitution." The powers of bodies whose jurisdictions are derived from consent or from canon law are not powers of government at all. In Re O'Farrell & Gorman, [1960] Ir. R. 239, 264, Mr. Justice Kingsmill Moore said: "[A] domestic tribunal with a jurisdiction based solely on contract . . . does not gain its efficacy from any action of the State or the Legislature, and is not a diminution or devolution of the judicial power of the State." The powers given to the organs of the EEC clearly are powers of government. The analogy can therefore be based only on the acceptance of the first principle suggested, namely, that arts. 34, 35, and 37 do not apply to jurisdictions which Irish law alone could not have established.

one, the more logical view is that the jurisdiction of the Court is unconstitutional in Ireland.

THE IRISH SUPREME COURT AS A COURT OF FINAL APPEAL

Under the Constitution, the Supreme Court is the court of "final appeal."[121] This is compatible with Article 177, because the Supreme Court would refer questions to the Community Court before giving its own decision. The Court would not be a court of appeal from the Supreme Court any more than the Department of External Affairs is a court of appeal when questions of the recognition of a foreign state under international law are referred to it.[122] However, if the Community Court held that a rule of law as laid down in a decision of the Supreme Court was contrary to the Treaty, Ireland would be "bound to take the measures required for the implementation of the judgment of the Court."[123] This might mean reopening, by legislation, the "final and conclusive"[124] decision of the Supreme Court, but it is probably unlikely that the Court would require a member state to reverse, by legislation, a decision of a national court, as distinct from altering the law for future cases.

Article 34(3)(3) provides that "no court whatever shall have jurisdiction to question the validity of a law . . . the Bill for which shall have been referred to the Supreme Court . . . under Article 26. . . ."[125] This provision could not prevent the Community Court from considering whether the act in question was contrary to the Treaty, but the exercise of the Community Court's jurisdiction in such a way seems to be contrary to the Constitution.[126] This again is unlikely to arise in practice, because it is unlikely that any bills referred to the Supreme Court under Article 26 would require consideration by the Community Court and because, if Ireland enters the EEC, the Supreme Court would presumably refer the bill to the Community Court under Article 177 before pronouncing it compatible with the Constitution.[127]

The EEC Commission

The Commission acts as a tribunal in connection with cases of discrimination

[121] Art. 34(4). Millner, "The Common Law and the Common Market," 15 Current Legal Prob. 18, 22 (1962), says that "in matters of Community law the House of Lords would have ceased to be the highest tribunal." This is perfectly accurate, because the House of Lords would be bound to obtain the decision of the Community Court and would be bound by it.

[122] This is the practice in Britain: Duff Dev. Co. v. Government of Kelantan, [1924] A.C. 797; Lyons, "The Conclusiveness of the Foreign Office Certificate," 23 Brit. Yb. Int'l L. 240 (1946). It is also the practice in the United States: Guaranty Trust Co. v. United States, 304 U.S. 126, 137 (1938). In France, apart from art. 177, the practice is that the courts refer *all* questions of treaty interpretation to the executive. The British practice is followed in Ireland: Zarine v. S.S. Ramava, [1942] Ir. R. 148.

[123] Art. 171.

[124] Art. 34(4)(5).

[125] Art. 26, corresponding to Act of March 12, 1951; art. 97, [1951] 1 Bundesgesetzblatt [BGBl.] 243, on the Federal Constitutional Court of Germany (now repealed), authorizes the President to refer any bill to the Supreme Court for an advisory opinion as to whether it is compatible with the Constitution.

[126] Technically, the Court would not be ruling on the validity of the act, which would be a question of national law, but rather would be deciding whether Ireland was in breach of the Treaty.

[127] Art. 26 does not, of course, require and might not permit the Supreme Court to consider directly whether the bill was contrary to anything other than the Constitution, i.e., contrary to the Treaty. However, it seems that the customary rule of international law that treaties should be obeyed is embodied in art. 29(3) of the Constitution; Saorstát & Continental S.S. Co. v. De Las Morenas, [1945] Ir. R. 291, 298; The State (Duggan) v. Tapley, [1952] Ir. R. 62.

in transport,[128] dumping,[129] state aids,[130] and, most important, in antitrust matters.[131] There is an increasing number of cases in which it must decide if a regulation has been contravened and, if so, impose fines. If these are "judicial" powers, they would be unconstitutional unless they were "limited." [132] Even if they were limited, they would be unconstitutional if they are powers over "criminal matters."[133] If the Court's jurisdiction would be constitutional, which is doubtful, the Commission's jurisdiction presumably would be constitutional for the same reasons.

Has the Commission "Judicial" Powers?

Article 37 uses the phrase "functions and powers of a judicial nature," and Article 34 the phrase "justice shall be administered in public courts. . . ." Justice is the function of the judiciary,[134] as distinct from the executive power of the state[135] and from the legislative authority,[136] both of which involve considerations of policy.[137] Unfortunately, the meaning of the word "judicial" in Irish administrative law varies in accordance with the subject matter. De Smith suggests four main tests in English law to determine if a function is "judicial."[138] (1) The final decision in the matter must have conclusive effect, subject to an appeal; it cannot be merely advisory. (2) A judicial proceeding usually involves a dispute between two or more parties as to their legal rights, duties, powers, liabilities, privileges, or immunities. (3) A judicial matter is determined on the basis of a pre-existing legal rule or fixed objective standard. (4) A judicial act is binding and imposes obligations on or affects the rights of individuals.

The antitrust functions of the Commission would not be judicial if the Commission is to apply economic policy rather than legally defined criteria in making its decisions, but this is unlikely. The Commission approves an agreement if it "helps to improve the production or distribution of goods or to promote technical or economic progress, whilst allowing consumers a fair share of the resulting profit."[139] Although these phrases are imprecise and the Commission has discretion in certain respects, the phrases indicate that the Commission is expected to follow an objective standard. The Commission is to impose fines for breaches of the antitrust provisions, and "a tribunal authorized to inflict a penalty, especially a severe penalty, even in cases where the offense is not strictly criminal, should be regarded as administering jus-

[128] Art. 79.

[129] Art. 91.

[130] Art. 93.

[131] Art. 89; Reg. 17.

[132] Art. 37.

[133] Arts. 37, 38.

[134] See Re Irish Employers Mut. Ins. Ass'n, [1955] Ir. R. 176, 240 (per Murnaghan, J.). Art. 6 reads: "All powers of government, legislative, executive and judicial. . . ." Cf. British Tribunals and Inquiries Act, 1958, 6 & 7 Eliz. 2, c. 66, § 14(3), which speaks of "executive functions." In Re O'Farrell & Gorman, [1960] Ir. R. 239, 264–65, Mr. Justice Kingsmill Moore said: "Such a question can arise only where there is a written constitution embodying the theory of the separation of powers." See Lynham v. Butler (No. 2), [1933] Ir. R. 74, 99 (per Kennedy, C.J.).

[135] Arts. 28(2), 28(12), 29(4).

[136] Art. 15(2)(1).

[137] Arts. 28(5)(2), 45.

[138] Judicial Review of Administrative Action 37–51 (1959); Committee on Ministers' Powers, Report, Cmd. No. 4060, at 73–74, 93 (1932); Lynham v. Butler (No. 2), [1933] Ir. R. 74; Re O'Farrell & Gorman, [1960] Ir. R. 239; Fisher v. Irish Land Comm'n, [1948] Ir. R. 3; The State (Crowley) v. Land Comm'n, [1951] Ir. R. 250, 265–67.

[139] Art. 85(3).

tice"[140] within Article 37. There is no doubt that the functions of the Commission under the antitrust provisions are judicial.[141]

Are EEC Antitrust Questions "Criminal Matters"?

Decisions imposing fines for breaches of the antitrust provisions of the Treaty are not of a criminal nature.[142] This cannot be assumed to mean the same as "criminal matters" in Article 37. "A characteristic feature of criminal matters is the infliction of penalties. . . ."[143] Irish law does not draw a distinction between criminal and administrative, disciplinary, or regulatory penalties,[144] and the Constitution does not contemplate any classification of legal proceedings other than civil and criminal classifications. Most Irish criminal law is statutory and is enforced against companies by fines. Breaches of Articles 85 and 86 are punishable by extremely large fines.[145] The infringement of a restrictive practices order under Irish law is a criminal offense,[146] so even if Irish law did distinguish between criminal laws and economic laws enforced by fines, it seems that Articles 85 and 86 would be in the former category. It is, therefore, probable that the antitrust powers of the Commission relate to "criminal matters."

Are EEC Antitrust Powers "Limited"?

If the powers of the Commission under Articles 85 and 86 do not relate to criminal matters, they would be constitutional if they were "limited functions and powers of a judicial nature." In the leading case of *Re O'Farrell & Gorman*,[147] Mr. Justice Kingsmill Moore said:

> It is not a question of "limited jurisdiction" whether the limitation be in regard to persons or subject-matter. Limited jurisdictions are specially dealt with in Article 34, 3, 40. It is the "powers and functions" which must be "limited" and not the ambit of their exercise. Nor is the test of limitation to be sought in the number of powers and functions which are exercised. The Constitution does not say "powers and functions limited in number." Again it must be emphasized that it is the powers and functions which are in their own nature to be limited. A tribunal having but a few powers and functions but those of far-reaching effect and importance could not properly be regarded as exercising "limited" powers and functions. The judicial power of the State is by Article 34 of the Constitution lodged in the Courts, and the provisions of Article 37 do not admit of that power being trenched upon, or of its being withdrawn piecemeal from the Courts. The test as to whether a power is or is not "limited" in the opinion of the Court, lies in the effect of the assigned power when exercised. If the exercise of the assigned powers and functions is calculated ordinarily to affect in the most profound and far-reaching way the lives, liberties, fortunes or reputations of those against whom they are

[140] Re O'Farrell & Gorman, [1960] Ir. R. 239, 263, 275 (per Kingsmill Moore, J.); Waterside Workers' Fed'n v. J. W. Alexander, Ltd. 25 Commw. L.R. 434, 445 (Austl. 1918) (per Griffith, C.J.). The question whether the powers of the Disciplinary Committee were "criminal matters" did not directly arise in Re O'Farrell & Gorman, which was decided on the grounds that the power was judicial within art. 34 and not "limited" within art. 37.

[141] The powers of the Commission under other provisions of the Treaty are similar, and it is not thought worthwhile to discuss them separately. They are less clearly "judicial."

[142] Reg. 17, art. 15(4).

[143] Re O'Farrell & Gorman, [1960] Ir. R. 239, 263, 275 (per Kingsmill Moore, J.); Melling v. O Mathghamhna, [1962] Ir. R. 1.

[144] Mr. Chief Justice Kennedy in Lynham v. Butler (No. 2), [1933] Ir. R. 74, uses the traditional dual classification. See the cases cited by Mr. Justice Kingsmill Moore in Re O'Farrell & Gorman, [1960] Ir. R. 239, 274.

[145] Reg. 17, art. 15. This is not to say that the size of a fine is to be determinative.

[146] Restrictive Trade Practices (Amendment) Act, 1959 Acts 1015, § 12.

[147] [1960] Ir. R. 239. See also Conroy v. Attorney General & Keaveney, decided Dec. 1964 (High Court) and Feb. 1965 (Supreme Court).

exercised they cannot properly be described as "limited."[148]

[T]he existence of an appeal to the Courts cannot restore constitutionality to a tribunal whose decisions, if unappealed, amount to an administration of justice.[149]

The exercise by the Commission of its powers will not normally affect "lives, liberties, . . . or reputations," but it will affect "fortunes." The power of the Disciplinary Committee of the solicitors' profession to end a lawyer's right to practice[150] is much more serious for the individual in question than the power of the Commission to fine is for enterprises infringing Articles 85 and 86. At most, the judicial powers of the Commission—which are numerous and not confined to antitrust matters—involve severe pecuniary penalties and cause alterations in business methods. However, there is no reason to make a distinction between powers which, if exercised, would have wide economic repercussions, and those which would more drastically affect a limited number of individuals. The Constitution protects the general interest[151] in the administration of justice by the judges, whose independence is guaranteed. Powers which may affect 225 million people[152] are not limited merely because they may not result in liquidations or in major changes in business methods.[153] It follows that the judicial powers of the Commission are incompatible with the Constitution, unless they can be justified on the basis that Article 34 does not apply to international bodies.

[148] [1960] Ir. R. at 263–64.

[149] [1960] Ir. R. at 275.

[150] The subject of Re O'Farrell & Gorman.

[151] See Re O'Farrell & Gorman, [1960] Ir. R. 239, 274–75.

[152] The approximate population of a Common Market containing the Six, the United Kingdom, and Ireland.

[153] See, however, the remarks of the Lord Chancellor, 243 H.L. Deb. (5th ser.) 419–20 (1962).

CONSTITUTIONALITY OF THE IRISH RESTRICTIVE PRACTICES AUTHORITY

The antitrust provisions of the Treaty are to be enforced by national authorities[154] as well as by the Commission. These national authorities will not be the national courts because ordinarily their structure will not permit the consultation with the Commission that is required[155] before ruling that a practice contravenes the Treaty.[156] The jurisdiction of the Irish cartel authority, therefore, would be constitutional only if it were within Article 37. Its jurisdiction, unlike that of the Commission, would be limited to cases in which the parties to restrictive practices were in Ireland or where the practices had effects in Ireland. It would have only the powers given to it by national law and not the Commission's power to fine. It thus would have a better chance of coming within Article 37 than the Commission, provided the sanctions it could impose

[154] Art. 88; Reg. 17, art. 9(3).

[155] Second General Report, para. 118 (1959).

[156] It is uncertain if it would be possible to constitute an administrative tribunal which would be a "court" within the meaning of the Constitution but which could consult and cooperate with the Commission, or (which amounts to the same thing) to reconstitute an Irish court under administrative rules of procedure so it could perform these functions. Unless the Irish courts insisted that the word "court" meant "court as normally constituted in a common law jurisdiction," this would probably be constitutionally possible, since the court's consultation with the Commission would be intended to assist the court to apply the law and so would be comparable to consultation with an amicus curiae and not contrary to art. 35(2). While this solution is in many ways attractive, it is highly unorthodox and unlikely to be adopted.

In France the ordinary courts alone enforce anticartel legislation; the Commission Technique des Ententes is only an advisory or investigatory body. See Deringer, "The Distribution of Powers in the Enforcement of the Rules of Competition Under the Rome Treaty," 1 Common Market L. Rev. 30, 38 (1963).

did not make its cases "criminal matters." If they did, it necessarily would be unconstitutional, since it would not be a court. Since the Commission expects a national authority to wield effective sanctions, it is doubtful if this could be avoided. Even though limited to the Irish economy, however, the powers of the national cartel authority would be important, and it is doubtful if they would be held to be "limited."

CONSTITUTIONALITY OF THE EEC'S TREATY-MAKING POWER

The problem arises whether the treaty-making power of the EEC[157] would be compatible with the Irish Constitution. The first question is whether Article 29(4)(2) permits the use of an organ which will have power under international law to bind the state without the consent of the government. Although the government may use any organ or method of procedure used by other states, its executive powers must be exercised in accordance with Article 28, which provides that the government is to be responsible to the lower house.[158] The government could hardly be "responsible" for a treaty which it could not legally prevent from binding the state in international law. Admittedly, the power of the Commission and the Council would be exercised "on the authority of" the government.[159] However, neither the government nor the Parliament could ever revoke this authority[160] without a breach of Ireland's international obligations to the other EEC member states and perhaps to the other parties to the treaty with the Community. The government could be dismissed from office, but only for the exercise of a power by two bodies in which the government had only a small vote.[161] The responsibility of the government would be the responsibility of a whipping boy. The fact that the treaty-making power was conferred on the Commission

[157] See p. 9.

[158] Art. 28(4)(1); see also art. 29(5)(1). Art. 29(4)(2) is wide enough to allow the government to assign to any international organ the treaty-making power of the state, if authorized to do so by law. However, it would be impossible to read art. 29(4)(2) separately from arts. 29(4)(1) and 28 and therefore from the requirement of the responsibility of the government to the lower house.

[159] Art. 6.

[160] Art. 240.

[161] The Irish member of the Commission would not in any way represent the interests of his country; art. 157. The question whether the government would be "responsible" is analogous to the question whether the Commission and the Council could be regarded as "subordinate" legislatures within art. 15(2)(2). In neither case could the Irish state unilaterally withdraw the power conferred, repeal the rules of law (whether a treaty or Community law), set up any authority to supervise the lawmaking one, give directions as to how the delegated powers should be exercised, or alter the constitution or powers of the lawmaking body. Both "responsibility" and "subordination" seem fictitious in these circumstances, and the responsibility of the government is even more unreal since the government is not even the lawmaking authority concerned. The Irish government would be responsible to the lower house for the misuse by its plenipotentiaries of their power to bind the state, if no right was reserved by the government to ratify any agreement entered into. In such a case the state would be irrevocably bound by the agreement for its duration. However, the government alone would have appointed the agent and provided him with powers which were, by hypothesis, excessive. The government could have withdrawn his authority, revoked the agreement under any of its terms which permitted its revocation, appointed a second plenipotentiary to act jointly with him, or altered his powers. In such a case, all of the requirements of subordination would have been fulfilled, except that of power to revoke immediately the rule objected to.

Art. 29(4)(2) of the Constitution was drafted to permit the continuation of the arrangements made pursuant to the Executive Authority (External Relations) Act, 1936 Pub. Stat. 1451. These arrangements were limited in scope and do not give any help in interpreting the provision.

with the consent of the lower house would not make it compatible with the Constitution.

The second question is whether the treaty-making power of the Council and the Commission can be reconciled with the constitutional provision[162] that treaties, other than "agreements or conventions of an administrative or technical character"[163] involving a charge on public funds, shall not bind the state until approved by the lower house. It seems quite clear that it cannot. However, the difficulty would not arise until such a treaty was concluded by the Council, and it might be possible for the lower house to approve it in time for it to come into force on the date fixed by the Council. The Commission would dislike any legal position which could lead to a breach of the Treaty, but since the problem would arise comparatively rarely, it is possible, though unlikely, that it would be prepared to accept such a solution.

CONSTITUTIONALITY OF AMENDMENTS TO THE TREATY

In general, amendments to the EEC Treaty must be ratified by all member states in accordance with their respective constitutional requirements before the amendments come into force.[164] However, Article 235 provides that:

> Where action by the Community appears necessary to achieve one of the objects of the Community, within the framework of the Common Market, and where this Treaty has not provided the necessary powers of action, the Council shall adopt the appropriate provisions by a unanimous decision [on the proposal of the Commission],[165] after consulting the Assembly.

There are also provisions for amending Articles 14 and 33 by similar procedure.

Even if Article 29(6) allows the Irish Parliament to confer on Community institutions the power to enact international legislation that will be directly applicable in Irish law, it could hardly permit the Parliament to confer the right to increase the delegated powers. To be constitutionally valid in Ireland, any decision of the Council under Article 235 whereby it obtained new powers would require the approval of the Parliament. This is clearly contrary to the Treaty and could not be overcome by any assurance to the Commission or the other member states that such approval would always be forthcoming.

NATIONAL INDEPENDENCE

One constitutional problem is politically, though not legally, of great importance for any state joining the EEC—the question of national sovereignty of member states. This is the external or international political sovereignty and is distinct from the internal sovereignty of the Irish Parliament under the Constitution. Article 5 provides that "Ireland is a sovereign, independent, democratic state." The words "sovereign" and "independent" are probably tautologous.[166]

The powers of the three Communities are limited to economic matters, including fiscal and monetary matters to the extent which the Council decides. The countries remain politically and legally independent in foreign policy, defense, police powers, education, and culture. Within the sphere of economics, powers

[162] Art. 29(5)(2).

[163] Art. 29(5)(3).

[164] Art. 236(3).

[165] The translation by Her Majesty's Stationery Office omits the reference to the proposal of the Commission. This is obviously an error. Since the unanimous vote of the Council is required, no difficulty arises under art. 28(4)(1) of the Irish Constitution; the government can properly be regarded as responsible to the lower house.

[166] See the remarks of Lord McNair, 243 H.L. Deb. (5th Ser.) 298 (1962). The nature or character of the state (e.g., republic) is not stated in the Irish Constitution.

have been transferred to the Community institutions only to a limited extent. Until these powers are exercised, the member states have considerable freedom to act, even in the economic sphere. The extent to which these powers are exercised will depend on the Council.[167]

Economic matters are often also political ones,[168] and entry into the EEC involves political commitments for the future.[169] However, national sovereignty and independence under international law concern the legal powers of the state. The most important legal powers surrendered to the EEC are those over matters affected by the common external tariff and the common commercial policy.[170] The power to make treaties may be delegated in international law without surrender of sovereignty,[171] and it seems clear that until further obligations are undertaken by EEC member states, they continue to be independent and sovereign in international law. Their freedom to exercise their external sovereignty has been limited, but it is limited *pro tanto* by any treaty. Since sovereignty is not a precise concept, it is not possible to say exactly at what point in the process of political integration member states would cease to be sovereign, but as long as foreign policy and defense are not assigned, the member states remain sovereign and independent.

CONCLUSION

It is not surprising that some of the EEC's powers are incompatible with the Irish Constitution, which is drawn up too precisely to allow it to be reconciled with international institutions exercising wide powers over national law. The Constitution sets up certain organs of government and gives them power limited only by the Constitution and by the system of mutual checks and balances set up by it. This system of checks and balances would be destroyed if the organs of government —even acting jointly—could irrevocably assign some functions of government to bodies that are not subject to the Constitution or to the democratic control of the Irish people.

[167] Gaudet, "The Legal Framework of the Community," in Legal Problems of the European Economic Community and the European Free Trade Association, Int'l & Comp. L.Q. Supp. No. 1, at 8, 9–12 (1961).

[168] Hallstein, United Europe: Challenge and Opportunity, The Politics of European Integration (1962).

[169] For an Irish view, see FitzGerald, "The Political Implications of the European Community," 51 Studies 44 (1962).

[170] "The essential difference between the common market and the free trade area lies precisely in this, that the free trade area leaves intact the sovereignty of the member states in their external economic relations." Pescatore, "Les Relations Extérieures des Communautés Européennes," 103(2) Recueil Académie D. Int. 9, 12 (1961). However, there is a difference between the relationship of the member states of a common market and that of the member states of a customs union, since a customs union does not affect economic laws other than those on tariffs and quotas.

[171] Report of the Fifth Committee (on Admission to the League) of the First Assembly of the League of Nations, Dec. 6, 1920, on Liechtenstein, quoted in part in 1 Hackworth, Digest of International Law 48–49 (1940). Liechtenstein was admitted to be a sovereign state but was denied admission to the League because she was regarded as unable to discharge the international obligations imposed on her by the Covenant. And see, by implication, art. 29(4)(2).

Part II

THE IRISH ECONOMIC BACKGROUND

Chapter 3

Some Aspects of the Irish Economy[1]

INTERNAL ASPECTS OF THE ECONOMY

Some background information on the Irish economy is necessary for the reader to understand the economic and legal questions to which the EEC would give rise in Ireland. Ireland was, until recently, primarily an agricultural country. Agriculture produced 22 per cent of the gross domestic product in 1964 and industry and construction 32 per cent. Although it has many natural advantages, such as good climate and a stable government, its agriculture (primarily beef cattle) is under-productive and undercapitalized, notwithstanding favorable credit facilities for agricultural loans.[2] Thirty-three per cent of employed labor was engaged in agriculture in 1964. There is relatively little processing of agricultural products.[3]

Ireland is underindustrialized, rather than underdeveloped, and has an efficient infrastructure. It has transport, electrical power (from water, turf, and oil), road, and shipping facilities which could

[1] Detailed economic information is available from the annual Statistical Abstract, the Irish Statistical Bulletin (Central Statistics Office), the National Income and External Trade Statistics, the Irish Banking Review, and the bulletins and reports of the Central Bank. See also Commission on Emigration and Other Population Problems, 1948–1954, Report [hereinafter cited as Commission on Emigration Report], Pr. 2541, ch. 3, "Economic Background" (1954); Commission of Inquiry into Banking, Currency, and Credit, Report, P. No. 2628 (1938) (strongly influenced by the late Dr. Per Jacobsson). See also O'Brien, "The Economic Progress of Ireland 1912–1962," 51 Studies 9–26 (1962); Nevin, "Ireland and the Common Market, " 50 Studies 271 (1961); IBEC Technical Services Corporation of New York, Appraisal of Ireland's Industrial Potential (1952); Biggar, "L'Industrie Irlandaise et Son Récent Développement," 197 Revue de la Société d'Etudes et d'Expansion 480 (1961); FitzGerald, "Mr. Whitaker and Industry," 48 Studies 138 (1959); Dewhurst, Coppock & Lamartine Yates, Europe's Needs and Resources 12, 33, 35, 39–40, 49, 55, 57, 70, 141, 471, 756–57 (1961); Jewkes, "An Outsider Looks at the Irish Economy," Irish Banking Rev., Sept. 1960, p. 16; Havens, "Impressions of the Irish Economy," Irish Banking Rev., Dec. 1959, p. 21; "The Irish Economy," Financial Times Supplement, Nov. 23, 1964; "Economic Achievement in the Republic of Ireland," Midland Bank Rev., Aug. 1965, p. 9. Supplement on the Republic of Ireland, May 28, 1965; "Survey: The Republic of Ireland," The Statist, Feb. 19, 1965; "Survey of the Republic of Ireland," Stock Exchange Gazette, May 8, 1964.

For business aspects, reference may be made to the supplement on Ireland, Investors Chronicle (London), Nov. 16, 1962, The Times (London) Review of Industry, Jan. 1963; Stock Exchange Gazette, Survey of the Republic of Ireland, May 8, 1964.

On related problems of Northern Ireland, see Joint Working Party on the Economy of Northern Ireland, Report [hereinafter cited as the Hall Report], Cmd. No. 1835 (1962); Economic Development in Northern Ireland, Cmd. No. 479 (1965); Isles & Cuthbert, An Economic Survey of Northern Ireland (1957) (the Isles Report).

[2] Through the Agricultural Credit Corporation, established by Agricultural Credit Act, 1927 Pub. Stat. 667.

[3] "Considerable scope seems to exist for the development of food-processing industries." OECD Economic Survey of Ireland, 1963, para. 38. See Lamartine Yates, Food, Land and Manpower in Western Europe 111, 148–50, 150–56 (1960). Food processing is now some 22% of total manufacturing industry.

support a greater measure of industrialization.[4] As was natural in a country which until recently had only small industries, this infrastructure was paid for primarily out of public funds. Recently it was decided to take advantage of the decline in demand for public funds for social infrastructure to expand public expenditure for increased productive investment and for education.[5]

The failure of private enterprise to contribute its full share to the economic development of the country has been due to various factors. Although some minerals have been discovered recently, Ireland is short of raw materials other than agricultural products. In the past, private enterprise has been handicapped to some extent by a shortage of capital.[6] Until 1966 public borrowing abroad had been used only twice—during the European Recovery Program and in 1927.[7] Company profits constitute a smaller percentage of national income than in many other countries. This reduces the amount of capital available for self-financed investment. Substantial amounts of foreign capital have been invested recently, and membership in the EEC would increase the amount of capital available for investment in Ireland.

An important cause of the failure of private enterprise to contribute fully to development seems to have been lack of initiative rather than lack of capital.[8] Shortage of entrepreneurial talent and energy was due in part to the lack of an industrial tradition and also in part to the strongly protectionist policy which was followed by successive Irish governments and which made profit-making on the home market easier than exporting competitively. Restrictions on freedom of establishment limited the amount of capital available for investment, although they provided protection for locally owned industry. Ireland's entry into the

[4] Johnston, Why Ireland Needs the Common Market 96, 99 (1962); OECD Economic Survey of Ireland, 1962, para. 24. In Ireland in the 1950's, investment in transport and communications was only slightly less than industrial investment; Murray, "Ireland and the European Free Trade Area," 5 Administration 25, 36 (1957). Ireland's economy has developed strikingly since 1957. In 1957, Ireland requested treatment as a less developed country in the proposed European Free Trade Area; in 1961, Ireland applied for full membership in the EEC. The feeling in Brussels that association might be initially more suitable may be attributed to a failure, due to preoccupation with the negotiations with Britain, to take adequate account of developments in Ireland.

For a brief but shrewd note on the Irish economy in 1958, see Report by the [OEEC] Group of Financial Experts to Working Party No. 23 of the Council on Financial Assistance for Less-Developed Countries Within the [Proposed] Free Trade Area, Annex, paras. 13–19, in Negotiations for a European Free Trade Area: Documents Relating to the Negotiations from July, 1956, to December, 1958, Cmd. No. 641, at 231–32 (1959).

[5] Programme for Economic Expansion, Pr. 4796 (1958); Second Programme for Economic Expansion, Pr. 7239 (1963).

[6] Very large amounts of capital were taken out of the Irish economy between 1800 and 1921, when the country became independent.

[7] For one method of financing for development of less industrialized countries which seems to have considerable merit, see U.N. Economic Survey of Europe in 1953, U.N. Doc. No. E/ECE/174, at 204–205 (1954).

[8] Lynch, "Economic Planning in Ireland," 8 Administration 180, 184 (1960). Commission on Emigration Report, Pr. 2541, para. 395 (1954); "Symposium on Economic Development," 20(2) Journal of the Statistical and Social Inquiry Society of Ireland [hereinafter cited as J. Stat. Soc.] 113, 116–17 (contribution of Ó Nualláin), 121–23 (contribution of Black), 131 (contribution of Nevin) (1958–59); U.N. Economic Survey of Europe, 1959, U.N. Doc. No. E/ECE/383, ch. VII, at 35–36 (1960); see Pincus, "Discussion Paper," in Regional Economic Planning 217–18 (Isard & Cumberland ed. 1961); Spengler, "Role of Competition and Monopoly in Economic Development," in Competition, Cartels and Their Regulation 7 (Miller ed. 1962); Ullastres, "New Methods of Integration and Economic Development," in Methods of Industrial Development 45, 48–49 (OECD, 1962); Henry & Heelan, "Capital in Irish Industry," 21 J. Stat. Soc. 135 (1963).

EEC would provide the "dynamic"[9] forces needed to put entrepreneurial energy to work and to add to the recent economic development.

Any country in the course of development must choose between maintenance of its external assets as reserves, to produce income to balance a trade deficit, and repatriation, to provide capital for investment and economic development. In Ireland it has been possible to use incoming capital to make good a deficit on current account. Ireland always has had substantial external assets,[10] and repatriation formerly provided the capital for much of the investment which took place. There have been tax incentives for Irish residents for repatriation and investment in new industry.[11] The scope for repatriation and portfolio investment has been limited by the small size of the Irish stock exchange.[12] Investment or unit trusts probably would have encouraged repatriation.

The small size of the home market—approximately 2,849,000 people in 1964—has been another factor inhibiting industrial expansion. Since the principal export market was Britain and since most foreign investment until recently was British, relatively few industrial enterprises were involved in exporting. No enterprises seem to have moved from Britain to Ireland to take advantage of reduced labor costs. Because of the small home market and the lack of industrialization, there was little scope for a capital goods industry until very recently, and most capital goods had to be imported. This inhibited economic growth, since industrialization usually progresses from consumer goods towards capital goods and since demand for agricultural products, especially when these products are unprocessed, is relatively inflexible. The small size of the home market prevented some protected industries from operating on an economic scale, further increasing costs already raised by tariffs. Except where there are high transport costs for a particular commodity, the disadvantage to Irish industry of the small home market would vanish on Ireland's entry into the EEC.

IRISH ECONOMIC POLICY

The small size of the home market would have been less important if the official policy on industrialization had not been to encourage industrial self-sufficiency wherever substantial protection could bring about adequate production by local enterprises. This policy resulted in an unfortunate concentration on consumer goods and contributed to the substantial disregard of export markets[13] by Irish industry un-

[9] Economic Development, Pr. 4803, ch. 1, paras. 18–19 (1958); Second Programme for Economic Expansion, Pr. 7239, para. 13 (1963).

[10] Commission on Emigration Report, Pr. 2541, para. 471 (1954), states that "the amount of Irish-owned capital invested abroad [is] . . . probably relatively larger than for any other country in the world." See OECD Economic Survey of Ireland, 1965, at 10–14, 16–20; OECD Economic Survey of Ireland, 1963, para. 48; Commission of Inquiry into Banking, Currency, and Credit, Report, P. No. 2628, para. 97 (1938). Ireland's liquid external assets rose by almost $140 million during 1956–62. See Second Programme for Economic Expansion, Pr. 7239, paras. 77, 85, 100 (1963). Total external assets in December 1961 were £224.5 million ($628.6 million); Statistical Abstract of Ireland, 1962, at 270. See Whitaker, "Ireland's External Assets," 18 J. Stat. Soc. 192 (1948–49); Geary, "Irish Economic Development Since the Treaty," 40 Studies 399, 414 (1951).

[11] Finance Act, 1932 Pub. Stat. 291, § 7, as amended; Finance Act, 1957 Acts 463, § 4.

[12] See Murray, "Some Aspects of the Industrial Capital Market in Ireland," 20(3) J. Stat. Soc. 97 (1959–60); "Irish Industrial Finance," Irish Banking Rev., Sept. 1960, p. 10.

[13] The Irish government did not expressly encourage industrial exports in the first few years after independence. Even the Irish legislation on freedom of establishment of non-nationals, which gave permission in detail for various activities, did not expressly permit until 1958 the establishment of foreign-owned industries exporting most of their products; In-

til 1958. Irish manufacturers preferred to make a high rate of profit per unit on a restricted output rather than expand, and this inhibited the growth of secondary industries supplying services and components. Protection was given by means of tariffs, quotas, and restrictions on freedom of establishment of foreign competitors, usually British. Protection was "indiscriminate" in Ireland and had a substantial effect on the cost of living and sometimes even on the cost of raw materials and thus on the cost of exports.[14] No effort was made to limit the period for which protection would be given, and thus to insure that the industries became competitive in due course. The business interests produced by protectionism were antipathetic to free competition, and the introduction of free trade was made difficult. Ireland's economy is not one which would naturally encourage attempts at self-sufficiency, and the reasons for protectionism were mainly political,[15] although the policy was first adopted at a time of widespread protectionism after the depression of 1930. Tariffs increase income but not productivity, and they may well reduce the incentive to increase productivity.

Since the home demand was not always adequately supplied, even when the small home market permitted economic levels of production, the policy of industrial self-sufficiency was not wholly successful even on its own terms. Many licenses were granted to import duty-free goods which home production should have been able to supply.[16]

However, according to the Committee on Industrial Organization,

> [B]y the early nineteen-fifties the industrial products which were still being imported were mainly goods for which the home market was too small to support the manufacture [in Ireland] on a minimum economic scale. At the same time it was becoming apparent that a faster rate of economic growth and increased employment would have to depend on increased exports—mainly industrial exports. Since the tariff is not an effective method of directly promoting an increase in industrial exports the emphasis shifted to other means, notably capital grants and export tax relief.[17]

Ireland probably has gone further now than any other western European country to encourage export industries and to attract private foreign capital for this purpose.[18]

The changes in the official attitude toward economic development in Ireland

dustrial Development (Encouragement of External Investment) Act, 1958 Acts 351. For a review of Irish tariffs and quotas, see Committee of Inquiry into Taxation on Industry, Report, Pr. 3512, App. I (1956). See also U.N. Economic Survey of Europe Since the War, U.N. Doc. No. E/ECE/157, ch. 12, at 215 (1953).

[14] Johnston, Why Ireland Needs the Common Market 66–67, 74–75 (1962); U.N. Economic Survey of Europe, 1959, U.N. Doc. No. E/ECE/383, ch. VII, at 38 (1960); FitzGerald, "Mr. Whitaker and Industry," 48 Studies 138, 145–48 (1959); see also "Some Aspects of the Development of Irish Manufacturing Industry," Irish Banking Rev., Sept. 1959, p. 10; Commission on the Registration of Shops, Report, P. No. 1313, paras. 21, 55–57, 60 (1934).

[15] On the political reasons for favoring protectionism and the official attitude to the report of the Fiscal Inquiry Committee (1923), see O'Brien, "The Economic Progress of Ireland 1912–1962," 51 Studies 9, 14 (1962); Geary, "Irish Economic Development Since the Treaty," 40 Studies 399, 403 (1951).

[16] Commission on Emigration Report, Pr. 2541, para. 386 (1954).

[17] Committee on Industrial Organization, Fourth Interim Report: Industrial Grants, Pr. 6924, para 1 (1962). The first legislation on capital grants, enacted in 1952, applied only to the less developed areas in the west. Similar legislation for the rest of the country was passed in 1956, the year the first export tax reliefs were given. See Johnston, Why Ireland Needs the Common Market 104 (1962); Second Programme for Economic Expansion, Pr. 7239, para. 7 (1963).

[18] U.N. Economic Survey of Europe, 1959, U.N. Doc. No. E/ECE/383, ch. VII, at 42 n.140 (1960).

were expressed in three documents[19] which stressed the need for productive investment.[20] The Capital Investment Advisory Committee suggested that the government organs preparing and co-ordinating economic policy should be reviewed and strengthened. The authorities responsible for grants, loans, subsidies, and services for industry, agriculture, and transport should concentrate on increasing production for export. Non-economic factors, such as prejudices for or against state enterprise, and special policies, such as the policy of decentralization and diversion of industry from Dublin to the west, should not interfere with economic projects. The productivity of state investments should be continuously and systematically reviewed. The Commission on Income Taxation should be asked to consider encouraging initiative by tax changes and increasing tax incentives for investment in Ireland.

The new policy described in the above quotation from the Committee on Industrial Organization should have been adopted earlier. Industrialization probably could have been effected by the maximum development of the natural resources, mostly agricultural, so as to increase production most effectively both for home consumption and for export. This approach would have increased agricultural purchasing power and therefore encouraged national industries to develop with the minimum of interference with free movement of goods and freedom of establishment.[21] This approach could well have been allied with the new policy just described, which has only recently made Ireland outward-looking in industrial trade. The Irish economy has expanded substantially since 1959,[22] with industrial production rising, up to the end of 1964, by 7 per cent per annum. This is expected to continue. Industrial exports increased by over 90 per cent during 1958–62.[23] It seems clear that free trade with state aid encourages economic development much more than protectionism, import-substitution, and industrial self-sufficiency based on the export of agricultural products (especially when these agricultural products are exported to Britain, which imports them at prices unfavorable to producers in Ireland and elsewhere).

Free trade with state aid where it is necessary and justifiable is the pattern of trade within the EEC. In a small national market already supplied with consumer goods, the only industries with

[19] Programme for Economic Expansion, Pr. 4796 (1958); Economic Development, Pr. 4803 (1958); Capital Investment Advisory Committee, Third Report, Pr. 4668 (1958); "Third Report of the Capital Investment Advisory Committee," Irish Banking Rev., Dec. 1958, p. 16. See also Second Programme for Economic Expansion, Pr. 7239 (1963) and Pr. 7670 (1964). The first program for economic expansion probably contributed more than anything else to Ireland's present prosperity.

[20] FitzGerald, "A Review of Three Recent Economic Publications," 6 Administration 193, 199 (1956). Two points with regard to agriculture have been omitted from this paragraph, summarizing Mr. FitzGerald's version of the three documents.

[21] Johnston, Why Ireland Needs the Common Market 45, 62–63, 74–75 (1962); Commission on Emigration Report, Pr. 2541, para. 386 (1954); Whitaker, "Capital Formation, Saving and Economic Progress," 19 J. Stat. Soc. 184, 191 (1955–56); Pincus, "Discussion Paper," in Regional Economic Planning 219–20 (Isard & Cumberland ed. 1961); Measures for the Economic Development of Under-Developed Countries, U.N. Doc. No. E/1986/ST/ECA/10, paras. 177–83 (1951).

This approach has been followed in New Zealand and Denmark with success.

[22] OECD Economic Survey of Ireland, 1962, paras. 1–8 passim. This growth was due in part to use of previously under-utilized capacity and to a high level of public investment.

[23] OECD Economic Survey of Ireland, 1963, para. 21. For comparative aspects, see U.N. Economic Survey of Europe in 1953, U.N. Doc. No. E/ECE/174, at 195–203 (1954). See also Beddy, Murray, FitzGerald & Walsh, "Industrial Promotion," 10 Administration 325 (1962).

really good prospects of growth are those with a substantial export potential.[24] Industries which cater only to the home market and which rely on protection to enable them to do so must be radically reorganized if they are not to disappear in the EEC. Because of this, the Irish government reduced non-revenue industrial tariffs unilaterally at the beginning of 1963 and of 1964 and is planning further reductions and the removal of the existing quota restrictions.

Ireland has carried out its industrialization mainly through private enterprise. As in most countries which are underindustrialized and in which both agricultural and industrial enterprises are small, government action has extremely important effects. Public authorities are responsible for over half of the total capital investment,[25] and government action has been necessary to bring about economic development in the private sector. Gross fixed investment during 1957–61 averaged only 14 per cent of the gross national product, though it rose to 21 per cent in 1965. Apart from protectionism and the improvement of infrastructure,[26] the Irish government acts through guarantees of the repayment of loans raised for capital investment;[27] through the Industrial Credit Company,[28] which provides loan financing for private enterprise; through the Industrial Development Authority,[29] which promotes investment; through the Grants Board,[30] which makes grants to finance new enterprises and expand existing ones; through the Export Board, which promotes exports; and through the Department of Industry and Commerce. A customs-free airport at Shannon was established,[31] and this subsequently became an industrial zone under the supervision of the Shannon Free Airport Development Company. In the peat, electricity, steel, sugar, railways, shipping, and air-transport sectors, state-owned commercial companies are in operation. The government has not tried to plan or coordinate private investment[32] or to exercise controls to insure

[24] OECD Economic Survey of Ireland, 1963, para. 29; OECD Economic Survey of Ireland, 1964, para. 27; Report by the [OEEC] Group of Financial Experts . . . , Annex, para. 15, in Negotiations for a European Free Trade Area: Documents . . . , Cmd. No. 641, at 231 (1959); see Myrdal, An International Economy 60 (1956). The Irish Central Bank, in its Annual Report, 1963, published before the publication of the Second Program for Economic Development, stressed that an annual 4% increase in the gross national product might require an annual increase in exports of 7–8%.

[25] OECD Economic Survey of Ireland, 1962, para. 14; Whitaker "Capital Formation, Saving and Economic Progress," 19 J. Stat. Soc. 184–94 (1955–56). In a phrase which has become well known, the Irish "are very much afraid of being called socialists but not of acting in some respects like socialists." Carter, "A Problem in Economic Development," 7 Administration 109 (1959). See generally FitzGerald, State Sponsored Bodies; Seán Lemass, Esq., T.D. (the present Prime Minister), "The Role of the State Sponsored Bodies in the Economy," 6 Administration 277, and 295 (comments by Andrews), 300 (comments by Beddy) (1958). See Measures for the Economic Development of Under-Developed Countries, U.N. Doc. No. E/1986/ST/ECA/10, paras. 41–52, 54, 58 (1951).

[26] Commission on Emigration Report, Pr. 2541, para. 416 (1954).

[27] Trade Loans (Guarantee) Act, 1939 Acts 177, and subsequent and previous legislation.

[28] Industrial Credit Act, 1933 Pub. Stat. 849; Industrial Credit (Amendment) Act, 1958 Acts 165.

[29] Industrial Development Authority Act, 1950 Acts 623.

[30] Undeveloped Areas Act, 1952 Acts 3. On state-sponsored bodies, see Chubb, A Source Book of Irish Government, ch. 10 (1964).

[31] See Johnston, Why Ireland Needs the Common Market 105–106 (1962).

[32] Economic Development, Pr. 4803, ch. 15, para. 5 (1958); OECD Economic Survey of Ireland, 1962, paras. 18, 29. The importance of government participation in industry in less developed countries and regions makes the relevant provisions of the EEC Treaty of crucial importance; see arts. 37, 92.

that private capital is used in the most efficient way.

The Irish government always has given guarantees against discrimination and against expropriation or nationalization and has permitted repatriation of capital, profits, and dividends at any time. No measures have ever been taken against industry already established in the country.

EXTERNAL ECONOMIC RELATIONS

Ireland's external economic relations are of very great importance; in 1964 exports equalled 37 per cent and imports 42 per cent of the gross national product.[33] Until recently, Irish exports have been predominantly agricultural products—about 35 per cent in 1964. These products have been exported primarily to the United Kingdom,[34] the largest importer of agricultural produce in the world, in return for a surprisingly large proportion of the United Kingdom's industrial products. The complementary character of the two economies and the trade connections between them make them an "almost classical" model for complete economic integration.[35] Because of its closeness and the ease of trade between the two economies,[36] the British market interfered with Irish industrialization. In recent years, exports to other countries have been an increasing proportion of Ireland's total exports.

Another aspect of Ireland's close economic connections with Britain is the virtually complete freedom of labor to move between the two countries, probably greater freedom than that of any other two countries in Europe. The amount of Irish emigration to Britain has been considerable. This has been due partly to the "demonstration effect"[37] of the British economy, which causes a desire for higher wages,[38] a high level of imports and consumption,[39] and until recently a low level of savings among Irish residents. Emigration to the United States and to Britain since 1930 has been at an extremely high rate, although since 1956 it has fallen below the natural increase in population.

In view of the importance of Ireland's trade connections with Britain, it is surprising that until recently steps have not

[33] OECD Economic Survey of Ireland, 1964, Basic Statistics; see Commission on Emigration Report, Pr. 2541, paras. 52–61 (1954); Tait, "The Public Sector in Ireland," 17 Nat'l Tax J. 22, 25 (1964).

[34] Seventy-two per cent of all exports went to the United Kingdom in 1966; OECD Economic Survey of Ireland, 1966, Basic Statistics. See Anglo-Irish Trade Agreement, April 25, 1938, Cmd. No. 5728, Irish Treaty Series [hereinafter cited as Ir. T.S.] No. 1 of 1938, Pr. 3104 (1938); Trade Agreement, July 31, 1948, 86 U.N.T.S. 38 (1951), Ir. T.S. No. 12 of 1948, Pr. 8983 (1948); Exchange of Notes, June 17, 1953, Ir. T.S. No. 4 of 1953, Pr. 1895 (1953); Trade Agreement, April 13, 1960, Ir. T.S. No. 4 of 1960, Pr. 5489 (1960); McManus, "Irish Trade Agreements," Irish Times, Oct. 28, 1964, p. 4; Irish Times, Oct. 29, p. 5; Irish Times, Oct. 31, 1964, p. 7.

[35] Lynch, "Economic Planning in Ireland," 8 Administration 180, 189, (1960); O'Mahony, "Economic Expansion in Ireland," 48 Studies 129, 130–32 (1959).

[36] Commission on Emigration Report, Pr. 2541, para. 392 (1954); Economic Development, Pr. 4803, ch. 2, para. 13 (1958). In December 1965 a treaty was concluded for the establishment of a free trade area between Britain and Ireland: U.K.-Irish Free Trade Agreement, Dec. 14, 1965, Cmd. No. 2858 (1965). The agreement is not yet in force.

[37] The demonstration effect is the tendency which knowledge of a highly industrialized economy has to cause expectations and demands in a less developed economy to imitate those in the highly industrialized economy.

[38] "Symposium on Economic Development," 20(2) J. Stat. Soc. 113–14 (1958–59) (contribution of Ó Nualláin); Whitaker, "Capital Formation, Saving and Economic Progress," 19 J. Stat. Soc. 184, 185 (1955–56); Economic Development, Pr. 4803, ch. 2, para. 7 (1958).

[39] Gross fixed capital formation averaged only 14% of the gross national product during 1957–61, though it rose to 19% in 1964.

been taken to insure that shipping routes between the two countries are entirely satisfactory.[40]

Ireland is in the sterling area, and the Irish pound has always had full parity of value with the pound sterling. There has always been free movement of capital between Ireland and the rest of the sterling area, and this has helped to insure that the usual deficit on visible trade in Ireland's balance of payments has been made up by invisibles such as tourism, emigrants' remittances,[41] and income from external assets. External assets are held almost completely in the sterling area and mainly in Britain.[42] Freedom of movement of Irish capital to the large London capital market has in the past reduced the amount of capital available for investment in Ireland and also reduced the size of the Irish capital market, since London shares were often more profitable than Irish investments. Since 1963, however, there has been considerable interest in the Irish stock exchange by foreign portfolio investors. The small number of Irish companies large enough to seek capital from the public and other factors also have contributed to the small size of the Irish capital market. In 1966 Britain introduced "voluntary" restrictions on exports of British capital to Ireland.

The main monetary aspects of completely free capital movements are clear.[43] There are very close links between the two banking systems. Interest rates in Ireland tend to follow the British rates. This has been unfortunate, both because the British bank rate has fluctuated since 1945, due to successive waves of deflation for balance-of-payments reasons, and because the Irish rate probably should be held at a lower level than the rate in Britain[44] to promote investment and growth.

With regard to capital and labor, a common market already exists between Ireland and Britain,[45] and the entry of both countries into the EEC would not make much difference in this respect. The relationship which has resulted and the nature and extent of its effects on the Irish economy are complicated and deserve more study than they have received, particularly in view of the significance of the lessons to be derived from them for the less developed areas

[40] See Naylor, "Cross Channel Transport," Investors Chronicle (London), Supp., Nov. 16, 1962; FitzGerald, "Irish Economic Problems," 46 Studies 271, 290 (1957); National Industrial Economic Council, Report on Measures to Promote Exports of Manufactured Goods, Pr. 8005, paras. 37–44 (1964).

[41] Except in war, there have never been exchange controls on remittances from the countries to which the Irish chiefly emigrate. Emigrants' remittances in 1961 were approximately $39.2 million, 2% of national income; Statistical Abstract of Ireland, 1962, at 265. See Ryan, "The Irish Balance of Payments," 4 Administration 49 (1956).

[42] Commission on Emigration Report, Pr. 2541, paras. 124, 61, 471 (1954); OECD Economic Survey of Ireland, 1963, para. 48. This has meant that Irish external assets were injured by increases in interest rates in Britain. See "The Sterling Area and Ireland," Irish Banking Rev., March 1958, p. 3.

[43] See OECD Economic Survey of Ireland, 1964, para. 39. See also Balogh, "Liberalization or Constructive Organization," 19 Bull. Oxford U. Inst. Statistics 39, 43, para. (v) (1957).

[44] See Commission on Emigration Report, Pr. 2541, Minority Report 395 (per Meenan) (1954).

[45] OECD Economic Survey of Ireland, 1962, para. 31; OECD Economic Survey of Ireland, 1963, para. 37. The rate of expansion in Ireland cannot be governed by monetary means. Irish balance-of-payments difficulties in 1955–56 were dealt with primarily by import restrictions and other measures to restrict domestic demand. On the other hand, the standard rate of tax is always kept below the British rate; see, however, Economic Development, Pr. 4803, ch. 3, paras. 7–8 (1958). On Ireland's connections with the international monetary institutions, see Menton, "Ireland and International Monetary Institutions," 20(1) J. Stat. Soc. 80, 92–98 (1957–58).

of the EEC. The "demonstration effect" on less developed regional economies will become stronger as economic and social integration proceeds.[46]

COMPARATIVE ASPECTS

There are sufficient similarities between the Irish economy and those of certain other areas in Europe, such as the south of Italy and the south and west of France, for conclusions to be drawn which may be applicable to all of them. This view has been indicated by the Irish Committee on Industrial Organization[47] and has been adopted by the United Nations Economic Commission for Europe, which in 1959 considered development problems in southern Europe and Ireland.[48] It was adopted by the Irish government in connection with the negotiations for a Free Trade Area in 1957,[49] though it since has been dropped. Per capita income in Ireland in 1964 was $918,[50] roughly halfway between that of Turkey, Greece, Yugoslavia, Spain, and Portugal, on the one hand, and that of the Six and Britain, on the other. Though more developed economically than the southern European countries just mentioned, Ireland is still a capital-importing country. In certain respects it resembles these countries in its lack of industrialization, and it has even higher rates of emigration.[51] All these economies have relatively large numbers of the population in agriculture and have considerable amounts of underemployment in agriculture and services, although underemployment is less com-

[46] Lynch, "The Economics of Independence," 7 Administration 91, 96 (1959); U.N. Economic Survey of Europe, 1959, U.N. Doc. E/ECE/383, ch. VII, at 1 n.1 (1960); Comité Intergouvernemental Créé par la Conférence de Messine, Rapport des Chefs de Délégation aux Ministres des Affaires Etrangères [hereinafter cited as Spaak Report] 65 (1956); Report by the [OEEC] Group of Financial Experts . . . , para. 28, in Negotiations for a European Free Trade Area: Documents . . . , Cmd. No. 641, at 223–24 (1959).

[47] Committee on Industrial Organization, Fourth Interim Report: Industrial Grants, Pr. 6924, para. 33 (1962).

[48] U.N. Economic Survey of Europe, 1959, U.N. Doc. No. E/ECE/383, chs. VII, VIII (1960). The following text material is taken largely from these chapters without detailed citation. The countries dealt with are Ireland, Greece, Turkey, Yugoslavia, Spain, and Portugal. None of these countries is at present in the EEC; Greece and Turkey each have a treaty of association with it. Portugal is in EFTA. Ireland is not in EFTA, because until recently the latter has not dealt with agricultural products. Yugoslavia is not in the OECD. The only remaining country in non-Communist Europe which is not in the EEC or EFTA and which is not included in the U.N. Economic Survey is Iceland, which, though in certain respects a less developed country, has a small population with very high level of per capita income. The Icelandic economy is also based very largely on a single type of product—fish and fish products. Of these seven countries, the economies of Ireland, Iceland, Greece, and Portugal are most dependent on international trade. See Johnston, Why Ireland Needs the Common Market, ch. II, "The Irish Economy in a European Perspective" (1962); U.N. Economic Survey of Europe in 1954, U.N. Doc. No. E/ECE/194, at 145 (1955); Murray, "Economies and Under-Developed Countries," 6 Administration 204, 216–17 (1958); Ryan, "The Prospect of Eire," The Times (London) Review of Industry, Jan. 1963, p. 12; Murray, "Ireland and the European Free Trade Area," 5 Administration 25, 36–37 (1957); FitzGerald, "Ireland and the Free Trade Area," 46 Studies 19 (1957); "Ireland's Bumpy Flight," The Economist, Sept. 11, 1965, p. 1013.

[49] See Report by the [OEEC] Group of Financial Experts . . . , in Negotiations for a European Free Trade Area: Documents . . . , Cmd. No. 641, at 217–36 (1959).

[50] See Economic Development, Pr. 4803, ch. 2, para. 2 (1958). The average weekly earnings of industrial workers in September 1965 were $31; OECD Economic Survey of Ireland, 1966, Basic Statistics.

[51] For a broad social study of Irish emigration, see Commission on Emigration Report, Pr. 2541 (1954); for the southern European countries, see U.N. Economic Survey of Europe in 1953, U.N. Doc. No. E/ECE/174, ch. 16 (1954).

mon in Ireland than in the other five. In all of them, standards of living can be raised and economic development encouraged most rapidly by industrialization, primarily by the establishment of new plants rather than by expansion of existing factories. Owing to the structure of industry, industrial output per capita in Ireland is now approximately half that of the Six and Britain, which have large-scale and capital-intensive industries. In the underindustrialized countries mentioned above, the percentage of gross national product going into fixed investment is substantially lower than in the Six, except in southern Italy. The low rate of fixed investment has until recently been one of the most serious impediments to economic development in Ireland.

All of these countries expect balance-of-payments difficulties for some years to come, and the U.N. Economic Commission has indicated two possible courses of action: diversification of industry and increase of industrial exports, or import restrictions and import-substitution. Ireland chose the former course of action in 1956 and had reasonable success. All these countries need to encourage higher rates of savings, investment, and capital formation, and it would require fiscal and other regional economic measures within the EEC to enable them to do this.

A high proportion of the total Irish revenue has always come from special indirect taxes. The agricultural sector pays little direct tax, personal incomes are lower than in the Six, and there is a fairly narrow industrial tax base, so rates of direct taxation have been undesirably high for a developing country.[52] It is not clear to what extent this has discouraged savings, investment, and higher production. Tax policy in a developing country should encourage investment and discourage consumption, especially in view of the importance of self-financing for small enterprises.

FOREIGN INVESTMENT IN AN EXPORT ECONOMY

In the seven years up to 1965, over 267 new manufacturing industries were established in Ireland, many of them with foreign capital. About one-third of these are British-owned;[53] the rest are owned by Germans, Americans, the Dutch, and others. The total capital involved in new enterprises with foreign shareholding in December 1965 was about $46.2 million. Many of these have received grants from public funds, and most of them are selling primarily in export markets to get the benefit of the tax relief for profits from exports.

There are certain advantages for investors in capital-importing countries. First, because of underemployment, there is usually an abundance of relatively cheap labor. In Ireland, the amount of labor potentially available is larger than the rate of unemployment indicates because of the high rate of emigration. The labor situation is particularly advantageous where the government is taking measures to limit wage increases to those justified by increases in production, as is now being done in Ireland.[54] Social security contributions by employers are also low. Since natural comparative advantages assume greater importance in conditions of free trade as

[52] Economic Development, Pr. 4803, ch. 3, paras. 7–8 (1958).

[53] A "List of New Industries with Foreign Participation" is published regularly by the Industrial Development Authority, Dublin. On external capital assistance, see U.N. Economic Survey of Europe in 1953, U.N. Doc. No. E/ECE/174, at 203–207 (1954).

[54] See Closing the Gap: Incomes and Output, Pr. 6957 (1963); National Industrial Economic Council, Report on Economic Situation 1965, Pr. 8552 (1965); Nolan, "Industrial Relations 1963," 1963 Irish Review and Annual 54 (1964).

competitive conditions are equalized, the advantages conferred by these reduced costs will be progressively accentuated by tariff reduction.

Second, the state aid which may be obtained for the establishment of new industry is considerable. Irish industries have tariff-free access to British markets and preferential tariff rates in the Commonwealth; comparable advantages exist with respect to the countries associated with the EEC and the less developed member countries of EFTA. The foreign investor can combine the cost and tax advantages of the less developed countries with access to large markets.

According to the OECD:[55]

> The structure of the [Irish] economy appears to be basically favorable to growth. Ireland is one of the rare countries in Western Europe to have a surplus of manpower at the present time. Yet in other respects the country is on a par with economies whose degree of development is more advanced, notably as regards educational standards, public and private attitudes to social and economic problems and the existence of an extensive infrastructure. Furthermore, the country is well placed geographically to serve the major European and North American markets. . . . The extent to which Ireland has been able to attract foreign capital and to increase exports of agricultural and, in particular, industrial products attests to the importance of these factors. It remains, however, that the problem of achieving an adequate rate of investment will become more urgent from now on and that further structural changes in industry and agriculture are called for.[56]

The less developed countries themselves benefit from foreign investment since it provides currency for imports of capital goods, furnishes capital and entrepreneurial talent for industrialization, results in employment and industrialization, and improves the balance-of-payments position if the products are exported. Private foreign investment can provide much larger amounts of capital more quickly than other methods of increasing investment, such as increased current saving,[57] increased exports, repatriation of external assets,[58] and to some extent, credit creation.[59] Projects financed by foreign investment are normally profitable, and foreign investors have an interest in the national prosperity.

If Ireland joins the EEC,[60] she will have four main problems. The first will be the competitive weakness of industry due to prolonged protectionist policies. If not remedied, this would necessitate either a slow rate of tariff reduction, which probably would not be acceptable to the Six, or some measure of dislocation. For this reason a unique and important series of studies of individual industries has been undertaken by the

[55] OECD Economic Survey of Ireland, 1961, para. 24.

[56] See also Fennell, Industrialization and Agricultural Development in the Congested Districts, Introduction (1962).

[57] Partly inhibited by the tax structure and the demonstration effect.

[58] This necessitates compensating increases in exports to maintain the balance-of-payments position.

[59] Commission on Emigration Report, Pr. 2541, Minority Report, paras. 57–70 (per Meenan) (1954); Capital Investment Advisory Committee, Third Report, Pr. 4668, para. 23 (1958). On the monetary aspects of economic expansion in Ireland, see Economic Development, Pr. 4803, ch. 3 (1958); on the benefits of foreign investment, see id., ch. 4, para. 35.

[60] For a summary of Ireland's position after the breakdown of the British negotiations with the EEC in January 1963, see Irish Banking Rev., March 1963, p. 10. For the problems of the EEC, see Lemass, FitzGerald & Maher, "The European Economic Community," 10 Administration 3 (1962); Council of Europe, The Position of Certain European Countries Other than the Six in the Event of the United Kingdom Joining the European Economic Community 43–46 (1961); Ryan, "The Need for Structural Change in Irish Industry," Irish Banking Rev., March 1961, p. 9.

Committee on Industrial Organization. State aids for adaptation and modernization have been provided, and tariffs have been reduced unilaterally. It was the relative weakness of Irish industry which caused doubts on whether Ireland should be admitted to full EEC membership at once or after an intermediate period of association similar to, but presumably much shorter than, that of Greece. The relatively undeveloped state of Irish industry would make Community policy on state aids, regional economic policy, and Community and national measures to encourage economic development of special importance, as they are in other less developed regions and countries in the EEC or likely to become associates or members of the EEC.

The second problem will be the compatibility of the existing Irish state aids to exports and to industry generally with the provisions of the EEC Treaty. This is discussed in Chapter Fifteen of this book.

Third, the small Irish market with its small industries[61] will be peculiarly vulnerable to dumping. The existing Treaty provisions and the implementing rules of law are discussed in Chapter Eighteen.

The fourth problem concerns state trading and will be less serious in Ireland than in other less developed countries. The Treaty of Rome regulates[62] but does not forbid state trading. Exactly what the Treaty provisions will mean in practice is not yet clear, but it does not appear that any major adjustments will have to be made by any of the Irish state-owned or statutory bodies. Owing to the difficulties of being precise at this time and to the specialized and limited interest of this problem, it is not treated in this book.

[61] The average number of employees of Irish enterprises is somewhat larger than that of enterprises in Belgium and Norway and much the same as that of enterprises in Italy, France, and Sweden. However, Irish industry is more labor-intensive than industry in more highly industrialized countries. See Linehan, "The Structure of Irish Industry," 20(5) J. Stat. Soc. 220 (1961–62).

[62] Arts. 37, 92.

Part III

COMPANY LAW AND FREEDOM OF ESTABLISHMENT

Chapter 4

Harmonization of Company Law and Comparative Aspects of Irish Company Law[1]

Company law has not the obvious economic implications of tax or antitrust law, and the company laws of the Six are more like one another and like the laws of Ireland and Britain than, for example, their tax laws. However, since company law deals with the type of enterprise which is most important in business and which is almost universally used by the investors of one state when establishing business operations in another, it was natural for the Treaty to contemplate harmonization of company law. For the same reasons it must be dealt with here.

THE SPECIFIC PROVISIONS OF THE TREATY

Article 220 requires member states to enter into negotiations to insure for their nationals reciprocal recognition of companies and maintenance of the companies' legal personalities if their registered offices are transferred from one state to another. Article 220 also requires member states to make mergers of companies subject to different national laws possible. Firms or companies constituted under either civil or commercial law (in countries such as France, where that distinction is made), cooperative societies, and other legal persons (*personnes morales*) under public or private law are to be dealt with. Firms or companies not intended to make profits are not within the Article.[2]

A company in one state cannot do business in the other member states unless it is recognized as validly incorporated, but this recognition alone does not give it freedom of establishment in the recognizing country.[3] The development of the Common Market will cause increased reciprocal investment among member states if freedom of establishment permits. Mergers between companies incorporated in different countries will be necessary to obtain the economies of scale possible in a large market. A company should be able to move all its activities to another member state without dissolution and its serious tax consequences.

[1] This chapter outlines the Treaty provisions and the work of the Community on harmonization of company law and then gives a comparative analysis of Irish company law. Differences among the laws of Ireland, Britain, and the Six are indicated where they would be likely to be significant for the foreign investor or to require harmonization in the EEC. As explained in the Introduction, no effort has been made to set out the laws of all of the Six on each topic. The chapter does not speculate how the different rules of law would be harmonized if the Commission considered harmonization necessary.

[2] Arts. 58, 220; EEC Commission, Direction Générale Concurrence, Reconnaissance Mutuelle des Sociétés, maintien de la personalité juridique en cas de transfert du siège de pays en pays, fusion des sociétés relevant de legislations nationales différentes, Doc. No. 3196/IV/62–F (1962); see also id., Doc. No. 6878/IV/64–F (1964) (the draft convention under art. 220). On the importance in French company law of whether a company is intended to make profits, see Church, Business Associations Under French Law 3 (1960).

[3] Loussouarn, "Droit International de Commerce," 12 Revue Trimestrielle de Droit Commercial 246, 251 (1959).

Recognition of companies

THE LAWS OF THE SIX

The present laws of the Six cause no important technical difficulties in practice with regard to recognition of most types of companies. However, the Six generally recognize as validly incorporated only a company which is incorporated in the country where it has its central office or principal place of management (*siège social*).[4] The *siège social* must be the real central office (*siège réel*) and not just a formal registered office (*siège statutaire*). This is the position in Belgium,[5] Luxembourg,[6] Germany,[7] and France.[8] Italy regards companies incorporated abroad which have their principal activity or their place of administration in Italy[9] as Italian companies, and they must comply with the requirements of Italian law. Although the position is disputed, it appears that a company with its registered office in the Netherlands is validly incorporated under Dutch law even if its principal place of management is elsewhere.[10]

France, Belgium, and Luxembourg decide what foreign law a company is subject to by the same test they use to determine whether it is subject to their own laws.[11] Germany probably also regards a foreign company as subject to the law of the place of its central office, but some authors argue for the law under which it was incorporated.[12] In the

[4] As to France and Belgium, see Hauser & Hauser, A Guide to Doing Business in the European Common Market 122–36 (1960). On corporations generally in conflict of laws, see 2 Rabel, The Conflict of Laws, chs. 18–23 (2d ed. 1960); as to the possibility of renvoi in recognition of foreign companies, see id. at 50–51. The differences in meaning of the various phrases in national laws here translated as "central office" or "principal place of management" are "negligible." Id. at 37. See Loussouarn, "La Condition des Personnes morales en Droit international privé," 96(1) Recueil Académie D. Int. 443, 475–83 (1959).

[5] Arreté Royal, Dec. 30, 1935, coordonnant les lois sur les sociétés, art. 197, speaks of the *principal établissement;* this means the administrative center or place where the company's records are kept, where the general meetings are held, or where the management makes decisions, not the principal place of business. Companies are liable to Belgian tax as residents if their legal situs, their principal administrative establishment, or their place of management is in Belgium.

[6] Law of Aug. 15, 1915, art. 159. The place where the company's records are kept may also be the *principal établissement.*

[7] Gesetz über Aktiengesellschaften, Jan. 20, 1937 [hereinafter cited as Aktiengesetz], art. 5.

[8] See Ordonnance No. 59–123, Jan. 7, 1959, 1959 Journal Officiel de la République Française [hereinafter cited as J.O.R.F.] 640; art. 73 of the new draft Civil Code is to the same effect. See Batiffol, "Observations sur le problème de la nationalité des sociétés," in 1 La Società per Azioni alla metà del Secolo XX, 65 (1962); Loussouarn, "Droit International de Commerce," 12 Revue Trimestrielle de Droit Commercial 246 (1959).

[9] Civil Code, arts. 2505, 2509.

[10] Thibièrge, "Le Statut des Sociétés Etrangères," in 1 Le Statut de l'Etranger et le Marché Commun [hereinafter cited as Le Statut de l'Etranger] 239, 335 (57th Congrès des Notaires de France, 1959). The Law of July 25, 1959, has confirmed that only a formal registered office is needed; Chesné, L'Etablissement des Etrangers en France et la Communauté Economique Européenne 277 (1962). See also Leleux, "Companies, Investment and Taxation in the European Economic Community," in Legal Problems of the European Economic Community and the European Free Trade Association, Int'l & Comp. L.Q. Supp. No. 1, at 23, 24, 26 (1961).

[11] The principle of recognition of companies if they are validly incorporated under the law of the country where they are managed is accepted by statute in Belgium; Commercial Code, bk. I, tit. IX, arts. 196, 197.

See Piot, "Du réalisme dans les conventions d'établissement," 88 Journal du Droit International 38 (1961); Thibièrge, "Le Statut des Sociétés Etrangères," in 1 Le Statut de l'Etranger 239, 250, 251; Loussouarn, Les conflits de lois en matière de Sociétés (1949).

[12] The phrase "law of incorporation" is used in the text for convenience to mean the law in accordance with which the company is constituted or incorporated.

Netherlands opinion is divided between the law of the place of the company's registered office and the law of the central office. The Italian law is not settled.

Recognition in the strict sense involves acceptance of the legal personality of the foreign company and of its capacity *inter alia* to contract in its own name and to sue and be sued. Belgium, Luxembourg,[13] Germany, and the Netherlands[14] give full recognition to any company with legal personality under the law to which they regard it as subject. Italy recognizes a company as having full legal personality if it is, under Italian law, subject to the law of a country which gives full recognition and the resulting privileges to Italian companies—the principle of reciprocity. France gives full recognition to foreign equivalents of French *sociétés anonymes* and *sociétés à responsabilité limitée,* but she gives recognition to the former only pursuant to a decree or a treaty.[15] Although some treaties recognize companies "constituted in conformity with the law" of the other country, recognition of foreign *sociétés anonymes* is usually given on the basis of the principal place of management. Reciprocal recognition of companies is dealt with by a number of bilateral treaties among the Six.[16]

The rule requiring a company to have a genuine link, usually its principal place

[13] Law of Aug. 15, 1915, art. 158.

[14] For Germany and the Netherlands, see the authorities gathered in Pennington, Companies in the Common Market 57 (1962).

[15] Decrees have been made in respect of companies from nineteen countries, including all the Six; Thibièrge, "Le Statut des Sociétés Etrangères," in 1 Le Statut de l'Etranger 239, 275; 2 Niboyet, Traité de Droit International privé français, No. 805 (1951). Draft Civil Code, art. 38, provides for full recognition of a company if the law where it is created gives it legal personality. The general principle that a decree or treaty is required for recognition is stated in the Law of May 30, 1857, No. 4578, art. 2; 1 Hamel & Lagarde, Traité de Droit Commercial 944-95 (1954). *Sociétés anonymes* are the more widely held of the two types of company recognized by French company law. *Sociétés à responsabilité limitée* correspond to United States close corporations; see pp. 110–12. See Chesné, L'Etablissement des Etrangers en France et la Communauté Economique Européenne 291–302 (1962). Irish companies have not been dealt with by decree.

See Ordonnance No. 59–123, Jan. 7, 1959, which equates change of nationality with change of registered head office (*siège social*) in the case of a stock company (*société anonyme*). Judgment of June 20, 1870, Cass. Civ., [1870] Sirey Jurisprudence [hereinafter cited as S.] I. 373; Judgment of Dec. 22, 1896, Cass. Civ., [1897] S. I. 84; Judgment of July 17, 1935, Cass Civ., [1936] S. I. 41; Judgment of July 7, 1947, Cass. Civ., [1947] J.C.P. II. 3871; Draft Civil Code, art. 73.

[16] Belgium-Italy Treaty of Commerce and Navigation, 1882, art. 4, [1882] Moniteur Belge 5021, [1882] Gazzetta Ufficiale, No. 305; Belgium-Netherlands Convention on Establishment and Work, 1933, art. 10, [1934] Moniteur Belge 338, [1936] Staatsblad, No. 83, at 4; France-Germany Convention on Establishment and Navigation, Oct. 27, 1956, art. 6, 1959 J.O.R.F. 8850, [1957] 2 Bundesgesetzblatt [hereinafter cited as BGBl.] 1662; France-Italy Convention on Establishment, Aug. 23, 1951, art. 7, 1958 J.O.R.F. 620, [1953] Gazzetta Ufficiale, No. 85(3); France-Luxembourg Convention on Establishment, 1930, art. 3, 1931 J.O.R.F. 9230, [1931] Mémorial du Grande Duché de Luxembourg 579; Germany-Italy Treaty of Friendship, Commerce and Navigation, 1957, arts. 7, 12, 33, [1959] BGBl. 950, [1961] Gazzetta Ufficiale, No. 134, Supp.; Germany-Netherlands Treaty on Companies, 1907, art. 1, [1908] Reichsgesetzblatt 65, [1952] BGBl. 435, [1908] Staatsblad, Nos. 11, 96; Luxembourg-Netherlands Convention on Establishment, Aug. 26, 1933, art. 10, [1933] Mémorial du Grande Duché de Luxembourg 610; Belgium-France Convention on Establishment, Nov. 5, 1927, arts. 5–7, 1927 J.O.R.F. 11270.

See Ireland-Germany Treaty of Commerce and Navigation, May 12, 1930, art. 13, Cmd. No. 4017 (1932), Ir. T.S. No. 9 of 1931. U.S.-France Convention on Establishment, Nov. 25, 1959, arts. XII, XIV, [1960] 2 U.S.T. & O.I.A. 2398, provides for reciprocal recognition of companies incorporated in either signatory state, unless they are controlled by nationals of a third state.

of management,[17] with the country under whose laws it is incorporated—the *siège réel* rule—is intended to prevent evasion. However, if the Common Market is to constitute a single economy, a company incorporated in any EEC member state should be able to have its principal place of management in any part of the EEC.

Recognition of Foreign Companies in Irish and English Law

The rules of Irish and English law on the recognition of foreign companies are different from those of the Six. In Irish and English law, as in United States law, the law under which the company is incorporated determines the legal personality of the company.[18] Irish law does not regard any company as invalidly constituted if it is properly incorporated according to the law of any other country, even though the principal place of management is not in that country. In general, the power of the company to sue and be sued and to contract and the powers and duties of its organs are governed by the law of incorporation. However, if the company is invalidly incorporated under its law of incorporation because its place of management is in another jurisdiction, the company will not be recognized by Irish law.

Proposals of International Bodies

Recognition of foreign companies has been the subject of various international

[17] *Siège social* is best translated as "central place of management" or "actual head office," but the phrase may mean also "formal head office." When the distinction between "actual head office" and "registered head office" is necessary, this book uses *siège réel* and *siège statutaire*, respectively. In France, the *siège social* is the place of principal management and control of the company; Judgment of Oct. 28, 1945, Cass. Reg., [1942] Gazette du Palais [hereinafter cited as Gaz. Pal.] I. 18. Weber v. Société générale anglaise et française, Commercial Court of Nancy, Feb. 18, 1907, 34 Journal de Droit International Privé 765–68 (1907), holds:

> The nationality of a commercial company or partnership (*société de commerce*) is determined by the country where it has its head office (*siège social*); but the choice of this head office must be serious and sincere and must correspond to the place where the directors actually direct the company (*où la direction de la société est réellement exercée par ses administrateurs*), where its business is centralized, from where all the branches of the company get their instructions and on which all the results of their activity converge; if the head office does not satisfy these conditions; . . . if the company, except for the choice of a foreign country as the place of its head office, has all the features of a French company; . . . if nowhere and under no circumstances can any evidence of transactions done by the foreign head office be found; if the business of the company is carried on exclusively in France, it is right to say that the designation of the head office is but a fiction and has been made only in order to remove the company from the requirements of French law; . . . therefore [this company] is a French and not an English company: it has been created in violation of French law and is void.

Translation, with certain changes, from Katz & Brewster, International Transactions and Relations: Cases and Materials 190–93 (1960).

Thibièrge, "Le Statut des Sociétés Etrangères," in 1 Le Statut de l'Etranger 239, 254–55, lists the following advantages for the *siège social* principle: a company can have only one *siège;* therefore, there is no difficulty in identifying the law which governs the company; the *siège*, unlike the place of operations, is permanent; the law of the place of the *siège* is more appropriate than the law of the place of the company's operations for governing the company as an entity, and it is the law that the directors know best; the law governing the company is the law with jurisdiction over the company; the company can operate abroad without altering its constitution. On the law of the place where the company is incorporated, see id. at 253, and for a comparison of the two principles, see id. at 258–64. See also Chesné, L'Etablissement des Etrangers en France et la Communauté Economique Européenne 259–60, 261–62, 267–71 (1962).

[18] Dicey, Conflict of Laws, ch. 16 (7th ed. 1958); 2 Rabel, The Conflict of Laws 31 (2d ed. 1960).

studies.[19] The draft convention of the Hague Conference on Private International Law in 1951 provides that a company will be recognized only if it has legal personality according to the law of incorporation.[20] The registered office must be in the country of incorporation, but the principal place of management need not be. However, recognition can be refused if the principal place of management is in a country which uses the *siège réel* rule, including the country deciding whether to recognize the company. The Council of Europe draft convention on establishment embodied much the same compromise.[21]

[19] Draft rules proposed in 1891 by the Institute of Private International Law, 11 Annuaire de l'Institut 171 (1892); Resolution of the Institute of International Law, 36th Sess., 1929, [1929] 2 Annuaire de l'Institut de Droit International 301.

[20] Conférence de la Haye de Droit International Privé, "Projet de Convention concernant la reconnaissance de la personalité juridique des sociétés, associations et fondations etrangères," [1952] 1 Actes de la Septième Session, 1951, at 126–38, 385–88.

Art. 1 of the draft convention reads, in part: "The legal personality acquired by a firm or company (*société*), an association or a foundation by virtue of the law of a contracting state where the formalities of registration or of publication have been fulfilled and where the company has its registered office (*siège statutaire*) will be fully recognized. . . ."

Art. 2 reads, in part: "However, the personality acquired pursuant to Article 1, need not be recognized in a contracting state the law of which involves consideration of the principal place of management (*siège réel*), if the principal place of management is considered as being in its territory . . . [or] in a state the law of which takes [the principal place of management] . . . into consideration. The company . . . is considered as having its *siège réel* in the place where its central management (*administration centrale*) is established." Id. at 385, author's translations. See Offerhaus, "La septième session de la Conférence de La Haye de Droit International Privé," 79 Journal du Droit International 1071, 1091 (1952); [1935] 2 Mémoires de l'Académie Internationale de Droit Comparé 630–66.

At the Conference of the International Law Association in 1960,[22] the common law influence was stronger than in the Six. The Conference hoped to allow flexibility in the management of large international companies, which is impossible if the principal place of management must be in the country under whose laws the company was constituted. The Conference also hoped to prevent fraud, which may occur if a company can be incorporated under the laws of a country with which it has no connection, a possibility under the Anglo-Irish principle. It was suggested[23] that the law of the country of incorporation should govern the legal personality of the company provided the company has some connection with that country. If the company has no effective link with the country of incorporation, the law of the principal place of management should govern. It was unanimously agreed that the law primarily applicable is the law under which the company was incorporated, and most experts now take this view.

Under these three solutions,[24] a com-

[21] Council of Europe Committee of Experts on the Treatment of Legal Entities, Draft Convention on the Establishment of Companies, art. 1, Doc. No. C.M. (62)36 (1962), applies to all companies incorporated for profit and having full legal personality or capacity to sue and to contract which have been incorporated in and have their *siège statutaire* in the jurisdiction of a signatory state. However, a signatory state can also require an effective and continuing connection with the relevant state if it so wishes.

[22] Forty-Ninth Conference, Hamburg; see Committee on International Company Law, Report 62–95 (1961); see also International Law Association, Forty-Eighth Conference [New York, 1958], Committee on International Company Law, Report 629–52 (1959).

[23] International Law Association, Forty-Ninth Conference, Committee on International Company Law, Report 62, 65 (1961).

[24] I.e., the recommendations of the Hague Conference on Private International Law, the Council of Europe Committee of Experts, and the International Law Association.

The Seventh International Congress on Lim-

pany which has no effective connection with the country of incorporation would be treated differently by countries which use the *siège réel* rule and by countries which look only to the law of incorporation.[25] This is clearly undesirable. Problems also arise if the country where the *siège réel* was situated and the country to which it has been moved differ on whether the move alters the company's governing law.[26] EEC member states must have a uniform rule on the law governing a company. The Anglo-Irish rule has the merit of insuring certainty, but some compromise along the lines of the Council of Europe draft, requiring at least a connection with the law of incorporation, is almost certain.

All the Six recognize a company which is validly incorporated under the law of the member state where it has its principal place of management. However, the exact legal position depends on case law. Case law is a source of law inferior to statute in the civil law countries, and a treaty on the recognition of foreign companies is desirable for this reason also. Each of the Six may refuse recognition on the grounds of public policy. They have different views as to the position to be taken where a company has legal personality under the law of incorporation but a similar company would not have legal personality in the recognizing country.[27] The concept of the *siège social* is not entirely clear, nor is it precisely the same in the laws of each of the Six. These matters need to be dealt with.

Recognition of Foreign Companies and the Freedom of Establishment Provisions of the Treaty

The question arises whether Article 58(1) modifies the rules of conflict of laws in the Six which have been stated above. If this Article prescribes a uniform rule that companies within its terms must automatically be recognized by member states, its exact meaning would be important.[28] Since Article 58 may not be directly applicable in national law,[29] it is possible that it does not affect recognition of companies,[30] but the view that it does so has been authoritatively expressed.[31] Recognition of the legal personality of a company confers the right to sue and to contract but not the right

ited Liability Companies at Cologne in 1962 took the view that recognition should be based on the law of incorporation but that these companies might be treated differently from the larger and commercially more important stock companies.

[25] International Law Association, Forty-Ninth Conference, Committee on International Law, Report 62, 67 (1961) (stressed by Mr. A. Philip of Denmark).

[26] Id. at 69–70, 91 (stressed by Professor Batiffol). Under the 1956 Hague Draft Convention on the Recognition of Companies, art. 3, all countries must regard the transfer as effective if the laws of both states involved so regard it.

[27] See Conférence de la Haye de Droit International Privé, "Projet de Convention . . .," [1952] 1 Actes de la Septième Session, 1951, at 385, 386.

[28] See pp. 146–58.

[29] The other provisions on freedom of establishment (arts. 52–58) are not directly applicable, since they contemplate their own implementation by directive. However, art. 53 may be directly applicable; see Costa v. ENEL, 10 Recueil 1141, [1964] C.M.L.R. 425.

[30] Art. 54 makes it clear that the other Treaty provisions on freedom of establishment are not directly applicable in national laws. Art. 220 refers to "companies within the meaning of Article 58(2)" but does not refer to art. 58(1). See Audinet, "Le droit d'établissement dans la Communauté économique européenne," 86 Journal du Droit International 982, 1012–24 (1959).

[31] Loussouarn, "Droit International de Commerce," 12 Revue Trimestrielle de Droit Commercial 246, 253 (1959); Chesné, L'Etablissement des Etrangers en France et la Communauté Economique Européenne 300–302 (1962); Thibièrge, "Le Statut des Sociétés Etrangères," in 1 Le Statut de l'Etranger 239, 334–37.

of establishment. If Article 58 prescribes a uniform rule on recognition of companies from other member states, it does so only for the purposes of establishment and rendering services, not, for example, for the purposes of litigation. If Article 58 requires recognition of a company with only a *siège statutaire* in the EEC, it supersedes to this extent the *siège réel* rule, which is in force in five member states.

Transfer of the *siège social* of a company and change of nationality

The existing laws of the Six present much greater difficulties with regard to the transfer of a company's place of management than with regard to recognition of the company. Since of the Six only the Netherlands permits a company incorporated under its law to have its place of management elsewhere, a company loses its nationality if it moves its place of management to another member state. This involves liquidation and its serious tax consequences and may prejudice the title of the company to trademarks and other industrial and commercial property. Liquidation is necessary in Belgium and Germany and probably in the Netherlands when a company changes its nationality by reorganizing under another nation's law. France permits a general meeting to change the nationality of the company and to move the place of management to a country with which France has a treaty allowing the legal personality of the company to be preserved in such circumstances.[32] No such treaty has yet been signed. In Italy[33] some and possibly, by analogy, all types of company may legally transfer their places of management to another country. In Italian law the legal situation resulting from a company's moving its place of management *to* Italy depends on the law under which the company was incorporated. The law of Luxembourg apparently allows a company to move its place of management into, but not out of, Luxembourg. The fact that the place of management of a company cannot be moved from one part of the Common Market to another inhibits freedom of establishment.

A treaty between the Six could make it possible for companies to change their nationality and reorganize without losing their legal personality or going into liquidation.[34] Even if the transfer of the place of management did not involve liquidation, it would involve reorganization of the company according to the law of the member state to which the company had moved, if the civil law rule that the law of a company's place of management governs the company is retained.[35] Eva-

[32] Ordonnance No. 59-123, Jan. 7, 1959, art. 31, 1959 J.O.R.F. 640. A two-thirds majority of the general meeting is required. See Thibièrge, "Le Statut des Sociétés Etrangères," in 1 Le Statut de l'Etranger 239, 318–23; Chesné; L'Etablissement des Etrangers en France et la Communauté Economique Européenne 307–11 (1962); Loussouarn, "La Condition des Personnes morales en Droit international privé," 96(1) Recueil Académie D. Int. 443, 489–503 (1959).

[33] Civil Code, arts. 2369, 2437. See also Civil Code, arts. 2365, 2486, 2505.

[34] This is easier to visualize in theory if one regards incorporation as a contractual act (broadly, the traditional French view) rather than as an administrative one (broadly, the German and Anglo-Irish views and the view which the French proposed to adopt in 1965).

[35] Since, in Irish law, the validity of the incorporation of a company does not depend on its place of management, it may transfer its central management to another state without any consequences. A company incorporated in Ireland is liable to corporation profits tax on its world income even if it has no other connection with Ireland. See also U.K. Income Tax Act, 1952, 15 & 16 Geo. 6 & 1 Eliz. 2, c. 10, §§ 412–13, 468. Except for tax reasons, it is unlikely that a company would need to change its nationality if it were free to move its place of management without doing so. If a company chooses to change its nationality, Irish law requires liquidation.

sion of national company laws could be prevented better by harmonization of their requirements rather than by conflict-of-laws rules. The *siège réel* rule on recognition could be retained for companies incorporated outside the EEC. Evasion of the *siège réel* rule might be possible if a company carried on business through a branch operation in the state whose requirements it wished to avoid, even though branch operations are usually subject to some local rules. If the Anglo-Irish rule on the law governing a company were adopted, a company could move its place of management to another state and still retain its original nationality and charter. No special rules as to the transfer of the place of management would be necessary.

Any legal system which permits a change in the nationality of a company[36] must specify the proportion of the shareholders who must consent to the change, and it must protect creditors and dissenting minorities. In the country to which the company moves, few provisions are necessary if the law accepts the continuity of the legal personality of the company. However, the company must make changes in its charter to comply with the new law.

Merger of companies of different nationalities

Ireland and the Six

The problem of merger of companies of different nationalities also presents difficulties, in particular from the point of view of the company being absorbed. A true merger in the laws of the Six is the sale of the assets and business of a company to a purchasing company in return for shares in the purchasing company, which are distributed to the shareholders of the selling company instead of the cash proceeds of its liquidation. Italy permits the acquisition of a local company by a foreign company by way of merger, and Belgium also permits this if the local company is put into liquidation. The acquisition of a foreign company by a local company seems to be possible under the laws of all of the Six, since the local company does not lose its nationality. The company absorbed in a merger in the strict sense changes its nationality, and this involves its liquidation under the laws of France, Germany, the Netherlands, and Belgium. A unanimous vote of the shareholders of the company absorbed is required in the laws of Belgium, France, and Luxembourg. Of the Six, only France has legislation permitting mergers of companies of different nationalities,[37] but she permits them only if she has a treaty regulating such mergers with the other country involved. In effect, if national laws permit merger of companies of different nationalities, the shares in the company absorbed are replaced by shares in a foreign company.[38] Legislation therefore is required to protect the shareholders' interests. Probably an auditors' report to

[36] The same problems arise in English or Irish law if a company needs to change its country of incorporation as arise in civil law if it needs to change the country of its *siège réel*.

[37] Ordonnance No. 59-123, Jan. 7, 1959, 1959 J.O.R.F. 640. See Thibièrge, "Le Statut des Sociétés Etrangères," in 1 Le Statut de l'Etranger 239, 324–27; Chesné, L'Etablissement des Etrangers en France et la Communauté Economique Européenne 311–12 (1962).

On the subject generally, see Rapports au Colloque international de droit européen, pt. I, "Fusion des Sociétés," 7-124 (1962).

[38] Judgment of Jan. 20, 1923, Commercial Court of Nancy, 1927 Revue des Sociétés 315, required unanimous approval of the shareholders of the company involved and has been criticized, notably by Professor Houin in "Le Traité de Rome et les fusions en droit commercial français," 34 Annuario di Diritto Comparato e di Studi Legislativi 84 (1960). See also Renauld, "Les Fusions de Sociétés en Droit Belge," 39 Revue de Droit International et Droit Comparé 217 (1962). It is important that unanimity of the shareholders should not be required in the EEC.

the shareholders of the company absorbed is necessary. Legislation is also necessary to protect creditors. In particular, both shareholders and creditors need full information. If a merger involves liquidation of one company and the sale of its assets to another, company tax on the capital gains involved is payable under the present law of the Six. Though mergers may not always be consistent with restrictive practices and monopoly policy,[39] they should be directly regulated, not inhibited by tax or other measures.

Both mergers of companies of different nationalities and transfers of the principal place of management of companies involve recognition by the company law of one country of rights and duties conferred by the company law of another country. Harmonization of company law in the EEC would therefore minimize some of the practical difficulties involved in both matters. It is not yet clear how either will be regulated in the EEC.

At present, the laws of the Netherlands, Luxembourg, Italy, and Germany on the supervision of mergers of local companies are fairly similar. In the Netherlands the control is administrative, and in Italy and Germany it is exercised by the court.[40]

In Ireland, apart from reorganization of a company, which may require the approval of the High Court,[41] mergers take place in three ways. The first and most common way is for one company to acquire all the shares in the other. This, which is not a merger in the civil law sense,[42] presents no difficulties under Article 220. Apart from exchange controls or restrictions on freedom of establishment, which would have to be repealed upon Ireland's joining the EEC, Irish law does not regulate the acquisition of Irish shares by foreign companies or the acquisition of foreign shares by Irish companies. The second way is for the assets of a company in liquidation to be sold for shares in the purchasing company, which are distributed to the shareholders of the selling company. In this case, the interests of the latter's shareholders and creditors are safeguarded.[43] In the third way, the assets of a company can be sold without putting the selling company into liquidation. In this case the creditors retain their rights against the selling company, and in certain circumstances they and the shareholders may have the directors restrained from selling the company's business. In all three cases the act can be carried out by the vote of a majority of the shareholders; unanimity is not required in Irish law. In Ireland mergers involve no serious tax consequences.[44] A merger of legal entities can be effected only in a company reconstruction with the approval of the High Court, and the court's powers apply only to companies incor-

[39] See EEC Commission, Action Programme for the Second Stage, paras. 26, 45 (1962).

[40] Houin, "Rapport général sur la fusion des sociétés," in Rapports au Colloque international de droit européen 9, 16 (1962).

[41] Companies Act, 1963 Acts, No. 33, §§ 201–203. Throughout this chapter, all references to sections, unless otherwise indicated, are to this Act. See National Bank of Greece v. Metliss, [1958] A.C. 509; Adams v. National Bank of Greece, [1961] A.C. 255.

[42] Houin, "Rapport général sur la fusion des sociétés," in Rapports au Colloque international de droit européen 9, 15 (1962); Houin, "Le Traité de Rome et les fusions en droit commercial français," 34 Annuario di Diritto Comparato e di Studi Legislativi 84, 85 (1960).

[43] See § 260; Gower, The Principles of Modern Company Law 556–60 (2d ed. 1957). Cf. U.K. Companies Act, 1948, 11 & 12 Geo. 6, c. 38 [cited in this chapter as U.K. Act].

[44] If a capital gains tax were introduced, this would not remain true. The sale of a business is not subject to the turnover tax under the Finance Act, 1963 Acts, No. 23.

porated in Ireland.[45] The latter rule would probably require amendment in the EEC to permit the courts to approve mergers with companies of other member states. If the proposed convention on mergers implementing Article 220 requires the safeguards in mergers of companies of different nationalities to be administered by a public body and not by private auditors, this could be done by a court.

PROPOSALS OF INTERNATIONAL BODIES

Both transfers of place of management and mergers of companies of different nationalities are treated in a draft convention of the Hague Conference on Private International Law.[46] Under it, all signatory states must recognize the continuity of the legal personality of a company in the case of transfer of its *siège social* if the two states directly concerned recognize it, and similarly treat mergers between companies of different nationalities. The draft convention does not affect the problems arising in domestic law, however. At a meeting in Brussels in 1961 a resolution was passed calling for a convention allowing mergers between companies of different EEC member states.[47] The resolution also called for non-discriminatory tax treatment of mergers; for acceptance of the principle that by the merger itself the new company succeeds to all the rights and liabilities of the old companies; for scrutiny of all mergers by a court, an administrative authority, or inspectors in the interests of creditors and shareholders; for advance publication of proposed mergers; and for establishment of a time limit for creditors to obtain security or payment, after which time the validity of the merger would be unchallengeable.

Harmonization of creditor and shareholder protection and freedom of establishment

To carry out the general program on freedom of establishment, the EEC Treaty requires the Council and the Commission to insure that, as far as necessary, the laws of member states give the same amount of protection to the interests of shareholders and creditors[48] of the types of company to which Article 220 applies.[49] Under this provision, directives now can be issued by a qualified majority of the Council, but harmonization of national laws under Article 100 requires a unanimous vote. Almost all principles of company law can be regarded as protecting shareholders or third parties.[50] However, the provision should be seen in the context of the other Articles on facilitating freedom of establishment. Article 54(3)(g) requires the same amount of protection for shareholders and third parties under each nation's law, but the methods by which the protection is given need not be uniform. Security requires, for example, that the

[45] Section 203 empowers the High Court to make orders facilitating the amalgamation of companies and applies only to companies incorporated in Ireland; see § 203(5) and § 2(1), definitions of "company" and "existing company." Cf. §§ 201–202, especially § 201(7); § 328(2); § 344. On the Companies Bill, 1962, as originally introduced, see Proceedings of the Special Committee on the Companies Bill, Report [hereinafter cited as Special Committee's Proceedings], Dáil Eireann, Parl. Deb., April 10, 1963, col. 596.

[46] Conférence de la Haye de Droit International Privé, "Project de Convention . . .," arts. 3, 4, [1952] 1 Actes de la Septième Session, 1951, at 385.

[47] Resolution, Rapports au Colloque international de droit européen 123–24 (1962). This resolution refers to arts. 54(3)(g) and 100, as well as to art. 220.

[48] Art. 54(3)(g); Thibièrge, "Le Statut des Sociétés Etrangères," in 1 Le Statut de l'Etranger 239, 343–48.

[49] Those defined in art. 58(2).

[50] Iannuzzi, "L'évolution du droit des sociétés par actions dans le territoire du Marché commun," 34 Annuario di Diritto Comparato e di Studi Legislativi 77, 79 (1960).

capital subscribed should be adequate for the company's business, that subscriptions for shares made in kind rather than in cash should not be overvalued, and that accurate balance sheets and profit and loss accounts should be published. Priority will be given to altering those rules which most seriously endanger legal and economic security.

The Commission concentrated initially on the protection of third parties but is now concerned with shareholders also. Three questions have been considered in particular so far:[51] the consequences when a company has not been validly incorporated; the protection of parties dealing with a company when the management exceeds its authority under the charter of the company; and the regulation of publication of information about a company's management, capital structure, and finances.

The validity of incorporation of a company

The validity of the incorporation of companies is of basic importance in safeguarding international business transactions. To insure that the company is properly incorporated, control by some administrative or judicial authority is desirable. If control is insured, the dissolution of the company is still possible, but not a retroactive declaration that the company is invalidly incorporated. This is the position in Italy and Germany[52] and also in the Netherlands, where invalid incorporation is almost unknown. In Belgium and Luxembourg, a notary is required for incorporation, and this reduces the risk of invalidity resulting from the lack of any public supervision. In Belgium and Luxembourg, hardly any grounds of nullity remain for the two main types of company, though the promoters may be personally liable if a company is irregularly constituted. In France, there are various grounds of nullity which can frequently be invoked against outsiders with retroactive effect but which may be curable. There are differences between the national laws even where they follow the same principles, and different types of company are not always treated alike.

In Ireland[53] and Britain, a certificate of incorporation is conclusive evidence that the company is validly incorporated. Legal personality is acquired on the date of incorporation shown in the certificate.[54] The position is the same for both "public" and "private" companies.[55] Unless its objects are illegal, there is no such thing as a defectively formed company. The dissolution of a company has no retroactive effects.[56] Irish law therefore provides security for outsiders dealing with a company and will need no alteration in the EEC. The EEC rules may merely reduce the grounds of nullity to a few clearly specified cases; limit the type of person who can plead nullity; lay down a short time limit, after which the

[51] Committee on Foreign Law, "Current Legal Developments in the European Economic Community," 18 Record of N.Y.C.B.A. 329, 342 (1963); EEC, Direction Générale, Doc. No. 2829/III/c/62-F (1962); EEC, Marché Intérieur, Doc. No. 7098/III/c/62-F (1962); EEC, Coordination des garanties exigées des Sociétés, Doc. No. 6960/III/c/62-F (1962). See EEC Commission, Proposal for a Council Directive . . . on Article 58, second paragraph . . ., 1964 Journal Officiel 3245/64, 1964 EEC Bull. No. 3, Supp. 10.

[52] See Levy, Private Corporations and Their Control 441-49 (1950). On the French law, see Church, Business Associations Under French Law 152–53 (1960).

[53] § 19; U.K. Act, § 15(1). See, however, Gower, The Principles of Modern Company Law 249–54 (2d ed. 1957).

[54] § 18(2).

[55] See pp. 110–15.

[56] §§ 249, 273. Under the Commission's proposals, 1964 Journal Officiel 3245/64, 1964 EEC Bull. No. 3, Supp. 10, incorporation is to be void only if the objects of the company are illegal or if no charter is drawn up. Third parties are not to be prejudiced by the nullity.

validity of incorporation will be conclusively assumed; and abolish the retroactive effect of decisions holding a company invalidly incorporated. Verification of validity of incorporation by a public authority, whether a court or an administrative authority, would be preferable to verification by a notary, if delays could be prevented and if the verification was conclusive. Some verification is essential. At present, the delays in the Netherlands, where incorporations are dealt with by the Ministry of Justice, are excessive.

Ultra Vires Acts by the Management

There is a conflict of interests between third parties and shareholders when the management of a company exceeds its powers.[57] The two principles possible are the strict ultra vires rule and the rule that management binds the company if it contracts within its apparent authority. The principle of apparent authority provides more protection for the outsider dealing with the company. The EEC solution will probably be to make all acts which are ultra vires the management but within the objects of the company binding on the company. Several types of case may arise: where the person purporting to contract on behalf of the company has not been validly appointed or has had his appointment cancelled, where the contract is ultra vires the company, and where the contract is outside the powers of the individual or is made for the personal benefit of the individual, not for the benefit of the company. These cases may involve questions as to how far the public can ascertain the personnel and the powers of the organs of the company.

In all the Six, a company has power to do anything, so no act is ultra vires the company. However, in the Six except Germany, a contract may be ultra vires the management if it is outside the objects of the company, but the outsider gets the benefit of the rules of apparent authority, unjust enrichment, and good faith.[58] In Germany, the management may validly contract outside the objects of the company. France has the strictest rule; the effective objects of the company, not the numerous objects listed in the charters, govern questions of ultra vires (*excès de pouvoir*).[59] In varying degrees, duly published restrictions on the powers of management may be pleaded by a company against a person alleging the existence of a contract. Each of the Six has argued for the adoption of its own rule. Probably the inaccuracy of any information published as required by law cannot be pleaded by the company. Except in France, where the rule just mentioned causes difficulty, the rule that management cannot validly contract ultra vires the company's objects causes little difficulty in practice, since objects clauses are very widely drawn.[60]

In Ireland, the case of an act ultra vires the company is regulated by stat-

[57] Van Ommeslaghe, Le Régime des Sociétés par actions et leur administration en droit comparé 449–503 (1960).

[58] Although somewhat similar rules exist in Irish law, they do not adequately protect a person contracting with the company.

[59] See 1 Hamel & Lagarde, Traité de Droit Commercial 566–68 (1954). A law of March 7, 1925, states that a limited liability company cannot plead any restrictions on the powers of managers; id. at 936–37. See Church, Business Associations Under French Law 377 (1960).

[60] Under the draft directive submitted to the Council, 1964 Journal Officiel 3245/64, 1964 EEC Bull. No. 3, Supp. 10, a third party in good faith may always rely on the acts of the officers whose names are published. A company is liable for acts of its officers unless they are ultra vires the company and the third party had no good reason to believe that the acts were within the company's powers. A company cannot plead statutory restrictions on its officers' powers against third parties, but it may rely on provisions in its charter making the consent of several officers necessary for the validity of an act.

ute.[61] Previously, objects clauses had been worded so broadly that the ultra vires rule gave no real protection to shareholders and was merely an occasional danger to third parties. The new rule permits any shareholder or debenture holder to obtain an injunction to prevent any ultra vires act but not to have the act revoked after it is completed. Directors are liable to the company for loss caused by an ultra vires act for which they are responsible. An act ultra vires the company is valid in favor of a person relying on it, unless he is shown to have known that the act relied on was not within the powers of the company. Even if an express prohibition exists, a party dealing with a company is not obliged to inspect its charter or prejudiced by his failure to do so.[62] This rule gives greater protection to a party contracting with the company than does the British law. It is similar to the recommendation of the Jenkins Report in Britain.[63] Shareholders should keep management within the objects of the company if anyone is to do so, but foreign shareholders may feel that the Irish rule gives too much scope to local management.

Unfortunately, no statute deals with the situation where the act is ultra vires the officers of the company but not outside the powers of the company itself. A company is generally bound by those acts of its officer which are within the scope of his authority, as it appears from published company documents,[64] or those which would have been within the scope of his authority if internal formalities, evidence of which normally would not appear in the published documents, had been complied with.[65] Unless there

[61] § 8. In England everyone dealing with a company is deemed to know the extent of the company's powers because they are published; Gower, The Principles of Modern Company Law, ch. 5 (2d ed. 1957). See Re Jon Beauforte (London), Ltd., [1953] Ch. 131. This rule has been criticized; see Company Law Committee, Report [hereinafter cited as Jenkins Report], Cmd. No. 1749, paras. 35–42 (1962), which recommended a modification.

For the disastrous consequences to a third party who knows that his contract is ultra vires the company, see Re M. J. Cummins, Ltd. (Barton v. Bank of Ireland), [1939] Ir. R. 60.

[62] See Special Committee's Proceedings, Dáil Eireann, Parl. Deb., Jan. 19, 1963, cols. 36–44. Section 8 reads: "Any act . . . done by a company shall, notwithstanding that the company had no power to do such act, . . . be effective in favor of any person relying on such act . . . who is not shown to have been actually aware, at the time when he so relied thereon, that such act . . . was not within the powers of the company . . . ."

[63] Cmd. No. 1749, para. 42 (1962). Committee on Company Law Amendment, Report [hereinafter cited as Cohen Report], Cmd. No. 6659, para. 12 (1945), had recommended that a company be given the same powers as an individual. The reason the Cohen Committee's recommendation was not accepted was that it would have been necessary to alter the rule on acts outside the powers of the directors though within the powers of the company. See Jenkins Report, Cmd. No. 1749, para. 38 (1962). In Ireland some experts felt that it would be illogical to abolish the doctrine of ultra vires for companies when it continued to apply to state corporations. Irish Company Law Reform Committee, Report [hereinafter cited as Irish Company Law Report], Pr. 4523, para. 50 (1958), merely notes that the Cohen Committee's recommendation was rejected in Britain and that one "must assume that there were strong reasons for this decision." This is hardly convincing.

[64] It is not clear exactly which of the documents available for inspection in the office of the Registrar of Companies can be pleaded against third parties.

[65] Gower, The Principles of Modern Company Law, ch. 8 (2d ed. 1957). The principle is known as the Rule in Turquand's Case, from Royal Brit. Bank v. Turquand, 6 E. & B. 327, 119 Eng. Rep. 886 (1856). See also Mahony v. East Holyford Mining Co., L.R. 7 H.L. 869 (1875); Thompson, "Company Law Doctrines and Authority to Contract," 11 U. Toronto L.J. 248 (1956). Since these matters were not dealt with by the 1963 Act, the anomaly now exists that only actual notice of a limitation on the powers of the company will prejudice a third party, but he has constructive notice of most, but apparently not all, of the

are suspicious circumstances, the party contracting with the company is entitled to assume that the company has given all necessary authorization whose existence he cannot verify from the documents available in the Office of the Registrar of Companies. If the officer purports to exercise powers not usual for one in his position, the company is bound only if it held him out to the other party as having these powers. These rules apply to cases where the invalidity or the termination of the appointment of the officer, or a limitation on his powers, is the vitiating element.[66] Where the act in question is a crime or a breach of the officer's duties to the company, the position is not clear.[67] Irish law has no concept of abuse of rights. The Companies Act of 1963 should have clarified the whole position, but it did not; clarification would be necessary for harmonization of company law in the EEC.

Publication of Information About Companies

The laws of the Six vary with regard to publication of the charters and names of the officers of companies. Publication may be by filing copies of the documents or abstracts of the information in an office, by inscribing them in a register, or by publishing them in an official or unofficial newspaper; sometimes by all three methods in the same country. All of the Six, in practice, require publication of the charters of all companies. In Luxembourg[68] this is not required by law. Alterations in a company's charter also must be published.[69] The objects of the company (in France, the effective objects of the company) as recited in its charter are set out in the commercial register. In each of the Six the amount of the share capital of a company must be published and the names of the company's directors, officers, and auditors must be filed, inscribed in a register, or published in a newspaper. Only Belgium and Germany require all three operations. The requirements on filing and publishing annual profit and loss accounts vary; in France, Belgium, and Germany, different types of company are treated differently. At present only France requires publication of information about companies in more than one journal; the other member states have only one. Only France and Italy have a single centralized commercial register. Criminal sanctions are the only method of enforcing publication of certain information, such as accounts. Civil sanctions, such as nullity of the unpublished act or the inability to rely on it against third parties, are possible in other cases. The sanctions vary among the Six, as does the extent of verification of the completeness and accuracy of the information published.

Centralization of the means of publication of information is needed. A single Common Market commercial register or register of companies has been sug-

---

limits on the powers of its officers which he could have ascertained from inspection of the documents in the Companies' Office. This anomaly is not important in practice for most Irish companies because they are closely held "private" companies. See Campbell, "Contracts with Companies" (pts. 1–2), 75 L.Q. Rev. 469 (1959), 76 L.Q. Rev. 115 (1960).

[66] Section 178 reads: "The acts of a director shall be valid notwithstanding any defect which may afterwards be discovered in his appointment or qualification." Cf. U.K. Act, § 180. See Irish Act, 1963, Table A, art. 108; Morris v. Kanssen, [1946] A.C. 459.

[67] See 1 Hamel & Lagarde, Traité de Droit Commercial 566–67 (1954), on *abus de raison sociale.*

[68] See Law of Aug. 10, 1915, art. 9, which contemplates publication but does not require it.

[69] In France and in Luxembourg, certain alterations need not be published.

gested[70] and may be set up. National registers containing the same information may be set up also. For harmonization the same information must be published in each country about each type of company, and at least the civil results, if not the criminal sanctions, for failure to publish information should be uniform. Information published in a journal cannot be officially checked to insure its adequacy and accuracy; filing or inscription in a register is required. Publication in a journal which has no comprehensive up-to-date index is of little use to outsiders gathering information about a company.

Several of the Six are considering improving their laws, towards a common high standard of protection for third parties, and this may be done before the terms of the EEC directives are agreed on.[71]

The law on publication in Ireland is fairly simple. The Registrar of Companies' Office is the only one concerned; and it has a file on every company. All documents which must be filed can be inspected. These documents include the charter (called the memorandum and articles) of the company, any changes in the name or the charter of the company, the prospectus of any shares or debentures being offered to the public, details of mortgages on the company's property, an annual return including a list of officers and shareholders, certain resolutions,[72] and some others. Some of this information is also published in an unofficial journal.[73] The company can plead against third parties the contents of most of the documents filed, and third parties can assume that all documents which should have been filed are filed and available for inspection.[74] In all cases except an act ultra vires the company, these rules apply whether the third party actually inspected the file or not. The Registrar of Companies does not verify the accuracy of documents filed, but the stock exchange may do so if a public issue of shares is made.

Methods of harmonizing company law

Company law is subject to all the EEC's methods of harmonizing laws. Harmonization of laws on protection of shareholders and third parties can be carried out by a directive approved by a qualified majority under Article 54. Harmonization of other rules of company law can be done by a directive approved unanimously under Article 100. Article 220 contemplates new treaties supplementing the EEC Treaty. The establishment, by a new treaty, of an international company law which allows the incorporation of European-type companies, as distinct from national companies, is another plan which has been

[70] See Rault, "Le registre européen de commerce," 34 Annuario di Diritto Comparato e di Studi Legislativi 105 (1960); Thibièrge, "Le Statut des Sociétés Etrangères," in 1 Le Statut de l'Etranger 239, 352–53. The draft directive submitted to the Council, 1964 Journal Officiel 3245/64, 1964 EEC Bull. No. 3, Supp. 10, requires each member state to maintain a national register which contains an up-to-date text of the company's charter, the names of its officers and managers, the names of its auditors if auditors are required, the registered office's location, and the company's balance sheet and profit and loss account for each financial year. Since it applies only to stock companies, it tends to discriminate against Dutch companies, all of which are of this type.

[71] See Hay, "Four Lectures on the Common Market: Trade Provisions—German and French Company Law—Establishment," 24 U. Pitt. L. Rev. 685, 732–34 (1963).

[72] §§ 10, 17, 23, 47, 99–108, 125, 143.

[73] Stubbs Gazette.

[74] Irvine v. Union Bank of Scotland, 2 App. Cas. 366 (1877); Ernest v. Nicholls, 6 H.L.C. 401 (1857). The principles are the same as those summarized above in connection with the authority of organs of the company.

discussed.[75] These companies would coexist with, rather than replace, companies incorporated under national company laws. The Commission is interested in this proposal because it would stimulate economic integration and facilitate the establishment of companies large enough to achieve maximum competitiveness on a worldwide scale.

IRISH COMPANY LAW: COMPARATIVE ASPECTS

Ireland has a bad tax system,[76] but a good company law. Until 1963 the British Companies (Consolidation) Act of 1908, as modified, was in force in Ireland. In 1963 a new act revised and consolidated the Irish statutes on company law. The 1963 Act does not embody all the judge-made principles of company law, and it leaves certain aspects of company law to development by the courts—notably, the duties of directors as trustees for the company.[77] It is very similar to the present British act; the principal differences are noted in this chapter as they arise. British textbooks and precedents may be used where the Irish Act does not deal with a point.[78] Two reasons for this similarity are that it would assist foreign investment, since British company law is likely to be familiar to American and European investors, and that trading connections between Ireland and Britain and the volume of British invest-

[75] This proposal was for a "federal" company code, not a uniform company law in each member state as France has suggested. A European court might have been needed to insure a uniform interpretation of the treaty. The proposal was made in academic and legal circles. One objection was that either such a company would have had labor representation on the managing board, in which case it would have been unattractive to promoters from countries where this is unknown, or it would not have had labor representation, in which case it would have been unacceptable to labor groups in countries such as Germany, where labor representation is required in some companies. Businessmen felt that creating such a company was pointless unless it offered tax advantages, which was impossible. Tax factors would lessen the value of such companies. It was felt that the possible benefits would not compensate for the difficulties of obtaining agreement on the terms of the European company law. See Ordre des Avocats á la Cour de Paris, Congrès International pour la création d'une Société commerciale de type européen, 3 Revue du Marché Commun, No. 27, Supp. (1960); Thompson, "The Project for a Commercial Company of European Type," 10 Int'l & Comp. L.Q. 851 (1961); EEC Commission, Third General Report, para. 165 (1960); Council of Europe, Compagnies Européennes, Doc. No. SG/R(53)4 (1953), and an earlier study, Doc. No. AS/EC-(49)20 (1949); Seidl-Hohenveldern, "European Companies," 1959 J. Bus. L. 120; Goldman, "Le droit des sociétés internationales," 90 Journal du Droit International 320, especially at 372–88 (1963); Thibièrge, "Le Statut des Sociétés Etrangères," in 1 Le Statut de l'Etranger 239, 360–62; 1959 Journal Officiel 1272/59; EEC Commission, Objet: Type de Société uniforme pour la Communauté Economique Européenne, Doc. No. IV/2139/60-F (1960). The last document gives as the advantages of a European-type company law the following: it would be easier to achieve than harmonization of existing company laws; it would facilitate cooperation of private interests from different member states, especially for aid to less developed countries; similar companies could be set up in different member states; an international type of company could be more easily financed internationally; it would solve the difficulties raised by art. 220 and the freedom of establishment provisions of the EEC Treaty.

[76] That is, unsuitable for the needs of the country, complicated, and in need of revision. It is extremely favorable to the exporter. The recommendations of commissions on company law, in contrast to those on taxation, have been acted on in both Ireland and Britain.

[77] See Keeton, "The Director as Trustee," 5 Current Legal Prob. 11, 18–29 (1952). The codes in British law—e.g., Sale of Goods Act, 1893, 56 & 57 Vict. c. 71; Marine Insurance Act, 1906, 6 Edw. 7, c. 41; Partnership Act, 1890, 53 & 54 Vict. c. 39—date from the time when British businessmen were interested in codification.

[78] On the Irish law, see Irish Company Law Report, Pr. 4523 (1958); Rules and Regulations of the Dublin Stock Exchange (1945) and supplements; Abd El-Motaal, "Some Aspects of the

ment in Ireland are so close that similar company laws were felt to be necessary.[79]

Company law in Ireland should be as simple as possible, in the light of Irish experience, and definitely much less complex than the present British legislation. At present there are some 380 "public" companies and some 11,000 "private" companies in Ireland. The expense to business interests of complying with elaborate antifraud legislation would not be justified by the additional protection obtained. Upon entering the EEC, any country with its company laws based on the British principles must make them harmonize with the laws of other member states. However, these changes should not make the laws too complex for the country's conditions; this is especially true of the laws on closely held companies in less industrialized countries, where most companies are small companies of this type.

[Irish] Companies Act, 1963," 12 Administration 119 (1964). See also Registration of Business Names Act, 1963 Acts, No. 30; Stock Transfer Act, 1963 Acts, No. 34; annual reports of the Department of Industry and Commerce on companies. On the British law, see Jenkins Report, Cmd. No. 1749 (1962); Cohen Report, Cmd. No. 6659 (1945); Committee on Shares of No Par Value, Report [hereinafter cited as Gedge Report], Cmd. No. 9112 (1954). On the Irish law before the 1963 Act, see Healy, "Reflections on Comparing the Irish and English Companies Acts," 20 J. Stat. Soc. 170 (1953–54).

See also Northern Ireland Department Committee on Company Law Amendment, Report, Cmd. No. 393 (1958). The standard works on British company law, widely used in Ireland, are Palmer, Company Law (20th ed. 1959); Palmer, Company Precedents (17th ed. 1956); and Buckley, The Companies Acts (13th ed. 1957).

For a company law code similar to the British and Irish systems, see Final Report of the [Ghana] Commission of Enquiry into the Working and Administration of the Present Company Law of Ghana (1961) [hereinafter cited as Final Report on the Present Company Law of Ghana]. A draft of this report received particular praise from the United States Department of State; id., para. 33.

For comparative studies, see Levy, Private Corporations and Their Control (1950); van Ommeslaghe, Le Régime des Sociétés par action et leur administration en droit comparé (1960); Gower, "Some Contrasts Between British and American Corporation Law," 69 Harv. L. Rev. 1369 (1956); Loss, Securities Regulation (2d ed. 1961); Schneider, "The American Close Corporation and Its German Equivalent," 14 Bus. Law. 228 (1958); McFadyean, "The American Close Corporation and Its British Equivalent," id. at 215; Houwink, "The American Close Corporation and Its Dutch Equivalent," id. at 250; de Sola Canizarès, La Constitution de la Société par Actions en Droit Comparé (1959); Keenan, "Companies and Taxation in the Common Market," 10 Int'l & Comp. L.Q. 454 (1961); Delany, "Reports of Committees: Company Law Reform in Ireland," 22 Modern L. Rev. 304 (1959); van Wynendaele & Wouters, Le Droit des Sociétés Anonymes dans les Pays de la Communauté Economique Européenne (1961); Banca di Credito Finanziaro, The American Investor's Digest of Italian Corporate Law (1957); Church, Business Associations Under French Law (1960); Steefel, Trading Under the Laws of Germany (1956); Sarabia, "Company Forms Under Civil Law," 43 Chicago B. Record 324 (1962); Hay, "Four Lectures on the Common Market . . . ," 24 U. Pitt. L. Rev. 685 (1963); Stobl, "Principles of the German Law of Partnership and Corporation," in 1 Doing Business Abroad 114 (Landau ed. 1962); Torem, "Business Organization and Operation in France," in id. at 138; Pavia, "Business Organization in Italy," in id. at 150; Steefel, "Selection of Form of Business Organization and Problems of Control and Operation in the Federal Republic of Germany," in id. at 219; Djian, Le contrôle de la direction des sociétés anonymes en France et dans les pays de l'Europe des Six (1963).

Translations into French of the company laws of the Six will be found in 1(1–3) Recueils Pratiques de Droit des Affaires dans les pays du Marché commun (Editions Jupiter, 1958, 1959).

[79] Irish Company Law Report, Pr. 4523, paras. 47, 188 (1958). The 1963 Act embodies most of the complexities of the U.K. Act. See also Northern Ireland Departmental Committee on Company Law Amendment, Report, Cmd. No. 393, paras. 3–4 (1958). Para. 5 of this report said that, although the law on public companies in Northern Ireland should be the same as in Britain, to facilitate British portfolio investment, efforts should be made to make Irish private companies more attractive to local capital than the British public companies in which the

The two principal types of company in Ireland and the Six

The company laws of Ireland, Britain,[80] and the Six (except the Netherlands[81]) allow two main types of company. Basically, these are the large company which obtains capital from the public and is operated for absentee owners by professional businessmen, and the small company which does not obtain capital from the public and is owned and operated by the same persons.[82] The legal distinction is roughly the same as the factual distinction in the United States between publicly held corporations and close corporations. The differences between the two types are much greater in the Six (except the Netherlands) than in Ireland;[83] on the Continent the smaller, closely held company is treated much like a partnership, but the widely held one is regulated almost as strictly as its counterpart in the United States is. In Britain and Ireland, the two types are regulated in rather different ways by the same legislation. The Six (except the Netherlands) have separate legislation for the two types of company.

In Ireland, the charter of a private company must restrict in some way the right to transfer its shares and must prohibit it from issuing shares or debentures to the public and from having more than fifty shareholders in addition to employees.[84] If it complies with these requirements, a private company may have a minimum of only two members, instead of the minimum of seven required in a public company.[85] It need not file its balance sheet for public inspection;[86] how-

---

capital would otherwise be invested. Irish company law probably should differentiate more between public and private companies than British law. In Ireland, tax incentives have been given for investment by local investors in public companies; Finance Act, 1937 Pub. Stat. 235, § 7, and Finance Act, 1956 Acts 353, § 7.

[80] In Britain the Jenkins Report, Cmd. No. 1749, paras. 55–67 (1962), has recommended ending the distinction between exempt private companies (i.e., exempt from the obligation to file accounts), private companies, and public companies. Cf. Irish Company Law Report, Pr. 4523, paras. 109–20 (1958).

[81] The Netherlands permits only one type of company, but this type may vary in size in a manner similar to the United States corporation.

[82] The larger type is called *société anonyme* (S.A.), *Aktiengesellschaft* (A.G.), *società per azioni* (S.p.A.), or *naamlose vennootschap* (N.V.). This type and its Irish equivalent, the public company, are here called "stock companies." The smaller type is called *société de personnes à responsabilité limitée* (SPRL, SARL) or *Gesellschaft mit beschränkter Haftung* (GmbH). This type and its Irish equivalent, the private company are here called "limited liability companies." See Conard, "Organizing for Business," in 2 American Enterprise in the European Common Market: A Legal Profile 1, 46–61 (Stein & Nicholsen ed. 1960). As well as public and private companies, other forms of companies are possible in Irish law; see §§197–98, Tables C, D, E. In Ireland, a company limited by guarantee rather than by shares cannot be a private company. Industrial and provident societies (a type of cooperative body based on the Industrial and Provident Societies Act, 1893, 56 & 57 Vict. c. 39) are important; Irish Company Law Report, Pr. 4523, para. 38 (1958). See also Limited Partnerships Act, 1907, 7 Edw. 7, c. 24.

[83] See Pennington, "Company Law Reform in Great Britain," 1 Common Market L. Rev. 58, 61–62 (1963); Hemard, "Le rapprochement entre le régime des sociétés à responsabilité limitée et celui des sociétés par actions dans la législation française contemporain," in 1 La Società per Azioni alla metà del Secolo XX, 331 (1962); Becker, "The Société Anonyme and the Société à Responsabilité Limitée in France," 38 N.Y.U.L. Rev. 835 (1963).

[84] § 33. If the company ceases to comply with these requirements, it loses its privileges; § 34. The corresponding provision in Britain is U.K. Act, § 28. In Britain a private company can have only one director, U.K. Act, § 176, but in Ireland two directors are always necessary, § 174. A public company may restrict the right to transfer its shares.

[85] §§ 5, 36. The maximum number of members of an unincorporated trading body is twenty.

[86] § 128. In Britain this applies only to a British exempt private company. In both countries a company must file details of certain charges over its assets; § 99.

ever, this privilege may have to be ended if Ireland joins the EEC. Some of the formalities of registration are dispensed with for a private company.[87] It can commence business as soon as it is incorporated,[88] and the holding of a formal meeting after incorporation and the publication of a report are unnecessary.[89] Private companies can allot shares without any minimum subscription having been paid.[90] For tax purposes there is no significance in the distinction.[91] A private company may be converted into a public company,[92] but not vice versa. There are some other minor differences in treatment.

In the Six (except the Netherlands) and in Ireland, limited liability companies are used more often than stock companies. Limited liability companies in the Six and private companies in Ireland cannot issue bearer shares. Bearer shares are very rare in Ireland, since they are difficult to reconcile with the legislation on exchange control and on freedom of non-nationals to own Irish manufacturing companies. They are very common in the Six as fully paid-up shares of stock companies, except in Italy, where they are not permitted. Neither private companies in Ireland nor limited liability companies in the Six may raise money from the sale of shares or debentures to the public. Unlike limited liability companies in the Six, a private company in Ireland is not regarded as being less worthy of credit than a public company, although a listing on the Irish stock exchange improves the commercial standing of a company. Restrictions on share transfers and a low minimum number of shareholders are common to private companies in Ireland and limited liability companies in the Six. In France, shares in a limited liability company are transferable only with the consent of a majority of shareholders holding 75 per cent of the capital, unless the company's charter provides otherwise. Irish law lays down the same requirements on management—a minimum of two directors, one of whom may be the secretary—for both private and public companies.[93] In the Six a stock company must have an elaborate management structure, particularly in Germany. In Germany one-third of the members of the supervisory board (*Aufsichtsrat*) of a stock company or a limited liability company with over five hundred employees must be labor representatives. In France any stock company with over fifty employees must set up a committee of employees, whose representatives may speak at all directors' meetings. In Ireland there are no requirements for labor participation in management or for workers' councils, even in public companies. Unlike a limited liability company in France, a private company in Ireland can have different classes of shares, and unlike a Belgian limited liability company, it can have corporate shareholders.

Other than as to the right of transfer, there is no difference between the nature of shares in a public and a private company in Irish law. In the Six a limited liability company is really a partnership

[87] §§ 179, 54.

[88] § 115.

[89] § 130; § 181 applies to private companies, unlike § 183 of the U.K. Act. In Britain only an exempt private company is free to make loans to its directors and need not have a qualified auditor; U.K. Act, § 190. It is a curious defect that neither the British Act nor the Irish Act collects all the provisions relating to private companies together.

[90] Section 53 applies only to public issues, which only public companies can make. A public company not making a public issue can allot shares at once.

[91] See, however, Finance Act, 1921, 11 & 12 Geo. 5, c. 32, § 22, dealing with unreasonable accumulation of profits by a closely owned company to avoid surtax.

[92] § 35 and Second Schedule.

[93] §§ 174–75.

with limited liability, and in Germany and Italy the shareholders have only one "share" each and "shares" need not have the same nominal value.[94]

The most important disadvantage of an Irish private company is its inability to raise capital from the public. However, although there is no maximum capital for a private company, most private companies would be rather small to use the capital market.[95] An Irish subsidiary can usually be financed in part by equity or loan capital from its parent company and in part by the Industrial Credit Company, government grants, bank loans, or accumulated profits, particularly if capital accumulation has been accelerated by tax concessions. If a public issue is not planned, a private company is usually preferable and is almost always the form adopted for a wholly owned subsidiary or a "one-man company."

Irish law does not distinguish between civil and commercial law, and they are administered together in the same courts. In France and Germany this separation exists, and stock companies and limited liability companies are always subject to commercial law, irrespective of the nature of their activity.

Public control over companies

"It is now widely recognized in all countries that the only effective way of preventing impropriety in the management of corporate enterprise is to ensure effective supervision by some government agency. The idea that shareholders can be relied upon to supervise management and to take effective steps to protect themselves is an anachronism."[96] So far, European countries have minimized the need for government control by requiring the company's own organs to supervise the management. Irish law relies on publicity and on civil remedies, rather than on administrative supervision, for the protection of shareholders and creditors of both private and public companies. Only the stock exchanges verify the accuracy of published information.[97] Apart from cases in which criminal offenses are alleged, there are powers of investigation in certain circumstances[98] where the shareholders suspect improper actions or where they have not been

[94] Gesetz betreffend die Gesellschaften mit beschränkter Haftung, April 20, 1892 [hereinafter cited as GmbH Gesetz], art. 5; Italian Civil Code, art. 2474. Hay, "Four Lectures on the Common Market . . .," 24 U. Pitt. L. Rev. 685, 734–35 (1963), lists some of the principal differences between an *Aktiengesellschaft* and a GmbH in German law as follows: (1) there is no judicial examination of the regularity of incorporation of a GmbH; (2) no annual financial statement is required; (3) decisions of a GmbH's shareholders' meeting do not require attestation by a notary; (4) the constitution may require shareholders to contribute money beyond their original subscription; (5) every shareholder is liable for the amount of the unpaid balance of the shares of every other shareholder; (6) shares may be transferred only by notarized instrument and thus cannot be sold on the stock exchange; and (7) shareholders may be liable for dividends not paid out of net profits, even if accepted in good faith.

[95] On the different effects of company tax on small and large enterprises, with particular reference to limited liability companies, see Cosciani, The Effects of Differential Tax Treatment of Corporate and Non-corporate Enterprises 59–60 (1959). OECD Economic Survey of Ireland, 1963, para. 48, says it might become necessary to take steps to encourage Irish private industry to finance itself more through public issues. See OECD Economic Survey of Ireland, 1962, para. 30.

[96] Final Report on the Present Company Law of Ghana 163, para. 1 (1961). See "How Much More Disclosure?" The Economist, Oct. 5, 1963, p. 77.

[97] Gower, The Principles of Modern Company Law 288–89 (2d ed. 1957).

[98] §§ 165–73; U.K. Act, §§ 164–75. Shareholders holding 10% or more of the share capital may request the Department of Industry and Commerce, which has functions similar to those of the Board of Trade in England, to appoint an inspector, or the Department can appoint one on its own initiative. There is nothing in Ireland corresponding to U.K. Act, §§ 172–74, on inves-

given "all the information . . . which they might reasonably expect" to obtain. These powers of investigation have no real parallel in the Six, where lesser functions are exercised on a more regular basis by a company's auditors. The nearest parallel in the Six is the power of an auditor in Italy.[99] The mere existence of these powers of inspection in Ireland is usually sufficient, and they are not often exercised. In theory, they are greater than the powers of the United States Securities and Exchange Commission.[100] In general, the flexibility of Irish company law and the freedom from official supervision which it gives make it satisfactory to direct investors. Its defects relate to the protection of small shareholders and creditors. Since these are precisely the persons whom the EEC is anxious to protect, in the EEC Irish company law would have to be strengthened in certain respects. Its defects are unlikely to cause difficulties for direct investment.

A startling feature of British and Irish company law in American eyes is the lack of legal regulation of the stock markets of the two countries. They are not completely unregulated,[101] but there is no legislation corresponding to the United States Securities Act or the Securities Exchange Act. Although investors are protected by requirements for full information and there are both civil and criminal sanctions[102] for misstatements, the law requires no official verification of information published. The explanation lies in the differences between the securities markets in the United States and the United Kingdom[103]—there is no organized "over-the-counter" market for securities in Britain as there is in the United States.

Branch operations in Ireland

Since there are few difficulties in incorporating a subsidiary in Ireland, branch operations of foreign companies are unusual in Ireland. The advantages and disadvantages of branch operations and subsidiary companies in Ireland do not normally depend on questions of company law. If the law of the investor's country of residence exempts foreign-source profits of foreign subsidiaries from taxation, then subsidiaries are preferable to branch operations. Only Irish-incorporated companies can obtain certain tax concessions for mines,[104] and only com-

tigation of ownership. See Jenkins Report, Cmd. No. 1749, paras. 213–18, 141–47 (1962). In Germany inspectors may be appointed by the court at the request of shareholders holding 10% of the share capital; Aktiengesetz, § 118. The Northern Ireland Departmental Committee on Company Law Amendment, Report, Cmd. No. 393, para. 24 (1958), strongly criticizes the British sections relating to investigation of ownership.

[99] Civil Code, arts. 2397–409; cf. also the supervision of public issues of shares by the Commission bancaire in Belgium, Arrêté Royal, July 9, 1935.

[100] See 2 Loss, Securities Regulation 1027–34 (2d ed. 1961); 3 Loss, Securities Regulation 1945–75 (2d ed. 1961); see also U.S. Securities Act, 48 Stat. 74, 15 U.S.C. § 77a (1933), as amended; U.S. Securities Exchange Act, 48 Stat. 881, 15 U.S.C. § 77b (1934), as amended.

[101] Prospectuses are regulated by Irish Act, §§ 43–52 and Third Schedule, and by U.K. Act, §§ 37–46 and Fourth Schedule, and U.K. Prevention of Fraud (Investments) Act, 1958, 6 & 7 Eliz. 2, c. 45, which provides that to carry on business stock exchanges must be recognized by the Board of Trade.

[102] §§ 49–50. See the remarks of Mr. G. Sweetman, T. D., on the Registration of Business Names Bill, 204 Dáil Eireann, Parl. Deb., col. 96 (1963).

[103] Gower, "Some Contrasts Between British and American Corporation Law," 69 Harv. L. Rev. 1369, 1381–82 (1956); Gower, "Business," in Law and Opinion in England in the 20th Century 143–72 (Ginsberg ed. 1959).

[104] Finance (Miscellaneous Provisions) Act, 1956 Acts 807, §§ 4–9; Finance Act, 1960 Acts 483, § 32; Finance (Profits of Certain Mines) (Temporary Relief from Taxation) Act, 1956 Acts 113.

panies managed and controlled in Ireland get the advantages of Ireland's double taxation conventions.[105] Whether a branch operation in Ireland is taxable there depends on the nature of its activity and the terms of any double taxation convention with the country of residence of the company. In Ireland, branch operations are regarded as less permanent and less likely to be vigorously developed than subsidiaries, and this may reduce the likelihood of obtaining state aid.

No permission is required to establish a branch in Ireland. A foreign company which establishes a "place of business" in Ireland must file a copy of its charter in English; a list of the names, addresses, and occupations of the directors and secretary; and the name of some person residing in Ireland who is authorized to accept service of process.[106] Curiously, a foreign company need not publish the names of local managers and need not give the address of its head office. Unless it would qualify as a private company if it were incorporated in Ireland, a foreign company annually must file balance sheets and profit and loss accounts of the company as a whole,[107] even if the company need not publish its accounts in its country of incorporation. Even if its accounts are not in the form usual in Ireland, they may be accepted without alteration.[108] A foreign company must state on all its documents its name, its country of incorporation, and the fact that the liability of its shareholders is limited.[109]

Formation of companies

There is, in form, only one procedure for incorporating a company in Ireland and in France. In German law there are two different procedures, depending on whether shares are offered to the public before incorporation with the necessary formalities.[110]

The documents relating to the incorporation of an Irish company are filed with the Registrar of Companies. A notary is not necessary; however, one of the documents filed is a statutory declaration by a solicitor or an officer of the company which must be made formally before a Commissioner for Oaths.[111] Ac-

[105] E.g., Irish-German Double Taxation Convention, Dec. 18, 1962, art. II, Double Taxation Relief (Taxes on Income and Capital and Gewerbesteuer [Trade Tax]) (Federal Republic of Germany) Order, 1962, S.I. No. 212 of 1962, Pr. 6792, Law of March 25, 1964, [1964] 2 BGBl. 266, 632. See pp. 272–81.

[106] § 352. See Jenkins Report, Cmd. No. 1749, para. 516 (1962). There are fines for failure to file these documents; § 358. In Ireland a company has express power to revoke the appointment of the person named to accept service of process.

[107] § 354. An Irish private company will be bound to file accounts in the United Kingdom if it has a place of business there, even if it would be an exempt company if incorporated there; U.K. Act, § 410.

[108] § 354(3); Explanatory Memorandum on the Companies Bill, 1962, Comment on § 354, at 29.

[109] §§ 351, 355.

[110] Levy, Private Corporations and Their Control, ch. 2 (1950). Belgian law contemplates two methods of incorporation; Commercial Code, bk. I, tit. IX, arts. 31–33. The first corresponds approximately to the normal Irish method of incorporation, only the signatories to the memorandum and articles being shareholders. Under the second, a public invitation to subscribe for shares is made, and the company is actually incorporated only at a meeting of those who have subscribed. The second method, like the German method of "incorporation in installments" (*Stufengründung*), is rarely used, except for increases of capital. This German method is used if the initial capital is issued partly to the public; Aktiengesetz, art. 30; Hay, "Four Lectures on the Common Market . . .," 24 U. Pitt. L. Rev. 685, 719–21 (1963); de Sola Canizarès, La Constitution de la Société par Actions en Droit Comparé, ch. VII (1959).

[111] § 19(2). As to the documents which must be filed on or shortly after incorporation, see §§ 17, 19(2), 113, 179, 195. In addition, a Declaration of Nominal Capital, the only func-

countants are not permitted to form companies. Before filing the documents, the name of the company must be approved as not being so similar to that of another company as to confuse the public or to lead the public to believe the two companies are connected.[112] If the company carries on business under any other name, the other name must be registered also;[113] the name of a company need not indicate its business.[114] Also, exchange-control permission must be obtained for the issue of any shares to a company outside the sterling area;[115] if this company is not a signatory[116] to the charter of the company, permission may be obtained later.

Since in Irish law a company need not issue all its authorized share capital, the usual practice is to incorporate with the minimum number of shareholders required by law and issue the bulk of the shares to the public or to the intended shareholders after incorporation. No shareholders' meeting is needed to incorporate a company.

Although a public company must hold a statutory meeting[117] at which the directors report to the shareholders on the capital subscribed, the charter can be changed only by formal procedures once the certificate of incorporation has been issued. In France, until the organizational meeting, the constitution of a company is merely provisional. The organizational meeting is held after the shares have been offered and subscribed for, and it ratifies the company's charter, the appointment of the directors and auditors, the issuing of the capital, the valuation of any assets transferred to the company in return for shares, and the issuing of founders' shares.[118] There are elaborate rules with regard to voting at the organizational meeting, [119] and the contrast with an Irish statutory meeting, which is usually a formality,[120] is striking. In Belgium the corresponding meeting is less important and less formal than

tion of which is to bear the stamp duty on the creation—not the issue—of the nominal capital of a limited company, must be filed. This stamp duty is at the rate of 0.25%, with a maximum of $140 on a nominal capital of $1.47 million. Fees other than stamp duty are set out in the Eighth Schedule to the 1963 Act; they are unimportant.

[112] §§ 21–24. Compare U.K. Act, § 18. See also Central Bank Act, 1942 Acts 445, § 41. There is a similar rule in Belgium.

[113] § 22. See Registration of Business Names Act, 1963 Acts, No. 30. In Germany, a company apparently can carry on business only under the name by which it is incorporated; Levy, Private Corporations and Their Control 338 (1950). This was regarded as unworkable in Ireland.

[114] In Germany, the name of a GmbH must either include the name of one of the partners or describe the business carried on.

[115] Exchange-control permission is not required for the sale of the business of a company to an enterprise outside the sterling area.

[116] § 7.

[117] § 130.

[118] The last two functions require two meetings, with the company being incorporated at the second. The first meeting is to appoint persons to value the assets subscribed in kind and the founders' shares or other special benefits conferred on a class of shareholders. See Hauser & Hauser, A Guide to Doing Business in the European Common Market 110 (1960). In practice, an organizational meeting separate from the meeting of the company's promoters at the notary's office is unusual.

[119] Escarra, "Some Points of Comparison Between the Companies Act, 1948, and the French Law of Companies," 11 Camb. L.J. 15, 23 (1951). These rules cause difficulty in practice because they cause the company to go temporarily out of the control of the majority shareholders who hold large blocks of shares.

[120] Final Report on the Present Company Law of Ghana 114, para. 6 (1961). However, at the statutory meeting the auditors report on the capital of the company and on any business taken over; § 130. It is therefore a safeguard. In Irish law the statutory meeting is likely to be the first meeting of the shareholders of a public company which has made a public issue of shares at once on incorporation.

in France.[121] In Germany, if the promoters of a stock company have not subscribed for all the share capital themselves, a meeting to pass the resolution incorporating the company is necessary.

Pre-incorporation contracts

Under English law and apparently also under French law, contracts made on behalf of a company before its incorporation are not binding on it.[122] Under the Irish Act[123] the company may ratify such a contract and become entitled under and bound by it. Until ratification, the promoters or other contracting parties are bound. A public company can ratify effectively only after it is entitled to commence business.[124] The Irish rule is an improvement on the English and the French laws. In Germany, a stock company may adopt contracts made on its behalf before incorporation.[125]

The memorandum and articles of an Irish company[126]

The principal task in forming a company in Ireland is the drafting of its charter, called its "Memorandum and Articles of Association." Model forms of memoranda and articles for the different types of company are set out in the 1963 Act.[127] The memorandum sets out the name, objects, and share capital of the company and formally states whether the company is limited; it is a document separate from the articles, which correspond to the bylaws of a United States corporation. A company must have its own memorandum, but it can adopt by reference the appropriate model set of articles or can have a few of its own articles and incorporate by reference some of the statutory model set. It is perhaps unfortunate that the Irish Act does not set out a list of standard minimum powers of a company and allow them to be adopted by reference, since this would reduce the present excessive length of objects clauses in memoranda.[128] The only importance of the distinction between the memorandum and the articles is that the articles can be altered by a "special resolution"[129]

[121] Hauser & Hauser, A Guide to Doing Business in the European Common Market 111 (1960).

[122] Kelner v. Baxter, L.R. 2 C.P. 174 (1866); Newborne v. Sensolid (Gr. Brit.), Ltd., [1954] 1 Q.B. 45. See, however, Jenkins Report, Cmd. No. 1749, paras. 44, 54 (1962).

[123] § 37.

[124] § 115(4).

[125] Aktiengesetz,, art. 34(2). In Belgian and Italian law, where there is no official supervision of the incorporation of companies, no difficulties arise with pre-incorporation contracts.

[126] For the contents of the constitution of a company in the laws of the Six, see the Netherlands Commercial Code, arts. 36a–36d, 39d, 40, 48; Italian Civil Code, art. 2328; German Aktiengesetz, art. 16; GmbH Gesetz, art. 3; French Law on SARLs, March 7, 1925, arts. 6, 11, 14, 18; Belgian Commercial Code, bk. I, tit. IX, arts. 28–30; Luxembourg Law Concerning Commercial Companies, Aug. 10, 1915, arts. 25, 27, 76, 99.

[127] First Schedule. Table A, Part I, sets out articles for a private company, as defined in § 33. Table B sets out a model form of memorandum for a company limited by shares, whether public or private. Table C gives a form of memorandum and articles for a company limited by guarantee (in practice, usually a company not intended to make profits) without a share capital. Table D deals with a company that is limited by guarantee with a share capital. Table E gives the form for an unlimited company, i.e., a company of which the shareholders have unlimited liability. This book deals only with limited companies having a share capital. The form of articles is dealt with in § 12 and § 14 and the content of memoranda in § 6. The memorandum and articles must be "printed," which apparently includes typing; § 2.

[128] See Jenkins Report, Cmd. No. 1749, paras. 43, 54 (1962).

[129] § 15. A special resolution is defined in § 141; twenty-one days' notice and a three-quarters majority of the votes cast are required.

of the shareholders, but the memorandum can be altered only with more difficulty.[130] A company must have official approval if it wishes to change its name.[131] If a company alters its objects, the alteration may be challenged in court within twenty-one days,[132] and the court has discretion in approving it and will consider, for example, whether it prejudices some of the shareholders. Even if it is part of the memorandum, the amount and classification of the nominal share capital of the company may be altered by an ordinary resolution of a general meeting,[133] but reduction of the share capital requires the confirmation of the court.[134]

The minimum number of shareholders in a company

At the time of incorporation and at all subsequent times, the minimum number of shareholders in an Irish private company is two, and in a public company, seven.[135] The signatories to the memorandum and articles may be nominees. No notice of any trust may be entered on a company's register of members,[136] and a company's articles normally provide that it need not recognize any interest in any shares except the absolute right of the registered shareholder.[137] A company's articles may give it power to inquire into the beneficial ownership of its shares to determine its position under the legislation on exchange control or freedom of establishment. Shares in a public company normally are freely transferable, but a manufacturing company's articles often give it power to refuse a transfer of shares if the transfer would alter the ownership of the company so as to deprive it of its right to manufacture in Ireland. Nominee shareholders are accepted for the purposes of company law, and a one-man company or a wholly owned subsidiary with one real shareholder is permissible as long as there are two—or in a public company, seven—nominal shareholders. Nominees can be controlled by options, trusts, and share transfers signed in advance.[138] If the number of shareholders is below the minimum for six months, the limited liability of the remaining shareholders is lost, and the company can be terminated on the application of a shareholder or creditor.[139]

French and Belgian law do not permit a one-man company, but Germany and the Netherlands do.[140] The whole ques-

[130] However, under § 28, any provision in the memorandum which could have been included in the articles can be altered as if it were part of the articles. In view of this section, the distinction between the memorandum and the articles no longer serves any useful purpose and should be abolished.

[131] § 23.

[132] § 10. Cf. U.K. Act, § 5.

[133] § 68.

[134] § 72.

[135] See, however, Jenkins Report, Cmd. No. 1749, para. 31 (1962). The minimum number of shareholders in a Netherlands company and in a German GmbH is two, and in a German A.G., five. The minimum number of shareholders in a French or Belgian stock company is seven.

[136] § 123; U.K. Act, §§ 3, 117. This is different from the rule in most states of the United States. See Irish Company Law Report, Pr. 4523, paras. 103–108 (1958); cf., however, § 32(7).

[137] See Table A, art. 7.

[138] The word "nominee" has no legal significance; the concept used is that of beneficial ownership, which equates a nominee with a trustee. See Jenkins Report, Cmd. No. 1749, paras. 141–47 (1962), and Irish Act, § 190. There is nothing in the Irish Act corresponding to U.K. Act, §§ 172–74, on investigation of ownership.

[139] §§ 36, 213, 215. The term "contributory" in § 215 is defined by §§207–208.

[140] See Conard, "Organizing for Business," in 2 American Enterprise in the European Com-

tion of nominee shareholders and one-man companies will have to be examined in the EEC to arrive at a common solution which will reconcile legitimate business interests with the protection of creditors. The question is one of principle, and it is important because the common law, the French law, and the German law differ on the matter.

Capital

An important feature of Irish and British company law, convenient for the foreign investor, is that forming a company and financing it are different processes.[141] This is due to the distinction between nominal, or authorized, share capital and issued share capital. In the Six this distinction is made only in the law of the Netherlands. In the rest of the Six all the shares of the company must be issued on or shortly after incorporation, but they need not be fully paid up. In Belgium unissued shares are not permitted. In Ireland a company can be incorporated and can remain in existence indefinitely with only those shareholders who signed the memorandum and articles, the balance of its nominal capital remaining unissued. Although this is not necessary, issued shares are normally paid up; therefore, there is usually no difference in Ireland between the issued and the paid-up capital of a company.

The 1960 Conference concerned with establishing a European-type company recommended that authorized but unissued shares should be permitted.[142] If they are permitted, debentures convertible into shares at the option of the debenture holder[143] and options to purchase shares can be given. Convertible debentures are a valuable method of safeguarding lenders in conditions of inflation, and stock options enabling employees to buy shares in their company below market prices are economically desirable since they encourage employees to work harder and to remain with the company. However, stock options are open to abuse since they reduce the value of other shares and since they frequently are used as tax avoidance

mon Market: A Legal Profile 1, 76–79 (Stein & Nicholson ed. 1960); Salomon v. Salomon & Co., [1897] A.C. 22. The trend in Europe is towards permitting one-man companies, and especially wholly owned subsidiaries. See Kahn-Freund, "Some Reflections on Company Law Reform," 7 Modern L. Rev. 54 (1944); on disregard of corporate entity, see Gower, The Principles of Modern Company Law, ch. 10 (2d ed. 1957); Irish Act, §§ 114(4), 150–55, 297.

[141] Kahn-Freund, "Some Reflections on Company Law Reform," 7 Modern L. Rev. 54, 57 (1944); van Ommeslaghe, Le Régime des Sociétés par actions et leur administration en droit comparé 26–27 (1960); Escarra, "Some Points of Comparison Between the Companies Act, 1948, and the French Law of Companies," 11 Camb. L.J. 15–17 (1951). See, however, Aktiengesetz, art. 169(1), which gives directors power to increase the capital without a general meeting. This power must be exercised within five years of the adoption of a charter, or of an amendment to the charter, which expressly gives this power. See generally Cole, Morley & Scott, "Corporate Financing in Great Britain," 12 Bus. Law. 324–77 (1957).

[142] Congrès International pour la création d'une société commerciale de type européen, 3 Revue du Marché Commun, No. 27, Supp. at 38 (1960). However, Rault, "Le statut européen des sociétés," 34 Annuario di Diritto Comparato e di Studi Legislativi 93, 103 (1960), holds that, for the protection of creditors, the assets of a company should not be worth less than its capital, and therefore that unissued capital should not be permitted. The principle is sound, but the conclusion seems valid only if the creditors of a company rely on the amount of the nominal capital in countries where the distinction between nominal and issued capital is made, which is doubtful; but see Jenkins Report, Cmd. No. 1749, paras. 233–34 (1962). Requirements on minimum capital should apply to issued capital where unissued capital is permitted.

[143] These have existed in France since World War II, for stock companies only; they also exist in Germany. For the French law, see Law of Feb. 25, 1953, and Decree of Sept. 3, 1953.

devices.[144] Permitting authorized but unissued share capital avoids numerous difficulties if a public issue is undersubscribed.

In the Six, except the Netherlands and except under certain statutory provisions in Germany and Italy, the prohibition on unissued shares makes it impossible for new shares to be issued without a resolution of a general meeting increasing the company's capital. In Ireland, a resolution of a general meeting is required to increase the company's nominal share capital,[145] but articles often allow directors to issue the unissued shares whenever they think desirable in the interest of the company.[146] Whether a stock dividend ("bonus issue") can be paid without the consent of a general meeting depends on whether all the authorized share capital has already been issued; if not, the directors can use their power to issue shares up to the amount of the authorized capital. The Irish Act does not require new shares to be offered to the existing shareholders before the balance of voting power is altered or outsiders brought in,[147] but this can be required by the company's articles. Giving preemptive rights to the shareholders prevents the use of convertible debentures.[148] In Ireland the directors or shareholders of a private company can be given the right of first refusal of shares being sold; this is frequently done in the Six. Unless it has issued shares to the public through a stock exchange, a public company also may restrict the right to transfer its shares.[149]

In Ireland a public company cannot commence business unless the directors have paid the minimum due on allotment on their shares.[150] Also, a prospectus of all shares issued, or a statement in lieu of prospectus if no public issue has been made,[151] must be filed with the Registrar of Companies. If a public issue has been made, business cannot commence until the minimum subscription has been subscribed, i.e., until an amount which will be adequate to pay for any property to be bought and for preliminary expenses, underwriters' commission, and working capital[152] has been paid up on the shares subscribed for. Although there is a minimum number of shareholders, there is no legal minimum par value of shares and no legal minimum capital.[153] Private companies and pub-

[144] See "When Is a Perquisite?" 104 Sol. J. 221 (1960); "Share Options as Perquisites," id. at 518; Samuels, "Tax on Shares from Employers," 26 Conveyancer and Real Property Lawyer (n.s.) [hereinafter cited as Convey.] 411 (1962).

[145] § 68. A special resolution is not required by law, though the company's articles may require it; if they do not, a simple majority is sufficient.

[146] This clause is from Table A, art. 5.

[147] Cf., e.g., French Décret-loi of Aug. 8, 1935; Aktiengesetz, art. 153; Italian Civil Code, art. 2441. There is no rule of law giving preemptive rights to shareholders in the Netherlands, but they are required in most cases in Belgium.

[148] In France the shareholders' meeting which authorizes the issue of convertible debentures (obligations) must waive the shareholders' preemptive rights; Decree of Sept. 3, 1953, art. 4. See Rice, "The Effectiveness of a Pre-emptive Rights Clause in a Company's Articles," 23 Convey. 42 (1959).

[149] On freedom to transfer shares, see Re Hafner (Olhausen v. Powderly), [1943] Ir. R. 426; Irish Company Law Report, Pr. 4523, para. 122 (1958).

[150] § 115.

[151] § 54.

[152] §§ 53, 115; Third Schedule, para. 4.

[153] Since English and Irish company law protect third parties by requiring disclosure of information, it is surprising that companies have never been required to disclose their actual assets or even their issued capital on their notepaper; Special Committee's Proceedings, Dáil Eireann, Parl. Deb., Jan. 9, 1963, cols. 58–64. In France 25% of the capital must be paid up before incorporation, and the rest must be paid within five years; Law of March 4, 1963. There is a similar rule in Germany; Aktiengesetz, arts.

lic companies which have never made a public issue can do business with a wholly inadequate share capital. This is startling to EEC lawyers. The position of third parties giving credit to Irish and British companies is not adequately protected; this would probably have to be remedied if Ireland joined the EEC. Since it is convenient to permit authorized capital to remain unissued, the introduction of a minimum issued capital for all companies is probably necessary. In France, Belgium, and Luxembourg there is no legal minimum capital for a stock company. In the Netherlands no minimum capital is required for any company but at least 20 per cent of the nominal capital must be issued at once. The Netherlands has not accepted the view of the other member states that a minimum capital of $20,000 should be required for stock companies.

Types of shares and voting rights

Shares in both public and private Irish companies are divided generally into ordinary shares (common stock) and preferred shares, each type having variations according to the provisions of the companies' articles. Bearer shares are rare in Ireland. The only types of capital expressly contemplated by the Irish Act are ordinary shares, stock, and redeemable preferred shares.[154] There are no classes of shares corresponding to "beneficial shares" or to "interest-paying shares" in French law. Redeemable preferred shares[155] are intermediate between debentures and equity shares. Since a company generally may not reduce its capital, these shares may be redeemed only out of profits or the proceeds of a new issue. In the former case, a fund of a sum equal to the nominal value of the redeemed shares is created and subsequently treated as capital.[156]

Irish law and British law permit non-voting equity shares[157] and weighted voting. Although allowing non-voting shares may mean that a minority of the equity shareholders can exercise control over a company, the unusual flexibility of the Irish law in this respect does not appear to have been abused.

The laws of the Six are much stricter. All equity shares in stock companies must have votes; Belgian, German,[158]

28, 49. If Irish law required a minimum capital, it would be impossible for the promoters of a company to finance it by means of a secured loan giving them priority over ordinary creditors. This would be an improvement on the present law. It is difficult in any country to insure that every company has a capital adequate in relation to the size of its operations.

[154] § 64; cf. U.K. Act, § 58. Section 68(1)(c) contemplates the conversion of shares into stock, and vice versa. In British and Irish law, "stock" is similar but not identical to "shares." The only difference between shares and stock is that if fully paid-up shares are converted into stock, they lose their numbers and are referred to according to the total par value held by a holder, not according to individual numbers, and they can be sold in fractions of the previous par value of one share. See also § 80; U.K. Act, § 74.

[155] §§ 64–65; cf. U.K. Act, § 58. See Commission of Inquiry into Banking, Currency, and Credit, Report, P. No. 2628, para. 621 (1938). For some problems, see Rice, "Capital Rights of Preference Shares," 26 Convey. 115 (1962).

[156] Redemption of preferred shares issued before 1959 (when they first were permitted in Ireland) is permitted. This was at least partly to allow companies to discharge their debts to the Industrial Credit Company.

[157] Jenkins Report, Cmd. No. 1749, paras. 123–40 (1962), discusses the controversy as to their merits. Although non-voting shares tend to widen the gap between ownership and management, the majority Report did not recommend their abolition but merely suggested that further publicity should be given to their disadvantages.

[158] Aktiengesetz, arts. 12, 114(1). A cumulative preferred share need not be given a vote, unless its dividend is in arrears. In a GmbH, non-voting shares and shares with multiple votes are permitted.

Dutch, and French[159] law all require votes to be in proportion to the capital represented by the voting shares. In addition, in Belgium, a single shareholder, whatever his holding, may not cast a majority vote in any meeting. However, in the Six founders' shares, which receive dividends but do not share in the capital on winding up, need not have voting rights. In Belgium they cannot have voting rights equal to the equity shares as a whole.

Irish law does not permit shares having no nominal or "par"[160] value, and in the Six only Belgium and Luxembourg permit them. The Irish Company Law Committee recommended them,[161] as did the Jenkins[162] and the Gedge reports in Britain. The Irish government, however, concluded that there was no advantage in permitting them. One factor presumably was that if no-par-value shares were authorized, the acts restricting freedom of establishment of aliens and imposing a penal stamp duty on the transfer of agricultural land to aliens[163] would have had to be entirely revised. Since Ireland's entry into the EEC would involve the repeal of this legislation, the matter should be reconsidered.

In Irish law share certificates are evidentiary documents, and ownership is conveyed by a separate document of transfer; a share certificate is not transferable by endorsement, as it is in the Six. This is a technical difference between common law and civil law with some important results.[164]

Subscription in kind for shares

Ireland permits shares to be issued in return for assets. This is important to the foreign investor who may wish to use machinery and know-how acquired elsewhere, rather than cash, in the establishment of a subsidiary operation. If shares are not issued for cash, the contract under which the assets, patents, or services are sold or supplied to the company and a statement of the number of shares allotted and the extent to which the shares are treated as paid up must be filed in the Registrar of Companies' Office.[165] The valuation of the assets by the company is not questioned[166] unless there is evidence of fraud or the payment is obviously inadequate. The valuation can be questioned by creditors, and in fact very little injury seems to have resulted. Thus the principle that shares

[159] In France, voting rights must normally be in proportion to the amount of capital which the shares represent; Law of Nov. 13, 1933. However, the company's bylaws may limit the number of votes which any one shareholder may exercise; Law of July 24, 1867, arts. 27, 31. This is the rule at the organizational meeting. There are other exceptions to the principle of equal capital, equal voting rights; Law of Nov. 13, 1933, art. 1; 1 Hamel & Lagarde, Traité de Droit Commercial 671–72, 819 (1954); Church, Business Associations Under French Law 428–31 (1960).

[160] § 6(4).

[161] Pr. 4523, paras. 63–72 (1958).

[162] See Jenkins Report, Cmd. No. 1749, paras. 32–34 (1962).

[163] Finance (No. 2) Act, 1947 Acts 619, § 13, and later legislation.

[164] Levy, Private Corporations and Their Control 303–305 (1950). On bearer shares, technically called "share warrants to bearer," see Gower, The Principles of Modern Company Law 359–61 (2d ed. 1957); Palmer, Company Law 313–16 (20th ed. 1959). On the practice known as "certification of transfers," designed to facilitate the sale of part of a shareholder's interest, see Irish Company Law Report, Pr. 4523, paras. 85–86 (1958); § 85; U.K. Act, § 79. In Ireland and Britain, shares (except bearer shares) cannot be transferred orally; § 81; U.K. Act, § 75. The register of members of an Irish company cannot be kept outside Ireland; § 116(6). On share transfers, see Stock Transfer Act, 1963 Acts, No. 34.

[165] § 58. If a prospectus is issued, see Third Schedule, paras. 8–14, 16, 22–24. If a statement in lieu of prospectus is issued, see Fourth Schedule.

[166] Re Wragg, [1897] 1 Ch. 796.

cannot be issued by the company at less than their nominal value is accepted[167] but not always enforced. The emphasis of Irish and British company law on publicity without official or other verification is here carried very far. If Ireland joined the EEC, some official verification of the value of assets subscribed for shares would probably be introduced. In the Six a variety of rules prevent assets from being overvalued. An independent valuation of the assets in question is necessary in France, Belgium, Germany, and Italy, and the promoters of a French limited liability company are personally liable for inadequacy.[168] In France two meetings are required before incorporation, one to appoint valuers and another to accept the valuation made by them.[169] Publicity may not itself indicate any overvaluation, and some other protection for creditors and shareholders eventually will be required in the EEC.[170] In Ireland and Britain a shareholder who has no preemptive rights under the company's articles is not protected from having the value of his shares reduced by the issuing of further shares at a price below their market value.[171] In Germany all the arrangements for subscriptions in kind for shares must be set out in the company's charter. Failure to do this does not make the incorporation void, but the subscription must be paid up in cash. Full details of the assets provided must be given to the shareholders, and the court may refuse to permit incorporation if the assets are overvalued.[172] In Belgium, Germany, and France, shares cannot be issued in return for labor and services;[173] this is possible in Ireland.[174]

[167] See, however, §§ 59, 63; U.K. Act, §§ 53, 57. These statutory rules derogating from the principle of conservation of capital seem to have adequate safeguards. When shares are issued at a premium § 62 requires the premiums to be treated substantially as share capital.

[168] In Belgium the founders, including the real promoters, of the company are personally liable for any clear overvaluation. In the Netherlands and Luxembourg there is no official valuation. In Belgium the valuation must be certified by a valuer appointed by the Commercial Court. In Italy the directors review the valuation of the assets, and the number of shares allotted is reduced if there has been an overvaluation; Civil Code, art. 2343.

[169] Décret-loi of Aug. 31, 1937, requires a public valuer where the company makes a public issue. On the two shareholders' meetings in France, see van Ommeslaghe, Le Régime des Sociétés par actions et leur administration en droit comparé 83–84 (1960); Church, Business Associations Under French Law 200–203, 205–209 (1960).

[170] In Ireland and Britain, if the company pays the price of the assets to the shareholder who then invests the money in shares, he is regarded as having subscribed in cash, and the valuation of the assets cannot be questioned unless fraud is alleged; In re Harmony & Montague Tin & Copper Mining Co. (Spargo's Case), 8 Ch. App. 407 (1873). This is an obvious method of avoiding the law.

[171] Except by the principle that the directors must always act in the interests of the company and possibly by § 205.

[172] Aktiengesetz, arts. 26, 29, 31; Levy, Private Corporations and Their Control 417–19 (1950). In the case of a GmbH, no verification is necessary.

[173] However, in France founders' shares, which do not represent any capital value but which are rights to share in profits, may be issued in return for services. As an additional protection, founders' shares and shares not issued for cash are not transferable, in general, for two years.

[174] § 58(1)(b). In Germany both the supervisory board (*Aufsichtsrat*) and public auditors verify the value of the assets subscribed; see Aktiengesetz, arts. 25, 45.

Dr. Beddy, who is the chairman of the Irish Industrial Development Authority, the Grants Board (An Foras Tionscal), and the Industrial Credit Company, has suggested that the consideration for foreign technical assistance or management agreements with Irish companies could be the issue of ordinary shares (i.e., common stock) in the Irish companies. These shares could be issued fully paid, up to the value of

In Ireland, the circumstances under which a company can purchase, even indirectly, its own shares are strictly limited,[175] and as in the rest of Europe, shares can be issued at a discount only in strictly regulated circumstances.[176]

Maintenance of a company's capital

The Jenkins Report recommended stricter rules on the distinction between profits, which are distributable as dividends, and capital, which must be retained in the company. In Ireland a company may not distribute profits resulting from the revaluation of unsold fixed assets; it is not clear whether this is permitted in Britain.[177] The Report also recommended that a realized capital profit should be distributable only if the directors are satisfied that the net value of all the remaining assets is not less than their book value and thus that the remaining assets fully represent the share capital and reserves. Profits should be distributable only to the extent to which they exceed net losses of past years.[178] These changes would bring British and Irish law more into line with that of the Six. Even when a company owns depreciating assets, Irish law does not require accumulation of reserves before payment of dividends. In France and Belgium every stock company must establish a reserve fund equal to 10 per cent of its capital.[179] In France statutory provisions regulate distribution of profits to insure that the profits are fairly divided between the shareholders, the directors, and the holders of founders' shares. In Ireland the only protection for shareholders in this respect is that details of all remuneration paid to directors must be given in the accounts.[180] In Germany at least 5 per cent of the profits of a stock company must be put to reserve each year until the reserve is equal to 10 per cent of the share capital. An Irish company can reduce its capital[181] only in very carefully limited circumstances.

---

the services to be rendered to the Irish company. An alternative method of remuneration would be to give the managing company a share in the profits of the Irish company, on the condition that it was used only to buy shares in the latter. Both methods insure that the company providing the management or technical assistance has a financial interest in the success of the Irish company. Both methods could be used by privately owned Irish companies as well as by companies which the state might find it necessary to establish with public capital; Dr. Beddy was discussing the latter. Beddy, Murray, FitzGerald & Walsh, "Industrial Promotion," 10 Administration 325 (1962).

[175] § 60. See Irish Company Law Report, Pr. 4523, paras. 73–77 (1958); see also § 32; U.K. Act, § 27. For the English law, see Victor Battery Co. v. Curry's, Ltd., [1946] Ch. 242. Cf. Aktiengesetz, art. 65. German law generally prohibits a company's buying its own shares, but this can be done in cases of "danger" to give a minority interest a controlling vote; Schneider, "The American Close Corporation and Its German Equivalent," 14 Bus. Law. 228, 240 (1958). A French company may purchase its own shares under certain circumstances. For the Belgian law, see Commercial Code, bk. I, tit. IX, art. 206.

[176] §§ 59, 63. See Irish Company Law Report, Pr. 4523, paras. 61–62 (1958); Aktiengesetz, art. 9.

[177] § 149(6); Westburn Sugar Refineries, Ltd. v. I.R.C., 1960 Scots L.T.R. 297; Dimbula Valley (Ceylon) Tea Co. v. Laurie, [1961] Ch. 353.

[178] Jenkins Report, Cmd. No. 1749, paras. 335–50 (1962); Gower, The Principles of Modern Company Law 107–13 (2d ed. 1957).

[179] Hauser & Hauser, A Guide to Doing Business in the European Common Market 112 (1960); Law of March 4, 1943, art. 11. However, a French stock company may in some circumstances pay interest on shares even if it cannot do so out of profits. Irish law requires dividends on shares to be paid out of profits, but not interest on debentures, since the latter is a trading expense for company law purposes. In Germany, Aktiengesetz, art. 52, requires dividends to be paid out of net profits.

[180] § 191.

[181] §§ 72–77; cf. U.K. Act, §§ 66–71.

Charges on a company's trading stocks

One common method of giving security for loan capital in Ireland and England is a "floating charge." This is a charge on the company's current assets and stock, but it does not affect the freedom of the company to trade until the owner of the floating charge takes action. For technical reasons, an unincorporated enterprise cannot give a charge over stock-in-trade and remain free to trade. A floating charge is particularly useful where the company has few capital assets but large quantities of stock. The fact that a company has given a floating charge can be ascertained from the Registrar of Companies' Office.[182] These charges are unknown in the EEC, but because of their usefulness they should probably be introduced.

Issuing shares to the public

Whenever shares are offered to the public, a prospectus must be issued. The contents of all prospectuses are regulated carefully by law.[183] A prospectus must comply with the stock exchange rules if a listing is sought. If no public issue is made, a "statement in lieu of prospectus" must be filed before the shares are issued.[184]

If no shares or debentures are being issued, public solicitation of deposits of cash for any purpose is not regulated by Irish law. This clearly needs to be dealt with, as it has been in Britain by the Protection of Depositers Act, 1963.[185] In Ireland, there is no legislation corresponding to the British Prevention of Fraud (Investments) Act, 1958,[186] which is intended to prevent public invitations to buy or sell shares unless made with a proper prospectus or through a reputable bank or stockbroker; this legislation has not been needed.

Public issues of shares in Ireland by all foreign companies are regulated[187] in substantially the same way as public issues by Irish companies. A foreign company must comply with the rules of the Irish stock exchanges if the issue is made through them. Freedom of establishment and free movement of capital are not affected by any of these provisions.

[182] § 99. See Gower, The Principles of Modern Company Law 73–75 (2d ed. 1957).

[183] §§ 43–52, and Third Schedule; see U.K. Act, §§ 37–46, Fourth Schedule; van Ommeslaghe, Le Régime des Sociétés par actions et leur administration en droit comparé 22 (1960); Jenkins Report, Cmd. No. 1749, paras. 235–52 (1962); Irish Company Law Report, Pr. 4523, paras. 97–99 (1958). On the German law, see Levy, Private Corporations and Their Control 396 (1950). On what constitutes a prospectus, see Government Stock Co. v. Christopher, [1956] 1 All E.R. 490.

[184] § 54, Fourth Schedule. This does not apply to a private company. A prospectus in Irish law corresponds in substance both to the "notice" published in the French Bulletin des annonces legales obligatoires à la charge des sociétés financières (BALO) and the *prospectus d'émission,* although the latter is in theory merely an advertisement; see Loi des Finances, Jan. 30, 1907; Décret-loi of Aug. 8, 1935.

Banks in Britain and Ireland do not normally provide long-term financing for industry and do not underwrite shares (though they may sub-underwrite an issue). See Heenen, "Les souscriptions publiques en droit belge," in 1 La Società per Azioni alla metà del Secolo XX, 317 (1962).

On financing of companies in general in Ireland, see OECD Economic Survey of Ireland, 1962, para. 30; Murray, "Some Aspects of the Industrial Capital Market in Ireland," 20(3) J. Stat. Soc. 97 (1959–60). On the rules on prospectuses, see Dublin Stock Exchange, Permission to Deal and Official Quotations: Regulations and Requirements.

[185] 11 & 12 Eliz. 2, c. 16.

[186] 6 & 7 Eliz. 2, c. 45.

[187] §§ 361–67. Cf. U.K. Act, §§ 417–23; Chesné, L'Etablissement des Etrangers en France et la Communauté Economique Européenne 305–307 (1962). In Ireland, a wider range of people may be liable for failure to furnish a proper prospectus in the case of a foreign company than in the case of an Irish company; cf. §§ 49, 362.

Except incidentally, where a public issue is made on an English stock exchange, few companies incorporated outside Ireland are likely to seek capital in Ireland; however, regulation of issues by companies of other EEC member states is important in the EEC. Companies must be able to take advantage of free movement of capital. Public issues are not regulated with equal strictness in each member state, and a public issue might be made in all member states by a company incorporated in the state with the laxest laws. Most states require prospectuses distributed by foreign companies to comply with the same or substantially the same rules governing prospectuses of local companies.[188] This is sufficient to insure protection of investors if the issue is made through the local stock exchange, but it is difficult to enforce if the prospectus is distributed by mail or through a newspaper. The company may be committing no offense in its country of incorporation or may not be prosecuted there—perhaps the only place where it has assets. If a civil action for damages is brought in Britain or Ireland, no action will lie unless giving misleading information or distributing a prospectus deficient in some other respect is actionable under both the law of the forum and the law where the tort was committed.[189] Under this rule, if the prospectus is adequate under the law of the origin of the prospectus, no action lies unless the tort is held to have been committed in the jurisdiction of the forum; that is, where the prospectus is read rather than where it is posted or written. The whole situation is unsatisfactory.[190] One difficulty is that EEC member states may not restrict foreign prospectuses more than local ones because of the rule against discrimination on the grounds of nationality. Even when uniform laws on prospectuses exist, it may be impossible to prosecute a company in its country of incorporation for a crime committed in another member state and impossible to enforce penalties in the country where the crime was committed. It may be necessary to make a major modification in the present rule against extraterritorial criminal jurisdiction by enabling courts to exercise criminal jurisdiction over companies of other member states or over local companies who commit crimes against foreign law. This will be desirable especially if member states retain different laws to suit local conditions. It would be useful to clarify the private international law rule on the place of the tort and to adopt a rule more satisfactory than the Anglo-Irish rule on the law under which an act must be tortious to be actionable in other member states. Harmonization of the criminal and civil rules in each member

[188] This is the position in Ireland, §§ 361–67, and in the United Kingdom, U.K. Act, §§ 417–23. See 1 Loss, Securities, ch. 1 passim (2d ed. 1961).

If Ireland joined the EEC, exchange-control permission would have to be made automatic for the issue of shares to any person residing in any EEC member state. The EEC Commission, Memorandum of the Commission on the Action Programme for the Second Stage, para. 21 (1962), said that it would cooperate with member states to eliminate "legislative and administrative obstacles above and beyond exchange controls governing the floating of loans by foreign firms on domestic capital markets, the introduction of foreign securities on domestic stock exchanges and the placing of foreign securities with savings institutions." In particular, government directives to big institutional investors on their investment policies, if given, must not direct the investors to discriminate between companies of different member states. The Commission has submitted to the Council a draft directive on these questions.

[189] See Dicey, Conflict of Laws, ch. 28 (7th ed. 1958). This is not the rule in the Six.

[190] See George Munro, Ltd. v. American Cyanamid & Chem. Corp., [1944] K.B. 432; Bata v. Bata, [1948] Weekly N. 366; Cheshire, Private International Law 385–86 (1947); Cook, Logical and Legal Bases of the Conflict of Laws, ch. 13 (1942); 2 Rabel, The Conflict of Laws, ch. 24 (2d ed. 1960).

state relating to the protection of investors is also desirable.[191]

In Ireland a shareholder to whom shares are issued by a company has an action in cases of fraud[192] or inaccuracies in a prospectus[193] against those responsible and, in some instances, may rescind the contract to buy the shares.[194] There is a presumption that inaccurate statements in a prospectus are due to the negligence of the directors and promoters.

Although the position is not wholly clear, the rules in the Six are broadly similar[195] with relation to actions for damages. In France directors are personally liable for errors in prospectuses, under the general principles of the Civil Code on tort liability.[196] However, rescission of the contract to take up shares is difficult in France; in Germany, it is impossible.[197]

Management[198]

Any company law should try to reduce the effects of the separation between ownership and management, especially in large, widely held companies. Article 54(3)(g) of the Treaty does not refer to this problem; but in general, shareholders in the Six have greater powers over management than do shareholders elsewhere. In Germany, however, the powers of holders of bearer shares in corporations are largely exercised by the banks in which the shareholders have deposited the shares.

The essential organs of an Irish company are the directors, the secretary,[199] the general meeting, and the auditors.

Qualifications of Directors

Every Irish company must have at least two directors;[200] neither need be a full-time director, but managing direc-

[191] On these questions in Britain, see 3 Loss, Securities Regulation 1863–71, 2004–2005 (2d ed. 1961). On the proposal to set up an EEC Securities and Exchange Commission, see Nicholson, "Assimilation in the European Common Market of Laws Affecting Companies," 9 Am. J. Comp. L. 358 (1960).

[192] Gower, The Principles of Modern Company Law 294–99 (2d ed. 1957); Palmer, Company Law, chs. 20, 23 (20th ed. 1959).

[193] § 49; U.K. Act, § 43. See also §§ 44, 53(4).

[194] Gower, The Principles of Modern Company Law 299–304 (2d ed. 1957). Professor Gower criticizes the law as being "muddled and uncoordinated," primarily because it is not clear whether an action lies for omissions from a prospectus and because the law on rescission by a person who did not buy shares direct from the company is unsatisfactory; id. at 314–15. On the first point, see Re Wimbledon Olympia, [1910] 1 Ch. 630; Re South of England Natural Gas Co., [1911] 1 Ch. 373; Nash v. Lynde, [1929] A.C. 158. On the rights of a transferee, see Peek v. Gurney, L.R. 6 H.L. 377 (1873); Andrews v. Mockford, [1896] 1 Q.B. 372.

[195] Loss, Securities Regulation 1111–12 (1951); see the materials cited in 3 Loss, Securities Regulation 1876 n.75 (2d ed. 1961).

[196] Law on Stock Companies of July 24, 1867, art. 15, amended by Décret-loi of Aug. 8, 1935, art. 1, and Décret-loi of Aug. 31, 1937, art. 3.

[197] Levy, Private Corporations and Their Control 380, 397, 438–40 (1950). See Aktiengesetz, art. 40, with regard to damages.

[198] For a detailed comparative study of the law relating to management of stock companies in the United States, the United Kingdom, and most of the Six, see van Ommeslaghe, Le Régime des Sociétés par Actions et leur administration en droit comparé, Pt. II (1960).

[199] Every company must have a secretary; § 175. His duties are mostly administrative, and he may also be a director. He is primarily responsible for keeping the company's file in the Companies' Office up to date. Usually his signature is required by the articles when the company's seal is used; Table A, para. 115. Where an act requires the cooperation of a director and the secretary, the same person cannot fill both roles; § 177.

[200] § 174. In Ireland neither a body corporate, § 176 (cf. U.K. Act, § 178), nor an undischarged bankrupt, § 183, may be a director. The court can prohibit certain people from being directors; § 184. In the United Kingdom a private company may have one director.

tors are common, as elsewhere in Europe. The company's articles need not specify the exact number of directors. The Irish Companies Act does not regulate the method of appointing directors;[201] in practice they are appointed initially by the signatories to the charter and thereafter by the general meeting. They can be appointed for any length of time. The power of dismissal is the only real sanction for the shareholders' control over the directors. Shareholders can always remove a director, even without cause, notwithstanding any provision either in the company's articles or in its contract with him,[202] but he must be given a hearing[203] and may be entitled to damages. This power of dismissal results from the principle, more fully accepted in the Six, that the directors are the shareholders' agents. In Ireland a director need not be a shareholder,[204] and there is no age limit. Directors are not required by Irish company law to be Irish nationals, but this may be required by the legislation on freedom of establishment. It is usual and advisable to have at least one Irish director on the board of a foreign-owned Irish subsidiary.

In Ireland the chairman of the board of directors does not have an overriding vote unless the articles of the company so provide. In France a Président-Directeur-Général is personally responsible for the management of the company and is the chairman of the board of directors and the principal executive of the company.[205] In Belgium there is no such statutory position; either a director or an outsider may be appointed manager.

In Ireland there is no legal limit to the number of directorships which one may hold. One may even be a director in competing companies; however, if the conduct of another business with which the shareholders or directors are associated causes loss to the company, the conduct may constitute oppression of the minority.[206] In France, a director generally may not be director of more than eight companies, and no president of a board of directors can hold more than two presidencies.[207] A French board of directors must consist of at least three, and not more than twelve, directors.

Powers of Directors

In principle the directors exercise their powers as a group; the Irish Act does not require the creation of an executive position or group subordinate to the directors.[208] The company's articles can

[201] Section 181 prevents shareholders' being forced to vote on the appointment of a group of directors as a whole.

[202] Directors for life of private companies cannot be removed; § 182 (1); U.K. Act, § 184. In France the managers of limited liability companies can be removed without cause only if the constitution of the company so provides. The Irish rule appears to be the same as that in Italy; Civil Code, art. 2383. In Germany the members of the supervisory board can be dismissed only by a 75% majority of the shareholders, Aktiengesetz, art. 87; and the members of the executive board can be dismissed by the supervisory board only for good reason, Aktiengesetz, art. 75(3). The managers of a GmbH can be dismissed without cause, GmbH Gesetz, art. 38; and they are subject to the shareholders' instructions.

[203] § 182(2).

[204] But if the articles so provide he must take up his shares promptly; §§ 179, 180. In France, directors must hold shares.

[205] Law of Nov. 16, 1940, art. 2.

[206] § 205; Scottish Cooperative Wholesale Soc'y v. Meyer, [1959] A.C. 324; London & Mashonaland Exploration Co. v. New Mashonaland Exploration Co., [1891] Weekly N. 165. See Aktiengesetz, art. 79(1). In Italy a director may not engage in competition with his company; Civil Code, art. 2390.

[207] Law Relating to Stock Companies, Nov. 16, 1940, art. 3, amended by the Law of July 7, 1953. The rule does not apply to a limited liability company.

[208] Table A, art. 112, empowers the directors to confer all their powers on a managing director even "to the exclusion of their own powers."

authorize the directors to delegate their powers and may set up and regulate the activities of executive committees, governing directors, and managing directors. A two-tier management, of which the directors are the supervisory group, thus can be set up in an Irish company if desired. A German corporation[209] must have a supervisory board and an executive board. Like Irish directors, the supervisory board is elected by the shareholders, and the board in turn appoints the executives. Unlike Irish directors, who can make contracts with third parties on the company's behalf, the supervisory board cannot; this is the function of the executive board. In this respect the supervisory board resembles a shareholders' committee rather than a board of directors. The president of the executive board corresponds to the managing director of an Irish company. One important difference between the two systems is that the full-time executives of an Irish company are usually directors to whom functions have been delegated, but no one may be a member of the supervisory and the executive boards of a German company simultaneously. The shareholders in an Irish company are thus more directly in contact with the executives than are the shareholders of a German corporation, but unlike the supervisory board they have no facilities for exercising control over the executives except at general meetings. In the absence of any legal separation in Ireland between policy-making and executive functions, policy-making and supervision are carried out in practice by the directors, and execution is by a full-time officer, who may be a manager or a director not formally distinguished from his colleagues.

Irish law reserves to the general meeting various powers which, in theory, enable shareholders to exercise a reasonable degree of control over directors. The powers to alter the company's charter,[210] to increase or reduce its share capital,[211] and to dismiss directors before the expiration of their term of office[212] cannot be delegated by the general meeting. There are provisions to insure that the shareholders are fully informed at annual intervals. However, important acts such as the sale of the company's business and the issuance of unissued capital can be done without consulting the shareholders[213] if the articles of the company permit. Normally the directors decide the amount of dividends, and the general meeting approves their decision. The extent of the powers of the directors depends on the company's articles, in particular, the clause which empowers the directors to manage the company's business. This flexibility is one weakness of shareholder protection in Irish law which probably would have to be remedied if Ireland joins EEC. In theory, ultimate control over the directors should be exercised by the share-

[209] Aktiengesetz, arts. 70, 86. See von Caemmerer, "Les Pouvoirs Respectifs de l'Administration et de l'Assemblée dans le Droit Allemand," in 1 La Società per Azioni alla metà del Secolo XX, 151 (1962); see also Mees, "Le Pouvoir Respectif de l'Administration et de l'Assemblée Générale dans les Sociétes par Actions en Droit Neerlandais," in id. at 237; Limpens, "Les Pouvoirs Respectifs du Conseil d'Administration et de l'Assemblée Générale dans les Sociétés par Actions en Belgique," in id. at 521.

[210] §§ 10, 15, 28.

[211] §§ 68, 72. The extent of the directors' borrowing powers is usually limited by the articles.

[212] § 182.

[213] Even if a take-over bid is being made. The only restrictions derive from the principle that the directors must act in the interests of the company as a whole; see Jenkins Report, Cmd. No. 1749, paras. 100–22, especially para. 113 (1962). The sale of a company's business by the directors is not possible in French or in German law; see Aktiengesetz, art. 255. In Germany, legislation is proposed which will give the shareholders the power to decide the amount of the dividend, up to 50% of the year's net profit.

holders, but this is obligatory in Ireland only in limited respects.[214] In Britain the clause in Table A[215] prescribing the directors' powers has been held to leave the general meeting no power to direct the board of directors on the conduct of the company's affairs except by an alteration in the company's articles.[216] In Ireland the corresponding provision of Table A[217] states that "the business of the company shall be managed by the directors . . . subject . . . to such directions, not being inconsistent with the [articles] or provisions [of the Act], as may be given by the company in general meeting." If a company adopts this provision, the general meeting may even demand, subject to the payment of damages, the dismissal of an employee or manager of the company whom the directors have employed, just as they may dismiss individual directors. The shareholders in a German corporation have no such power over the members of the executive board.[218]

Duties of Directors

The duty of care imposed on directors in the Six is stricter than that imposed by Irish law. The Jenkins Report states that "the basic principles underlying the relationship" of directors to their company should be set out.[219] The Report recommends that certain duties should be owed by directors to the shareholders (not now the case), not merely to the company as a separate entity.[220] "There is a striking contrast between the directors' heavy duties of loyalty and good faith and their very light obligations of skill and diligence."[221] A director need show only the skill that can reasonably be expected of someone with his knowledge and experience. He ought to attend directors' meetings when he reasonably can, but failure to attend meetings is not in itself a breach of his duty.[222] He may trust another officer to carry out his functions honestly if there is no reason for suspicion and if the circumstances permit or require the function in question, for example, a technical matter, to be left to the officer.[223]

[214] Jenkins Report, Cmd. No. 1749, Note of Dissent 207, para. 3 (1962). In Ireland, the power to dismiss directors is the only real inalienable right of control over policy.

[215] U.K. Act, Table A, para. 80.

[216] Quin & Axtens v. Salmon, [1909] A.C. 422.

[217] Para. 80. The change in the wording from the U.K. Act makes it clear that the curious interpretation of the House of Lords in Quin & Axtens v. Salmon, [1909] A.C. 422, is rejected.

[218] Aktiengesetz, art. 103.

[219] Cmd. No. 1749, paras. 87, 99 (1962). The Report recommends that, in addition to all other duties, a director should be expressly required to observe the utmost good faith towards the company in any transaction with it or on its behalf and should act honestly in the exercise of his powers and the discharge of the duties of his office. A director should also be prohibited from making use of any money or other property of the company or any information acquired by virtue of his position as director or officer of the company to gain, even indirectly, an improper advantage at the expense of the company. The Jenkins Committee seems to have regarded these statements as largely declaratory of the existing law. See Gower, The Principles of Modern Company Law, ch. 23 (2d ed. 1957); Gower, "Corporation Law in England and America," 4 U. Chi. L.S. Record 1, 21 (1955).

[220] Percival v. Wright, [1902] 2 Ch. 421.

[221] Gower, The Principles of Modern Company Law 497 (2d ed. 1957); Palmer, Company Law, ch. 56 (20th ed. 1959).

[222] Since mere failure to attend meetings cannot normally be shown to have caused any particular loss to the company, liability for failure to attend meetings would be difficult to enforce, but the standard required seems too low.

[223] Re City Equitable Fire Ins. Co., [1925] Ch. 407. See, however, Table A, para. 91(g), which provides that a director will lose his office if he is absent from meetings for more than six months without the permission of the other directors. See also Table A, para. 138, and § 200.

German law requires a full-time director, that is, a member of the executive board, to display the skill and care of an ordinary conscientious manager of a business.[224] However, the members of the executive board are appointed by the supervisory board, not the shareholders, and they are full-time executives. In the Netherlands directors must display the care which they would use in their own affairs,[225] and in Italy and Belgium, the care displayed by a commercial agent.[226]

To prevent directors from conducting the affairs of the company for their own benefit, the approval of the shareholders is required by Irish law for payment of compensation to a director for loss of office.[227] Tax-free payments to directors are prohibited, and particulars of all payments and loans to directors must be given in the company's accounts.[228] There is no legal maximum for directors' remuneration in Ireland. A company must keep a register of all shares in it or in an associated company held by or in trust for a director or one of his family, and a director is in theory obliged to furnish information to the board in connection with these shares and with loans or payments to him.[229] The most important provision, however, requires a director to disclose to the other directors and shareholders his interest in contracts to be made by the company.[230] If this is not done, it seems that the contract can be set aside by the company and that it can recover any profit made by the director. In the unlikely event that the company's articles do not deal with conflicts of interest, the contract must be approved by the general meeting. Conflicts of interest are important and will require regulation in the EEC. Contracts involving directors with

[224] Aktiengesetz, art. 84(1). The burden of proof is on the manager.

[225] Civil Code, art. 1743.

[226] Italian Civil Code, art. 2392.

[227] § 186. Section 187 provides that payments made as compensation for loss of office to the directors of a company selling all or part of its property are to be regarded as having been made in trust for the company, unless the payments are approved by the general meeting. Compare the French rule of *abus de la raison sociale*; 1 Hamel & Lagarde, Traité de Droit Commercial 566–67 (1954). This rule prevents the directors' being paid part of the purchase price properly due to the company in return for their approval of the sale. Section 188 deals with the same problem where the shares in the company are sold; see U.K. Act, §§ 191–94. See Jenkins Report, Cmd. No. 1749, paras. 92–99 (1962). In Germany loans to directors of a corporation require the approval of the supervisory board; Aktiengesetz, art. 80(1).

[228] §§ 185, 191, 192. These detailed sections are important because most directors prefer to receive fees rather than dividends, to obtain tax relief for earned income. In the United Kingdom, except in the case of private companies of the closely held type, which are exempt from the obligation to file accounts, most loans to directors are prohibited; U.K. Act, § 190. Details of loans to officers other than directors must be given in the accounts; U.K. Act, § 197.

[229] §§ 190, 193; cf. U.K. Act, § 195. The shareholder's protection here is inadequate in certain respects.

[230] § 194; cf. U.K. Act, § 199. Compliance with § 194 does not relieve a director from complying with the common law rules on conflicts of interest, though the articles may do so. Paragraphs 83–84 of Table A nullify a vote of a director on a contract in which he has an interest. Section 200 invalidates a company's articles insofar as they purport to exempt any officer of the company from liability for breach of duty or breach of trust. The Irish stock exchange rule for companies dealing with the exchange is that a director may not vote on a contract in which he has an interest. For technical criticisms of U.K. Act, § 199, see Final Report on the Present Company Law of Ghana 150 (1961).

Irish law contains no rule invalidating the votes in general meeting of director-shareholders who could not, under Table A, para. 84, vote in a directors' meeting, on a contract in which they had an interest. Shareholders are thus in a vulnerable position as to conflicts of interest, and the extent of their protection depends on how § 205 is enforced by the courts; see p. 135. Some of the Six (but not France or Bel-

conflicts of interest require the approval of the general meeting in France[231] and the approval of the supervisory board in Germany.

Shareholders' meetings[232]

Under Irish law, annual shareholders' meetings must be held by all types of companies,[233] and other meetings must be held if demanded by shareholders owning 10 per cent of the voting capital[234] or if called by the directors. Annual general meetings and meetings at which special resolutions[235] are to be passed require a minimum of twenty-one days' notice. Extended notice is required if it is proposed to remove a director or to appoint different auditors.[236] Other general meetings require fourteen days' notice or, in the case of a private company, seven days' notice. If the company's auditors and all the shareholders (90 per cent, in the case of a special resolution) agree, shorter notice is permitted. Curiously, there are no statutory requirements as to how notice shall be given.[237] The notice normally must give details of all business, except the ordinary business of an annual meeting under Table A. A company is not required to assist shareholders by sending out notice of their resolutions with the notice of the meeting.[238]

Any shareholder entitled to attend and vote may appoint a proxy, who need not be a shareholder.[239] The right to appoint a proxy cannot be taken away by the company's articles, and every notice of a meeting must state that members have this right. A proxy has the same rights to speak and vote as the member appointing him.[240] The directors may not require the documents by which proxies are appointed to be sent in more than forty-eight hours before the time of the meeting. If the directors send out proxy forms for signature, they must be sent to all shareholders.

---

gium) have a rule to this effect; e.g., Netherlands Commercial Code, art. 44c; Italian Civil Code, art. 2373. A rule similar to that in the Netherlands and Italy exists in Germany with regard to a GmbH, but it can be set aside by the company's charter.

[231] Law of July 24, 1867, art. 40; Law of March 4, 1943, art. 10; Church, Business Associations Under French Law 379–80 (1960).

[232] The statutory meeting of shareholders, which is held within three months of incorporation of a public company, § 130, need not be held by a private company or a private company converted into a public company.

[233] § 131. See Table A, para. 53.

[234] § 132. General meetings other than the annual statutory general meetings are referred to in the Act as extraordinary general meetings. See also § 134(b).

[235] § 141. See § 143(5)(b), and Jenkins Report, Cmd. No. 1749, para. 460 (1962).

[236] §§ 142, 161, 182. This is called "special notice" in U.K. Act, §§ 160, 184. "Extraordinary" resolutions still exist in England but have been abolished in Ireland.

[237] See § 134; Table A, paras. 51–52, 133–36; cf. U.K. Act, § 133. See Jenkins Report, Cmd. No. 1749, para. 467 (1962). In the Netherlands a notice in a newspaper is sufficient; this is the only possible type of notice to the holders of bearer shares.

[238] U.K. Act, § 140. This is unfortunate, because to Americans even the British rule is inadequate, and Irish directors are in other respects in a much stronger position than the shareholders; see Re Dorman Long & Co., [1934] 1 Ch. 635, 657–58 (per Maugham, J.); Gower, The Principles of Modern Company Law 437, 440, 443 (2d ed. 1957). In France a draft law to permit shareholders to propose resolutions is to be introduced.

[239] § 136. In France a proxy in a stock company should be a shareholder.

[240] U.K. Act, § 136(1), gives a proxy statutory right to speak only at a meeting of a private company. In Ireland a proxy and the duly appointed representative of a company exercise the same rights in all circumstances; § 139. There are no rules regarding the contents of documents sent out by the directors under which proxies can be appointed, and this lack is a defect.

Subject to the company's articles, two shareholders of a private company, or three shareholders of a public company, present in person are a quorum.[241] In France, for ordinary meetings, shareholders holding 25 per cent of the capital are a quorum; in Italy, shareholders representing 50 per cent of the capital are a quorum.[242] There are no quorum requirements in German law.

Contracts to vote in a particular way or not to vote and voting trusts, though unusual, are legal and may be enforced by injunction.[243] The shareholders' meetings may be held outside Ireland if the shareholders wish.[244]

Unless a special resolution[245] is required or the company's articles so require, decisions normally are made by simple majority.[246]

Accounts

British and Irish law require directors to have prepared annually a balance sheet and a profit and loss account which must give a "true and fair" view of the company's financial affairs and must contain a large amount of detailed information specified by law.[247] These accounts need not estimate the company's net worth or the total value of its assets[248] nor give even a total figure for turnover or a rate of return on capital. Professionally qualified auditors must make a report and certify that these accounts comply fully with the law,[249] and the accounts must be signed by the directors.[250] Proper records, from which the accounts are made, must be kept during the accounting year;[251] it is unsatisfactory that shareholders have no right to see these records, since the right to obtain information is essential to shareholders' protection. These records may be kept outside Ireland. Before the general meeting, the accounts and the directors' and the auditors' reports must be sent to all shareholders and debenture holders.[252]

[241] § 134(c). Table A, pt. II [private companies], para. 5, allows two members present only by proxy to be a quorum. The quorum must be present when the resolution is passed; Hennessy v. National Agricultural & Industrial Dev. Ass'n, [1947] Ir. R. 159.

[242] Italian Civil Code, art. 2368; in France, Law of July 24, 1867, art. 30. At a meeting to alter the articles of a stock company, one-half of the capital should be represented and a majority of two-thirds is required.

[243] Puddephatt v. Leith, [1916] 1 Ch. 200.

[244] § 140.

[245] § 141.

[246] In Germany, changing the company's bylaws, approval of the dissolution, merger, and reorganization of the company, the acquisition of assets exceeding in value 10% of the capital within two years of formation, and the transfer of the company's assets require three-quarters majorities; Aktiengesetz, arts. 45, 145, 203, 234, 255, 257, 263.

[247] § 149 and Sixth Schedule; U.K. Act, § 149 and Eighth Schedule are very similar. Analysis of trading accounts between the various activities of a company is not required.

[248] Jenkins Report, Cmd. No. 1749, paras. 333, 353 (1962). In Germany, accounts must show wages and salaries and total material costs. Legislation is proposed which would prohibit the creation of hidden reserves.

[249] Seventh Schedule; § 162 deals with the qualifications of auditors.

[250] § 156.

[251] § 147; see Butt v. Kelson, [1952] Ch. 197. See Aktiengesetz, arts. 131–32; Belgian Commercial Code, bk. I, tit. IX, art. 77; French Law of Companies, July 24, 1867, arts. 27–35, and Law of March 14, 1943, art. 11; Italian Civil Code, art. 2423; Luxembourg Law of Aug. 10, 1915, art. 72; Netherlands Commercial Code, art. 42; see also Blondeel, "Problems Involved in Operating Within the EEC," in Doing Business in the Common Market 15, 19 (Commerce Clearing House, 1963); Weismann, "Profit and Loss Accounts in the German Federal Republic," 2 J. Common Market Studies 185 (1963). In the Netherlands, no accounts need be published unless bearer shares are issued. Group accounts and figures on turnover are compulsory in France.

[252] § 159.

Even after making allowances for differences in techniques of legislative drafting, the provisions of Irish and British law are more detailed and stricter than those of the Six. In the Six, difficulties occur because the accounts are brief and because sums put to reserve need not be properly shown. However, figures for turnover normally are given; this is not required in Ireland or Britain.

Since private companies in Ireland need not publish their accounts, there are provisions to prevent public companies from setting up private companies as subsidiaries to keep particular aspects of their total business secret. If a public company controls another company through the latter's directors, or equity or voting capital, or through an intermediate holding company,[253] group accounts covering the parent company and all subsidiaries must be published. If group accounts would be impracticable or misleading, any shareholder in the parent company is entitled by Irish law to see the accounts of a subsidiary.[254] If the parent company is a private company, group accounts are not required in Ireland, but shareholders are entitled to see the accounts of subsidiaries if group accounts are not prepared.[255] In Britain, group accounts are required even where the holding company is a private company. If group accounts are not required, the shareholder has no right to information on the subsidiaries.[256] Group accounts are unusual in the Six.[257]

Irish law has gone further than British law in the matter of accounts in two other respects. In view of the complexity of accounts of the balance-sheet type—as opposed to the "narrative" type of accounts—almost always used in Ireland, "fair and accurate summaries" of the accounts and of the auditors' report may be issued in addition to full accounts.[258] A more important measure requires the directors' report, which must be presented with the accounts to the shareholders, to state any change in the nature of the company's business, in the business of its subsidiaries, or in the classes of business in which the company has an interest, whether as a shareholder in another company or otherwise.[259] The report must list the names, places of incorporation, and the nature of the business[260] of all companies in which the

[253] § 155. The U.K. Act does not apply if the voting shares held are not equity shares; cf. Irish Act, § 155(1)(a)(iii). See Irish Company Law Report, Pr. 4523, paras. 180–88 (1958). Neither Act applies to a company owned to the extent of exactly 50% each by two other companies if neither of the parent companies has control, as defined, for some other reason. Other devices are possible to avoid the sections. In Ireland directors are not entitled to withhold information which they think will harm the business of the company or where the operations of the parent and the subsidiary are entirely different; cf. U.K. Act, §§ 150(2), 157(2). Presumably the principal cases where disclosure might be harmful would be those where it would prejudice the competitive position or financial standing of the company. These are the cases where disclosure is most necessary for the protection of the public.

[254] § 150(3).

[255] § 154. There is no similar provision in Britain.

[256] See, however, § 166(b)(iii).

[257] In Germany, legislation has been proposed which would require consolidated accounts from certain types of company.

[258] § 156(4).

[259] § 158(3). In Britain the directors need not give this information if they believe that it would harm the company; U.K. Act, § 157(2). In Ireland, the Industrial Credit Company will not reveal the companies in which it holds over 20% of the shares; § 158(6). See 206 Dáil Eireann, Parl. Deb., cols. 816–19 (1963).

[260] §§ 158(4), 158(5); there are no corresponding provisions in the U.K. Act. Jenkins Report, Cmd. No. 1749, paras. 114, 122 (1962), recommends that more complete directors' reports should be required by law for the information and protection of shareholders. It points out that the modern practice is to put the useful information in the report of the chairman of the board of directors and that some safeguards are required for this practice.

company owns more than 20 per cent of the voting capital. This rule applies to all companies, including those not required to produce group accounts and including private companies. There is no such rule in Britain.

Adequate accounts are important for the protection of shareholders and, if they are made available to the public, of creditors. While certain criticisms have been made of the present requirements on the contents[261] of accounts, the most important defect in the Irish law is the exemption for private companies—the great majority of companies in Ireland—from the obligation to publish any accounts at all. Only the fact that a private company owes money to a secured creditor is apparent from the file in the Registrar of Companies' Office.[262]

Even more information than is now given in the accounts of British and Irish public companies is probably desirable if the efficiency of the European capital market is to be improved and interstate portfolio investment is to be encouraged and safeguarded. There is little point in giving tax preference for distributed profits of companies unless the shareholders can make a well-informed judgment about where to reinvest. One expert[263] has said that details of a company's turnover in its principal lines of activity, a valuation of its fixed assets on the basis of replacement cost, less depreciation on the basis of replacement cost,[264] and details of the company's main activities[265] should be given in its published reports and accounts.

Auditors

Auditors are appointed at the first directors' meeting, and thereafter, by each annual general meeting.[266] An auditor must be a qualified accountant.[267] Unlike the rule in the Six, appointment is made annually; however, reappointment is automatic unless some contrary step is taken.[268] If an auditor is not reappointed, he must be given an opportunity to present his case to the shareholders.[269] Irish shareholders need not have serious grounds for removing auditors from office, as French and Italian shareholders apparently must.

[261] Jenkins Report, Cmd. No. 1749, paras. 353–97 (1962). The most important recommendation is that the company's turnover should be disclosed; id., paras. 393–94. This would be an important indication of the company's efficiency and would enable pressure to be put on inefficient managements—a useful contribution to economic development.

[262] § 99; Irish Company Law Report, Pr. 4523, paras. 117, 153–61 (1958).

[263] Rose, Disclosure in Company Accounts (1963). See also Chorley & Wolff, "Commercial Law and Company Law," in Law Reform Now 150 (Gardiner & Martin ed. 1963); Lawson, "The Banker and the Jenkins Report on Company Law: Accounts," 84 J. Inst. Bankers 272 (1963).

[264] Only depreciation on the basis of original cost is permitted for tax purposes under Irish law.

[265] See, however, § 158.

[266] § 160(6). Section 160(7), which is peculiar to Ireland, provides that the appointment of a firm of accountants as auditors has the effect of an appointment of whoever may be the qualified partners of that firm from time to time.

[267] § 162. A person convicted of a crime in connection with duties as an auditor, an officer of the company, a partner or employee of the company or of an associated company, and a corporate body are ineligible. Except in the case of a private company, a partner or employee of an officer of the company or of an associated company also is ineligible, § 162(3)(b); otherwise, there is no relaxation in Ireland of the requirements in the case of a private company. Unlike France, there is no restriction on relatives of directors being appointed. France requires no qualifications if a company does not make a public issue; if it does make a public issue, one auditor must come from a public panel. There are similar rules in Belgium, Italy, and Germany. On the French law, see Law on Companies, July 24, 1867, as amended.

[268] § 160(2).

[269] § 161.

The Netherlands is the only one of the Six which does not insist on auditors' being appointed. In Germany, they are not required for a limited liability company, and in the other four member states they are required only for stock companies and some limited liability companies.[270]

In Ireland, as in the rest of Europe, auditors are watchdogs with statutory powers, not outsiders brought in by the directors to verify the accuracy of the bookkeeping. They have a responsibility to the company and the shareholders to see that the company is run according to law.[271] However, unlike French, Belgian, Italian, and Luxembourg auditors, Irish auditors may not call a general meeting of a stock company. The auditors make a report on the company's or group's records and accounts. The contents of this report are regulated by law,[272] and the report must certify that the Companies Act has been complied with. The auditor's report must be attached to any copy of the accounts distributed. It guarantees their accuracy, and it must be read at the general meeting and must be available to any shareholder. Shareholders are probably as well protected in Ireland as in states where the duties of auditors extend beyond verification of accounts; it seems difficult in practice to combine more extended duties with independence from the management.

Italy goes further than any other EEC member state by requiring auditors to attend all directors' and shareholders' meetings and to investigate the complaints of shareholders holding 5 per cent or more of the share capital and by making the auditors liable for losses which with due care they could have prevented. They must carry out quarterly checks and may investigate the legality of any aspect of the company's management and policy on their own initiative,[273] so they function as a type of supervisory body as well as accounting experts. This is also true in France and Luxembourg to a lesser extent; but in France, at least, the powers of the auditors to control the management are "obviously inadequate,"[274] although auditors must report irregularities to the office of the prosecutor.

Protection of minorities

An Irish shareholder (but not a debenture holder) or the personal representative of a deceased shareholder may apply to the High Court if he considers that the company's affairs are being conducted or the powers of the directors exercised in an oppressive way or "in disregard of his interest" as a shareholder.[275] The Minister for Industry and Commerce

[270] See Conard, "Organizing for Business," in 2 American Enterprise in the European Common Market: A Legal Profile 1, 107 (Stein & Nicholson ed. 1960).

[271] Confusingly, auditors are officers of the company for some purposes but not for others; cf. §§ 162(3), 168(6), 200. On whether the auditors are responsible to the shareholders individually, see Gower, The Principles of Modern Company Law 429 (2d ed. 1957).

[272] § 163, Seventh Schedule.

[273] Civil Code, arts. 2397–409; Conard, "Organizing for Business," in 2 American Enterprise in the European Common Market: A Legal Profile 1, 108 (Stein & Nicholson ed. 1960); Pennington, Companies in the Common Market 37 (1962); van Ommeslaghe, Le Régime des Sociétés par Actions et leur administration en droit comparé 101–102, 129–30, 219–20 (1960).

[274] Thibièrge, "Le Statut des Sociétés Etrangères," in 1 Le Statut de l'Etranger 239, 349. A new law is being introduced to strengthen the auditors' powers. In Belgium the law is unsatisfactory, since some companies need not have official auditors.

[275] § 205. U.K. Act, § 210, does not expressly cover cases where misuse of the directors' powers is complained of. See Scottish Cooperative Wholesale Soc'y v. Meyer, [1959] A.C. 324; Re H. R. Harmer, Ltd., [1959] 1 Weekly L.R. 62; Pennington, "Company Law Reform

may apply to the court if an investigation reveals any of these circumstances.[276] In Ireland there is no need for the facts to be serious enough to justify the company's being wound up.[277] The court has discretion to direct or prohibit any act and to cancel or vary any transaction. For example, it may require the purchase of the aggrieved shareholder's shares, regulate the conduct of the company's affairs in the future, or require an alteration in the company's articles. The mere existence of these provisions has a salutary effect. They provide protection for minorities similar to, and perhaps greater than, that given by the principle of abuse of legal rights in the Six.[278]

Another provision protecting minorities concerns the rights of shareholders owning a particular class of shares. In principle these rights could be altered by a change in the articles of the company.[279] Articles usually provide for variation of class rights upon the approval of a specified majority of the shareholders of the class in question, voting separately.[280] The Irish Act,[281] however, gives the holders of 10 per cent of the shares affected the right to appeal to the court on the grounds that they are being "unfairly prejudiced." Although this gives a degree of protection, the voting rights of preferred shareholders are not regarded as "varied" by a stock dividend which increases the total voting power of the ordinary shareholders and alters the balance of voting power between the two

---

in Great Britain," 1 Common Market L. Rev. 58 (1963). This is one of the important differences between British and Irish law. It is one of the numerous situations where the High Court has discretion in dealing with the affairs of a company. For other situations, see §§ 28, 73–75, 78, 135, 166(a), 201, 203, 204. See Re Dorman Long & Co., [1934] Ch. 635, 657 (per Maugham, J.); Scottish Ins. Corp. v. Wilson & Clyde Coal Co., [1948] Sess. Cas. 360, 375–77 (per Cooper, L.), aff'd, [1949] A.C. 462. In addition to the sections mentioned, the courts are involved in numerous matters in winding-up proceedings.

[276] §§ 170(3), 205(2).

[277] In both countries a company can be wound up if it would be "just and equitable" to do so; § 213(f); U.K. Act, § 222(f). This also constitutes a protection for minorities. However, winding up might unfairly prejudice some shareholders and in such cases U.K. Act, § 210, gives a remedy. See Jenkins Report, Cmd. No. 1749, paras. 199–212 (1962), for recommendations on the United Kingdom law, most of which have been embodied in the Irish Act. Jenkins Report, para. 205, suggests three cases where the court's power under U.K. Act, § 210, could be used: where the directors increase their fees and deprive shareholders of a dividend, where the directors refuse to accept a share transfer to personal representatives of a deceased member and thus force the sale of the shares to themselves at a low price, and where the directors issue shares to themselves on advantageous terms. See also Northern Ireland Departmental Committee on Company Law Amendment, Report, Cmd. No. 393, para. 12 (1958), on which § 205 of the Irish Act is largely based.

[278] For the French law, see 1 Hamel & Lagarde, Traité de Droit Commercial 826–27 (1954); Janne d'Othée, "Du droit des minorités dans les sociétés anonymes," in 1 La Società per Azioni alla metà del Secolo XX, 359 (1962).

[279] Which can be passed by 75% of the votes cast; § 141.

[280] Table A, para. 3, gives the usual form of the provision just mentioned, requiring the consent of the holders of three-quarters of the shares of the class. Section 28(3) protects class rights if they are protected in the memorandum. This is the rule in German law for stock companies, Aktiengesetz, art. 146(2); and this also applies to increases and reductions in the share capital, arts. 149, 175.

[281] § 78; U.K. Act, § 72, gives this right to 15% of the shareholders of the class affected. The Irish Act thus carries out the important recommendation of para. 198 of the Jenkins Report. It is an unjustifiable omission to give no protection to minorities in the absence of a provision in the articles on the subject, since statutory protection is needed more in such circumstances.

classes.[282] Other than carefully drawn articles, there is no protection in Irish law for a class of shareholders, and thus foreign portfolio investors are likely to be deceived. Moreover, minorities are not protected, as they are in Belgium and Luxembourg,[283] by a limitation on the number of votes which can be exercised by any one shareholder. The Six seem to give fuller protection to classes of shareholders and to regulate class meetings more closely than Ireland. Unlike in French and Belgian law,[284] there is no general principle in Irish law that changes in a company's charter must not discriminate between classes of shareholders.

Any minority holding at least 10 per cent of the paid-up voting shares has the important right to insist on a general meeting's being called.[285] This right cannot be abrogated by the company's articles.

A less satisfactory area of Irish company law is that dealing with the rights of a shareholder to bring a derivative action against the directors for breach of a duty owed by them to the company.[286] These actions are rare in Britain and Ireland. Since Irish shareholders can request the court to examine objectionable company dealings, the derivative action may cease to be of practical significance.[287] In France shareholders holding 5 per cent of the capital may bring a derivative action for damage done to the company, but the damages are payable to the shareholders personally. In France and Belgium directors are liable for damage done to shareholders as individuals, but there is no shareholders' derivative action in Belgium. However, directors are liable to anyone injured by a breach of the company's constitution. In the Six, the doctrine of abuse of rights gives protection somewhat similar to that given by a derivative action.

Cumulative voting, insuring minority shareholders of representation on the board of directors, is unknown in Britain, Germany, and Ireland.[288] Cumulative voting is legal in Belgium and has been used to protect minorities. The same effect can be achieved by having several classes of shares.[289] Cumulative voting is probably more appropriate in public companies than in closely held companies because the directors are supervisors rather than managers in public companies and divergent interests may need to be represented.

Voting agreements are legal in Germany, and sometimes take the form of

[282] Greenhalgh v. Arderne Cinemas, [1946] 1 All E.R. 512; White v. Bristol Aeroplane Co., [1953] Ch. 65; Re MacKenzie & Co., [1916] 2 Ch. 450; Re John Smith Tadcaster Brewery, [1953] Ch. 308.

[283] In stock companies, but not in limited liability companies; Belgian Commercial Code, bk. I, tit. IX, art. 76; Luxembourg, Recueil des lois concernant les Sociétés Commerciales (1956); Law of Aug. 10, 1915, on Commercial Companies, art. 71(2).

[284] See Law of July 14, 1867, art. 31; Law of May 1, 1930; Belgian Commercial Code, bk. I, tit. IX, art. 71.

[285] § 132. In Germany the corresponding proportion of shareholders in a stock company is 5%. In Italy, it is 20%; Civil Code, art. 2367.

[286] See Koestler, "The Stockholders' Suit: A Comparative View," 46 Colum. L. Rev. 238 (1946); Gower, The Principles of Modern Company Law 528–38 (2d ed. 1957); Palmer, Company Law 496–504 (20th ed. 1959). On the United Kingdom law, see Wedderburn, "Shareholders' Rights and the Rule in Foss v. Harbottle" (pts. 1–2), 1957 Camb. L.J. 194; 1958 Camb. L.J. 93.

[287] Cf. Pavlides v. Jensen, [1956] Ch. 565.

[288] Section 181 requires directors to be appointed individually and not collectively. This tends to empower 51% of the shareholders to elect 100% of the directors. See "The Conflict of Cumulative Voting and Staggered Directorships," 24 U. Cinc. L. Rev. 560 (1955); Williams, Cumulative Voting for Directors (1951).

[289] Blondeel, "Problems Involved in Operating Within the EEC," in Doing Business in the Common Market 15, 19 (Commerce Clearing House, 1963).

voting trusts, especially in connection with the peculiarly German institution known as a shareholders' protective association.[290] Voting agreements are permitted in the Netherlands. Although voting agreements are generally illegal[291] in France, the French courts have allowed agreements between groups of shareholders by which each group obtained the right to appoint a certain proportion of the board of directors but the individuals to be appointed were not specified.[292]

While this book is concerned with direct rather than portfolio investment and while United States direct investors tend to use wholly owned subsidiaries, the protection of minorities in the company laws of the EEC member states is important. Joint ventures with local interests are often the best method of doing business. In Irish law, minority protection does not interfere with the operation of the company; the same probably cannot be said for the laws of the Six. Even where the legal protection of minorities does not interfere (for example, in the voting structure of a company), the United States investor, as the minority shareholder, may be concerned. This may arise in Ireland as long as the restrictions on the freedom of aliens to hold controlling interests in manufacturing companies continue. Management agreements and executive committees to whom the directors have delegated functions may cause difficulties in settling the rights of minority and majority groups. Protection for minorities is essential to insure free movement of capital in the EEC and to encourage small investors to invest in companies in less industrialized regions.

[290] Schneider, "The American Close Corporation and Its German Equivalent," 14 Bus. Law. 228, 233, 239 (1958).

[291] Décret-loi of Aug. 31, 1937.

[292] Hauser & Hauser, A Guide to Doing Business in the European Common Market 118 (1960).

Take-over bids

Unlike in Britain, take-over bids have been infrequent in Ireland, and the only provisions affecting them relate to the buying-out of a dissenting minority by the new owners[293] and to payments to directors.[294] The Jenkins Report recommended improvements in the British law.[295] While the effort to follow and improve on the U.K. Act has resulted in legislation which is probably unnecessarily complicated for Ireland, it was decided in this matter to omit complicated and rarely used provisions. The Irish Minister for Industry and Commerce does not have even the limited power of the British Board of Trade to adopt regulations having the force of law to control take-over bids. Further legislation, at least to protect offeree shareholders when take-over bids occur, will probably be required if Ireland enters the Common Market.

This chapter analyzes the law relating to the form of business entity most frequently used by investors establishing operations abroad. But in practice, they may not be free to set up these operations. The next chapter deals with the effect of the EEC on restrictions which may prevent them from doing so.

[293] § 204; cf. U.K. Act, § 209. See In re Bugle Press, [1960] Weekly L.R. 956. Section 204 provides both protection of the new owners from the minority and protection for the minority, who may elect to be bought out. The power to acquire compulsorily the shares of a small dissenting minority is apparently unpopular with United States investors, but it is unlikely to affect them in practice. See Boyle, "The Sale of Controlling Shares: American Law and the Jenkins Committee," 13 Int'l & Comp. L.Q. 185 (1964); U.K. Prevention of Fraud (Investments) Act, 1958, 6 & 7 Eliz. 2, c. 45; Licensed Dealers (Conduct of Business) Rules, 1960, [1960] 1 Stat. Instr. 386 (No. 1216).

[294] §§ 187–89. See Gower, The Principles of Modern Company Law 488–95 (2d ed. 1957); Palmer, Company Law 683–84, 754 (20th ed. 1959).

[295] Cmd. No. 1749, paras. 265–94 (1962).

Chapter 5

Freedom of Establishment

GENERAL CONSIDERATIONS

Disadvantages of foreign investment

Restrictions on freedom of establishment are of two types—one that involves or permits discrimination on the grounds of nationality and one that does not.[1] Before looking at the effects of the EEC on each type, the disadvantages of freedom of establishment for non-nationals should be stated.[2] This chapter does not attempt to weigh the advantages and disadvantages of foreign investment but merely states some of its disadvantages both in less developed and in highly industrialized economies. An understanding of these disadvantages is important not only to governments but also to investors negotiating for concessions or for permission to establish operations.

Drain on Main Sources of National Wealth

First, there is the situation in which a particular industry is one of the chief sources of wealth in the country, and nationals cannot afford to share more of the wealth with non-nationals than is necessary to obtain the capital or knowledge required for proper exploitation. This situation is particularly likely to arise in a less developed economy. The prosperity of Iceland, to take a European example, depends on the fishing industry. Iceland

[1] Non-discriminatory restrictions on freedom of establishment are rules of law or administrative practice imposed on both nationals and non-nationals to prevent the entry of all enterprises not financially or otherwise qualified or to insure the optimum use of national resources. Restrictions may be due to the nature of the business, the form of the enterprise, or the existence of a state monopoly. See Le Droit d'Etablissement dans le Marché Commun, 1958 J.O.R.F. 1000; the French law, as of 1958, and a summary of the legal position in the other member states is given at 1004–10. Obvious examples are the requirements of professional qualifications for doctors and lawyers and of financial standing for banks and insurance companies. In addition, there may be social reasons for restrictions in some areas, e.g., acquisition or subdivision of land. So long as these restrictions are not discriminatory, they may be justified in the EEC by the circumstances of the member state in question. For example, in its present form, the Irish penal stamp duty—a 25% transfer tax on the alienation to a non-national of land not bought for industrial purposes— is contrary to art. 7, but some restrictions on freedom of individuals from outside the immediate rural areas to acquire agricultural land could probably be justified, if they were non-discriminatory, on the grounds of the social, economic, and agrarian problems of rural areas in Ireland; see arts. 39(2), 54(3)(e).

[2] See Streeten, Economic Integration, ch. 4 (1961); MacDougall, "The Benefits and Costs of Private Investment from Abroad: A Theoretical Approach," 22 Bull. Oxford U. Inst. Statistics 189 (1960); Economic Development, Pr. 4803, ch. 4, para. 36 (1958); Manning, "Private Foreign Investment," in Methods of Industrial Development 257 (OECD, 1962). Streeten states the question: "Whether a country should, from a national point of view, discourage capital exports and encourage capital imports will depend on the relation between the divergence of private profits and national gains at home and abroad." Streeten, Economic Integration 80 (1961).

cannot allow non-nationals to participate in its fishing industry, since there are no known alternative sources of wealth adequate to compensate for the profits which would be lost to Icelandic nationals by such participation. Also, fishing grounds are uniquely capable of being exploited by non-nationals who make no contribution to the local economy.

Unwanted Competition with Locally Owned Industry

Second, at a certain stage in the development of a country's economy, restrictions on the right of foreign nationals to establish industries may aid economic development. But protectionist devices such as tariffs and quotas do not prevent foreign enterprises from establishing local manufacturing operations inside the tariff and quota barriers and exploiting the national market.[3] Therefore, where locally owned industry is able to meet national demand, restrictions on the freedom of establishment of non-nationals are a necessary supplement to protective tariffs and quotas. Protection enables locally owned industry to achieve economies of scale and protects it from dumping and from competition in its early stages of development, when its experience and technical skill do not enable it to compete, even on the home market, with foreign-owned firms. In some sections of the economy, such as retail distribution, restrictions on freedom of establishment are the only possible measures of protection, though protection is hardly ever necessary.

Inflationary Effects

Third, substantial amounts of foreign capital entering a country often have an inflationary effect because they flood the capital market or raise the prices of commodities sought by foreigners beyond the prices nationals are prepared to pay. The first effect has occurred notably in Switzerland, which receives recurring waves of foreign money in time of international political or financial crises. The second effect has occurred in Ireland, where foreigners have raised the prices of agricultural land.

Foreign investment adds to the capital and expertise available for economic development in a country.[4] Any new industry will give employment,[5] reduce emigration, and broaden the industrial

[3] Ullastres, "New Methods, Integration and Economic Development," in Methods of Industrial Development 45, 50 (OECD, 1962), points out that foreign investment in a country is more likely if foreign-made products are excluded by tariffs.

[4] This is important because the necessary capital may be available in the developing country (if it is available at all) only out of public funds or from a large number of small investors. Wide diffusion of ownership and the resulting power over management may be economically undesirable. "One [illusion] is that a locally-owned business is better than a foreign one; the opposite is the truth, for advanced technical knowledge flows readily from a great firm to its subsidiaries and a plant which is paid for by foreign capital is a great deal better than one which has to be paid for out of the scanty savings of the Republic." Carter, "The Irish Economy Viewed from Without," 46 Studies 137, 140 (1957).

The Commission of Inquiry into Banking, Currency and Credit, Report, P. No. 2628, para. 424 (1938), said in connection with the Irish legislation on freedom of establishment:

> While it is conceivable that external ownership of a high proportion of capital may be undesirable in certain cases, the question would seem to merit examination whether the stringent provisions of these Acts do not go further than is reasonably required in the public interest . . . . [T]hese Acts . . . have the effect of excluding certain capital investments in industry which might otherwise take place and of concentrating more fully on the domestic market the burden of finding such capital as is required.

[5] Measures for the Economic Development of Under-Developed Countries, U.N. Doc. No. E/1986/ST/ECA/10, paras. 177–83 (1951). A criticism often made of foreign investors is that they make inadequate efforts to appoint local nationals to senior posts. Management contracts in underdeveloped countries often require the managers to train local nationals for senior man-

base. The experience brought in by foreign investment would be obtainable otherwise, if at all, only at greater cost, because businessmen and technicians normally require higher salaries to work for enterprises owned and controlled in countries other than their own. The know-how acquired by employees in a foreign-owned firm could normally be acquired only by emigration. However, "in a developed country an increase in foreign-owned capital may have unfavorable effects unless it occurs in a competitive industry, unless it raises the productivity of labor for a given amount of natural resources, or unless technical knowledge and experience are diffused from foreign firms to the rest of the economy."[6] It does not benefit the local economy if it only buys up existing enterprises. Apart from tax factors, the economic difference between a local operation's having local or foreign owners is the amount of net profits which the latter will withdraw from the local economy and repatriate if exchange controls permit. The extent to which the industry is capital-intensive or labor-intensive and the extent to which it will need to acquire capital goods, raw materials, and services from abroad will be important. A foreign-owned operation will be more likely to obtain raw materials and component parts from its parent company abroad at a later stage of production, and therefore at a higher cost, than a locally owned enterprise, which will be as vertically integrated as is economically reasonable.

Effects on Balance of Payments

The fourth disadvantage concerns effects of foreign investment on a country's balance of payments. This is particularly important if the profit-making capacity of the investment depends on the terms of an agreement or concession made between the host government and the investor. Enterprises investing abroad require higher rates of profit than they demand from investments at home,[7] initially as an incentive to invest in an unfamiliar country, where they often regard the risks of investment as being higher. Where high profits are made on the national market of the capital-importing country and are consistently repatriated, they constitute a considerable drain on the balance of payments. The private profits of the investor may even exceed the social benefits of the investment, i.e., the economic benefits derived by the national economy from increased production, wages, and other local expenditures.

The effects of decisions by the foreign investor are important in connection with balance of payments. Foreign investment is much less stable than local investment, and the capital-importing country may have to maintain liquid reserves, with a consequent loss of yield, to finance repatriation of profits and capital[8] in the currency originally invested. The experience of Britain as banker to the sterling area shows that deflation may be necessitated by such pressure. The cost in foreign exchange of external borrowing by the government is not reduced by the amount of tax charged on the interest, as is the case with external borrowing by private interests, at least in the absence of a double taxation convention.[9]

---

agement and technical posts. On account of the standards of education, management contracts are almost unknown in Ireland.

[6] Streeten, Economic Integration 94 (1961).

[7] Measures for the Economic Development of Under-Developed Countries, U.N. Doc. No. E/1986/ST/ECA/10, paras. 48, 108, 225 (1951); Streeten, Economic Integration 92 (1961).

[8] Id. at 91.

[9] Economic Development, Pr. 4803, ch. 4, para. 36 (1938). However, the interest rate may be raised to take into account the tax deducted at source by the payor.

Another disadvantage of foreign-owned industry is that if demand on the national market falls to a level at which continued operation is uneconomic, a foreign-owned operation will go into liquidation more quickly than a locally owned enterprise, since the former will normally be a subsidiary or branch operation of an enterprise in the same sector of industry,[10] not an operation owned directly by individuals. Capital from the liquidation of a locally owned operation may be reinvested in another sector of the national economy so as to provide employment in place of the operation wound up. If a foreign-owned operation is liquidated, however, the proceeds of liquidation are withdrawn from the national economy.[11] This normally does not represent a net loss of capital to the national economy, since foreign-owned concerns are established with foreign capital. However, in a country such as Ireland, the result of a liquidation has often been the emigration of the former employees, which is a social misfortune and a loss to the national economy of their productive capacity.

The natural but unfortunate response of foreign-owned operations to serious deterioration in conditions of trade applies whether the operation is selling only on the national market or is exporting. However, a foreign-owned operation often does not export.[12] It normally does not export to the country where its parent company is situated, and it usually exports to third countries only if cheap labor, tax or other incentives, or tariff preferences make exporting more profitable for the branch or subsidiary operation than for the parent. Unless the foreign-owned operation exports enough to produce as much foreign exchange as is repatriated as profits, it results in a net drain on the balance-of-payments position of the host country.[13]

Semi-Economic Disadvantages

Apart from the dislike of foreigners by nationalists and the desire to preserve the national identity by preventing the buying up of the country by foreigners, there are other disadvantages, not purely economic, to freedom of establishment. Enterprises involved in the establishment of foreign operations are usually large, at least when compared to existing enterprises in countries which restrict the right of establishment. Especially when the foreign investor is a single large enterprise, governments dislike importing a large amount of foreign-owned capital representing great economic (and therefore, in some circumstances, political)

[10] Especially if it has been set up to retain local markets from which the products of the foreign parent had been excluded by tariffs and quotas. One may agree with Professor Carter that "it is the efficiency of a business which determines whether it will continue in a slump, not the site of its head office" ("The Irish Economy Viewed from Without," 46 Studies 137, 143 [1957]), without denying that in a recession a branch office is likely to be closed before the head office. See Thibièrge, "Le Statut des Sociétés Etrangères," in 1 Le Statut de l'Etranger 239, 302, for the view that it is in the foreign investor's interests to establish a local subsidiary rather than a branch operation; see also Chesné, L'Etablissement des Etrangers en France et la Communauté Economique Européenne 244 (1962).

[11] See Streeten, Economic Integration 91 (1961).

[12] Especially if established behind tariffs or quotas which exclude the products of the parent from the national market. The fact that foreign subsidiary or branch operations often do not export may mean that they are not set up in sectors where the national demand alone would be too small for economical production, or it may mean that in essential sectors, where local production on an uneconomic scale is preferable to importation, the product, by hypothesis of substantial economic importance and in substantial demand, is sold on the national market at an excessive price. See Irish Committee on Industrial Organization, Report into the Motor Vehicle Assembling Industry (1962).

[13] Economic Development, Pr. 4803, ch. 4, para. 36 (1958).

power.[14] This dislike is not confined to newly independent, small, poor, or socialist states; examples of it have occurred in Canada and in France in recent years. The way in which the economic power might be used will vary with the circumstances. Apart from potential diplomatic intervention, this economic power will not be greater than the same amount of capital in the hands of the same number of nationals, but it will be more difficult to subject to governmental control. Substantial foreign investment in a small number of industries is more likely to be disliked than foreign investment evenly distributed throughout the economy.

Governments dislike having important economic sectors,[15] such as basic industries, and "sensitive" sectors, such as agriculture and public services,[16] in the hands of foreign enterprises. This is especially so when the investing enterprise comes from a country which is economically and politically powerful, even if the two governments are on good terms. This consideration is probably less important in Ireland than in most other capital-importing countries likely to become connected with the EEC.

In addition, a government which implements economic plans by financial inducements rather than by direct controls, like the French government, dislikes being unable to influence the international planning of a world-wide enterprise not dependent on local capital. Such planning may even be contrary to local anti-inflationary policy. A government can exercise informal pressure on important financial and policy decisions of a company if the management is composed of nationals whose interests are in the country, but it cannot exercise influence through local boards of a company whose top management is elsewhere and whose concern is for the interests of the group as a whole.

These constitute the principal economic and semi-economic disadvantages of having local operations foreign-owned or financed where local capital and enterprise are prepared to undertake the same operation. However, local capital and enterprise are not always available.

Advantages of foreign investment

If local capital and initiative are not available to undertake the operation, many of the disadvantages of foreign investment still exist, but its advantages, particularly import substitution, will normally outweigh them. Locally manufactured products may be cheaper for the local consumer than the imported commodity, especially if local raw materials are used, if transport costs are high, or if local labor is cheap, as it is likely to be in a developing country. This anti-inflationary effect benefits the balance of payments, and it is especially important if tariffs have been imposed for balance-of-payments reasons.[17] Any exports from local operations also have favorable balance-of-payments effects. On the other hand, repatriation of profits by the operation, usually in foreign currency, may offset this. The government may have made a substantial capital grant to the

[14] See Fatouros, Government Guarantees to Foreign Investors 37 (1962), and the authorities cited there; "Companies Outgrow Countries," The Economist, Oct. 17, 1964, p. 271; and see generally Howe Martin, International Business: Principles and Problems (1964).

[15] See, in this connection, arts. 55, 56; Reply of the Commission in Dec. 1964 to question No. 83/64 in the European Parliamentary Assembly.

[16] Other examples taken from the laws now in force in various European countries are transportation, armaments, energy, publishing, banking, insurance, and shipping. See U.S.-French Convention on Establishment, Nov. 25, 1959, art. V, [1960] 2 U.S.T. & O.I.A. 2398, T.I.A.S. No. 4625.

[17] On the other hand, if local production is not adequate to meet demand, tariffs have an inflationary effect.

new industry, so the additional capital obtained from abroad may not be very great. If tax concessions are given, there may be little immediate revenue advantage from the operations, and the economic benefits to the country will be only the wages paid and the employment given, the demand for local raw materials and services, and the reduced price of the finished product for the local consumer. If shortage of local experience or knowledge, rather than capital, is the difficulty, some of the economic disadvantages can be avoided by having the local operation managed by a foreign enterprise for a fee or royalty under a management agreement or by having local participation in an operation controlled by foreign shareholders. If local experience is available but local capital is not, fixed-interest and non-voting participation by foreign interests would partially solve the problems. But since private foreign investors normally require substantial profits, it is usually impossible to obtain foreign capital in such a way as to limit the share of the profits obtained by the foreign interests.

Incentives to foreign investment

If no exports are contemplated or if successful exporting depends on a guaranteed home market, a government with a small national market may give a foreign or local investor a monopoly of the national market to persuade him to establish a local manufacturing operation.[18] This may also be done if the local market is barely large enough for economies of scale. The increase in the size of the market for local enterprises when a country joins the EEC would reduce the need for protection to insure economies of scale. In theory, restrictions on freedom of establishment should be less necessary in sectors where substantial amounts of capital are required and where economies of scale are greatest, since in these sectors competitors are less likely to enter the market. However, it is in those sectors that businessmen most often ask for a guaranteed monopoly position. Even if there is no law restricting the right of establishment, concession agreements may be given in underdeveloped countries. These agreements often include a provision preventing the government from giving aid to competitors of the concessionaire and may require the government to introduce a tariff to protect the investor from foreign competition. A promise not to give state aid to the investor's competitors may be equivalent in practice to a restriction on the right of establishment, because few investors set up factories in underdeveloped countries without negotiating an agreement for a tax concession or some other state aid.[19] Also, a government may feel obliged to refuse permission for the establishment of, or to refuse state aid to, an enterprise likely to compete on the home market with existing enterprises. Alternatively, the government may make state aid conditional on a guarantee by a new investor that only a specified percentage or a specified number of units of its total production will be sold on the home market. Freedom from even the threat of competition from a new entrant is economically important, whether it is derived from an official assurance or from natural factors such as the small size of the home market or the amount of capital required to commence operations. It means that the only external stimulus to the economic progress of the enterprise concerned will be consumer resistance or an official policy against misuse of monopoly power. The break-up of the monopoly will be impos-

[18] See Measures for the Economic Development of Under-Developed Countries, U.N. Doc. No. E/1986/ST/ECA/10 (1951).

[19] This is, of course, not true of Ireland. In Ireland state aid to export industries is given automatically by way of tax concession, and no negotiation is necessary.

sible, and prevention of abuse of monopoly power is probably the field of restrictive practices in which an effective policy is most difficult to achieve.[20]

This difficulty must be faced if it is really necessary to assure foreign or local interests a monopoly position to induce them to establish industries in a country. In Ireland the government has never felt bound not to aid the establishment of industries which would compete in export markets with existing industries which had received state aid. If state aid is available to existing industry, reluctance to assist new industry to compete on the home market would constitute discrimination and distort competition. It normally would be difficult to ascertain the extent to which administrative discretion was being exercised in this way except where the potential investor is told why the government is unwilling to assist him or where the government has insisted that a specified percentage of the products of the new factory be exported.

There is no substantial distinction between a general incentive to export that is open to any investor within its terms, which Articles 92 or 98 of the Treaty might permit, and state aid to a new enterprise on the condition that it does not compete on the home market with existing enterprises. It is submitted that the Community rules on state aid to existing enterprises by way of protection from competition on the home market should be the same as the rules of Article 85(1) and 85(3) on the territorial division of markets by the enterprises themselves. Article 92 is wide enough to cover this form of state aid. A difficulty arises if the government has a legal obligation, under its concession agreement with the original enterprise, to protect it from competition, and if the enterprise could not continue contributing successfully to economic development unless protected against competition within the national market. It is submitted that if the government is obliged under the Treaty to alter the status quo, the national market should be opened to free competition, except where a market-sharing agreement between the enterprises concerned comes within Article 85(3), and that the government's covenant to protect the enterprise from competition on the national market should be replaced by state aid to the enterprise of approximately the same economic value, which state aid then would be subject to Article 92. Although the Treaty contemplates a regional policy on state aids to industry, economic integration requires complete freedom of establishment and freedom of movement of goods, subject only to the terms of the Treaty.[21]

Many of the above arguments give grounds for controlling the establishment of foreign-owned enterprises rather than prohibiting it. In comprehensive national legislation, the government has considerable administrative discretion to favor establishment of foreign-owned industries which will process local raw materials and provide substitutes for imports, thereby reducing dependence on foreign supplies and raw materials.[22] A license for a foreign investor to establish may be conditional on the use of local construction materials, fuel, raw materials, or advertising services, or on the employment of a specified proportion of local nationals, an important point often dealt with specifically by legislation. However, businessmen dislike having to negotiate for permission to establish or for a tax concession and they prefer—at least in

[20] International Conference on Control of Restrictive Business Practices 142–48 (1960).

[21] E.g., arts. 36, 55, 56.

[22] Potential investors should examine import statistics to ascertain the value and volume of imports of the product which they intend to manufacture, as an argument in favor of permission to establish and for favorable treatment under tax concession and other state aid legislation.

developed countries—to operate under legislation which operates automatically.

FREEDOM OF ESTABLISHMENT IN THE EEC

The nature of the right of establishment and the need for freedom of establishment[23]

To allow economic integration, Article 7 of the EEC Treaty prohibits discrimination on the grounds of nationality among nationals and enterprises of mem-

[23] Various studies of this subject are mentioned in footnotes to this section. See generally, Chesné, L'Etablissement des Etrangers en France et la Communauté Economique Européenne (1962); Everling, The Right of Establishment in the Common Market (1964); Le Statut de l'Etranger et le Marché Commun (57th Congrès des Notaires de France, 1959); Commission du Marché Intérieur of the Parliamentary Assembly, Report [hereinafter cited as the Kreyssig Report], A.P.E. Doc. No. 1 (1961); Vignes, "Le droit d'établissement et les services dans la Communauté Economique Européenne," 7 Annuaire Français de Droit International 668 (1961); Hay, "Some Problems of Doing Business in the Regional Markets of Europe," 17 Rutgers L. Rev. 305, 311–26 (1963); Hay, "Four Lectures on the European Common Market . . .," 24 U. Pitt. L. Rev. 685, 751–66 (1963). See also Loussouarn, "La Condition des Personnes morales en Droit international privé," 96(1) Recueil Académie D. Int. 447 (1959); Pourvoyeur, "La Suppression des Restrictions au Libre Etablissement dans la C.E.E.," 33 La Vie Economique et Sociale 130 (1962); Thompson, "Subsidiary Companies and the Right of Establishment in the Common Market," 1963 J. Bus. Law 119; van Damme, "L'harmonisation du droit d'établissement dans les different groupes régionaux d'Etats," 39 Revue de Droit International et de Droit Comparé 105 (1962). A considerable amount of work has been done by the Council of Europe on freedom of establishment; see European Convention on Establishment, Dec. 13, 1955, European Treaty Series No. 19 (1956). This, however, relates only to individuals and not to legal persons. It has been ratified by several states and came into force in February 1965.

The provisions of EFTA Convention, Jan. 4, 1960, 370 U.N.T.S. 3, on establishment are as follows:

Article 16: Establishment

1. Member States recognise that restrictions on the establishment and operation of economic enterprises in their territories by nationals of other Member States should not be applied, through accord to such nationals of treatment which is less favourable than that accorded to their own nationals in such matters, in such a way as to frustrate the benefits expected from the removal or the absence of duties and quantitative restrictions on trade between Member States.

2. Member States shall not apply new restrictions in such a way that they conflict with the principle set out in paragraph 1 of this Article.

3. Member States shall notify to the Council, within such period as the Council may decide, particulars of any restrictions which they apply in such a way that nationals of another Member State are accorded in their territories less favourable treatment in respect of the matters set out in paragraph 1 of this Article than is accorded to their own nationals.

4. The Council shall consider not later than 31st December, 1964, and may consider at any time thereafter, whether further or different provisions are necessary to give effect to the principles set out in paragraph 1 of this Article, and may decide to make the necessary provisions.

5. Nothing in this Article shall prevent the adoption and enforcement by a Member State of measures for the control of entry, residence, activity and departure of aliens where such measures are justified by reasons of public order, public health or morality, or national security, or for the prevention of a serious imbalance in the social or demographic structure of that Member State.

6. For the purposes of this Article:
   - (a) "nationals" means, in relation to a Member State,
     - (i) physical persons who have the nationality of that Member State and
     - (ii) companies and other legal persons constituted in the territory of that Member State in conformity with the law of that State and which that State regards as having its nationality, provided that they have been formed for gainful purposes and that they have their registered office and central administration, and carry on substantial activity, within the Area of the Association;
   - (b) "economic enterprises" means any type of economic enterprise for production of or commerce in goods

ber states.[24] Discriminatory restrictions on the freedom of nationals and enterprises of other member states to establish business operations must be abolished, even if they are unintentional or if they result from administrative practice.[25] If discrimination results, even from measures designed for legitimate purposes, it is incompatible with the Treaty if its effect is to place nationals of other member states in a position different from that of local nationals. Freedom of nationals and enterprises of member states to establish themselves throughout the EEC fuses the national markets and insures the most efficient use of Community resources, and it insures that managerial, labor, scientific, and technical skills all can operate where the costs of raw materials and transport are most advantageous. The need for freedom of establishment in the EEC is more important than its disadvantages outlined above. Freedom of nationals of member states to establish themselves throughout the Common Market is politically the most important measure of economic integration required by the EEC Treaty and also the most difficult to implement. Foreign ownership of local industry involves political reactions which do not occur in the case of free movement of imported goods or even freedom to render services.[26]

The EEC Treaty provides for free movement of capital and for freedom to use it in the establishment of industrial, commercial, and professional enterprises.[27] Freedom of establishment and freedom to render services are interdependent, and it is not easy to draw a clear distinction between them in law or in economics. Freedom of establishment includes freedom to enter all non-wage-earning activities and freedom to set up and to operate enterprises on a permanent basis.[28] It includes[29] the right to set up a factory, a farm,[30] or any business activity, and to set up an agency, branch operation, or subsidiary company. Freedom to render services is the freedom to carry on business other than merely buying or selling goods on a temporary basis. Services were intended to be in a residual category comprising all activities not under other provisions.[31]

The EEC Treaty does not contemplate unrestricted freedom to establish all forms of enterprise. What it requires is that nationals of all member states be on the same footing in each member state with regard to freedom of establishment (national treatment) and that the requirements for establishment in a given

---

which are of Area origin, whether conducted by physical persons or through agencies, branches or companies or other legal persons.

[24] This applies also in the association of Greece; see Accord créant une association entre la C.E.E. et la Grèce, July 9, 1961, art. 5.

[25] See, e.g., art. 54(3)(c). General Program on Freedom of Establishment, tit. III, 1962 Journal Officiel 36/62, lists the types of provision or practice which constitute restrictions on freedom of establishment. Restrictions on freedom of establishment which result from exchange-control restrictions are dealt with under arts. 67–73. Private restrictions on freedom of establishment are prohibited by art. 7 if they are based on nationality and may be incompatible with arts. 85 and 86 if they are not. Regulations to implement these articles are contemplated by the Treaty.

[26] First General Report, para. 76 (1958).

[27] Schlachter, "Le droit d'établissement dans le Marché Commun et ses problèmes," 30 Annuaire de l'A.A.A. 70, 76–77 (1960).

[28] Le Droit d'Etablissement dans le Marché Commun, 1958 J.O.R.F. 1000. On services, see arts. 59–66.

[29] Vignes, "Le droit d'établissement et les services dans la Communauté Economique Européenne," 7 Annuaire Français de Droit International 668, 675 (1961).

[30] Arts. 54(3)(e), 39(2).

[31] See art. 60; Schlachter, "Le droit d'établissement dans le Marché Commun et ses problèmes," 30 Annuaire de l'A.A.A. 70, 75–76 (1960). Cf. EFTA Convention, art. 16; see note 23.

sector be the same in each member state (harmonization of law).[32] These are quite separate requirements, and both must be carried out to fulfill the demands of the Treaty. To insure equal conditions of competition, non-discriminatory restrictions on freedom of establishment must be harmonized so that artificial factors do not divert investment in a given sector into one member state rather than another.

Freedom to render services throughout the Common Market is enough for small enterprises, in practice; they cannot contemplate the establishment of a branch operation or a subsidiary company, and they are unlikely to move their operations into another member state. For a large enterprise, trading in goods or rendering services in a particular area will normally precede the establishment of a branch operation or a subsidiary there. In these circumstances the exact distinction between establishment and services is academic. This book deals only with establishment because, among other reasons, it deals only with industrial activities of companies and not with individuals.

The scope of and limitations on the right of establishment

Freedom to acquire and freedom to make direct and portfolio investment in companies of all member states is an essential aspect of economic integration. Member states have given nationals of other member states national treatment in regard to financial participation in the capital of Article 58 companies, as is required by Article 221.[33]

Article 220 provides for negotiations between member states to insure, for the benefit of their nationals, national treatment with regard to protection of persons and the enjoyment of rights. This general provision covers national treatment under tax laws, compulsory acquisition of property, public and private (i.e., professional) social security and pension funds, standing in litigation, credit and loans, and all rights with regard to land and personal, industrial, and commercial property. The Treaty does not deal specifically with many of these matters; they do not affect the right of establishment directly, but they have some bearing on it.

The Treaty, in Article 54(3)(f), specifically contemplates freedom of establishment "as regards . . . the entry of personnel belonging to the main establishment into managerial or supervisory posts in . . . agencies, branches and subsidiaries." Freedom to bring in management staff from elsewhere in the Common Market is an aspect of freedom of establishment rather than of free movement of labor. To allow the entry of necessary management staff, the laws of member states relating to residence permits and work permits must be altered to give national treatment to nationals of member states.[34]

If nationals of the member state in question are not free to carry on a particular occupation because it is reserved to the state or prohibited, foreign enterprises cannot undertake the occupation there.[35] Member states may maintain

[32] Schlachter, "Nouveaux Aspects de la liberté d'établissement dans le Traité de Rome," 4 Revue du Marché Commun 75, 76 (1961); Audinet, "Le Droit d'établissement dans la Communauté économique européenne," 86 Journal du Droit International 982, 996 (1959).

[33] See 1961 Journal Officiel 1150/61.

[34] See, however, Committee on Foreign Law, "Current Legal Developments in the European Economic Community," 18 Record of N.Y.C.B.A. 329, 344 (1963); art. 54(3)(d).

[35] Art. 55; see arts. 90, 37. With regard to individuals, art. 55 is of considerable importance since public positions may be reserved for nationals of the member state in question. Art. 55 seems to have little effect on industrial and commercial enterprises, though it might affect some, e.g., banks.

state trading monopolies, but the monopolies may not discriminate between nationals of member states or use their position to replace tariff barriers or quantitative restrictions, and they are subject to the rules on competition. If, instead of a state monopoly, a monopoly has been granted to an organization in which nationals can be members, establishment of enterprises in competition with the monopoly can be prohibited, but nationals of other member states must get national treatment with regard to joining the monopoly organization.

The Council, on the proposal of the Commission, may decide that the Treaty provisions on freedom of establishment shall not apply to specified sectors or activities,[36] and member states may limit freedom of establishment in the interests of public policy, public security, and public health.[37] For enterprises, as distinct from individuals, this is important primarily because member states may adopt measures distorting conditions of competition with respect to goods used for military purposes.[38] The general provision[39] allowing the Commission to derogate from the obligations of a member state under the Treaty by authorizing protective measures may be used if freedom of establishment is causing serious difficulties likely to persist in one sector of the economy of a member state or if there are difficulties which may cause grave economic hardship to a region. The Commission may exercise this power only on the application of a member state. The protective measures must disturb the operation of the Common Market as little as possible and must be necessary to rectify the position and to adapt the sector concerned to the Community economy. The Commission has not suggested the exclusion of any sector from the program on freedom of establishment, and the safeguard provision has not been invoked. The Commission has prepared a list of the sectors regarded by member states as falling within the other provisions.

The right of establishment under the EEC Treaty applies to the sectors of industry under the ECSC[40] and Euratom[41] only in principle and is subject to the provisions of the other two Treaties. Transportation,[42] agriculture, and fisheries are subject in principle to the provisions on freedom of establishment and are dealt with in the Annexes to the General Program on freedom of establishment, discussed below.

The persons and companies entitled to the right of establishment

National treatment with regard to the right to establish is given to nationals (*ressortissants*) of member states.[43] The national law of the member state in question decides whether the individual is a national. Differences between national laws on the nationality of an individual claiming the right of establishment must be settled by private international law or by agreement between the states con-

[36] Ibid.

[37] Art. 56; cf. art. 36, especially the proviso in the last sentence.

[38] Art. 223.

[39] Art. 226.

[40] EEC Treaty, art. 232. For the rules governing freedom of establishment in the field of nuclear energy, see Euratom Treaty, arts. 10, 12, 14, 15, 17, 49, 97, 98, 100, 144.

[41] It is agreed that freedom of establishment must be created in the sectors of coal, steel, and nuclear energy; Gaudet, "Aspects Juridiques de la liberté d'établissement dans le Marché Commun," lecture to the Association Néerlandaise des Juristes Européens, April 29, 1961, at 12.

[42] Kreyssig Report, A.P.E. Doc. No. 1, paras. 51, 64 (1961).

[43] Art. 52. For a discussion of the connotations of *ressortissants*, see Vignes, "Chronique juridique des Communautés européennes," 40 Revue de Droit Internationale et de Droit Comparé 9, 24 (1963).

cerned. Article 58 assimilates certain companies and firms to nationals of member states for the purposes of the right of establishment and freedom of services.[44] The legal entities which are given these rights may be constituted under civil law, commercial law, or public law, and they include cooperative societies and at least some unincorporated associations. State trading companies, including those which are not fiscal monopolies and are not intended to make substantial profits at the expense of the public, are given the right of establishment, but private companies not intended to make profits are not.

The Basic Principles

The provisions relating to freedom of establishment of companies are based on two principles. First, the Treaty does not lay down any requirements as to the nationality or residence of the directors or shareholders.[45] The right of establishment can be claimed if there is an existing economic link with the economy of a member state. If national laws do not permit this link to be created, the Treaty gives no right of establishment to enterprises of non-member states. Second, since the whole Community is to be a single market, a company established in one part of the Common Market is entitled to establish itself in any other part. The latter principle overrides any national law discriminating against companies owned by nationals of non-member states, at least if the connection of the foreign-owned company with the Common Market is a genuine economic one. The Treaty does not prevent the enactment of a uniform law in all member states restricting the freedom of nationals of non-member states to establish companies in the Common Market.[46] However, unless such a law is enacted, the Treaty gives an absolute right to Americans and other nationals of non-member states to establish companies if they can bring themselves within the Treaty's terms.

Establishment of Primary and Secondary Operations

A legal entity, usually a company, enjoys the right of establishment[47] only if it is formed under the law of a member state[48] and has within the Common Market either[49] its central administration, its

[44] See Chesné, L'Etablissement des Etrangers en France et la Communauté Economique Européenne 219–36 (1962); Scholz, Bruns-Wuestefeld, Le Tallec & Bronsart, "The Right of Establishment in the EEC," in International Manual on the European Economic Community 233, 243, 246 (Junckerstorff ed. 1963).

[45] See Piot, "Du réalisme dans les conventions d'établissement," 88 Journal du Droit International 38, 76 (1961).

[46] Such a law would be forbidden by art. 7 if the broad interpretation that art. 7 prohibits discrimination against the nationals of non-member states on the grounds of nationality is correct. More important, such a uniform law might be a breach of treaties on freedom of establishment, including the United States treaties of friendship, commerce, and navigation.

[47] As to services, see arts. 59, 66.

[48] The phrase *constituées en conformité de la législation* in art. 58 literally means "constituted in conformity with the law" of a member state. In practice it would be almost impossible for a company to be constituted in conformity with the law of a member state if it were incorporated under the law of a non-member state.

[49] The official view is that these are alternative requirements. The requirement of incorporation and a registered office in a member state may be repetitious. In the text the phrases "principal place of management," *siège réel,* and "central administration" are used interchangeably. See Audinet, "Le droit d'établissement dans la Communauté Economique Européenne," 86 Journal du Droit International 982, 1016 (1959). Chesné, L'Etablissement des Etrangers en France et la Communauté Economique Européenne 279–81 (1962), argues that since *administration centrale* and *principal établissement* mean the same thing in the laws of several member states, the word *ou* between them means "in other words," not "alternatively." On

principal establishment (*principal établissement*),[50] or its registered office.[51]

A company formed under the law of a member state and fulfilling one of the three alternative requirements of Article 58 has the right to establish its primary operations, such as its principal place of production or operations or its place of central management, anywhere in the Common Market. If Article 58 is satisfied by a formal registered office, a company which is incorporated in a member state and which has a formal registered office anywhere in the EEC theoretically may establish its primary operations anywhere in the Common Market, even if it has no real economic link with the EEC. However, in the absence of a convention on recognition of foreign companies, the national laws of the Six govern a company's freedom of establishment. The Six

---

this view all three phrases are synonymous and repetitious, and *siège statutaire* means "head office." Art. 2 of the Hague draft convention on the recognition of companies, Conférence de la Haye de Droit International Privé, "Projet de Convention . . .," [1952] 1 Actes de la Septième Session, 1951, at 385, identifies the central administration of a company with the *siège réel*. Compare the Irish and English tax concept of "management and control."

[50] *Principal établissement* probably means primarily the "principal place of management," but it also includes a company's principal place of business operations. If it did not, a company incorporated and doing business entirely within the EEC would be denied the right of establishment merely because it was managed outside the EEC. This seems unlikely, since the Treaty does not discriminate against companies owned or managed by nationals of non-member states. Chesné, L'Etablissement des Etrangers en France et la Communauté Economique Européenne 279–81 (1962), regards the *principal établissement* as the place where the board of directors and the general meeting of the company assemble, and regards the three phrases in art. 58(1) as synonymous.

[51] There has been controversy as to whether art. 58 requires only a formal registered office or the genuine head office (*siège réel*) of the company. The matter is not free from difficulty, and the alternative interpretations must be kept in mind. The official interpretation is that a formal registered office is sufficient; see General Program on Freedom of Establishment, tit. I, 1962 Journal Officiel 36/62. M. Gaudet, the Directeur Général au Service Juridique des Executifs Européens, said that the Commission took this view, and he pointed out that under the national laws, as they then stood, the transfer of a registered office from one member state to another would involve the dissolution of the company; "Aspects Juridiques de la liberté d'établissement dans le Marché Commun," lecture to the Association Néerlandaise des Juristes Européens, April 29, 1961, at 10. The Commission must know the intention of the framers of the Treaty. The General Program avoids stating this view expressly, since the Commission avoids prejudging issues which can be settled only by the Court.

However, according to the General Program, for a company to obtain the right to establish branches, subsidiaries, and agencies throughout the EEC, if it has not its central administration or principal place of business there, it must show that its operations involve an effective and continued connection (*un lien effectif et continu*) with the economy of a member state (or of an overseas territory), and "this connection cannot be based on nationality, even the nationality of the shareholders, the directors or the auditors or the supervisors or the individuals holding the company's capital."

The General Program is not always correctly understood; it requires an "effective and continued connection" with the economy of a member state only where the Treaty requires that the company be "established" in connection with the right to establish branches, and not pursuant to art. 58. Notwithstanding the official view, it seems reasonable that the phrase *siège statutaire* should be understood to mean the concept as it exists in the national laws of five of the member states. The Treaty often uses precise technical terms from one legal system without intending their technical meaning. This interpretation permits the three phrases in art. 58 to be interpreted *eiusdem generis* with each other. It is not inconsistent with the General Program, which in connection with primary operations merely repeats the Treaty provision. It is open, however, to the objection that the drafters of the Treaty could have said *siège réel* if they had meant it.

Art. 58 fulfills a positive and a negative function; it grants the right of establishment to some companies owned by nationals of non-member states, and it deprives some companies of the right to establish themselves even if they

(except the Netherlands[52]) do not recognize a company as validly formed unless it has a genuine office (*siège réel*) in the state where it is incorporated.[53] Thus, a right of establishment based on incorporation and only a formal registered office has little practical importance before the advent of the convention contemplated by Article 220.[54]

To have the right to establish secondary operations such as branches, subsidiaries, and agencies throughout the EEC, a company must comply with Article 58 and must also be "established,"[55] i.e., have an "effective and continued connection"[56] with the economy of a member state. This requirement has been explained[57] as requiring continuing business activities in the relevant sector of the economy of the member state and permanent premises occupied by the enterprise. A company which had its central administration or principal business operations in a member state would automatically be "established" in the Common Market.

The Question of What Constitutes a Registered Office Within Article 58

A difficult and important question is whether the Treaty gives a company with a merely formal registered office in a member state the right to establish its central administration in another member state, thereby permitting it to avoid restrictions on establishment under the laws of the second state, or whether this is prevented by the Treaty, not merely by national laws. If a formal registered office satisfies Article 58, the proposed

are incorporated in a member state. Nationals are deprived of the right to establish a company which they own if it is incorporated outside, or has its central administration and its principal place of business outside, the Common Market. This may well have been intended, for example, to hinder tax-haven operations. The negative function of art. 58 with regard to nationals of non-member states could only be to prevent such people's avoiding the strict provisions of the national law of one member state by acquiring a purely formal relationship with the economy of another. If it does not do this, it does not effectively limit the freedom of nationals of non-member states to set up companies in the EEC. Viewed in this light, the literal interpretation of art. 58, which makes the phrase *siège statutaire* largely unnecessary in view of the need for incorporation and which makes it contrast with the alternative requirements of a real economic link, seems odd.

On the whole problem, see Chesné, L'Etablissement des Etrangers en France et la Communauté Economique Européenne 276–87 (1962); Scholz, Bruns-Wuestefeld, Le Tallec & Bronsart, "The Right of Establishment in the EEC," in International Manual on the European Economic Community 233, 244 (Junckerstorff ed. 1963).

[52] See Law of July 25, 1959, cited by Chesné, L'Etablissement des Etrangers en France et la Communauté Economique Européenne 277 (1962).

[53] Vignes, "Le droit d'établissement et les services dans la Communauté Economique Européenne," 7 Annuaire Française de Droit International 668, 693 (1961); Audinet, "Le droit d'établissement dans la Communauté économique européenne," 86 Journal du Droit International 982, 1014–20 (1959).

[54] The Committee on Foreign Law, "Current Legal Developments in the European Economic Community," 18 Record of N.Y.C.B.A. 329, 344 (1963), says: "Since a company organized in one member state cannot completely transfer itself to another, the right of 'principal establishment' provided for by Article 52 may primarily benefit individuals. Companies are primarily benefited by the right to establish branches and subsidiaries."

[55] Art. 52.

[56] The quotation is from the explanation given in the General Program on Freedom of Establishment, 1962 Journal Officiel 36/62, of the meaning of art. 52 in the case of companies.

[57] Gaudet, "Aspects Juridiques de la liberté d'établissement dans le Marché Commun," lecture to the Association Néerlandaise de Juristes Européens, April 29, 1961, at 11; see also Scholz, Bruns-Wuestefeld, Le Tallec & Bronsart, "The Right of Establishment in the EEC," in International Manual on the European Economic Community 233, 246 (Junckerstorff ed. 1963).

convention on reciprocal recognition of companies will raise issues which are of considerable economic importance and are more than merely technical legal questions. Harmonization of national laws on freedom of establishment might be a prerequisite to the convention's being ratified. The laws of Ireland and Britain allow a company to be incorporated in a country where it has only a formal registered office. If Ireland and Britain join the EEC, companies incorporated under their laws but with no real economic connection with either country will have the right of establishment throughout the EEC if the Treaty does not require more than a formal registered office in the EEC.[58]

If a convention establishing a federal, European-type company is adopted, this issue will have to be considered. When the conditions under which companies can be established in each member state are harmonized, there will be no question of investors' avoiding the law of one state by incorporating elsewhere in the EEC and carrying on their operations in the first state.

This situation is unlikely to arise as long as national laws make it impossible to have the registered office and the principal place of management of a company in different member states. Also, even if a company cannot establish itself in the state in which it wishes to operate, if it has its principal place of management anywhere in the EEC it can establish a subsidiary there. Since Articles 58 and 52 can be satisfied by a holding company which itself has few real business functions but is "established" and has its principal place of management in a member state,[59] there is little object in denying a company with only a registered office in the EEC the same rights. The real question may be whether companies owned by nationals of non-member states are to have the right of establishment. If so, the answer is that the Treaty cannot be interpreted so as to deprive them of it effectively, but that the Treaty does not prevent their being deprived of it by a uniform law adopted by all member states. This will become very important for United States investors in Europe if France continues to press for Community measures to restrict United States investment in European industry.

ARTICLE 52 AND ARTICLE 58

If a company which is incorporated but not "established" (within the meaning of Article 52) in a member state has one of the three types of operation specified in Article 58, it can establish itself.[60] If Article 58 adds anything to the right to establish branches and subsidiaries conferred by Article 52, as distinct from merely stating the conditions in which companies can exercise that right, either

[58] If the national laws of member states are used to interpret art. 58 and if the laws of new member states may be so used, the accession of Ireland and Britain will alter the consensus of national laws in favor of the view that a merely formal connection with a member state would be sufficient to give a company the right of establishment provided by the Treaty. See Chapter Four.

[59] Gaudet, "Aspects Juridiques de la liberté d'établissement dans le Marché Commun," lecture to the Association Néerlandaise des Juristes Européens, April 29, 1961, at 11, says that to be "established" within the meaning of art. 52 a company must have business activities in "the relevant sector" of the economy of a member state. This could mean that a company will be regarded as being "established" only if its operations in the EEC are in the sector in which it wishes to establish branch operations, but the Treaty gives no support to such a strict view. It would be reasonable, however, to prevent an enterprise from acquiring the right to establish itself in some particularly "sensitive" or important sector by establishing itself in some entirely different sector.

[60] On the connection between arts. 52 and 58, see Audinet, "Le droit d'établissement dans la Communauté économique européenne," 86 Journal du Droit International 982, 1020 (1959).

it must confer a right to establish something more than a mere branch or its three alternatives do not necessarily amount to being "established." Article 58 clearly gives a company which is within its terms the right, subject to the present rules of national law, to establish its central administration or its principal operations in or to move them to any part of the EEC; it does not merely confer the right to establish branch operations. The interpretation of Article 58 that the three alternatives do not necessarily constitute being "established" is unlikely, unless a nominal registered office satisfies the Article, in which case this interpretation becomes necessary.[61] If "principal establishment" in Article 58 includes a principal place of operations, the Treaty gives a company with its principal place of operations in the EEC the right to have its principal place of management anywhere else in the EEC. However, a company may not be able to exercise this right because most national laws require it to have its principal place of management in the country in which it is incorporated. Unless a formal registered office satisfies Article 58, a company within Article 58 will automatically be "established" and have the right to establish branches. Even if a formal registered office is within the meaning of Article 58, a company with only a formal registered office in the EEC will not have the right to establish branches throughout the EEC.[62] A company which is incorporated in a member state and "established" within the Common Market through a branch will have the right to establish its head office or branch operations throughout the EEC only if it comes within Article 58.[63] However, if such a company incorporates a subsidiary within the Common Market and if the subsidiary has its principal place of management there, the subsidiary, but not the parent, will have the right of establishment. The fact that an enterprise has the right to establish even branches only if it has its central administration in the EEC has the presumably inevitable effect of differentiating between incorporated and unincorporated branch operations in the EEC of companies outside it.

THE POSITION OF NATIONALS OF NON-MEMBER STATES

In view of the importance of the right of establishment for the future, it is useful to analyze it from the point of view of a new company whose shareholders are not nationals of a member state. If the law of the member state where it is intended to locate the principal operations and the management permits the establishment of the company there, no difficulty arises. If this state's law does not permit the company to be established there without claiming the benefit of the Treaty, the company must comply with

[61] If *principal établissement* means the same thing as *administration centrale* and *siège réel*, all the company's operations, other than the place where it is managed and controlled, are branches, agencies, or subsidiaries within the meaning of art. 52. See Gaudet, "Aspects Juridiques de la liberté d'établissement dans le Marché Commun," lecture to the Association Néerlandaise des Juristes Européens, April 29, 1961, at 11.

[62] Information Service of the European Communities, The Right of Establishment and the Supply of Services 6 (1962).

[63] Companies come under art. 52 only by virtue of and in accordance with the terms of art. 58. If art. 58 requires only a formal registered office, then having an unincorporated branch operation in the EEC will confer the right to establish on a company incorporated in a member state. If this is not the correct interpretation of art. 58, only a company whose primary operations are within the Common Market would have the right to establish branches under art. 52. This seems incompatible with art. 52, which, though it requires an establishment, does not require the company to have its principal establishment in the Common Market for it to have the right to set up branches. It also makes art. 52's requirement of an establishment tautologous.

Article 58. It must be incorporated in some other member state, and under most national laws it probably will have to locate its central administration there. If it wishes to have only its central administration in the first member state and if that state's law does not prevent this, it sets up its principal operations, and this apparently gives it the right of establishment under the Treaty. If it wishes to obtain the right of establishment to set up its principal operations, all it needs to do is to set up its central administration in another member state. It can establish both its business operations and its principal place of management in the first member state, whose restrictions on freedom of establishment are causing the difficulty, only if that state's law allows it to move its principal place of management into that state after it has been set up elsewhere. The principal place of management must be set up elsewhere in order to give the company the right to establish its business operations in the first member state. If a company with only a formal registered office in the EEC has the right of establishment under Article 58, then by setting up this office a company could acquire the right to establish both its business operations and its principal place of management in the first member state, subject only to its national law. The question arises whether the central administration or *siège réel* of a company with no other place of business in the EEC is a real enough economic link to be the basis of the right of establishment. If it is not, the company could probably set up a small place of business which would be its "principal establishment" which it would be entitled to transfer to the desired country, the small establishment then being wound up. This result is so odd that one is forced to the conclusion that the establishment of the *siège réel* or central administration of a company which has no actual place of production is sufficient to satisfy Article 58.[64]

Because of the rules of national law already mentioned, if the right to establish operations is claimed for a company incorporated in another country, care must be taken to prevent the *siège réel* of the company from being moved from that country when the operations are set up.

Implementing the Treaty provisions on freedom of establishment[65]

The Treaty prohibits discriminatory restrictions on the right of establishment.[66] Drawn pursuant to Article 54(1), the General Program[67] for the abolition of existing restrictions lists the individuals and companies which have the right of establishment, the types of provision which constitute restrictions on freedom of establishment, and the timetable and the conditions for the achievement of freedom of establishment in the various sectors. It is not legally binding, except probably on the organs of the Commu-

[64] This means that no great difference in practice would be made by accepting the literal and officially endorsed interpretation of the phrase *siège statutaire* in art. 58.

[65] See Scholz, Bruns-Wuestefeld, Le Tallec & Bronsart, "The Right of Establishment in the EEC," in International Manual on the European Economic Community 233, 238–42 (Junckerstorff ed. 1963); Oppermann, "L'application des programmes généraux de la C.E.E. concernant la liberté d'établissement et la libre prestation des services," 7 Revue du Marché Commun 544 (1964).

[66] Art. 53. There is no requirement that new non-discriminatory provisions should be coordinated, unless, as seems reasonable, art. 54(3)(b) is interpreted as creating an obligation that binds the national authorities to collaborate effectively with one another and with the Commission in respect of the measures they adopt; cf. art. 102.

[67] 1962 Journal Officiel 36/62.

nity themselves,[68] in the sense that it can be altered or departed from only by a unanimous vote. The Program is being carried out by directives issued by the Council;[69] this must be done gradually because of the disruptive effects which would result from suddenly introducing unlimited competition[70] and because of the different methods used in the member states for limiting freedom of establishment in various sectors. Some states limit freedom of establishment by preventing non-nationals from establishing themselves, but impose no restrictions on nationals; some impose comprehensive restrictions on the freedom of both nationals and non-nationals to establish themselves.[71] Merely giving national treatment to nationals of member states would have different effects according to the principle on which the laws of the country were based. National treatment for nationals of all member states could be assured in each of the Six by fairly simple directives, but in order to insure the maximum freedom of establishment for all nationals of member states,[72] directives must harmonize the conditions of establishment in all member states in each sector. Coordination of legislation, regulations, and administrative rules of member states on freedom of establishment will involve a number of directives and will eventually affect all the laws relating to economic and professional activity in the Community. Directives could be so specific about the result to be achieved that they would almost result in uniform laws in each member state, but it is unlikely that this will be necessary in connection with freedom of establishment.[73]

If entering into or carrying on business in a sector is regulated by legislation in one member state, because of the importance of the sector to the economy or social structure of the state concerned, the voting in the Council must be unanimous. Directives to coordinate national laws on protecting savings, granting credit, and carrying on banking also must be approved unanimously.[74] In

[68] Vignes, "Le droit d'établissement et les services dans la Communauté Economique Européenne," 7 Annuaire Français de Droit International 668, 669 (1961); Gaudet, "Aspects Juridiques de la liberté d'établissement dans le Marché Commun," lecture to the Association Néerlandaise des Juristes Européens, April 29, 1961, at 22. The argument is that since the Council had to adopt the General Program unanimously, a qualified majority may not adopt a directive inconsistent with it, and that if a directive pursuant to it was issued by a qualified majority of the Council, one of the minority states could challenge the validity of the directive on the grounds that it was incompatible with the General Program.

[69] See, e.g., 1963 Journal Officiel 466/63, 1323/63, 1326/63, 1609/63; 1962 Journal Officiel 46/62, 167/62; 1961 Journal Officiel 147/61.

[70] Le Droit d'Etablissement dans le Marché Commun, 1958 J.O.R.F. 1000.

[71] Gaudet, "Aspects Juridiques de la liberté d'établissement dans le Marché Commun," lecture to the Association Néerlandaise des Juristes Européens, April 29, 1961, at 5; Schlachter, "Nouveaux Aspects de la Liberté d'Etablissement dans le Traité de Rome," 4 Revue du Marché Commun 75–76 (1961); Audinet, "Le droit d'établissement dans la Communauté Economique Européenne," 86 Journal du Droit International 982, 1025–26 (1959); Piot, "Du réalisme dans les conventions d'établissement," 88 Journal du Droit International 38, 70 (1961); Schlachter, "Le droit d'établissement dans le Marché Commun et ses problèmes," 30 Annuaire de l'A.A.A. 70, 79 (1960).

[72] See art. 54(3)(c).

[73] Art. 54(3)(g) uses the phrase "coordinating to the necessary extent and rendering of equal value." See Gaudet, "Aspects Juridiques de la liberté d'établissement dans le Marché Commun," lecture to the Association Néerlandaise des Juristes Européens, April 29, 1961, at 6, 18, 19, 24.

[74] Unanimity is also required for the coordination of the national laws on the medical, paramedical, and pharmaceutical professions, and the obligation to extend national treatment to non-nationals is conditional on this coordination's being carried out; art. 57(2), 57(3). The

other cases, the Council may act by qualified majority. The Council and the Commission are to insure collaboration between national authorities and the establishment of a system of priorities,[75] pursuant to the Program on freedom of establishment. Freedom of establishment might coexist with unequal conditions of competition if the member states gave aid to encourage establishment to all enterprises or if they gave aid on a discriminatory basis. State aids must be abolished insofar as they affect conditions of establishment, subject to the provisions with regard to less developed regions.[76]

Freedom of establishment in new member states

The Birkelbach Report[77] stated that on the accession or association of a new member state more companies from the new member state would establish branches in the existing member states than vice versa. Enterprises already operating in the Common Market would give only part of their attention to the new national market. For the enterprises of the new member state, the enlargement of the market would be relatively much greater, and they would be led to strengthen their connections with the existing member states. This tendency would be more pronounced if the new member state was a small market, unless it was acceding with a larger new member state, for whose markets the small state would be an advantageous base of operations, as Ireland could expect to be. The tendency would be less pronounced if at the time of the accession of the new member state it was clear that state aids to investment in the new member state would be permitted by the Commission to encourage the flow of capital into the new member state.

Any state acceding to the Treaty must accept the provisions with regard to freedom of establishment and free movement of capital. Freedom of establishment between the new member state and the existing member states will be brought about by gradual, reciprocal liberalization. If the existing member states at once gave the acceding state the benefit of the liberalization they had achieved at the date of accession and if the new member state liberalized its laws only gradually, the tendency for capital to flow from the new state into the existing member states would be accentuated. While apparently to the advantage of the new member state, this policy might cause balance-of-payments difficulties. If the acceding states were highly industrialized, this policy would expose the existing member states to the full force of competition from the acceding state's industry. Gradual, reciprocal liberalization is appropriate because the right of establishment must be coordinated with freedom of movement of goods, labor, and capital, and this cannot be suddenly or unilaterally liberalized. For example, freedom of establishment under the treaty of association of Greece is to be brought about "gradually and in a balanced fashion."[78] Never-

---

Council must also issue directives for the reciprocal recognition of qualifications and degrees; art. 57(1).

The Council has a residuary power to harmonize by unanimous vote laws affecting the Common Market; art. 100. Under arts. 54(2), 55, 56(2), 57(1), 57(2), the Council may act by a qualified majority vote.

[75] Art. 54(3)(a) provides that priority must be given to insuring freedom of establishment where it would make a particularly valuable contribution to the development of production and trade.

[76] Art. 92; General Program on Freedom of Establishment, 1962 Journal Officiel 36/62, 39/62.

[77] Birkelbach Report, A.P.E. Doc. No. 122, para. 49 (1961–62).

[78] Accord créant une association entre la C.E.E. et la Grèce, July 9, 1961, art. 47.

theless, the Commission will try to assimilate the position of acceding states to that of existing states as quickly as possible because of administrative convenience and because of the fact that having special arrangements reduces the importance of the common policies and rules and vitiates the idea of a community. The Commission therefore will try to avoid reopening arrangements made, for example, for the coordination of both conditions of entry into non-salaried activities[79] and laws on public policy, public security, and health.[80] Since some of these matters will be dealt with in the negotiations, the Council will be able to act by a qualified majority only within the framework of the agreement reached, and the provisions relating to consultation of Community organs[81] will be modified *pro tanto*. It is not clear how far it is necessary to consult the Assembly and the Economic and Social Committee before agreeing on arrangements with the acceding state involving effects on the internal regimes of the existing member states.[82]

Associated countries contemplating full membership must eventually liberalize their laws and assimilate them to those of member states. For example, the treaty of association with Greece[83] provides that reciprocal freedom of establishment for residents of Greece and of the Common Market, in accordance with the principles of the EEC Treaty, will be effectuated but that the time limits and the General Program and directives in force in the Six will not apply. The time limits and the methods of achieving freedom of establishment between the EEC and Greece are to be settled by the Council of Association for each sector after the directives dealing with that sector have been issued by the EEC Council, and are to take into consideration the special economic and social circumstances of Greece.

Since freedom of establishment under the EEC Treaty involves gradual suppression of all restrictions on freedom of establishment of nationals of member states throughout the Common Market,[84] it is different in nature and in scope from the rights given by traditional treaties on establishment, and it is difficult to analyze it further. For countries which have no treaties of establishment with member states, accession to the Treaty will involve a much greater enlargement of the rights of their enterprises and of enterprises of member states than for those countries which already have treaties of establishment with the Six.

FREEDOM OF ESTABLISHMENT IN IRELAND

The objects of the present legislation

The Irish legislation[85] restricting the freedom of establishment of aliens was enacted to protect both foreign-owned and locally owned enterprises against competition from foreign-owned factories in Ireland, as an incentive to investment. The Irish government still recognizes a moral obligation to protect the industries set up on this basis.[86] Ireland has made few treaties of establishment, and the

[79] Art. 58(2).

[80] Art. 56.

[81] The Assembly and the Economic and Social Committee; arts. 54(1), 54(2), 56(2), 57(1), 57(2).

[82] Arts. 54(1), 237.

[83] Arts. 47, 48.

[84] Gaudet, "Aspects Juridiques de la liberté d'établissement dans le Marché Commun," lecture to the Association Néerlandaise des Juristes Européens, April 29, 1961, at 4.

[85] Primarily, Control of Manufactures Act, 1932 Pub. Stat. 427, and Control of Manufactures Act, 1934 Pub. Stat. 721 [hereinafter cited as 1932 Act and 1934 Act, respectively], as amended by Industrial Development (Encouragement of External Investment) Act, 1958 Acts 351 [hereinafter cited as 1958 Act].

[86] See, for example, 165 Dáil Eireann, Parl. Deb., col. 532 (1958).

government has not made exceptions to the legislation[87] which was enacted after the country became independent. Owing to the liberal tradition derived from British law, there were few discriminatory restrictions on freedom of establishment, and therefore a comprehensive and complex measure was regarded as necessary. The debates in the Irish Parliament indicate some confusion on the reasons for the legislation, one of a series of protectionist measures commencing with the raising of tariffs, and the functions it could be expected to perform. No control was exercised over competition from Irish-owned industries or the freedom of Irish nationals to establish industries. In spite of the potentially inflationary effect of high tariffs and production on an uneconomic scale, the legislation did not prevent duplication and waste of resources or establishment of uneconomic enterprises.[88] Foreign-owned branch manufacturing operations set up to avoid Irish tariffs were regarded as less desirable than the kinds of industry permitted by the legislation.

The aim of the 1958 Act was to allow foreign investment which would increase exports but to retain some protection for firms already established and for Irish-owned enterprises on the home market. Consequently, a foreign-owned company which intends to export most of its products is free from all restrictions. The acts have been largely preventive, and no prosecutions under them have ever been brought.

The scope of the legislation

Although a company must be incorporated in Ireland to take advantage of some of the provisions of the 1958 Act, it applies to all companies wherever incorporated; it ends the restrictions on manufacturing by individuals and partnerships.[89] The act applies only to "manufacturing processes," which are defined[90] as making, altering, finishing, or adapting for sale[91] by the use of mechanical power any article, material, or substance. Repairs and industrial activities not involving the use of mechanical power are not subject to any restriction.

Permission to Manufacture Any Commodity

(1) A company may[92] carry on any "manufacturing process" if it exports at least 90 per cent in value of its total output.[93] The 1958 Act allows a company to carry on business "primarily" for export, in which case its sales on the Irish market of each commodity on which it uses mechanical power must be "incidental" to its export trade in that com-

[87] See, for example, U.S.-Irish Treaty of Friendship, Commerce and Navigation, Jan. 21, 1950, art. VI(4), [1950] U.S.T. & O.I.A. 785, T.I.A.S. No. 2155, Ir. T.S. No. 7 of 1950, P. No. 9791, 206 U.N.T.S. 269 (1955), and the Minutes of Interpretation, under which the Control of Manufacturers Acts continue to apply to United States citizens. The Irish legislation would have needed to perform this function if emigration had not prevented the Irish population from rising.

[88] This is one of the functions of the corresponding legislation in Greece and is the object of the restrictions on freedom of establishment enacted in the Netherlands in 1933.

[89] 1958 Act, § 5(4)(a). The Act does not apply to industrial and provident societies under the Industrial and Provident Societies Acts, 1893, 56 & 57 Vict. c. 39, which are a type of cooperative company which is important in Ireland. Surprisingly, no foreign investors seem to have taken advantage of this.

[90] 1958 Act, § 2.

[91] Adapting for sale includes packing, bottling, and labeling for sale. See 1932 Act, § 1. There is no restriction on a retailer's altering an article intended to be sold at retail or on agriculture or the processing of certain agricultural products (milling wheat, adapting any product of milled wheat for sale, and working slaughterhouses—1958 Act, § 11), or manufacturing cement. All of these are dealt with by other legislation.

[92] 1934 Act, § 9(1); 1958 Act, § 5.

[93] 1958 Act, § 5(1)(a), 5(3).

modity, or "taking one year with another,"[94] it must export at least 90 per cent in value of all the commodities it manufactures.[95]

Aliens can always form a separate company to export a commodity which they have not previously manufactured in Ireland, and the new company will come under this provision. Like any other arrangement which enables a company to increase its exports, this will have official approval. This is the most important and attractive provision in the whole legislation; no permission to manufacture is required. Since most foreign investors take advantage of the tax concessions for profits from exports, it provides the natural basis for foreign investment in Ireland. A company established on this basis will be in a strong position when negotiating for grants and will get the maximum amount of assistance from the Irish government. The company may be of unlimited size, and no Irish participation in the ownership or in the management or control[96] is necessary at any stage.

(2) An "excluded company"[97] may manufacture any commodity. An excluded company is a public company[98] that is incorporated, managed, and controlled[99] in Ireland and limited by shares, not by guarantee. One of the principal objects of the company must be to manufacture a commodity intended for export, and the charter of the company must so provide. Each class of its voting shares[100] must have been listed on one of the Irish stock exchanges, and the stock exchange must be satisfied that at least 50 per cent of each class of voting shares have been bona fide issued for public subscription in Ireland and have been made available "primarily"[101] to Irish citizens or to companies incorporated, managed, and controlled in Ireland. However, these shares need not have been bought or held by them. Each prospectus must mention that one of the company's principal objects is manufacturing for export, and the company must act on this. Since the 1958 Act requires only that a listing on the stock exchange be granted, the loss of a listing will not involve loss of status as an "excluded" company.[102]

[94] This phrase is not intended to require a mathematical average. See 169 Dáil Eireann, Parl. Deb., col. 878 (1958).

[95] No test for "incidental" sales is suggested by the 1958 Act. Presumably, a factory producing a quantity of high quality products could sell faulty but marketable products or byproducts on the home market even if these sales were over 10% of its total sales. Such a percentage is high in most industries, particularly over a period of more than one year. Any company which exported, on the average, less than 90% of its total output would probably be deprived of the advantage of freedom from the need for administrative approval, especially in view of the ambiguity of the phrase "taking one year with another."

[96] It may be advisable to have at least one Irish director to take part in negotiations with the government or the Grants Board to lend substance to the contention that the company is managed and controlled in Ireland for tax purposes. This is advantageous whatever the basis on which the company is entitled to establish manufacturing operations.

[97] 1958 Act, § 4(2), 4(3).

[98] As distinct from a private or closely held company. See pp. 110–12.

[99] In tax law, the phrase "controlled in Ireland" means in effect that the directors' meetings are held in Ireland, and it presumably has the same meaning in the context of this chapter.

[100] But not debentures; 1932 Act, § 1.

[101] Any public issue of shares on Irish stock exchanges only would be "primarily" available to Irish citizens. If a public issue so made was over-subscribed, it is not clear whether it would be necessary to give preference to Irish citizens or companies in allotting the shares. It is submitted that no such preference is required by the Act; it would be inconsistent with ordinary commercial practice, and the Act requires only that shares "have been made available primarily" to Irish subscribers.

[102] This was certainly the intention; see 166 Dáil Eireann, Parl. Deb., col. 989 (1958). Since questions of the contravention of these Acts are

This provision allows foreign investors to establish an Irish company with Irish participation and thereafter to sell on the Irish home market. It also enables foreign investors to acquire, on the stock exchange, a controlling interest in an existing Irish manufacturing company, which will remain free to manufacture any commodity.

(3) A company may manufacture any commodity if the "fixed assets" used in its entire business do not exceed £5,000 ($14,000) in value,[103] regardless of ownership of the assets.

(4) A company which has been manufacturing any commodity in Ireland for five years, up to 1964, may manufacture any commodity even if it has passed into the ownership of non-Irish interests.[104]

(5) A company which is Irish-owned and controlled is "qualified" to manufacture any commodity. A "qualified" company[105] must have over 50 per cent in nominal value of its issued shares[106] beneficially owned by Irish citizens, Irish-born persons, Irish residents, or companies which themselves have over one-half of all shares, at least two-thirds of all voting shares,[107] and at least two-thirds in nominal value of each class of voting shares so owned, directly or indirectly. A majority of its directors, excluding a full-time managing director, must be Irish citizens, Irish-born, or Irish residents for five years. A full-time managing director need not meet any of these qualifications.

The company's paid-up share capital must be at least one-half the value or the original cost of the fixed assets used in the business, whichever is less, after deducting government grants, reserves provided out of profits, sums due on short-term[108] hire purchase agreements, and loans guaranteed by a Minister, made by Irish citizens or Irish-controlled companies, or made or guaranteed by the Industrial Credit Company.[109]

The object of the last provision is to prevent evasion of the shareholding requirements by having a company with a small equity capital held by Irish citizens and fixed assets purchased with large loans made by a foreign enterprise, which thus could dominate the Irish company. There is nothing in the Act to prohibit a foreign enterprise from making a loan to an Irish citizen or an Irish-controlled company which then could re-lend to the manufacturing company and assign its rights under the loan agreement to the foreign enterprise. The

---

more likely to be considered in the Department of Industry and Commerce than in the courts, the importance of legislative history (which is not used by the courts) is considerable, especially if the interpretation intended was the more liberal one.

It is normal to insert in the charter of an Irish public company a provision enabling the directors to inquire about the beneficial ownership of any shares; this is to insure that the required proportion of the shareholding is in the hands of Irish citizens or companies. No such provisions would be required in the case of a company which was "excluded."

[103] 1958 Act, § 5(1)(h).

[104] Control of Manufactures Act, 1964 Acts, No. 40, § 1. The same applies to a company which has at least one-half of all its shares and two-thirds of its voting shares held by a company which manufactured in Ireland in the five years preceding 1964.

[105] 1958 Act, First Schedule, pt. I.

[106] But not debentures, which can be held by foreigners, subject to the requirement of adequate capital; 1932 Act, § 1.

[107] This probably does not include preferred shareholders entitled to vote only if their dividend is substantially overdue.

[108] I.e., less than five years.

[109] If a company's paid-up share capital is less than one-half the cost or value of its fixed assets, calculated as stated, and if it has notified the Minister for Industry and Commerce that it was manufacturing a particular commodity in 1958, it may continue to do so, but it will not be entitled to manufacture other commodities; 1958 Act, § 5(2).

1958 Act does not prevent an Irish company's being managed by a foreign enterprise pursuant to a management agreement if the above technical requirements are met. Because each class of shares having voting rights must be owned by Irish persons or companies, it is not possible to avoid the Act by having a class of shares with multiple votes.[110]

Permission to Manufacture Particular Commodities

(1) A company may manufacture a particular commodity if the company carries on the manufacturing process under a "new manufacture license."[111] The issue of this license is at the discretion of the Department of Industry and Commerce, which takes into consideration the requirements of the Irish market as compared with the capacity of existing Irish enterprises, the size and nature of the existing producers, the volume of exports, and the amount of employment likely to result from issuing the license. An increasing number of these licenses have been issued recently to existing and new companies, even where the demands of the home market are largely met, especially if a proportion of the resulting products will be exported. With the permission of the Minister, a new manufacture license may be transferred together with the business.[112] Once granted, a license cannot be revoked except for a "serious offense" under the 1932 Act,[113] for failure to commence manufacturing within the time limit specified in the license,[114] or on the cessation of business or the refusal by the Minister of permission to transfer the license.[115]

(2) A company may manufacture a particular commodity under a certificate of exemption. This provision allows certain companies already established in Ireland to manufacture for export, even if they are owned or financed by non-Irish interests or if they wish to finance themselves from foreign sources. To obtain a certificate of exemption, a company must be incorporated, managed, and controlled in Ireland[116] or must be incorporated in Ireland and have had its shares listed on one of the Irish stock exchanges for at least five years.[117] One of the company's main objects in carrying on the manufacturing process permitted by the certificate must be to develop an export trade in the commodity concerned. Certificates of exemption[118] are granted by the Department of Industry and Commerce.

[110] In addition, there is a provision which authorizes companies which have been in operation since 1934 and which are Irish-controlled to manufacture by the use of mechanical power. This provision is complex and is of little interest to the foreign investor. It applies to a company which has been operating continuously since July 1934 (1958 Act, § 5(1)(e) and First Schedule, pt. II) and which was then and is at the time of manufacture the subsidiary of a company which was then and is at the time of manufacture 51% beneficially owned by shareholders who were Irish citizens in 1934, who were born in Ireland, or who had been resident in Ireland for the previous five years, or owned by a "grand-parent" company itself so owned.

[111] 1958 Act, §§ 5(1)(g), 7; 1932 Act, §§ 4–10. It is usual to include in a new manufacture license any provisions regarded as necessary to protect existing Irish industry, such as a requirement that the factory licensed should export a specified proportion of its products.

[112] 1932 Act, § 8.

[113] 1932 Act, § 10(2), 10(3).

[114] 1934 Act, § 11(3).

[115] 1932 Act, § 9.

[116] 1958 Act, §§ 5(1)(c), 6.

[117] 1958 Act, § 6(2).

[118] They always require the company to commence the manufacturing process within a specified time; 1958 Act, § 6(3). They are transferable together with the business of the company, with the approval of the Department, if the transferee (which must also be a company) will maintain or develop the export trade. A certificate is revocable only if the permitted manufacturing process is ended, if permission

(3) If the Minister of Industry and Commerce declares a commodity "excepted,"[119] anyone may manufacture it. A commodity can be excepted if it is not being manufactured in Ireland to a substantial extent.[120] It was intended that commodities would be excepted to permit their manufacture by a particular company, rather than as a general measure to encourage foreign investment. It is difficult to define adequately a category of commodities, and therefore it might be difficult to decide if a commodity is within an order making similar commodities excepted. Since excepted commodities may be manufactured by foreign-owned competitors of the enterprise for whose benefit the commodity is excepted, a new manufacture license would usually be more favorable to the investor.

(4) A business which is under substantially the same ownership as in 1932 may manufacture commodities which would have been a reasonable extension of its business at that time. In more detail, the rule is that if the business of a company has been carried on continuously since June 1932,[121] either by the company itself or by a company which is over 50 per cent owned by the company or the individuals who owned the business in 1932, and if some manufacturing process was carried on either in 1932 or in January 1958, it may manufacture a commodity if doing so would have been a reasonable extension of the company's business in 1932.

Foreign investors may acquire a controlling interest in a company authorized to manufacture a limited range of commodities if the company has a certificate of exemption and remains managed and controlled in Ireland or if the company has a new manufacture license which does not contain a restriction on the ownership of the company.

A company may apply to the High Court for a declaration that it is entitled to carry on a manufacturing process.[122] The Minister for Industry and Commerce may serve a notice requiring information as to whether a company comes within the provisions of the Act.[123]

Changes in Irish law which would be necessitated by entry into the EEC—

The position of nationals of non-member states

When Ireland joins the EEC, the provisions discussed above—the most important discriminatory restrictions on freedom of establishment in Ireland—will have to be repealed insofar as they apply to nationals of EEC member states. The Treaty, however, does not require them to be entirely repealed, unless Article 7 prohibits discrimination on the grounds of nationality against nationals of non-member states. This is unlikely.[124] In fact, the Irish government has repealed these Acts entirely, as of January 1968, even if Ireland has not joined the EEC by then.[125] The repeal of the legislation outlined above will create a liberal regime in Ireland with regard to freedom of establishment for foreign investors, including those from non-member states.

---

to transfer is refused, or if the company has failed to commence manufacture within the time limit specified; 1958 Act, § 6(7).

[119] 1958 Act, § 3; 1934 Act, § 17.

[120] 1958 Act, § 3(1).

[121] 1958 Act, § 5(1)(f) and Second Schedule.

[122] 1934 Act, § 9; 1958 Act, § 10.

[123] 1934 Act, § 14(2)–14(8); 1958 Act, § 8.

[124] See van Hecke, "The Prohibition Against Discrimination in the European Economic Community," in 1 Cartel and Monopoly in Modern Law 341, 343 (Institüt für ausländisches und internationales Wirtschaftsrecht an der Johann-Wolfgang-Goethe-Universität, 1961). See art. 234.

[125] Control of Manufactures Act, 1964 Acts, No. 40, § 2; see Second Programme for Economic Expansion, Pr. 7239, para. 57 (1963).

However, Irish legislation requiring residence permits for all aliens[126] residing in Ireland would have to be repealed[127] with regard to nationals of member states if Ireland joined the EEC.

The most-favored-nation clause

THE U.S.-IRISH TREATY OF FRIENDSHIP, COMMERCE, AND NAVIGATION[128]

This treaty permits Ireland to continue to regulate the establishment of and the acquisition of interests in manufacturing and insurance[129] enterprises.[130] Freedom to acquire interests in manufacturing enterprises must not be restricted more than under the Control of Manufactures Acts of 1932 and 1934,[131] and these Acts "will be applied in a liberal spirit." United States nationals are granted most-favored-nation treatment with regard to establishment and acquisition of manufacturing enterprises.[132] If Ireland entered the EEC and repealed the existing Acts only insofar as they applied to nationals of member states, the question would arise whether the most-favored-nation provision[133] entitled United States nationals to the same rights. In spite of the prospective repeal of the existing restrictions on freedom of establishment, this problem would arise in connection with the other most-favored-nation provisions of the treaty.[134] There is no provision that the obligation to provide most-favored-nation treatment shall not apply to advantages accorded by either contracting party by virtue of a customs union.[135] If the new EEC member state in question is not a member of GATT,[136]

[126] E.g., Aliens Act, 1935 Pub. Stat. 221, § 5.

[127] This can be done by statutory instrument (i.e., regulations having the force of law) without the enactment of legislation by the Irish Parliament.

[128] Jan. 21, 1950, [1950] U.S.T. & O.I.A. 785, T.I.A.S. No. 2155, Ir. T.S. No. 7 of 1950, P. No. 9791, 206 U.N.T.S. 269 (1955). See Connell, "United States Protection of Private Foreign Investment Through Treaties of Friendship, Commerce and Navigation," 9 Archiv des Völkerrechts 256 (1961–62).

[129] See Insurance Act, 1936 Pub. Stat. 1027, §§ 11, 19, and Insurance Act, 1964 Acts, No. 18, which must be amended in the EEC insofar as they affect EEC nationals. There are other restrictions on freedom of establishment in Ireland under Agricultural Produce (Cereals) Act, 1933 Pub. Stat. 29; Industrial Alcohol Act, 1938 Acts 337; Sugar (Control of Import) Act, 1936 Pub. Stat. 187; and Tea (Purchase and Importation) Act, 1958 Acts 285.

[130] Art. VI, especially VI(4).

[131] Minutes of Interpretation of art. VI(4).

[132] Art. VI(3).

[133] Most-favored-nation treatment is defined in art. XXI(2) of the treaty as "treatment accorded within the territories of a Party upon terms no less favorable than the treatment accorded therein, in like situations, to nationals, companies, products, vessels or other objects, as the case may be, of *any* third country." (Emphasis supplied.) Art. XX(3) specifically provides that the most-favored-nation provisions of the 1950 Treaty with regard to free movement of goods shall not apply to advantages accorded by Ireland to the British Commonwealth or by the United States to certain territories. This provision adds some weight to the argument that an exception for entry into a customs union should not be read into the 1950 Treaty.

[134] E.g., arts. I(1), VIII(3), IX(1), XI, XII(1), XII(3), XIV(2), XVI, XVII(2), XVII(3), XVIII(3), XVIII(4).

[135] For a provision so providing, see U.S.-Netherlands Treaty of Friendship, Commerce and Navigation, March 27, 1956, art. XXII(3), [1957] 2 U.S.T. & O.I.A. 2043, T.I.A.S. No. 3942 (effective Dec. 5, 1957). This provision deals only with the "advantages accorded by virtue of a customs union" and presumably therefore deals only with tariffs and quotas; Nicholson, "The Significance of Treaties to the Establishment of Companies," in 2 American Enterprise in the European Common Market: A Legal Profile 153, 182 (Stein & Nicholson ed. 1960). Ireland has entered into an Exchange of Notes, July 2, 1951, Ir. T.S. No. 2 of 1951, Pr. 630, 100 U.N.T.S. 54, with Norway, constituting an agreement on commercial relations and providing for most-favored-nation treatment.

[136] Art. XX(2) of the U.S.-Irish Treaty provides that "the provisions of the present Treaty relating to the treatment of goods shall not pre-

FCN treaties such as the U.S.-Irish Treaty raise the general question whether the most-favored-nation clause requires EEC member states to give nationals of non-member states the same privileges as nationals of member states.

Under GATT, the creation of customs unions or the adoption of interim agreements necessary for the attainment of a customs union is not incompatible with a most-favored-nation clause with regard to movement of goods if the common external tariff is not higher than the average of the previous national tariffs and if an interim agreement involves a definite plan for achieving the full customs union within a reasonable time.[137] The same principle may be used to analyze the situation with regard to freedom of establishment, freedom of movement of persons, and the other aspects of economic integration.[138] If the EEC were a political union in which the constituent states had ceased to be sovereign in international law, it seems clear that the EEC would not be bound to give member-state treatment to nationals of non-member states.[139]

clude action by either Party which is . . . specifically permitted by the General Agreement on Tariffs and Trade . . . during such time as such Party is a contracting party to the General Agreement. . . . Similarly, the most-favored-nation provisions of the present Treaty shall not apply to special advantages accorded by virtue of the aforesaid Agreement. . . ." However, Ireland is not yet a member of GATT, though negotiations are in progress. Art. XX(2) deals only with "the treatment of goods" and not with freedom of establishment or other matters arising out of the EEC Treaty. Art. XXIV of GATT deals only with customs unions and does not specifically permit economic unions.

[137] GATT, art. XXIV.

[138] Art. 59 provides that the Council may give freedom to render services to nationals of non-member states who are established within the Community.

[139] See Chesné, L'Etablissement des Etrangers en France et la Communauté Economique Européenne 18 (1962).

The EEC Treaty

EEC member states are certain to resist pressure to extend to nationals of non-member states the rights given to nationals of member states by the Treaty. Article 234 provides that, in carrying out previous treaties with non-member states, member states are to "take into account the fact that the benefits granted under this Treaty by each member state form an integral part of the establishment of the Community and are thereby inseparably linked with the creation of common institutions, the conferring of powers on such institutions and the granting of the same advantages by all other member states."[140] In other words, member-state treatment is not to be extended to non-member states, because the obligations and privileges of member states are intimately involved in the entire process of economic integration, the reciprocal privileges deriving from it, and the balance of voting power and the assurance of impartiality built into the institutions of the Community. A most-favored-nation clause, it is argued, is not intended to guarantee membership in, without obligations of, any future customs unions or economic unions which the states bound by the clause may join.

Non-member states are in general unlikely to attempt to obtain member-state treatment for their nationals under most-favored-nation clauses.[141] If they did so, the effect certainly would be the cancellation and renegotiation of the clauses in question. At most they will argue that they are entitled to member-state treat-

[140] See EEC Commission v. Italy, 8 Recueil 1, [1962] C.M.L.R. 187; 1961 Journal Officiel 1273–75/61.

[141] Nicholson, "The Significance of Treaties to the Establishment of Companies," in 2 American Enterprise in the European Common Market: A Legal Profile 153, 182–83 (Stein & Nicholson ed. 1960); Hay, "The European Common Market and the Most-Favored-Nation Clause," 23 U. Pitt. L. Rev. 661, 683 (1962).

ment in order to obtain concessions from the member states.

Although these two considerations reduce the practical importance of the question, member states cannot abrogate the rights of non-member states by agreement among themselves. The Treaty provides that it is not to abrogate them;[142] if Treaty obligations are incompatible with previous obligations, the earlier treaty must be terminated in accordance with its provisions or the principles of international law. The EEC Treaty is to prevail vis-à-vis member states and their nationals, and the member state concerned is to regularize the situation. If necessary, member states must assist each other; for example, by agreeing mutually to terminate previous treaties made among themselves and not involving a non-member state and by adopting a common attitude toward these problems. GATT makes an exception to the most-favored-nation clause in favor of customs unions on the presumption that customs unions do more good by freeing trade on a comprehensive and reciprocal basis than they do harm by causing discrimination. The same argument is applicable to nations which agree to free movement of the factors of production and to insure the most efficient use of their resources by equalizing conditions of competition, but GATT does not mention economic unions. An economic union involves something different in kind from a customs union, since it eliminates the characteristics which make the national market an economic unit. This makes it impossible for one member state to give member-state rights under a most-favored-nation clause without also giving unrestricted access to the economies of other member states.[143] However, the fact that a new economic entity has been created does not mean that the older political entities which still exist are no longer bound by the most-favored-nation clause.[144] Freedom to obtain capital and to establish enterprises and freedom of movement of labor are involved much more intimately in the economy of the host member state than are its tariffs or quotas. Since some of these freedoms could hardly be given without the cooperation of the non-member state, if nationals of the non-member state were entitled to them,[145] it could be argued that the most-favored-nation clause is inapplicable because its nature is to confer on nationals of the beneficiary state an automatic benefit in the name of non-discrimination.

The basis for the operation of the most-favored-nation clause is that the state under the obligation could have insured reciprocal benefits for itself either by negotiating for them in the treaty which contains the clause or by inviting the beneficiary state to join in the negotiations for the later treaty. But even when the most-favored-nation clause is part of a treaty on establishment, the state bound by it cannot have obtained a bargain adequate to compensate for its obligations if the clause applies in the case of economic unions, nor can it insure

[142] Art. 234.

[143] This is not true during the transitional period of the EEC, when the origin of goods imported from outside the EEC still affects the tariff paid on goods passing from one member state to another.

[144] Hay, "The European Common Market and the Most-Favored-Nation Clause," 23 U. Pitt. L. Rev. 661, 668–71 (1962).

[145] For example, a worker's right to transfer his rights under social security legislation in one country to a country to which he migrates could not be given without the cooperation of the state which the worker was leaving. Since freedom of establishment and services is bound up with harmonization of laws, it is argued that a non-member state which has not agreed to harmonize its laws is not entitled to freedom of establishment for its nationals; Piot, "Du réalisme dans les Conventions d'établissement," 88 Journal dù Droit International 38 (1961); Audinet, "Le droit d'établissement dans la Communauté economique européenne," 86 Journal de Droit International 982, 1008–10 (1959).

that the other member states will accept the beneficiary state as a member of the economic union, or even if they do, that the economic union would be reasonable or possible for the beneficiary state. Since the weight of diplomatic practice seems to be against reading an exception on economic unions into the most-favored-nation clause, the point cannot be regarded as settled,[146] but for the reasons given it seems clear that nationals of non-member states will not, in fact, be given member-state treatment in the EEC. Most of the United States and British authorities, both before and after the conclusion of the EEC Treaty, seem to favor the view that nationals of non-member states are entitled to member-state treatment from customs and economic unions, but most of the European authorities take the opposite view.

[146] Hay, "The European Common Market and the Most-Favored-Nation Clause," 23 U. Pitt. L. Rev. 661, 682 (1962), concludes: "[T]he establishment of the EEC has not affected the most-favored-nation treatment accorded U.S. nationals and companies except in matters of trade. In the latter area, the application of the most-favored-nation clause would seem precluded by virtue of the customs union exception." Professor Hay points out that the customs union exception only deals with most-favored-treatment in matters of trade; id. at 671–76. He cites the authorities for and against the view that the customs union exception can be implied in most-favored-nation clauses (id. at 677–78) and holds that it can be implied as between signatories of GATT; cf. Vignes, "Le droit d'établissement et les services dans la Communauté Economique Européenne," 7 Annuaire Français de Droit International 668, 690 nn.80–82 (1961). M. Vignes cites various European authorities for the view that the customs union exception should be read into most-favored-nation clauses and deduces that an exception for economic unions also should be read in. Chesné, L'Etablissement des Etrangers en France et la Communauté Economique Européenne 18 (1962), takes the same view, on the ground that the EEC is an inchoate political union. See also de Lacharrière, "Aspects récents de la clause de la nation la plus favorisée," 7 Annuaire Français de Droit International 107, 109–13 (1961); Kiss, "La Convention Européenne d'établissement et la clause de la Nation la plus favorisée," 3 Annuaire Français de Droit International 478 (1957); Jahnke, "The European Economic Community and the Most-Favored-Nation Clause," 1 Can. Yb. Int'l L. 252 (1963).

Part IV

TAXATION

Chapter 6

Harmonization of Taxation: Indirect Taxes[1]

After market prospects, probably the next most important consideration in establishing a foreign business operation is the incidence of taxation. The following chapters deal with the tax aspects of the EEC most important to investors. The phrase "indirect taxes" describes taxes on the employment of income, i.e., taxes on consumption and expenditure, such as sales and excise taxes, and taxes on the factors of production. The phrase "direct taxes" describes taxes on income or the formation of income and taxes on capital, including company taxes. Social security payments and special taxes on capital gains and on capital movements do not fall readily into either category.

CUMULATIVE TAXES AND THE TREATY PROVISIONS

When the EEC Treaty was signed, each member state imposed a general indirect tax on almost all sales and services. These taxes were paid by the seller at a rate equal to a specific percentage of the payment made and were similar to sales taxes in the United States. The tax paid on sales of goods before they were exported was refunded to the exporter, and at the point of import a charge was imposed equivalent to the tax on locally made goods at the same stage of production or distribution. This is the "destination principle," by which the only indirect taxes borne by the consumer are those of the country of destination of the goods and not those of the country of their origin. Under this principle, goods of a given type in a given country bear the same amount of tax, whatever their origin.

[1] See Chrétien, "Les divers problèmes fiscaux des trois Communautés Européennes," in Les Problèmes Juridiques 255 and the studies cited at 272; Sannwald & Stohler, Economic Integration, ch. V (1959); "Les doubles impositions internationales en matière de taxe sur le chiffre d'affaires," 28 Cahiers de Droit Fiscal International 157 (1955); Galeen, "An Outsider's Views on EEC Tax Problems," 2 European Taxation 127 (1962); Meade, Case Studies in European Economic Union 310–36 (1962); Vedel, "Les Aspects Fiscaux du Marché Commun," 12 Bull. Int'l B. Fiscal Documentation 321 (1958); ECSC High Authority, Rapport remis à la Haute Autorité le 8 avril, 1953, 3243/1 F. PP. 1–36A; Zimmermann, "Les Problèmes Fiscaux du Marché Commun," 100(2) Recueil Académie D. Int. 595 (1960); Shoup, "Taxation Aspects of International Economic Integration," in Aspects Financiers et Fiscaux de l'Intégration Economique Internationale 89 (L'Institut International de Finances Publiques, 1954); Reboud, Systèmes Fiscaux et Marché Commun 77–102 (1961); Belassa, The Theory of Economic Integration 238–48 (1961); Committee on Turnover Taxation, Report, Cmd. No. 2300 (1964); Sullivan, The Search for Tax Principles in the European Economic Community 12–35, 63–66, 85–90 (1963); Sixth General Report, paras. 60–62 (1963); van Hoorn & Wright, "Taxation," in 2 American Enterprise in the European Common Market: A Legal Profile 343 (Stein & Nicholson ed. 1960); Dosser, "Welfare Effects of Tax Unions," 31(3) Rev. Econ. Studies 179 (1964). For an analysis of all the existing indirect taxes in the Six, see Taxes Indirectes perçues à l'importation dans les six pays de la C.E.E. (Eurolibri, 1962); Due, "Sales Taxation in Western Europe: A General Survey" (pts. 1–2), 8 Nat'l Tax J. 171, 300 (1955); see also Federation of British Industries, Value-Added Turnover Tax (1963); OEEC, The Influence of Sales Taxes on Productivity (1958).

To prevent subsidies, the EEC Treaty provides that the refund at the time of export may not exceed the total tax imposed;[2] to avoid a protective tariff effect, the charge imposed on imported goods may not exceed the tax borne by local goods.[3] This means theoretically that the effect of all indirect taxes would be neutral and that no distortion of competition would occur. However, administrative complications due to the refund and compensatory charge on the goods, called "tax frontiers," and the resulting psychological barrier remain. Under this system, if the tax rate is high, large amounts of capital may be tied up until the refund is paid.

The indirect taxes of all the Six (except France) were cumulative, that is, were charged at each sale on the sale price, including the tax passed on from each previous transaction. Therefore, the total amount of tax in the price of goods was limited only by the number of times which the goods had been sold. Purchasers kept no record of the proportion of the purchase price which was made up of tax. One could not calculate how much tax had been borne by any particular items at the point of export; refunds were based on the average amount of tax borne by goods of the type and at the stage of distribution in question. The charges on imported goods had to be calculated in the same way. Article 97 permitted these averages to be used, to obtain approximately equal conditions of competition, but their operation could never be accurate.

Cumulative multistage sales taxes also gave an advantage to vertically integrated enterprises, which own the goods from the raw material stage to the retail stage and so have little tax to pass on. This effect existed even between firms in the same national market, and complicated special arrangements were made in Germany, Italy, Luxembourg, and the Netherlands to counteract it. Cumulative taxes did not permit tax on capital machinery and raw materials to be credited against the tax on the product sold, and thus they inhibited technical development and specialization in the manufacture of components and machinery for production.[4] They also prejudiced capital-intensive enterprises and benefited labor-intensive ones.

ADDED-VALUE AND SINGLE-STAGE TAXES

The general sales tax in France is a non-cumulative multistage tax called an added-value tax. Like the cumulative, or "cascade," turnover tax, it is charged on the value of the payment made with each sale or service. However, the seller credits against the tax on the sale the tax which he paid on the purchase of the object sold or its raw materials or component parts (the "physical deduction"). In this way the tax is paid in installments, but it cannot exceed the gross tax (before the credit) on the final sale to the consumer; each owner pays tax only on the difference between the cost price to him and the sale price—the value added. The yield of an added-value tax is thus the same as the yield of a single-stage tax imposed at the final stage (e.g., wholesale or retail stage) at which

[2] Art. 96. The provisions on indirect taxes are arts. 95–97, 99. The Treaty assumes the destination principle and regulates its operation.

[3] Art. 95. See EEC Commission, Rapport du Comité Fiscal et Financier [hereinafter cited as Neumark Report] 77 (1962). English translations of the Neumark Report appear in 1 Commerce Clearing House, Common Market Reporter 2401 (1965) [hereinafter cited as CCH], and in International Bureau of Fiscal Documentation, The EEC Reports on Tax Harmonization (1963). Cites to the French and the CCH versions of the Neumark Report are given herein as, e.g., Neumark Report, Rapport 77, CCH 2473.

[4] Antal, "Harmonization of Turnover Taxes in the Common Market," 1 Common Market L. Rev. 41, 52–53 (1963); Committee on Turnover Taxation, Report, Cmd. No. 2300, para. 15 (1964).

the added-value tax is payable, if the rate of the two taxes is the same. However, the single-stage tax is cheaper to administer.

This added-value tax gives no incentive to vertical integration. It is easy to collect, since each purchaser insures that the tax on all previous transactions has been paid in order to reduce the tax he owes. It is more complex than a cumulative tax and has many more points of collection[5] than a single-stage tax. Its great advantage for international trade and the reason for its adoption is that the tax borne by particular goods at the point of export and the tax to be levied by the importing country can be calculated simply and accurately. Exports cannot be subsidized or doubly taxed, since the refund is exactly the tax included in the total price of the goods at the point of export. In practice, to simplify administration, exporters acquire raw materials tax-free and pay tax only to the extent to which the finished products are not exported. The tax paid on the acquisition of capital machinery and other amounts of tax borne "indirectly"[6] by goods can be deducted from the tax on the finished product (the "financial deduction"), so technical development is not hindered except where the finished product is tax-free. An added-value tax in all member states would enable the destination principle to achieve, for all practical purposes, complete neutrality between the products of different member states and to end all trade-diverting effects.

The amount of tax to be refunded on exports and to be levied on imports can also be calculated accurately if there is a single-stage non-cumulative tax. Some member states perhaps could have a single-stage and others a non-cumulative multistage system without distorting conditions of competition. Certain difficulties arise, however, in connection with even single-stage excise taxes.[7] Single-stage taxes make special rates and exemptions simpler to operate than added-value taxes. Using an added-value tax means greater difficulty in retaining tax relief for particular commodities for social reasons, even prior to the adoption of the principle of taxation in the country of origin; the tax operates much better if there are few special rates and exempt commodities. Thus an added-value tax tends to unify the indirect tax structure and to result in a broad tax base. As compared with a single-stage tax of the same rate imposed at the last stage where the added-value tax is payable, an added-value tax is less likely to cause economic disturbance since the tax is spread. The taxpayer can more easily pass the tax on to the buyer of the goods or services, and the risk of evasion is reduced.

With either an added-value tax or a single-stage tax (other than a single-stage tax at the retail stage), the destination principle involves the retention of tax frontiers after tariff frontiers have

[5] See Antal, "Harmonization of Turnover Taxes in the Common Market," 1 Common Market L. Rev. 41, 47–48 (1963); Committee on Turnover Taxation, Report, Cmd. No. 2300, paras. 31–60 (1962); Wheatcroft, "Some Administrative Problems of an Added Value Tax," 1963 Brit. Tax Rev. 348; Prest, "Value Added Tax Coupled with a Reduction in Taxes on Business Profits," id. at 336. Stout, "Value Added Taxation, Exporting and Growth," id. at 314, 320, points out that an added-value tax is more favorable to growth than a tax on net business profits, since it does not hinder capital accumulation by successful firms and since it encourages worthwhile investment in capital machinery and economy in the use of labor and other costs, especially if the tax is not fully shifted. See generally Sullivan, The Tax on Value Added (1965).

[6] Art. 96.

[7] Rapport fait au nom de la commission du marché intérieur sur la proposition de la Commission de la C.E.E. au Conseil (doc. 121, 1962–1963) concernant une directive en matière d'harmonisation des législations des Etats membres relatives aux taxes sur le chiffre d'affaires, A.P.E. Doc. No. 56, at 63 (1963–64).

been abolished. A single-stage retail tax theoretically allows the abolition of tax frontiers and the retention of the destination principle.[8] Otherwise, tax frontiers can be ended only by the use of the origin principle. Under the origin principle, there is no refund at the point of export and no import levy, and tax is paid in the country of destination only if a taxable transaction takes place there.[9] Subject to this, goods with the same origin pay the same tax, regardless of destination. Under the origin principle, a buyer resident in a member state with a retail tax could avoid paying the tax by buying his goods in another state, so the retail tax might have to be supplemented by a "use tax" in the member state in question on goods bought elsewhere. The need for a use tax would be less likely to arise if both states imposed added-value taxes. Even if the member states adopted the origin principle for intra-Community trade, they would have to apply the destination principle to imports from non-member states.

THE PROPOSALS OF THE EEC COMMISSION

After detailed studies[10] of various types of taxes, the Commission decided that the existing cumulative indirect taxes in the five member states should be changed to the system already in force in France. In 1963 Germany introduced a draft law establishing an added-value tax. Also in 1963, Belgium decided to adopt a single-stage tax at the wholesale level, but this change has been postponed indefinitely.

The proposals of the Commission[11] are embodied in two draft directives submitted to the Council. The first step in the proposed plan is the replacement of cumulative turnover taxes with an added-value tax based on similar principles in each member state.[12] Rates and exemptions will not need to be uniform. The new added-value tax normally will be imposed on all transactions up to and including the retail stage, but member states need not apply it to the retail stage or may impose a separate single-stage retail tax to maintain revenue. Taxes at the retail stage do not affect conditions of competition of goods originating in different states. The steps by which the non-cumulative taxes are modified will depend on the type of tax in ques-

[8] Neumark Report, Rapport 41, CCH 2440. A single-stage retail tax is the simplest form of turnover or sales tax; an added-value tax is inherently the most complicated.

[9] The change from the destination principle to the origin principle would cause an increase in the price of exports. On the removal of physical controls at frontiers, see EEC Commission, Rapport Général des Sous-Groupes A, B et C créés pour examiner différentes possibilités en vue d'une harmonisation des taxes sur le chiffre d'affaires [hereinafter cited as Rapport des Sous-Groupes A, B et C]. Rapport du Sous-Groupe A (1962). An English translation of the General Report of Sub-Groups A, B and C appears in International Bureau of Fiscal Documentation, The EEC Reports on Tax Harmonization (1963).

[10] Rapport des Sous-Groupes A, B et C; Neumark Report, Rapport 40–45, 76–81, CCH 2439–44, 2472–77. Art. 99 expressly contemplates harmonization of indirect taxes to end the distortions of competitive conditions due to cumulative taxes. According to the Belgian Finance Minister, the Commission chose an added-value tax to avoid taxing capital goods, to make possible a high tax rate, and to facilitate abolition of tax frontiers; Dequae, "Les Impôts indirects dans le Marché Commun," 19 Bull. Int'l B. Fiscal Documentation 23 (1965).

[11] Proposition de la Commission de la C.E.E. au Conseil relative à une directive en matière d'harmonisation des législations des Etats membres relatives aux taxes sur le chiffre d'affaires, A.P.E. Doc. No. 121 (1962–63); 1965 EEC Bull. No. 5, Supp. at 17. See Fourth General Report, paras. 63–66 (1961); Fifth General Report, paras. 60–62 (1962). The modified proposals are found in 1964 EEC Bull. No. 7, Supp.

[12] The Neumark Committee considered that harmonization would be necessary even if the origin principle were not adopted.

tion and on the type of added-value tax adopted.[13] A uniform sales tax system would greatly simplify interstate trade.

The second step is the adoption of the origin principle. To preserve equal competitive conditions, substantial uniformity in tax rates and, in particular, in the exemptions from tax under each national law will be necessary. This directly involves budgetary policy and possibly involves new taxes, higher tax rates, or payments by the other member states to a state which has lost a large amount of revenue.

To adopt the origin principle, either an added-value tax or a single-stage tax at the same stage will have to be adopted by all states. An added-value tax is not required by the origin principle, but it may minimize budgetary changes caused by the adoption of that principle. Converting the existing multi-stage taxes into an added-value tax will be easier than converting them into single-stage taxes. Unfortunately,[14] of the numerous possible forms of added-value taxes,[15] there is no one clearly preferable form. The French version, the only one in actual operation, is agreed to be too complicated, even though any form of added-value tax requires complex accounts for all taxpaying enterprises.

The original proposals of the Commission involved setting up transitional non-cumulative taxes which were intended to be short-lived. The Neumark Report[16] contemplates agreement on the details of the added-value tax before abolition of cumulative taxes. This minimizes the work involved, but it has caused delay. Two European bodies[17] also considered the propositions that the existing systems should be converted directly into an added-value tax and that the principles of the latter should be settled before any changes are made. The Commission's proposals contemplate a common system of added-value taxes, the merits of which are not known. Also, while essential to create a single market, the abolition of tax frontiers may not be practicable unless the social, tax, budgetary, economic, and monetary policies of member states

[13] The type of added-value tax to be adopted is to be broadly based and is to apply at the usual rate to services, capital goods, and overhead expenses. This implies a high tax rate for services. Special arrangements may be made for small retailers. See Rapport des Sous-Groupes A, B et C 103–32; the "Opinion" of the Commission on the structure of a common added-value tax, 1964 Journal Officiel 1800–802/64, now embodied in a second draft directive, 1965 EEC Bull. No. 5, Supp. at 17.

[14] Antal, "Harmonization of Turnover Taxes in the Common Market," 1 Common Market L. Rev. 41, 53–54 (1963); Sullivan, The Search for Tax Principles in the European Economic Community 90–94 (1963).

[15] Neumark Report, Rapport 42, CCH 2441. Two systems of calculating an added-value tax are the "base on base" system and the "tax on tax" system. Under the "base on base" system, the tax is paid on the difference between the price of raw materials and the price of the finished product. Under the "tax on tax" system, the tax paid on the price of the raw materials is credited against the tax on the price of the finished product. The "tax on tax" system is usually preferred and has been chosen by the Commission. Unless rates and exemptions are uniform, the "base on base" system results in some difficulties in calculating the amount of the tax accurately and thus results in distortions in competition. In Germany it is disliked because it could be held to be a tax on gross profits, which would have to be shared by the federal government with the Länder; "West Germany: New Thoughts about Turnover Tax," 3 European Taxation 119–20 (1963). The two systems produce different results only if different tax rates for different goods are involved.

[16] Neumark Report, Rapport 44, CCH 2444. See also 1963 Journal Officiel 2631–33/63.

[17] The Commission on the Internal Market of the Parliamentary Assembly and the Economic and Financial Committee; see Rapport . . . concernant une directive . . . [relative] aux taxes sur le chiffre d'affaires, A.P.E. Doc. No. 56 (1963–64). The same view was taken by the German federal legislature. The Commission's original proposals were intended to assist Italy.

are harmonized.[18] Since it makes changes in tax rates impossible, abolition of tax frontiers involves a major surrender of financial control. However, the advantages of abolition of tax frontiers may appeal sufficiently to business interests to make it politically attractive. It is not universally agreed that an added-value tax is the best form of tax in a market free from tax frontiers. One important point is that, since agricultural products probably would be subject to a lower added-value tax rate than industrial goods, countries exporting industrial goods would obtain a higher yield from the common tax than countries exporting agricultural products if the origin principle were adopted. In fact, the "special" treatment for agricultural products might be more important than the "normal" treatment of other goods.

The Internal Market Commission supported the complete abolition of tax frontiers; therefore, it criticized the inconsistency of the Neumark Report in this respect and said that excise taxes should be harmonized simultaneously with turnover taxes.[19] Tax frontiers for special or excise taxes cannot be ended[20] for a long time, however.

Even though tax frontiers could be abolished and the destination principle retained under a single stage retail tax, the Neumark Committee rules out a common retail tax because of the large number of collection points that would be needed and because of political reasons. They consider, therefore, that an added-value tax is necessary to abolish tax frontiers on the basis of the principle of origin. A single-stage tax at the wholesale or production stage was held incompatible with the elimination of tax frontiers by a previous study.[21] Both general retail taxes and general added-value taxes on all stages are neutral in their effect on competition.

INDIRECT TAXATION IN IRELAND—THE "TURNOVER TAX"

The Irish Commission on Income Taxation in 1960[22] sought to broaden the indirect tax base[23] and recommended a

[18] Judging from the Neumark Report, harmonization of all these policies is contemplated, and indeed it should be. However, it cannot be expected to come about for a considerable length of time. See Dequae, "Les Impôts indirects dans le Marché Commun," 19 Bull. Int'l B. Fiscal Documentation 23 (1965), for a criticism of the Commission's proposals in this respect. The Netherlands has been reluctant to adopt an added-value tax, at least until the abolition of tax frontiers is certain. France has been reluctant to agree to the elimination of tax frontiers, but the German federal legislature has supported it strongly.

[19] Rapport . . . concernant une directive . . . [relative] aux taxes sur le chiffre d'affaires, A.P.E. Doc. No. 56 (1963–64). The Neumark Report contemplates retention of tax frontiers for excise taxes but not for turnover taxes, because excise taxes will be difficult to harmonize due to their importance as sources of revenue, especially in Italy.

[20] Neumark Report, Rapport 49, 79–80, CCH 2448, 2475.

[21] Rapport des Sous-Groupes A, B et C, Rapport du Sous-Groupe B, especially at 59–60, 63–64, 67; Rapport du Sous-Groupe C, pt. B. See also Neumark Report, Rapport 40, 41, CCH 2440; Rapport . . . concernant une directive . . . [relative] aux taxes sur le chiffre d'affaires, A.P.E. Doc. No. 56, paras. 45–49, 168–72 (1963–64); Committee on Turnover Taxation, Report, Cmd. No. 2300, ch. 5 (1964). The principal objection to such a tax is that if it is to produce the same revenue as an added-value tax it must be imposed at a fairly high rate, especially if capital goods and services are exempted to avoid a cumulative effect. This means that the producer or wholesaler paying the tax must find a fairly large sum—much larger than in the case of an added-value tax—which his credit terms to purchasers might not permit him to recover promptly. Evasion of the tax is also easier than evasion of an added-value tax.

[22] Third Report, Pr. 5567 (1960).

[23] In the British tradition, Ireland relied for revenue on excise taxes, taxes on income (income tax, surtax, and corporations profits tax),

sales tax.[24] In its comment on the Tax Commission's report,[25] the Irish government reservedly[26] agreed that a sales tax would be appropriate and unavoidable if a substantial increase in taxation was necessary.

The tax as finally adopted in 1963[27] is a single-stage, 2.5 per cent retail tax,[28]

---

and death taxes. See Shoup, "Some Distinguishing Characteristics of the British, French, and United States Public Finance Systems," 47(2) Am. Econ. Rev. 187, 189, 191–92 (1957). In Britain there is a selective, single-stage, multirate sales tax on consumer goods called a "purchase tax," imposed at the wholesale stage, and used to regulate consumption in a way unknown in the Six. See OEEC, The Influence of Sales Taxes on Productivity, ch. VII (1958); Committee on Turnover Taxation, Report, Cmd. No. 2300, chs. 4–5 (1964). The base of purchase tax has been enlarged in Britain and the number of rates reduced.

As is the case with most underindustrialized countries, the proportion of public revenue in Ireland derived from indirect taxation—68%—was already higher than that in Italy—65.6%—and Italy depends on indirect taxation more than the other EEC member states. The Irish figure includes local taxes on the use of land and buildings ("rates"). See Commission on Income Taxation, Third Report, Pr. 5567, at 7, 73 (1960); Broderick, "An Analysis of Government Revenue and Expenditure in Relation to National Accounts," 20(3) J. Stat. Soc. 132 (1959–60). Tait, "The Public Sector in Ireland," 17 Nat'l Tax J. 22, 24 (1964), gives 71%. For the current figures, see the annual Statistical Abstract of Ireland. The figures given in the text are not strictly comparable. For the proportions in the Six, see Neumark Report, Rapport 25, CCH 2426; EEC Commission, Les recettes et les dépenses des administrations publiques dans les pays membres de la C.E.E. (1965). The Irish central government receipts for the financial year 1961–62 were composed of taxes on income, £35 million; capital taxes on death, £2.9 million; excise taxes, £33.5 million; customs duties, £45 million; and other taxes, £35.3 million. Total receipts from local taxes were £23.2 million ($65 million). Customs and excise duties together constituted 52% of total central government revenue, which was £151.6 million ($424.3 million). Statistical Abstract of Ireland, 1962, at 271, 284. In Britain indirect taxes produce 45.6% of the total revenue, including social security contributions; see Committee on Turnover Taxation, Report, Cmd. No. 2300, para. 6 (1962).

[24] They called it a purchase tax; Third Report, Pr. 5567, ch. IV (1960). The Tax Commission considered briefly a tax on capital gains, an annual tax on wealth, an expenditure tax, and certain other taxes. The Tax Commission pointed out that the phrases "purchase tax" and "sales tax" are indiscriminately used for taxes on the value of goods bought and sold, including multistage taxes. For convenience, the phrase "turnover tax" has been used for the form of tax introduced by the Finance Act, 1963 Acts, No. 23, since this is the current nomenclature in Ireland. It has been usual to refer to the multistage systems in force in the Six as turnover taxes. See Direct Taxation, Pr. 5952, para. 34 (1961). Nortcliffe, Common Market Fiscal Systems 87–88 (1960), points out that the United Kingdom purchase tax has been primarily an instrument of economic control, while the multistage taxes in the Six have been revenue raisers. The selectivity of purchase tax, as constituted at present, and its use as a regulator have involved frequent changes of rate. Like all taxes imposed at the wholesale stage, difficulties arise in situations where there is no wholesale stage, e.g., when a manufacturer sells to the consumer. See OEEC, The Influence of Sales Taxes on Productivity 5 n. (1958).

[25] Direct Taxation, Pr. 5952 (1961).

[26] Id., paras. 32–43 (1961). See Commission on Income Taxation, Third Report, Pr. 5567, Minority Report (1960). The government stated that a sales tax would be regressive and socially undesirable and that it might cause wage, salary, and cost increases and affect competitive capacity.

[27] Finance Act, 1963 Acts, No. 23, §§ 46–56; Finance Act, 1965 Acts, No. 22, pt. VI; Turnover Tax Regulations, S.I. Nos. 157, 162–65, 201–208 of 1963. See also Irish Revenue Commissioners, Guide to the Turnover Tax (1963).

[28] The Minister for Finance said that a cumulative multistage tax had been rejected on the ground that the retail price of commodities would be increased not only by the tax but by the trade profit on the tax as well as the cost price. An added-value tax was ruled out as being too complex for a country with no previous experience of general sales taxation. A single-stage tax at the wholesale stage on selected commodities at a variety of rates was rejected on the grounds that it would disturb patterns of trade and might threaten particular industries. Also, it would have a narrower base than a retail tax and could not extend to services; a

called a "turnover tax," which resembles the taxes in Norway[29] and Sweden. The tax base is gross turnover less receipts from other registered dealers and other exempt transactions, plus stock withdrawn for personal use. Acquisition of capital goods and raw materials is tax-free. For simplicity, the tax is imposed on total cash receipts, not on individual sales, so that retailers need not make uniform increases in the price of each commodity. It is expected, however, that competition will prevent disproportionate price increases on particular commodities and distortion of trade. The tax is unusual among single-stage taxes in that it applies to services. Certain services and goods are exempt from the tax,[30] but the tax is very broadly based. Imports are taxed on entry into Ireland, unless they have been imported by "registered" enterprises for resale.

Tax is paid on the gross proceeds from sales of goods and services by registered sellers, including retailers, wholesalers, and manufacturers, to unregistered buyers. Transfers of goods between registered persons involve no tax. Retailers must register and pay tax on all sales of non-exempt goods. Since registration is necessary to obtain tax-free supplies, manufacturers, wholesalers, and retailers have an incentive to register. Small traders who need not and do not register can obtain only taxed goods.[31]

The advantage of this system is its simplicity in relation to each collection point, since all goods are either taxable or exempt. However, it is more difficult for a retailer to keep the necessary accounts than for a wholesaler and, since most retailers are taxable, the system has the disadvantage of having a large number of collection points.[32] Taxation at the

---

higher rate would therefore be required. This would increase the trade "markup" and the price to the consumer with no benefit to the Revenue, and extra capital would be needed because the tax would be paid before retail sale. The government's comments on the regressive effect of the tax "hardly accorded with orthodox economic theory." Tait, "The Public Sector in Ireland," 17 Nat'l Tax J. 22, 24 (1964). It was also said that the selective application of the wholesale tax would involve complexities in bookkeeping; this, in fact, may not have been avoided by the system adopted, 202 Dáil Eireann, Parl. Deb., cols. 83–84 (1963). For a variant of the scheme adopted which would have more favorable economic effects, see Johnston, Why Ireland Needs the Common Market 16 (1962). For the controversy over the turnover tax in Ireland, see notably 205 Dáil Eireann, Parl. Deb., cols. 544–676 (1963).

[29] On the Norwegian retail sales tax, see Due, Sales Taxation, ch. XII (1957); Federation of British Industries, Taxation in Western Europe 174–75 (4th ed. 1962).

[30] Exempt sales are: sales of goods for export; sales by farmers of their own produce; and sales of live animals, animal foods, veterinary supplies, farming and fishing equipment, hydrocarbon oils, certain building and construction materials, and certain capital machinery. Exempt services are: banking, insurance, services under contracts of employment, professional services, hospital services, building, transport, hotel-keeping, moneylending, advertising, and certain services in which no goods are sold retail; Finance Act, 1963, No. 23, First Schedule. See "Tax Development in Ireland," 3 European Taxation 121, 122 (1963). The goods exempt from the turnover tax are considerably fewer than those suggested by the Commission, which included food, fuel, books, non-durable household goods, and goods subject to heavy excise taxes.

[31] Small traders need not register, but if they do they pay a special reduced rate on the first $280 of their gross receipts.

[32] The Tax Commission recommended taxation at the wholesale stage to make collection easier and to prevent evasion; Third Report, Pr. 5567, paras. 113–15, and Appendix (1960). The number of small retailers who need not register means that many manufacturers not otherwise concerned with the tax have to pay it on sales to these retailers. To this extent, the tax is in fact paid at the wholesale stage. One difficulty with taxes at the retail stage is that, unless accurate records of stock are kept, it is hard to insure that tax is paid on the sale value of goods used by the retailer himself. Evasion is also possible if a registered buyer uses his registration to buy tax-free goods for purposes for which he is not registered, e.g., for his own use.

retail level prevents distributors from calculating their profit on the tax as well as on the tax base and avoids discrimination between products, if the tax is fully passed on. Much of the opposition to the tax came from retailers who feared liability to additional income tax, as well as turnover tax, if accurate accounts were required for the purpose of the latter. Taxing total receipts deprives retailers of a rule of thumb for calculating the rate appropriate to individual sales, but it prevents problems arising from bad debts and discounts. It also involves collective agreements on the price increases needed to take the tax into account. This would be troublesome if the tax rate were frequently changed, and might cause price increases on some commodities greater than the rate of tax.

HARMONIZATION

This book is not concerned with harmonization of excise taxes, which is necessary to insure that imported goods, including goods that can be functionally substituted for local goods, bear the same amount of tax as local goods in all member states. Harmonization would involve substantially reducing the present Irish excise tax rates. The main difficulty of harmonizing the Irish turnover tax with taxes in the Six lies not in altering its structure or even in converting it into an added-value tax, but in the fact that at present it produces such a small proportion of total revenue. A common rate of added-value tax in all member states would mean a large increase in the rate of the existing Irish tax, probably to about 15 per cent. The increased revenue might permit reductions in direct taxes, and it would have to finance compensating concessions to lower-income groups to meet the well-known social objections to a regressive tax. A change in this respect would not be urgent, and for internal reasons, including social policy, the Irish government may move in this direction. However, harmonization is the most important fiscal problem of the EEC for Ireland, and it would be politically explosive. A major shift to a general indirect tax could be seriously inflationary unless it were carefully handled,[33] possibly by price control. Tax systems will not be harmonized until the over-all incidence of direct and indirect taxation in all EEC member states is roughly the same. Since Britain's and Ireland's indirect taxes produce higher proportions of revenue from much narrower tax bases than the taxes of most of the Six, this would involve a considerable fiscal, social, and economic change.[34]

Single-stage retail taxes, such as the Irish turnover tax, involve fiscal frontiers but would be compatible with the abolition of these frontiers if rates were uniform. If the Commission's proposal for a common added-value tax is accepted, Ireland and Britain eventually would have to change their present single-stage taxes to an added-value tax. Since the tax base of the Irish turnover tax is wider than that of the British purchase tax, Ireland is slightly closer to an added-

[33] Economist Intelligence Unit, Taxes for Britain 26–27 (1962); OECD Economic Survey of Ireland, 1965, at 16. On a wage policy in Ireland, see Closing the Gap: Incomes and Output, Pr. 6957 (1963). A uniform-rate added-value tax in the Six would mean rate increases in all the member states except France. Because of the conversion to a noncumulative tax, the increases in the cost of living and the revenue yield would not be as great as the rate increase. The alternative to such a shift towards regressive taxation in the Six would be a decrease in the French rate, necessitating an increase in direct taxation to maintain revenue, and this might be politically or economically undesirable.

[34] The Commission is well aware of the relationship between direct and indirect taxes and of the extent of the problems which would be involved for Britain and Ireland. See Nortcliffe, Common Market Fiscal Systems 78–79 (1960); Committee on Turnover Taxation, Report, Cmd. No. 2300, para. 6 (1964).

value tax in this respect.[35] The only objection to an added-value tax per se in Ireland would be its complexity for taxpayers and the number of points of collection, even if the retail stage is excluded.

[35] The French added-value tax, however, is not imposed on retailers.

Chapter 7

Harmonization of Taxation: Direct Taxes[1]

THE IMPORTANCE OF DIRECT TAXES

Harmonization of direct taxation is mentioned only twice in the EEC Treaty, while indirect taxation is dealt with carefully insofar as it affects exports and imports between member states.[2] Article 98 requires approval from the Council for relief from direct taxation for exports. Article 220 requires member states to make arrangements for the avoidance of double taxation within the Community. Article 99 refers only to harmonization of indirect taxation, and harmonization of direct taxes can be accomplished only under Article 100. This disregard of direct taxation seems to have occurred because the problems of harmonizing direct taxes are less urgent and more complex than those of harmonizing indirect taxes and could not be specifically dealt with in the Treaty. There seems to

[1] These chapters on taxation deal with three main topics: the EEC's work on harmonization of taxation, some changes likely to be made in the Irish tax system for harmonization and "fiscal transparency" (that is, sufficient similarity of concepts, rules, and structure of different tax systems for valid comparisons to be made directly), and some aspects of the Irish tax system which are of interest to investors. These chapters discuss only taxes which affect investors and do not discuss all the budgetary and other changes in national fiscal systems which would be involved in the proposals of the EEC. "The budgetary problems of an integrated area are largely dependent on the extent to which decision making is delegated to central [federal] agencies or to a federal government. The spectrum runs from a free trade area with relatively few centrally solved tax problems to complete integration, where the importance of the federal budget overshadows that of the state budget." Belassa, The Theory of Economic Integration 231 (1961). The EEC proposals (the Neumark Report) are far-reaching, and it is not certain how far they will be adopted nor whether any action arising from them is likely in the near future. The range of possibilities if the proposals are not followed is too great for discussion here. See Shoup, "Taxation Aspects of International Economic Integration," in Aspects Financiers et Fiscaux de l'Intégration Economique Internationale 89, 108–12 (1954).

On harmonization of taxation in general, see id. at 89; Zimmermann, "Les Problèmes Fiscaux de Marché Commun," 100(2) Recueil Académie D. Int. 595 (1960); Mersmann, "Le Système Fiscal Allemand et la C.E.E.," 1 La Fiscalité du Marché Commun 16 (1962); Kauffman, "La Législation fiscale du Grand Duché de Luxembourg confrontée avec les tendences vers une harmonisation des fiscalités," 3 La Fiscalité du Marché Commun 59 (1962); Moss, "Tax Burdens in Common Market Countries," 12 Nat'l Tax J. 216 (1959); Reboud, Systèmes Fiscaux et Marché Commun (1961); Strasma, "Comparing Taxes in a Common Market," 13 Nat'l Tax J. 184 (1960); Moss, "Reply," 13 Nat'l Tax J. 186 (1960); Schmölders, "The Principle of Competition in Tax and Finance Policies," in 2 Cartel and Monopoly in Modern Law 509 (1961); Dale, Tax Harmonization in Europe (1963); ECSC High Authority, C.E.C.A. 1952–1962, at 412–30 (1963); Shoup, The Theory of Harmonization of Fiscal Systems (1963); 2 Meade, The Theory of International Economic Policy, ch. 25 (1955); EEC Commission, Schéma des Impôts existant dans les Etats membres de la CEE, Edition 1964, Doc. No. 9499/IV/63-F (1963); Dosser, "Theoretical Considerations for Tax Harmonization," in Papers of the International Institute of Public Finance (1964); Rädler, Corporate Taxation in the Common Market (1965).

On taxation and related matters, see van Hoorn & Wright, "Taxation," in 2 American Enterprise in the European Common Market: A Legal Profile 343 (Stein & Nicholson ed. 1960).

[2] Arts. 95–97, 99.

have been no real agreement as to the extent to which it would be necessary to harmonize direct taxes. Harmonization of direct taxes involves a common tax policy and thus similar economic and budgetary policies, which could seriously encroach on the independence of member states.[3]

Experts realized that differences in direct taxes could distort competition, apart from state aids or double taxation. As M. Uri[4] puts it:

> The Common Market should protect the right of all firms to choose their location freely, the opportunity for each firm to obtain the capital which it needs . . . not necessarily within the boundaries of the country where it is located, and finally, the opportunity for each firm to make investments whether purely financial or in the form of the creation or acquisition of manufacturing facilities in areas where the profits seem most favorable. In addition, these movements of capital, whether or not they are associated with the practice of a free choice of manufacturing sites, must correspond to the basic earning ability of the investments and not to fiscal advantages. This does not exclude the possibility that important differences in assessment rates may reverse the relationship between net income after taxes compared to profits before taxes. To avoid this distortion there is no other solution than to effect a radical convergence not only of tax rates but also of the tax bases with particular attention to authorized deductions, amortization provisions, and capital gains provisions. For this harmonization will not come about of itself, at least not in the desirable sense of the word. If no deliberate action is taken, there will be cumulative pressures to favor the inflow of capital through competitive lowering of tax rates which would in the end destroy direct taxes and the financial resources of the countries [of the Common Market].

The Neumark Committee was set up to consider to what extent differences in the fiscal systems of member states impede competition and economic expansion and the establishment of a common market similar to an internal market.

If direct taxes are passed on, they directly affect conditions of competition and prices. If not passed on, they affect profit-making capacity and therefore the likelihood of new investment.[5] Different types or rules of direct taxation affect enterprises in different ways. Competition is distorted primarily by differences in the structure of taxes rather than in rates of taxes in different countries; tax differences affect competition between industries in different countries, not competition between economies. Taxes hindering distribution of profits interfere with movement of capital. In conditions of free movement of capital, differences in effective tax rates cause capital migration, shifts of residence, and diversion of

[3] Bille, La Souveraineté Fiscale des Etats et l'Intégration Economique Internationale (1958). One reason for not dealing with direct taxes in the Treaty is that direct taxes, unlike indirect taxes, are not necessarily passed on, so differences in direct taxes do not necessarily affect the prices at which goods are sold across national frontiers. For a discussion see Reboud, Systèmes Fiscaux et Marché Commun 112–14 (1961); Cosciani, The Effects of Differential Tax Treatment of Corporate and Non-Corporate Enterprises, ch. 1 (1959); Meade, Case Studies in European Economic Union 334–35 (1962); Rapport . . . concernant une directive . . . [relative] aux taxes sur le chiffre d'affaires, A.P.E. Doc. No. 56, at 61, 62 (1963–64); see Irish Commission on Income Taxation, Third Report, Pr. 5567, at 44 n.32 (1960). The British views are influenced by the Colwyn Committee, Committee on the National Debt and Taxation, Report, Cmd. No. 2800 (1927), which believed that marginal enterprises prevent the shifting of direct tax by their profit-making competitors. See Committee on Turnover Taxation, Report, Cmd. No. 2300, paras. 206–17 (1964).

[4] "Economics and Politics of the Common Market," in Competition, Cartels and Their Regulation 378, 396 (Miller ed. 1962).

[5] Von der Groeben, "Systèmes fiscaux nationaux et Marché Commun," 1 La Fiscalité du Marché Commun 6, 12 (1962); Kauffman & Kunitzki, "Le Programme d'harmonisation fiscale de la C.E.E.," 4 La Fiscalité du Marché Commun 86, 93 (1963).

investment into low-tax countries.[6] Taxation of capital gains may also cause capital movements or inhibit investment, especially if they are taxed at normal income tax or company tax rates. Tax treatment of capital gains in the country of source or in the country of residence of the potential investor, depending on the terms of the double taxation treaty between the two countries, is specially important to expanding enterprises in underdeveloped regions anxious to attract capital. As tariffs come down, the relative importance of different effective rates of direct taxation will increase.

The Neumark Report effectively avoids the controversy about the extent to which direct taxes[7] could be passed on. The Report says that it is possible to pass on company taxes and taxes on net wealth, at least partially, as well as real property taxes and taxes on business operations.[8] Indirect taxes are almost always passed on by increased prices, since they are genuine cost factors; taxes on net income or profits are passed on in some degree,[9] at least in the long run, even in conditions of competition.

THE TAX REQUIREMENTS OF A COMMON MARKET

A common market which is a single economy ultimately involves the abolition of tax frontiers and differences in tax treatment based on nationality, residence, and place of control.[10] The question of tax frontiers relates only to indirect taxation, including the important excise taxes. The abolition of discrimination requires substantial uniformity of structure and rates in national tax systems.[11]

[6] Meade, Case Studies in European Economic Union 333 (1962); Rapport . . . concernant une directive . . . [relative] aux taxes sur le chiffre d'affaires, A.P.E. Doc. No. 56, at 61 (1963–64). Until recently, capital migration in the Six has been prevented by exchange controls, institutional difficulties, and non-economic factors. See the remarks on the need for a Community regional economic policy on pp. 304–308. Taxes, except possibly death taxes, do not seem to have caused much capital migration between Britain and Ireland since Ireland became independent, although there have never been exchange controls in peacetime. This may be due to the unusual double taxation convention on income tax. See Merrett, "Taxation in a Shrinking World," 114 The Banker 422 (1964). Taxation only in the country of residence would cause tax-inspired capital movements only when the taxpayer was willing to change residence.

[7] The Neumark Report tentatively classified taxes into, first, taxes on income, the production of income, and net wealth; second, taxes on the consumption or use of income, including taxes on production factors; and third, taxes on capital gains and capital movements; Rapport 24, CCH 2425. The emphasis of this book on the type of tax which exists in Ireland has meant that it omits discussion of the other types of tax mentioned at this point in the Neumark Report; i.e., taxes on land and buildings, on royalties and interest, and on professional income.

[8] Rapport 62, CCH 2460.

[9] Neumark Report, Rapport 26–27, 62, CCH 2427, 2460. See generally Cosciani, The Effects of Differential Tax Treatment of Corporate and Non-Corporate Enterprises, ch. 1 (1959). He concludes: "In an advanced economy, like that of Western European countries, the [corporation] tax is more or less substantially passed on to consumers both in the short-run and the long-run." Id. at 36. See also Merrett & Sykes, "Incomes Policy and Company Profitability," Dist. Bank Rev., Sept. 1963, p. 18; Krzyzaniak & Musgrave, The Shifting of the Corporation Income Tax (1963). If marginal costs are equal, a company competing with enterprises paying lower direct taxes cannot pass on its direct taxes fully. Harmonization of taxes would reduce tax-shifting.

[10] See, however, Sullivan, The Search for Tax Principles in the European Economic Community 11 (1963), who uses the phrase "tax fair play." See Vedel, "Les Aspects Fiscaux du Marché Commun," 43 Droit Fiscal 1 (1958).

[11] Fair apportionment of the tax base for revenue purposes between member states also is required, and differences in tax treatment between incorporated and unincorporated operations, including branches and subsidiaries in other member states, must be minimized.

The basic requirement of a common market is freedom of movement for goods and for the factors of production. Taxes must not encourage or inhibit movements of capital. This means double taxation must be eliminated and taxes on the movement of capital eliminated or harmonized. Dissimilar technical rules and concepts, even where the economic effects are substantially the same, interfere with doing business between member states; harmonization in technical respects therefore is required.

For complete economic integration there must be increased interstate co-operation and substantial similarity in tax policies with regard to balance of payments, counter-cyclical measures, and policies for investment and growth.

THE NEED FOR EQUAL CONDITIONS OF COMPETITION AND THE FACTORS WHICH DISTORT THEM

Given free movement of capital and other factors, a common market requires substantially equal conditions of competition so that available resources can be used most efficiently. Equity between individual enterprises also demands that tax burdens should be effectively similar throughout the Community, if it is to be like a single national economy.

The Neumark Report does not insist on uniform taxes.[12] Taxes can continue to reflect different national policies on the extent of redistribution of income and other social and political ideals, on growth, and on the use of benefit-matched taxes (taxes which involve no redistribution but pay for a benefit to the same body of taxpayers) and differences in economic structure, e.g., consumption patterns. Hopefully, the EEC Commission will remember this.

The Neumark Report says[13] that the complete absence of an income tax or a general turnover tax in one country will clearly distort competition, even if the proportion of the national income taken in tax is the same in each state, and that it is desirable to reduce gradually the differences in the structure of and the proportions of revenue derived from the main types of tax.[14] In Germany, the Netherlands, and Luxembourg, direct taxes produce a much greater proportion of total revenue than in Belgium or particularly France and Italy. In France, the general added-value tax is more important, and in Italy,[15] as in Ireland, special consumer or excise taxes are.

There will be differences of national outlook on the desirability of having the total revenue of each member state derived in similar proportions from direct and indirect taxes.[16] Because indirect

[12] Rapport 9, 30, 34, 62–63, CCH 2412, 2430, 2434, 2460. That uniformity of tax laws is not necessary for economic and political integration is proved by most federations and confederations. See Barrère, "L'influence de la croissance économique des Etats membres sur les problèmes d'harmonisation fiscale," Neumark Report, Annexe E, 124, 127–28; Nasini, "Progress on Tax Harmonization in the Common Market," 2 European Taxation 163, 164 (1962).

[13] Rapport 29–30, CCH 2430.

[14] For an analysis of the structure of the fiscal systems of the Six according to total revenue produced, see Neumark Report, Rapport 25, CCH 2426; Wincott, "The Future of Taxation," in Conference on Taxation and the Common Market 1 (International Fiscal Association, U.K. Branch, 1962); Committee on Turnover Taxation, Report, Cmd. No. 2300, para. 6 (1964); EEC Commission, Schéma des Impôts, Appendice (1964).

[15] In some of the Six, notably Italy, state monopolies of certain commodities take the place of special excise or consumer taxes.

[16] One of the Neumark Committee's reasons for thinking that it is desirable to derive equal proportions of total revenue in each member state from direct and from indirect taxes is, presumably, that heavy direct taxes penalize an exporting enterprise in competition with an enterprise paying indirect taxes which are refunded at the point of export. This problem is discussed on pp. 297–99.

taxes are regressive, they are regarded in Ireland and Britain as socially undesirable. However, they are simpler to collect than direct taxes, and this is important in southern Europe, where standards of honesty in tax matters are apparently lower than elsewhere.

THE PRACTICAL MEANING OF UNEQUAL CONDITIONS OF COMPETITION

Article 100 speaks of provisions which affect the establishment and operation of the Common Market, and Article 101 speaks of "distortion" of conditions of competition. Direct taxes do not directly alter the marginal production costs of goods or services supplied, though they may do so indirectly. Differences in the effective rates of direct taxes alter the effective return on capital, whether the taxes affect the company's profits or the dividends which it pays.[17] Since both personal income tax and company tax are general taxes taken into consideration in fixing rates of exchange, differences in the tax rates may to some extent be nullified by the exchange rates.[18] A company in a country with a low effective tax rate may be able to reduce its selling price and maintain its net profits after tax. It can have greater profits for reinvestment,[19] perhaps permitting reduction of marginal costs, or for diversification, and it may pay larger dividends to its shareholders.[20] Its competitor, bearing a higher effective tax rate, has a lower capacity for self-financing or capital formation. It can acquire additional capital for investment only by reducing its dividend or by borrowing or increasing its capital, in which case it will also increase its commitment to produce a minimum profit. The enterprise with the higher tax rates may be less able to obtain capital or may be able to obtain it only at greater cost to itself, especially if the state in question also imposes the highest over-all rate of tax on distributed profits.[21] In such a case there is a difference in the possibilities both for self-financing and for obtaining outside capital. In other cases the methods of financing most favorable to the companies differ, again distorting movement of capital.

GENERAL FACTORS LIKELY TO DISTORT COMPETITIVE CONDITIONS

Similar effective tax rates for similar activities cannot be achieved on a wide scale until all types of tax have been harmonized so as to cause substantially similar economic effects.[22] The question

[17] So, of course, do differences in monetary policy, but free movement of capital throughout the EEC will tend to equalize the cost of capital.

[18] Dale, Tax Harmonization in Europe 28 (1963), points out that since exchange rates do not fluctuate freely and in fact are rarely altered, competitive disadvantages may persist for long periods. Exchange rates can only eliminate the effect of general differences in tax treatment and not disadvantages suffered by individual enterprises. These were the conclusions reached when the matter was discussed in the ECSC. See also Day, "Financial Implications of the Common Market," in Political and Economic Planning, Aspects of European Integration 128 (1962).

[19] This effect may be caused by investment allowances or large initial allowances and neutralized if they are provided in the higher-rate country.

[20] See generally Hearings Before the [United States] Senate Committee on Finance on H.R. 10650, 87th Cong., 2d Sess., pt. 1, at 200–203 (1962); Sullivan, The Search for Tax Principles in the European Economic Community 59–60 (1963).

[21] Cosciani, The Effects of Differential Tax Treatment of Corporate and Non-Corporate Enterprises 80 (1959).

[22] Neumark, "Tax Harmonization in the Common Market," 147 The Accountant 700 (1962). "Federal" taxes could be substituted for national taxes only if the latter had been made uniform. If the need to harmonize effective tax rates conflicts with the aim of having similar proportions of total revenue derived from each

is the net burden of taxation on the relevant industries. If residents of one country have to pay directly for services, while similar services are paid for in another country from general tax revenue, the residents of the former country are at a disadvantage, and this must be taken into account before their net tax burdens can be compared. Social services and social security are provided in some countries primarily out of employers' or employees' contributions. Therefore, social security contributions as well as taxes must be considered in comparing the burden of public revenue and the benefits obtained from it for similar enterprises in different countries.

The important factor in calculating net tax burdens is the extent to which fiscal policies redistribute income rather than return it to the taxpayers who provided it. The extent of taxation is not the same as the extent of redistribution. The Neumark Report concludes that the general tax burden on enterprises is not proportionate to the proportion of the national income taken in taxes, because the funds drawn off are returned to the economy for the general benefit. Industries in countries with high total taxes are thus not necessarily at a competitive disadvantage, unless revenue is used for developing underdeveloped regions; this expenditure shows only long-term returns to the economy, especially if the revenue is used on infrastructure, which is not directly productive. The same disadvantage to the economy is caused by a long delay between collection and expenditure.[23] It follows that to equalize competitive conditions the Community as a whole should bear some of the cost of developing less developed regions. Rich countries can afford a higher relative tax level than poor ones.[24]

From the viewpoint of an individual enterprise, only taxes not passed on to the consumer or shifted back are an actual cost to the enterprise, and in return for these taxes the enterprise benefits from the public services and state expenditures,[25] including public contracts. These benefits may be impossible to calculate accurately and have no direct relationship to the amount of taxes borne. It is impossible to calculate in the abstract the individual enterprise's tax burden. Benefits from public spending are rarely taken into account in calculating the operating costs of an enterprise, even with taxes matched specifically to benefits. To the individual enterprise, the progressive or regressive effect of taxes is obviously important.[26]

The Neumark Report considers tax rates and structure separately. Both alter the relative amount of revenue from the tax. The same tax may have different economic effects in different countries if there are differences in the structure of industry, the level and distribution of

type of tax, as it would if differences in economic structure persist, the harmonization of rates presumably will be given priority.

[23] Neumark Report, Rapport 14, 23, CCH 2416, 2424. The Report concludes that the differences in the proportions of GNP taken in tax and in social security contributions in the Six are not significant.

[24] Neumark, "Tax Harmonization in the Common Market," 147 The Accountant 700, 701 (1962). Less-wealthy countries obtain relatively less revenue from a given direct tax and need to rely more on indirect taxes.

[25] Neumark Report, Rapport 14, CCH 2416. The extent to which sectors such as construction and armaments are able to obtain government contracts and the extent of public spending on tourism, export stimulation, and research are thus important. In the EEC, discrimination on the grounds of nationality in awarding public contracts is prohibited.

[26] All taxes on capital are regressive in relation to the income produced by the assets taxed, even if the capital taxes themselves are progressive. A tax on the factors of production encourages efficiency because it is regressive in relation to profits.

the national income, the incidence of self-financing, the capital- or labor-intensive nature of the enterprise paying tax, the relative importance of economic sectors, the corporate or non-corporate nature of the enterprises, and consumer habits. Important also are the extent of tax evasion and the efficiency of tax administration.[27] The extent to which ordinary commercial accounts are accepted by law and in practice as the basis for imposing taxes varies throughout the Six, and this would alter the effective tax rate even if the legal rules and the tax rates were identical.

Even where identical rates, structure, and administration exist, the scope for passing on direct taxes may be greater in one state than in another.[28] It would probably be impossible deliberately to effect even similar net tax burdens by means of different rates or structures, since the factors influencing effective rates of tax are so complex and so changeable. Substantial equalization of total tax burdens[29] involves, in practice, substantial equalization of the structures and, to a lesser extent, the rates of all taxes.

TREATY PRINCIPLES OTHER THAN EQUAL COMPETITIVE CONDITIONS

The Treaty requirement of equal conditions of competition is to be read as subject to the other requirements of balanced expansion, increased stability, and improved standards of living.[30] Equal conditions of competition throughout the EEC are only the means to insure the optimum use of available resources, and they will not be sought at the cost of harmful economic side effects or sought so rapidly as to cause structural difficulties. EEC member states may modify their taxes for the sake of growth or business cycle policy. Effects on balance of payments and social effects, such as the regressive or progressive nature of the modified taxes, must be considered. The norm to which existing tax systems will be assimilated will not be merely a compromise between them but rather will be designed to aid growth and stability and to be compatible with welfare as well as with equity.

COMPARING TAX LEVELS

The Neumark Committee concludes that differences in the tax laws of the Six distort competition. However, in making comparisons between existing levels of direct taxation in the Six, various pitfalls must be avoided. Effective tax rates depend on so many factors that general comparisons are of very little

[27] Rapport 27–28, CCH 2428.

[28] Neumark, "Tax Harmonization in the Common Market," 147 The Accountant 700 (1962).

[29] Subject to measures of regional economic policy, for example. The Neumark Report did not discuss the use of either "federal" EEC taxes or harmonized national taxes as positive measures of Community economic policy. Taxes in each member state may be used for policy purposes before their rates and structures have been made similar. National or Community policy considerations may make it preferable not to harmonize existing taxes with corresponding taxes elsewhere in the Common Market. The Neumark Committee's terms of reference were merely to "study if and to what extent the differences currently existing in the finances of Member States partly or even entirely hinder the establishment of the Common Market bringing into being and guaranteeing conditions analogous to those of an internal market," and to "study how far it is possible to eliminate those differences which more considerably hinder the development and functioning of the Common Market." Cf. art. 100; see Barrère, "L'influence de la croissance économique des Etats membres sur les problèmes d'harmonisation fiscale," Neumark Report, Annexe E, 124, 129–30.

[30] Preamble and arts. 2, 104. Many other provisions could be cited. This is stressed in the Neumark Report, Rapport 13, 83–88, CCH 2415, 2478–83. EEC Commission, Action Programme for the Second Stage (1962), says that taxes must be "economically rational and socially coherent."

value.[31] The effective rates, not the nominal rates of tax, must be compared. The effective rate of tax depends on the computation of the taxable income or other tax base, and this is made in varying circumstances according to different rules in the different member states. It is necessary to compare the effective rates of capital tax, municipal tax, turnover tax, and company tax or income tax. If the collection of revenue is decentralized to some extent, local taxes must be taken into account; in Ireland, however, they are only 13 per cent of total tax revenue. To calculate these, it would be necessary to decide how far each could be passed on and how much the enterprise could expect to benefit from government spending and financial policy. These two factors cannot be considered except from the point of view of a particular enterprise. It is unreal to generalize about effective rates of tax without making detailed assumptions about the type of enterprise under consideration and without considering economic double taxation and the cumulative effect of several taxes.[32]

However, even comparisons between the tax position of the same enterprise in different countries may be misleading, since the tax system itself alters the capital structure and organization of an enterprise in a particular sector of industry in a given country. In some countries enterprises minimize tax by financing themselves with borrowed capital; in others they are normally self-financing.[33] Whether an enterprise is capital- or labor-intensive also affects its tax position, according to whether direct tax rates or social security contributions are high. Changes in the market for the products of an enterprise influence the extent of profit distribution, which affects the amount of tax borne by the company. Tax borne by the shareholders is also important and depends on their number, the extent of their shareholdings, their other wealth, and their tax domicile. The extent to which tax law and its administration permit tax avoidance also affects the real tax position. Taxes on other enterprises may decrease the amount of income they have available for expenditure on goods and services provided by the enterprise, but an increase in their capital allowances may enlarge the market for these goods or services.

UNIFORM TAXES: TAXATION OF COMPANIES

To consider the economic effects of taxation of companies it is necessary also to discuss taxation of dividends.[34] Each of the Six imposes a company tax separate from the tax on individuals.[35] In Ireland and (until 1965) in Britain,[36] companies pay a tax peculiar to themselves and also pay the income tax paid

[31] Van Hoorn, Tax Aspects of European Economic Cooperation 1 (1958); Company Taxation in Western Europe 4–7 (Mees & Zoonen 3d rev. ed. 1962); see Committee on Turnover Taxation, Report, Cmd. No. 2300, paras. 159–79 (1964).

[32] For example, the provision making corporation profits tax no longer deductible for income tax purposes in Ireland—Finance Act, 1961 Acts 671, § 7—substantially neutralized the simultaneous reduction in the rate of income tax, as far as companies liable to income tax in Ireland were concerned.

[33] Van Hoorn, Tax Aspects of European Economic Cooperation 4 (1958); Sullivan, The Search for Tax Principles in the European Economic Community 39–40 (1963).

[34] Taxation of individuals and unincorporated entities is not dealt with directly in this book.

[35] Such a tax was introduced in Belgium only in 1962. In Italy, the company tax is a "complementary" or supplementary tax.

[36] See U.K. Finance Act, 1965, 13 & 14 Eliz. 2, c. 25.

by individuals. The Neumark Committee recommends[37] the introduction in each country of a standard, flat-rate company tax with the same allowance for depreciation and the same rules with regard to items such as losses, capital gains, valuation of stock, and payment of provisional installments of tax. Similar tax rates are valueless unless the tax bases are the same. The Report recommends that the rate of tax on undistributed profits be substantially similar in each member state; otherwise, large companies doing international business, for which the tax on undistributed profits is important and which the Neumark Committee regarded as more mobile than small companies, would alter their tax domicile to the country with the lowest rate of company tax.[38] Without uniform company taxes, no double taxation treaty can prevent a company engaged in trade between member states from paying taxes different from some of its competitors.

Similar treatment in each member state for undistributed profits is required also to prevent a company resident in the member state with tax laws most favorable to self-financing from accumulating profits for the benefit of a group.[39] This uniform rate should be similar to the maximum income tax rate to prevent use of the corporate form for purely tax reasons.[40] The Neumark Committee suggests an undistributed profits tax rate at 50 per cent.

The Neumark Report suggests that the rate for distributed profits should be approximately half of that for undistributed profits and at least 15 per cent, but this is controversial. The member states could vary the rate for distributed profits as part of their growth and business cycle policies and coordinate it with their personal income taxes. The Neumark Committee recommends a withholding tax on dividends, royalties, and interest high enough to prevent evasion and low enough to minimize repayment claims and other administrative complications. This tax would be at two rates: a low rate between 10 per cent and 20 per cent, if the recipient's identity is known and he is a resident of the EEC, and a higher rate of at least 25 per cent, if his identity is unknown and if it might be impossible

[37] Neumark Report, Rapport 37–39, 66–68, 90, CCH 2437–39, 2463–65, 2484–85. Where schedular taxes are retained, as at present in Italy, they should be credited against the company tax. The Report admitted that there are "theoretical arguments" for a single tax on both companies and shareholders (the Irish system) but said that as the trend in the Six was towards separate company taxes it would be easier to harmonize taxes on the latter basis; Rapport 38, CCH 2438. Professor Neumark's personal preference is for a flat-rate tax on company profits and a progressive complementary tax graduated according to the proportion of profits to the working capital of the company; "Tax Harmonization in the Common Market," 147 The Accountant 700, 706 (1962). Nevin, The Irish Tax System (1963), has suggested a tax on the factors of production, including labor as well as capital; this would encourage growth and efficiency but would not be very different in effect from the net wealth tax proposed by the Neumark Report, if the latter were imposed on companies and combined with higher social security contributions. For a list of the possible ways of treating company profits, see Forte, "Report," 27 Cahiers de Droit Fiscal International 143–44 (1954).

[38] Neumark Report, Rapport 65, CCH 2462. The Report considers that large companies find it easier to pass on their tax, since it is usually at a flat rate, and are more likely to choose their location purely on the basis of commercial and financial considerations; Rapport 63, CCH 2460. In most countries the company tax is progressive at low profit levels.

[39] Neumark Report, Rapport 38, CCH 2437. This could be prevented by tax measures discriminating against companies of other member states, which would be incompatible with the Treaty.

[40] Neumark Report, Rapport 66, CCH 2462–63. At present the maximum rate of personal income tax in Ireland is 72.5%, and in Britain it always has been substantially higher.

for member states to impose further tax.[41] The higher rate would be uniform in each member state, but the lower rate would not need to be. Repayment would be made if the recipient was not liable to tax at the rate withheld. The withholding tax would be paid to the state of residence of the company and repaid by it to the state of residence of the recipient, since it would be a prepayment of the recipient's own tax.

To avoid distortions of competition due only to corporate form, the Neumark Committee recommends that intercorporate dividends be exempt from withholding tax unless the shareholding company is residing outside the EEC, its identity is unknown, or it is a holding company paying an artificially low rate of tax.[42] If the company receiving the dividends does not redistribute them within a reasonable time, it would pay tax at the rate for undistributed profits. The exemption from withholding tax would apply only if the parent company had held a large proportion of the shares (at least 15 per cent or 20 per cent is suggested) in the subsidiary for at least two years. Discrimination against small shareholdings by companies is a natural corollary of tax differentiation in favor of distribution of profits. For example, the present German system applies the principle of tax discrimination against undistributed profits to a group of companies, allowing time for redistribution of intercorporate dividends and penalizing speculation in shares and portfolio investment by companies.[43] The Neumark Report states that redistributed intercorporate dividends should not be taxed more heavily than those paid by a company out of its own trading profits; this is the principle in Ireland.

The Report does not mention one important aspect of the German system—the special treatment for "small" companies, with a net worth of under DM 5 million ($1.25 million), which are regarded as dependent on self-financing if more than 75 per cent of their shares are owned by individuals. This special regime consists of progressive tax rates on undistributed profits, rising at one point to 59 per cent, and a fixed rate of tax of 26.5 per cent on distributed profits.[44] Similar treatment for small companies will be essential if the Neumark Report's proposals are adopted. The suggested tax rate for undistributed profits is probably too high for underindustrialized regions because in these regions there should be no incentive to distribute profits. Most companies in these regions are either small or medium-sized locally owned

[41] Rapport 62, 67, CCH 2459, 2463. This is now the rule in Belgium. The identity of the shareholder is often unknown in the case of bearer shares.

[42] Neumark Report, Rapport 39, 67–68, CCH 2439, 2464. The withholding tax would not be imposed if a double taxation convention provided otherwise. It is curious that the Report should contemplate that low rates of tax for holding companies should continue, since these rates facilitate tax avoidance and, therefore, distortion of conditions of competition. The exception may have been made to avoid prejudging the question whether Luxembourg would be required to alter its present laws on holding companies. The limitation of freedom from withholding tax to parent companies in the EEC is an interesting example of the Neumark Committee's concept of the EEC as one fiscal jurisdiction. On the law in Luxembourg, see Kauffman, "Régime fiscal des holdings, sociétés de placements et fonds communs de placements," Neumark Report, Annexe D. See "Holding Companies," 1 European Taxation, No. 3, at 6 (1961); id., No. 4, at 3; id., No. 8, at 7; id., No. 10, at 5.

[43] The recipient of the dividends must have held 25% of the capital of the subsidiary company for twelve months to receive the tax relief under German law.

[44] Harvard University Law School, Taxation in the Federal Republic of Germany 629–30 (1963). Since the rate for the distributed profits of this special type of small company has been left rather high, they may choose to be taxed at the usual rates.

companies or large subsidiaries of foreign enterprises. The former normally are too small to use the capital market and thus are dependent on self-financing; because of juridical double taxation or other reasons, the latter may not be likely to seek capital outside the region and, because of their reluctance to let in outside interests, they are not likely to use even an adequate local capital market.[45] Thus, they may also be dependent on self-financing. It could be argued that differentiation in favor of distributed profits would enlarge the Irish or regional capital market and so make equity financing possible in place of self-financing; this is the object of the German law. However, no capital market can be open to a company too small to make a public issue successfully,[46] and Irish law has differentiated in favor of profit distribution for years. Throughout the EEC, self-financing should be encouraged by reduced tax rates on undistributed profits of small companies, and in underindustrialized areas there should be special tax rates for distributed and undistributed profits of all companies, to facilitate expansion and capital formation and to eliminate the incentive to distribute profits. Presumably, reduction of the rate of company tax on undistributed profits would be one aspect of a regional economic policy[47] intended to encourage wholly owned subsidiaries in areas in which they seem the preferable form of operation for at least foreign investment.[48] In less developed regions self-financing is probably preferable to equity or loan financing, even by the existing shareholders.

It is difficult to reconcile encouragement of new investment and expansion of existing enterprises in underdeveloped regions with an increased return after taxes for the investor. One possibility is to impose the usual rates of tax on dividends paid by these enterprises but to exempt from taxation capital gains on sale of the shares. Another method is to have the same rate of company tax for distributed and undistributed profits in order to give the company no incentive for distribution but to reduce the personal income tax on dividends paid by companies in less developed regions.

The Neumark Committee does not refer to group accounts of associated companies, another aspect of treating associated companies as a single enterprise for tax purposes, so that it is not clear whether they would permit the losses of a parent company or wholly owned subsidiary to be set off against the profits of the other.[49]

Similar treatment in each member state for dividends paid to individuals is

[45] Even if the foreign parent company has ample capital resources, it usually prefers that the subsidiary in a less developed region finance itself rather than make demands on the parent's liquidity, especially before the subsidiary has proved itself to be profitable. Cosciani, The Effects of Differential Tax Treatment of Corporate and Non-Corporate Enterprises 98–99 (1959), criticizes the type of company tax proposed by the Neumark Committee as being unsuited to developing economies because it penalizes expanding firms. See also Merrett, "Will the New Taxes Spur Investment?" 115 The Banker 149 (1965); Royal Commission on Taxation of Profits and Income, Final Report, Cmd. No. 9474, Memorandum of Dissent, para. 103 (1955).

[46] Cosciani, The Effects of Differential Tax Treatment of Corporate and Non-Corporate Enterprises 60 (1959).

[47] Regional policies are mentioned but not discussed in the Neumark Report; Rapport 4, 12, 23, CCH 2407, 2414, 2424. See Chapter Twelve. Large depreciation allowances encourage self-financed expansion more effectively than do low tax rates on undistributed profits.

[48] See European Investment Bank, Annual Report, 1959, at 15; Vasseur, Le droit de la réforme des structures industrielles et des économies régionales 167–77, 364–75 (1959).

[49] In Germany, integrated companies may unify their accounts for tax purposes; Harvard University Law School, Taxation in the Federal Republic of Germany 387–90, 789–92 (1963).

required only to the extent to which personal income taxes need to be harmonized in the EEC. The rate of company tax on distributed profits will decide the extent to which the system recommended by the Neumark Committee will favor distribution of company profits[50] in practice. If dividends paid to individuals were not subject to the proposed unitary income tax at a reduced rate, shareholders controlling a company would have an incentive to distribute profits only until their personal rates of tax approached within 15 per cent (if this is the rate of company tax chosen for distributed profits) of the rate on undistributed profits.

The company tax on distributed profits causes economic double taxation[51] and, like the general tax on net wealth proposed by the Neumark Committee, causes differentiation in favor of earned income.[52] To avoid economic double taxation and discrimination against capital-intensive enterprises, this net wealth tax would not be imposed on companies. Since the Six have divergent policies on this, it is curious that the Neumark Committee discusses neither the merits of a lower rate of tax for distributed profits nor the type of economic situation in which the lower rate is appropriate. Economic double taxation deters investment and distribution of company profits. So, however, does differentiation in favor of earned income as against investment income, and the rules on this in Britain, Ireland, and the Six[53] will need to be harmonized. Only a policy favoring distribution of profits will encourage reciprocal investment throughout the EEC and will insure that capital moves freely into the enterprises which can use it most profitably, thus maximizing growth. However, this policy may cause companies to overcapitalize or use loan capital obtained by reborrowing distributed profits, and increases the number of holding companies in countries with low tax rates on undistributed dividend income. Free intersectoral flow of capital should be aided by taxes favoring distributed profits, since legal and business

[50] See Schendstok, "Harmonisation de l'impôt prélevé sur les bénéfices des sociétés de capitaux et sur les dividendes distribués ou perçus," Neumark Report, Annexe F, 136. There are several ways to avoid economic double taxation of distributed company profits. Only a comparison of the rates of tax in each case can decide the extent to which economic double taxation has been eliminated and the extent to which the tax system discriminates in favor of distribution of company profits. For an excellent comparative analysis, see Nortcliffe, Common Market Fiscal Systems 83–85 (1960). Two less orthodox methods are to tax the shareholders in full on the undistributed profits of the company and to tax them at the full rate on the capital gain in the value of their shares when realized. See Merrett, "Capital Gains Taxation: The Accrual Alternative," 16 Oxford Economic Papers 262 (1964).

[51] "Economic double taxation" is used in the text to mean subjection of the same income to two types of tax or to tax in the hands of two legal persons, and thus to a total burden of tax greater than it otherwise would have borne. A tax policy for less developed regions of the EEC could adopt the Greek method of exempting distributed profits from all company tax; this would equate income from the taxpayer's own activities with income invested in a less developed area.

[52] "Net Worth Taxes in Europe," 1 European Taxation, No. 16, at 5 (1961). See Wheatcroft, "What About a Wealth Tax?" 184 The Statist 81 (1964); Peacock, "Economics of a Net Wealth Tax for Britain," 1963 Brit. Tax Rev. 388; Tress, "A Wealth Tax Is a Wealth Tax," id. at 400; Wheatcroft, "The Administrative Problems of a Wealth Tax," id. at 410; Irish Commission on Income Taxation, Third Report, Pr. 5567, ch. VI (1960). The wealth-tax structure suitable for a given country depends vitally on the distribution of wealth; see Nevin, The Ownership of Personal Property in Ireland (1961). A wealth tax might have to be supplemented by a gift tax.

[53] See Nortcliffe, Common Market Fiscal Systems 79–81 (1960). In a country in need of capital investment, such as Ireland, this differentiation involves a conflict between growth and equity.

factors tend to limit diversification. The German system was adopted to end economic double taxation, to enlarge the capital market, and to widen public ownership of large companies;[54] the first two reasons and perhaps also the third reason should have influenced the Neumark Committee.

TAXES ON CAPITAL MOVEMENTS

Capital transfer taxes inhibit freedom of movement of capital. These are taxes or stamp duties on the creation of companies with share capital, on increases in the capital of a company, and on the issuance and transfer of shares. These transactions may be subject to double taxation if shares of a company of one country are issued on the stock exchange of another. Differences in these taxes may influence the nature and place of investment and, particularly, the choice of a capital market. The Neumark Committee concludes that differences in capital transfer taxes are especially likely to affect fixed-yield securities and that double taxation should be eliminated and these taxes made uniform and eventually abolished.[55] The Commission compromised with the views of member states and in 1965 submitted to the Council a draft directive providing for replacement of existing taxes by a common tax on capital movements (other than share transfers, which would be liable to a separate tax) at 0.5–1 per cent. Because of the deficiencies in European capital markets, the Commission considered these taxes more urgent than the Neumark Committee did.

SUMMARY OF THE NEUMARK REPORT'S RECOMMENDATIONS

Since only the recommendations of the Neumark Committee which affect taxation of companies and company profits are discussed here, a summary of the recommendations of the Committee[56] is necessary. Disregarding preparatory work, they are, in order of urgency:

First Stage: (1) Cumulative turnover taxes are to be abolished and replaced by an added-value tax or possibly a single-stage tax. Supplementary single-stage retail taxes may be introduced. Fiscal frontiers ultimately should be abolished by adoption of the origin principle, and this will necessitate harmonization of excise and special consumer taxes. Adjustments in excise taxes may involve compensatory or equalization payments between member states.[57] This view confirmed the detailed views of the Sub-

[54] Cosciani, The Effects of Differential Tax Treatment of Corporate and Non-Corporate Enterprises 95 (1959), says that the choice of policies depends on "considerations of financial policy in general, on the desire to increase or diminish or not to influence the public's purchasing power, on the desire to augment national savings in order to create greater capital investment in the national economy, or on the desire to slow down capital investment." He points out that heavier taxes on undistributed profits increase the importance of interest rates and monetary policy for companies requiring finance and may result in prejudice to equity shareholders, who indirectly bear the company's tax, as against debenture holders, who do not.

[55] Neumark Report, Rapport 52–54, CCH 2450–52. At present, share transfers in Ireland are taxed at the rate of 1% of the value, in the case of Irish shares, and 2% for foreign shares; the creation of share capital is taxed at 0.25%. The proposed EEC common tax is to be imposed on the formation of a company with a share capital, on contributions of assets in return for shares, and on movement of a company into the EEC. Mergers would be taxed at the lower rate. States would have the option to tax certain other transactions. See 1965 EEC Bull. No. 2, Supp. 11–14.

[56] See Rapport 89–92, CCH 2483–87. It is not possible to say how many years each stage will last or whether all the recommendations will be carried out as planned or at all.

[57] Rapport 40–45, 51–52, CCH 2439–44, 2449–50. The origin and destination principles are discussed in the Neumark Report at Rapport 76–82, CCH 2472–78.

Groups discussed in the previous chapter. (2) The uniform withholding taxes on dividends and interest, already discussed, should be adopted. (3) All existing double taxation conventions should be revised to resemble the OEEC-OECD model convention to prepare for a single multilateral double taxation convention.

Second Stage: (4) The company tax already discussed should be introduced. This will have the same rates and tax base and give similar treatment for distributed profits in each state. (5) A unitary personal income tax should be introduced with a uniform structure and rules, though not necessarily with uniform rates.[58] At the same time, schedular or "real" taxes with economic effects similar to company and income taxes should be integrated into those taxes. Taxation of capital gains should be standardized. It is not clear whether the proposed tax on net wealth should be introduced at this stage or at the same time as measure (10),[59] below. This net wealth tax, like that in the Netherlands but unlike those in force in Germany, Luxembourg, and Italy,[60] will not apply to companies. (6) A multilateral double taxation convention should be concluded. (7) Special consumer taxes not levied in all member states and not important as revenue raisers should be abolished.[61]

Third Stage: (8) Capital transfer taxes should be abolished.[62] (9) The taxation of transport and sources of energy must be harmonized. (10) Common tax institutions, an information agency, a common fund for supranational equalization payments, and a European tax court to settle questions which cannot be settled by national courts should be set up. (11) Estate and succession taxes on death should be harmonized. (12) Policy and techniques for obtaining revenue and for providing social security will have to be harmonized. (13) Special consumer taxes common to all member states and important as revenue raisers must be harmonized. This will not be necessary until tax frontiers have been ended for these taxes by adoption of the origin principle. In the course of carrying out all of these reforms, a common financial policy would be adopted by all member states.

The Committee's proposals would tend to put control of the revenues of member states into the hands of EEC institutions, and this strong centripetal tendency may make the proposals unacceptable to the governments of some member states. If accepted, these proposals will involve changes in the national tax systems to maintain revenue, which changes are not discussed in this book. The Neumark Committee does not discuss whether the Community should continue to be financed out of payments made by national governments out of national taxes[63] or by a "federal" tax payable to the Community itself.[64]

CHANGES IN EXISTING TAX SYSTEMS TO ACHIEVE HARMONIZATION

Differences in the rates and structure of direct taxes affect interstate trade primarily through their effect on the cost

[58] Rapport 32–36, 57–62, CCH 2432–36, 2455–59.

[59] Rapport 46–47, CCH 2445–46.

[60] In Italy the tax on capital is an element in the company tax.

[61] Rapport 45–46, 30, 49–51, CCH 2444–45, 2431, 2448–49.

[62] Rapport 52–54, CCH 2450–52.

[63] Nasini, "Progress on Tax Harmonization in the Common Market," 2 European Taxation 163, 164 (1962).

[64] Nor did they discuss subsidies or tax factors affecting agriculture, although these not only distort conditions of competition in agricultural products but also, by affecting the cost of food and therefore wage levels, distort conditions of competition in other sectors as well. This is particularly important in Britain; see Federation of British Industries, Export Incentives 4 (1962).

and supply of capital, and they are not as important as differences in indirect taxes, but it is not possible to achieve equal competitive conditions by means as simple as the destination principle. Harmonization, not a technical remedy, is required. Due to changes in the structure and rates of direct taxes, changes in the rates of indirect tax probably will have to be made to maintain revenue. Some changes would be required anyway for harmonization. Major changes from direct to indirect taxation involve serious consequences and cannot be carried out abruptly. The Neumark Report does not suggest any timetable for carrying out its recommendations.

States now without taxes of the kinds recommended will introduce them and will reduce their dependence on the types of tax which they will later have to abolish. The Six will probably make piecemeal alterations in the tax bases of their direct taxes to assimilate them to the proposed uniform taxes by introducing common principles and concepts aimed at fiscal transparency. Consequential changes in tax rates may be necessary. Piecemeal alterations of taxes which already exist in each member state, such as company taxes, are most likely to affect investors in the immediate future. Even when the details of the uniform taxes have been agreed on by member states, they could only be introduced gradually. Fiscal transparency will permit questions of economic and juridical double taxation to be dealt with efficiently and will facilitate comparison of tax burdens, thereby aiding further harmonization. The popular demand for harmonization of taxation would be increased by fiscal transparency on the grounds of equity between EEC residents. Even where effective tax rates are similar, interpenetration of economies is inhibited by purely technical differences between tax systems. This would be important for Ireland and Britain, since their tax systems differ technically, as well as economically, from those of the Six.

Ultimately, the establishment of similar tax structures and rates in all member states will involve coordinated policies on public spending. The permissible variations in the common taxes may not prevent them from producing amounts of revenue which are totally different, both relatively and absolutely, in different member states. The revenue produced may be excessive or inadequate for the member state in question, so equalization payments between member states, resulting ultimately in a common budget, would be required. Because free movement of capital may result in net capital emigration, thus causing a reduction in the tax base,[65] these payments will be necessary, especially since under conventional international tax law the country of source, not the capital-exporting country, has the primary right to tax. The Neumark Report does not discuss the changes in national tax systems due to revenue considerations which would arise from paying the proposed uniform taxes to a supranational tax authority. The alternative to pooling tax receipts would be to try to divide the tax base equitably between the member states. This would be possible without altering competitive conditions, e.g., by adopting special rules as to source of income in order to allocate taxes to the member state in difficulties. It does not matter to which state an enterprise pays taxes if the effective tax rate is the same. This is a complicated method of achieving the same result as a sharing of revenue receipts, but it might be adopted in a country which is less developed than other member states.

[65] Neumark, "Tax Harmonization in the Common Market," 147 The Accountant 700, 702 (1962). These movements of capital would tend to increase because the reduction in the tax base would necessitate either increased tax rates or reduced social services.

THE CONCEPT OF TAXABLE INCOME

Taxable profits of business enterprises in the Six are the difference between the value of the net assets at the beginning and the end of the accounting period, after making allowances for capital invested or withdrawn.[66] In Ireland (and in Britain until 1965), tax is charged on "trading profits" or "income from specified sources."[67] Taxable trading profits are the difference between gross income receipts and the expenditures wholly and exclusively incurred to produce them. The most important results of the difference between Ireland and the Six are that in the Six capital gains, even if non-recurring, are included in taxable business profits and capital expenditure and capital losses are deducted in computing taxable income. The effect of the difference is lessened by the fact that in Ireland most deliberately made or recurring capital gains are taxed as income.[68] In Britain a special tax on certain short-term capital gains was introduced in 1962 and a tax on all capital gains in 1965;[69] in Ireland capital gains up to the amount of depreciation already allowed but not in excess of the actual cost of the asset are taxed. Nevertheless, the tax base in Ireland is narrower than in the Six. In Ireland, the Six (except Belgium), and Britain, there is no special rate of tax on companies' capital gains; they are taxable, if it all, at the full tax rate. The Irish principle that taxable income must come from a specific source necessitates special provisions where no source exists when the income is received; for example, before the commencement or after the cessation of trading. Since the tax base must be the same in all member states, adoption in Irish law of the broader EEC concept of the tax base will be necessary. This adoption would facilitate simplification of the existing legislation, which sacrifices both simplicity and principle to remedy the anomalies due to the net-trading-profits and source-of-income principles. The distinction between income and capital gains would no longer be crucial to tax liability. Apparent capital gains due to inflation must not be taxed.

Under Irish law and under British law until April 1965, miscellaneous types of irregular or non-recurring capital gains are exempt from tax. Therefore, it is difficult to state in general how the competitive position of Irish and British industry benefits from their exemption, except that it will be aided most during periods of economic expansion or inflation.[70] The introduction of the EEC

[66] On the new Belgian rules, see Decree of April 19, 1963; for a statement of the German principle, see Einkommensteuergesetz, Aug. 15, 1961, art. 4. See generally "Computation of Taxable Profits," 3 European Taxation 182 (1963). Capital gains are not normally taxed until the assets in question are sold.

[67] See Economic Intelligence Unit, Taxes for Britain (1962); Baker, "Income Tax Planning for Common Market Operations," in 2 Institute on Private Investments Abroad 382–83 (Southwestern Legal Foundation, 1961); Davies, "Britain into Europe: The Prospect of Tax Reform," 1962 Brit. Tax Rev. 81, 88. The difference between the principle in the EEC and that in Britain (until 1965) is "fundamental." Wheatcroft, "Direct Tax," in Conference on Taxation and the Common Market 7 (International Fiscal Association, U.K. Branch, 1962); Dale, Tax Harmonization in Europe, ch. VIII (1963); Royal Commission on Taxation of Profits and Income, Final Report, Cmd. No. 9474, para. 109, and Memorandum of Dissent, paras. 2–84 (1955); Head, "The Case for a Capital Gains Tax," 18 Pub. Fin. 220 (1963); Irish Commission on Income Taxation, Third Report, Pr. 5567, ch. V (1960); Ilhersic, The Taxation of Capital Gains (1962).

[68] This and some detailed consequences of Irish law adopting the EEC concept are discussed on pp. 212–13.

[69] Finance Act, 1962, 10 & 11 Eliz. 2, c. 44. §§ 10–16 and Ninth and Tenth Schedules; Finance Act, 1965, 13 & 14 Eliz. 2, c. 25, pt. III.

[70] Committee of Inquiry into Taxation on Industry, Report, Pr. 3512, at 35 (1956).

principle would increase the level of company tax since some depreciation is already deductible. The distortion of competitive conditions cannot be dealt with satisfactorily without introducing a new concept of the tax base.[71] Those investment trusts and insurance companies which do not turn over their portfolios fast enough to be taxed as dealers benefit greatly from the Irish principle.

DEDUCTIBLE EXPENSES[72]

It is difficult also to classify clearly the circumstances in which Irish industry is prejudiced by the refusal of Irish law to permit capital expenditure or losses on capital assets to be deducted in computing taxable income. Since capital expenditure on industrial buildings and machinery and on patents and certain scientific research can be deducted in one year, as a result of special legislation,[73] the difference between the Irish and the Continental systems is again not as great in practice as it is in principle. In the Six all capital expenditure is deductible over varying periods. The practical difference is in the treatment of assets which have not been specially made depreciable in Ireland, the most important being intangible and wasting assets and commercial buildings.

The distinction between capital and revenue expenditure in Irish law is not based on accounting principles, and its application in practice is difficult and unsatisfactory. In general, the test of a non-deductible capital expense is that it is made "once and for all . . . with a view to bringing into existence . . . [a new] asset or advantage for the enduring benefit" of a business.[74] Expenditure on fixed capital, as distinct from circulating capital,[75] is normally capital expenditure and not deductible. If the object of the expenditure is to bring a new capital asset or advantage into existence, the making of the payment in installments or the fact that the asset is not in fact created or the advantage acquired is irrelevant.[76] If expenditure is held to be capital expenditure, it is made out of taxed profits unless it comes within one of the classes for which depreciation is allowed.

In many cases of payments allowed as revenue expenses, the substance of the transaction is indistinguishable from payments held elsewhere to be capital payments. A capital expense to the payor is not necessarily a capital gain in the hands of the payee, in spite of the possibility of double taxation if the tax treatment of the receipt is not coordinated with that of the expense. Recommendations were made in the United King-

[71] The nearest thing at present in Irish law to the express provisions of the fiscal laws of the Six is Income Tax Act, 1918, 8 & 9 Geo. 5, c. 40, Schedule D, Cases I and II, Rule 3. In the EEC the member states would put pressure on each other to rationalize and improve the efficiency of their tax systems, so as to avoid having to make compensation payments unnecessarily to maintain each other's revenue.

[72] See 1 British Tax Encyclopedia 1256–83 (Wheatcroft ed. 1962).

[73] See generally Harvard University Law School, Taxation in the United Kingdom 179–81 (1957). For provisions on scientific research, see Finance Act, 1946 Acts 657, § 5, and Finance Act, 1965 Acts, No. 22, § 2. Depreciation allowances, patents, and know-how are dealt with in Chapter Eight.

[74] Atherton v. British Insulated & Helsby Cables, Ltd., [1926] A.C. 205, 213, 10 Tax Cas. 155, 192 (per Cave, L.). See Southern v. Borax Consol., 23 Tax Cas. 597 (1940); Bolam v. Regent Oil Co., 37 Tax Cas. 56 (1956); see, however, Vale v. Martin Mahoney & Bros., Ltd., 2 Ir. Tax Cas. 331 (1947); Commission on Income Taxation, Seventh Report, Pr. 6581, para. 194 (1962).

[75] Anglo-Persian Oil Co. v. Dale, 16 Tax Cas. 253 (1931).

[76] United States Steel v. Cullington (No. 1), 23 Tax Cas. 71 (1939); Southwell v. Savill Bros., 4 Tax Cas. 430 (1901); Countess of Warwick v. Ogg, 8 Tax Cas. 652 (1924); cf. Anglo-Persian Oil Co. v. Dale, 16 Tax Cas. 253 (1931).

dom[77] for rationalizing the position with regard to lump-sum payments for the hire or use of an asset, payments for assets or rights of only limited duration, payments for enduring trade advantages not actually assets in the normal sense, and unsuccessful payments; no similar recommendations have been made in Ireland, and the law is still in the unsatisfactory position indicated.

Since the difference between deductible revenue expenses and disallowed capital payments may turn on the formal nature of the transaction, it may be argued that a well-advised Irish enterprise can avoid the competitive disadvantage resulting from these rules; however, case law proves that it cannot. In any case, the emphasis on form rather than substance is objectionable in a rational tax system and has been condemned by the Neumark Committee, as a matter of principle, in other connections in the context of harmonization of tax law.[78] Because there normally is a connection between the tax treatment of the payment in the hands of the payor and of the payee, there normally is a conflict of interest as to who is to be given the tax benefit resulting from the rule of law. The difficulty of ascertaining the result is itself an impediment to business decisions.

In addition to special rules relating to capital expenditure on the acquisition of patents[79] and the fact that any revenue expenditure on the acquisition of technical information is deductible on ordinary principles, there is a special Irish provision[80] making capital expenditure on scientific research deductible in full in the year of the expenditure. A special study made for the OECD[81] indicates that the tax treatment of research varies widely. Harmonization of these provisions is likely to take place by giving more favorable treatment to such expenditure, comparable to that now given by France—where one-half the expenditure is deductible in the first year—and Britain.

In calculating the profits of an Irish business, only expenses "wholly and exclusively"[82] for the purposes of the trade are deductible. This rule has caused excessively large directors' fees and salaries paid to controlling shareholders and their relatives as a distribution of profits,[83] not as remuneration for services, to be disallowed. The "wholly and exclusively" rule is an anti-avoidance provision, since it limits deductible expenses to those which are incidental to the trade and are for business purposes.[84] It seems nar-

[77] Committee on Taxation of Trading Profits, Report, Cmd. No. 8189, paras. 246–64 (1951). See Irish Commission on Income Taxation, Seventh Report, Pr. 6581, ch. III passim (1962); Second White Paper on Direct Taxation, Pr. 7024, paras. 47–48 (1963).

[78] Rapport 53, CCH 2451. See Royal Commission on Taxation of Profits and Income, Final Report, Cmd. No. 9474, Memorandum of Dissent, paras. 12–18 (1955).

[79] Finance Act, 1959 Acts 681, § 47.

[80] Finance Act, 1965 Acts, No. 22, § 2.

[81] Van Hoorn, Tax Treatment of Research and Development (1962).

[82] Income Tax Act, 1918, 8 & 9 Geo. 5, c. 40, Schedule D, Cases I and II, Rule 3(a). This rule was discussed by British Committee on Taxation of Trading Profits, Report, Cmd. No. 8189, paras. 149–62 (1951); ch. IV of this report deals generally with the basis of computation of taxable income in British tax law, which, until 1965, was substantially similar to that of Ireland. See also Usher's Wiltshire Brewery, Ltd. v. Bruce, [1915] A.C. 433, 6 Tax Cas. 399; Income Tax Codification Committee, Report, Cmd. No. 5131, paras. 76–79 (1936); Kealy v. O'Mara Limerick, Ltd., [1942] Ir. R. 616; Davis v. M., [1947] Ir. R. 145.

[83] Stott & Ingaham v. Trehearne, 9 Tax Cas. 69 (1924); Copeman v. William Flood & Sons, Ltd., [1941] 1 K.B. 202, 24 Tax Cas. 53 (1940). Curiously little use has been made of this principle by the revenue authorities in Ireland and Britain.

[84] See Committee on Taxation of Trading Profits, Report, Cmd. No. 8189, paras. 148–62

rower in practice than similar rules in the Six, owing to the difference in the statutory method of calculating the tax base. In France and the Netherlands, directors' fees are more heavily taxed than normal salaries, and all of the Six distinguish in principle between payment of fees and withdrawal of profits. In Ireland, however, the company law does not limit the remuneration of directors.[85]

THE RELEVANCE OF THE CORPORATE FORM

Similarity of tax treatment for incorporated and unincorporated enterprises is unimportant in practice in the EEC, except in connection with double taxation of distributed corporate profits. Little business is done by unincorporated enterprises. Existing national tax laws appear to impose substantially different total amounts of tax on incorporated and unincorporated enterprises, although the result is difficult to estimate since the technical treatment may be radically different.[86] Distortion of competition by choice of the form of enterprise can be dealt with on a national basis.

VALUATION OF STOCK

Treatment of stock is in general more flexible and more liberal in the Six than in Ireland, where the "first in, first out" or the average cost methods are normally used. Valuation in Ireland is on the basis of the original cost or present market value, whichever is lower.[87] Unlike the methods used in the Netherlands and Italy, the base-stock method is not used in Ireland. The "last in, first out" method, which is permitted in Italy, the Nether-

---

(1951); Royal Commission on Taxation of Profits and Income, Final Report, Cmd. No. 9474, paras. 123–28 (1955).

[85] The Netherlands intends to abolish the special tax on directors' fees; "New Tax Proposals in the Netherlands," 3 European Taxation 91 (1963). The extent to which fees are deductible is to be limited. For the Irish provisions relating to benefits in kind to directors and senior employees, see Finance Act, 1958 Acts 553, §§ 23–30. On pension schemes, see Finance Act, 1958, §§ 31–43; Wheatcroft, "The General Principles of Tax Planning," 1963 Brit. Tax Rev. 36. For other aspects of tax avoidance in connection with retiring directors, see Beak v. Robson, [1943] 1 All E.R. 46; Associated Portland Cement Mfrs. v. I.R.C., [1946] 1 All E.R. 68; Henley v. Murray, [1950] 1 All E.R. 908; Hunter v. Dewhurst, 16 Tax Cas. 605 (1932); Dale v. de Soissons, [1950] 2 All E.R. 460. See, however, Finance Act, 1964 Acts, No. 15, §§ 7–9.

[86] See Cosciani, The Effects of Differential Tax Treatment of Corporate and Non-Corporate Enterprises (1959).

[87] See Commission on Income Taxation, Seventh Report, Pr. 6581, at 197–98 (1962); Royal Commission on Taxation of Profits and Income, Final Report, Cmd. No. 9474, ch. 18 (1955); Committee on Taxation of Trading Profits, Report, Cmd. No. 8189, paras. 280–83 (1951). In France, Luxembourg, and Germany, valuation of stock is, broadly, on the basis of original cost or the market price, whichever is lower. In France and Germany there are provisions to counteract the effect of rising prices. In Belgium almost any commercially acceptable method of valuing stocks is permitted for tax purposes. Germany and Luxembourg permit the *Teilwert* method. By this method stock is valued at that proportion of the total price of the business as a going concern which would be attributable to the stock in question. This method can be used only if the price so calculated is lower than the cost price.

In practice, differences in methods of valuing stock or in the number of years of life of a capital asset for depreciation purposes and in other tax rules may divert capital and distort competitive conditions between different sectors in the same country. This may occur without any formal differentiation in fiscal law and may or may not be intentional. For example, in Ireland investment allowances, as distinct from initial allowances, are given for ships; Finance Act, 1957 Acts 463, §§ 17–23.

See Wheatcroft, "The General Principles of Tax Planning," 1963 Brit. Tax Rev. 20, 32–33; Talbot, "Tax Aspects of Stock Valuation," 1957 Brit. Tax Rev. 229; Edey, "Valuation of Stock in Trade for Income Tax Purposes," 1956 Brit. Tax Rev. 23; "Comparative Analysis of Depreciation Allowances and Inventory Valuation in the Common Market," 5 European Taxation 114 (1965).

lands, and in some circumstances in Luxembourg, is not permitted. In Ireland, treatment of stock is governed by rules of practice and not by statute, and the general rule is that any normal commercial method of dealing with stock (other than those mentioned) is permissible, if consistently used. Once again, the exact effect on competitive conditions must be considered in relation to an individual enterprise rather than from a general viewpoint. The most liberal treatment of stock in the EEC is given in Belgium.

LOSSES, JOINT VENTURES, AND RESERVES

In Ireland and Britain losses may be carried forward and set off against future profits without any time limit.[88] In the Six losses may be carried forward only for limited periods.[89] The principal that tax should be paid only on the total net profits over the whole life of a business is a reasonable one and is important to a cyclical[90] or a large industry, which cannot readily contract and expand again when conditions improve. If the unemployment situation is serious, it should not be aggravated by liquidations if tax policy can prevent it. In this respect the tax laws of the Six should be brought into line with those of Ireland and the United Kingdom.[91]

One source[92] recommends that it should be made possible to set off losses of joint marketing or manufacturing companies against the profits of parent companies. One provision of Irish law[93] allows joint subsidiary companies incorporated before March 1, 1965, to treat as income payments made to them by their parent companies to recoup their

The Irish provisions on dividend stripping are Finance Act, 1958 Acts 553, §§ 51–53 and Third Schedule; corresponding British provisions are Finance (No. 2) Act, 1955, 4 Eliz. 2, c. 17, § 4; Finance Act, 1958, 6 & 7 Eliz. 2, c. 56, §§ 18–19; and Finance Act, 1960, 8 & 9 Eliz. 2, c. 44, § 31. See also Shoup, "Tax Tension and the British Fiscal System," 14 Nat'l Tax Rev. 1, 8–11 (1961).

[88] Finance Act, 1960 Acts 483, § 3. See generally Commission on Income Taxation, Seventh Report, Pr. 6581, ch. XIV (1962). The Income Tax Commission states the four principal rules relating to losses. First, a loss in a business or profession, including farming, can be set off against income from other sources in the same year. Second, a loss in one trade may be set off against a profit in another carried on by the same taxpayer. These two rules apply to income tax and surtax. The same principles apply to corporation profits tax, which is imposed on net total income, not on income from a number of sources or trades. Third, a loss can be set off against income in later years from the same source, with no time limit; Finance Act, 1960, § 3. This rule has applied to corporation profits tax only since the Finance Act, 1964 Acts, No. 15, § 25. Fourth, a loss in the closing year of a business which exceeds income from other sources in that year can be carried back and set off against the income of the three previous years; Finance Act, 1960, § 4. The time limitation on this "carry-back" is contrary to the principle of paying tax only on the total profits over the whole life of a business, but it is probably justified by administrative convenience.

Of the Six only the Netherlands permits losses to be set off against the profits of previous years. This carry-back is limited to one year but is not limited to the last year of trading.

See Wheatcroft, "The General Principles of Tax Planning," 1963 Brit. Tax Rev. 20, 33–34.

[89] In Italy, Belgium, Germany, and France, five years; Luxembourg, two years; the Netherlands, six years or, in some cases, a longer but specified period.

[90] See Machlup, The Political Economy of Monopoly 56–62 (1952).

[91] Nortcliffe, Common Market Fiscal Systems 82 (1960).

[92] Irish Committee on Industrial Organization, Interim Report on State Aid to Be Granted to Industry to Adapt Itself to Meet Common Market Conditions [hereinafter cited as Interim Report on State Aid], Pr. 6510, at 16, 18 (1962); cf. Commission on Income Taxation, Seventh Report, Pr. 6581, at 198–99 (1962); Committee on Taxation of Trading Profits, Report, Cmd. No. 8189, ch. VII (1951).

[93] Finance Act, 1962 Acts 563, § 13; cf. U.K. Finance Act, 1953, 1 & 2 Eliz. 2, c. 34, § 20.

losses and allows the parent companies to deduct the payments. Losses include capital allowances for depreciation and for interest and royalty payments.[94] This is an important step in treating joint ventures as enterprises integrated with their parent companies. It is also a step towards tax concessions, other than unlimited carry-over of losses, to new enterprises. In spite of the lack of industrial initiative and the scarcity of entrepreneurs in Ireland, no tax incentives have ever been given to a new manufacturing business as such, except to a new export business. Such incentives, if temporary, distort competition only long enough to enable new enterprises to establish themselves, without interfering with competition between other enterprises in the same sector, and are useful to implement regional development policy and to encourage capital formation. Such incentives assist (and might be limited to) small manufacturing or service firms and do not prejudice competing large, international firms. Too many Irish business enterprises are engaged in distribution and too few in manufacture. However, such incentives are not valuable to the large enterprises most needed to take advantage of the large European market.

In general, commercial accounts are more readily accepted as an accurate statement of taxable income in the Netherlands than in the rest of the EEC, in Ireland, or in the United Kingdom. The Netherlands permits accumulation of tax-free reserves to spread recurring costs, to replace certain fixed assets, and to cover risks normally insured against, and Belgium allows them for bad debts and certain future expenditures.[95] In Ireland reserves can be accumulated only out of taxed profits. Fiscal transparency can hardly be achieved without substantially uniform accounting techniques.[96]

THE PRECEDING YEAR BASIS OF ASSESSMENT

The Irish income tax system is complicated by the "preceding year" basis of assessment. Income tax on the profits of a business is based on the profits made in the year preceding the one for which the tax is assessed. This involves complicated calculations which cause irrational increases or decreases in tax liability. If one business is stopped and another commenced, between one and two years' profits of the old business are not taxed, and between one and two years' profits of the new business are taxed twice. The same thing occurs when a company alters its accounting year. The opportunity for tax avoidance is obvious.[97] The present

[94] Finance Act, 1962 Acts. 563, § 13(6).

[95] In France some tax concessions were given for reserves to offset inflation. Germany also allows this and also permits tax-free retention of the excess of the compensation for a lost or damaged asset over its written-down value if the asset is to be replaced. A Belgian decree, Arrêté Royal, May 30, 1963, permits the formation of tax-free reserves for future business losses if clearly specified and due to special risks, for the overhaul of depreciating assets, and for protection in cases of future damage. Reserves for losses are limited to a specified proportion of the annual profits which can be put to reserve.

[96] Nasini, "Progress on Tax Harmonization in the Common Market," 2 European Taxation 163, 167 (1962). See Neumark Report, Rapport 37, CCH 2436–37; Schendstok, "Les méthodes de coordination interne en matière fiscale doivent être harmonisées," 3 La Fiscalité du Marché Commun 67 (1962); Heerkens, "Patterns of European Taxation," in Doing Business in the Common Market 54, 60 (Commerce Clearing House, 1963).

On the difference between business profits for tax purposes and profits according to the ordinary principles of accountancy, see U.K. Income Tax Act, 1918, 8 & 9 Geo. 5, c. 40, Schedule D, Cases I and II, Rule 3; Charlton, "The Taxation of Business Profits," 19 J. Stat. Soc. 45, 49–50 (1956–57).

[97] Wheatcroft, "The General Principles of Tax Planning," 1963 Brit. Tax Rev. 20, 31–32. There is nothing in Ireland corresponding to

system has been severely criticized[98] on various other grounds; in particular, it results in loss of double taxation relief in certain circumstances.[99] In spite of the disadvantages which it pointed out,[100] the Irish Income Tax Commission decided against any change in the system of personal income tax which would involve advance estimates of profits and payments on account. The Income Tax Commission, however, did recommend that company income tax should be payable on the income of a company's accounting period,[101] like corporation profits tax. Adoption of this recommendation is essential to the principle that over the life of a business as a whole the total taxed profits should equal the total profits made. There is no point in accepting this principle for carry-over of losses and not for assessment of initial and final years.[102] Its adoption is a prerequisite to the creation of a unified company tax along Continental lines.

PRETRADING EXPENSES

Irish law should be altered to harmonize with EEC rules on the treatment of expenses incurred before the commencement of trading. At present the new enterprise can deduct these expenses after it commences trading only if they relate to training staff for manufacturing operations or to dredging.[103] It is not always enough that these expenses may be deductible by the promoting company. Economic considerations[104] as well as harmonization of taxation necessitate making all pretrading expenses deductible.

SOCIAL SECURITY

Social security in Ireland and Britain is financed much more out of general taxation and less out of direct contributions by employers and employees than in the Six.[105] This gives labor-intensive firms an advantage over similar firms in

British Finance Act, 1953, 1 & 2 Eliz. 2, c. 34, § 19, and Finance Act, 1954, 2 & 3 Eliz. 2, c. 44, § 17. See also Nelson, "The Opening Years' Provisions: Uses and Abuses," 1958 Brit. Tax Rev. 244; Lynch, "Some Aspects of Tax Planning," 69 Accountants' Magazine 114, 115 (1965).

[98] See Charleton, "The Taxation of Business Profits," 19 J. Stat. Soc. 45, 54–55 (1956–57).

[99] British Royal Commission on Taxation of Profits and Income, Final Report, Cmd. No. 9474, at 209–30 (1955); Irish Commission on Income Taxation, Sixth Report, Pr. 6039, at 38 (1961); Committee on Taxation of Trading Profits, Report, Cmd. No. 8189, paras. 19–66 (1951). See A Scheme for an Accounts Basis for Income Tax on Company Profits, Cmd. No. 2347 (1964); Nelson, "The White Paper on an Accounts Basis for Company Income Tax," 56 Accountants' J. 304 (1964).

[100] Seventh Report, Pr. 6581, ch. XXVI, at 218 (1962). See also Sixth Report, Pr. 6039, chs. XI, VII (1961); Davidson, 45 Cahiers de Droit Fiscal International 127, 136 (1961).

[101] Sixth Report, Pr. 6039, ch. X (1961). The same recommendation was made by the British Royal Commission on Taxation of Profits and Income, Final Report, Cmd. No. 9474, para. 776 (1955), with regard to Schedule D, Cases I and II.

[102] British Committee on Taxation of Trading Profits, Report, Cmd. No. 8189, at 11 (1951).

[103] Finance Act, 1959 Acts 681, §§ 74, 57, respectively. This odd pair of exceptions is a good example of the piecemeal derogation from principle which adoption of the concept of taxable income of the Six would avoid. See also Finance Act, 1956 Acts 353, § 23(2).

[104] Irish Commission on Income Taxation, Seventh Report, Pr. 6581, para. 192 (1962); Committee on Taxation of Trading Profits, Report, Cmd. No. 8189, para. 169 (1951).

[105] Jaysay, "Fiscal Harmonization and British Company Earnings," 1 J. Common Market Studies 56, 58 (1962); Economist Intelligence Unit, Taxes for Britain 18–22, 37 (1962); Davies, "Britain into Europe: The Prospect of Tax Reform," 1962 Brit. Tax Rev. 81, 85; EEC Treaty, arts. 117–18; Statistical Abstract of Ireland, 1962, at 225. While the figures are not strictly comparable, social security seems to be financed out of tax revenue to the extent of 10–25% in the Six and about 65% in Ireland and 60% in Britain.

the Six, but it prejudices capital-intensive firms and reduces the incentive to economize in the use of labor. In 1962 industrialists in the Six complained that social security in Britain was subsidized by the general taxpayer. Changes are likely to raise contributions in Britain and Ireland substantially and to relate employees' contributions more closely to individual earnings than at present.

GENERAL CONCLUSIONS

The changes which probably will be necessary in the Irish tax system if Ireland joins the EEC involve broadening the tax base of both direct and indirect taxation. Both changes should be welcomed in Ireland, although the regressive effect of increased indirect taxes will have to be counteracted by wage increases, with their inflationary tendencies, as well as by increased social security benefits and decreased personal direct taxation. Both changes might permit reduction of direct taxes, with their disincentive effects on the economy. A decrease in present rates of company taxation would be desirable to encourage self-financing in countries such as Ireland with small capital markets. It is unfortunate that so much of the revenue from the added-value tax will have to be used to make up that lost by reducing the principal excise taxes; if it could be used to reduce the principal excise taxes or company taxes, economic growth would be encouraged. Like the other innovations, a tax on net wealth[106] would encourage growth and efficiency and counteract the regressive effects of the indirect taxes. Since both Ireland and Britain at present have progressive death taxes which will need to be reduced, this seems an obvious way of insuring social justice. Alternatively, the revenue from a wealth tax could be used to reduce the higher rates of personal income tax. To avoid economic ill-effects, an increase in the social security contributions of companies would have to be offset by relief from direct taxes. In present conditions of unemployment in Ireland, increased social security contributions by employers in the form of a payroll tax are less suitable than they are in the Six. Relief to labor-intensive enterprises to counteract the effects of increased social security contributions would nullify both the economic advantages and the object of harmonizing tax burdens. Tax concessions to lower-income groups would prevent wage claims due to increases in employees' contributions and correspondingly would benefit companies. The whole question is connected with tax methods of supporting a wages policy.[107]

THE ACTIVITIES OF THE COMMISSION

Working groups have been set up to study, first, the tax base and effective tax rates for direct taxation of businesses in each of the Six, especially with regard to depreciation, measures to promote investment, stock evaluation, capital gains, and business losses; second, tax measures particularly favorable to, for example, holding companies or manufacturing companies, and to "tax havens";[108] and, third, the influence of taxes on external investment in the Community. The

[106] In Britain the possibility of such a tax has been officially raised by the National Economic Development Council, Conditions Favourable to Faster Growth, § E, para. 170 (1963).

[107] See Closing the Gap: Incomes and Output, Pr. 6957 (1963); "How to Reform Taxes," The Economist, Feb. 9, 1963, pp. 481–82; OECD Economic Survey of Ireland, 1964, paras. 15–16, 40.

[108] Nasini, "Progress on Tax Harmonization in the Common Market," 2 European Taxation 163, 167 (1962); von der Groeben, "Systèmes fiscaux nationaux et Marché Commun," 1 La Fiscalité du Marché Commun 6, 13–14 (1962). Apparently the working group paid particular attention to the problem of "base company" subsidiaries of United States companies, since most of the external investment in the EEC is by United States interests.

Fiscal Committee of the OEEC-OECD is studying double taxation.[109] Taxation of insurance policies and indirect taxes on the movement of capital are being studied by other working groups but are not considered in this book.

RECIPROCAL ENFORCEMENT OF TAX LAWS

It is a principle of private international law that the courts of one state will not enforce the revenue laws of another. This principle applies in Ireland[110] and in Continental Europe,[111] subject to bilateral treaties for reciprocal assistance in enforcement of taxes[112] by way of extradition, collaboration in the collection of taxes, and exchange of information.

Ireland has no treaties dealing with enforcement of foreign taxes, even with the United Kingdom. Irish practice has been to enter into only provisions for exchange of information in treaties on double taxation and tax evasion.[113] This is also the practice of the United Kingdom. Full exchange of information between EEC member states will of course be essential.

In the EEC it will probably be necessary to override the principle that revenue laws of foreign states will not be enforced, since the problem of tax evasion will arise in the same way as the need for reciprocal enforcement of bankruptcy decrees. The reasons for the principle—that revenue laws are purely a matter for the foreign state and that local courts must not enforce objectionable foreign laws and should avoid drawing invidious distinctions between them[114]—are unconvincing in the context of the EEC. Double taxation conventions recognize foreign taxes, and the revenue authorities cooperate to prevent evasion; Ireland must conclude agreements for reciprocal enforcement as well. If international

[109] The next chapter discusses the Irish law on the main topics considered by these groups. Subsequent chapters deal with the problems of double taxation in the EEC and with the Irish double taxation conventions most important to the United States investor.

[110] Buchanan, Ltd. v. McVey, [1954] Ir. R. 89; Dicey, Conflict of Laws 161–62, 793–94 (7th ed. 1958). See, however, Regazzoni v. Sethia, [1958] A.C. 301, 324.

[111] Kuhn, Comparative Commentaries on Private International Law 48–49 (1937); Caisse Générale Locale de Secours contre la Maladie de la Commune de Julich v. S.A. des Ateliers de Godarville, trib. civ. Charleroi (France), Jan. 8, 1930, 57 Journal de Droit International 1097 (1930).

[112] See generally League of Nations Economic and Fiscal Committee, London and Mexico Model Tax Conventions: Commentary and Text 44–48 (1946); Ehrenzweig & Koch, Income Tax Treaties 229–32 (1959); Albrecht, "The Enforcement of Taxation Under International Law," 30 Brit. Yb. Int'l L. 454 (1953). See, however, 2 U.S. Joint Committee on Internal Revenue Taxation, Legislative History of United States Tax Conventions 1593, 1602 (1962).

[113] U.K.-Irish Double Income Taxation Agreement, April 14, 1926, art. 6, U.K. Income Tax Act, 1952, 15 & 16 Geo. 6 & 1 Eliz. 2, c. 10, Eighteenth Schedule, pt. I, Irish Finance Act, 1926 Pub. Stat. 401, 441, First Schedule, pt. I; U.K.-Irish Corporation Profits Tax Agreement, May 18, 1949, art. 8, [1949] 1(3) Stat. Instr. 3536 (No. 1434), Irish Finance Act, 1949 Acts 75, 143, Fifth Schedule, Ir. T.S. No. 4 of 1949, Pr. 9433; U.S.-Irish Double Taxation Convention, Sept. 13, 1949, art. XX, [1951] 2 U.S.T. & O.I.A. 2303, T.I.A.S. No. 2356, Irish Finance Act, 1950 Acts 369, 411, Second Schedule, Ir. T.S. No. 7 of 1951, Pr. 1081, 127 U.N.T.S. 89 (1952); Irish-German Double Taxation Agreement, Dec. 18, 1962, art. 23, Ir. S.I. No. 212 of 1962, Pr. 6792, German Law of March 25, 1964, [1964] 2 BGB1. 266, 632.

[114] See "International Enforcement of Tax Claims," 50 Colum. L. Rev. 490 (1950); Moore v. Mitchell, 30 F.2d 600 (2d Cir. 1929). In the United States, where the problem relates only to relatively unimportant indirect taxes and some property taxes, the old rule is being modified; see State ex rel. Oklahoma Tax Commission v. Rodgers, 238 Mo. App. 1115, 193 S.W. 2d 919 (1946), and the other cases cited by Albrecht, "The Enforcement of Taxation Under International Law," 30 Brit. Yb. Int'l L. 454, 464 (1953).

equalization payments are to be made to supplement the revenue of a member state, it would be ridiculous for other member states to refuse to execute decrees for the payment of taxes to that state.

Eventually it will be necessary to permit the revenue authorities of a member state to sue directly for tax due and not merely on a judgment of the courts of the member state. This means that the courts of the enforcing state must decide the question of liability if it is contested; once the law in question is common to each member state, there will be no difficulty about this, and in any case, it is not much more difficult than any other case of proof of foreign law.

TAXATION OF INDIVIDUALS: EARNED AND INVESTMENT INCOME

An expert has concluded[115] that the Six differentiate more than the United Kingdom in favor of earned income of individuals and against dividends. This book does not consider the tax position of individuals, but apart from directors and employees, business enterprises have an interest in this question because high taxes on unearned income encourage consumption rather than investment; substantial turnover taxes may neutralize this effect. In small enterprises it may be advantageous to withdraw profits, as far as possible, in the form of salaries and directors' fees, and there may be tax reasons for preferring an unincorporated partnership to an incorporated company where this involves liability to individual income tax instead of company tax. High direct taxes on earned income, however, may increase salary costs by causing pressure for higher wages and by increasing the demand for benefits in kind.[116]

In general, it is easier to compare the tax treatment of the income, and particularly the earned income, of individuals in different countries than to compare the treatment of company profits.

TAX TREATMENT OF NON-RESIDENTS

The tax treatment of non-residents is an important influence on trade among EEC member states at present, although it eventually will be governed primarily by double taxation conventions. In general, permanent establishments of non-resident enterprises are taxed on local-source income in substantially the same way as locally resident individuals or companies, regardless of any double taxation convention. There may, however, be a special rate of tax for permanent establishments of foreign enterprises or a remission of the supplementary income tax on individuals. These special rates, which exist in Belgium, the Netherlands, and Germany, distort competition, and whether they favor or prejudice foreign enterprise, they must eventually be abolished in the EEC. Income from foreign sources other than the country of residence of the enterprise is also usually taxed in the same way as local-source income, if it is remitted to the country in question or if the shares or property from which the income arises form part of the working capital of a permanent establishment there.

If no permanent establishment or "fixed base" exists, local-source business income of non-residents—other than dividends, interest, and royalties—is subject to tax in the Six, except France, in more limited circumstances than in the United Kingdom or Ireland. In the Netherlands and Italy, the provisions of domestic law are generally similar to the provisions of double taxation conventions[117] on per-

[115] Nortcliffe, Common Market Fiscal Systems 81 (1960).

[116] Which may be taxable in Ireland in the hands of the recipients; Finance Act, 1958 Acts 553, pt. IV.

[117] Nortcliffe, Common Market Fiscal Systems 11, 41–42 (1960). See also "German Taxation of Foreign Corporations, Aliens and Non-Residents," 1 European Taxation, No. 16, at 3

manent establishments, and substantially the same situation prevails elsewhere in the Six.

Whether a double taxation convention applies or not, dividends, interest, and royalties paid to a foreign enterprise and not attributable to a local branch or permanent establishment are usually subject, in the country of source, to a withholding tax at a flat rate which may be more than the ordinary rate of withholding tax on dividends. The Netherlands imposes no withholding tax on interest and royalties paid to a foreign resident unless they are attributable to a permanent establishment or are paid by a subsidiary company owned to the extent of at least 25 per cent of the share capital by the parent company or shareholder in question. Italian tax law does not seem to impose a withholding tax on dividends paid to foreign residents. France is the only country which taxes the dividends paid by a foreign-resident company to the extent to which they are paid out of French-source profits. Belgium has given special tax concessions for foreign managers and employees under the new tax law of 1962.[118] While it may be unpopular to give special tax concessions to foreigners, this is an incentive to experts to visit a country to give technical advice. Whether it is effective depends on the rules of the experts' country of residence with regard to foreign-source income.

To insure freedom of movement of labor and professional services, the Neumark Committee recommends that foreign-resident individuals should be given the same family and personal allowances and exemptions as residents.[119] This is an important application of the principle that there should be no discrimination on the grounds of residence for tax purposes.

(1961); id., No. 17, at 5; id., No. 18, at 3; den Boer, "Taxation des enterprises etrangères aux Pays-Bas," 1963 La Fiscalité du Marché Commun 155; "The Concept of Permanent Establishment in Germany," 5 European Taxation 16 (1965).

[118] Circular Letter No. Ci. R. 9 USA/217.882, Feb. 2, 1963, discussed in "Special Ruling for Foreign Individuals Employed Temporarily in Belgium," 3 European Taxation 122 (1963).

[119] Rapport 35, CCH 2434.

Chapter 8

Some Aspects of the Irish Tax System[1]

TYPE OF TAX SYSTEM

The Irish system of direct taxation is unitary[2] both for companies and for individuals, and not schedular, in spite of its method of classifying income. In the Six, only Italy has a schedular system,[3] though it is combined with a progressive supplementary tax on individuals. In Ireland, "income tax" is paid by individuals and companies at the same rate.[4] It is supplemented by two taxes imposed on substantially the same income used for income tax purposes; these are surtax, a deferred installment

[1] The books on Irish law frequently used by practitioners include a compilation of statutes and case law: H. W. Robinson, Irish Statute Law Relating to Income Tax, Sur-Tax and Corporation Profits Tax (1953); British Inland Revenue, Income Taxes Outside the Commonwealth, pt. II, "Summary of Income Tax Laws in the Republic of Ireland" (1956) (this publication has annual supplements); Grogan, The Principles and Practice of Irish Income Tax (1952); Wilson & Kelly, Irish Income Tax and Corporation Profits Tax (1957) (this publication has annual supplements). For a more detailed statement of the law, it is necessary to refer to works on the British tax system, on which Harvard University Law School, Taxation in the United Kingdom (1957), is excellent. The principal practitioners' books are: Simon, Income Tax (2d ed. 1952); Konstam, The Law of Income Tax (11th ed. 1950); and British Tax Encyclopedia (Wheatcroft ed. 1962). On tax avoidance, see Potter & Monroe, Tax Planning (1959). See also International Bureau of Fiscal Documentation, "Guide to Taxes in Ireland," 4 European Taxation 115 (1964). Practical and quite detailed information and valuable statements of principle are obtainable from the following reports of Irish and British government commissions of inquiry. *Irish:* Committee of Inquiry into Taxation on Industry, Report, Pr. 3512 (1956); Commission on Income Taxation [hereinafter cited as Irish Income Tax Commission], First Report, Pr. 4891 (1958); Second Report, Pr. 5119 (1959); Third Report, Pr. 5567 (1960); Fourth Report, Pr. 5731 (1960); Fifth Report, Pr. 6033 (1961); Sixth Report, Pr. 6039 (1961); Seventh Report, Pr. 6581 (1962). The views of the government on the proposals made in these seven reports are in Direct Taxation, Pr. 5952 (1961), and Second White Paper on Direct Taxation, Pr. 7024 (1963). See also the annual reports of the Revenue Commissioners. *British:* Royal Commission on Income Tax, Report, Cmd. No. 615 (1920); Income Tax Codification Committee, Report, Cmd. No. 5131 (1936); Royal Commission on Income Tax, Draft Income Tax Bill, Cmd. No. 5132 (1936); Committee on Taxation of Trading Profits, Report, Cmd. No. 8189 (1951); Committee on Taxation of Provisions for Retirement, Report, Cmd. No. 9063 (1954); Royal Commission on Taxation of Profits and Income [cited in this chapter as Royal Commission], First Report, Cmd. No. 8761 (1953); Second Report, Cmd. No. 9105 (1954); Final Report, Cmd. No. 9474 (1955).

For a discussion of the economic aspects of the British tax system up to 1954, see Hicks, "The Economic Effects of British Income and Profit Taxes," in Enquête sur l'Imposition des Revenus Industriels Commerciaux et Professionels (Morselli ed. 1954). For a criticism of its legal structure, see Income Tax Codification Committee, Report, Cmd. No. 5131, Introduction and passim (1936); Royal Commission,

of income tax at progressive rates, payable by individuals with incomes over a specified minimum, and corporation profits tax, a flat-rate tax with a special low rate on company profits below a specified figure.

The Irish taxes on income are fundamentally those taken over from Britain in 1922 with only one substantial change.[5] This system has been modified in Britain. Only one effort[6] has been made to consider its suitability for Ireland or to modern conditions. Since its principles are those of the British Income Tax Act of 1803,[7] it is doubtful if it is suitable for either.

As in other fields of law, Irish tax legislation has followed British legislation fairly closely. The Irish legislation has consisted mostly of detailed anti-

---

Final Report, Cmd. No. 9474, Memorandum of Dissent (1955).

Irish Income Tax Commission, Sixth Report, Pr. 6039, ch. III (1961), recommends ending the division of income for income tax purposes into Schedules and Cases, which division is based on the fundamental income tax act, Income Tax Act, 1918, 8 & 9 Geo. 5, c. 40. (For brevity, in this chapter, citations of Irish and British Finance and Income Tax Acts are given only with the first reference to a given act.) In this chapter the reader is, as far as possible, untroubled with this division, although the recommendation has not been accepted; Second White Paper on Direct Taxation, Pr. 7024, para. 14 (1963). The most important Schedule for the investor is Schedule D. Case I of Schedule D deals with income from a trade or business; Case II deals with income from a profession. These two are treated together for almost all purposes. Schedule E deals with wages and salaries, including directors' fees, and certain pensions. Schedules A and B deal with income deemed to be received from land. Schedule A income tax is paid at the standard rate on an artificial and now obsolete valuation of an owner's interest in land in Ireland. This has now been superseded in Britain; Finance Act, 1963, 11 & 12 Eliz. 2, c. 25. Under Schedule B, income tax is charged on an artificial value of the occupation of farm and other lands. Taxes on fictitious income, like Schedule A and B tax, will have to be abolished in the EEC. Schedule C income tax is a withholding tax on certain securities issued by state or semi-public bodies. Schedule D, Case III, deals primarily with passive income—i.e., income from capital, untaxed interest, dividends and annual payments, certain foreign-source income, income from property leased for business purposes—but also with certain dairying profits and some income of foreign life insurance offices. Cases IV and V have been repealed in Ireland. Case VI covers all types of taxable income not taxed under any other Case or Schedule. In Britain a short-term capital gains tax under Schedule D, Case VII, was introduced by Finance Act, 1962, 10 & 11 Eliz. 2, c. 44, and a full-scale capital gains tax by Finance Act, 1965, 13 & 14 Eliz. 2, c. 25, pt. III.

The Schedules are sets of rules relating to the tax base in the case of income of different kinds. The tax rate is the same in all cases, subject to personal allowances and deductions. Income under all Schedules forms a single taxable fund in the hands of each taxpayer, who is taxed only on his net income; see London County Council v. Attorney General, [1901] A.C. 26, 35–36 (per Macnaghten, L. J.).

[2] In a unitary tax system, in principle a single tax is paid on the net amount of a single fund of taxable income; in a schedular system, different taxes are imposed on different types of income, irrespective of the amount of the taxpayer's income or losses from other sources.

[3] In Italy a committee has been appointed to consider the revision of the whole tax system; 3 European Taxation 24 (1963).

[4] Although personal reliefs and allowances for earned income and for children graduate the effective rate of income tax on individuals with smaller incomes.

[5] The most important recent change in the Irish income tax structure is the tax exemption given to profits from exports, discussed on pp. 337–43.

[6] The reports of the Irish Income Tax Commission reassessed the system technically but did not fundamentally reconsider it. For some strong and cogent criticisms, see Royal Commission, Final Report, Cmd. No. 9474, Memorandum of Dissent (1955).

[7] 43 Geo. 3, c. 122. See Shoup, "Tax Tension and the British Fiscal System," 14 Nat'l Tax J. 1, 15 (1961); 1 British Tax Encyclopedia, Introduction, pt. 2 (Wheatcroft ed. 1962); Shoup, "Some Distinguishing Characteristics of the British, French, and United States Public Finance Systems," 47(2) Am. Econ. Rev. 187, 190–94 (1957).

avoidance provisions, sections remedying specific injustices, and tax incentives to economic growth. Both tax systems are radically different from that in the United States and from those elsewhere in Europe.

GENERAL TECHNICAL CRITICISM

A consolidation of the Irish income tax statutes is now in progress.[8] No effort has been made at codification of the case law. The Income Tax Act of 1918 was the last consolidation of Irish statute law, and numerous changes since then have added to its complexity.[9] There is not even an official volume of all the statute law now in force which incorporates amendments. The simple structure of the Irish economy,[10] the smaller amounts of money involved, and the lower incidence of sophisticated tax avoidance and evasion should permit a rationalization of the Irish tax system, but no effort has been made to rationalize it.[11]

Since knowledge of tax law increases in proportion to the total sums liable to tax, the implications of Irish law have not been as fully analyzed as the laws of wealthier and more highly industrialized countries. In Britain and Ireland the Revenue Commissioners have considerable discretion, and litigation is less frequent than in the United States; tax matters are often handled as accounting problems rather than as matters of law. For these reasons many points of Irish tax law have not been decided by the courts. There is only a small demand for published material on the law of any country with a small population and a small national income, and law teachers in the British tradition have failed to regard tax law as worthy of attention.[12] The lack of critical analysis has resulted in uncertainty on questions which United States lawyers regard as being of basic importance. Such uncertainty need not inhibit investment, but it can cause certain practical problems to arise, just as uncertainty on questions of greater detail can cause practical difficulties in more sophisticated tax systems.

ECONOMIC CRITICISM

The total tax burden in Ireland in 1964 was 26 per cent of gross national product, which is fairly high in an underindustrialized country. Although much of this tax burden comes from expenditure taxes, the income tax rates are higher than is economically desirable, since high rates of direct tax are a heavier burden

[8] Direct Taxation, Pr. 5952, at 20 (1961); Income Tax Bill, 1964; Income Tax Bill, 1966. Earlier inaction was due in part to the extreme conservatism of the Irish Revenue Commissioners, the shortage of skilled personnel who could carry out rationalization, and the scarcity of well-informed critics outside Revenue circles. As to the first, see OEEC, The Influence of Sales Taxes on Productivity 80–81 (1958).

[9] British Income Tax Codification Commission, Report, Cmd. No. 5131, para. 43 (1936), said that "the existing classification of income cannot be defended on any logical ground." See also Irish Income Tax Commission, Sixth Report, Pr. 6039, para. 26 (1961).

[10] In comparison with that of Britain.

[11] Compare Finance Act, 1920, 10 & 11 Geo. 5, c. 18, § 53(3); Finance Act, 1944 Acts 201, § 14; and Finance Act, 1962 Acts 563, § 13, with the fact that there is no general right to amalgamate the accounts of parent and subsidiary companies for income tax purposes. See Second White Paper on Direct Taxation, Pr. 7024, para. 14 (1963).

[12] This is "astonishing." Shoup, "Tax Tension and the British Fiscal System," 14 Nat'l Tax. J. 1, 2, 15–16 (1961). As well as those reasons mentioned in the text, Professor Shoup lists other reasons for anomalies in the British fiscal system: the outdated structure of the taxes, the relative unimportance given to equity between taxpayers in comparison with revenue considerations, the failure of the revenue authorities to interest themselves in policy, the pressure of time on Parliament, the conservatism of Royal Commissions, and the reluctance to delegate power to the executive. Another factor is the lack of interest in codification, which would have compelled rationalization. All Professor Shoup's comments apply equally to the Irish tax system.

if the average per capita income is low. The Irish tax system has too narrow a tax base, is difficult to enforce against the small self-employed taxpayer, and encourages economic growth only through special measures. In the latter connection a tax on the factors of production has been unofficially suggested;[13] this would have the effect of encouraging enterprises whose profits were high in proportion to their capital and labor costs. Company profits taxes tax success and should be minimized in a country seeking rapid economic growth, but if alterations were made in the Irish tax system to encourage economic growth, many further changes would be necessary to avoid unduly regressive effects and to insure proper allocation of financial resources.

WEALTH TAXES

Like Britain, Ireland has death taxes, but no tax on capital, such as exists in Germany, Luxembourg, and the Netherlands. Land and buildings are taxed locally at less than 2 per cent of the capital cost and nationally at approximately 1 per cent of that cost. Rationalization on entry in the EEC and implementation of the recommendations of the Neumark Report for a tax on net wealth probably would result in the substitution of that tax, at least in part, for the present death taxes, which are easily avoided and which are intended to have social rather than economic effects.

JURISDICTION TO TAX UNDER IRISH LAW

Jurisdiction to tax under Irish law is based on two general principles. First, the world income of an Irish resident is taxable even if it is not remitted to Ireland. This is full, or unlimited, liability to tax.[14] Second, Irish-source income of a non-Irish resident is taxable, but other income is not.

Residence of companies:[15] Subjective liability to Irish tax

Under Irish law, a company is resident where its "central management and control" is located,[16] regardless of its country of incorporation.[17] This concept is substantially the same as that of the place of "effective management" used in the

[13] Nevin, The Irish Tax System (1963). Similar suggestions have been made in Britain by the National Economic Development Council; see National Economic Development Council, Conditions Favourable to Faster Growth (1963); Kaldor, An Expenditure Tax, ch. VI (1955).

[14] Compare the principles of "unlimited" and "limited" liability to German company tax of German and foreign companies, respectively, under Körperschaftssteuergesetz, Nov. 18, 1958, arts. 1–2. See Albrecht, "The Taxation of Aliens Under International Law," 29 Brit. Yb. Int'l L. 145, 152–69 (1952).

The concept in the Six of the domicile of an individual is radically different from that in Ireland and Britain; Royal Commission, First Report, Cmd. No. 8761, paras. 8–20 (1953); Davies, "Taxes in the Common Market," 146 The Accountant 148, 153 (1962).

In Belgium, a company operating for profit is liable to the company tax if it has its registered office, principal establishment, or its central control and management in Belgium.

[15] On the rules relating to residence of individuals, see Irish Income Tax Commission, Seventh Report, Pr. 6581, ch. XII (1962). Residence of a company is also relevant to the source of its trading profits; Royal Commission, First Report, Cmd. No. 8761, para. 12 (1953). See 1 British Tax Encyclopedia, Introduction, paras. 1-088–1-094 (Wheatcroft ed. 1962).

[16] DeBeers Consol. Mines, Ltd. v. Howe, [1906] A.C. 455; Egyptian Delta Land & Inv. Co. v. Todd, [1926] A.C. 1. The more usual phrase "managed and controlled" is used in U.K.-Irish Double Income Taxation Agreement, April 14, 1926, art. 4, U.K. Income Tax Act, 1952, 15 & 16 Geo. 6 & 1 Eliz. 2, c. 10, Eighteenth Schedule, pt. I, Irish Finance Act, 1926 Pub. Stat. 401, 441, First Schedule, pt. I. For another statutory definition of residence, see U.K. Income Tax Act, 1952, § 468.

[17] However, see p. 220 on the residence of a company for corporation profits tax purposes.

OECD Fiscal Committee's draft article on fiscal domicile.[18] The main test is where the directors' meetings are held.[19] If an executive committee of directors controls routine business but policy is decided by all the directors, the place where the full board meets determines the place of residence,[20] except in cases of dual residence.[21]

The residence of a trading company is unlikely to be questioned unless it does most of its business in or from a base in Ireland but argues that it is taxable only on Irish-source income. If the size of the Irish-based operations justifies it, the usual practice is to incorporate a subsidiary in Ireland which is clearly managed and controlled in Ireland.

Residence of companies: Practical aspects

Control means management and direction of the company's business, not voting power. Even a wholly owned subsidiary of an Irish-resident company is not itself resident in Ireland if its directors make their own decisions at meetings outside Ireland and if they are not controlled by the directors of the parent company.[22] If most of the directors of a company are Irish residents, some explanation may be necessary for holding directors' meetings abroad. In Irish law, a company generally may alter its residence, and consequently its tax character, only if it has new shareholders who are residents abroad or if the present shareholders or directors change their own residence.[23] Some questions as to the place of management and control may arise if the directors pass resolutions only by signing them and without holding meetings.

Irish-source income of non-residents[24]

A non-resident is liable to tax only on Irish-source income, i.e., profits from property or from a business in Ireland.

[18] OEEC Fiscal Committee's Draft Double Taxation Convention, art. III, in The Elimination of Taxation, First Report (1958); see id., Annex C, para. 19; OECD Fiscal Committee, Draft Double Taxation Convention on Income and Capital (1963), art. 4.

[19] Cesena Sulphur Co. v. Nicholson, 1 Ex. D. 428, 1 Tax Cas. 88 (1876); DeBeers Consol. Mines, Ltd. v. Howe, [1906] A.C. 455. The place of central management and control is a question of fact to be decided on the basis of the whole business operations of the company, so the place of the trading and the place of incorporation may be important. New Zealand Shipping Co. v. Stephens, 24 T.L.R. 172, 5 Tax Cas. 533 (1907); Iveagh v. Revenue Comm'rs, [1930] Ir. R. 386; Agricultural Corp. v. Vale, [1935] Ir. R. 681.

[20] American Thread Co. v. Joyce, 6 Tax Cas. 163 (1913); New Zealand Shipping Co. v. Thew, 8 Tax Cas. 208 (1922). See, however, Union Corp. v. I.R.C., [1952] 1 All E.R. 646. The place of meetings of the supervisory board of a German company probably is the place of residence; cf. Hood v. Magee, [1918] 2 Ir. R. 34, 7 Tax Cas. 327; 1 Simon, Income Tax 367 (2d ed. 1952).

[21] A company has dual residence if it is managed and controlled in two jurisdictions; Swedish Cent. Rail Co. v. Thompson, [1925] A.C. 495, 9 Tax Cas. 342, 370. See also Apthorpe v. Peter Schoenhofen Brewing Co., 4 Tax Cas. 41 (1899); Union Corp. v. I.R.C., [1952] 1 All E.R. 646, 657, 662.

[22] Gramophone & Typewriter Co. v. Stanley, [1908] 2 K.B. 89. See generally 2 Simon, Income Tax 55–56 (2d ed. 1952).

[23] There may, of course, be exchange-control problems as well as the problem discussed here. In Ireland there is nothing corresponding to U.K. Income Tax Act, 1952, §§ 412, 468, which prohibits the transfer of income without permission to people outside the United Kingdom and the transfer of the residence of a company to avoid United Kingdom income tax. Similar provisions exist in the Netherlands. *Quaere* whether these provisions will ultimately be regarded as incompatible with freedom of movement of capital in the EEC.

[24] On the United Kingdom law, see generally the excellent study by Schipper, The Liability to Tax of Non-Resident Companies, pt. I (1958). For a summary of the corresponding British law, which points out the influence of British law on the concept of a permanent establishment, see Hellgar, 34 Cahiers de Droit Fiscal International 249 (1957).

Business income[25] is taxable only insofar as it is derived from a business "exercised" or "carried on" in Ireland.[26] A distinction is made between trading "with" Ireland, which involves no tax liability, and trading "within" Ireland, which involves tax liability.[27] These rules are superseded when a double taxation treaty applies.

A company is not "carrying on a business" in Ireland unless there is some regularity or repetition in its operations there; isolated transactions are not taxable. If a non-resident company's Irish activities are confined to purchasing goods for resale abroad or soliciting orders to be accepted and carried out abroad, no liability to Irish tax arises, even if the company has a fixed place of business or an employee or an agent permanently residing in Ireland.[28] The main test is whether the contracts of sale or for services are made in Ireland.[29] If contracts are made abroad on behalf of a principal who subsequently adopts the contracts in Ireland, the principal is not doing business in Ireland.[30]

The mere fact that the contracts are not made in Ireland may not be sufficient if delivery of the goods or performance of the services and payment of the price are made and the terms of the sale negotiated in Ireland, especially if the goods have been manufactured there.[31] However, there has been no case in which a foreign company has been held to be taxable when the contract was not made in Ireland.

The concepts of income[32] and capital gains

Income has not been defined by legislation or by the Irish courts. For most business operations, normal accountancy practice is followed,[33] but only the types of income set out in the five "Schedules" are taxable. Capital gains are omitted

[25] Taxable under Schedule D, Cases I and II, as distinct from income from property which is taxed under Schedules A and B (profits deemed to arise from land) or D, Cases III and VI, or income from employment (Schedule E); see note 1 above.

[26] Income Tax Act, 1918, Schedule D, General Rule 1(a)(iii). The corresponding provision in the United Kingdom is Income Tax Act, 1952, § 122. Finance Act, 1920, § 52(2)(b) makes "the profits of a foreign company carrying on in [Ireland] . . . any trade or business . . . so far as those profits arise in [Ireland]" liable to corporation profits tax.

[27] Grainger v. Gough, [1896] A.C. 325, 335, 3 Tax Cas. 462 (per Herschell, L. J.); see 1 British Tax Encyclopedia, paras. 1-446, 1-447 (Wheatcroft ed. 1962); Royal Commission, Final Report, Cmd. No. 9474, para. 675 (1955).

[28] Attorney General v. Sulley, 5 H. & N. 711, 157 Eng. Rep. 1364, 2 Tax Cas. 149 (1860).

[29] Grainger v. Gough, [1896] A.C. 325, 3 Tax. Cas. 462; F. L. Smidth & Co. v. Greenwood, [1922] 1 A.C. 417, 8 Tax Cas. 193; Maclaine v. Eccott, [1926] A.C. 424, 10 Tax Cas. 481.

[30] Cunard S.S. Co. v. Revenue Comm'rs, [1931] Ir. R. 287; see also Weiss Biheller & Brooks, Ltd. v. Farmer, [1923] 1 K.B. 226.

[31] Maclaine v. Eccott, [1926] A.C. 424, 10 Tax Cas. 481; F. L. Smidth & Co. v. Greenwood, [1921] 3 K.B. 583, 593, 8 Tax Cas. 193, 199, 203, aff'd, [1922] 1 A.C. 417, 423, 8 Tax Cas. 193, 205, 206. See also Muller & Co. v. C.I.R., [1928] A.C. 34.

[32] Brudno & Hollman, "The Taxation of Capital Gains in the United States and the United Kingdom," 1958 Brit. Tax. Rev. 26, 134, point out that capital gains are more narrowly defined in Britain and Ireland than in the United States, where they are taxed at a reduced rate. See also Peacock, "Some Observations on the Reports of the Royal Commission on the Taxation of Profits and Income," 10 Nat'l Tax. J. 255 (1957). Royal Commission, Final Report, Cmd. No. 9474, Memorandum of Dissent, para. 5 (1955), advocates the Continental concept of taxable income—the "net accretion of economic power between two points of time"—on the grounds, *inter alia,* of equity between taxpayers. This was adopted, in effect, by U.K. Finance Act, 1965, pt. III.

[33] For a discussion of this statement and the extent to which it is not accurate in practice, see Charleton, "The Taxation of Business Profits," 19 J. Stat. Soc. 45, 52–53 (1956–57).

from the Schedules and therefore[34] exempt from income tax, surtax, and corporation profits tax. The rule that capital gains are not taxed applies even to business assets.[35]

The fact that business enterprises in Ireland are not taxed on capital gains, as enterprises are in the Six,[36] offsets in some degree the failure of Irish law to allow deductions from taxable income for capital expenditure, losses, depletion allowances on wasting assets or depreciation on administrative and commercial (as distinct from industrial) buildings, and intangible capital assets. Since the difference between capital gains and income is a question of degree[37] masquerading as a question of principle, the distinction has resulted in a body of irrational and complicated law.[38]

However, two types of capital gain are taxable. The first is that received from the sale of patent rights.[39] The second is the gain from the sale of property sold in the regular course of business or even from an isolated sale "in the nature of trade."[40] In theory this is not an excep-

[34] Pearn v. Miller, 11 Tax Cas. 610 (1927).

[35] Although depreciation deductions may have to be adjusted.

[36] France and Belgium defer taxation of capital gains if the profits are reinvested; for a comment on the French law, see Vasseur, Le droit de la réforme des structures industrielles et des économies régionales 366–68 (1959). Germany and the Netherlands alter the normal tax rates in taxing capital gains.

[37] Admitted by the Irish Income Tax Commission, Seventh Report, Pr. 6581, paras. 123, 127 (1962); see Royal Commission, Final Report, Cmd. No. 9474, Memorandum of Dissent, paras. 2–33, especially paras. 12–18 (1955).

[38] One of the principal means of avoiding tax is to substitute a deductible income payment for a non-deductible capital payment (although the capital payment may qualify for a capital allowance) or to substitute a non-taxable capital receipt for a taxable income receipt; Wheatcroft, "The General Principles of Tax Planning," 1963 Brit. Tax Rev. 20, 29, 34–35. See Lynch, "Some Aspects of Tax Planning," 69 Accountants' Magazine 22, 30–32 (1965); Royal Commission, Final Report, Cmd. No. 9474, Memorandum of Dissent, paras. 22–23, 45–48 (1955). The Majority Report surprisingly makes no reference to tax avoidance arising from the exemption of capital gains from tax. This useful means of tax avoidance would have to be changed in the EEC, especially since this change would bring the Irish system into line with the laws of the Six and with sound tax principles.

[39] Dealt with in Finance Act, 1959 Acts 681, ch. III. There is a slight difference in the treatment of an Irish-resident vendor and a non-resident vendor. See Dublin Society of Chartered Accountants, Changes in Industrial and General Taxation, 1950–61, at 87–91 (1961); see also pp. 234–35.

[40] Leeming v. Jones, 15 Tax Cas. 333 (1930); see O'Dwyer v. Irish Exporters, Ltd., [1943] Ir. R. 176. Royal Commission, Final Report, Cmd. No. 9474, paras. 80–117, at para. 116 (1955), says that circumstances in Britain where a profit from an isolated transaction or from sporadic transactions is classified as income are as follows:

1) If the object of the purchase and resale is normally the subject of trading and not of investment.

2) If the object in question does not yield income or any benefit as a result of ownership. In this case, it is likely to have been bought with a view to resale.

3) If the object is resold after a short period, trading is likely to have been intended. This is never the sole ground of a decision. Compare the short-term capital gains tax introduced in Britain by Finance Act, 1962, 10 & 11 Eliz. 2, c. 44, §§ 10–16, Schedules 9–10; 1 British Tax Encyclopedia, ch. 9, pts. 1–2 (Wheatcroft ed. 1962); see also U.K. Finance Act, 1965, pt. III.

4) If there has been a series of sales of the same kind of property, all of them are likely to be regarded as business transactions. Where, in fact, a number of sales have been made, this is important evidence of a taxable business transaction, but even a single transaction may, in accordance with the other criteria, be taxable. See Kealy v. O'Mara Limerick, Ltd., [1942] Ir. R. 616.

5) If the property sold is improved or made more marketable, or if an organized effort, such as opening an office or starting large-scale advertising, is made to obtain purchasers.

6) If there is no explanation for the sale,

tion to the rule that capital gains are not taxable; the gains are from a "trade" in the assets in question, even if they are, e.g., buildings, which are normally capital assets rather than stock in trade.[41] If the asset is not of a kind usually dealt with in the taxpayer's business, the profit is normally regarded as a capital gain. Unlike the tax laws of the Six, Irish tax law does not presume conclusively that any sale by a trading company is made in the course of business, and this is the crucial difference.

Broadly, the Irish rules produce the reasonable result that income tax and corporation profits tax are payable if a series of transactions results in capital gains. An isolated transaction which results in a windfall is not normally taxed. This is contrary to equity but is not likely to inhibit growth. If a company's principal business is investment in securities, whether sales at a profit are incidental to reinvestment or are the principal purpose of the original investment is a question of fact.[42] Insurance companies and companies dealing in investments are taxed on profits from resale of investments.

With respect to capital gains made by individuals, Irish law does not use the concept of so-called "speculative" (i.e., short-term) capital gains used in the laws of Germany, Italy, and Luxembourg.[43] In France, the principle is that capital gains are not taxable unless they are made by an enterprise carrying on a business. Capital gains made by companies are normally taxable, and with one exception relating to associated companies, this is the position in Germany and in the Six generally.[44]

TAXATION OF COMPANIES[45]

Income tax and distributed profits

Companies, like individuals, are liable to income tax at the "standard" rate on

such as a sudden emergency or opportunity requiring sale to obtain cash or otherwise, which would negative the idea that the original purchase was prompted by an intention to resell.

7) If the object of buying the property was primarily to resell it at a profit, at least if some of the other criteria for a taxable transaction exist. The mere hope that an investment can be sold at a profit is not enough to make the proceeds taxable. Under Finance Act, 1965 Acts, No. 22, pt. VII, all profits from "developing land" as defined are liable to tax.

[41] However, payments, even if from profits, made to a shareholder of a company in liquidation are not taxable, since they are capital in the hands of the shareholder. For an extension of this principle, see Rae v. Lazard Inv. Co., [1963] 1 Weekly L.R. 555. With regard to types of receipts which may be treated as either capital or income in varying circumstances, see Harvard University Law School, Taxation in the United Kingdom 236 (sums received by an employee on termination of employment), 252–53 (loan discounts and premiums), 259–63 (annuities), 263 (proceeds of life and accident insurance policies) (1957).

[42] See Income Tax Act, 1918, § 33; Howth Estate Co. v. Davis, 70 Ir. L.T.R. 79 (1936).

[43] For the German law, see Harvard University Law School, Taxation in the Federal Republic of Germany 467–70 (1963).

[44] In Belgium the same principle applies to capital gains and losses made by any industrial or commercial enterprise, whether incorporated or not. In France, although capital gains are taxed at the ordinary income tax rates, there are provisions for spreading large capital gains over four years. In France and the Netherlands, there are relief provisions in the case of reinvestment, revaluation, and transfer and amalgamation of a business.

[45] See Schendstok, "Double Tax Burden on Earned and Distributed Profits of Limited Companies in the United Kingdom," 29 Cahiers de Droit Fiscal International, 30 (1955); Royal Commission, Final Report, Cmd. No. 9474, chs. 2, 20, 27, and Memorandum of Dissent, paras. 85–111 (1955); Kaldor, An Expenditure Tax, ch. V (1955); Wheatcroft, "The Tax Treatment of Corporations and Shareholders in the United States and Great Britain," 1961 Brit. Tax Rev. 51; Committee on Turnover Taxation, Report, Cmd. No. 2300, paras. 125–73 (1964).

For a brief summary of the treatment of company profits in the United Kingdom, West Germany, and France, see Canadian Tax Foundation, Report 147–70 (1962).

taxable profits (at present 35 per cent, or 7 shillings on the pound).[46] To this extent the company is, for tax purposes, separate from the shareholders. A company is likely to pay a higher rate of income tax on undistributed profits than a partnership with the same income[47] because of the effect of personal allowances and earned-income relief given to partners.

The principle of the separate taxable entity is modified as to dividends.[48] The company pays the same amount of income tax whether its profits are distributed or not. Dividends are paid (or are deemed to be paid)[49] after making a deduction from the gross amount of the dividend at the standard rate of income tax. The tax withheld remains the company's and is not paid to the revenue authorities. The recipient bears the proportion of the income tax paid by the company which is appropriate to his dividend. The company actually bears income tax only on undistributed profits, including that proportion of the taxable profits which is paid in tax.[50] This principle is quite different from that by which the company and the shareholder are subject to separate taxes and the company must withhold the shareholders' tax from dividends and pay it to the revenue authorities,[51] which in various forms is the law in the Six[52] (except Luxembourg). The Irish principle, whereby the income of a company is treated as the income of its shareholders, applies to all types of company, not only to closely held private companies. It is a rough-and-ready method of avoiding taxing the income for a second time, when it is in the hands of the shareholders, because tax is deducted from dividends at the standard rate even if the company did not pay tax at that rate.[53]

The authorities collect only surtax from shareholders on their dividend income; the company has paid, in economic terms, the whole of their income tax.[54] If the shareholder is liable to income tax at less than the standard rate, he may obtain a refund, but he has no redress if the company distributes no profits, even though he is bearing, through his shares, income tax to which he is not liable.

[46] Finance Bill, 1966, § 1.

[47] A partnership, however, would involve the individual partners in surtax, in addition to income tax on their shares of the total profits. A partnership is not a separate legal entity for the purposes of Irish law. There is no provision by which a partnership may elect to be taxed as a company, as there is in France; see Code des Impôts, art. 206(1), 206(3).

[48] See Income Tax Act, 1918, General Rule 20; Finance Act, 1925 Pub. Stat. 397, § 13; Finance Act, 1940 Acts 301, § 5.

[49] Dividends can be paid, at the option of the company, "free of income tax." This means that the company makes a payment of the full amount of the dividend declared, instead of declaring a theoretical figure from which tax is deducted to arrive at the actual amount paid. (As to surtax, see Cull v. C.I.R., [1940] A.C. 51.) If this is done, the shareholder is deemed for surtax purposes to have received a gross dividend of the sum which, after deduction of tax at the standard rate, would yield the net amount actually paid—the "grossed-up" dividend. In either case, income tax in Ireland on companies is an "apparent" and not a genuine corporation tax; Schendstok, "Double Tax Burden on Profits Earned and Distributed by Limited Companies," 29 Cahiers de Droit Fiscal International 1–2 (1955).

[50] The company also bears the corporation profits tax, since it cannot be deducted from dividends.

[51] The former principle exists in Irish law under Income Tax Act, 1918, General Rule 21, which is discussed on pp. 232–36. See Schendstok, "Les méthodes de coordination interne en matière fiscal doivent être harmonisées," 3 La Fiscalité du Marché Commun 67, 69–70 (1962).

[52] See "The Italian Dividend Tax," 3 European Taxation 152–56 (1963).

[53] Economic double taxation occurs to the extent of the corporation profits tax paid by the company.

[54] But not in strict legal analysis; Biddle v. Commissioner, 302 U.S. 573 (1938).

There is no practical or economic reason why the "standard rate" of tax for companies and for individuals should be the same. Differentiation due to incorporation is not avoided, since company profits bear a tax not imposed on individual shareholders and since the effective tax rate of individual shareholders is rarely the standard rate.[55] The effective rate of tax borne by the company depends on its rate of corporation profits tax and the extent to which its profits are distributed.[56] The greater the distribution of profits, the higher is the ratio of the tax borne by the company to the amount of the undisturbed profits, so if most of the profits are distributed to preferred shareholders, the equity shareholders bear most of the tax. This occurs wherever there is a differentiation in favor of distributed profits.

Practical results

One odd result of the Irish system is that if a company has distributed profits on which it has paid no tax because of initial allowances or reasons other than export tax reliefs, it nevertheless may deduct tax from the gross dividend at the standard rate. If the shareholder is not liable to tax, he may recover from the Revenue the tax withheld from the payment.[57]

Dividends paid out of capital gains, on which a company is not taxable, are not subject to tax, by deduction or other-

[55] At present, 72.5% is the highest total tax rate, including income tax and surtax. In practice, an individual who is not liable to surtax never pays tax at the "standard rate" on his whole income, owing to earned income relief, personal allowances, and other factors.

[56] The company tax rate is made up of the standard rate of income tax at the time (at present, 35%, corporation profits tax being deducted) plus the lower rate of corporation profits tax (7.5%) on its undistributed profits up to £2,500 decreasing in proportion to the percentage of profits distributed, and a second rate (at present, 23%) on its profits over £2,500, also decreasing in proportion to the extent of distribution.

Shareholders pay the same amount of income tax and surtax on the gross dividends they receive that they would pay if they had received the same amount of income from a non-corporate source; so when calculating the incidence of tax on distributed company profits, the tax borne or paid by the shareholders can be ignored.

If a company which pays no corporation profits tax distributes all of its net profits after tax, deducting tax from the dividends paid, it bears tax on its total profits at a rate equal to the square of the standard rate of income tax. The square of the present standard rate is almost exactly 12.25%. Almost all companies now pay corporation profits tax as well as income tax.

Where P is net profits before tax, R is income tax rate, C is the higher rate of corporation profits tax, and S is the lower rate of corporation profits tax (R, C, and S all being expressed as decimals); then on profits on which only the lower rate of corporation tax is payable, the total tax borne by the company, if the profits are fully distributed, is $P(S+R^2-SR^2)$. At present the rate of tax borne by the company on profits over £2,500 that have been completely distributed is $100(C+R^2+CR^2)\%$. Under the system proposed by the Neumark Report, the minimum rate of company tax, payable when the net profits are fully distributed, is $100(T^2+L-LT)\%$ where T is the tax rate for undistributed profits and L is the tax rate for distributed profits.

In theory, the company could distribute the whole of its profits after tax by paying a dividend "free of tax," that is, by paying out the net amount of the dividend declared without deducting tax from it. Assuming for simplicity that the company pays no corporation profits tax, the shareholders would then be regarded as having received a gross sum equal to the net profits of the company before tax and as having borne income tax on it. In this case, therefore, the effect of the corporate form vanishes, and the company bears no tax at all. The company is left with the same liquid assets as it had at the beginning of the year.

These calculations are based on the assumption that the taxable income for the purposes of income tax and of corporation profits tax is the same, which is not always the case. It also assumes that neither tax is deductible in computing the other. This is not now the law; Finance Bill, 1966, when enacted, will make corporation profits tax deductible for income tax purposes.

[57] See Cobb, "Investment Allowances," Investors' Chronicle, Nov. 16, 1962, pp. 560–61;

wise, when paid to the shareholders.[58] However, this does not apply to dividends paid by companies not resident in Ireland[59] to an Irish resident.

Since dividends are not taxed in the hands of the shareholders, no saving in income tax[60] can be obtained from capitalizing the profits of the company by increasing its authorized capital and distributing shares as a stock dividend, although these shares are not taxable.[61] In the case of a parent company taxable in another country where the tax rate on capital gains is lower than the rate for income, some over-all tax saving may be achieved.[62] Bonus issues of debentures[63] or preferred shares, even if redeemable,[64] are not taxable. Bonus issues are taxed in the Six only by Luxembourg and the Netherlands. They probably should not be liable to income tax at all, since they are not properly regarded as income.

Companies' income tax: Comparative aspects and economic realities

By changing both the rates and the scales of income tax, surtax, and corporation profits tax,[65] a wide range of economic effects could be achieved under the present Irish system, although with formal and technical complications.[66] The principle of a single tax for companies was rejected in Britain, though it

---

Lynch, "Some Aspects of Tax Planning," 69 Accountants' Magazine 114, 116 (1965). This result is less startling in Ireland, where investment allowances are available only for ships, than it was in Britain, since the gain is less significant with initial allowances, which are in effect only interest-free loans from the state. See also Committee of Public Accounts, H.C. Paper No. 221 (1963–64); U.K. Finance Act, 1965.

[58] Neumann v. I.R.C., [1934] A.C. 215, 18 Tax Cas. 332; Gimson v. I.R.C., [1930] 2 K.B. 246, 15 Tax Cas. 595. This rule was criticized strongly in Britain; Royal Commission, Final Report, Cmd. No. 9474, paras. 803–809 (1955); Income Tax Codification Committee, Report, Cmd. No. 5131, paras. 98–110 (1936). See also Cenlon Fin. Co. v. Ellwood, [1962] 2 Weekly L.R. 871, 1962 Brit. Tax Rev. 320. This is another anomaly due to the distinction between taxable income and tax-free capital gains.

[59] Reid's Trustees v. C.I.R., [1949] A.C. 361, 30 Tax Cas. 431. This case would probably be followed by the Irish courts, especially as it is more consistent with principle than is the rule respecting "capital profit dividends" paid by Irish companies.

[60] If the shareholders are individuals, there may be a saving of surtax.

[61] I.R.C. v. Blott, 8 Tax Cas. 101 (1921); "Capital Distributions," 104 Sol. J. 59, 78 (1960). For comparisons in the treatment of bonus issues, see Dale, Tax Harmonization in Europe 74–76 (1963).

[62] Although not necessarily; if the Irish tax on the dividend can be credited against the foreign tax, the over-all rate may be lower than the Irish income and corporation profits tax rates and the foreign capital gains tax rate on the bonus shares. There may be exchange-control difficulties in repatriating capital (in Ireland, these are unlikely), and the parent company would lose any tax reduction for intercorporate dividends.

[63] C.I.R. v. Fisher's Ex'rs, 10 Tax Cas. 302 (1926). Royal Commission, Final Report, Cmd. No. 9474, para. 800 (1955), recommends the alteration of the rule with regard to debentures.

[64] Whitemore v. I.R.C., 10 Tax Cas. 645 (1925). See, however, Ackroyd v. I.R.C., 24 Tax Cas. 515 (1942). For the Netherlands law, see "Income Taxes on Normal and Stock Dividends in the Netherlands," 2 European Taxation 112 (1962).

[65] The small number of surtax rates and the absence of "reduced rates" of income tax make the whole present Irish system simpler than the British system.

[66] A few results cannot be achieved by altering the rates of income tax and corporation profits tax; e.g., the tax rate on undistributed profits cannot be made lower than the "standard" rate of income tax. This could be done only by altering the scale of income tax rates on individuals, which would effectively separate company income tax from income tax on individuals and would make the existence of two separate taxes on companies pointless. It is also impossible to reduce or increase the extent to which a company can pass on tax, which might be necessary to alter the differential between

has since been adopted.[67] In Ireland,[68] the government has said that company tax should be separated from personal taxation "to secure greater flexibility in relation to economic and fiscal policy." What it suggested was a single company tax on undistributed profits and a separate tax on personal income, including dividends. Presumably, economic double taxation will be avoided by having different rates of company tax for distributed and undistributed profits.[69] A single company tax was one of the most important measures recommended by the Neumark Report, so upon joining the EEC Ireland would have to introduce such a tax. The present Irish system of taxing dividends is important because of its unusual nature and the problems it causes in double taxation treaties. Economically, like most other systems, it results in a reduced rate of tax on distributed profits.

German law imposes a high rate (51 per cent) of tax on undistributed company profits and a low rate (15 per cent) on distributed profits.[70] The rates and the technical means used are different, and the difference in the effective rate of tax on distributed and undistributed profits is much greater than in Ireland, but the economic effect is the same. Unlike Ireland, the Six, except the Netherlands and France, treat dividends paid to residents and non-residents differently, and this discrimination is, in principle, incompatible with the Common Market. The Netherlands, Italy, and Belgium reduce the tax on dividends. The Netherlands is considering a reduced rate of company tax for distributed profits and since 1965 France allows shareholders a credit for company tax paid. In Italy, the schedular tax on profits is not paid by the shareholder on dividends. In Belgium, under the 1962 tax reform, there is a reduced rate of tax for distributed profits, and half of the company tax payable on profits later distributed is credited against the personal income tax.[71] Relief for dis-

---

distributed and undistributed profits, without reducing or increasing the level of personal income tax. Even under the existing system, there is no reason why the standard rates of income tax for company profits, for deduction of tax from dividends, and for individuals should not be different.

[67] Finance Act, 1965, pt. IV. It was rejected mainly for administrative reasons connected with giving a credit to the shareholder for tax paid by the company; Royal Commission, Final Report, Cmd. No. 9474, paras. 541–47 (1955). See, however, id., Reservation 345–47, and id., Memorandum of Dissent, ch. III, especially para. 91. The present Irish system is essentially that recommended by the Royal Commission. The first step to official revival of the idea of a single company tax in Britain was in 1964; A Scheme for an Accounts Basis for Income Tax on Company Profits, Cmd. No. 2347 (1964).

[68] For the problems involved in such a change, see generally Irish Income Tax Commission, Seventh Report, Pr. 6581, ch. XXV and Appendix III. The government's policy is set out in the Second White Paper on Direct Taxation, Pr. 7024, paras. 89–91 (1963).

[69] The alternative is a tax on company profits at a rate so low that the effective burden of cumulative taxation on distributed profits would be reduced to an acceptable level, and this would completely alter the financial structure of Irish industry. Another alternative would be to reduce the personal income tax rate on dividends.

[70] Nortcliffe, Common Market Fiscal Systems 83–85 (1960). The real rate on distributed profits is about 23% because the tax paid is treated as undistributed profits and taxed at the 51% rate. See Körperschaftssteuergesetz, Nov. 18, 1958, arts. 9, 19; Harvard University Law School, Taxation in the Federal Republic of Germany 624–34 (1963).

[71] See Schendstok, "Les méthodes de coordination interne en matierè fiscale doivent être harmonisées," 3 La Fiscalité du Marché Commun 67, 69 (1962). On the proposed new laws in the Netherlands, see International Bureau of Fiscal Documentation, Annual Report, 1962, at 23 (1962). Under the French tax reform law of July 12, 1965, although there is no special company tax rate for distributed profits, economic double taxation is minimized by a credit system similar to, but simpler than, that in Belgium.

tributed profits will be given under the harmonized systems of direct taxation in the EEC, but the Irish method of giving this relief is unlikely to be adopted and would have to be altered in due course. At present it gives more complete relief against double taxation than the method of any of the Six. Whether differentiation in favor of distributed profits is desirable depends on the economic advantages of profit retention and self-financing which result from the pre-1965 French system. Questions of economic policy are therefore involved. The economic double taxation resulting from the pre-1965 French system penalizes distribution rather than encourages self-financing, and it causes the growth of large companies and monopoly problems.

Tax differentiation in favor of undistributed company profits does not necessarily have any effect on the general level of savings, investment, or capital formation, which Ireland and other less developed countries must do their utmost to encourage. Undistributed profits are not necessarily used for capital investment,[72] while accelerated depreciation allowances, for example, encourage fixed capital formation directly. However, a low rate of tax on undistributed profits or tax concessions facilitates self-financing.[73] Tax concessions may be necessary for investment if tax rates are high because the tax base is small.

Intercorporate dividends

No special legislation was required in Ireland to exempt dividends paid to a parent company from further income tax. Since corporation profits tax is not paid on behalf of shareholders, dividends had to be exempted from that tax.[74] Unless a subsidiary company is exempt from corporation profits tax, its profits after income and corporation profits tax are not taxable again, even if they pass through several companies and even if they are not finally distributed to individual shareholders.[75] In Germany the dividend is exempt from the usual withholding tax only if the recipient company holds 25 per cent of the payor's share and if it redistributes the dividend received, withholding the required tax on the amount distributed.[76] In Luxembourg, the dividend is always exempt from tax in the hands of the recipient company if the latter's shareholding is 25 per cent; there is no requirement of further distribution.[77] In Belgium and Italy, dividends are not completely exempt from double taxation, but the payee company need not hold any particular proportion of the payor company's shares. In Belgium, the withholding tax on the "grossed-up" div-

[72] Vogel, "Tax Incentives for Industrial Development," in Methods of Industrial Development 271, 272–76 (OECD, 1962).

[73] Irish Income Tax Commission, Seventh Report, Pr. 6581, ch. XV (1962), discusses the whole question. It has often been argued that undistributed profits should be more lightly taxed, owing to the difficulty of equity financing on the small Irish capital market.

[74] This was done by Finance Act, 1920, § 53(2)(a).

[75] Dividends paid by a company which would be liable to corporation profits tax at the higher rate if its profits reached £2,500 are exempt from that tax in the hands of a shareholding company, even if the profits of the latter exceed £2,500. See Wilson & Kelly, Irish Income Tax and Corporation Profits Tax 253 (1957). The result of the rule stated in the text is that the Irish tax system has no further claim (except surtax) on the distributed profits of a company liable in principle to corporation profits tax. Consequently, in negotiating double taxation treaties there is only surtax to be waived on profits distributed to non-Irish residents.

[76] Körperschaftssteuer-Durchführungsverordnung, art. 29; see Harvard University Law School, Taxation in the Federal Republic of Germany 432–39 (1963); see also "Taxation of Intercorporate Dividends Received in Europe," 4 European Taxation 135 (1964).

[77] There are special rules for holding companies; see Chapter Eleven on unilateral relief.

idend (15 per cent)[78] is still payable, but the recipient company pays further company tax only on a small proportion of the dividend. In France, Germany, and the Netherlands, intercorporate dividends are very heavily taxed if there is no substantial shareholding. In the absence of a double taxation treaty, only France and the Netherlands give relief from economic double taxation for intercorporate dividends paid by foreign companies.

Corporation profits tax[79]

In addition to income tax at the prevailing standard rate, Irish companies pay corporation profits tax at a flat rate of 23 per cent on profits over £2,500,[80] and at 7.5 per cent on profits below £2,500. This tax cannot be passed on to the shareholders, but since it is now an allowable deduction in calculating profits for income tax, some economic double taxation results. Almost all trading companies[81] are liable to corporation profits tax.[82]

The rules with regard to the residence of companies for corporation profits tax purposes differ from those relating to income tax. Any company incorporated in Ireland is liable to corporation profits tax on its world profits, even if it is managed and controlled abroad.[83] A company incorporated abroad pays corporation profits tax only on profits arising in Ireland, even if it is managed and controlled in Ireland. This difference is important with regard to double taxation, in particular when considering the suitability of Ireland as a locale for a "base," or holding, company. There seems to be no justification for differentiating between income tax and corporation profits tax in this way.

A company is liable to corporation profits tax on the profits on any trade or business, including income from investments.[84] In general, for corporation profits tax purposes, income is computed according to normal accountancy principles, and the rules are less complex

[78] In the Belgian system, company tax is paid at the rate of 30%. One-half of this is credited against the personal income tax of the shareholder receiving a dividend. The other half is added to the dividend, and the company then deducts the withholding tax at 15% of the amount of the grossed-up dividend. If the identity of the shareholder is not known to the company, the rate of withholding tax is 30%. If the shareholder is a company, 85% of the net dividend received after the withholding tax has been deducted is exempt from the company tax (strictly, is a deduction from taxable income). If the recipient is a manufacturing company, 95% of the net dividend is exempt. See generally "Survey of Belgian Income Taxes," 4 European Taxation 145, 185–94 (1964).

[79] A general study, unfortunately complete only up to 1946, is Winder, Irish Corporation Profits Tax (1946).

[80] Corporation profits tax is now deductible in calculating income tax; Finance Act, 1961 Acts 671, § 7; Finance Bill, 1966. The present rates stated in the text are proposed by Finance Bill, 1966.

[81] Building societies (Finance Act, 1956 Acts 353, § 22) and a variety of non-profit and semipublic companies of no interest to the investor are exempt from corporation profits tax. A list of companies which are exempt is given in Wilson & Kelly, Irish Income Tax and Corporation Profits Tax 246–47 (1957), and in British Inland Revenue, Income Taxes Outside the Commonwealth 261–62 (1956).

[82] Unlimited liability companies were made liable to it by Finance Act, 1964 Acts, No. 15, § 26.

[83] Finance Act, 1920, § 52(2), 52(3), adapted by Inland Revenue (Adaptation of Taxing Acts) Order, Executive Council Order No. 4 of 1923 and E.C.O. No. 3 of 1924.

[84] Finance Act, 1920, § 52(2). The phrase "including the holding of investments" does not appear in the provision dealing with companies incorporated outside Ireland, but profits made by these companies from Irish investments appear to be liable to corporation profits tax.

than those for income tax.[85] Only actual profits are taxable, not profits treated as arising from interests in land, which are liable to income tax. Dividends or interest paid by a company are not liable to corporation profits tax in the hands of the company receiving them,[86] except in some circumstances where the latter owns over 50 per cent of the shares in the payor company and the profits of the companies are amalgamated.[87]

Anti-avoidance provisions[88]

To prevent tax avoidance, there are certain restrictions, peculiar to corporation profits tax, on expenses which are deductible both for it and for income tax purposes. For income tax the only limit on deductible remuneration of directors or of any officers of the company is that it must be "wholly and exclusively laid out for the purposes of the business."[89] This provision is interpreted fairly liberally. For corporation profits tax purposes, no remuneration[90] over £2,500[91] paid to a director by a company of which the directors[92] have control may be deducted, unless the director in question is a full-time employee and controls no more than 5 per cent of the ordinary shares (i.e., common stock) in the company.[93] The deductible remuneration of anyone connected with the management of the company who has a controlling interest in it is also limited to £2,500 a year.[94] These rules apply even if a salary of more than £2,500 is reasonable by commercial standards.[95] However, if a director carries on a business entirely separate from the company, the company can deduct payment for work done in that capacity which is not related to his directorship.[96] Deductions are not permitted for interest or royalties paid to anyone having a controlling interest in the company[97] or for interest on per-

[85] Irish Income Tax Commission, Sixth Report, Pr. 6039, paras. 30, 139 (1961); Lynch, "Some Aspects of Tax Planning," 69 Accountants' Magazine 114, 119 (1965).

[86] Finance Act, 1920, § 53(2)(a).

[87] Finance Act, 1944, § 14. This section applied only if the parent company was incorporated before, and the subsidiary after, May 1941; it ceased to apply in December 1964; Finance Act, 1965 Acts, No. 22, § 34.

[88] The rule against artificial and fictitious transactions and transactions mainly intended to avoid corporation profits tax does not apply to income tax; Finance Act, 1920, §§ 53(2)(d), 55(4); Finance Act, 1944, § 15. This is an example of unwillingness to delegate discretionary fiscal power to the executive. Under Finance Act, 1920, § 55(4), fines may be imposed for fictitious and artificial transactions.

[89] Income Tax Act, 1918, Schedule D, Cases I and II, Rule 3(a); see Copeman v. William Flood & Sons, Ltd., [1941] 1 K.B. 202, 24 Tax Cas. 53.

[90] Defined comprehensively by Finance Act, 1944, § 12.

[91] Raised to this amount by Finance Act, 1964, § 27.

[92] See Associated Properties, Ltd. v. Revenue Comm'rs, [1949] Ir. Tax Cas., No. 75; Himley Estates, Ltd. v. C.I.R., [1933] 1 K.B. 472, 17 Tax Cas. 367 (1932).

[93] Finance Act, 1941, § 36(4). There is no restriction on the number of directors who may be paid £2,500 each, as there is in Britain; British Finance Act, 1937, 1 Edw. 8 & 1 Geo. 6, c. 54, Schedule 4, § 11, as amended by Finance Act, 1952, 15 & 16 Geo. 6 & 1 Eliz. 2, c. 33, § 34.

[94] Finance Act, 1920, § 53(2)(c); Finance Act, 1964, § 27; Second White Paper on Direct Taxation, Pr. 7024, para. 26 (1963); Irish Income Tax Commission, Sixth Report, Pr. 6039, paras. 164–67 (1961).

[95] Id., para. 164.

[96] Committee of Inquiry into Taxation on Industry, Report, Pr. 3512, at 142, para. 11 (1956).

[97] The prohibition on deductions applies even if the control is indirect or is joint control with another person or company; Finance Act, 1920,

manent loans paid to anyone[98] if the loans are secured on the assets or income of the company and repayable at more than three months' notice.[99] Interest on secured loans repayable at short notice is deductible. These are the only restrictions on the freedom of a company to deduct from taxable income, for corporation profits tax purposes, remuneration of directors and interest, royalties, and any other payments on which income tax is withheld at the source.[100]

The tax year for corporation profits tax

Income tax is charged for each tax year, ending on April 5, on the profits of the previous tax year, but corporation profits tax is charged for each actual accounting period of the company on the taxable income of that period. The tax base is substantially the same for both taxes, so this differentiation is unnecessary. The Income Tax Commission recommended[101] its abolition with respect to taxation of companies, but this has not yet been carried out. The anomalies are in the rules relating to income tax, and their abolition would help to unify the two taxes.

Consolidation of the accounts of parent and subsidiary companies

For the purposes of corporation profits tax, a parent company may treat the profits of a wholly owned subsidiary as if they were the profits of a branch;[102] for example, to set off the losses of one company against the profits of the other. By an anomaly, this does not apply to income tax except in special circumstances.[103] The parent company must hold, directly or through a nominee, the whole of the subsidiary's capital.[104] There is no need for actual control over the subsidiary's operations or for similarity of activities.

No restriction is placed on the division of a substantial concern into several companies, each of which can earn £2,500 profit a year subject to corporation profits tax at the lower rate and deduct £2,500 as fees for each director, even if the same directors are common to all of them.[105] Other tax avoidance devices, such as separate deductions for payments made to an associated com-

---

§ 53(2)(g). See Revenue Comm'rs v. Associated Properties, Ltd., [1959] Ir. Tax Cas., No. 96.

[98] Neither of these prohibited deductions applies to mortgage interest charged on lands if half or more of the gross income of the company is derived from rents or profits from the lands charged, unless there is a mortgage debenture on all the company's assets; Finance Act, 1921, 11 & 12 Geo. 5, c. 32, § 57. In Belgium, under the new tax law of 1962, interest is not deductible to the extent that it exceeds 9%; art. 11(3) 1.

[99] Finance Act, 1920, § 52(3). Companies normally give security by a mortgage debenture or a floating charge.

[100] However, dividends, interest, royalties, or other payments paid out of profits, on which income tax is retained by the company and not handed over to the revenue authorities, are not deductible; see pp. 231–37.

[101] Sixth Report, Pr. 6039, ch. X (1961). See Second White Paper on Direct Taxation, Pr. 7024, paras. 91–93 (1963).

[102] Finance Act, 1920, § 53(3). For the German rules, see Harvard University Law School, Taxation in the Federal Republic of Germany 387–90, 789–92 (1963).

[103] Finance Act, 1962, § 13. See Irish Income Tax Commission, Sixth Report, Pr. 6039, paras. 165–67 (1961); Committee on Industrial Organization, Interim Report on State Aid, Pr. 6510, para. 34 (1962); cf. French Decree No. 60-381 of April 22, 1960.

[104] Finance Act, 1944, § 53(3), recognizes the ambiguous legal position of the nominee shareholder in Irish (and British) law. A nominee is an independent shareholder for the purposes of company law but is not usually recognized as a separate shareholder for tax purposes.

[105] For other tax avoidance devices involving several companies, see Wheatcroft, "The General Principles of Tax Planning," 1963 Brit. Tax Rev. 20, 35–36.

pany for the use of the same patents or know-how, are also possible if a business can be divided between separate corporate entities.

DEPRECIATION[106]

Depreciation allowances and the concept of taxable income

The traditional principle in the Irish tax system and, until 1965, in the British tax system—that taxable business profits are the excess of income receipts over current non-capital expenditures necessary to earn them—necessitates specific provision for depreciation of capital assets, especially because of inflation, heavy taxation, and the increasing number of industries requiring large amounts of capital investment. Depreciation is an exception to the principle that capital gains are not taxable and that other capital losses are not deductible expenses.[107] The result is a compromise, embodied in complex legislation, which the concept of taxable profits as the increase in net worth would avoid.

Economic aspects of depreciation allowances

The Irish tax system does not give investment allowances.[108] In Ireland, in the year when the asset is acquired, an accelerated depreciation allowance called an "initial allowance" is given, and it is followed by annual allowances by which the balance of the cost is written off. The effect is that of an interest-free loan; the amount of the subsidy thus depends on the rate of interest otherwise payable. Initial allowances automatically provide finance for capital expenditure and permit a greater degree of liquidity than would be possible if no extra capital allowance were given. They facilitate investments by small companies which cannot use the capital market, so these companies need not wait until self-financing has provided the necessary cash.[109] Initial allowances are important both for the Irish investor who needs capital and for the foreign investor who is reluctant to tie up large sums of liquid capital in an Irish subsidiary.

Initial allowances were increased in 1962, on the recommendation of the

[106] Tax treatment of capital assets is a most important element in a tax system designed to encourage investment and expansion. See Vogel, "Tax Incentives for Industrial Development," in Methods of Industrial Development 271, 272–74 (OECD, 1962); Committee on Taxation of Trading Profits, Report, Cmd. No. 8189, ch. V (1951). On the Irish law, see Charleton, "Capital Allowances for Plant and Machinery," in Dublin Society of Chartered Accountants, Changes in Industrial and General Taxation, 1950–1961 (1961). On the position in the EEC, see ECSC High Authority, Direction Générale Economie-Energie, Régimes Fiscaux d'Amortissements (1961); EEC Commission, Direction Générale de la Concurrence, Etude déscriptive et comparative des amortissements fiscaux normaux et spéciaux applicables aux biens sujets à dépréciation dans les pays membres de la C.E.E., Doc. No. IV/7053/61-F (1961); Richman, "Depreciation and the Measurement of Effective Profits Tax Rates in the European Common Market and United Kingdom," 17 Nat'l Tax J. 86 (1964). See "Comparative Analysis of Depreciation Allowances and Inventory Valuation in the Common Market," 5 European Taxation 114 (1965).

[107] Royal Commission, Final Report, Cmd. No. 9474, chs. 15, 16 (1955); Irish Income Tax Commission, Seventh Report, Pr. 6581, ch. II (1962). See also Committee on Taxation of Trading Profits, Report, Cmd. No. 8189, ch. V (1951).

[108] Except in the special case of shipping; Finance Act, 1957 Acts 463, §§ 17–23. "Investment allowances" are special allowances resulting in a permanent relief from tax; they are given in addition to the annual depreciation allowances, which cover the total cost of the asset. Britain introduced investment allowances in 1954; Finance Act, 1954, 2 & 3 Eliz. 2, c. 33.

[109] Cosciani, The Effects of Differential Tax Treatment of Corporate and Non-Corporate Enterprises 58–59 (1959).

Committee on Industrial Organization,[110] because accelerated depreciation encourages re-equipment by allowing the cost to be set off against tax soon after purchase instead of during the life of the asset. The Committee concluded that the greatest incentive to invest is a large depreciation allowance in the early life of the asset and that investment allowances are not significantly more effective than initial allowances.

Comparative aspects

In Britain the scale and availability of investment allowances has varied greatly since their introduction because, unlike in Ireland, they have been used as an economic regulator.[111] The importance of investment allowances in anticyclical and growth policy in the EEC will be considerable. The investment allowances in Britain under the Finance Act of 1963[112] are comparable to the present initial allowances in Ireland.

In general, Germany does not give investment or initial allowances, but annual allowances are given on all buildings and other capital assets. Initial allowances of 20 per cent are now given on most industrial equipment in France, and a number of selective allowances are also given. They are given in Italy in the less developed areas. In 1964 the Netherlands, for cyclical reasons, suspended initial allowances of one-third of the value of the asset spread over four years; the allowances had not applied to automobiles or office equipment, and investment allowances of 10 per cent had been given instead on certain types of assets. Investment allowances are given in Belgium and Luxembourg, and initial allowances of up to 33⅓ per cent in certain sectors in Belgium. Unlike in Ireland, annual depreciation allowances are permitted on all types of assets in each of the Six.

Harmonization of depreciation allowances requires both uniform principles and uniform depreciation periods in each member state for each sector. Since even depreciation allowances, which are the same for all sectors in a given country, are not necessarily equitable between capital-intensive and labor-intensive industries, it is difficult to say how the Irish tax system compares with those of the Six in its effects.[113]

Depreciation allowances in Britain and Ireland are based on the original monetary cost (the "historic" cost) of the asset concerned and, unlike in France, the effect of inflation is not recognized by statutes permitting revaluation or substitution of current replacement cost.[114] The effect of depreciation allowances is substantially the same as if they were deductible business expenses. They may be carried forward indefinitely if they

[110] Committee on Industrial Organization, Interim Report on State Aid, Pr. 6510, para. 24 (1962).

[111] Bird, "Countercyclical Variations of Depreciation Allowances in the United Kingdom," 16 Nat'l Tax J. 41 (1963). The variations have been so frequent and so substantial that, since initial and investment allowances are given as of the time the goods are paid for rather than the time they are ordered, business planning has been rendered uncertain. Because of the previous-year basis of assessment, capital allowances are given against income tax only in the year of assessment, after the year when the expenditure was incurred; this reduces the incentive effect.

[112] On new machinery, 30%, and on industrial buildings, 15%.

[113] See Economist Intelligence Unit, Taxes for Britain 24 (1962). For a summary of the laws of the Six, see "Computation of Taxable Profits," 3 European Taxation 182 (1963). The "life" of secondhand machinery and motor vehicles is important for depreciation purposes since they do not qualify for initial allowances.

[114] On the French system, see van Hoorn & Wright, "Taxation," in 2 American Enterprise in the European Common Market: A Legal Profile 371–72 (Stein & Nicholson ed. 1960); Vasseur, Le droit de la réforme des structures industrielles et des économies régionales 368–75 (1959).

are not used.[115] Technically, however, they are allowed for the income tax year in question and not for the basis year.[116] They all apply to corporation profits tax for the appropriate accounting period.

Industrial buildings and hotels

INITIAL ALLOWANCES

Initial allowances on industrial buildings are now 20 per cent of the construction cost.[117] The buildings must be used in a trade carried on in a factory or similar premises, but since qualifying constructions need not be *in* the factory, roads, parking space, and walls qualify.[118] A part of the building not used for industrial purposes may be disregarded if its capital cost is less than 10 per cent of the total.[119] Additions to existing buildings qualify for allowances, since parts of buildings can be treated independently. Showrooms, office space, office canteens, employees' welfare rooms, repair shops, or commercial buildings should be physically part of a factory building. Stores and warehouses are, in practice, treated as factories for the purpose of annual allowances.[120] The cost of acquisition of land is not eligible, but the cost of cutting or leveling land for the foundation of a factory and the cost of installation of machinery are included.[121] The Income Tax Commission[122] recommends that commercial buildings[123] should be made eligible for capital allowances, along revised lines suggested by it, in the same way as industrial buildings. This recommendation

[115] Income Tax Act, 1918, Rule 6(3), Cases I and II, Schedule D (Machinery). Finance Act, 1963, § 5, provides that capital allowances can be taken into account to augment or create a trading loss. Germany is the only one of the Six which does not permit the carry-forward of unused depreciation allowances. Losses and depreciation allowances which are unused can be carried forward indefinitely in Ireland.

[116] This results from the previous-year basis of assessment for income tax; Irish Income Tax Commission, Sixth Report, Pr. 6039, ch. VIII (1961). See also Finance Act, 1956, §§ 23(1)(d), 23(4), 27. In the case of a company, it always is best to claim initial allowances where possible.

[117] Finance (Miscellaneous Provisions) Act, 1956 Acts 807, pt. IV; Finance Act, 1962, § 11(2).

[118] Finance (Miscellaneous Provisions) Act, 1956, § 17(1). Factory canteens qualify, since they are used for the purposes of a trade carried on in a factory.

[119] Finance (Miscellaneous Provisions) Act, 1956, § 17(3)(5). If the disqualified portion exceeds 10%, there is an apportionment. Allocation of cost may be made on the basis of floor area. Because of the wording of the section, an addition of non-industrial premises to existing qualifying buildings will qualify for the initial allowance if the whole of the addition costs 10% or less of the original cost of the completed structure.

[120] Irish Committee of Inquiry into Taxation on Industry, Report, Pr. 3512, para. 120 (1956). They would probably be held to be eligible for initial allowances, which are available for any "building or structure in use for the purposes of a trade carried on in a factory . . ."; at least they would be eligible if they were on the same site as the factory and were used for manufacturing or handling rather than distribution or sales promotion.

[121] Finance (Miscellaneous Provisions) Act, 1956, § 19. Para. (b) and the proviso were repealed by Finance Act, 1959, § 73(2), but the present state of the law is as indicated in the text. The cost of preparing the site is treated as expenditure on an industrial building, while the machinery receives the higher initial allowance; Finance Act, 1959, § 73(3).

[122] Seventh Report, Pr. 6581, paras. 143–46 (1962). The Commission recommended that existing commercial buildings, as well as new ones, should be eligible for capital allowances. Cf. the similar recommendation of the Royal Commission, Final Report, Cmd. No. 9474, paras. 379–82 (1955). For the Irish government's attitude, see the Second White Paper on Direct Taxation, Pr. 7024, para. 42 (1963). In Belgium commercial buildings may be written down at 3% per annum.

[123] Buildings or structures for a dock undertaking, including harbors and jetties for merchandise or passengers, are eligible under Finance Act, 1959, §§ 24(4), 73(1).

has not been carried out. The failure to give depreciation allowances for commercial and administrative buildings other than hotels[124] is a striking fault in the tax laws of Ireland and Britain.

ANNUAL ALLOWANCES

In Ireland, annual allowances for the same type of buildings as those which qualify for initial allowances are given to the first owner at the rate of 2 per cent on the actual construction cost.[125] This is the straight line method, which is used by all the Six for buildings. Since the 2 per cent is calculated on the basis of the actual cost, not the value as written down by the initial allowance, the effect is that the building will be entirely written off after forty years. The corresponding period is fifty years in Germany, but twenty years is usual in France, Belgium, Luxembourg, and Italy. However, Irish initial allowances are larger than those given in the Six.

Annual allowances are given on a building only if it was constructed since 1956[126] and is an "industrial building." If the building is subject to a lease,[127] the taxpayer entitled to the allowance is the one who incurred the capital expenditure concerned, or his assignee, but not his lessee.[128]

If the building is sold during the years in which annual allowances are available, the annual allowances after the sale are calculated by dividing the written-down value by the number of years remaining out of a fifty-year period which begins with the date of first use of the building.[129] The written-down value for this purpose[130] is the sale price or the original construction cost, whichever is less. Therefore, if the sale price[131] is greater than the construction cost, the purchaser receives annual allowances which permit him to write off the entire construction cost, but not the entire price paid by him, within the balance of the fifty years. In the Six, the construction cost is relevant only for the first owner. If the purchaser buys at less than the seller's written-down value, the seller gets a balancing allowance (see material immediately following) of the amount of the difference.[132]

The principle by which the purchaser of a secondhand building cannot obtain depreciation allowances on the basis of a cost greater than the original construction cost penalizes such a purchaser if the price of the building has risen for any reason.[133] In order to calculate the true cost of a secondhand building, the

[124] See Finance Act, 1960 Acts 483, § 33.

[125] Finance Act, 1959, § 25(1). The straight line method must be used; for machinery, the declining balance method is the one normally, but not necessarily, used.

[126] See, however, Finance Act, 1959, § 2.

[127] Finance Act, 1959, § 25(2).

[128] If the building is used for industrial purposes, the lessee may deduct the rent from taxable profits in the usual way. If the lessee adds a qualifying structure to the premises, he and the assignees of the leasehold interest get initial and annual allowances in respect to it. Also, the lessee may add non-qualifying additions up to the value of 10% of the *whole* building even if he has not added any qualifying additions; Finance (Miscellaneous Provisions) Act, 1956, § 17(4).

[129] Finance Act, 1959, § 25(3).

[130] Called the "residue of expenditure." Finance Act, 1959, § 27. It is explained as the capital cost of construction, less the initial and all annual allowances (including those deemed to have been allowed for years during which the building was not used for industrial purposes), but plus any balancing charges made on the sale.

[131] On a first sale. The principles are the same for subsequent sales.

[132] Finance Act, 1959, § 27(5). On balancing allowances, see p. 227.

[133] This is unfortunate since, even in an expanding industrial economy, there are secondhand industrial buildings which can be efficiently used, and the sale price of such buildings may be more than the original cost. Fear of speculation in used factories seems an

purchaser must find out the construction cost, and this is often difficult before the contract is signed. The rule is also anomalous because the excess of the sale price over the construction cost is a tax-free capital gain.[134] Even apart from this, the system of depreciation allowances may harm the seller.[135] Because of large initial allowances, the written-down value may be much less than the sale price. The balancing charge will be made on the difference, at the seller's effective tax rate, in one year, while the allowances which caused it to arise were spread over several years.[136]

All of the aspects which are criticized in this discussion of the capital allowances on industrial buildings must be reconsidered in due course, to achieve a rational tax system of the sort on which harmonization of tax burdens among member states of the EEC must be based.

inadequate reason for discriminating against taxpayers who, for sound business reasons, prefer not to construct a new one. Presumably the reason for the rule is unwillingness to make the state bear the cost of inflation. This rule does not apply to machinery.

[134] The government has accepted the Income Tax Commission's view that sums received on the disposal of capital assets should be taxable; Second White Paper on Direct Taxation, Pr. 7024, para. 43 (1963); Irish Income Tax Commission, Seventh Report, Pr. 6581, paras. 156–62 (1962); cf. Royal Commission, Final Report, Cmd. No. 9474, paras. 391–92 (1955). See Finance Act, 1965, pt. VII. The changes recommended would bring Irish law substantially into line with the laws of the Six on this point.

[135] Irish Income Tax Commission, Seventh Report, Pr. 6581, paras. 163–71 (1962).

[136] This is much more serious in the case of an individual, who will be liable to progressive surtax on the amount of the excess in addition to his ordinary income, than for a company, which pays tax at a flat rate of 50% on profits over £2,500, but the effect is still serious. A change in the existing law was recommended by the Irish Income Tax Commission only with regard to surtax.

Balancing Allowances and Charges

If the owner[137] of an industrial building[138] sells his interest, he receives a balancing allowance or charge to adjust the written-down value for tax purposes to the amount he receives.[139] If the proceeds of sale[140] are less than the written-down value,[141] a balancing allowance is given to allow him a deduction against tax for the extra depreciation which he has suffered. If the proceeds of a sale exceed the written-down value, the excess, called a "balancing charge," is added to taxable income for the year of sale, in order to withdraw the excess depreciation allowed.[142] If the proceeds of sale exceed the construction cost of the building, a balancing charge of the difference between the written-down value and the construction cost is made. The excess of the sale price over the construction cost is disregarded for the purpose of balancing allowances and charges, as well as for annual allowances.

Machinery and equipment

Initial Allowances

Initial allowances for new plants and machinery are now 40 per cent of the cost.[143] The balance is written off in annual allowances. The equipment must

[137] Strictly, the person entitled to the annual allowances, called the owner of the "relevant interest" in Finance Act, 1959; for the definition of this term, see § 29.

[138] Finance (Miscellaneous Provisions) Act, 1956, § 17(1); Finance Act, 1959, § 26(1).

[139] Finance Act, 1959, § 26(1).

[140] The proceeds of sale, insurance moneys, salvage, and compensation are treated in the same way.

[141] Finance Act, 1959, § 27.

[142] Finance Act, 1959, § 26(2), 26(3). Allowance is made for years in which annual allowances were not given because the building was not used for industrial purposes; § 26(4).

[143] Finance Act, 1962, § 11(1).

be new[144] and may include a wide variety of apparatus and assets of a durable nature,[145] but not road vehicles for carrying goods or passengers.[146] Installation and transport costs are included in capital expenditure on machinery.[147] In Britain initial allowances have been given on secondhand machinery. Therefore, if a company has British income, it may be advantageous to buy secondhand machinery for use in Britain before bringing the machinery to Ireland, to obtain an initial allowance which can be set off against British income tax.

Even though an item of machinery may be fixed to a building, it should be claimed as machinery rather than as part of a building, since the initial and annual allowances for machinery allow the cost to be written off faster.[148] Machinery will qualify for an initial allowance even if it is not in an industrial building and would not qualify for one as part of a building.

If machinery is bought on an installment basis,[149] each installment is divided into principal and interest, the latter being deductible in the ordinary way as a revenue expenditure. The capital sum involved in each installment is the subject of a separate initial allowance for the tax period during which it is paid.

In general, only the taxpayer who actually carries on the business in which the machinery is used and to whom the machinery belongs is entitled to an annual allowance. However, if the burden of maintaining the machinery falls on a lessor, he may obtain the initial and annual allowances due, as if the trade were carried on by him.[150] If the lessee of machinery is carrying on the trade, the machinery belongs to him for the purpose of initial and annual allowances only if he is bound to maintain it at his own expense and return it in as good

[144] Except in the case of ships; Finance Act, 1957, §§ 17–23. The exclusion of secondhand machinery is important if the promoters of a company want to use in an Irish factory machinery which they have already used elsewhere. Secondhand machinery and vehicles are eligible for annual allowances.

[145] "Plant . . . includes whatever apparatus is used by a businessman for carrying on his business—not his stock in trade which he buys or makes for sale, but all goods and chattels, fixed or movable, live or dead, which he keeps for permanent employment in his business." Yarmouth v. France, 19 Q.B.D. 647, 658 (1887) (per Lindley, L.J.), adopted in Hinton v. Maden & Ireland, Ltd., [1959] 3 All E.R. 356, 363, 369, 38 Tax Cas. 391, 417, 424 (per Reid, L.J., and Jenkins, L.J., respectively). See Jarrold v. John Good & Sons, Ltd., [1962] 1 Weekly L.R. 1101, 1962 Brit. Tax Rev. 327. Small tools and implements are normally not eligible.

[146] Finance Act, 1956, § 23(1).

[147] Finance Act, 1956, § 23(1), allows any "capital expenditure incurred on the provision of new machinery or plant for the purposes of the trade . . . ."

[148] What is in question here includes elevators, lighting, water supply, and ventilation and air conditioning systems. The test, in general, is whether the item is part of the building and cannot be moved without substantial damage, or whether it is a machine which happens to be slightly attached to the building and can be relatively easily moved. If machinery is fixed to the land or building, a stamp duty will be payable on sale.

[149] The distinction between hire purchase and credit sale is a technical one based on the time of passing of the property in the machinery, the hire purchase form giving somewhat greater security to the transferor. See generally Hire-Purchase Act, 1946 Acts 713. In hire purchase transactions, the revenue and capital elements are, in form, payment for hire and for the option to purchase, respectively.

[150] Income Tax Act, 1918, Schedule D, Cases I and II, Rule 6(2); Finance Act, 1944, § 2; Finance Act, 1957, § 2(4): The last was applied to initial allowances by Finance Act, 1956, § 24(2). All leases of machinery must be carefully drafted with wear-and-tear allowances in mind. The words "provided the burden of the wear and tear will fall on him" in Finance Act, 1944, § 2, seem to have no effective meaning except in the circumstances suggested, which are unlikely. Since Rule 6(2) and Finance Act, 1959, § 43, do not correspond, the position seems to be as stated in the text.

condition as he received it or if he is obliged to contribute towards its replacement, in addition to paying rent.

ANNUAL ALLOWANCES

Annual depreciation allowances for machinery and plant—wear-and-tear allowances—vary with the type of equipment and are calculated on the basis of percentage rates intended to write down the cost of a piece of machinery to its expected scrap value[151] over its useful life.[152] No specific percentage rates are prescribed by law. The actual allowances given are 125 per cent of each annual sum[153] so calculated, except in the case of vehicles,[154] so the total cost is written off before the end of the useful life of the asset. The total of initial and annual allowances may not exceed the actual cost, including capital expenditure on renewal and improvement.[155] The method used is the declining balance method,[156] under which the percentage, calculated without reference to any initial allowance, is applied each year to the written-down value, i.e., the cost less any initial allowance[157] and annual allowances previously given. The percentage rates usually allowed are published and are negotiable if they are inappropriate,[158] as, for example, in the case of intensive use.[159] The Income Tax Commission recommended that[160] the periods over which annual allowances are granted and the number of rates used should be gradually reduced. Since the actuarial purchase value of all the annual allowances to be given in the future is substantially less than the actual cost of an asset with a long expected life, this would improve the position of industry.[161] It would also bring Irish depreciation allowances more into line with those of the Six.

The usual periods for depreciation of machinery in the Six are from five to ten years, except in Luxembourg, where the usual period is twenty years. There are numerous special depreciation allowances for particular types of assets.

[151] Usually 10% of cost.

[152] In addition to companies, wear-and-tear allowances for machinery are available to individual taxpayers carrying on a profession or employed by another; Finance Act, 1949 Acts 75, § 3(1). Balancing charges and allowances also apply; Finance Act, 1959, § 58.

[153] Finance Act, 1957, § 2.

[154] Finance Act, 1957, § 2(5)(a).

[155] Income Tax Act, 1918, Schedule D, Cases I and II, Rule 6(6); Finance Act, 1956, § 24(3). This rule is important if the machinery cost the taxpayer nothing, e.g., if it was received in a distribution in kind on liquidation.

[156] For machinery, the declining balance method is used in France (see the Law of Dec. 28, 1959), Germany, Luxembourg, and the United Kingdom, and in the Netherlands for the first four years. The straight line method is used in Italy and Belgium, but see art. 13 of the 1962 Belgian tax law; see also "Computation of Taxable Profits," 3 European Taxation 182, 183 (1963).

[157] Finance Act, 1956, § 24(1). Under the straight line method, which is used in Ireland in calculating depreciation on ships and buildings, the total of all the annual allowances is spread evenly over the life of the assets, subject to changes in the relevant historic cost due to sale of the asset.

[158] Committee of Inquiry into Taxation on Industry, Report, Pr. 3512, para. 99 (1956), says that appeals against negotiated percentages are almost unknown.

[159] Intensive use is recognized in all of the Six either by reductions in the depreciation period (Italy, Luxembourg, France, the Netherlands) or by percentage increases in the depreciation allowances according to the number of additional shifts worked.

[160] Seventh Report, Pr. 6581, para. 142 (1962). This recommendation has not been implemented, and the only statement made with regard to it was noncommittal; Second White Paper on Direct Taxation, Pr. 7024, para. 41 (1963).

[161] Irish Income Tax Commission, Seventh Report, Pr. 6581, para. 120 (1962).

The usual Irish rates[162] give longer depreciation periods, but this is offset by the Irish initial allowances and to some extent by the use of the declining balance method, which has the effect of accelerating the annual allowance.

The annual allowances for machinery are based on a principle different from and preferable to that for annual allowances for industrial buildings. The actual cost to each purchaser is the basis on which annual wear-and-tear allowances are calculated,[163] even if it exceeds the cost to the first owner. This cost is spread over the remaining anticipated life of the asset and gives the amount of the annual allowances to which the purchaser is entitled. However, if an owner sells machinery for more than he paid for it, the excess is a tax-free capital gain, although he suffers a balancing charge on the difference between the written-down value and the price which he originally paid.[164] In both Ireland and Britain recommendations have been made[165] that this anomaly should be abolished by taxing the vendor on capital gains from the sale of machinery, but no legislation has yet been passed in Ireland. The number of occasions on which such gains are made are probably comparatively few, except where inflation exists.

Balancing Allowances

A balancing allowance or charge for machinery[166] is made of an amount equal to the difference between the written-down value[167] and the sale price or, in the case of sales to associated persons or companies[168] and certain other transactions,[169] the market value. The harshness of imposing in a single year a balancing charge equivalent to the depreciation allowed over a longer period is mitigated by the option to reduce the initial and annual allowances available for the machine being bought in replacement by the amount of the balancing charge.[170] Balancing allowances and charges are assessed upon termination of ownership of the asset, termination of use for the trade, or permanent discontinuance of the trade.[171] There are provisions[172] dealing with a machine which

[162] Set out in Committee of Inquiry into Taxation on Industry, Report, Pr. 3512, at 130–33 (1956). They are based on the British rates. For the usual rates in the Six, see Economist Intelligence Unit, Taxes for Britain 24 (1962); evidence given by Secretary of Treasury Dillon, Hearings Before the [United States] Senate Committee on Finance, 87th Cong., 2d Sess., pt. 1, at 82, 396.

[163] In Ireland the turnover tax is not normally payable on capital goods. Indirect taxes are included in the cost base in Italy, Luxembourg, the Netherlands, Belgium, and Germany, but not in France.

[164] Finance Act, 1959, § 34(4). See, however, Second White Paper on Direct Taxation, Pr. 7024, paras. 42–43 (1963).

[165] Irish Income Tax Commission, Seventh Report, Pr. 6581, para. 155 (1962); Royal Commission, Final Report, Cmd. No. 9474, paras. 385–91 (1955).

[166] Finance Act, 1959, §§ 33–45.

[167] Finance Act, 1959, § 62.

[168] Finance Act, 1959, § 39; for other anti-avoidance provisions, see § 62.

[169] The "capital expenditure unallowed" will be the written-down value, except when renewal allowances have complicated the position or when annual wear-and-tear allowances have not been claimed.

[170] Finance Act, 1959, § 35.

[171] Finance Act, 1959, § 34(1); see also §§ 39, 61, 64, 67.

[172] Finance Act, 1959, § 38. A balancing allowance or charge is given in proportion to the degree of trade use of the machinery. If a company gives or sells a machine, usually in practice a motor car, to one of its directors at a price below the market value, the director will be liable to tax on the benefit in kind thus given him; Finance Act, 1958 Acts 553, pt. IV. But the company is entitled to a balancing allowance on the loss it has sustained, in spite of the departure from the market price; Finance

is used partly for the trade and partly for private use.

DEDUCTION OF INCOME TAX AT SOURCE

Deduction of income tax at source, or indirect collection, is an important feature of the British and Irish tax systems. It is an administrative device designed "to safeguard the collection of revenue by using taxpayers as collectors from other taxpayers, and to reduce the costs of administration,"[173] and has only an indirect effect on tax liability. It takes different forms with regard to the deduction of tax from dividends, from salaries and wages (known in Ireland and in Britain as Pay-As-You-Earn or P.A.Y.E.),[174] from rents,[175] from public securities,[176] and from the type of payments now to be discussed.

Tax may be charged by deduction in two main ways. The person paying income to the taxpayer may deduct the tax and pay it to the revenue authorities, or he may deduct the tax and keep it to recoup himself. The first principle is widely used in Europe and is advocated in the Neumark Report; the second principle is peculiar to Irish and English law. In either case the tax is that payable by the payee on the income in question.

If the payor cannot deduct the payment in computing his taxable income and therefore makes it wholly out of taxed profits,[177] he may deduct tax, at the standard rate, from the payment and retain the sum deducted to recoup himself and may pass the tax on to the payee.[178] If the payor's taxed profits exceed the gross amount of the payment, the tax liability of the payor is not affected. If the payment is an allowable deduction or is not paid wholly out of taxed profits, e.g., when the payments exceed the payor's taxable income, tax must be deducted from the payment and paid over to the revenue authorities;[179] the payor has no option as to whether to make the deduction. This form of deduction is similar to withholding taxes in other countries. If the payment is made partly out of taxed profits, deduction of tax is compulsory, but only the tax on the part not paid out of taxed profits need be paid to the revenue authorities. In all cases payment of the sum in question, after deducting or retaining tax, is a good discharge to the payor for the full amount which he is liable to pay. Since the payee has borne income tax at the

---

Act, 1959, § 39(3). In the case of a director-controlled company, this may sometimes enable an over-all tax saving to be made.

[173] Royal Commission, Final Report, Cmd. No. 9474, para. 985 (1955).

[174] In Ireland this was introduced by and is regulated by Finance (No. 2) Act, 1959 Acts 1117; see generally Income Tax Commission, First Report, Pr. 4891 (1958). Surtax may be deducted in certain cases from salaries; Finance Act, 1961, § 11. See Tait, "The Public Sector in Ireland," 17 Nat'l Tax J. 22, 31–32 (1964); Income Tax, Pr. 5276 (1959).

[175] Under Income Tax Act, 1918, Schedule A.

[176] Under Income Tax Act, 1918, Schedule C.

[177] That is, out of net profits after payment of tax. See Irish Income Tax Commission, Sixth Report, Pr. 6039, ch. IX (1961).

[178] Income Tax Act, 1918, General Rule 19. In these cases, other than those involving dividends, the United States doctrine in the *Biddle* case, 302 U.S. 573 (1938), still applies where Irish-source interest or royalties are taxable in Ireland. Distributed profits could be made deductible; Kirkpatrick, "Impôt annuel et précomptes dus par les sociétés belges par actions," 1963 Journal des Tribunaux 57, 61.

[179] Income Tax Act, 1918, General Rule 21. An assessment on the payor for the tax on a deductible payment is possible; Moss Empires, Ltd. v. I.R.C., [1937] A.C. 785, 21 Tax Cas. 264. If the tax is not deducted by the payor or if he does not pay it to the revenue authorities, the payee may be directly assessed. By an anomalous rule, a payor who does not deduct tax when making the payment cannot subsequently recover the tax from the payee; Taylor v. Taylor, [1938] 1 K.B. 320. See, however, 1 Konstam, The Law of Income Tax 268 (11th ed. 1950).

standard rate on the annual payment, he is not liable to any further tax on it except surtax.

Tax cannot be deducted from any annual payment unless it is in itself net income of the payee[180] and a slice of the payor's profits. If the annual payment is a trading expense to the payor or a trading receipt to the payee, tax cannot be deducted. As in Germany, deductions are permitted for interest which originates in a business venture but not from interest which is "pure" income from capital.

Subject to the provisions of any double taxation treaty on the liability of the recipient to Irish tax, deduction of tax at source applies to payments to both residents and non-residents.

Capital expenditure is not a deductible expense for tax purposes. Tax cannot be deducted from any capital payment, except one made to a non-resident for the use of a patent,[181] or from the capital part of an annual payment. The distinction between capital payments and income may be an artificial and difficult one. For example, if the purchase price of a capital asset is payable in installments, the vendor pays no tax on it; but if the price is paid in the form of an annuity payable at the same times, over the same period, and in the same amounts as the installments of capital, it is taxable. If a capital asset is paid for by installments and each installment consists partly of capital and partly of interest, tax is deductible from that portion of the payment which represents interest.[182]

Corporation profits tax cannot be deducted at source or otherwise passed on to the recipient of any annual payments. This results from the principle that corporation profits tax is payable only once on distributed company profits and should be borne by the company paying it. Interest on debentures and loans is deductible for the purposes of corporation profits tax.

Interest payments

The provisions regarding both the deduction of tax from interest payments and the deductibility of the interest payments are confused, but it will be seen that this in no way results from the principle of deduction at source and retention of the tax on interest. Interest on or an annual payment for capital lent to or invested in a business is not deductible in computing the taxable profits of the business.[183] The theory behind this is that dividends and interest on fixed and loan capital—as distinct from interest on temporary fluctuating overdrafts—are shares in net profits. If according to commercial accounting principles the interest, annuities, and other annual payments would be charges on net profits after the latter have been ascertained, rather than revenue expenses to be taken into account in ascertaining them, they are not deductible.[184] Whether interest

[180] Re Hanbury (Conisley v. Hanbury), 20 Ann. Tax Cas. 333, 38 Tax Cas. 588 (1939); London Corp. v. I.R.C., [1952] Tax. R. 267, 272, [1953] 1 All E.R. 1075; 1 British Tax Encyclopedia 1155–57 (Wheatcroft ed. 1962); see also Forsyth v. Thompson, [1940] 2 K.B. 366; Ashey v. London Film Prods., [1944] K.B. 133, 140; Committee on Taxation of Trading Profits, Report, Cmd. No. 8189, para. 10 (1951).

[181] Under Finance Act, 1959, ch. III.

[182] Secretary of State v. Scoble, [1903] A.C. 209.

[183] Income Tax Act, 1918, Schedule D, Cases I and II, Rule 3(f); European Inv. Trust Co. v. Jackson, 18 Tax. Cas. 1 (1932); Bridgewater v. King, 25 Tax Cas. 385 (1943). In the EEC, the taxable income of a company is the difference in the net worth at the beginning and the end of the tax year, so payments of capital into and out of the enterprise must be taken into account when computing taxable income.

[184] Income Tax Act, 1918, Schedule D, Cases I and II, Rule 3(1). The circularity of the expression in Rule 3(1), "in computing the amount of [taxable] profits . . . no sum shall

on what is usually called circulating, or working, capital is deductible is a question of fact; interest on temporary accommodation in the course of business is deductible,[185] but interest on debentures is not.[186]

If "yearly interest" is payable wholly out of taxed profits, the payor has an option of deducting tax at the standard rate[187] and retaining it. Even if he does not deduct tax, no further income tax[188] is payable by the recipient. "Yearly interest . . . or any other annual payment"[189] has been interpreted broadly; it means interest which is calculated by periods of at least a year, even if the obligation to pay it may cease before the first year is over,[190] or if the annual payments vary in amount, or if they are payable only on a contingency which may not arise. The interest may be paid more often than once a year, and the only essential requirement seems to be that the payments are capable of recurring,[191] but the law is not clear.

If interest is payable out of taxed profits but is not "yearly," the payor cannot deduct tax and pass it on to the payee.[192] The quite arbitrary distinction between "yearly" interest and other interest is

---

be deducted for . . . any annual payment *payable out of profits,*" (emphasis supplied) is explained, in part, in Income Tax Codification Committee, Report, Cmd. No. 5131, at 144–45 (1936). Some annual payments are deductible on commercial accounting principles and are also deductible under Rule 3(1) because of the words emphasized; Gresham Life Assur. Soc'y v. Style, 3 Tax Cas. 185 (1892). "An annuity to the widow of a deceased partner, interest on capital advanced by a partner or upon money borrowed for the purposes of the business are . . . payable out of [taxed] profits" and not deductible; 3 Tax Cas. at 192. However, "the dividing line between money used as capital and money which represents mere financial facilities is difficult to draw." Schipper, The Liability to Tax of Non-Resident Companies 68 n.2 (1958). See Alexandria Water Co. v. Musgrave, 11 Q.B.D. 174, 1 Tax Cas. 521 (1883); British Sugar Mfrs. v. Harris, [1938] 1 All E.R. 149. One advantage of the Irish tax treatment of debenture interest is that there is no tax preference in favor of loans and against equity capital.

[185] Farmer v. Scottish No. Am. Trust, [1912] A.C. 118, 5 Tax Cas. 693, commented on in European Inv. Trust Co. v. Jackson, 18 Tax Cas. 1 (1932). The law is confused and uncertain; see 2 Simon, Income Tax 244 (2d ed. 1952).

[186] Alexandria Water Co. v. Musgrave, 11 Q.B.D. 174, 1 Tax Cas. 521 (1883).

[187] The standard rate in force during the period in which the interest accrued, not the rate in force at the time of payment of the interest; Income Tax Act, 1918, General Rule 19. The recommendations of the Irish Income Tax Commission, Sixth Report, Pr. 6039, paras. 116–18 (1961), have been accepted, and legislation to rationalize the position will be enacted; Second White Paper on Direct Taxation, Pr. 7024, para. 24 (1963).

[188] And no further corporation profits tax, if the payor is a company which is liable to it; Finance Act, 1920, § 53(2)(a). If the payor company can deduct the interest for corporation profits tax purposes, the payee company must include the interest in its income liable to corporation profits tax.

[189] Income Tax Act, 1918, General Rule 19.

[190] Re Craven, [1907] 2 Ch. 448 (per Warrington, J.).

[191] Moss Empires, Ltd. v. I.R.C., [1937] A.C. 785, 21 Tax Cas. 264. The distinction between annual and other payments has been justly criticized by the Irish Income Tax Commission, Seventh Report, Pr. 6581, ch. XI (1962).

[192] This piece of fiscal wisdom is because General Rule 19 applies only to "yearly interest" and General Rule 21 applies to "any interest," whether "yearly" or not. The reason tax must be deducted at source if the payments are not made out of taxed income is that the Revenue has an interest in insuring that tax is deducted in such cases, while deduction at source is irrelevant to the tax yield if the payment is made out of income which has already borne tax. See Irish Income Tax Commission, Seventh Report, Pr. 6581, ch. XI (1962); Income Tax Codification Committee, Report, Cmd. No. 5131, paras. 93–97 (1936).

therefore relevant to tax liability and not merely to mechanics. Tax may always be deducted from annuities and annual payments which are not interest.

If interest (except bank interest), whether "yearly" or not, is not paid out of profits which have been taxed, tax must always be deducted and paid to the Revenue. "Yearly" interest paid to a bank may have tax deducted from it, and short-term bank interest can be deducted in computing taxable profits. If it is deducted, tax need not be withheld when paying it. Even if the interest is not taken as a deduction and is paid without deduction of tax, the tax on the interest can be repaid.[193] Thus the tax on bank interest need never be borne out of taxed profits.

Interest payable to finance houses other than banks, notably hire purchase finance houses, is not deductible. The Irish tax system therefore discriminates in favor of loans from banks, discount houses, and stockbrokers. The Income Tax Commission recommended that all interest payable on capital and loan advances used for a business should be deductible for income tax;[194] this recommendation has not been accepted.

Patent royalties

The cost of purchase and the proceeds of sale of a patent, formerly considered capital expenditure and capital receipts, have been assimilated to deductible expenses and taxable income, respectively, by recent legislation.[195] The cost of acquiring patent rights by way of license or assignment is allowed as a deduction to the purchaser over seventeen years or over the remaining life of the patent or the period of the license, whichever is shorter. As in the case of annual allowances for other capital expenditure, balancing allowances and charges are made if the purchaser resells or allows the rights acquired to lapse.[196]

[193] Income Tax Act, 1918, § 36. Repayment of tax on interest payable to a discount house or a stockbroker is given in the case of interest which is not "yearly" interest. If tax is not deducted from "yearly" interest paid to a discount house or stockbroker, no repayment claim can be made; in the case of bank, a claim can be made. This is the effect of the words "not being yearly interest" in § 36(2). This provision was enacted so that interest paid to payees of these types would not need to be paid out of taxed income, to encourage investment in government stock being issued at that time.

[194] Seventh Report, Pr. 6581, paras. 402–406 (1962); Second White Paper on Direct Taxation, Pr. 7024, para. 63 (1963). The Income Tax Commission seems to have recommended the abandonment of more of the existing law than would be necessary to rationalize it. A taxpayer should not bear tax on interest paid by him to another. This can be achieved either by allowing the interest as a deduction or by allowing the taxpayer to pass on the tax by deducting and retaining it. In either case, the payee should be taxed and is now taxed. The Income Tax Commission contemplated a case where interest was payable even if profits were not sufficient to meet it. In such a case it is logical to treat the interest as a deductible expense. However, if interest were made payable only when profits were available from which it could be paid, then and only then should one retain the existing principle that interest is not deductible because it represents a share of profits. If this were accepted, it would avoid the confusion symbolized in the Income Tax Act, 1918, Schedule D, Cases I and II, Rule 3(1). See Income Tax Codification Committee, Report, Cmd. No. 5131, at 144–45 (1936). In practice, in Ireland interest is usually payable irrespective of the amount of profits. The only difficulty in making all deductible interest subject to a withholding tax at the standard rate is the nuisance of compulsory withholding of tax, for payment to the Revenue, on small interest payments in respect of short periods. This is the reason for the special treatment of bank interest.

[195] Finance Act, 1959, ch. III. The corresponding provisions in the United Kingdom are Income Tax Act, 1952, §§ 316–22. The legislation is complicated and the text is only a summary.

[196] If the principle of increase in the balance-

The proceeds of sale of a patent are taxable in the hands of an Irish resident, usually over six years. If a non-resident sells an Irish patent, tax must be deducted by the purchaser from the capital sum and paid to the revenue authorities. The tax deducted is spread over six years by means of a repayment claim made by the non-resident seller.[197] In the case of a license, tax is deducted from the royalty[198] and will be retained or paid to the Revenue according to whether the royalty is paid out of taxed profits or not.[199]

The advantages of deduction of tax at source are retained for royalties and capital sums payable to non-residents, to insure that the tax is paid. The administrative complications of repayment claims would be unjustifiable in the case of residents. The spreading of the cost and the proceeds of sale over several tax years is the only derogation from their treatment as ordinary income and expenditure. Tax cannot be deducted from capital payments to residents, and the distinction between capital and income payments, which no longer affects tax liability, is still relevant to tax mechanics in this case.

Under the provisions of the U.S.-Irish Double Taxation Convention[200] and the Irish-German Double Taxation Agreement,[201] Irish-source patent royalties and royalties for the use of other industrial and commercial property are exempt from Irish tax if they are received by a United States or German resident company with no permanent establishment in Ireland.

Payments for know-how and unpatented secrets

Payments for technical assistance other than the use of patents are becoming increasingly important in the industrial and commercial world, and technical assistance is often more important than patents. A "sum paid in respect of the use of a patent"[202] is never deductible. Tax may be deducted from it, and if it is not paid out of taxed profits, tax must be deducted. The phrase seems to include payments for "rights [which] might only be considered incidental . . . such as the right to have any improvement of the patent made by the grantors during the currency of the agreement and the right to advice or assistance as to how best to avail . . . of the patent."[203]

---

sheet value of a business, used in the EEC as the measure of taxable income, were adopted, the complex legislation under discussion could be replaced by provisions permitting the "spreading" of the cost of purchase and the proceeds of sale over several tax years. Royal Commission, Final Report, Cmd. No. 9474, para. 32 (1955), points out that with steeply progressive tax rates single receipts must be "spread" and taxed over several years. In the British tax system this has resulted in unwillingness to tax such receipts at all; id., Memorandum of Dissent, para. 11.

[197] Finance Act, 1959, § 50.

[198] For the use of, but not for the acquisition of, the whole of the patent rights; Finance Act, 1959, § 46(2).

[199] The licensor may have the tax borne by deduction reduced to the amount which would be payable if the entire amount of the royalties had been paid over a six-year period; Finance Act, 1959, § 54. A patent royalty is always paid out of taxed profits unless the profits are less than the royalty, since a patent royalty is not deductible; Income Tax Act, 1918, Schedule D, Cases I and II, Rule 3(m).

[200] Sept. 13, 1949, art. VIII, [1951] 2 U.S.T. & O.I.A. 2303, T.I.A.S. No. 2356, Irish Finance Act, 1950 Acts 369, 411, Second Schedule, Ir. T.S. No. 7 of 1951, Pr. 1081, 127 U.N.T.S. 89 (1952).

[201] Dec. 18, 1962, art. VIII, Irish S.I. No. 212 of 1962, Pr. 6792, German Law of March 25, 1964, [1964] 2 BGB1. 266, 632.

[202] Income Tax Act, 1918, Schedule D, Cases I and II, Rule 3(m).

[203] Paterson Eng'r Co. v. Duff, 25 Tax Cas. 43, 50 (1943) (per Macnaghten, J.). The theory behind this is that, like patent royalties, such know-how payments are regarded as a share in the profits of the payor rather than as

Technical assistance (but not management services) is usually connected with a patent license. The extent to which the remuneration paid under the license agreement is related to the patent or is for technical assistance not related to the patent depends on the circumstances and cannot be settled by an agreement between the parties. If the remuneration is not connected with the patent and if it is payment for services rendered, rather than a concealed withdrawal of profits, it is an expense deductible by the payor. It is also an item of the gross income of the payee, who pays tax on it only if he is carrying on a trade in Ireland. If the contract was concluded, the payment made, and the services rendered outside Ireland, the payee is not liable to Irish tax.[204] This position is more doubtful if the services are rendered in Ireland. Normally only net profits from rendering services are taxable, so payments for services are not liable to tax deduction at source. The expenses incurred in rendering the services and an appropriate proportion of the expenses of obtaining the secret information transmitted are deductible.

Payment for technical assistance may not be in fact for services rendered but may be "income chargeable itself, as such, to tax,"[205] as a share of the payor's net profits transferred to the payee, not a mere gross receipt. In this case, if the payment is an "annual payment,"[206] tax may be deducted, since the payment is not deductible. It would be unusual to regard payments for technical assistance as a share in the payor's profits, however.

Capital receipts from the sale of know-how

Secret knowledge is an asset,[207] and payment for imparting it to others may be a capital payment on the sale of an asset or may be taxable income if the knowledge is exploited but not disposed of. If the company transferring the secret information loses its trade to the payor, at least in a particular geographical area, the transaction is the sale of a capital asset.[208] The difference is that between providing know-how as a service and parting with it.[209] A "once-for-all" trans-

an expense incurred by the payor before making a profit. Whether this theory corresponds to the facts depends on all the circumstances. If the license requires payment, even if the licensee's profits are less than the payment, the tax deducted must be paid to the Revenue, and the payor cannot deduct the payment, even though in the circumstances the payment is an expense and not a share of the profits. See Blanco White, "Agreement for the Sale of 'Know-How'" (pts. 1–2), 26 Convey. 366, 727 (1962).

[204] See Schipper, The Liability to Tax of Non-Resident Companies 96 (1958).

[205] London Corp. v. I.R.C., [1952] Tax. R. 269, 272, [1953] 1 All E.R. 1075; Re Hanbury (Conisley v. Hanbury), 20 Ann. Tax Cas. 333, 38 Tax Cas. 588 (1939).

[206] Income Tax Act, 1918, General Rules 19 and 21.

[207] Goodwill, another intangible, is also an asset under Irish tax law.

[208] Moriarty v. Evans Medical Supplies, Ltd., [1957] 3 All E.R. 718. This case emphasized that the payment was made for the disclosure of information and not for the performance of services and that the company had "parted with its property . . . a capital asset." The company parted with its privileged position in the market in question, and except where the company supplying the information contracts not to use the information itself in the future, it is hard to see how else a company can part with know-how. Viscount Simonds said it would be "difficult to separate the value of a secret imparted . . . and the value of the service rendered in imparting it." Id. at 727.

[209] If the transaction is a method of trading with and exploiting the knowledge, especially if it is an extension of the company's previous trade and not a substitute for it or a part of it, if the knowledge—the capital asset—is not diminished by the transaction, and if there is a series of transactions in each of which instruction and advice is given in return for payment, the payments will be taxable as income of the payee; Rolls-Royce, Ltd. v. Jeffrey, [1962] 1

action in which the supplier of the information is prevented from subsequently using the information supplied is probably a capital transaction. If the knowledge disclosed requires supplementary information to maintain its usefulness and keep it up to date, it is likely to be a service. The transmission of information, assistance, and advice which, though highly skilled, is not secret is unlikely to be a sale of an asset for a capital sum.

Know-how problems

The problem of how far technical assistance given simultaneously with a patent license will be equated with patent royalties and treated as a share of the licensee's net profits after tax arises only because the Irish tax system taxes annual payments of distributed profits by deduction and not directly.[210] The problem of the extent to which the foreign supplier of the information is taxed because it is trading within the jurisdiction is connected with the distinction between rendering services and sharing in profits. It arises under double taxation conventions and is not peculiar to the Irish or British tax systems. The problem whether, in any particular case, the transfer of know-how is to be regarded as the sale of an asset or the rendering of services is one of the many problems which arise, at least so far as business enterprises are concerned, only because the Irish tax system does not tax capital gains from the sale of the assets of a business. Payments for know-how are dealt with specifically in the U.S.-Irish Double Taxation Convention[211] and the Irish-German Double Taxation Agreement.[212]

All E.R. 801. Viscount Simonds quoted the test stated by Lord Justice Bankes, in British Dyestuffs Corp. (Blackley), Ltd. v. I.R.C., 12 Tax Cas. 586 (1924): "[I]s the transaction in substance a parting by the company with part of its property for a purchase price, or is it a method of trading by which it acquired this particular sum of money as part of the profits and gains of that trade?" [1962] 1 All E.R. at 803. See also Musker v. English Elec. Co., 1964 Tax R. 1929. On tax avoidance in this connection, see Wheatcroft, "The General Principles of Tax Planning," 1963 Brit. Tax Rev. 20, 34–35.

[210] The question is whether the income from technical assistance not connected with the patents is gross or net income in the hands of the payee; if the former, the expenses referable to it are primarily questions for the payee and the Revenue, not the payor. At present, only the expenses do not concern the payor.

[211] Art. VIII.

[212] Art. VIII. For a statement of policy by the U.K. Inland Revenue which would probably be followed in Ireland, see "Double Taxation Relief: Royalties and 'Know-How' Payments," 104 Sol. J. 610 (1960). See "Tax on Royalties for Know-How in the Netherlands," 1 European Taxation, No. 11, at 4 (1961).

Chapter 9

Double Taxation and Economic Integration[1]

ANALYSIS OF THE PRINCIPLES ON WHICH DOUBLE TAXATION TREATIES ARE BASED

The incidence of double taxation[2] on trade and investment between member states is the most important[3] problem of the EEC because economic integration will result in an increase in activity taxable in two or more jurisdictions.[4] Double taxation inhibits intra-Community trade and investment and hinders economic integration and the efficient use of European resources by restricting the freedom of capital to move to where it is most needed or can most usefully be employed.[5] It places enterprises taxable in two member states at a serious competitive disadvantage in both national markets vis-à-vis local enterprises, which are subject only to one set of taxes. Double taxation is important to investors in the EEC because they cannot take advantage of the large market brought about by the EEC without running the risk of being subject to it. It is vital that investors' tax lawyers insure that these competitive disadvantages are avoided and that the incidence of all countries' taxes is minimized. The problems of double taxation are especially important for capital-importing countries, since they tend to have few double taxation treaties. Double taxation questions are also important for capital-importing countries and regions

[1] For a full treatment of some of the problems discussed in this chapter, see Richman, Taxation of Foreign Investment Income: An Economic Analysis (1963); Barlow & Wender, Foreign Investment and Taxation (1955); Bittker & Ebb, Taxation of Foreign Income (1960). See EEC Treaty, art. 220—the only Treaty provision on double taxation.

[2] Most works on taxation distinguish between "economic" double taxation, liability of the same income to tax twice, usually within the same jurisdiction, and "juridical" double taxation, taxation of the same income in two jurisdictions.

If a double taxation treaty does not exempt the income in question from tax in one of the two jurisdictions, the total tax rate is usually the same as that in the country with the higher tax rate. (The exception is where the country of source has the higher tax rate and the country of residence gives a "full" tax credit.) The distinction between double taxation which does and that which does not result in a total rate of tax higher than in the country with the higher tax rate is important for clear thinking on this matter; only when the former occurs is double taxation in itself objectionable. See generally OECD Fiscal Committee, Draft Double Taxation Convention on Income and Capital 140–50 (1963). Payment of tax in a second jurisdiction, if the over-all rate is the same as the higher of the two national tax rates, is economically irrelevant to the taxpayer (except for the administrative costs). This chapter is not directly concerned with the revenue aspects of double taxation realities.

[3] Kauffman, "Les moyens propres à combattre, sur le territoire du Marché Commun, les doubles impositions en matière d'impôts directs," 16 La Revue Fiscale 169, 175 (1959), considers eliminating double taxation more important than harmonizing tax levels in member states.

[4] Van den Tempel, "L'élimination de la double imposition dans les pays de la C.E.E.," 6 La Fiscalité du Marché Commun 131 (1963).

[5] International Chamber of Commerce, Avoidance of Double Taxation (1955); Spaak Report 94; Oetterli, 41 Cahiers de Droit Fiscal International 135–38 (1959); Reboud, Systèmes Fiscaux et Marché Commun 185-94 (1961).

in the EEC because they need to have competitive conditions altered in their favor, and relief from double taxation is one method of doing this, and because by definition much of their capital is potentially taxable elsewhere.

If the tax rate in the country of source of income is higher than in the country of the taxpayer's residence, activities outside the country of residence are inhibited unless the "full" tax credit is given.[6] Only where the cumulative burden of tax is higher than the burden in the country with the higher tax rate is juridical double taxation a real inhibition on free movement of economic factors. It is generally agreed that double taxation as here described should be abolished. It has not always been successfully abolished, but its abolition is essential to economic integration.

Existing double taxation treaties have not been designed to give equal treatment to equals. The treaties carry the effect of different national tax rates across frontiers and so add to the distortion of competition produced by different national tax rates on enterprises taxable only in one member state. This chapter discusses the appropriateness in an economic union of the tax rates applied by treaties to various types of income, company profits, and capital gains.

Methods of giving relief from double taxation

There are four main methods of preventing double taxation of foreign-source income: exempting foreign income from local tax, crediting the amount of the foreign tax against local tax, deducting foreign tax from taxable income, and reducing the local rate of tax on the foreign income. The first two are the principal methods, the two recommended by the OEEC-OECD Fiscal Committee,[7] and the only two with which this chapter deals. Deducting foreign tax from taxable income does not reduce the total rate of tax to the higher of the two national rates; therefore, it is inadequate as relief. Reducing the tax rate on foreign-source income may be inadequate or excessive relief, depending on the rate of foreign tax involved and the extent of the reduction.

A tax credit is inappropriate if the foreign tax is partly or wholly passed on by the taxpayer, and it would be impossible in practice to decide whether the foreign tax was being passed on. Since the exemption method does not depend on the amount of foreign tax paid or borne, the same objection cannot be made against it, but it does not purport to achieve tax equality between individual taxpayers on an international basis.[8]

[6] Under the "ordinary" credit, the maximum credit for tax in the country of source is the amount of tax which, double taxation relief apart, would be payable in the country of residence on the income in question. The "full" credit is not so limited, and where the effective rate of tax in the country of source is the higher rate, the excess may be set off against tax on other income. See Sullivan, The Search for Tax Principles in the European Economic Community 66–69 (1963).

The United States and the United Kingdom are both tax credit countries, but the tax credit method of giving relief, whether unilateral or by treaty, is not widely used in Europe.

[7] Exemplified in arts. XXIV and XXIII, respectively, of the OEEC Fiscal Committee's Draft Model Taxation Convention; these are arts. 23A and 23B in OECD Fiscal Committee, Draft Double Taxation Convention on Income and Capital 54 (1963); see Chapter Ten, note 3. The remaining two methods are discussed by Kauffman, "Les moyens propres à combattre, sur le territoire du Marché Commun, les doubles impositions en matière d'impôts directs," 16 La Revue Fiscale 169, 179 (1959).

[8] The deduction method is most appropriate for dealing with taxes which are passed on, since gross income is increased by the extent to which the tax is shifted; Richman, Taxation of Foreign Investment Income: An Economic Analysis 32 (1963).

The effects of the exemption and credit methods on equal competitive conditions

The effect of a double taxation convention on conditions of competition in an economic union depends on the principle on which the convention operates with respect to particular types of income. If only one country taxes the income in question,[9] an enterprise is to that extent in the same competitive position as other enterprises in that country, even though it is not resident or its income is not from sources in that country. Whether the result is advantageous depends on the respective tax rates. Where the "ordinary" tax credit is used for the income in question, the enterprise is in the position of an enterprise in the country with the higher of the two tax rates, and if the "full" tax credit is given, it is in the position of an enterprise in the country of residence. The use of the "ordinary" tax credit thus does not always result in tax equality,[10] and therefore equal conditions of competition, between residents or result in neutrality between foreign- and local-source income—two virtues claimed for it.[11] If the "ordinary" tax credit is given and the tax rate is higher in the country of source, the company in question is at a competitive disadvantage in comparison with other companies selling the same commodity in the country of residence but

[9] OEEC Fiscal Committee's Draft Double Taxation Convention, arts. XXIII, XXIV; OECD Fiscal Committee, Draft Double Taxation Convention on Income and Capital 54 (1963), arts. 23A, 23B.

[10] That is, equal tax paid per unit of income. However, among other factors, an investor abroad or an exporter may be incurring risks not shared by an enterprise doing business only in its country of residence. These risks may be genuine in a less developed country for purely economic reasons, even if there is no political danger, such as that of expropriation. The risks are taken into account in calculating the amount of state aids. Carroll, 34 Cahiers de Droit Fiscal International 21 (1956), points out that circumstances may deter investment abroad even if a capital-exporting country insures tax equality. There are more theoretical reasons for holding that the apparent equality is not real equality; the benefits derived by an investor abroad from taxes paid to his country of residence may not be as valuable as those which he would obtain if he invested at home. Kauffman, "Les moyens propres à combattre, sur le territoire du Marché Commun, les doubles impositions en matière d'impôts directs," 16 La Revue Fiscale 169, 179 (1959), points out that it is unusual, except in the case of a branch operation, for the tax in the country of source, which is usually a withholding tax, to be higher than the progressive rate of tax on the total income of an individual in the country of residence.

Where the taxpayer has income from sources in more than one foreign country, the treatment may approximate either the "ordinary" or the "full" credit, depending on whether he may set a high rate of tax in one foreign country against a low rate of tax in another; see Oldman, "United States Tax Law and Treaties Affecting Private Foreign Investment," 19 Fed. B.J. 342, 346–47 (1959).

[11] Richman, Taxation of Foreign Investment Income: An Economic Analysis 27–29, 35–36 (1963), says that "the application of both source and residence principles combined with the foreign tax credit, is clearly the best compromise, for it is consistent with criteria of supranational equity of individual tax burdens, and capital-export neutrality," but she points out that this is based on the assumption, *inter alia,* that the "full" and not the "ordinary" tax credit is given. The third criterion, equity between nations, could be satisfied by arranging for the country of source to tax income of foreign capital at a rate which was a fixed fraction of the tax rate in the country of residence or, at least, a fixed rate or maximum rate of tax. In this connection, see Irish-German Double Taxation Agreement, Dec. 18, 1962, art. VI, Irish S.I. No. 212 of 1962, Pr. 6792, German Law of March 25, 1964, [1964] 2 BGBl. 266, 632. This treaty provides for an alteration in the maximum rate of tax which may be imposed on dividends in the country of source, if the tax differentiation in that country (Germany) between distributed and undistributed profits varies by specified percentages from the present differentiation. There seems to be no reason why the maximum rate in the country of source should not vary according to the general tax rate in the country of residence.

not in comparison with other companies operating in the country of source. This may be a poor reward for initiative in exporting or a legitimate deterrent to the export of capital; in either case, it is unfortunate from the Community point of view. Whichever type of credit is given, the higher rate of tax is paid on the income subject to double taxation if the country of source has the lower rate. This means that enterprises of the country of residence in question are always at a disadvantage in the country of source in comparison with residents of that country and probably also in comparison with residents of third countries trading in the country of source. Residents of the country of source would have a tax rate different from that of residents of third countries, unless the third countries exempted foreign-source income from tax.[12] Again this effect is undesirable from the point of view of the Community, since it permits interstate trade or investment with the benefit of the tax rates in the country of source only if the capital migrates entirely to that country. If this migration is impossible, the transaction may not take place; if it is possible, an artificially caused capital movement occurs.

The special effect of the "full" tax credit when the tax rate is higher in the country of source is a waiver by the country of residence of some of the tax on local income which it otherwise would have received, since the rate on all income is the lower national tax rate. The "full" credit system therefore gives to the taxpayer a subsidy which may or may not be justified, from the point of view of the country of residence, by the favorable effect of the foreign operations on its balance-of-payments position or for some other reason. Relief against double taxation might discriminate by giving the "full" credit in cases where a subsidy is justified and "ordinary" credit where it is not. From the Community point of view such a subsidy might be objectionable; for example, it might be considered a tax aid to exports, contrary to Article 98 of the EEC Treaty.

Prima facie, it is more important that conditions of competition for a foreign enterprise be the same as those for local enterprises in the state of source. Only the use of the tax exemption method in the country of residence is sure to achieve this. No method of giving relief can place the enterprise simultaneously in the same competitive position as enterprises in both countries. Until the effective tax rates in all member states are similar, a choice is therefore necessary.

The position of a foreign subsidiary company

What has been said applies only if the taxpayer is operating a branch operation in the country of source. The situation is different if the operations in the country of source are carried out through a subsidiary and if the tax law of the country of residence of the parent company permits deferral of the tax payable on the profits of the foreign operation until repatriation. The subsidiary is taxed in the same way as other similar companies in the country of source, assuming that it is resident for tax purposes in that country and that its capacity for self-financing is the same as theirs. Its foreign ownership does not normally affect its effective tax rate. As long as the subsidiary is taxable only in the country of source, no question of double taxation arises until repatriation of profits in the form of dividends. The independent

[12] The competitive disadvantage suffered by United States industry in Latin America and elsewhere was the main reason given by United States industry for demanding the introduction of the tax credit system in the United States (it replaced the system in which foreign tax was only a deduction). The same factor caused the creation of the British Overseas Trade Corporations; see Royal Commission, Final Report, Cmd. No. 9474, ch. 24 and Memorandum of Dissent 174–79 (1955).

question then arises as to the extent to which the law of the country of residence of the parent company allows credit to the parent for foreign tax. To equalize competitive conditions in an economic union, should the country of residence of the parent company treat the foreign-source dividends in the same way as the foreign-source profits of a branch or as the local-source profits of a subsidiary? Countries adopt different policies on economic double taxation of dividends as well as on relief from juridical double taxation. Equal treatment for the profits of a foreign subsidiary and a foreign branch is attractive because it looks to the substance rather than the corporate form. However, since a subsidiary is taxed in the country of source in the same way as its competitors there, it could be argued that, by the exemption principle, a branch should be treated like a foreign subsidiary. The second alternative is attractive because it maintains the economic distinction between dividends paid by a wholly owned or almost wholly owned subsidiary and dividends paid on a portfolio investment. It abolishes the tax frontier as far as tax measures affecting only the shareholder can do so. Harmonized treatment of intercorporate dividends and measures taking into account the tax in the country of source on both the dividends[13] and the subsidiary's profits are necessary. The taxation of dividends paid to the investor or shareholder is important because it affects the likelihood of the foreign subsidiary's being set up and the ease with which the foreign subsidiary can obtain capital. The subsidiary should be able to raise capital in other member states, and the parent company should be able to invest in the country of source on the same tax terms on which it can invest at home.

Therefore, even in the case of a foreign subsidiary operation, juridical double taxation may inhibit international investment and may influence the decision whether to incorporate the foreign operation, irrespective of the economic merits of the decision. Double taxation may also inhibit international trade by preventing the establishment of an operation[14] liable to direct tax in the country of destination of goods, although this occurs also when the tax rate in the country of destination is higher than that in the country of origin, i.e., the country of residence.

The extent of shareholding by the parent company in the foreign subsidiary also may distort competition. The Neumark Committee's proposals and the tax systems of some of the Six give relief from double taxation of distributed corporate profits only where the recipient holds more than a specified proportion of the capital of the distributing company. This proportion is necessarily arbitrary and the effective over-all rate of tax may vary considerably, depending on the proportion of shares held. In the absence of a treaty, none of the Six gives

[13] This question has given rise to controversy over the identity of the payor of the tax withheld from dividends under the United Kingdom and Irish fiscal systems; Biddle v. Commissioner, 302 U.S. 573 (1938). The rule in the *Biddle* case is rejected by U.S.-U.K. Double Taxation Convention, April 16, 1945, art. XIII, 60 Stat. 1377, T.I.A.S. No. 1546, Cmd. No. 6902 (T.S. No. 26 of 1946), [1946] 1 Stat. Rules & Orders 885 (No. 1327), 6 U.N.T.S. 189 (1947), and by U.S.-Irish Double Taxation Convention, Sept. 13, 1949, art. XIII, [1951] 2 U.S.T. & O.I.A. 2303, T.I.A.S. No. 2356, Irish Finance Act, 1950 Acts 369, 411, Second Schedule, Ir. T.S. No. 7 of 1951, Pr. 1081, 127 U.N.T.S. 89 (1952). The same question arose in the negotiations of the Irish-German Double Taxation Agreement and was solved by compromise—art. XXII.

[14] No tax disadvantage arises from having a permanent establishment if the relevant double taxation treaty provides for taxation only in the country of residence, the position of most treaties with regard to shipping companies and airlines.

relief from taxes for foreign tax paid by a subsidiary on its own behalf and not in respect of dividends paid by it, other than relief against economic double taxation of distributed profits.

Competition is distorted also if the country of source taxes local branches of non-resident enterprises at rates different from those used for local subsidiaries of foreign enterprises and for locally owned companies.

Extension of tax rate benefits across frontiers through the exemption principle

If the principle of exemption applies in either country, it is possible to take advantage of a low rate of tax in the single country taxing the income and still get the benefit of the business advantages of the other country, whether it is the country of source or of residence. The same principle applies to a company which obtains the benefit of a tax concession or a low rate of tax, such as a special rate of tax on foreign-source income in its country of residence, and which exports to other countries without incurring liability to tax there, for example, by not setting up a permanent establishment. The opposite case, exemption from tax in the country of residence, may also extend across national frontiers the effect of a low rate of tax in a country in which the company has a permanent establishment.

PRACTICAL ASPECTS OF DOUBLE TAXATION TREATIES

The effect of traditional double taxation treaties

From the viewpoint of states planning economic integration, existing double taxation treaties tend to equalize conditions of competition between groups of enterprises in an irrational way. They have never been intended to efficiently allocate resources. If a permanent establishment is to be treated as an enterprise separate from its parent, it seems reasonable to treat it on the same basis as other enterprises in the country in which it is situated. If a permanent establishment is not treated as a separate enterprise, it presumably should be placed on an equal footing with enterprises in the country of residence of the parent company. The former result is produced if the method of exemption is used by the country of residence, the latter if the method of tax credit is used.[15] The possible combinations involving different types of profits, high and low rates of tax in the countries of source and of residence, and relief by the exemption or the credit method[16] are too numerous to justify analysis in theory. In each case[17] the

[15] Except where the "ordinary" tax credit is used and the country of source has the higher rate of tax. A factory producing independently for a separate market and a sales office are both treated as permanent establishments, though the former might well be regarded as a separate enterprise and the latter could not. Investment companies are in different competitive circumstances according to whether the double taxation treaties of their countries of residence permit them to get the benefit of low rates of tax on distributed profits in the countries of source of dividends, interest, and royalties.

[16] Not to mention the effect of the "full" credit and the "exemption with progression" on other income not subject to the double taxation convention in question.

[17] Except where a compromise between different principles is reached, as in the case of the 18% tax credit given by Germany for Irish tax on dividends paid by Irish companies to certain German shareholders.

Situations arise in which there may be distortions of competition between two enterprises which are operating in the same country; for example:

(1) Between two enterprises, both exporting to a state where one has a permanent establishment and the other does not. Competition is distorted where the country of destination has the higher tax rate and only the "ordinary" credit is available, where the country of destination has the lower tax rate and the country of residence applies the exemption principle, and where no convention or unilateral relief exists.

competitive position of the taxpaying enterprise with respect to the particular item of income is equated with that of other enterprises either in the country of source or in the country of residence. Adoption of the country's standard which would minimize distortions of competition happens only by coincidence. Further questions arise in connection with deferral of tax until repatriation of the profits of a subsidiary which is neither incorporated nor taxed in the country of residence of the parent but which should be regarded from an economic point of view as part of the same enterprise. Because of its corporate form, which in itself should have no economic significance, a subsidiary is always treated as an enterprise separate from its parent if it is incorporated in a different country. Since astute tax lawyers seek competitive advantages through tax-avoidance schemes, the theoretical complexities have practical importance. However, techniques of preventing double taxation cannot solve the problems of harmonizing direct taxes in different countries, although a multilateral double taxation convention could enable the question of "base companies" to be dealt with.[18] The problem is rather to harmonize national laws on direct taxation and thereby enable a multilateral double taxation convention to be concluded. However, it is important to understand the effect of existing double taxation conventions, even if conditions of competition cannot be entirely equalized merely by changes in them.

The failure of traditional double taxation treaties to deal with double taxation

One way in which most existing double taxation conventions fail to deal with diverse tax systems is that the tax credit in the country of residence is usually given only for those foreign taxes which are similar to the direct taxes in the country of residence.[19] Capital-importing

---

(2) Between two enterprises, one of which exports to the other's state of residence but does not have a permanent establishment there. If the first enterprise is not taxable in the country to which it exports, distortions of competitive conditions can be eliminated only by harmonization of effective tax rates.

(3) Between two enterprises, one of which exports to the other's state of residence and has a permanent establishment there. Here competitive conditions will be distorted because of the tax burdens on the principal places of business of the enterprises, as in (2) above. Distortion will also occur in the second country if the tax rate in the exporting enterprise's country of residence is higher, unless the second country uses the principle of exemption.

(4) Between two enterprises resident in different countries, both exporting to the same country. If neither pays tax in the country of destination, the situation is the same as in (2) above. If both do, a distortion will exist unless (i) the tax rate in the country of destination is the highest of the three rates and either an ordinary credit or an exemption is given in both the countries of residence, or (ii) both the countries of residence apply the exemption principle. If one enterprise has a permanent establishment in the country of destination and the other does not, distortion of competitive conditions is inevitable, except where the effective rates of tax in the two different countries are identical. The latter case can safely be assumed not to exist and has been disregarded up to this point.

More complicated and less likely combinations of circumstances are possible. In this footnote, subsidiaries have been ignored completely. In principle it is irrelevant whether relief is given pursuant to a convention or by way of unilateral action. The effect of progressive taxes has been ignored, and also the incidence of arbitrary measures of relief, such as the Belgian method of unilateral relief.

[18] See OEEC Fiscal Committee, The Elimination of Double Taxation, Fourth Report 44, 55, 63 (1961).

[19] See Owens, The Foreign Tax Credit, ch. 2. (1961). Most double taxation conventions list the taxes in each of the countries involved which are covered by the convention and provide that similar taxes, if they are introduced, will be assimilated to the taxes listed. Exemption from taxes on capital gains and on capital is sometimes given to non-residents not carry-

countries often tax extractive industries by means of royalties on production rather than by taxes on net profits, and in many countries there are local or provincial taxes which may be based on capital or profits or both. Failure to deal with these types of tax is an important defect in many double taxation conventions, especially since economically less developed countries tend to place less emphasis on direct taxation and more on indirect taxes.

The difficulties of giving a tax credit (as distinct from a deduction) against direct tax in the country of residence for indirect tax paid or borne in the country of source are partly practical; it would be difficult to calculate or to verify the amount of indirect tax actually borne. The difficulties are partly theoretical, due to the structural differences between direct and indirect taxes. Failure to allow a credit for foreign indirect taxes is only one aspect of the general failure of international practice with regard to double taxation to relate direct and indirect taxes to one another. Modern double taxation treaties, such as the Irish-German Agreement, deal with taxes on capital and on capital gains but do not enable the taxes to be credited against tax in the country of residence unless the capital or the capital gain is itself liable to double taxation.

Another difficulty may arise. In most cases relief is given by the country of residence only on income arising in the country with which the treaty is made and taxed in that country. However, no relief is given for income taxed in that country but regarded by the tax law of the country of residence as arising in some third country.[20] This difficulty could be solved by a multilateral treaty. Another difficulty arises where the method of computation of the foreign-source income is different in the two countries which are parties to the treaty; credit cannot be given for foreign tax on income which is not liable to tax in the country of residence. Different views on the deductibility of certain items of expenditure or the availability of substantial depreciation allowances may make the "tentative" tax in the country of residence less than the foreign tax.[21] Other situations not clearly dealt with by existing double taxation treaties also exist.[22]

If the taxes of different countries are applied to the same income at different

ing on a trade or business; see, e.g., Irish-German Double Taxation Agreement, arts. X, XX; U.S.-U.K. Double Taxation Convention, art. XIV. See Walter, 41 Cahiers de Droit Fiscal International 150–52 (1959); Jansen, 46 Cahiers de Droit Fiscal International 72–73 (1961); Sullivan, The Search for Tax Principles in the European Economic Community 68 (1963).

[20] Royal Commission, Final Report, Cmd. No. 9474, ch. 24 (1955); Koch, 46 Cahiers de Droit International 55, 56–60 (1961); OECD Fiscal Committee, Draft Double Taxation Convention on Income and Capital 140 (1963). Owens, "United States Income Tax Treaties—Their Role in Relieving Double Taxation," 17 Rutgers L. Rev. 428 (1963), points out that double taxation treaties usually regulate the situation where there is liability to tax in two jurisdictions; they do nothing to alter the rules of national law which give rise to liability, e.g., the rules relating to residence and source of income. One important source of difficulty arises where goods have been manufactured in one country and sold in another. How much of the income is derived from manufacturing and how much from distribution?

[21] This does not result in taxation of the doubly taxed income at an over-all rate higher than that in the country with the higher tax rate; the difficulty is that the tax bases are different. It does result in a proportion of the foreign tax not being available as a credit against tax in the country of residence. The total tax paid in both jurisdictions on the whole of the income (the net profits of a permanent establishment, for example) which has been taxed in the country of source is more than the total tax payable in respect of the part of that income which is taxable in the country of residence, even if the country of residence has the higher rate of tax.

[22] See, for example, Shelbourne, "Double Taxation and Its Improvement," 1957 Brit. Tax Rev. 48, example (b) at 53.

times, full relief may not be available.[23] Timing problems would also be ended by "fiscal transparency," but they normally cannot be handled by double taxation conventions, except by provisions for consultation on an ad hoc basis. They can be handled, however, by provisions permitting a tax credit to be carried forward or back and set off against tax liability of other years.

Apart from the usual case where a person resident in one state derives income from sources in another, if each party to a double taxation treaty regards a taxpayer as being resident in its own territory, criteria are required for deciding with which state the taxpayer has the more substantial connection.[24]

The difficulty of negotiating double taxation treaties

Double taxation problems often are unresolved in the numerous cases[25] where no traditional double taxation treaty has been, or can be, negotiated between the countries involved. Apart from eliminating double taxation, prohibiting discrimination, and providing for administrative cooperation, tax treaties also allocate taxable income between the countries involved. Insofar as they deprive the country of source of jurisdiction to tax, they tend to prejudice capital-importing countries, since those countries will not benefit proportionately from the right to tax the income of their residents which arises in the other country.[26] This disadvantage to capital-importing countries is not always balanced by other provisions in tax treaties. This difficulty would be accentuated by the adoption of the proposals of the Neumark Committee, which, in the interests of a more rational tax system throughout the Community, recommends allocating further revenue to countries of residence.

POSSIBLE SOLUTIONS

"Co-ordination [of double taxation conventions between member states of the OEEC] would have many advantages: the application of common rules . . . in questions of double taxation would provide more stability than can be guaranteed by the existing bilateral Conventions which are negotiated or revised independently of one another. Such rules would in particular give more certainty to Member countries' residents doing business in other European countries and to investors, and this would be bound to have a favourable effect on the development of visible and invisible trade and intra-European investment. . . . Common rules would also simplify the work of the taxation authorities of Member countries."[27]

The OECD Fiscal Committee and the Neumark Committee hope in due course that among all European countries there will be a multilateral double taxation treaty based on the existing model bilateral treaty produced by the former committee.[28] Under this model, relief may be

[23] See id., example (c) at 53.

[24] OECD Fiscal Committee, Draft Double Taxation Convention on Income and Capital (1963), art. 3. See generally Folliet, "Le lieu d'imposition des personnes physiques en matière d'impôts directs," 17 Cahiers de Droit International 7 (1951).

[25] OECD Fiscal Committee, Draft Double Taxation Convention on Income and Capital 24 (1963).

[26] Froomkin & Wender, "Revenue Implications of United States Income Tax Treaties," 7 Nat'l Tax J. 177 (1954).

[27] OEEC Fiscal Committee, The Elimination of Double Taxation, First Report, para. 20 (1958); see also id., Fourth Report, para. 13 (1961); OECD Fiscal Committee, Draft Double Taxation Convention on Income and Capital, para. 3 (1963); van den Tempel, "L'élimination de la double imposition dans les pays de la C.E.E.," 6 La Fiscalité du Marché Commun 131 (1963).

[28] When taxes in each member country of the EEC are fully harmonized, a multilateral double taxation convention among EEC members will

given against double taxation by either the credit or the exemption method. In an economic union, harmonization of tax laws should insure the alteration of member states' existing rules on jurisdiction to tax, so that the number of cases in which income will be even tentatively liable to tax in more than one jurisdiction will be minimized. This is merely the application of the exemption principle to particular rules to insure that the tax jurisdictions of member states do not overlap. It might be necessary to divide the right to tax between two member states by providing, for example, a maximum rate of tax which could be imposed by the country of source. This might be necessary for inter-nation equity, but equity could be insured more simply by international compensation payments.

Taxation only in the country of source

Because exempting all income from tax in the country of residence would have the effect in many cases of lowering the total rate of tax payable, it is widely advocated.[29] It would not cause a substantially greater loss of revenue to the country of residence than the tax credit system if the tax rates in the two countries were similar—a state of affairs which the EEC will effect in due course. However, taxation only in the country of source is already the rule for undistributed profits of foreign subsidiaries of companies resident in countries which permit deferral of tax until repatriation.[30] Insofar as effective tax rates in the countries of source are lower than those in the country of residence, investment in the less developed countries would be encouraged, causing prejudice to the balance-of-payments position of capital-exporting countries. Since balance-of-payments problems could be handled by other means in an economic union, substantial simplification in the rules relating to double taxation certainly would be possible.

Taxation in the country of source is based on the benefit principle of taxation and corresponds to modern notions of inter-nation equity. In the context of an economic union, the first objection to the use of the principle of source, if coupled with the exemption method, is that it renders *pro tanto* ineffective efforts to apply progressive taxes or, indeed, any unitary or "synthetic" tax. It arbitrarily places unequal tax burdens on taxpayers in their country of residence, according to the countries in which the sources of their income are situated. This complicates the problem of harmonizing conditions of competition between them and the taxpayers of other member states. There are in effect as many tax rates as there are countries available for investment or, since the necessity of harmonizing tax conditions in non-member countries for the investments of EEC residents is not urgent, as many rates as there are member countries. This ob-

be a purely technical device for preventing multiple tax burdens on income which would be liable to substantially the same rate of tax, irrespective of the country of source. Until that time, however, the question whether the principle of residence or that of source should be applied still exists.

[29] At least for many types of income. Compare International Chamber of Commerce, Avoidance of Double Taxation (1955), with Shelbourne, "Double Taxation and Its Improvement," 1957 Brit. Tax Rev. 143. It is also advocated by Kauffman, "Les moyens propres à combattre, sur le territoire du Marché Commun, les doubles impositions en matière d'impôts directs," 16 La Revue Fiscale 169, 180–86 (1959).

[30] Application of the principle to foreign branches would make the corporate form irrelevant. Taxation of the profits of branch operations on the basis of "remittance" or "deferral" —the respective United Kingdom and the United States terms for substantially the same idea looked at in different ways—has been rejected by the British Royal Commission, First Report, Cmd. No. 8761, para. 38 (1953). See Sullivan, The Search for Tax Principles in the European Economic Community 66–67 (1963).

jection would lose its force if the tax systems of all member states were fully harmonized. It is less important with regard to proportional taxes than progressive taxes, and thus in practice it is not important with regard to company taxes, which are basically proportional.

Taxation only in the country of source, especially if not limited to cases where a permanent establishment exists, adds to the tax complications of a company which is operating in a number of countries,[31] as is often the case in the EEC. The extent to which this system departs from the goal of equality of tax burdens for similar activities and thus interferes with efficient allocation of resources and with capital-export neutrality depends on the national tax rates involved. Since the source principle would have the maximum effect of diverting portfolio and direct investment into the country with the lowest rate of tax on local-source income, it would increase the tax base there. This effect already occurs under the tax credit method, but only where the taxpayer finds it possible or worthwhile to establish a subsidiary company resident for tax purposes in the country of source. Harmonization of national tax laws, not elimination or deferral of local tax until repatriation, is the preferable method of eliminating the differences under most tax systems between a foreign branch operation and a foreign subsidiary. If the accumulated profits of such a subsidiary are taxed at the full income tax or company tax rates on repatriation, not at capital gains rates, the advantage gained is merely indefinite postponement of the tax in the country of residence. The deterrent to distribution of profits is greater where the country of residence gives no relief against economic double taxation of distributed corporate profits or intercorporate dividends. This deterrent is due to the higher rate of tax there and not to any flaw in the international rules on double taxation. The incentive to keep the profits accumulated in a subsidiary in the country of source may encourage either reinvestment and expansion through self-financing or investment in other local enterprises. Insofar as countries with low rates of direct taxes tend to be in need of capital, this effect is a fortunate one.

Taxation only in the country of residence

Modern tax theory and the Neumark Report favor a unitary progressive income tax on individuals and a unitary tax on companies. A company tax could be imposed by taxing EEC taxpayers entirely in their country of residence[32] or by completely harmonizing taxes so that every item of income is taxed in the same way in every member country. The latter alternative is incompatible with a progressive tax unless, in fixing the tax rate in each member country, the total amount of income from all other EEC sources is known. This would be administratively troublesome and it follows that a progressive tax should be imposed on each taxpayer's whole income in his country of residence.[33] If this is done, the use of the principle of source and the tax credit method apportions the total tax between the two countries but does not affect the total tax liability of the taxpayer, except where the tax rate in the country of source is different and only the "ordinary" credit is given. If, however, the taxpayer pays tax only in the country of residence, fair apportionment between countries can be carried out by direct international payments, if the requisite information is available from the records of the country of residence. Representatives of each member

[31] Richman, Taxation of Foreign Investment Income: An Economic Analysis 27 (1963).

[32] Assuming that each member country imposes taxes of the two kinds mentioned.

[33] See Irish Income Tax Commission, Sixth Report, Pr. 6039 ch. III (1961); Seventh Report, Pr. 6581, para. 439 (1962).

country can review the income allocated to sources within that country, on the pattern of the Anglo-Irish system of cooperation on double taxation questions. In an economic community the information required for apportionment need not be as accurate and detailed as that needed at present for a single enterprise taxable in two independent countries. When economic integration has reached the stage of common responsibility for the total revenue of each country, as it may do eventually, such information will no longer be needed. If apportionment of fiscal receipts can be arranged in other ways, the principle of taxation exclusively in the country of residence can be adopted for all progressive taxes, for administrative convenience.

A single tax assessment for each taxpayer is an administrative convenience, not a necessity, in the case of a flat-rate tax common to all member states. The taxpayer benefits from having to deal with only one revenue authority, and apportionment of the tax can take place on an international level.[34] This is the solution recommended by the Neumark Committee[35] as the ultimate ideal, when harmonization of taxation and close administrative cooperation between member states permit it. In the case of the recommended flat-rate company tax, taxation exclusively in the country of source automatically deals with both apportionment of tax between the member countries on a reasonable basis and differences in rate due to regional tax incentives, but causes difficulties if there are different rates for distributed and undistributed profits. Proof of distribution of profits would have to be supplied by the country of residence to the country in which the permanent establishment was situated, if the lower rate of company tax were to be applied to profits distributed in another member country and thus not subject to further tax in the country of source.

Taxation in the country of residence insures capital-export neutrality, except to the extent that tax in the country of residence on the foreign-source profits of a foreign subsidiary is deferred until repatriation. Only harmonization can provide capital-export neutrality in this respect.

Taxation of dividends

The usual practice in Europe is to tax the profits of a permanent establishment at the full local rate for undistributed profits, disregarding subsequent distribution elsewhere. This will have to be altered if a common EEC system of differentiation, for company tax purposes, in favor of distributed profits is adopted. The problem can be dealt with by taxation only in the country of residence, by differential rates of tax for permanent establishments, or by tax credits in the country of residence which would have to be balanced by payments made by the country of source.

Both the proposed OECD multilateral double taxation convention and the necessary harmonization in the tax treatment of non-residents and of foreign-source income are likely to be based as closely on existing practice as the requirements of economic integration will permit. There is some inconsistency therefore between the Neumark Report's recommendation of a multilateral convention based on the OECD model and its proposals for taxation of dividends. If double taxation conventions permit withholding taxes on dividends paid to shareholders resident outside the country of residence of the payor company or if, as under the British-type tax system in force in Ireland, tax paid by a company is passed on to shareholders, the tax withheld or passed on is paid to the country of the source

[34] If the double taxation treaties of the country of residence provided for it, a "matching credit" could be given for any reduction in tax given in the country of source.

[35] Rapport 71, 73, CCH 2467, 2469.

of the dividend. It is therefore a tax on the non-resident shareholder's income by the country of source. Since the Neumark Committee recommends that international tax matters in the EEC ultimately be dealt with by taxation only in the country of residence,[36] the Committee views withholding on dividends as an administrative method of insuring payment of a proportion of the tax payable in the country of residence of the shareholder, not as a method of paying tax to the country of source.[37] As between the revenues of member states, therefore, the Committee contemplates exemption of dividends from tax in the country of source. This is a radical departure from existing practice in Europe, except under the U.K.-Irish Double Income Taxation Agreement, and is all the more radical because of the proposed limitation on the rate of company tax to be imposed on distributed profits, which also restricts severely the revenue of the country of source.

The OEEC draft article[38] and most European double taxation conventions limit the rate of tax which may be imposed by the state of source on dividends paid to a non-resident parent company holding a substantial proportion of the shares of the payor company. The Neumark Committee[39] recommends complete elimination of economic double taxation of intercorporate dividends if certain prerequisites are fulfilled. To harmonize the tax laws of the member states of the EEC, the Neumark Committee recommends a further rule binding the state of residence of the parent to give the same exemption from tax to dividends from foreign subsidiaries that it gives to dividends paid by local subsidiaries. This is essential to secure tax harmonization and is one of the few limitations on the taxing power of the state of residence suggested by the Neumark Committee. Since the result of the Committee's proposals, in themselves desirable, will be to increase revenue for countries of residence, acceptance of the necessity for international compensation payments is of great importance for predominantly capital-importing countries. The EEC member states already have accepted the principle of international compensation payments for certain purposes in the sphere of agriculture by setting up the Agricultural Guidance and Guarantee Fund, and they also contemplate pooling the proceeds of the common external tariff.[40]

DOUBLE INDIRECT TAXATION

The Neumark Committee[41] points out that Article 220 covers "indirect international double taxation" as well as direct international or juridicial double taxation. This arises where two tax jurisdictions tax the same income in the hands of two taxpayers—as, for example, where a payment made out of taxable income by a resident of one country is taxed again in the country in which the recipient resides. The most important case of this, double taxation of dividends, has been separately discussed and is specifically treated by all double taxation treaties. Cases may also occur with respect to certain interest payments or voluntary payments made for the support of individuals. Another important case of double indirect taxation which has received the attention of the Commission is that connected with insurance contracts. Double indirect taxation will require the attention of the OECD Fiscal Committee in due course.

[36] Rapport 70–71, CCH 2467.

[37] Rapport 69, CCH 2465.

[38] OEEC Fiscal Committee's Draft Double Taxation Convention, art. XX; see OECD Fiscal Committee, Draft Double Taxation Convention on Income and Capital (1963), art. 10.

[39] Rapport 39, 66, CCH 2438–39, 2463.

[40] See EEC Treaty, art. 201.

[41] Rapport 69, CCH 2466.

Chapter 10

Irish Double Taxation Conventions

THE U.S.-IRISH DOUBLE TAXATION CONVENTION[1]

Permanent establishment

THE IMPORTANCE OF A PERMANENT ESTABLISHMENT

If it is not managed and controlled in Ireland and if it has no permanent establishment in Ireland, a corporation organized in the United States pays no Irish income tax or corporation profits tax on its industrial or commercial profits, i.e., on its business income, as distinct from its profits from investments.[2] If a United States company has a permanent establishment in Ireland, all its Irish-source income is liable to tax in Ireland, including income not derived from the permanent establishment. It is therefore

[1] Sept. 13, 1949, [1951] 2 U.S.T. & O.I.A. 2303, T.I.A.S. No. 2356, Irish Finance Act, 1950 Acts 369, 411, Second Schedule, Ir. T.S. No. 7 of 1951, Pr. 1081, 127 U.N.T.S. 89 (1952). All references in this section to articles are to the U.S.-Irish Double Taxation Convention, unless otherwise indicated.

[2] Arts. II(1)(h)–II(1)(j), III(2); see 2 U.S. Joint Committee on Internal Revenue Taxation, Legislative History of United States Tax Conventions 1579 (1962). See also id. at 2573 for a more detailed study of the similar U.S.-U.K. Double Taxation Convention, April 16, 1945, and Protocol, June 6, 1946, 60 Stat. 1377, T.I.A.S. No. 1546, Cmd. No. 6902 (T.S. No. 26 of 1946), [1946] 1 Stat. Rules & Orders 845 (No. 1327), 6 U.N.T.S. 189 (1947). (Additional Protocols to the U.S.-U.K. Convention were signed on May 25, 1954, [1955] 1 U.S.T. & O.I.A. 37, T.I.A.S. No. 3165, [1955] 1 Stat. Instr. 1013 (No. 162), 207 U.N.T.S. 312 (1955); and on Aug 19, 1957, [1958] U.S.T. & O.I.A. 1329, T.I.A.S. No. 4124, [1958] 1 Stat. Instr. 1274 (No. 1751), 336 U.N.T.S. 330 (1959).) See also Relief of Double Taxation (Taxes on Income: Ireland-U.S.A.) Regulations 1951, Ir. S.I. No. 381 of 1951, and Relief of Double Taxation (Taxes on Income: Ireland–U.S.A.) Regulations 1956, Ir. S.I. No. 87 of 1956. Owens, "United States Income Tax Treaties: Their Role in Relieving Double Taxation," 17 Rutgers L. Rev. 428 (1963), states that, due to unilateral relief by the United States, her income tax treaties play only a marginal role in relieving double taxation; most tax treaties do not deal with the problems which necessitate bilateral agreement, such as the definition of residence and source of income. Miss Owens concludes that a re-evaluation of the United States treaty program is required. The source-of-income question would be met in the EEC by harmonization of the rules relating to geographical source of income. Most United States treaties merely limit taxation in the country of source, make some foreign taxes creditable against United States tax which would not otherwise be so, and adjust source rules. Cases in which, under the United States Internal Revenue Code, benefits are dependent on reciprocal treatment in the other country are also dealt with. See also generally Owens, The Foreign Tax Credit (1961); "Treaties to Avoid Double Taxation of Income Between European Countries and Between European Countries and the United States, as of January 31, 1965," 5 European Taxation 21 (1965); Willis, "Great Britain's Part in the Development of Double Taxation," 19 Bull. Int'l B. Fiscal Documentation 418 (1965); Roberts, "Avoiding Double Taxation—A Reorientation of the Role of Tax Treaties," id. at 309.

For a discussion of the problems of permanent establishments in international fiscal law, see Bechinie, General Report, Rapports pour le XIième Congrès International de Droit Financier et Fiscal, 34 Cahiers de Droit Fiscal International 193 (1957). Much of this discussion has been embodied in the work of the OEEC and OECD Fiscal Committees.

not possible to avoid Irish tax by arranging for profits to be made under the supervision of a permanent establishment in such a way that they are not regarded as made by it.[3]

A company managed and controlled in Ireland and not incorporated in the United States is exempt from United States federal income tax unless it has a permanent establishment in the United States. A corporation incorporated in the United States but managed and controlled in Ireland is dealt with under the tax credit provisions of the treaty,[4] since it is subject to tax in both countries on its world income.

If a United States company has a permanent establishment in Ireland, its Irish tax is credited against the United States tax. The minimum over-all tax rate on the profits of an Irish permanent establishment is therefore the United States tax rate.[5] The credit given by United States tax law is the "ordinary" and not the "full" credit.[6] Only foreign income taxes are credited, including Irish income tax and corporation profits tax; indirect taxes, such as the Irish turnover tax, are not credited, whether they are borne by the branch operation or not.[7]

Except possibly in the initial stages of establishing a business in Ireland, a branch operation is unlikely to be advantageous either from the point of view of Irish or United States tax.

What Constitutes a Permanent Establishment

Since no Irish-source income is derived from it, a fixed place of business used exclusively for the purchase of goods is not a permanent establishment.[8] Any other type of branch operation with permanent premises, such as a factory, or any office where the business is managed, constitutes a permanent establishment. A permanent establishment is "a branch, [place of] management, factory or other fixed place of business . . ."[9] The words "other

[3] The principle adopted by the OECD is that only profits attributable to a permanent establishment may be taxed in the country of source of income; OECD Fiscal Committee, Draft Double Taxation Convention on Income and Capital (1963), art. 7. See the OEEC Fiscal Committee's draft art. XV in The Elimination of Double Taxation, Third Report (1960). This is the rule adopted in the Irish-German Double Taxation Agreement, Dec. 18, 1962, art. III(1), Irish S.I. No. 212 of 1962, Pr. 6792, German Law of March 25, 1964, [1964] 2 BGBl. 266, 632. This principle is regarded as more suitable in conditions of economic integration; OECD Fiscal Committee, Draft Double Taxation Convention on Income and Capital 81 (1963).

The OECD model double taxation convention on income and capital was prepared by the OEEC Fiscal Committee and completed by its successor, the OECD Fiscal Committee. The OEEC draft articles are numbered in Roman numerals. OECD Fiscal Committee, Draft Double Taxation Convention on Income and Capital 37 (1963), presents a table indicating the numbers given to the articles of the OEEC draft and the articles in the OECD final model.

[4] The civil law countries in Europe usually exempt income taxable in the country of source from tax in the country of residence.

[5] Art. XIII.

[6] U.S. Int. Rev. Code of 1954, § 904(1). This is the "per-country" limitation, which limits the amount of the foreign tax credit to the amount of United States tax which, but for the tax credit, would have been payable on the income from the country in question. The taxpayer may choose the "over-all" limitation, under which the amount of the tax credit is limited to the amount of United States tax which would have been payable on the total amount of his foreign income. In this way, foreign taxes with rates higher than the United States rate may be set off against other foreign taxes with lower rates.

[7] Export taxes, taxes on gross receipts, production taxes, taxes on capital, and taxes imposed for the right to do business cannot be credited against United States tax.

[8] Art. III(4).

[9] Art. II(1)(l). OECD Fiscal Committee, Draft Double Taxation Convention on Income and Capital 43 (1963), art. 5, lists as examples of permanent establishments, in addition to those given above, an office, a workshop, a

fixed place of business" must be construed *eiusdem generis* with the previous words, and a fixed place of business, to constitute a permanent establishment, probably must have a directly productive character. This interpretation fits in with Article III(4), and if it were accepted, research laboratories, showrooms, information bureaus, and public relations offices would be exempt from Irish tax. It is difficult to calculate the profits derived from these places, but the question whether they constitute permanent establishments is important, since on it depends the liability of other Irish-source income to Irish tax.[10] The test seems to be whether the activities at the premises in question are sufficiently closely related to the profit-making operations for the premises to constitute a "place of business."[11]

To be a "permanent" establishment, a place of business must be "fixed." A temporary place of business such as an office in a hotel room is not enough. Otherwise, the limitation of the permanent-establishment rule on the source country's power to tax would be largely eaten away. If the place of business of the enterprise itself is fixed, however, its size is irrelevant, and even isolated or infrequent sales will make it a permanent establishment.[12]

Even where a corporation incorporated in the United States is not managed and controlled[13] in Ireland it may have a place of management[14] there, and this constitutes a permanent establishment. However, a formal registered office in Ireland, created by the company's incorporation there, would not constitute a permanent establishment.[15]

---

mine, quarry or other place of extraction of natural resources, and a building site or construction or assembly project which exists for more than twelve months.

[10] A sales promotion office at which sales are made is a permanent establishment. A warehouse used only for storing goods for sale in Ireland is not a permanent establishment, since no business would be carried on there. A research unit which supplies "know-how" to Irish licensees probably is a place of business, but an office from which a sales campaign is launched is not, if the actual sales are carried out by independent agents of the company who are not based in the office.

[11] OECD Fiscal Committee, Draft Double Taxation Convention on Income and Capital 43 (1963), art. 5(3), reads:

The term "permanent establishment" shall not be deemed to include:

a) the use of facilities solely for the purpose of storage, display or delivery of goods or merchandise belonging to the enterprise;
b) the maintenance of a stock of goods or merchandise belonging to the enterprise solely for the purpose of storage, display or delivery;
c) the maintenance of a stock of goods or merchandise belonging to the enterprise solely for the purpose of processing by another enterprise;
d) the maintenance of a fixed place of business solely for the purpose of purchasing goods or merchandise, or for collecting information, for the enterprise;
e) the maintenance of a fixed place of business solely for the purpose of advertising, for the supply of information, for scientific research or for similar activities which have a preparatory or auxiliary character, for the enterprise.

[12] Regular sales are necessary for an agent to constitute a permanent establishment.

[13] Art. II(1)(g).

[14] The grammatical structure of the sentence "'[P]ermanent establishment' . . . means a branch, management, factory or other fixed place of business" is not elegant, and there is no parallel in any other Irish double taxation treaty. The wording used in United States double taxation treaties is not uniform, and it is not always clear whether the variations are intended to involve differences in meaning.

[15] Because a formal registered office is not in itself a place of management or a place of business, but merely an address for the service of process and for certain formal purposes. In fact, registered offices are often those of the lawyers or accountants of the companies concerned. See also art. II(1)(g), II(1)(h).

AGENTS AND SUBSIDIARIES AS PERMANENT ESTABLISHMENTS

Employment of an agent without the establishment of a permanent "agency" does not constitute a permanent establishment.[16] An agency is not a permanent establishment unless the agent habitually exercises a general authority to negotiate and conclude contracts on behalf of the foreign company or has a stock of merchandise from which he regularly fills orders on its behalf.[17] The agency is not a permanent establishment if the agent has to refer contracts to his principals for approval, even if he communicates their acceptance of the contracts to the purchaser.

Most independent agencies are not treated as permanent establishments because they are separate enterprises and receive taxable remuneration for their work. Any other rule distorts trade by causing transactions to be carried out in the form of purchase and resale, the *de facto* agent becoming *de jure* a purchaser of the goods, or by making agents liable to pay the tax due by companies with which they have only a business connection and from which repayment is uncertain. A "bona fide commission agent or broker acting in the ordinary course of his business" is not, as such, a permanent establishment;[18] if he has a stock of merchandise or the power to bind the United States company, he is not acting in the ordinary course of his business. There is no provision in the U.S.-Irish Treaty that agents having an independent status are not permanent establishments. Such a provision would cause some uncertainty in practice; but if there is no such provision, the scope for taxation in the country of source is increased, and consequently the occasions when the complicated system of tax credit[19] must be used become more frequent.

A subsidiary company in Ireland is not necessarily a permanent establishment of its United States parent. This is so whether the subsidiary is incorporated in Ireland or merely carries on business there and whether the subsidiary is taxable in Ireland because it has a permanent establishment there or for some other reason.[20] In general, even if the two companies are not associated, the parent company is liable to Irish tax only if the subsidiary is its permanent establishment, i.e., if the subsidiary concludes contracts on behalf of the parent or fills orders for the parent from a stock of goods.[21] If the subsidiary is incorporated in the United States and has no fixed place of business in Ireland, neither company will be liable to Irish tax, even if the subsidiary concludes contracts on behalf of its parent. No provision is made for the situation where the company in the country of source is the parent and not the subsidiary,[22] but presumably, similar rules apply.

For the purpose of calculating its taxable profits, a subsidiary, like a permanent establishment, is treated as if it

[16] Ehrenzweig & Koch, Income Tax Treaties 82 (1949).

[17] Art. II(1)(l); cf. OECD Fiscal Committee, Draft Double Taxation Convention on Income and Capital (1963), art. 5(3)(b).

[18] Art. II(1)(l). The OEEC Fiscal Committee's draft art. II(5) is to the same effect, although it adds the possibility of employing "any other agent of an independent status," without liability to local tax; OEEC Fiscal Committee, Taxation, First Report 34 (1958). See OECD Fiscal Committee, Draft Double Taxation Convention on Income and Capital (1963), art. 5(5).

[19] See Irish Income Tax Commission, Sixth Report, Pr. 6039, ch. VII (1961).

[20] Art. II(1)(l).

[21] See Firestone Tyre & Rubber Co. v. Lewellin, [1957] 1 All E.R. 561, 37 Tax Cas. 111.

[22] Cf. OECD Fiscal Committee, Draft Double Taxation Convention on Income and Capital (1963), art. 5(6).

were an independent enterprise dealing with its parent organization at arm's length.[23]

A subsidiary incorporated in Ireland but managed and controlled in the United States is not liable to Irish income tax on the part of its income arising outside Ireland, but it is liable to corporation profits tax on this income, subject to the tax concessions for profits from exports. A subsidiary company can shield the parent company from Irish tax[24] and give a tax advantage where the Irish operation is exporting and is liable to tax in a third country, since only an Irish company can take advantage of the double taxation agreements between Ireland and third countries[25] and since Irish tax saved by a branch operation will merely reduce the credit allowed against United States tax. Sales in Ireland normally are made through an Irish subsidiary as principal, not as agent for the parent. To insure this result, the dealings between the parent and subsidiary should always be sales, and the remuneration of the subsidiary should be profits made on resale, not commission. This is advisable even though both the commission and the profits of the subsidiary from resale may be revised if they do not represent the profits which would be obtained by enterprises dealing at arm's length.

[23] Arts. III(3), IV; see Income Tax Act, 1918, 8 & 9 Geo. 5, c. 40, General Rules 8 and 9.

[24] Except tax borne by deduction from dividends paid by the subsidiary.

[25] For a United States–owned subsidiary to operate in Britain and to benefit from the provisions of the U.K.-Irish Double Income Taxation Agreement, April 14, 1926, U.K. Income Tax Act, 1952, 15 & 16 Geo. 6 & 1 Eliz. 2, c. 10, Eighteenth Schedule, pt. I, Irish Finance Act, 1926 Pub. Stat. 401, 441, First Schedule, pt. I, the subsidiary must be managed and controlled as well as incorporated in Ireland. The same applies in the case of the Irish-German Double Taxation Agreement. See pp. 273–74.

A Subsidiary Carrying on Business for a Parent Company

Under the U.S.-Irish Treaty, a parent company cannot be liable to Irish tax merely on the grounds that it is doing business in Ireland through its subsidiary, even if it exercises the maximum amount of control and supervision over the subsidiary. The language of the treaty and the principles of Irish company and tax law[26] exclude this possibility, but it may arise under other systems of law.[27]

A problem whose solution is uncertain could arise where a United States company agrees to give know-how to an Irish company. Neither an agreement for the supply of secret information nor a cross-licensing agreement normally will make the Irish company a permanent establishment of the United States company. However, if the United States company provides employees or technicians from its own staff not only to advise on secret and technical matters but to give commercial and financial advice or management services, the Irish company might be held to be trading in an informal partnership with the United States company. The fact that the remuneration of the latter is said to be for the use of technical information will not be conclusive. If the United States company were "engaged in trade or business in Ireland,"[28] not only the remuneration for the know-how but any other Irish-source income would become liable to Irish tax, since the Irish company would be the "fixed place of business" of

[26] Gramophone & Typewriter Co. v. Stanley, [1908] 2 K.B. 89; Salomon v. Salomon & Co., [1897] A.C. 22.

[27] See Michel, "The Concept of Permanent Establishment in International Fiscal Law," 1 Cahiers de Droit Fiscal International 213, 217 (1939), Carroll, id. at 258 and 2 Cahiers de Droit Fiscal International 34–35 (1940).

[28] Art. III(1), III(2).

the United States company. The United States company would be liable to Irish tax only if the Irish company exercised authority to conclude contracts "on its behalf" or kept a stock of goods from which it filled orders "on its behalf."[29] An Irish company in which a United States company owns shares and to which it provides technical advice is more likely to be regarded as carrying out operations for the United States company than an independent company would be. To be an agent in Irish law it is not necessary to disclose either the identity or the existence of a principal. The problem[30] is an important one in international tax law, since it could arise under many double taxation conventions. It is perhaps unlikely to arise in Ireland, where the authorities are more anxious to encourage foreign investment and technical assistance than to obtain the last penny of tax. The question might arise if the payment for the know-how is excessive and is regarded as concealed participation in profits. In such a case part of the payment can be disallowed as a deduction.[31] If the Irish enterprise had not deducted the payment or if it were argued that other Irish-source income was taxable because the enterprise receiving the know-how was the permanent establishment of the United States enterprise providing it, the question would have to be decided. The way the question is resolved may depend on the exact wording of the relevant treaty in each case.[32]

Exemption from Irish Tax: Interest, Royalties, and Profits of Shipping Companies and Airlines

The rules relating to permanent establishments do not apply to profits derived by a United States corporation from ships or aircraft registered in the United States; these are exempt from Irish tax even if the company has a permanent establishment and sells tickets in Ireland.[33]

If a United States corporation has no permanent establishment in Ireland, the United States, as the country of residence, is exclusively entitled to tax certain types of income. Irish-source interest paid to a United States corporation[34] on any form of debt is exempt from Irish tax.[35] This is based on the principle that payment for loan capital should be taxed only in the country furnishing the capital, since the source of income is the capital, not the business operations, of the

[29] See Firestone Tyre & Rubber Co. v. Lewellin, [1957] 1 All. E.R. 561, 37 Tax Cas. 111.

[30] This is discussed by Michel, "The Concept of Permanent Establishment in International Fiscal Law," 1 Cahiers de Droit Fiscal International 213, 232 (1939).

[31] Art. IV. This article provides that any profits which would have accrued to an enterprise if its transactions had been on an arm's-length basis "may be included in the profits of that enterprise and taxed accordingly." Apparently an enterprise not otherwise liable to Irish tax on any of its income could not become liable to it merely because of this provision.

[32] Although the words are not the same, seemingly identical in substance with the U.S.-Irish Convention are: the OEEC Fiscal Committee's draft art. II, in The Elimination of Double Taxation, First Report 33 (1958), and draft art. XXII, in id., Fourth Report 31 (1961); OECD Fiscal Committee, Draft Double Taxation Convention on Income and Capital (1963), arts. 5, 12; and Irish-German Double Taxation Agreement, arts. II(1)(g), VIII (apart from the provision that, even where a permanent establishment exists, only royalties and know-how payments effectively connected with it may be taxed in the country of source).

[33] Art. V. This is the ordinary international rule.

[34] Provided the United States company is not managed and controlled in Ireland; art. II(1)(h). For the Irish concept of interest, see Income Tax Act, 1918, 8 & 9 Geo. 5, c. 40, Schedule D, Case III, Rule 1.

[35] Art. VII(2). This exemption is reciprocal; art. VII(1). The interest is exempt from Irish tax only if the recipient is liable to United States tax on it.

borrower.[36] However, if the company paying the interest is resident in Ireland and over 50 per cent of its voting shares are directly or indirectly controlled by the United States corporation to which the interest is paid, the interest may be taxed in Ireland. This prevents shares of profits or dividends on equity capital, which are taxable in the country of source, from being withdrawn under the guise of interest. Irish-source royalties paid to a United States company for the use of "copyrights, patents, designs, secret processes and formulae, trademarks, and other like property" also are exempt from Irish tax.[37] It is difficult to disguise equity capital to avoid Irish tax in such cases, so even royalties paid by a wholly owned subsidiary to its parent are exempted from Irish tax.[38] Since most royalties are not deductible by the paying company, tax cannot be avoided by paying large royalties, and the provision[39] allowing taxation of Irish companies on the profits which they would have made if their transactions with associated companies had been on an arm's length basis need not be invoked.[40]

[36] For internal purposes, however, interest may be treated as a share of profits under Irish law, not as compensation for the hire of capital, which would be a deductible revenue expense.

[37] Art. VIII. Rental payments for movie films are included also. The United States recipient must not be resident in Ireland and must be liable to United States tax on the royalties for the exemption from Irish tax to apply.

[38] Both the OECD provisions on interest and on royalties exempt from tax in the country of source only such sums as would have been agreed on in an arm's length transaction, the excess remaining taxable; OECD Fiscal Committee, Draft Double Taxation Convention on Income and Capital (1963), arts. 11(6), 12(4).

[39] Art. IV.

[40] Irish-source dividends, mining royalties, and rents from real property paid to individuals resident in the United States are exempt from Irish surtax; arts. VI(2), IX(2). There is no similar concession to United States companies (which are not liable to surtax) although the corresponding concession in the United States applies to Irish-resident companies.

United States taxation of foreign-source income

Prior to the Revenue Act of 1962,[41] foreign-source profits of a foreign subsidiary,[42] even one managed and con-

[41] 76 Stat. 960 (1962). The relevant parts of this are Int. Rev. Code of 1954, §§ 951–64, 970–71 [hereinafter cited as 1962 amendments]. See Nusbaum & Kaiser, "New 1962 Provisions on U.S. Taxation of Foreign Income," 1963 Brit. Tax Rev. 108. Apart from the considerable legislative history of the 1962 amendments, there is a large amount of literature on the subject of United States taxation of foreign income. See, in particular, Rado, United States Taxation of Foreign Investment—The New Approach (1963); Richman, Taxation of Foreign Investment Income: An Economic Analysis (1963); Gibbons, Tax Factors in Basing International Business Abroad (1957); Owens, The Foreign Tax Credit (1961); Barlow & Wender, Foreign Investment and Taxation (1955); van Hoorn & Wright, "Taxation," in 2 American Enterprise in the European Common Market: A Legal Profile 343 (Stein & Nicholson ed. 1960); 5 Institute on Private Investments Abroad and Foreign Trade (Southwestern Legal Foundation, 1963); Eichler, "Taxation of Foreign Subsidiaries Under the Revenue Act of 1962—A Note on Proposed Legislation," 30 Geo. Wash. L. Rev. 950 (1962).

[42] Except in the case of a foreign personal holding company; Int. Rev. Code of 1954, §§ 551–58. For a comparison between this form of company and the provisions of the 1962 amendments, see Wales, "Tax Policy in Relation to Foreign Business Income," 40 Taxes 961, 963 (1962). Sections 551–58 of Int. Rev. Code of 1954 correspond to U.K. Income Tax Act, 1952, 15 & 16 Geo. 6 & 1 Eliz. 2, c. 10, § 245.

The 1962 amendments are one of the few instances where a country has imposed its own taxes on foreign-source income of foreign-resident companies, apart from personal holding companies; however, other countries probably have avoided this by imposing exchange controls on the export of capital. Few countries have classified even income of residents for the purposes of double taxation relief on the basis of balance of payments and foreign economic policy, as has the United States. For example,

trolled in the United States, were not subject to United States tax. Profits could be accumulated indefinitely in foreign subsidiaries without any liability to United States tax until a dividend was paid to the United States parent company. Intermediate holding, or "base," companies[43] were established in countries[44] with low tax rates on income arising elsewhere.[45] The fact that United States enterprises established foreign subsidiaries to reduce their taxes,[46] instead of exporting from their home factories, increased the strain on the United States balance of payments.

The 1962 amendments are a compromise between the view that deferral of tax should be ended entirely[47] and the

---

a special reduced rate is given to United States–incorporated Western Hemisphere trade corporations which derive substantially all their income from manufacturing operations or from export sales in the Western Hemisphere outside the United States; Int. Rev. Code of 1954, §§ 921–22.

[43] In the tax law of the United Kingdom and that of most other countries, unlike in the United States tax law before 1962, the interposition of a base company has had an unfavorable effect, if it has any effect at all, on the amount of relief available in the country of residence against foreign tax, since no foreign tax credit is normally available for tax paid by a sub-subsidiary, or "grandchild" company. See U.K. Income Tax Act, 1952, 15 & 16 Geo. 6 & 1 Eliz. 2, c. 10, §§ 347–53 and Sixteenth and Seventeenth Schedules. The United Kingdom gives deferral to a special type of company, known as an overseas trade corporation, in respect of its trading but not its investment income; Royal Commission on Taxation of Profits and Income, Final Report, Cmd. No. 9474, para. 689 (1955); Finance Act, 1957, 5 & 6 Eliz. 2, c. 49, pt. IV, §§ 23–37 and Fourth through Eighth Schedules; Finance Act, 1959, 7 & 8 Eliz. 2, c. 58, § 27; Finance Act, 1962, 10 & 11 Eliz. 2, c. 44, § 19(6); see generally Stanford, Overseas Trade Corporations (1958); Bronheim, "Overseas Trade Corporations—A United Kingdom Experiment," 35 Taxes 771 (1957).

[44] The best known "base countries" are probably Switzerland, Luxembourg, Liechtenstein, Monaco, Panama, the Bahamas, and the Netherlands Antilles (the latter country has a double taxation convention with the Netherlands and is an associated territory of the EEC). See generally Gibbons, Tax Factors in Basing International Business Abroad (1957). Recent legislation has altered the position in Switzerland and in Monaco.

[45] From the countries where active business operations were carried on, profits were withdrawn in order to avoid taxes there on undistributed profits; to reinvest the profits in another foreign operation; to avoid expropriation, devaluation, or imposition of exchange controls or multiple exchange rates; to satisfy other shareholders in the manufacturing company; to attract subscriptions for a new issue of shares; or to receive tax concessions available only if profits were withdrawn within a specified time.

[46] See Dam, "Taxation of Foreign Income: Constitutional and International Law Aspects," in Krause & Dam, Federal Tax Treatment of Foreign Income 107 (1964). On foreign investment from the point of view of the capital-exporting country, see Balogh & Streeten, "Domestic Versus Foreign Investment," 22 Bull. Oxford U. Inst. Statistics 213 (1960).

A country which imposes low taxes on income from sources in other countries provides many opportunities for tax avoidance in international transactions. A company resident in such a country can export to other countries without paying tax to them or can carry out services in support of exports; receive interest and royalty payments from the licensing of patents, trademarks, and know-how; provide management services; or hold portfolio investments. Apparently, the EEC working party on tax-haven countries paid particular attention to investment in the EEC by United States interests operating through base companies.

[47] See Hearings Before the House Committee on Ways and Means, 87th Cong., 1st Sess. 3, 8–10 (1961); Hearings Before the Senate Committee on Finance on H.R. 10650, 87th Cong., 2d Sess., pt. 1, at 99–103, and pt. 10, at 4252–53 (1962).

The principal arguments made to Congress against the revenue bill as summarized by Eichler, "Taxation of Foreign Subsidiaries Under the Revenue Act of 1962—A Note on Proposed Legislation," 30 Geo. Wash. L. Rev. 950, 958–65 (1962), were: that the long-term indirect effects of foreign investment were favor-

previous law.[48] The amendments apply United States rates to various types of foreign income—broadly, those previously channeled through base companies—of United States–controlled foreign subsidiaries, even if the foreign income is not repatriated to the United States. The amendments thus increase the capital-export neutrality and taxpayer equality of the United States tax system, though these principles have been tempered by balance-of-payments considerations, by economic policy towards less developed countries, and by the value of direct investment abroad to the United States. Except by reducing the incentive to export capital, and thus reducing the United States tax base, the amendments do not affect inter-nation equity, i.e., fair apportionment of taxes and the tax base between nations; this equity cannot be obtained by the tax credit mechanism without a double taxation convention. The tax credit still causes United States tax claims to yield to the claims of foreign countries. No new incentives for foreign investment have been created. Deferral of United States tax until profits are repatriated, the largest concession, is continued for portfolio investment in less developed countries (including Ireland), for manufacturing operations, and to some extent for exports of goods and services from the United States. For direct and portfolio investment in underdeveloped countries, the tax credit is still computed in a way which results in payment of an over-all tax rate less than the normal United States rate. Although it is only a slight incentive for foreign investment, deferral for manufacturing subsidiaries abroad aids rapid capital accumulation, especially when combined with tax concession legislation, and reduces the initial capital investment, thus having favorable balance-of-payments effects on the United States capital account. From the point of view of the less developed countries, the 1962 amendments give an incentive to reinvestment and expansion; United States corporations still save United States tax by establishing manufacturing operations in countries to which they have been exporting, and thereby improve the balance-of-payments positions of these countries.

Tax credit and tax-sparing[49]

A much more important incentive for

able to the United States balance of payments, not unfavorable, as the Administration held; that, since foreign investment is often necessary to preserve access to a national market, the proposals interfered with legitimate investment as well as with investment undertaken only for tax reasons; and that United States foreign investment had to compete with local enterprises bearing lower tax rates. It was also argued that the provisions were unconstitutional, difficult to administer, unnecessary in view of the existing powers of the Treasury Department, and in violation of the spirit of double taxation treaties. For some other criticisms, see Rodgers, "Taxation on Private Investments Abroad—Economic Aspects," in 4 Institute on Private Investments Abroad 249 (Southwestern Legal Foundation, 1962).

[48] For a discussion of the whole system of United States unilateral relief against double taxation and its effect on foreign investment, see United States Income Taxation of Private United States Investment in Latin America, U.N. Doc. No. ST/ECA/18 (1953).

The 1962 amendments are complicated, and this book does not attempt a detailed analysis of them. For studies of the 1962 amendments, see Stone, "U.S. Taxation of Profits Withdrawn from Foreign Corporations," in 5 Institute on Private Investments Abroad 85 (Southwestern Legal Foundation, 1963); O'Connor, "United States Taxation of Earnings of American-Controlled Foreign Corporations," 42 Taxes 588 (1964); Guttentag, "Tax Aspects of Foreign Operations," 10 Wayne L. Rev. 529, 537–43 (1964); Ross, "The Impact of the Revenue Act of 1962 on Reorganizations and Other Rearrangements Involving Foreign Corporations," N.Y.U. 22d Inst. on Fed. Tax 761 (1964); Friedman & Silbert, "Final Regulations on Controlled Foreign Corporations and Less Developed Country Corporations," id. at 811.

[49] The American phrase "tax-sparing" means the same as the European "matching credit":

investment in capital-importing countries than those under the 1962 amendments could be given. The effect of the tax credit is that the rate of tax in the capital-importing country can be raised, at the expense of United States revenue, or lowered, to the benefit of United States revenue, without altering the over-all tax rate paid by investors who distribute their foreign profits.[50] The tax credit nullifies tax concessions offered by capital-importing countries if the profits are distributed to the United States shareholders. If profits are not distributed and are not subjected to United States tax, tax concessions are effective, and the tax credit and the 1962 amendments encourage reinvestment and expansion.[51] Even then, the result is only postponement of payment of tax, which amounts to an interest-free loan of the sum eventually payable. This is not true if the repatriated profits are taxed at the lower rate of tax for capital gains or if they are not taxed at all, as is the position with Irish tax concessions on profits from exports. If tax concessions in capital-importing countries are to be valuable when profits are repatriated, capital-exporting countries which use the tax credit system must give a credit for the foreign tax from which the foreign subsidiary has been relieved as a result of special legislation for favored industries. Not all investors can leave their funds abroad indefinitely, and there is little incentive to invest abroad if tax at the full rate will be due upon repatriation.

The 1962 amendments were the first tax measures enacted in the United States in recent years to encourage foreign investment in capital-importing countries specifically.[52] As such, they are significant; but the comprehensive measures for tax-sparing which were suggested but not enacted would have constituted a much greater benefit to the investor. Unfortunately, tax-sparing has the disadvantage of novelty in many

the country of residence gives, against its own tax on the foreign-source income, a credit which matches the amount of the foreign tax which has been remitted or spared by reason of a special exemption, instead of a credit only for the foreign tax actually paid.

On the merits of tax-sparing from the American point of view, see Surrey, "The Pakistan Tax Treaty and 'Tax Sparing,'" 11 Nat'l Tax J. 156 (1958); Kust, "The Pakistan Tax Treaty," 10 Tax Executive 103 (1958); Hollman, "The Pros and Cons of Tax Sparing for Waived Foreign Taxes," 9 J. Taxation 152 (1958); U.N. Economic and Social Council, International Tax Problems, U.N. Doc. No. E/2865 (1956); Richman, Taxation of Foreign Investment Income: An Economic Analysis, ch. V (1963).

[50] Under the 1962 amendments the same effect occurs, even if the foreign company does not distribute its profits, when the profits consist of "base company income," as defined in Int. Rev. Code of 1954, § 954(a).

[51] Richman, Taxation of Foreign Investment Income: An Economic Analysis 81 (1963), points out that the larger is country A's total accumulated profits in country B, and therefore the larger the volume of profits available for reinvestment, the more important it becomes to country B that reinvestment of profits from old capital should be stimulated rather than investment of new capital. Consequently, the less desirable it becomes to coordinate tax-sparing by A with B's tax concession. In an economic union or in a double taxation convention, it might be possible to provide for tax-sparing only after a specified number of years or after a specified proportion of profits had been reinvested. However, it is doubtful if it can be deduced from Dr. Richman's conclusion that an attempt should be made to bottle up accumulated profits by tax methods when these profits exceed the probable amount of new capital likely to be attracted. A gradual decrease in the amount of tax spared by the capital-exporting country would encourage prompt repatriation and discourage investment. Tax-sparing is strongly criticized by Heller & Kauffman, Tax Incentives for Industry in Less Developed Countries 74–78 (1963).

[52] In 1961 Germany passed a law providing tax incentives (not related to double taxation) for investment in less developed countries; Vogel, "Tax Incentives for Industrial Development," in Methods of Industrial Development 271, 280 (OECD, 1962).

countries; it would be easier to overcome certain technical difficulties in tax-sparing by bilateral treaties than by legislation.[53] The loss of revenue to the capital-exporting country is no greater in the case of tax-sparing than it is under the ordinary tax credit system, if the country of source of the income increases its rate of tax and obtains the total tax itself. The objection to tax-sparing is primarily on revenue grounds but also on the ground of equity; it is argued that all taxpayers in the capital-exporting country should pay tax at the same rates on their income, regardless of the source[54] and the proportions in which it is shared between the countries involved. However, using the tax credit for less developed country corporations results in different over-all tax rates according to the foreign tax rate paid; in this case foreign economic policy has been allowed to override taxpayer equality. The broader concession on the part of capital-exporting countries advocated by the International Chamber of Commerce—that capital-exporting countries should exempt income arising in capital-importing countries from tax[55]—is also contrary to taxpayer equality.[56] An advantage of taxation only in the country of source would be that it would give the same incentive to investment in a country in which the ordinary rates of direct taxation are low that tax-sparing would give in a country which lowers its ordinary rates specially to attract investment.

In Ireland and certain other countries, tax concessions are given only for profits from exports. Subsidies for exports by means of remission of direct taxes are contrary to GATT. The United States has been prominent in demanding adherence to the rules of GATT and might be reluctant to enact tax-sparing, which

[53] It would be difficult to frame legislation so as to prevent capital-importing countries from "exempting" investors from fictitious taxes, for example. In addition, the offer to "spare" taxes is, of course, a substantial bargaining point. Tax-sparing has legislative sanction in Britain under Finance Act, 1961, 9 & 10 Eliz. 2, c. 36, § 17; Nortcliffe, "Current Notes," 1961 Brit. Tax Rev. 219–20; Nortcliffe, "Current Notes," 1962 Brit. Tax Rev. 193–97; Royal Commission on Taxation of Profits and Income, First Report, Cmd. No. 8761, paras. 52–60 (1953). See Gal-Edd, 46 Cahiers de Droit Fiscal International 81–86 (1961); Brosh, id. at 101–104; Klimovsky, id. at 120–24. Analogous to tax-sparing, as it is normally conceived, would be a provision in the country of residence that, irrespective of the amount of tax imposed in the country of source, a credit of a specified amount would be given. This would have the advantage of simplicity. See van Hoorn, id. at 87. According to the testimony of Dan Throop Smith, Deputy to the Secretary of the Treasury (In Charge of Tax Policy), Hearings Before the Subcommittee on Foreign Trade Policy of the House Committee on Ways and Means, 85th Cong., 2d Sess. 51 (1958), summarized by Gordon, "Some Aspects of United States Policy in the Taxation of Foreign Income," 1959 U. Ill. L.F. 222, 231, four conditions for tax-sparing are required: (1) The capital-importing country should eliminate tax obstacles to private investment by entering into a double taxation convention which includes a provision prohibiting discrimination against United States investment. (2) The tax incentives should be general and not limited to United States investors. (3) The conditions under which the incentives would be given should be fully specified and administrative discretion minimized. (4) Tax incentives should be of a limited type. Only the first of these requirements is imposed primarily in the interests of the United States; they all are intended to insure that the tax concessions are effective. The third condition, that administrative discretion should be minimized, is incompatible with the preference of the EEC Commission for selective state aid.

[54] This assumption is more natural in a country such as the United States than in many other countries. If "proportional taxes" on particular types of income are not supplemented by a progressive tax levied on total income or if a substantial proportion of the tax paid by any taxpayer is paid in indirect taxes, the national tax law cannot produce taxpayer equality regardless of how it treats foreign-source income.

[55] International Chamber of Commerce, Avoidance of Double Taxation (1955).

[56] See Surrey, "The United States Taxation of Foreign Income," 1 J. Law & Econ. 72 (1958).

would increase the effectiveness of the Irish tax concessions.[57] This point does not seem to have arisen in connection with the existing Irish double taxation conventions which provide for tax-sparing,[58] but it is important since the Irish export tax concessions may also be contrary to the EEC Treaty and since tax-sparing is essential to an adequate, effective regional economic policy in the EEC.

THE U.K.-IRISH DOUBLE TAXATION AGREEMENTS

Income tax[59]

The arrangements between Ireland and the United Kingdom on double taxation and income tax are designed for a situation where there is a considerable degree of economic integration.[60] They are based on the principles which are advocated by the Neumark Committee and which raise special problems for capital-importing regions and countries in the EEC.

An individual resident in Ireland or the United Kingdom and not a double resident is liable to income tax and surtax only in the country where he is resident and is exempt from tax in the other country.[61] The same principle applies to companies, which pay income tax only in the country in which they are managed and controlled,[62] regardless of their country of incorporation, even if they have a permanent establishment in the other country or substantial trading profits or income from property situated there. The result, which is important from the investor's point of view, is that the tax liability of an Irish-resident company depends only on Irish law, and even if the company is exempt from Irish tax, it will not become liable to British tax on its British-source income. The principle of taxation only in the country of residence is unique in the general double taxation conventions of both Britain and Ireland. However, it has been widely used to avoid double taxation of shipping and aircraft companies, due to the impossibility of determining their sources of income on a geographical basis. To a considerable extent, the peculiar nature of the U.K.-Irish Agreement of 1926 is because at the time it was

[57] Ireland is not a member of GATT, but negotiations are in progress.

[58] Irish-German Double Taxation Agreement, art. XXII(2); Irish-Swedish Double Taxation Agreement, Nov. 6, 1959, art. XXIII, Ir. T.S. No. 11 of 1960, Pr. 5790 (1960).

[59] U.K.-Irish Double Income Taxation Agreement, April 14, 1926, U.K. Income Tax Act, 1952, 15 & 16 Geo. 6 & 1 Eliz. 2, c. 10, Eighteenth Schedule, pt. I, Irish Finance Act, 1926 Pub. Stat. 401, 441, First Schedule, pt. I; amended April 25, 1928, Irish Finance Act, 1928 Pub. Stat. 71, 101, First Schedule; amended July 21, 1947, Irish Finance Act, 1948 Act 281, 301, First Schedule; amended April 4, 1959, U.K. Finance Act, 1959, 7 & 8 Eliz. 2, c. 58, Seventh Schedule, Irish Finance Act, 1959 Act 681, 833, Second Schedule, Ir. T.S. No. 3 of 1959, Pr. 5009; amended June 30, 1960, U.K. Finance Act, 1960, 8 & 9 Eliz. 2, c. 44, Fifth Schedule, Irish Finance Act, 1960 Acts 483, 555, Third Schedule, Ir. T.S. No. 12 of 1960, Pr. 5847. The agreement and the first two amendments are in U.K. Finance Act, 1926, 16 & 17 Geo. 5, c. 22, Schedule II, pt. I; in Finance Act, 1928, 18 & 19 Geo. 5, c. 17, Fourth Schedule; and in Finance Act, 1948, 11 & 12 Geo. 6, c. 49, Ninth Schedule, respectively, and have been re-enacted by Income Tax Act, 1952. See also Irish Finance Act, 1953 Acts 235, § 3, the provision giving relief where double resident spends less than six months a year in Ireland and pays more than the full rate of British tax. See generally Mason, "United Kingdom–Eire Double Taxation Agreements and Assessments" (pts. 1–2), 1959 Brit. Tax Rev. 261, 339. The text does not take into account the changes proposed by the Irish Finance Bill, 1966, §§ 4, 19, and First Schedule.

[60] Ehrenzweig & Koch, Income Tax Treaties 10 (1949); 1 British Tax Encyclopedia 1396–98 (Wheatcroft ed. 1962).

[61] U.K.-Irish Double Income Taxation Agreement, as amended April 25, 1928, art. 1(a), 1(b).

[62] U.K.-Irish Double Income Taxation Agreement, art. 4.

made the country of residence was regarded as having the prior right to tax income; in spite of the detailed amendments, the agreement was not renegotiated until the British Finance Act of 1965[63] necessitated its partial renegotiation.

The advantage of the residence principle from the point of view of the two governments concerned is that once the residence of a taxpayer is established there is no further calculation involved in deciding liability to tax; all income tax borne in the country in which the taxpayer is not resident must be repaid, and no further tax may be imposed. In the country of residence the foreign source of the income is disregarded, and the taxpayer's liability is calculated essentially by reference to the ordinary law,[64] the principal difference being that since tax deducted in the country of source is repayable, it must be added to the net income received in order to calculate income tax liability in the country of residence. Computation of tax is thus greatly simplified.

Since the rule exempting companies from income tax in the country of source does not apply to double residents, they are treated in a more usual way. A provision, however, states: "For the purpose of this Agreement a company, whether incorporated by or under the laws of Great Britain or of Northern Ireland or of [Ireland] . . . or otherwise, shall be deemed to be resident in that country only in which its business is managed and controlled."[65] Since it is possible under English law and probably under Irish law for a company to be managed and controlled in two countries,[66] the question arises whether the provision quoted excludes this possibility in the case of a company whose management and control is divided between the United Kingdom and Ireland.[67] The better view is that a company cannot be a resident of both countries and that the provisions dealing with dual residents apply only to individuals. If an individual is regarded by both the United Kingdom and Ireland as being one of their own residents, no effort is made to decide[68] with which country he is more closely connected, and the rules relating to double residents are applied. This is contrary to the modern Continental practice, as expressed in the OECD Fiscal Committee's draft model convention, but except where the effective rate of Irish tax is higher than that in the United Kingdom, no hardship is caused.

A double resident is liable to income

[63] 13 & 14 Eliz. 2, c. 25.

[64] See Finance Act, 1926 Pub. Stat. 401, First Schedule, pt. II, for variations in the usual basis of assessment.

[65] U.K.-Irish Double Income Taxation Convention, art. 4.

[66] Swedish Cent. Rail Co. v. Thompson, [1925] A.C. 495, 9 Tax Cas. 342, 370.

[67] Since the Income Tax Act, 1918, 8 & 9 Geo. 5, c. 40, Schedule D, in force in both the United Kingdom and Ireland at the time of the 1926 Agreement, uses the words "residing" and "resident," art. 4 was not merely repeating the legislative provisions and is not deprived of effect by the interpretation that it permits management and control to be divided. However, the exempting provisions—art. 1(a) and 1(b)—do not apply to a double resident, and the word "only" in art. 4 seems to be superfluous if it does not exclude the possibility of a second country's being involved. (See, in this connection, the definition of the terms "resident of Ireland" and "resident of the United States" in the U.S.-Irish Double Taxation Convention, art. II.) The point does not seem to have been decided, and the practice in cases where the management and control are equally divided between the two countries is to regard the company as resident only in the country of incorporation. This practice has no statutory basis.

[68] Cf. the OEEC Fiscal Committee's Draft Double Taxation Convention, art. III; OECD Fiscal Committee, Draft Convention on Double Taxation of Capital and Income (1963), art. 4.

tax and surtax in each country on the whole of his income, but gets relief by way of credit in each country against the tax otherwise payable there. The tax credit is given at the same rate in each country on the income doubly taxed. This rate is half of the lower of the two effective rates of tax, making no deduction for any tax paid in the other country.[69] The effective[70] rate of tax in each country is the rate of income tax and surtax[71] which would have been payable on the total income taxable there if no question of double residence or double taxation had arisen. The result is that, on the income liable to double taxation, tax is paid in the country which has the lower of the two effective tax rates at half of the effective tax rate in that country. In the country which has, independent of double taxation relief, the higher effective tax rate, tax is paid at a rate which is the difference between half of the lower effective rate and the higher effective rate. The income subject to double taxation bears tax over-all at the higher of the two effective rates.[72]

Since Irish tax rates are irrelevant to the tax liability of a company resident in Britain, dividends paid by an Irish-resident subsidiary to a British resident parent are subject to British tax at the full rate, even if they and the profits from which they are paid are exempt from Irish tax. There is no tax-sparing or

[69] U.K.-Irish Double Income Taxation Agreement, as amended April 25, 1928, art. 2.

[70] Art. 2 of the U.K.-Irish Agreement used the phrase "the appropriate rate of . . . tax." The term "effective rate of tax" has been used in the text, as it seems more descriptive.

[71] U.K.-Irish Double Income Taxation Agreement, as amended April 25, 1928, art. 1.

[72] To calculate the tax payable, first calculate the total income taxable in each country. This includes all income subject to double taxation, and also includes sums such as those remitted to one of the two countries and taxable on a remittance basis, but not taxable in the other country. Then, disregarding double taxation, calculate the total tax payable in each country on the total income taxable there, giving the usual personal allowances. To find the effective, or "appropriate," rate of tax in each country, divide the total tax payable before double taxation relief by the total income (not the total taxable income, i.e., the total income after deduction of personal allowances) in that country. One-half of the lower of the two rates is the "rate of relief." Since the tax rates in Ireland are always lower than those in the United Kingdom, the Irish effective rate is usually the lower of the two.

If B is the total income which is taxable in both countries,

(B + Y) is the total income taxable in the country with the higher effective rate of tax,

(B + X) is the total income taxable in the country with the lower effective rate of tax,

S is the higher effective rate of tax (expressed as a decimal), and

T is the lower effective rate of tax (expressed as a decimal).

Then:	in the country with the higher effective rate	in the country with the lower effective rate
the total tax actually payable is:	$S(B + Y) - \frac{BT}{2}$	$T(B + X) - \frac{BT}{2}$
and the total tax payable in both countries is:	$SB + SY + TX.$	

Broadly speaking, relief for Irish income tax is given against British income tax for the same year, and relief for Irish surtax is given against British surtax in the year following the year in which the surtax arose; U.K.-Irish Double Taxation Agreement, as amended April 25, 1928, art. 2(1)(c), 2(1)(f), 2(2). In practice, relief is given as is most convenient.

For examples of calculations, see Wilson & Kelly, Irish Income Tax and Corporation Profits Tax 224–30 (1957); 1 Simon, Income Tax 299–300 (2d ed. 1952).

If, under U.K. Income Tax Act, 1952, 15 & 16 Geo. 6 & 1 Eliz. 2, c. 10, § 350, tax is deducted from a dividend paid by a United Kingdom company at the full United Kingdom standard rate but repayment is limited to the net rate of tax payable by the company after other double taxation relief has been taken into account, only a repayment of the amount of the net United Kingdom rate is given; U.K.-Irish Double Income Taxation Agreement, as amended April 25, 1928, and July 21, 1947, art. 1(a).

matching credit provision[73] in British tax law for dividends paid by an Irish export company, in the case of either a single resident or a double resident.[74]

If a company resident in one of the two countries receives dividends from a company resident in the other, it pays income tax at the full rate on the gross dividend and reclaims the income tax which it has suffered by deduction in the country of source.[75]

Corporation profits tax[76]

Corporation profits tax and the corresponding "profits tax" in the United Kingdom are treated separately from income tax and more conventionally. A company incorporated in Ireland—and therefore liable to Irish corporation profits tax on its world profits—and not managed and controlled in the United Kingdom—in which case it would be similarly liable to profits tax—is not liable to United Kingdom profits tax on its industrial and commercial profits unless it has a permanent establishment in the United Kingdom.[77] A company managed and controlled in the United Kingdom, if it is not incorporated in Ireland, pays no Irish corporation profits tax on its industrial and commercial profits unless it has a permanent establishment in Ireland.

A permanent establishment is defined in substantially the usual way.[78] The profits of a permanent establishment are calculated as if it were an independent enterprise dealing with its parent company. The existence of a permanent establishment is a criterion for liability to local tax and not the measure of the profits liable to tax, i.e., other income from sources in the same country becomes liable to local tax although it would not otherwise be so.[79] Any tax so payable is credited against the corresponding tax in the country of residence of the company.[80]

A company incorporated in Ireland and managed and controlled in the United Kingdom is a double resident, and its over-all liability is dealt with under the tax credit provisions of the agreement. If tax is payable in either country on profits arising there, a credit for that tax is allowed against the tax in the other

[73] U.K. Finance Act, 1961, 9 & 10 Eliz. 2, c. 36, § 17, permits tax-sparing or matching credit provisions in double taxation treaties, but there is no such provision in the U.K.-Irish Agreement.

[74] Until British Finance Act, 1965, 13 & 14 Eliz. 2, c. 25, a British-owned Irish exporting subsidiary could sometimes avoid United Kingdom tax by remitting profits only by way of capital gains. However, this could not be done by paying dividends out of capital profits; Reid's Trustees v. C.I.R., [1949] A.C. 361, 30 Tax Cas. 431. The other rules relating to the distinction between capital and income are the same in British and Irish tax laws. In Britain, however, there is now a tax on capital gains.

[75] If the dividend is paid without deduction of tax, it is deemed to be a dividend of the amount which, after deduction of tax at the standard rate, would give a net dividend equivalent to the dividend actually paid.

[76] U.K.-Irish Corporation Profits Tax Agreement, May 18, 1949, [1949] 1(3) Stat. Instr. 3536 (No. 1434), Irish Finance Act, 1949 Acts 75, 143, Fifth Schedule, Ir. T.S. No. 4 of 1949, Pr. 9433.

[77] U.K.-Irish Corporation Profits Tax Agreement, arts. II(1)(e)–II(1)(g), III(2).

[78] U.K.-Irish Corporation Profits Tax Agreement, art. II(1), II(1)(4). The wording is identical to that of U.S.-Irish Double Taxation Convention, art. II(1); cf. Irish-German Double Taxation Agreement, art. II(1)(g).

[79] Cf. OEEC Draft Double Taxation Convention, art. XV; OECD Fiscal Committee, Draft Convention on Double Taxation of Income and Capital (1963), art. 7.

[80] Under Irish law, a company is "resident" in Ireland for the purposes of corporation profits tax if it is incorporated in Ireland, irrespective of its place of management and control; Finance Act, 1920, 10 & 11 Geo. 5, c. 18, § 52(2), 52(3). The word "resident" is used in the U.K.-Irish Corporation Profits Tax Agreement.

country on the same profits.[81] The credit allowed may not exceed the amount of corporation profits tax which, but for the double taxation relief, would have been payable on the gross amount of the profits[82] before deducting the profits tax. In other words, a company cannot have both a deduction and a credit, and the credit is the "ordinary" and not the "full" credit. If the tax in the country of source cannot be credited against the tax in the country of residence, it is allowed as a deduction.

If a company resident in only one country under the agreement pays a dividend to a company which beneficially owns, directly or indirectly, 75 per cent or more of the ordinary share capital of the paying company, the shareholder company gets credit for the corporation profits tax or the profits tax paid by the subsidiary. The tax paid by the subsidiary is added back to calculate the amount of the profits from which the dividend was paid. The credit is that proportion of the tax paid by the subsidiary which is attributable to the part of the profits represented, after tax, by the dividend. If the whole dividend exceeds the profits of the period for which it was paid, the profits of the most recent accounting periods are looked at.[83]

A company operating ships or aircraft pays the taxes dealt with in the agreement only in the country in which it is resident.[84]

The agreement contains the usual provisions relating to transactions between associated companies and prohibiting discriminatory taxation.[85] There are no provisions with regard to interest or royalties.

The discriminatory effect of the U.K.-Irish Double Income Taxation Agreement

The question arises whether the U.K.-Irish Double Income Taxation Agreement is discriminatory, in that it gives Irish industry access to the large British market free of British tax, except for profits tax where a permanent establishment exists, and gives corresponding advantages to British industry in Ireland.

There are two aspects of the special situation created by the agreement. First, if the effective tax rate is higher in Britain than in Ireland or in a third country, the agreement allows an Irish company to pay the lower of the two relevant rates of tax instead of the higher, as is the case of most double taxation treaties. The agreement therefore gives an advantage to Irish-resident companies over companies resident in the third country, insofar as both are doing business in Britain through permanent establishments.

Second, and more important, if an Irish-resident company[86] has a perma-

[81] U.K.-Irish Corporation Profits Tax Agreement, art. VII; Irish Finance Act, 1949 Acts 75, Fifth Schedule, pt. II, para. 2. No credit is given for United Kingdom profits tax if the company is liable to Irish tax only on Irish-source income because it is incorporated outside Ireland; Irish Finance Act, 1949 Acts 75, Fifth Schedule, pt. II, para. 4.

[82] Irish Finance Act, 1949 Acts 75, Fifth Schedule, pt. II, para. 4.

[83] Finance Act, 1949 Acts 75, Fifth Schedule, pt. II, para. 6. It has been argued that no indirect credit should be given; Royal Commission on Taxation of Profits and Income, Final Report, Cmd. No. 9474, Memorandum of Dissent, paras. 167–70 (1955).

[84] U.K.-Irish Corporation Profits Tax Agreement, art. V.

[85] U.K.-Irish Corporation Profits Tax Agreement, arts. IV and VI, respectively.

[86] Owing to the residence principle in the agreement, an Irish branch of a company resident in England cannot benefit from the export tax relief, since it pays no tax in Ireland anyway; a subsidiary managed and controlled in Ireland is necessary. A United Kingdom overseas trade corporation cannot do business in Ireland; U.K. Finance Act, 1957, 5 & 6 Eliz. 2, c. 49, § 24(6). This is because such a company would be exempt from Irish tax under the agreement and from British tax under British law.

nent establishment in Britain, the profits tax payable on all profits from sources there constitutes its entire tax liability if it is exporting all of its products from Ireland. It may, therefore, get the best of both worlds by operating in Britain and benefitting from Irish tax concessions. This advantage does not result directly from the agreement, but from the tax concessions, which in the EEC must be compatible with Article 92 or Article 98.

The extent of the advantage conferred by the agreement itself—the freedom of Irish-resident enterprises to do business in Britain through permanent establishments free of British income tax—depends on the tax rates involved. If the effective tax rates were the same, there would be no advantage. Also, no advantage is given if a permanent establishment is not necessary for doing business in the sector of industry in question.

Unless one believes that having different definitions of permanent establishment under different double taxation treaties is discriminatory per se, it is inconsistent to maintain that the U.K.-Irish Agreement is discriminatory, since a narrow definition favors enterprises which are doing business in a foreign country if the tax rate in their country of residence is lower. Different definitions of permanent establishment are only matters of degree, in economic terms, although there is legally a difference of principle between taxation in the country of source and in the country of residence.

It is not possible to equalize competitive conditions between enterprises resident in countries with different tax rates by double taxation conventions. The peculiarity of the U.K.-Irish Agreement is that it allows either country to give tax relief to its own residents in respect of their operations in the other country and allows enterprises operating side by side in either country to pay different rates of tax if their respective countries of residence have different tax rates. This is incompatible with a rational tax system.

There is nothing inherently discriminatory about the agreement. However, it increases the importance of Irish tax concessions and other state aids to industry, since their effect is not limited to companies merely exporting to Britain, as would otherwise be the case. The 1926 Agreement therefore may make it more difficult to justify the tax concessions in the eyes of the EEC Commission. If Ireland joins the EEC, the proper course would be to consider the compatibility of the Irish tax concessions with Articles 92 and 98 in the light of the increased importance of the Irish tax concessions, not to abrogate the agreement. It would be unfortunate if a country such as Ireland, where the total revenue from direct taxes is relatively small, were deprived of the advantages of simplicity in administration for the sake of minimizing distortion of conditions of competition caused by differences in effective tax rates and not by the agreement. Harmonization of taxes would be necessary in the EEC even if the agreement were terminated, and tax harmonization would make its termination unnecessary.

The Neumark Report recommends, as a short-term measure, that the EEC member states adopt a multilateral double taxation convention based on the OECD model treaty.[87] However, the Report prefers the principle of taxation only in the country of residence when national tax laws have been harmonized and close cooperation can be insured.[88] It would therefore be undesirable and unneces-

[87] Rapport 71–74, CCH 2467–70.

[88] Rapport 73, CCH 2469. Both these requirements are fulfilled in the case of the U.K.-Irish Agreement. The principle of taxation only in the country of residence has been described as the "ideal solution." Vogel, 41 Cahiers de Droit Fiscal International 119 (1959).

sary to replace the U.K.-Irish Agreement by a conventional treaty, whether bilateral or multilateral, since the ultimate ideal in the EEC is a multilateral arrangement on the same principles as the U.K.-Irish Agreement.[89]

The operation of the U.K.-Irish Double Income Taxation Agreement and the applicability of conventions based on residence

The simplest method of avoiding double taxation of income is to exempt it from taxation in one country.[90] The U.K.-Irish Agreement is unusual because the exemption is given and the revenue waived by the country of source.[91]

The aims of a double taxation treaty are the prevention of double taxation[92] of income taxable in both countries and the fair allocation of the tax payable between the two countries involved.[93] Both functions are adequately performed by the provisions of the U.K.-Irish Agreement on double residents, as long as the tax rates are similar. With regard to single residents, double taxation is prevented by the U.K.-Irish Agreement, but any fair allocation of tax between the two countries is achieved not in respect of any individual but on the basis of the whole body of taxpayers taxable in both countries.[94] It follows that the way revenue is apportioned between the two countries is approximate at best and may vary from time to time. The permanent emigration to Ireland of a few British millionaires with British-source income would confer a much greater benefit on the Irish Revenue under the existing agreement than would be the case under a conventional treaty; a substantial increase in investment in Ireland by British residents, on the other hand, would have much less effect.

The result of the residence principle between two countries is fair only if substantially similar amounts of income accrue in each country to residents of the other country, i.e., if the reciprocal investment and trading are balanced. This is an inherent limitation on such treaties. The capital-importing country loses revenue under the residence principle, but it is not clear that Ireland is a net importer of capital from Britain. British-source income of Irish residents is, typically, dividends paid to Irish institutional and individual investors who have invested on British stock exchanges and wages paid to Irish residents who work in Britain. Irish-source income of British residents is more difficult to fit into categories.

[89] But presumably it would have some other treatment of double residents.

[90] In Memorandum Explaining the [U.K.-Irish] Agreement . . ., Cmd. No. 2654 (1926), the British government stressed that the principle of taxation only in the country of residence was described in the report of the Committee of Economists to the League of Nations as "the most desirable practical method of avoiding the evils of double taxation." The modern preference for taxation in the country of source is based on the view that the latter country should have the primary right to tax most kinds of income.

[91] If the difference in tax rates were large, in the case of a double resident the lower-rate country would continue to get half of the tax payable before double taxation relief, and the higher-rate country would receive a large percentage of the tax payable before relief. The British and the Irish tax rates have always been similar, although Ireland has always had the lower standard rates. See Economic Development, Pr. 4803, ch. 3, paras. 7–8 (1958).

[92] That is, taxation in both countries causing the payment of tax at an over-all rate higher than would have been payable in either of them separately.

[93] See Angelopoulos, 41 Cahiers de Droit Fiscal International 154–55 (1959).

[94] "The weakness of [the U.K.-Irish Agreement] . . . lies in the lack of a suitable and reasonable method of apportionment. To place the tax entirely on residence may also seem unduly favorable to a creditor state." Wang, "International Double Taxation of Income: Relief Through International Agreement 1921–1945," 59 Harv. L. Rev. 73, 106 (1945).

The agreement has been in force for over forty years, and presumably both countries think it preferable to any arrangement more likely to produce internation equity at greater administrative trouble and expense. Because of the difference in importance of a given amount of revenue in the two countries, owing to the relative sizes of their budgets, and because Ireland has always had the lower standard rate of tax, the Irish revenue authorities apparently believe that more British-source income accrues to Irish residents than Irish-source income accrues to British residents.[95] Accurate figures are difficult to obtain because the standard by which the existing arrangement should be judged would not be the total amounts of Irish- and British-source income on the basis of national tax laws, but the total amounts of income which would be taxable in each country on the basis of an orthodox double taxation treaty.[96]

If the over-all result is fair to both countries, the greater administrative convenience of double taxation treaties based only on residence makes them especially satisfactory where there is a large volume of investment and trade between the two countries, i.e., where there is a high degree of economic integration. They are therefore more suitable in the EEC than other types of treaty. Administrative expense is saved not only by the governments concerned but also by all residents with income from sources in the other country. Double taxation treaties based on residence allow taxation of world income in the state of residence, essential to progressive taxation,[97] to be combined with deduction of direct taxes at source,[98] the most satisfactory method of preventing tax evasion, without the complexities of the tax credit system and the consequent technical barriers to trade between member states.

Owing to the advantages given to enterprises in the country with the lower effective tax rate, a residence-principle treaty probably is suitable for use only between countries with similar tax rates. A residence-principle treaty does nothing to minimize differences in competitive conditions due to differences in the tax rates.

There is no reason why the process which prevents double taxation of an enterprise should be combined with that which apportions the tax between the two countries involved. The two processes traditionally have coincided simply because this insured that the enterprise which was interested in achieving the first result would thereby be made responsible for bringing about the second. But a well-balanced pattern of trade and investment between two member states would probably mean that, apart from the effect of special state aids, no great

[95] The presumably satisfactory operation of the U.K.-Irish Agreement is due to part to the absence of any important extractive industry in Ireland using British capital. Where such industries exist, capital-importing countries normally wish to tax them on the basis of the principle of taxation in the country of source. It may be that the agreement was intended to give Ireland somewhat more revenue than it would have received under a conventional double taxation treaty.

[96] The existing tax returns relating to corporation profits tax and profits tax could be used to get an estimate of the position as far as companies are concerned. Only a goverment-sponsored study using confidential information available to the revenue authorities could show whether either country has benefited disproportionately from the agreement.

[97] See generally the discussion in the Neumark Report on the relative merits of unitary and schedular income tax systems; Rapport 32–75, CCH 2432–71.

[98] Under the U.K.-Irish Agreement, income tax deducted in one country is repaid to the taxpayer on proof of payment of tax in the other. Under the proposals of the Neumark Committee, tax deducted in the country of source would be paid to the country of residence on the ground that the tax deducted was simply a prepayment of the tax there.

changes in the total revenue of either country would result from the adoption of a double taxation arrangement based on the principle of residence. If taxes have been at least partly harmonized, the task of calculating the extent of any advantage or disadvantage to a member state as a result of adopting a treaty based on residence should be less difficult than that of calculating tax credits in every individual case. Any advantage to a member state could be remedied by an international payment of the type which will be necessary if other proposals for harmonization of taxes are carried out.[99]

THE IRISH-GERMAN DOUBLE TAXATION AGREEMENT[100] AND THE OEEC-OECD MODEL DOUBLE TAXATION CONVENTION

The importance of the OECD model

Since the Irish-German Double Taxation Agreement follows the lines of the OEEC-OECD Fiscal Committee's draft model double taxation convention and since the latter is now widely used among OECD member nations,[101] they

[99] The precise effects of entry into the EEC on the revenues of member states cannot be foreseen accurately. There are no Treaty provisions dealing with the possibility of a substantial loss of revenue, although it might be considered as one of the difficulties which would permit the use of the safeguard provisions, such as art. 226. The plans for an eventual change from the destination principle to the origin principle as the basis for turnover taxes, and indeed any other proposals for substantial tax harmonization, probably will make it necessary for compensation to be paid to one member state by the others for loss of revenue due to these measures. The idea of payments being made by one government to another as a result of the uneven operation of a double taxation treaty is discussed in the League of Nations Economic and Financial Commission, Report on Double Taxation 48–51 (1923). The Neumark Committee mentions the possible need for sharing the revenue received between two or more countries and draws the analogy of the German trade tax, which sometimes is shared between several municipalities; Rapport 71, CCH 2467.

[100] Dec. 18, 1962, Irish S.I. No. 212 of 1962, Pr. 6792, German Law of March 25, 1964, [1964] 2 BGBl. 266, 632. References in this section are to the Irish-German Convention, unless otherwise indicated. Germany is the only one of the Six with which Ireland has a double taxation treaty.

[101] See OEEC Fiscal Committee, The Elimination of Double Taxation, Second Report, paras. 6–13 (1959); Third Report, paras. 6–8 (1960); Fourth Report, paras. 7–12 (1961); OECD Fiscal Committee, Draft Double Taxation Convention on Income and Capital [cited in this section as Final Report 1963] 22 and paras. 49–61 (1963).

On the work of the League of Nations on double taxation, see the publications of its Economic and Financial Commission: Report on Double Taxation (1923); Taxation of Foreign and National Enterprises (5 vols., 1932–33); London and Mexico Model Tax Conventions: Commentary and Text (1946). See also 4 U.S. Joint Committee on Internal Revenue, Legislative History of United States Tax Conventions, pt. I (1962); Seligman, Double Taxation and International Fiscal Cooperation (1928); Wang, "International Double Taxation of Income: Relief Through International Agreement 1921–1945," 59 Harv. L. Rev. 73 (1945).

The United States has expressed certain reservations about the OECD model. It reserved its right to tax on the basis of citizenship (in the case of corporations, on the basis of place of incorporation); this is not contemplated in the Fiscal Committee's studies. It also reserved its position with regard to taxation by political subdivisions and taxation of capital gains. It tentatively reserved its position pending further study on the following points: (1) the subordination of art. 7 (of the Final Report 1963; it is art. XV in the Fiscal Committee's Third Report), on taxation of commercial and industrial profits, to the articles dealing with specific types of income; (2) the exemption from tax of profits accumulated by foreign corporations, including foreign personal holding companies; (3) the imputation of income based on the use of immovable property; (4) the rejection of the principle that where a permanent establishment exists local-source income not derived from it may be subject to local tax where, as under United States law, jurisdiction to tax enterprises of the other contracting state is limited in any event by the source of income; (5) the use of 25% direct capital ownership as the criterion for reduction of the permissible rate of tax at source on intercorporate dividends; (6) the exemption from tax of income from independent

are discussed together. The Neumark Committee recommends that all conventions between member states of the EEC should be revised to correspond to the OECD model, with a view to concluding a multilateral convention for the whole Community.[102] The EEC Commission has accepted this,[103] and so United States investors doing business in the Common Market can expect to be subject in due course to double taxation conventions based on the OECD model.

Taxes and residence of companies

The Irish-German Agreement deals with Irish income tax, surtax, and corporation profits tax, and with German income tax, corporation tax, federal capital tax, and municipal trade tax. This chapter is, however, limited to the tax position of companies.[104] To qualify in Germany for the benefit of the agreement, a company must be managed and controlled in Ireland.[105] Either management and control or incorporation in Germany, however, gives a company the relief from Irish tax provided by the agreement. A company incorporated in Germany and managed and controlled in Ireland[106] is a double resident.[107]

If both Ireland and Germany regard a taxpayer as resident in their own jurisdiction, the agreement supplies no test for deciding in which country the taxpayer should be regarded as resident. Ireland has not accepted the OECD Fiscal Committee's article on fiscal domicile.[108] This is apparently because, as a predominantly capital-importing country, Ireland would lose revenue if cases of double residence were resolved by deciding with which country the taxpayer had the closest connection instead of by applying the tax credit method

---

services, where no fixed base is maintained in the taxing state, and the exclusion of entertainers from this provision. See Final Report 1963, paras. 39–40.

Ireland also has double taxation treaties with Denmark, Ir. T.S. No. 1 of 1965, Pr. 7576, S.I. No. 203 of 1964; with Sweden, Nov. 6, 1959, Ir. T.S. No. 11 of 1960, Pr. 5790; and with Canada, Oct. 28, 1954, Finance Act, 1955 Acts 403, First Schedule, Ir. T.S. No. 18 of 1955, Pr. 2760, 304 U.N.T.S. 317 (1958). Ireland also has agreements for the avoidance of double taxation of the profits of shipping and air-transport companies with Norway, Ir. T.S. No. 12 of 1955, Pr. 3266, S.I. No. 98 of 1955; with Denmark, Ir. T.S. No. 13 of 1955, Pr. 3267, S.I. No. 97 of 1955; with Switzerland, Ir. T.S. No. 14 of 1960, Pr. 5857, S.I. No. 211 of 1959; and with South Africa, May 1, 1958, Ir. T.S. No. 13 of 1960, Pr. 5802, S.I. No. 210 of 1959, 398 U.N.T.S. 3 (1961).

[102] Rapport 69–75, CCH 2463–71.

[103] EEC Commission, Memorandum on the Action Programme for the Second Stage, para. 37 (1962).

[104] Individuals only are dealt with under the following articles of the Irish-German Convention (parenthetical references are to corresponding articles in the OEEC draft, as embodied in the first four reports of the Fiscal Committee): art. III, on permanent establishments of partnerships; art. XI, on income from professional services (art. VI); art. XII, on salaries and wages derived from the exercise of employment in one of the two countries (art. VII); art. XIII, on government pensions (art. VIII); art. XIV, on directors' fees (art. IX); art. XV, on non-government pensions (art. X); art. XVI, on income of entertainers and athletes (art. XI); art. XVII, on income from teaching or research; art. XVIII, on income of students or apprentices (art. XII); art. XIX, on annuities; art. XXI, on personal allowances and reliefs; art. XXII(3), on source of income of professional men or operators of ships or aircraft (art. VII[3]). See also art. XXV, on discrimination on the grounds of nationality (art. IV).

[105] Only an Irish subsidiary, not an Irish branch, can obtain the Irish tax relief for mines; see art. XXV(3); Finance (Profits of Certain Mines) (Temporary Relief from Taxation) Act, 1956 Acts 113, §§ 5–6; Finance (Miscellaneous Provisions) Act, 1956 Acts 807, § 5; Finance Act, 1960 Acts 483, § 32.

[106] Such a company is liable to Irish income tax, not corporation profits tax, on profits from sources outside Ireland.

[107] Art. II(1)(d)(ii)–II(1)(d)(iv).

[108] First Report, art. III; Final Report 1963, art. 4 and at 69.

applicable to income taxable in both countries.

Taxation only in the country of residence: Shipping and airline profits, interest, royalties

Enterprises entitled to the benefit of the Irish-German Agreement are taxed on income from operating ships and aircraft in international traffic only in the country in which their places of effective management are situated.[109]

Enterprises resident in only one of the two countries are exempt in the other country from tax on loan interest from sources there, insofar as the interest is reasonable.[110] The OECD model gives a country the right to tax interest arising there at a maximum rate of 10 per cent.[111] Ireland advocates the policy that interest should be exempt from tax in the country of source, to encourage foreign investment as far as the tax law of the country of residence will permit.[112] Reciprocal exemption from tax in the country of source is provided for royalty payments; for payments for the alienation of, or the use of, any copyright, patent, trademark, design, or know-how; and for the use of scientific equipment and information on scientific experience.[113] Both the Irish-German Agreement and the OECD model exempt from tax in the country of source payments for the supply of information, even if not secret, on industrial and commercial experience, if the amount is "fair and reasonable" and is not in excess of the arm's-length value[114] and not a concealed withdrawal of profits. However, if the interest, royalty, or other payment is attributable to a permanent establishment in the country of source, it is taxable there.[115]

The definition of a permanent establishment

A "permanent establishment" in the Irish-German Agreement and the OECD model means "a fixed place of business in which the business of the enterprise is wholly or partly carried on." It includes a place of management and other kinds of office, a branch, a factory, extractive operations, and construction sites

[109] Art. V. OEEC draft art. V is identical; cf. Final Report 1963, art. 8. Irish shipping and aircraft companies are also exempt from the capital element of the German municipal trade tax, which is based partly on income and partly on the capital value of business assets.

[110] Art. VII.

[111] OEEC draft art. XXI; Final Report 1963, art. 11. For a discussion of this compromise solution, see OEEC Fiscal Committee, Fourth Report 51–54. Interest is defined in substantially the same way in the OECD model and in the Irish-German Agreement, except that the latter does not require other income from money lent which national law treats as interest to be assimilated to interest. Both articles prevent concealed extraction of profits in the guise of interest.

[112] Ehrenzweig & Koch, Income Tax Treaties 139 (1949). The argument is that if the country in which the borrower resides taxes the interest, the creditor will take this tax into account in fixing the rate of interest, which may therefore become prohibitively high. This view assumes that the creditor will not take into account the tax in his country of residence. This assumption, which has wider implications, describes an illogical attitude but nevertheless may well be correct. The argument disregards the possibility of changes in the rate of tax in the country of source.

[113] Art. VII(1)–VII(3); OEEC draft art. XXII(2); Final Report 1963, art. 12.

[114] Arts. VII(4), VIII(4); OEEC draft arts. XXI, XXII; Final Report 1963, arts. 11, 12. Unlike the OECD model article, the provision in the Irish-German Agreement applies even where the recipient of the royalties is not an associated company, but it is unlikely to be used in such a case. Payments for the rental of movie films are considered royalties under the OECD model but are treated as "industrial and commercial profits" under the Irish-German Agreement, art. II(1)(b).

[115] Art. VIII(5); OEEC draft art. XXII; Final Report 1963, art. 12. Royalties for information and know-how transmitted through, but not originally obtained by, the permanent establishment are taxable in the country of source.

in existence for over a year.[116] Agents who habitually exercise authority to contract on behalf of the foreign company as their principal are "permanent establishments." By altering the terms of the agency agreement, the parties can make or prevent the principal from being liable to tax in the country of source, so the tax position may change with no difference of substance.[117] A company is not liable to local tax even if it keeps a stock of goods or operates facilities for storage, display, or delivery.[118] There is no liability to local tax if the only purpose of the agent or the office is to purchase goods or collect information. Brokers and independent agents who sell goods on behalf of a foreign company in the ordinary course of their business are not "permanent establishments," even if they habitually conclude sales on behalf of the company. The fact that one company is a subsidiary of another or controls it does not of itself make either company a permanent establishment of the other. Offices carrying on preparatory or auxiliary activities, such as advertising, research, or supplying information, and offices maintaining stocks of goods only for processing by another enterprise are not permanent establishments.[119]

Taxation of local-source income where a permanent establishment exists

If a company has a permanent establishment in the country of source, it is liable to local tax on the profits attributable to the permanent establishment. Under the Irish-German Agreement and the OECD model, it continues to be exempt from local tax on all profits not attributable to the permanent establishment.[120] Apart from the purely theoretical question of tax jurisdiction, the OECD Fiscal Committee has decided that because of the number of companies carrying on business in more than one country and the variety of their activities it is preferable not to tax income from sources separate from a permanent establishment merely because a permanent establishment exists. This is especially so in the EEC, since the number of companies doing business in several member states will increase. To tax such income "might interfere seriously with ordinary commercial processes and so be out of keeping with the long-term aims of the [Fiscal] Committee itself."[121] The amount of trade between Ireland and Germany is small by European standards, and the agreement probably adopted the principle of taxing only profits attributable to permanent establishments because of the views of the Fiscal Committee.

Calculation of profits of permanent establishments and associated companies

The ordinary rule is that a permanent establishment is taxed on the profits which it would have made if it had been an independent enterprise dealing at

[116] Art. II(1)(g); OEEC draft art. II; Final Report 1963, art. 5.

[117] Neumark Report, Rapport 73, CCH 2469, commenting on OEEC draft art. II. If this definition is combined with the rule exempting income not attributable to the permanent establishment from tax in the country of source, the question may arise whether, in relation to particular profits, the agent is acting in his capacity as a permanent establishment. For a discussion of the German concept of a permanent establishment, see Vogel, 34 Cahiers de Droit Fiscal International 233 (1957), and see generally Thibièrge, "Le Statut des Sociétés Etrangères," in 1 Le Statut de l'Etranger 375–99. Neither the Irish-German Agreement nor the OECD model refers to agents who maintain a stock of goods for the taxpaying enterprise.

[118] Art. II(1)(g)(iii); OEEC draft art. II(3); Final Report 1963, art. 5(3); cf. U.S.-Irish Double Taxation Convention, art. II(1)(e).

[119] OEEC Fiscal Committee, First Report 49; Final Report 1963, at 73–74.

[120] Art. III(1); OEEC draft art. XV; Final Report 1963, art. 7(1). Cf. U.S.-Irish Double Taxation Convention, art. III.

[121] OEEC Fiscal Committee, Third Report 35; Final Report 1963, at 80–82.

arm's length with its head office, less its expenses, including executive and general administrative expenses.[122] These profits are calculated on the basis of the market value of the goods and services passing between the permanent establishment and its head office, although the OECD model allows variations from this principle if justified by commercial usage.[123] The permanent establishment's share of the administrative expenses of the head office may be deductible in computing its profits, but payments to the head office for patents or money lent or for management normally are not deductible. Commission paid to the permanent establishment for services rendered locally is not included[124] in its profits, at least unless the company includes it. Profits from the sale abroad of goods purchased by a permanent establishment cannot be attributed to it.

Any company may be taxed in either country on the profits which it would have made but for conditions imposed in its commercial or financial relations with an associated company which would not have been imposed in dealings between independent enterprises.[125]

Immovable property, capital gains, taxes on capital and directors' fees

Income from immovable property may be taxed by the state in which the property is situated.[126] In general, gains from the sale of capital assets may be taxed only in the country of residence. However, a capital gain is taxable in the country of source if it is attributable to a permanent establishment there.[127] Taxes on capital may be imposed if the assets taxed are immovable property in the taxing country or are the assets of a permanent establishment, or if the assets are ships or aircraft and the effective management of the company is in the taxing country. In other cases taxes on capital may be imposed only in the country of residence of the taxpayer.[128]

Directors' fees may be taxed in the country in which the company is resident.[129] A German-resident director of an Irish-resident company will not be liable to German tax on his director's fees, even if the Irish personal allowances cause the effective rate of Irish tax to be very low. The tax credit system prevents this advantageous position's existing also in the case of an Irish-resident director of a German company.[130]

Dividends

The most important and most controversial provisions in any double taxation convention are the provisions dealing with interest and dividends and with income which is subject to taxation in both countries.[131] The problem of interest is solved if one accepts the view of the Irish government that interest should be taxed

[122] Art. III(3), III(4); OEEC draft art. XV; Final Report 1963, art. 7. See International Chamber of Commerce, Double Taxation in the Atlantic Community 9 (1962).

[123] The Irish-German Agreement has no provision corresponding to Final Report 1963, art. 7(4), or OEEC draft art. XV (4).

[124] These statements are based on the Fiscal Committee's comments; Third Report 37–39; Final Report 1963, at 83–85.

[125] Art. IV. See OEEC draft art. XVI, and Final Report 1963, art. 9, to the same effect.

[126] Art. IX; OEEC draft art. XIII; Final Report 1963, art. 6.

[127] Art. X; see Final Report 1963, art. 13.

[128] Art. XX; OEEC draft art. XIV; Final Report 1963, art. 22.

[129] Art. XIV; OEEC draft art. IX; Final Report 1963, art. 16.

[130] Under art. XXII, Germany exempts from tax Irish-source income which may be taxed in Ireland; Ireland merely gives a credit against Irish tax paid in Germany.

[131] See Brosh, 41 Cahiers de Droit Fiscal International 129–31 (1959); International Chamber of Commerce, Double Taxation in the Atlantic Community 10 (1962).

only in the country of residence. Dividends under the Irish-German Agreement are treated in different ways by the two countries.

Irish Taxation of Irish-Source Dividends

The right of Ireland to tax Irish-source dividends is limited only by the fact that dividends paid to individuals are exempt from Irish surtax.[132] No limit is placed on the extent to which Irish companies may pass on their income tax to German-resident shareholders, nor is there a limit on taxation of local-source profits of local companies. Since the tax deducted from Irish-source dividends is not, in German tax theory, a tax on the shareholder, Germany did not ask for a clause such as that in the OECD model[133] limiting the right of the country of source to tax dividends.

German Taxation of Irish-Source Dividends

A German-resident limited company is exempt from German tax on a dividend paid by an Irish-resident company in which the German company owns 25 per cent or more of the voting shares. Also, no German tax is payable on the shares on which the dividend is paid. The exemption from German tax applies whether the Irish company has retained the income tax on the dividend or paid the declared amount of the dividend in full, "free of tax."[134] If the German shareholder owns less than 25 per cent of the voting shares in the Irish company or is an individual, 18 per cent of the net dividend received is credited against German tax on the dividend. The credit against German tax varies in relation to the gross dividend, in accordance with the effective rate[135] at which Irish tax is deducted from the dividend.

A German company which receives a dividend from an Irish subsidiary pays no tax on it, whether it is redistributed or not. If it is redistributed, the shareholders are liable to tax on it in the ordinary way.

The Problem of Irish Tax on Dividends

From the point of view of Irish tax law, the 18 per cent credit against German tax does not give the German shareholder full relief against double taxation. Irish law regards the income tax paid by the company as having been paid on behalf of the shareholders.[136] Whether the Irish company deducts tax from the gross dividends which it declares or not, Irish tax law holds that income tax on the dividends has been borne by the shareholders at the standard rate in force and that the credit should equal the tax at the standard rate on the gross amount of the dividend or, if the declared amount

[132] Art. VI(1). Dividends are dealt with by Irish-German Agreement, arts. VI, XXII; cf. OEEC draft art. XX; Final Report 1963, art. 10.

[133] OEEC draft art. XX(2); Final Report 1963, art. 10. In the OECD model, it is expressly stated that the provisions dealing with dividends shall not affect the taxation of the company paying them. The OECD model proposes that the country of source should be allowed to impose tax at a maximum rate of 5% of the gross amount of intercorporate dividends if the shareholder company owns at least 25% of the capital of the payor company, and 15% in all other cases.

[134] A German-resident individual receiving a dividend from an Irish-resident company is exempt from Irish surtax; art. IV(1). See also art. XXII(2)(b).

[135] Apart from changes in the standard rate itself, the rate at which tax may be deducted from the dividend by the Irish company varies with the proportion of the profits derived, free of any liability to tax, from exports. The credit is 18% of the gross dividend, where the dividend is paid wholly out of profits from exports from Ireland and so is exempt from Irish tax.

[136] See the analysis of the effect of the Irish system of deduction of tax from dividends in Chapter Eight.

is paid in full, on the "grossed-up" amount of the dividend.[137] At current Irish tax rates, 18 per cent of the net dividend is a smaller percentage[138] of the gross or "grossed-up" dividend than the tax deducted from the latter.

The German tax system does not give a German shareholder in a foreign company a credit for the tax paid by the company on its profits, as distinct from a "direct" credit for the foreign tax paid by withholding or otherwise by the shareholder on the dividend itself. A shareholder needs no credit for the German company tax paid by a German company because a reduced rate of company tax is paid on distributed profits. Continental tax theory distinguishes sharply between taxes on the company and taxes on the shareholder. Although under the Irish system the shareholder bears the economic burden of income tax on distributed profits if the tax is deducted by the company, tax lawyers from Continental Europe are reluctant to regard the tax deducted from the dividend as being a tax on the shareholders because the income tax is, in law, paid by the company. They therefore regard the gross or "grossed-up" amount of the dividend under the Irish system as little more than a fiction. The real amount of the dividend is regarded as the net amount, on which no tax has been paid by the shareholder and in respect of which, therefore, no direct tax credit can be given.[139] The shareholder gets only a deduction from taxable income instead of a credit for tax paid. Legally, the reasoning is correct. The compromise agreed on is that a fixed percentage of the net dividend received is to be credited against German tax. In looking at the two systems from the point of view of harmonization of tax laws, the economic position, not the legal technicalities, will be considered. The problem of Irish-source dividends arises only because of technical differences in the laws of the two countries involved, and harmonization of tax techniques and laws within the EEC should help to solve it.[140] Substantially similar provisions dealing with dividends in bilateral treaties are essential for the adoption of a multilateral double taxation treaty.

German Taxation of German-Source Dividends

The maximum German tax on a dividend paid by a German company to an Irish-resident company holding at least 25 per cent of its voting shares is now 25 per cent. Dividends paid to an Irish-resident individual and to an Irish company holding less than 25 per cent of the payor company's voting shares may be taxed at a maximum rate of 15 per cent.[141] Under the agreement or the

[137] The "grossed-up" amount of the dividend is that sum which, after deduction of tax at the standard rate, would yield the net amount paid.

[138] How much smaller depends on the standard rate in force. Eighteen per cent of the net dividend is 18(1-R)% of the gross or "grossed-up" dividend, where R is the standard rate of income tax (expressed as a decimal) in force in Ireland.

[139] Cf. Biddle v. Commissioner, 302 U.S. 573 (1938).

[140] See OEEC Fiscal Committee, Fourth Report, para. 14, and Neumark Report, Rapport 69–75, CCH 2465–71. In Final Report 1963, para. 33, the OECD Fiscal Committee points out that its provision on dividends (art. 10; OEEC draft art. XX) must be supplemented by special clauses in the case of the United Kingdom, Ireland, Belgium, and Germany, among others, because these countries relieve economic double taxation of distributed profits. The Neumark Report suggests that all EEC member states should give such relief. For a general review of tax treatment of dividends in Britain, the United States, and the Six, see "Overseas Taxes and Investors," The Economist, July 7, 1962, p. 62; see also "Stiffer Taxes on Foreign Dividends?" The Economist, March 13, 1965, p. 1162.

[141] But see art. VI(2). In Germany, distributed profits of large companies now are taxed at 15% and undistributed profits at 51%. See U.K.-German Double Taxation Convention,

OECD model, there is no limit to the tax which may be imposed on dividends paid on shares effectively connected with a permanent establishment in the country of source of the dividends.[142] The exemption from German tax for dividends paid to a company which owns 25 per cent or more of the voting shares of the payor company effectively extends to Irish parent companies the exemption from economic double taxation given to inter-corporate dividends by German law. Germany now imposes company tax at the relatively low rate of 15 per cent on distributed profits and imposes fairly high taxes on shareholders. If the shareholder is not a German resident, Germany must recoup from the shareholder the tax which it has waived by imposing a low rate of tax on distributed profits.[143]

The maximum German tax on German-source dividends paid to an Irish company holding at least 25 per cent of the payor company's voting shares is determined by the amount that the German company tax rate on distributed profits is less than the rate for undistributed profits.[144] The OECD model has a similar scheme.[145]

Irish Taxation of German-Source Dividends

Ireland gives a credit against Irish tax for the German tax paid on a German-source dividend[146] and for the German company tax. If the dividend is paid on shares entitled to a fixed rate of interest and a share of the profits (in Ireland, called "participating preference shares"), the German company tax is taken into account insofar as the dividend exceeds the fixed rate.[147] The amount of the credit for German company tax is that proportion of the company tax on the profits from which the dividend is paid, which was paid on the proportion of those profits represented by the dividend, i.e., which was paid on the amount of the dividend "grossed-up" by the company tax.[148] At present the German taxes are

---

Aug. 18, 1954, art. VI, Cmd. No. 9570 (T.S. No. 59 of 1955), [1955] 1 Stat. Instr. 972 (No. 1203), replaced by U.K.-German Double Taxation Convention, Nov. 26, 1964, Cmd. No. 2547 (ratifications not yet exchanged).

[142] Art. VI(5); OEEC draft art. XX(4); OEEC Fourth Report 37; Final Report 1963, art. 10(4) and at 94. The wording differs slightly; the Irish-German provision reads: "[if] such dividends are attributable to that permanent establishment"; the OECD model reads: "attributable to that permanent establishment with which the holding by virtue of which the dividends are paid is effectively connected." This is explained in the Fiscal Committee's Fourth Report at 45–46 as referring to dividends paid on holdings forming part of the permanent establishment's assets or otherwise effectively connected with it; cf. Final Report 1963, at 103. The definitions of dividends differ; see art. II(h); OEEC draft, art. XX(3); Final Report 1963, art. 10(3).

[143] See OEEC Fiscal Committee, Fourth Report 50; Final Report 1963, at 105. In the U.K.-German Convention of 1954, the maximum rate of German tax on dividends was fixed at 15%, subject to a similar provision for alteration if the rates of company tax on distributed and undistributed profits ceased to differ from each other by one-third; S.I. No. 1203 of 1955, art. VI.

[144] If at least 28% less, the maximum rate is 25%; if 20%–28% less, the rate may be from 15%–20%; if 5%–20% less, the rate is 15%; if less than 5% less, the rate is 10%; art. VI(3).

[145] Under the OECD model, the corresponding maximum rate of tax on dividends in the country of source is 5% and the maximum rate is also 15% for dividends paid to individuals or to companies directly holding less than 25% of the capital shares of the payor company; OEEC draft art. XX; Final Report 1963, art. 10.

[146] Including a dividend paid by a GmbH and distributions on investment trust certificates; art. II(h).

[147] Art. XXII(1). Neither of the two German capital taxes—the capital tax itself or the capital element in the municipal trade tax—may be credited against Irish tax.

[148] After having been grossed up by the amount of tax withheld on the dividend itself; Finance Act, 1958 Acts 553, Second Schedule, paras. 7–10.

a company tax on distributed profits at 15 per cent, a municipal trade tax, and a withholding tax on the dividend at 25 per cent, the maximum rate permitted by the agreement[149] and the usual withholding rate in Germany for non-residents.

Relief from double taxation for income taxable in the country of source

Double taxation arises if there is no provision to resolve cases of double residence[150] and if income is subject to taxation in the country of source. Dividends, income of permanent establishments, and certain types of individual income other than interest are taxable in the country of source, under the Irish-German Agreement.

Under the agreement, Germany deals with income which "may be taxed" in Ireland in two ways. In the first, dividends paid to companies with small shareholdings or to individuals, Irish-source income of double-resident individuals, and Irish government pensions paid to German nationals are all dealt with by the tax credit method, by which unilateral relief is given in Germany. The full Irish tax is credited, except in the case of dividends. In the second, dividends paid to German companies with large shareholdings in Irish companies and all other income liable to Irish tax are exempted from German tax. They may, however, be taken into consideration in determining the appropriate rate of the progressive German taxes on individuals and on small private companies owned by individuals.[151] Germany therefore departs from the principle of equal tax treatment of German residents irrespective of source of income, first, by giving a tax exemption instead of a tax credit, and second, by giving a credit against German tax for certain dividends which have not, in German tax theory, borne Irish tax.

Any Irish-source income[152] of a taxpayer resident in Germany and not a double resident, which under the agreement "may" be taxed in Ireland, is exempt from German tax.[153] Since the Irish-source income need not have actually borne Irish tax to be exempt from German tax, this is a tax-sparing or matching credit provision. The entire profits of an Irish operation of a German company are exempt from German tax, even if they have borne no Irish tax because they were derived from exports. An Irish branch of a German company can therefore get the full benefit of the Irish tax concessions and an Irish subsidiary is unnecessary. However, to be exempt from German tax, it is essential that the income should be regarded by German law as income from sources within Ireland.[154]

Ireland gives credit against Irish tax for German tax on German-source income,[155] whether the German tax is imposed directly or by deduction, but Ire-

[149] Art. VI.

[150] Such as OEEC draft art. III on fiscal domicile; Final Report 1963, art. 3.

[151] Known as "exemption with progression." If the Irish-source income were not taken into account in computing the German rate of tax, this would be "full exemption."

[152] And "any item of capital situated in Ireland which according to this Convention *may be* taxed in Ireland." Art. XXII(2)(a)(aa). (Emphasis supplied.) Capital gains are not taxed as such in Ireland, but the German capital tax, in the absence of a convention, would be payable on the Irish assets of a German resident. Due to the words emphasized, the fact that Ireland does not impose a capital tax is irrelevant.

[153] Art. XXII(2).

[154] The location of the source of income is often a problem in international fiscal law; see Richards, 42 Cahiers de Droit Fiscal International 175, 178 (1960); Owens, "United States Income Tax Treaties: Their Role in Relieving Double Taxation," 17 Rutgers L. Rev. 428 (1963).

[155] Art. XXII(1).

land does not give an exemption from tax for any such income.[156] The credit given is the "ordinary" credit,[157] under which the total tax is paid at the higher of the two effective tax rates. For companies, the most important cases where this credit is given are German-source dividends and income of German permanent establishments.

Alternative methods of relief

The OECD model contemplates[158] the use of either the "exemption with progression" method or the "ordinary" credit method. Exemption with progression produces the same result as does the method by which the state of residence gives up its right to tax *part* of the income. Relief from taxation in the country of residence for income specially exempt from tax in the country of source, as an investment incentive, can be given either by corresponding exemption in the country of residence or by providing that credit will be given in the country of residence for the tax "spared" in the country of source. In the latter case the extent of the tax concession must be clearly ascertainable. The OECD model leaves the choice between the exemption and tax credit methods to the states concerned. If the amount of investment and lending in one country by enterprises of the other is substantially greater than the amount moving the other direction, the predominantly capital-exporting country, as the country of residence, usually is unwilling to waive the right to tax repatriated profits.[159]

[156] Except under art. V, on profits from ships and aircraft, and art. IX, on immovable property.

[157] Finance Act, 1958 Acts 553, Second Schedule, paras. 4, 5.

[158] OEEC draft arts. XXIII, XXIV; Final Report 1963, arts. 23A, 23B. The wording permits simple alterations to provide for the "full exemption" method and the "full credit" method.

[159] On double taxation between debtor and creditor countries, see League of Nations Economic and Financial Commission, Report on Double Taxation 45–51 (1923). In the U-K.-German Double Taxation Convention, where the technical problems were essentially the same as in the case of the Irish-German Convention but the amount of reciprocal investment was better balanced, Germany agreed not to use the tax credit method. Germany exempted from her tax all United Kingdom–source income subject to United Kingdom tax, including dividends paid by United Kingdom companies and United Kingdom–source income of double residents; Double Taxation Relief (Taxes on Income) (Federal Republic of Germany) Order, 1955, art. XVI, [1955] 1 Stat. Instr. 972 (No. 1203).

The principle of exemption may be becoming less popular. Even when the volume of reciprocal investment and trading is substantially the same for the two countries, the exemption method is unsuitable if the effective tax rates differ substantially, since it diverts investment and taxable activities into the country with the lower tax rates if exchange controls, freedom of movement of labor, and other legal rules permit. Such capital movements may cause balance-of-payments difficulties, reduce the tax base, and slow capital formation and fixed investment in the country with the higher tax rate.

If local tax is not imposed or if foreign-source profits of foreign companies owned by residents and the profits are not repatriated, double taxation cannot arise, and profits can be accumulated and reinvested and full advantage taken of tax concessions, even if no double taxation relief exists. (Some tax concession legislation applies only if the profits benefiting from it are distributed within a limited period. This is not the position in Ireland, except apparently with regard to surtax.) It is a question of policy whether a tax incentive should benefit distributed profits, since the result may not be reinvestment but a deterrent to investment if it does not do so. If the country of residence has no tax-sparing provisions, it may be possible to finance a foreign manufacturing subsidiary through loans made to a foreign holding company. Profits up to the amount of the initial capital invested can then be repatriated by way of repayment of the loan, and later by way of a loan from the holding company to the parent. The feasibility of this depends on the national law of the shareholder's country of residence.

Chapter 11

Unilateral Relief from Double Taxation

WHEN UNILATERAL RELIEF IS NECESSARY AND ADVANTAGEOUS

States usually give their residents unilateral relief against double taxation of foreign-source income subject to foreign tax.[1] In an economic union where there is no double taxation convention between the country of source and the country of residence, this relief is necessary to prevent cumulative double taxation and to avoid seriously inhibiting freedom of establishment and interstate trade and is desirable to insure capital-export neutrality. Since it is often difficult for capital-importing and capital-exporting countries, whose interests with regard to the taxation of income are different, to negotiate double taxation conventions, unilateral relief in the latter type of country[2] is important.

Unilateral relief is most often given by capital-exporting countries because of its effect on profits from foreign investment. Double taxation treaties are less common among capital-importing countries than among capital-exporting countries. Countries which are short of capital seldom analyze the effects of different types of foreign-source income on balance of payments and economic development, and they seldom give unilateral relief, since it may encourage investment abroad instead of in local industry and thus reduce their revenues. Relief may not have this latter effect in practice, since the countries most attractive for portfolio investment usually have high taxes on local-source income. Unilateral relief by a country short of capital may merely result in the substitution of a fairly high tax rate in the potential country of source for a very high over-all tax rate due to cumulative double taxation. However, residents of capital-importing countries sometimes are prepared to accept high taxes on investment elsewhere rather than low taxes on investment at home because of non-fiscal factors such as the small size of the domestic capital market or political instability.

Residents of a capital-importing country who are potential investors abroad are, typically, institutional investors or small portfolio investors, not direct investors. They are seldom in a position to decide whether the profits of a foreign company in which they are shareholders should be distributed, so they usually cannot avoid tax in their country of residence by accumulating profits in the foreign company. Denial of unilateral relief is therefore likely to be more effective as a deterrent to foreign investment by portfolio investors than by a large manufacturing company, which can accumu-

[1] Only where a country taxes income from foreign sources is unilateral relief necessary. The term unilateral relief does not include tax concessions for local-source income flowing abroad.

[2] Owens, "United States Income Tax Treaties: Their Role in Relieving Double Taxation," 17 Rutgers L. Rev. 428, 430 (1963), says that United States treaties play only a "marginal" role in relieving double taxation, because of the United States unilateral relief.

late the profits of a foreign subsidiary. However, it may be important to maintain the foreign portfolio of institutional investors, which may be a substantial part of the external assets of a capital-importing country. The lack of a large capital market at home on which portfolio investments could be made may make it inequitable to deny unilateral relief to a resident who invests abroad or may divert investment into unproductive domestic assets.

Even in countries which typically do not export capital, unilateral relief is necessary to avoid double taxation of profits from exports subject to tax in the country of destination. Unilateral relief should prevent double taxation of foreign-source income of individuals temporarily resident abroad[3] or of foreign-source income derived from services performed abroad. Even if a double taxation convention exists, the right of the country importing the goods to tax the profits of a permanent sales establishment of the exporting enterprise is unlimited; relief is even more necessary if no convention exists. Unlike unilateral relief for foreign-source investment income, unilateral relief in these cases benefits the country giving it, even if no reciprocal concession of any kind is available.

In practice, unilateral relief is usually given in both capital-importing and capital-exporting countries if there is some compensating factor, such as exports, if the balance-of-payments position is strong and there is pressure in favor of foreign investment, or if there are political reasons for unilateral relief. A sound system of unilateral relief relieves profits from exports from double taxation[4] and distinguishes between foreign investment in the national interest, e.g., that which aids the balance of payments, and foreign investment of funds which could be used at home. In a country with a high rate of direct taxation, equality between taxpayers and the need to avoid unduly inhibiting foreign investment may make a more comprehensive system of unilateral relief necessary.

METHODS OF UNILATERAL RELIEF

Unilateral relief usually is given in a particular country by the same method as relief under a convention. There is no reason in principle why unilateral relief must be given by way of exemption or credit directly related to the incidence or the amount of foreign tax borne by the income in question. Exemption from local tax on foreign-source profits avoids double taxation.[5] A simple but less effective method is to impose tax in the country of residence on foreign-source income only at a reduced rate, regardless of the incidence or the amount of the foreign tax.[6] None of these methods normally is called unilateral relief, but their function is identical.[7]

[3] OECD Fiscal Committee, Draft Double Taxation Convention on Income and Capital (1963), art. 15(2), is intended to facilitate the international movement of qualified personnel; para. 22. See also "Stiffer Tax on Foreign Dividends?" The Economist, March 13, 1965, p. 1162; "Should Britain Tax Overseas Investment?" The Economist, Feb. 13, 1965, p. 687.

[4] This is not contrary to the rules of GATT.

[5] This is the system used in France for industrial and commercial profits of a business carried on outside France. This is the practical effect of the Irish tax concessions for profits from exports, although the concessions apply only to foreign-source income derived from exports and although they are given irrespective of the place of the sale (and thus the "source" of the profits) and of liability to foreign tax.

[6] This is the system used in Belgium.

[7] Klimowsky, "Unilateral Measures for the Avoidance of Double Taxation, Especially as Regards Fiscal Aspects of the Relationship Between Capital Exporting Countries and Countries in the Process of Development," 43 Cahiers de Droit Fiscal International 7, 13–14 (1961).

Countries can give unilateral relief merely by allowing the foreign tax as a deduction from the gross foreign income. This method treats the foreign tax as an expense of obtaining the income taxed, and it seems reasonable if no more extensive allowance, taking into account the fiscal nature of the payment, is to be given. However, it is unfortunately doubtful if foreign tax is even allowable as a deduction in Britain and Ireland in the absence of a treaty provision,[8] and in practice the point is dealt with expressly in double taxation conventions.

Certain countries, such as the United States, the United Kingdom, and France, give a greater measure of unilateral relief or have special tax provisions for income from countries with which they are or have been closely associated. In some countries companies whose function is only to hold shares or to do business abroad are subject to special tax provisions.

If adequate unilateral relief is given, double taxation treaties merely simplify administrative and accounting tasks and so facilitate international trade and investment.[9] They also provide guarantees, e.g., against discriminatory taxation.

Unilateral tax-sparing or matching credit provisions are unusual.[10] Unilateral tax-sparing provisions would transfer the control of the tax position to the less developed countries, create practical difficulties of computation and greater likelihood of evasion by the less developed countries, and contradict the principles of jurisdiction to tax of some capital-exporting countries. These difficulties do not arise if tax-sparing is dealt with in a double taxation treaty. Tax-sparing is not relief against double taxation but unilateral action to encourage investment abroad.

UNILATERAL RELIEF

Ireland

The U.K.-Irish Double Income Taxation Agreement[11] deals with most of the investment abroad by Irish residents and with exports to the country which has been the largest buyer of Irish exports.[12] Ireland concluded no other double taxation treaty until 1950.[13] Few other European countries have had so few treaties, so the inadequacy of the unilateral relief given by Ireland can be ascribed to the giving of priority, somewhat shortsightedly, to revenue considerations.

Unilateral relief is given, on a discretionary basis, for income from employment performed wholly abroad where Irish tax at the full rate would cause

[8] See I.R.C. v. Dowdall O'Mahoney & Co., 33 Tax Cas. 259 (1952).

[9] Treaties may provide that credit may be given for foreign taxes not within the scope of unilateral relief. See Klimowsky, "Unilateral Measures . . .," 43 Cahiers de Droit Fiscal International 7, 23–26 (1961). The same rule usually applies even in the case of a convention, though special provisions may deal with taxes on capital and on capital gains.

[10] Greece grants its tax concessions only to enterprises from countries whose unilateral relief methods do not nullify the concessions; Klimowsky, "Unilateral Measures . . .," 43 Cahiers de Droit Fiscal International 7, 29 (1961). The subsequent remarks are based largely on Klimowsky, id. at 31ff. See Royal Commission on Taxation of Profits and Income, Final Report, Cmd. No. 9474, ch. 25 and Memorandum of Dissent, paras. 167–73 (1955).

[11] April 14, 1926, U.K. Income Tax Act, 1952, 15 & 16 Geo. 6 & 1 Eliz. 2, c. 10, Eighteenth Schedule, pt. I, Irish Finance Act, 1926 Pub. Stat. 401, 441, First Schedule, pt. I.

[12] Although the fact that the world income of an Irish resident is liable to Irish tax makes unilateral relief all the more necessary where no treaty exists, it also means that the authorities have no incentive to give unilateral relief in order to encourage remittances; cf. Brosh, 41 Cahiers de Droit Fiscal International 197 (1959).

[13] U.S.-Irish Double Taxation Convention, Sept. 13, 1949, [1951] 2 U.S.T. & O.I.A. 2303, T.I.A.S. No. 2356, Irish Finance Act, 1950 Acts 369, 411, Second Schedule, Ir. T.S. No. 7 of 1951, Pr. 1081, 127 U.N.T.S. 89 (1952).

"hardship."[14] This allows relief from double taxation for Irish residents working abroad or living on foreign-source pensions which are liable to tax abroad. Further relief against double taxation is given to "returned emigrants"— individuals who have resided for ten years in the United States, various countries of the British Commonwealth, or some British possessions, but who have become residents[15] of Ireland. The relief is discretionary and is limited to the amount of the foreign tax or the amount of Irish tax at the individual's effective rate of tax on the income in question, whichever is less.[16]

Neither of these provisions applies to companies, so even foreign operations which benefit the Irish balance of payments may be doubly taxed. Ireland is therefore unsuitable as a site for "base company" operations, except where it is possible to accumulate profits from equity participation in foreign companies in an Irish-incorporated company not managed and controlled in Ireland. This can be done only if the Irish company can hold its directors' meetings in a country which does not regard this as making the company resident there. Under this arrangement the foreign-source income of the Irish company would be liable only to corporation profits tax[17] in Ireland. Ireland has never tried to attract holding companies.[18]

Belgium[19]

A double taxation treaty between Ireland and Belgium is being negotiated. Until it comes into force, relief from double taxation of Irish-source income is given unilaterally in Belgium. Belgium does not use the tax credit in giving treaty relief or unilateral relief.

The profits of a foreign branch of a Belgian company are liable to Belgian tax, and relief against double taxation is given by reducing the rate of Belgian company tax to one-quarter of its normal rate, i.e., to 7.5 per cent. On distributed profits in excess of 5 million francs ($100,000), this is raised to 8.75 per cent.[20] The income must have borne some foreign tax similar to the Belgian company tax, but the reduction is given irrespective of the rate of foreign tax paid; the relief therefore may be either excessive or inadequate. The system has the advantage of administrative simplicity. Income from foreign immovable property and from services, including provision of know-how, is treated in the same way as ordinary business income.

[14] Finance Act, 1931 Pub. Stat. 405, § 5. Relief might well be given as a matter of policy to individuals who have gone abroad for training, since hardship is likely to result in such cases.

[15] To obtain relief, individuals must be domiciled and "ordinarily resident" in Ireland, as well as being merely resident; Finance Act, 1941 Acts 215, § 3.

[16] Ibid., limited by Finance Act, 1943 Acts 197, § 2, and extended by Finance Act, 1954 Acts 571, § 11, and by Finance Act, 1955 Acts 403, Second Schedule, pt. II, para. 5(3).

[17] Now 23%; Finance Bill, 1966.

[18] Solo, "Economics of the International Base Company," 14 Nat'l Tax J. 70, 76–78 (1961), points out that a country has little to gain by persuading companies merely to incorporate there. However, there may be substantial advantages to a country's giving tax incentives to companies to set up their headquarters there, although taxes will be only one element in headquarters costs. See Kauffman, "Régime fiscal des holdings, sociétés de placements et fonds communs de placements," Neumark Report, Annexe D.

[19] For the position prior to the reform of 1962, see van Rolleghem, 41 Cahiers de Droit Fiscal International 214–16 (1959), and van Hoorn, id. at 216.

[20] "Survey of Belgian Income Taxes," 4 European Taxation 175, 196 (1964). On the new Belgian Law of Nov. 20, 1962, see generally [1962] Moniteur Belge 10674 n.1; Chambre des Représentatifs, Projet de Loi partant réforme des Impôts sur les Revenus-Exposé des Motifs, Doc. No. 264 (1961–62). Law of June 21, 1927, gives special treatment to Belgian companies for income from sources in the Republic of the Congo.

A foreign subsidiary of a Belgian company generally is not liable to Belgian tax on its profits from foreign sources, but it may be taxed on any unusual or gratuitous profits which it has received directly or indirectly from the Belgian parent.[21] To be a foreign company, under Belgian tax law, the subsidiary must be incorporated elsewhere and must have its head office outside Belgium.

Dividends paid by a foreign company to a Belgian company are liable, after allowing a deduction for any foreign tax paid on the dividend, to a prepayment of tax at the rate of 15 per cent. They are not liable to substantial further tax in the hands of the parent company or to the ordinary withholding tax when the parent company distributes them;[22] this rule is the same as the one on distribution of profits by a Belgian subsidiary. The rule for foreign companies is the same, regardless of the extent of the Belgian company's shareholding.

Interest and other income from moveable property, such as debts and patents, are liable to a similar prepayment of 15 per cent, which is credited against the tax payable by the recipient. The recipient also gets a credit of a fixed amount of 15 per cent of the net sum received in Belgium for foreign tax, if some foreign tax has been paid on the income in question.

France

In principle a French-resident company is not liable to French tax on foreign-source profits of independent establishments abroad, if the foreign operations form a complete "commercial cycle." However, foreign-source dividends, interest, and royalties are liable to French tax. No unilateral relief is given, except that the foreign taxes are allowed as a deduction from taxable income. A double taxation convention probably will soon be concluded between France and Ireland.

Italy

At present there are no Irish-Italian double taxation treaty negotiations, and so the liability to double taxation of the Irish-source income of an Italian-resident company is governed by Italian law. Italy has concluded few double taxation treaties since the territoriality principle is generally the basis of tax jurisdiction there. However, some foreign-source income is liable to Italian tax. There is no provision for unilateral relief as such, but foreign taxes are deductible.

The company tax is imposed on the entire income of a company, including foreign-source dividends, subject to the usual tax reduction for inter-corporate dividends. Income tax is not imposed on dividends, but is imposed on interest which, though paid from abroad, is regarded as Italian-source income because it is paid under a contract made in Italy or because the debt is secured by a mortgage on property situated in Italy. Class "B" income tax is imposed on commercial and industrial profits, including royalties, wherever made, unless they are made by

[21] Law of Nov. 20, 1962, art. 6(4), [1962] Moniteur Belge 10674. There is the usual provision for the rewriting of the accounts of a company on an arm's-length basis where a Belgian company controls or is controlled by a foreign company, or both are under the same ownership or under the same management even if the ownership is different.

[22] Law of Nov. 20, 1962, art. 34, [1962] Moniteur Belge 10674, defines manufacturing companies as those whose principal activity is extracting, manufacturing, or transforming raw materials and products and which have less than 50% of their paid-up capital invested in other companies. Such a company pays company tax at 30% on only 5% of the net dividends received by it. Trading or investment companies pay company tax on 15% of the net dividends they receive. This is the effect: in theory, they have a deduction of 95% or 85% of the net dividend (i.e., after deduction of the 15% prepayment) against their taxable income.

a foreign permanent establishment with its own administration and accounts.[23]

Luxembourg

Luxembourg has few double taxation treaties, and none is contemplated with Ireland at present. Companies are liable to three taxes: the national income tax, which is the most important; a flat-rate tax on wealth; and a municipal tax based on profits, wealth, and sometimes payroll. In general, foreign-source profits of a Luxembourg company are liable to national income tax, and foreign taxes are merely deductible. A draft law presently before the Luxembourg Parliament exempts from the national income tax half of the foreign-source income of a permanent establishment abroad and of foreign mines, certain agricultural activities, and rents from foreign sources, but it gives no relief for dividends from foreign sources.

In Luxembourg a company which holds at least 25 per cent of the shares of another Luxembourg company is exempt from tax on the dividends it receives from the subsidiary. This is merely to avoid economic double taxation of inter-corporate dividends. There is a special provision[24] for holding companies. They may own any kind of shares, bonds, or debentures, and may own and license industrial and commercial property. They are subject only to an annual tax based on the value of the shares they hold and two taxes on their own capital, all at low rates. Such a company may be either a stock company or a limited liability company, but to be eligible for the most favorable tax regime, the former must be used. This regime[25] applies only to Luxembourg companies which have assets in excess of $20 million and which have been set up by a foreign company. These are subject to special low taxes on interest and dividends paid out, and foreign directors and managers are taxed on their salaries.

The Netherlands

At present, a double taxation convention is being negotiated between Ireland and the Netherlands. Until it comes into force, relief from double taxation for Irish-source income is given in the Netherlands by an unusual type of unilateral relief. Treaty relief in the Netherlands is usually given by the same method. Resident companies and individuals are liable to Netherlands tax on their world income. Even if no foreign income tax is in fact payable, because of allowances or reliefs, relief is given if the income remains in principle liable to tax; but no relief is given if the income is exempt from foreign tax. The application of this principle to the Irish tax concessions for profits from exports is not clear, because export profits are completely tax-free, but there is no concession for profits made on the Irish market by a company which is primarily engaged in exporting.[26] However, unilateral relief would probably be given for profits exempt from Irish tax. If the foreign income is not liable to a tax analogous to Dutch income tax or company tax, the foreign tax is deductible, and no unilateral relief is given.

[23] Law on Direct Taxes, Jan. 29, 1958, art. 82. See Croxatto, "Taxation of Foreign Income in Italy," 16 Bull. Int'l Bur. Fisc. Doc. 193 (1963).

[24] Law of July 31, 1929 (Loi sur le régime fiscal des sociétés de participations financières); see Kauffman, "Régime fiscal des holdings, sociétés de placements et fonds communs de placements," Neumark Report, Annexe D.

[25] Law of Dec. 27, 1937; Decree of Dec. 17, 1938.

[26] "Facilities granted by developing countries for stimulating investments will not, as a rule, constitute an impediment to exemption" from Dutch tax; H. Baron van Lawick, 44 Cahiers de Droit Fiscal International 211, 214 (1961). See also id. at 216, 217, and 41 Cahiers de Droit Fiscal International 216–19 (1959).

Unilateral relief is given by calculating the tentative Dutch tax on the total income from all sources, no relief being given for double taxation. The foreign-source income is given a credit at the effective rate of tax so calculated for the whole income.[27] For the flat-rate company tax, this means that all foreign-source income is free of Dutch tax. The exemption cannot be greater than the tax which would have been payable on the foreign-source income in the absence of unilateral relief. For income from business carried on abroad through a permanent establishment[28] or a permanent representative, profits from land and buildings and mortgages on land and buildings situated abroad,[29] and certain foreign-source income of individuals, the relief is given irrespective of the rate of foreign tax. The unilateral relief does not apply to foreign-source royalties, interest, or dividends, but if the foreign company pays a tax similar to the Dutch company tax and the Dutch parent company owns at least 25 per cent of its paid-up capital,[30] the dividends are exempt from Dutch company tax. If the Dutch parent owns less than 25 per cent of the shares, relief will be given only if the shares are part of the assets of a permanent establishment abroad. In this case the dividends are part of the permanent establishment's trading income, and Dutch tax will be imposed on its net profits.[31]

[27] Decree of Aug. 30, 1962, [1962] Staatsblad, No. 344, substantially re-enacting Decree of Feb. 11, 1953, No. 186, [1953] Staatsblad, No. 30, amended by Decree of June 23, 1958, No. 1, [1958] Staatsblad, No. 121, art. 3, which provides that the calculation is as follows:

$$\frac{\text{Relief}}{\text{Tentative tax on total income}} = \frac{\text{Foreign taxable income}}{\text{Total income}}$$

Therefore, the relief is:

$$\text{Foreign income} \times \frac{\text{Tentative tax on total income}}{\text{Total income}}$$

Foreign losses or "unused" foreign profits (i.e., where there is a foreign profit which exceeds a loss on Netherlands-source income) may be carried forward for up to six years; art. 3(2), 3(3). A translation of the 1953 and 1958 decrees is given in "Unilateral Double Taxation Relief Provisions in the Netherlands," 1 European Taxation, No. 4, at 7 (1961), and some explanatory notes are found in id., No. 8, at 3.

[28] Defined in art. 6 in substantially the same manner as in double taxation treaties.

[29] Art. 1(2)(b), 1(2)(g), 1(2)(h). The relief is given also for income from various activities abroad of individuals resident in the Netherlands.

[30] Provided the shares have been held for a year. Two types of investment company are also exempt from Dutch tax on foreign-source dividends. This percentage may be reduced to 5%; see International Bureau of Fiscal Documentation, Annual Report, 1962, at 23–24.

[31] Double taxation arrangements with Germany are discussed on pp. 272–81.

Part V

STATE AIDS

Chapter 12

State Aids and Regional Economic Policy in the EEC

TAX CONCESSIONS FOR EXPORTS[1]

The profits made by a foreign investor in a less developed region or country are vitally affected by the extent to which the local economic development policy results in the giving of state aid, in particular, in the form of tax concessions for exports, which are specially advantageous to the investor but present special problems under the EEC Treaty.

Only one of the tax provisions[2] of the EEC Treaty, Article 98, mentions direct taxation. The systems of indirect taxes with refunds on exports and levies on imports which existed in the member states in 1958[3] were likely to aid exports artificially and to impede imports of virtually all commodities. Therefore, action was necessary in spite of the problems involved. Within the Six, no rule of direct taxation affected exports or imports in such a direct or important way,[4] so no special provisions were necessary.

The scope of Article 98

Article 98 prohibits giving relief for exports by exemption from charges other than turnover taxes, excise taxes, and other indirect taxes, and it deals primarily with direct taxes such as income tax and company tax.[5] It prevents member states from evading the other fiscal provisions by giving relief from direct taxes for exports,[6] which distorts competition just as much as relief by means of indirect taxation.

Institutional provisions of Article 98

An exemption from direct taxes on profits from exports to other member states may be given only to the extent that the exemption has received the prior approval of a qualified majority of the Council[7] on the proposal of the Commission. The approval must be only for

[1] Neither the EEC Treaty nor the authors who have considered competition in the EEC deal at length with state aids. It is therefore necessary to look at the economic position to formulate the legal criteria to decide what types of aid are compatible with the Treaty. This is a legal matter, not a question of policy.

[2] Arts. 95–99; cf. EFTA Convention, Jan. 4, 1960, art. 6, 370 U.N.T.S. 3 (1960).

[3] Described on pp. 171–73.

[4] Both EFTA, in its convention, art. 13 and Annex C, as amended by EFTA Council decision No. 8 of 1961, adopted March 15, 1961, and the OEEC, in a decision adopted at its 270th meeting on January 14, 1955, prohibit state aid to exporters. See OECD Decision No. C(59)202. See also GATT Declarations of Nov. 19, 1960, GATT Basic Instruments and Selected Documents (Ninth Supp. 1961, at 32–36, 185); GATT Working Party on Subsidies, Report, 17th Sess., Nov. 19, 1960, Ref. No. L/1381. See Federation of British Industries, Export Incentives 4, 8–13, 30 (1962).

[5] 1 von der Groeben & von Boeckh, Kommentar zum EWG-Vertrag 326 (1958). The word in the French text *impositions* and the corresponding word in the German text *Abgaben* include direct as well as indirect taxes. See Sullivan, The Search for Tax Principles in the European Economic Community 35–38 (1963).

[6] Art. 98.

[7] Relief from direct taxes for exports is a political matter for the Council because of the effect of this measure on the reality of exchange

a limited time, and reasons for the approval must be given. Article 98 is stricter than Article 93[8] and Article 102(1).[9] An appeal to the Court against the Commission's decision to propose, for the Council's approval, measures contemplated by a member state lies only on the grounds that the measures are not under Article 98 and therefore do not need the approval of the Council or that a regulation involved has been infringed or that powers have been misused.[10] Under Article 93 the Council can, in exceptional circumstances, overrule the decision of the Commission, but it cannot overrule a decision of the Commission not to propose measures under Article 98. The Council's decision can be made by a qualified majority of twelve votes,[11] but the Council can alter the proposal of the Commission only by a unanimous vote.[12] It may, however, criticize the proposal and refer it back, and the Commission is then free to submit it again, appropriately modified.

The "extent" of the export aid presumably means the percentage change in the tax imposed[13] or the number of commodities or taxes to be affected. The length of time for which the tax relief is permitted must be fixed by the Council's decision, but there is no legal limit on this length of time. To estimate the likelihood and the duration of permission under Article 98, it is necessary to know why the permission for tax relief for exports is to be given. Permission is given only for the period for which relief is essential to fulfill the objects of the article.

Balance of payments

In contrast to Article 92, Article 98 gives no indication of the purposes for which tax relief for exports should be approved. The discretion of the Commission

rates. (This is, of course, true also of relief from indirect taxation, which is dealt with specifically in the Treaty; arts. 95–97, 99. See Spaak Report 60, 71; Sullivan, The Search for Tax Principles in the European Economic Community 52–57, 61 [1963].) Both the rate of exchange and the rate of direct tax in the country of residence of the enterprise (i.e., the country of origin of goods exported) affect net profits from exports. Relief from direct taxes for exports is a political matter also because it involves the Community in joint responsibility for a breach of art. XVI of GATT. Ireland and Japan are the only countries mentioned in the study by the Federation of British Industries, Export Tax Incentives, ch. III (1962), as giving relief from direct taxes for exports. Possibly a tax concession under art. 98 would be regarded more favorably if it were one of the types of state aid permitted by art. 92, but in that case the strict provisions of art. 98 certainly would apply.

[8] Which merely requires member states adopting state aids to inform the Commission and allows the Commission to prevent the proposals' coming into force if they are incompatible with the Common Market.

[9] Which requires member states to consult with the Commission "where there is reason to fear the introduction or amendment of a legislative or administrative provision may cause distortion" of competition.

[10] Art. 173.

[11] Art. 148.

[12] Art. 149.

[13] It cannot mean the duration of the tax relief. In practice, the Commission, by agreement with the member state, could impose restrictions or conditions on the operation of the relief proposed. If it did so, the member state might withdraw its proposal entirely and fall back on the safeguard provisions of art. 22, during the transitional period, or arts. 108, 109, or 226, or possibly art. 73. As a practical matter the relief cannot be limited to exports to a particular member state. Although this would correct an imbalance in the payments position of one member state vis-à-vis another, it would divert trade excessively and be impossible to administer. The Council probably cannot alter or decide the duration of the export aid, except by unanimous vote, but it is bound by the time suggested by the Commission. The literal interpretation of the provision seems to leave this matter to the Council, but the Commission's function as the impartial guardian of the general Community interest applies to the duration as well as to the extent of the export aid.

and the Council is absolute; but permission is plainly not intended to be given often. The obvious justification for tax relief for profits from exports is the balance-of-payments position of the member state desiring to reduce the tax.[14] A protocol to the EEC Treaty "concerning certain provisions affecting France" specifically permitted the (then) French system of import taxes and repayment of taxes on exports. Ireland has not the political power of France, and the franc zone made French devaluation a very serious step. Nevertheless, this protocol is an important precedent for temporary continuation of tax measures to relieve balance-of-payments difficulties. However, protocols derogating from the terms of the Treaty must be exceptional and temporary.[15]

Neither the balance-of-payments provisions nor the related provisions relating to free movement of capital[16] refer to Article 98. Article 108 allows a member state in such a position to make "use of all the means at its disposal," and these means certainly include tax concessions for exports. Export subsidies are one method of reconciling the frequently inconsistent aims of Article 104.[17] However, Article 108 is not nearly so stringent as Article 98. If the "mutual assistance" agreed on by the Council proves inadequate, protective measures may be determined by the Commission alone;[18] in an emergency, the member state may

[14] This was, in fact, one reason for the Irish tax concession legislation. In the debates on the Finance (Miscellaneous Provisions) Bill, 1956, the Minister for Finance said it was "to stimulate production and exports arising out of increased production" and to counteract the temporary worsening in Ireland's terms of trade; 160 Dáil Eireann, Parl. Deb., cols. 1605–606 (1956). See also id., cols. 1624, 1696–97; 46 Seanad Eireann, Parl. Deb., cols. 1469–79, 1485, 1490, 1493, 1518 (1956). The country had recently been in balance-of-payments difficulties on current account, and special import levies had been imposed. More important, in 1956 it was decided that industrial expansion could come only from exports and not from production for the home market. See also Committee of Inquiry into Taxation on Industry, Report, Pr. 3512, para. 171–72 (1956).

Quaere whether the need for tax relief for exports from Ireland was due to the exchange rate between the Irish and British pounds (which were and have always been at full parity). An exchange rate which overvalued the Irish currency vis-à-vis the pound sterling would reduce the effective yield obtained by the Irish exporter from repatriated profits. A reduction in direct taxes on profits from exports would increase the effective yield. Devaluation of the Irish pound was never seriously considered although it has been mentioned for the Northern Ireland pound in unofficial circles; "Split over Ulster," The Economist, Oct. 27, 1962, pp. 331–32. This is a matter of importance for less developed countries sharing a currency with capital-exporting countries. See Verloren van Themaat, "Competition and Restrictive Business Practices in the European Economic Community," in Institute on Legal Aspects of the European Community 99, 107 (Federal Bar Association, 1960). U.N. Economic Survey of Europe in 1956, U.N. Doc. No. E/ECE/278, ch. IV, at 15–16 (1957), points out that "insofar as loss of tariff protection brings about a worsening of the balance of payments of a former high-tariff country, exchange rates will have to be adjusted to restore equilibrium; and the adjustment will have an incidental effect equivalent to some restoration of protection." See Harrod, "Common Market in Perspective," 19 Bull. Oxford U. Inst. Statistics 51, 54 (1957); Martin, "The Economic Basis of Industrial Development," in Methods of Industrial Development 55, 58 (OECD, 1962); Gibson, "An Amended Irish Monetary System," 19 J. Stat. Soc. 137 (1956–57), and comments therein; ECSC High Authority, Rapport remis à la Haute Autorité le 8 avril, 1953, 3243/1 F. PP. 1-36A, at 11–12; Belassa, The Theory of Economic Integration 239 (1961).

[15] OEEC Special Working Party, Report on the Possibility of Creating a Free Trade Area in Europe 15 (1957).

[16] Arts. 39, 104–109 and 67–73, respectively. These are in sections of the Treaty separate from the fiscal provisions (arts. 95–99).

[17] The aims of art. 104 are frequently inconsistent, especially in developing countries and regions.

[18] Art. 108(3).

take protective measures without a decision of the Council or even without informing the Commission and the other member states until the measures come into force.[19] During the transitional period, mutual assistance may be given by special reductions of tariffs or increases in quotas benefiting the member state in difficulties. These measures merely accelerate liberalization of trade.[20] In spite of its broad provisions, there is no indication that Article 108 authorizes derogation from the Common Rules of the Treaty.[21] On the other hand, balance-of-payments difficulties "should be cured by means which do not prevent a continuing expansion of over-all output in each country."[22] Deflation or exchange rate fluctuation would be even less desirable than import restrictions[23] or interference with conditions of competition. The advantage of tax aids to exports is that they increase trade, rather than reduce it, but they improve balance of payments only over a fairly long period. Only enterprises already organized for exporting can take prompt advantage of the relief. The effect of tax relief is therefore difficult to judge, and it must necessarily be maintained longer than more direct measures.

Article 226 applies in the case of difficulties in a particular sector or a particular region and does not clarify the interpretation of Article 98. Protective measures, such as exchange controls and changes in interest rates, are permitted under Article 73 with the approval of the Commission, in case of disturbances in the capital market in any member state. The relationship to balance of payments is obvious, but there is no reference to Article 98. The better view is that Article 98 does not permit tax relief to deal with balance-of-payments difficulties,[24] except perhaps in an emergency.

Advantages and disadvantages of relief from direct taxes

Relief from direct taxes for exports cannot be limited to sectors which need assistance without the administrative difficulties of creating a special tax category.[25] This is not an objection if the relief is intended to deal with balance-of-payments difficulties. Relief affects conditions of competition between the whole economies of states, not merely between particular enterprises or regions,

[19] Art. 109. Since only in an emergency can measures to deal with balance-of-payments difficulties be taken unilaterally, member states have made a major surrender of national monetary sovereignty.

[20] Cf. art. 226(3).

[21] Arts. 85–102.

[22] U.N. Economic Survey of Europe in 1956, U.N. Doc. No. E/ECE/278, ch. IV, at 28 (1957).

[23] Ibid. State aids generally do not interfere with economic integration, and the extent to which they alter competitive conditions can be calculated easily.

[24] In fact, it might even be improper if art. 98 was so used; cf. Compagnie des Hautes Fourneaux de Chasse v. High Authority, 4 Recueil 129, 147 (1958), where the Court said that it would constitute misuse of powers if a provision of the Treaty meant for one purpose was used for another purpose where other provisions expressly applied. See Valentine, "The Jurisdiction of the Court of Justice of the European Communities to Annul Executive Action," 36 Brit. Yb. Int'l L. 174, 194 (1960); EEC Commission v. Luxembourg, 8 Recueil 813 (1962), [1963] C.M.L.R. 199. See, however, Sullivan, The Search for Tax Principles in the European Economic Community 36 (1963).

[25] Van Hoorn, 41 Cahiers de Droit Fiscal International 25, 29 (1959). For a less usual view, see Wemelsfelder, "A Rehabilitation of Export Subsidies," 46(1) Am. Econ. Rev. 880 (1956). See also Federation of British Industries, Export Incentives 30 (1962), where direct tax incentives are described as "arbitrary and discriminatory and . . . against one of the canons of taxation, . . . equity. . . . [T]hey would require complicated legislation and would be difficult to administer."

and it is politically undesirable.

Article 98 prohibits all relief from direct taxes for exports, unless specifically authorized, and does not use the concept of a subsidy, as do the provisions of GATT.[26] There is therefore no question of arguing that remission of direct taxes is not a subsidy and is not prohibited because it does not affect marginal costs.[27] Even if this is true, it is irrelevant under Article 98. In fact, since direct taxes are normally passed on, relief from direct taxation enables enterprises to reduce selling prices even if marginal costs are not affected.

In a common market with free movement of capital, tax relief for exports diverts trade and investment into the state giving the relief.[28] The results of this will outlast the relief itself. Tax relief for exports subsidizes exporting enterprises at the expense of other taxpayers and diverts capital artificially within the national economy. As economic integration progresses, more large enterprises will be exporting to other member states and will be eligible for tax relief for exports if it is given. Export tax relief affects all enterprises exporting to other member states, while tariffs affect conditions of competition only in the national market of the member state imposing them.

On the other hand, economic interpenetration is more important than exactly equal conditions of competition, and tax relief for exports helps to remedy trade imbalance. Where this imbalance is due to artificial factors, tax relief seems legitimate if it equalizes competitive conditions. If difficulties appear temporary, it is obviously preferable to devaluation.

Harmonization of tax burdens
ARTICLE 98

When cumulative multistage indirect taxes have been abolished, the price of exports will not be affected by indirect taxes; to that extent, imports and local products will be on an equal footing in all member states. Direct taxes, however, are not remitted in respect of exports; they are borne by the enterprise or passed on. In either case, an exporting enterprise resident in a member state with high direct taxes and low indirect taxes will be at a disadvantage compared with an enterprise in a country with low direct taxes and high indirect taxes, since the effect of the indirect taxes will be neutral. This disadvantage will be in pro-

[26] Art. XVI, "Subsidies"; see also art. III. In any case, GATT Declaration of Nov. 19, 1960, GATT Basic Instruments and Selected Documents (Ninth Supp. 1961, at 32–33), and the Report of the Working Party on Subsidies, Ref. No. L/1381, adopted on the same date, Ninth Supp., at 185, both state that relief from direct taxes for exports constitutes a "subsidy." "Policy measures which directly frustrate the effects of removing tariffs and quota restrictions (e.g., export subsidies or discriminatory turnover taxes) will be prohibited in the Common Market." U.N. Economic Survey of Europe in 1956, U.N. Doc. No. E/ECE/278, ch. IV, at 4 (1957).

[27] It is argued on pp. 181–83 that direct taxes which are not passed on will affect marginal costs indirectly. The Irish revenue commissioners described remission of direct taxes on exports as a "concealed subsidy" in spite of the fact that they regarded tax as "something posterior to the completion of trading operations." Committee of Inquiry into Taxation on Industry, Report, Pr. 3512, para. 171 (1956).

[28] This is less likely in a sector where transport costs are high, if the state granting the concession is geographically separated from some or all of the other member states, if the duration of the concession is brief, and if the costs of moving an establishment or setting up a new one are substantial in relation to the total amount of profits which would be affected by the concession. Nevertheless, the tendency certainly exists.

In capital-intensive industries, because the ratio of sales to capital is low, the profit margin on sales must be high to insure a normal rate of return. The ratio of income tax to sales is thus high, and tax exemption allows a greater percentage price reduction; Shoup, The Theory of Harmonization of Fiscal Systems 13 (Institut International de Finance Publiques, 1963).

portion to the difference in the effective rates of direct taxation. It will exist in connection with both sales on the national market of one of the enterprises concerned and sales in a third member state.[29] This disadvantage can be removed only by reducing direct taxes on profits from exports; compare Article 92's permitting state aids to the extent to which they compensate for an artificial disadvantage. The positive function of Article 98 is to provide the machinery by which relief from direct taxes can be permitted, when it is justified for this reason.[30] While the reasoning behind Article 98 is undoubtedly sound, the extent of the disadvantage, and therefore the extent to which taxes should be reduced, is difficult to calculate.[31] The disadvantage depends on the controversial question of the extent to which the enterprises are passing on their direct taxes and thus converting them into taxes on consumption and on the extent to which the enterprises benefit from the use of revenues collected. The object of Article 98 is to equate the average net burden of direct and indirect taxes on all exporting enterprises in all member states. To attempt an accurate statement of the result to be achieved illustrates the problems. The indirect taxes borne by enterprises in the country proposing to give the tax concession, e.g., on the purchase of capital machinery, must be taken into account, if they are not completely repaid in respect of exports. Rather than an estimate of the over-all levels of direct taxation, an estimate must be made of the burden of direct taxation on enterprises exporting from the country in question in comparison with enterprises of other member states. To be accurate, this comparison requires a degree of "fiscal transparency" which does not now exist.[32] Presumably, an assessment of the correctness of the rate of exchange must be made. Presumably, the object is to calculate the mean rather than the median burden of tax on the exporting enterprises. The level of taxation sought is the appropriate level in all the other member states, because there would be no point in equalizing tax burdens between two member states if, in doing so, conditions were distorted further in comparison with a third. The possibility of more than one member state's wishing to remit some direct taxes on exporting enterprises cannot be excluded. Difficulties arise, in theory, in deciding with which enterprises in the other member states the comparison should be made. The comparison should be with all enterprises of the other member states, not only with those which are themselves exporting. Presumably, since it is conditions of competition which are to be equalized, the comparison should be made only with enterprises in the same sectors as the exporters, or principal exporters, of the member state proposing to reduce taxes. The question whether the mean or the median burden of taxation in other member countries should be the standard of comparison depends on the extent to which the enterprises in the sectors in

[29] Van Hoorn & Wright, "Taxation," in 2 American Enterprise in the European Common Market: A Legal Profile 343, 434 (Stein & Nicholson ed. 1960). The statement in the text assumes that there is no double direct taxation. If double taxation arises, the over-all tax rate paid by each enterprise should be examined to determine its competitive position. See Stout, "Value Added Taxation, Exporting and Growth," 1963 Brit. Tax Rev. 314, 320.

[30] 1 von der Groeben & von Boeckh, Kommentar zum EWG-Vertrag 326 (1958).

[31] The Neumark Report, Rapport 58, CCH 2455, says that the application of the principle of taxation in the country of destination to income taxes is impossible, because there is no practical possibility of calculating the amount to be refunded on export. See also Dale, Tax Harmonization in Europe 25–27 (1963); Sullivan, The Search for Tax Principles in the European Economic Community 36 (1963).

[32] Except possibly between countries with tax systems as similar as Britain's and Ireland's.

question in those countries are themselves exporting. If they export on a large scale, a decision must be made as to whether tax relief for their exports is possible from a budgetary or administrative point of view. If they do not export, it must be decided whether similar tax levels can be achieved by general harmonization of direct taxation or by special treatment for the enterprises in the sectors in question without disorganizing the national economy. This in turn depends on the size of the sector in question, relative to the whole of the national economy, and on the political question of how far a major fiscal upheaval in a small state is to be preferred to an upheaval—relatively smaller but absolutely larger—in a big one.

Other methods

Any member state at any time can achieve the same result as removing direct taxes on exports by lowering direct tax rates and increasing its revenue from indirect taxes, subject only to Article 102. Any state which wants to make this change and which collects over half of its revenue in direct taxes probably will have the approval of the Commission. On the other hand, a member state which collects more than half of its revenue from indirect taxes has no incentive for decreasing that proportion.

Another solution to the difficulty is to impose direct taxes on profits derived from exports only in the country of destination of the goods.[33] This is practicable only if the taxpaying enterprises have property in the country of destination against which payment of tax can be enforced, or if exemption from tax in the country of residence of the enterprises is conditional on payment of tax in the country of destination. This arrangement converts an export incentive into double taxation relief and, of course, may thereby defeat its object. However, it insures fairly equal conditions of competition between imports and local goods. Both methods of making this solution administratively possible permit the enterprises to arrange their affairs so as to avoid some tax. This scheme is an application not of the destination principle but rather of the principle of origin, as applied to income arising from sources in two different states.

The differences in the extent to which the Six rely on direct and indirect taxes are considerable,[34] and one of the largest single fiscal problems in the EEC is to correct the situation so that total revenue is derived in substantially equal proportions from direct and indirect taxes in each member state.[35] Such an equilibrium is necessary for tax harmonization. Although it will be a lengthy and difficult process to achieve it, the Commission prefers to equalize the burdens of direct and indirect taxes in this way rather than by concessions under Article 98. In theory, the latter would solve the problem at once, but their use will certainly be exceptional, especially in light of the political questions involved, including breach of Article XVI of GATT. The practice of most international trade organizations is strongly against them. Since tax relief for exports normally has to apply to a broad range of goods,[36] it cannot be related to the needs of the enterprise or the industry involved, as a

[33] Shoup, "Taxation Aspects of International Economic Integration," in Aspects Financiers et Fiscaux de l'Intégration Economique Internationale 101 (1954); Sullivan, The Search for Tax Principles in the European Economic Community 45–52, 62–63 (1963); Shoup, The Theory of Harmonization of Fiscal Systems 6 (1963).

[34] See Neumark Report, Rapport 58, CCH 2455–56.

[35] The rates of direct tax in Ireland are comparable to those in the Six, but the proportion of total revenue derived from direct taxes is not.

[36] This is not true if the tax measure is a specific one such as, for example, the provision of French tax law which gives exporting enter-

state aid should be.

Article 98 is the only provision in the Treaty dealing with the problem of harmonizing direct with indirect taxation. If a member state has not done something to put its exporters on equal terms with those of other countries[37] before it enters the EEC, it is unlikely to be permitted to do so under Article 98. The EEC is a pragmatic organization and is more likely to tolerate existing inequalities than to introduce new ones by way of partial remedy.

The application of Article 98 to tax concessions of the type in force in Ireland

Detailed rules of direct taxation which favor exports and are in force in present or future member states can be dealt with under Article 100. Either the applicant state or the member states are almost certain to raise the question of a comprehensive measure such as the Irish tax relief for exports (analyzed in Chapter Sixteen, on state aids in Ireland) in the course of negotiations for assession to the EEC. If nothing is said during the negotiations, then since the legislation is clearly contrary to Article 98, the new member state will be bound either to repeal the legislation, to amend it in order to bring it outside Article 98, or to obtain the approval of the Council and the Commission for it before the Treaty comes into force in the new state. It could be approved unanimously in the negotiations by the existing member states without the approval of the Commission, which, under the Treaty, has no veto over the terms of accession of a new member state. In practice, the Commission is likely to object to the existing legislation, and the Council is unlikely to overrule its objections, except as a political concession. If the legislation had not been approved in the negotiations, it is unlikely that the Council and the Commission would approve it unless it was modified. However, since both the Commission[38] and the Council[39] can make their decisions under Article 98 without unanimity, it is theoretically possible that the legislation is more likely to be approved after the new member state enters the Community than in the course of negotiations. The chance of approval even then seems remote. The Council and the Commission might even regard need for tax concessions as evidence that the new state was not prepared for full membership in the EEC. Legislation such as that in Ireland would therefore have to be amended so as to take it outside the scope of Article 98.

Conversion to State Aid Not Directly Related to Exports

Article 98 does not prohibit a state from giving tax concessions for profits from exports to non-member states; these are affected by the Treaty only under the provisions relating to the common commercial policy,[40] which probably involves their eventual abolition. Article 98 does not prohibit relief from direct taxation for profits from sales on the home market, although this alters conditions of competition between the enterprises which benefit from it and residents of other member states in the same way that conditions are altered in other national markets in respect of goods exported. Such relief will be dealt

prises an additional depreciation allowance calculated by a formula based on the proportion of the export profits to total turnover. The Commission required this provision to be repealed.

[37] In spite of the fact that the competitive advantage described above is admitted to exist, exemption or relief from direct taxation for exports is apparently contrary to GATT, arts. III(1), XVI. GATT does not contain any provision comparable to art. 98.

[38] Art. 163.

[39] Art. 148.

[40] Arts. 3(b), 110–16, especially art. 112.

with under the less stringent provisions of Article 92.

Article 98 prohibits only tax relief given specifically for exporting, and therefore it does not prohibit tax relief given to exporting enterprises on some other basis. Article 98 merely does for direct taxes what the other tax provisions are intended to do for indirect taxes. Any other interpretation would limit Article 92 to state aids to enterprises given only in their own national markets and to nonfiscal state aids, since Article 92 applies to state aids only insofar as they affect trade between member states. Article 92 is not expressed to be subject to Article 98, yet state aids which are likely to benefit exporters are more common than those which are not. However, tax relief for exporting enterprises which is guaranteed them even if they cease exporting might be within Article 98. This depends on the facts of the situation rather than the words of the legislation; but if the legislation does not expressly confine the relief to profits from exports, there is a strong presumption against applying Article 98. The Commission has not, in practice, regarded tax concessions which affect exports to other member states as within Article 98. The state aids permitted by Article 92(2) and 92(3) are not limited to those unlikely to affect exports. In a country having a fairly small population and especially in a region near a frontier, most state aid affects exports. Indeed, the most useful type of state aid in a less developed region may be aid which is likely to assist exports, since increasing exports is often the best method of encouraging economic expansion.

Since only a tax concession directly proportionate to the exports of the enterprises concerned is within Article 98, existing legislation contrary to that article could be amended so as to define the profits exempt from tax in a way unrelated to exports; e.g., by limiting the concession to enterprises suffering from temporary difficulties or newly established or established in a region or sector requiring substantial investment and expansion. A region or sector may be entitled to tax relief under Article 92, and Article 98 may not apply even if the enterprises concerned sell very little on the home market.

If this modification of tax concessions for exports were adopted, it would aid certain enterprises in selling both on the home market and elsewhere in the EEC. This would insure that the state would be careful not to assist one enterprise at the expense of another which was already operating in the state but which was not to benefit from the concession.

Conversion to Relief Against Double Taxation

As an alternative method, the existing tax exemption for export profits can be converted into a means of giving unilateral relief against double taxation. The only essential difference between a tax incentive for exports and unilateral relief from double taxation is that with the latter the income must be liable—at least in principle—to foreign tax. However, except with the tax credit method, no foreign tax need have been paid. This method probably is not within Article 92, but it may be within Article 98.

In practice, tax concessions for exports are normally temporary and selective; but they need not be, if the state concerned is prepared to make a greater sacrifice of revenue. Although tax concessions for exports are usually given if the goods are physically exported, even if the transaction resulted from the initiative of the foreign buyer and not that of the local seller, it is worthwhile to discriminate between a seller who takes the initiative and carries on activities abroad and an enterprise which remains at home and is lucky enough to receive foreign orders which it can fulfill. This distinction corresponds somewhat to the distinction between those enterprises whose activities may involve them in liability to foreign tax and those whose activities cannot do so. Tax exemption given to the former class of enterprises may constitute exemption for exporting within Article 98 or unilateral relief against double taxation, which is not mentioned by the Treaty and can be dealt with only under Article 100. The economic substance of the matter should be looked at rather than the legal form. Unilateral relief which is conditional on activities in the country to which the goods are exported does not become relief for exporting, even if it is an exemption from tax that is given automatically in specified circumstances, if those circumstances are reasonably likely to give rise to liability to foreign tax. To decide if liability to foreign tax is likely, one must look to international tax law in the absence of a treaty preventing the country of destination of the goods from imposing tax where no permanent establishment exists. Since unilateral relief should apply regardless of the country of source of the income, it is no objection to say that no liability to tax arises in particular countries or that the state giving the relief is a party to double taxation conventions with particular countries.

It may be objected that this is an attempt to reintroduce tax relief for exports under another name. But if the existing tax relief is repealed, some measure of relief against double taxation of profits from exports will have to be introduced at once. Systems of unilateral relief do not always distinguish between foreign-source income from direct or portfolio investment, that from sales activities, and that from capital or patents hired out abroad. However, countries which are short of capital should draw these distinctions, and most double taxation treaties do so. By the 1962 amendments to the Internal Revenue Code and previous legislation, the United States has classified foreign-source income partly on the basis of balance-of-payments criteria. EEC member states are entitled to distinguish between those types of foreign-source income which they wish to encourage and those which they do not. New member states will be under a moral duty to existing foreign investors to alter the terms of their tax concession legislation as little as possible, and if they do not maintain tax incentives for exports, they are free, subject to Article 100 or Article 102, to organize their tax systems as they see fit. By exempting foreign-source income from local tax and giving another state power to exempt it from tax completely, they would do no more than many countries which have entered into double taxation conventions or than those countries which base their jurisdiction to tax on the territoriality principle.

NON-FISCAL STATE AIDS TO EXPORTS

Since Article 98 has no application to state aids to exports other than exemptions from or repayments of direct taxes and any types of tax not covered by Articles 95–97 and 99, other state aids—even though given explicitly to exports—are within the more liberal provisions of Article 92. However, state aids such as cash grants for export operations constitute a subsidy, in the sense that they reduce marginal costs of production or distribution of goods. Article 98 and the other fiscal provisions make it clear that aids to exports are to be considered more strictly than other tax measures, and this principle applies equally to non-fiscal state aids. However, Article 92(3)(b) permits state aid "to remedy a serious disturbance in the economy of a member state," and this phrase is broad enough to include balance-of-payments difficulties. State aids which, in practice, aid exports may be proper and necessary and indeed more advantageous from the point of view of the Community than state aids which merely protect local producers from competition from imports. Non-fiscal state aids for exports to non-member states will be subject to the common commercial policy.

The Commission has done some work on non-fiscal measures to encourage exports.[41] Arrangements for giving information to exporters are permitted, because they encourage economic development and integration and overcome difficulties without distorting conditions of competition. Credit facilities for establishing branches in non-member countries do not distort trade between member states and should not be incompatible with the common commercial policy. The Commission has also worked on coordinating policy with regard to credit insurance guarantees and financial credits. Work is continuing on medium-term credit facilities for interstate trade, some guarantees against business risks, and market-prospecting insurance.

REGIONAL ECONOMIC POLICY IN THE EEC

Regional economic policies deal with two main types of region: regions which are underdeveloped and which have never been industrialized, and regions which, though formerly prosperous, are suffering from underemployment and a decline in standards of living, perhaps due to the local industry's having suffered a depression, become obsolescent, or used up the available natural resources.[42] Most of the Republic of Ireland is in the first category; Northern Ireland is in the second.[43]

The regional economic policy of the EEC will be important to Ireland because, first, in the context of a single European economy, the whole of Ireland is a less developed region. Second, the western regions of Ireland are undeveloped in comparison with the eastern half of the country. Ireland has a per capita income very much higher than southern Italy, but lower than any of the Six or Britain as a whole, and lower than northern Italy.[44] Even in the unlikely event of Ireland's being associated with the EEC before obtaining full member-

[41] Fifth General Report, para. 51 (1962); Sixth General Report, para. 49 (1963).

[42] First General Report, paras. 56–59 (1958). See also the series of reports of the Irish Committee on Industrial Organization on particular sectors of industry likely to be affected by free trade conditions. An EEC group studying regions in decline classified them into (1) those suffering from general economic and social obsolescence, (2) those whose major activities are declining, and (3) those with an infrastructure unsuitable to a changed pattern of business; see the Commission's three reports—Les problèmes, objectifs et méthodes de la politique régionale dans la C.E.E. (1964); L'adaptation des régions d'ancienne industrialisation (1964); and Moyens de la politique régionale dans les Etats membres de la C.E.E. (1964). See also EFTA Secretariat, Regional Development Policies in EFTA (1964).

[43] Fennell, Industrialization and Agricultural Development in the Congested Districts 5 (1962). The EEC Conference on Regional Economies also considered problems of over-populated areas and problems arising from the division of economic regions by national frontiers. There is also the wider question of insuring a division of activity among the regions of the EEC which would be economically and politically reasonable and which would prevent overconcentration of industry; Rapport fait au nom de la commission économique et financière sur la politique régionale dans la C.E.E., A.P.E. Doc. No. 99, paras, 13, 27, 34 (1963–64). See also A.P.E. Doc. No. 54 (1958–59) and A.P.E. Doc. No. 24 (1958).

[44] For figures for regional per capita income in Ireland, see Attwood & Geary, Irish County Incomes in 1960 (1963); U.N. Economic Survey of Europe, 1959, U.N. Doc. No. E/ECE/-383, ch. VII, chart II (1960); Chase Manhattan Bank, The European Markets 33 (1964). The economic development of a state presents much the same problems as a region with a similar industrial and agricultural structure, especially in conditions of free trade; Martin, "The Economic Basis of Industrial Development," in Methods of Industrial Development 55, 61 (OECD, 1962).

ship, the same questions, at least in modified form, would arise during the interim and on full accession to the Treaty.

"The possible entry of Greece and Turkey, or of any other country in the course of industrialization . . . raises problems of coordinating trade, investment, employment, and other economic policies which are quite different from those applicable to countries at a roughly similar stage of development . . . ."[45]

The need for a Community regional economic policy

Regional economic policies are necessary in the EEC, first, because there are serious differences between the levels of economic development and prosperity of various regions of the existing member states.[46] Second, the expansion of the Community economy would be retarded by less developed regions[47] but would be accelerated if these regions became prosperous through industrialization.[48] Third, the operation of the EEC itself might accentuate existing disparities or create difficulties in particular areas.[49]

One advantage of an enlarged market is that competition will insure the disappearance of inefficient enterprises. In

[45] U.N. Economic Survey of Europe, 1959, U.N. Doc. No. E/ECE/383, ch. VII, at 39 (1960); see Belassa, The Theory of Economic Integration 202–95 (1961); U.N. Economic Survey of Europe in 1956, U.N. Doc. No. E/ECE/278, ch. IV, at 19 (1957).

[46] First General Report, paras. 52–59 (1958); European Investment Bank, Annual Report, 1962, at 16–17; Chase Manhattan Bank, The European Markets 33 (1964); Spaak Report 18. The standard of living in southern Italy, Sicily, Corsica, Sardinia, and parts of southwest and southern France is substantially lower than elsewere in the EEC, and no major economic plan could omit some provision for its improvement.

[47] Johnston, Why Ireland Needs the Common Market 99 (1962); Marjolin, in 1 Documents de la Conférence sur les économies régionales 19, 21 (EEC Commission, 1961).

In his summary of the likely effects of the EEC on less developed regions, M. Marjolin says that some regions formerly handicapped by being on the periphery of their national markets are now in a central position in the Common Market; id. at 26–28. The conversion of certain areas to new industries will be aided by the increased demand in an enlarged market and by their attractiveness to new investment due to sound infrastructure and abundant labor. The position is more complex for regions still on the periphery of the enlarged market. These will suffer from loss of protection and will benefit less than industrialized areas from increased interstate trade. Enterprises in the outlying regions are not large enough to attract outside capital for development. Large movements of labor out of Italy are essential, but emigration harms the regions from which it occurs. M. Marjolin concludes that without a regional economic policy the less developed regions would develop faster than hitherto but not fast enough to diminish the gap between them and the industrialized regions.

[48] See generally British National Economic Development Council, Conditions Favourable to Faster Growth (1963). For British regional economic policy, see, e.g., Central Scotland: A Programme for Development and Growth, Cmd. No. 2188 (1963), and The North East: A Programme for Regional Development and Growth, Cmd. No. 2206 (1963).

[49] For an illustration of the difficulties of a regional economy in a common market with Great Britain, i.e., Northern Ireland, see Isles & Cuthbert, An Economic Survey of Northern Ireland (1957), and the Hall Report, Cmd. No. 1835 (1962), discussed in "Split over Ulster," The Economist, Oct. 27, 1962, p. 331, where the wider relevance of the experience of Northern Ireland (which has very limited control of its regional economy) is emphasized. Like Ireland, Northern Ireland has endeavored to encourage outside investment by reducing the cost of capital. See Ryan, "Indivisible Ills," 5(4) Administration 63 (1957); Carter, "The Unity of the Irish Economic Problem," 47 Studies 379 (1958).

On the wider problems of free trade for less developed regions, see Myrdal, An International Economy 224 (1956); Murray, "Ireland and the European Free Trade Area," 5 Administration 25, 33–35 (1957); Report by the [OEEC] Group of Financial Experts . . ., in Negotiations for a European Free Trade Area: Documents . . ., Cmd. No. 641, at 217, 218–20 (1959). The latter makes the important point:

regions where the principal industry is inefficient, hardship may result if no other industry can increase employment in the same region. This is particularly likely in agricultural and underindustrialized areas, where there may be very few industries or only industries that are too small to be efficient or that are able to compete only with the benefit of protection.

Where different regions are at substantially different stages of economic development, economic integration may accentuate the differences, unless a regional economic policy is adopted.[50] Less developed areas may be far from markets and suffer from added transport costs even if the infrastructure and other economic elements are adequate. Lack of industrialization often means lack of technical, repair, and information serv-

---

Since, during the . . . [transitional] period, productivity will be continuing to develop in other countries, . . . no system of derogations [from the ordinary obligations of member states] could, by itself, serve to correct the fundamental disequilibrium between the two groups of countries. To achieve such a purpose it is essential that the less developed countries should (a) draw up long-term development plans which take account of the progressive fulfilment by those countries of the obligations of membership . . . and (b) achieve the additional capital formation necessary for the execution of these plans and for the stimulation of a self-generating process of development.

The view that a regional economic policy is needed to prevent the EEC's causing an increase in the divergence in standards of living between the industrialized and the less developed regions of the EEC was adopted by Dr. Mansholt; 2 Documents de la Conférence sur les économies régionales 7, 9–10 (EEC Commission, 1961). The European Investment Bank says:

[T]he difference between the various countries [in increase in gross national product] was somewhat reduced with regard to per capita product. It seems, however, that the same does not yet apply to the regional differences that exist within each country; the few known facts indicate that in certain countries it is the already well-developed regions that played the biggest part in the general expansion whereas the rate in the less developed districts remained *below average.*

Annual Report, 1961, at 18. (Emphasis supplied.)

See Action Programme for the Second Stage, paras. 121–23 (1962). See also the works of Perroux cited by Belassa, The Theory of Economic Integration 192–93 (1961); Rapport . . . sur la politique régionale dans la C.E.E., A.P.E. Doc. No. 99, para. 30 (1963–64); Hoffman, "Underdeveloped Areas and Economic Integration," 1954 Les Cahiers de Bruges 280; Damaskenides, "Le développement économique de la Grèce et son intégration à la zone de libre échange," in Marché Commun, Institutions Communes 59 (1960); Neumark Report, Rapport 8, CCH 2411; Bourguinat, Espace économique et intégration européenne: Essai de détermination de l'incidence du Marché Commun sur les inégalités régionales de développement (1961).

[50] This occurred notably in Italy after unification; U.N. Economic Survey of Europe Since the War, U.N. Doc. No. E/ECE/157, ch. 12, at 218–19 (1953). Capital was more readily available and communications were better in the industrialized north than in the agricultural south, and since industrial areas are the best markets for industrial products, transport costs were reduced. Dr. Gunnar Myrdal has called this the "law of cumulative causation." Although capital is inherently more mobile than labor, southern workers migrated to the north, and since profits were greater in the north and labor more skilled, capital from both north and south was invested in the north. The southern economy, self-sustaining in a small market, could not compete for capital, labor, and markets against interests from elsewhere in Italy, and northern industry expanded to take over southern markets; Deniau, The Common Market 24–25, 38–41 (1962); Pincus, "Discussion Paper," in Regional Economic Planning 217, 218 (Isard & Cumberland ed. 1961). Enterprises contemplating investment in the south decided that the advantages of low wages, abundant labor, and higher marginal productivity would be offset, as far as their profit-making capacity was concerned, by the economic disadvantages of inadequate infrastructure and housing, shopping centers, schools, hospitals, local raw materials (since one reason less developed regions fail to prosper is shortage of raw materials), and sources of energy; id. at 218–20; Uri, "Economics and Politics of the Common Market," in Competition, Cartels and Their Regulation 367–98 (Miller ed. 1962).

ices for industry. This unfortunate effect of economic integration is accentuated by linguistic and psychological differences, and business caution due to ignorance of conditions in other member states. It is therefore partly due to classical economic factors and partly due to non-economic factors.

A large, capital market, unified and equally accessible to all interested parties, helps to reduce the inequality of development in the various countries which stems from their differing capacity for capital formation. International movements of capital therefore favor the elimination of the underemployment which characterizes certain areas, and do this without the social and economic disadvantages which would result from transfers of labor.[51]

This is true, but as the author quoted recognizes, the favorable influence of free capital movement on regional economic development will not necessarily be effective.

It is generally conceded that to finance all the investment necessary for a reasonable rate of development in southern Italy and, still more, in the other countries of southern Europe out of their own resources would impose a heavy, and in some cases intolerable, strain on the economies of those countries. They therefore need to import capital. In a situation in which differences in interest rates from country to country reflect the influence of individual governments' monetary and credit policies rather than differences in the real rate of return on capital, however, there is little reason to hope for a noticeably more economic pattern of international capital movements as a result of removing restrictions. There is certainly little reason to suppose that the removal of restrictions on capital movements within the Common Market . . . during the next few years would by itself induce a more rapid flow of funds towards the under-developed regions; and indeed the possibility of a perverse flow from the poorer to the richer members cannot be ruled out.[52]

Due to freedom of movement of capital[53] or to deliberate efforts to harmonize monetary and credit policies, interest rates in the Common Market will tend towards approximately the same level in each member state.[54] This level may not be low enough to maximize economic expansion in less developed areas, and even if it is, some differentiation in their favor will be required to bring them to the degree of development of the rest of the EEC. Regional development must be aided through special credit institutions, direct subsidies, or tax concessions. These will be needed because the flow of capital from the poorer to the richer regions is not necessarily "perverse." In regions where capital is scarce, the high cost of facilities external to the company itself may mean that its productivity is lower than in other regions.[55] On the other hand, from the viewpoint of the economy as a whole, the company's pro-

[51] Segré, "Capital Movements in the European Economic Community," 60 Banca Nazionale del Lavoro Rev. (March 1962). Capital must be deliberately encouraged to move into less developed regions, because the effect of banking systems is to collect regional savings and invest them on national markets, thus depriving regions of the benefit of their savings; U.N. Economic Survey of Europe in 1954, U.N. Doc. No. E/ECE/194, at 153 (1955); European Investment Bank, Annual Report, 1958, at 16; EEC Commission, Moyens de la politique régionale dans les Etats membres de la C.E.E. 112, 121–22 (1964).

[52] U.N. Economic Survey of Europe in 1956, U.N. Doc. No. E/ECE/278, ch. IV, at 19 (1957).

[53] Movements of "hot money" are not yet liberalized throughout the EEC.

[54] This is in fact the position between Britain and Ireland; see Economic Development, Pr. 4803, ch. 3, para. 12 (1958).

[55] U.N. Economic Survey of Europe in 1953, U.N. Doc. No. E/ECE/174, ch. 15, at 184 (1954); Report by the [OEEC] Group of Financial Experts . . ., in Negotiations for a European Free Trade Area: Documents . . ., Cmd. No. 641, at 217, 223–24 (1959). For a theoretical discussion of the whole question of the effect of freer trade on less developed regions, see Meier, International Trade and Development (1963).

ductivity may be higher than in other regions, in that the company may be producing more at a smaller profit to itself but at a greater profit to the whole economy; hence the economic justification for a regional economic policy. The "infant industry" argument is valid for less developed areas; however, the case for regional policies concerns not merely economic development but also "the fundamental lack of balance between industry and agriculture"[56] in poorer regions and countries. Agricultural labor surpluses cause the money costs of industrial production to be higher in relation to those of agriculture than is justified by the comparative real costs in the two sectors.[57] Hence, the exchange rate at which the foreign account of the state is roughly in balance is one at which industrial costs tend to be non-competitive with foreign costs, and agricultural costs competitive.[58] In these circumstances, agriculture suffers from underproduction, and agricultural workers suffer from underemployment and low per capita income. Where this is so, economic integration without a regional economic policy contributes to intra-European specialization only in the sense that it perpetuates the role of the less developed regions as exporters of agricultural products and importers of industrial products. This perpetuates and indeed increases differences in the levels of economic development and per capita income. At least where agriculture is competitive, the state concerned need not introduce new tariffs or feel compelled to associate with the EEC before joining it. Nevertheless, the Community must formulate regional economic policy to deal with the difficulty.

Underdeveloped countries, unlike less developed regions of industrialized countries, have not coexisted with highly developed areas in free market conditions, and therefore they may be more severely affected by competition from the latter.[59] For example, Irish industry has been protected from competition and needs state aid to enable it to adjust to free trade conditions. Ireland is on the edge of Europe; this location is less disadvantageous than in the past, due to the nature of modern industry, but it inhibits industrialization.[60] While wages and prices of branded and other products tend to become standardized in a large common market, transport costs operate against the remoter areas,[61] and this slows their development. Regional economic policies also may be required because of sea and land barriers separating member states from each other and from outlying regions.

While the EEC makes regional economic policies even more necessary, it encourages the economic expansion which is a necessary precondition of effective

[56] U.N. Economic Survey of Europe Since the War, U.N. Doc. No. E/ECE/157, ch. 12, at 219 (1953), of which the rest of the paragraph in the text is a paraphrase; see also id., ch. 8, at 153–55. See Myrdal, An International Economy 224, 278–80 (1956); Streeten, Economic Integration 90 (1961).

[57] Agricultural labor surpluses mean that underemployment can be reduced with little sacrifice of agricultural output if industry takes labor from agriculture, or that the real cost of increasing industrial output is relatively low.

[58] This is less true for a region, which is not a unit for exchange rate purposes, than for a country.

[59] U.N. Economic Survey of Europe in 1956, U.N. Doc. No. E/ECE/278, ch. IV, at 19 (1957), on southern Italy.

[60] U.N. Economic Survey of Europe in 1954, U.N. Doc. No. E/ECE/194, at 138 (1955).

[61] "Symposium on the Report of the Commission on Emigration," 19 J. Stat. Soc. 104, 105–106 (1955–56). The "demonstration effect" is likely to be very strong in the EEC and will tend to raise wage rates in less developed regions, especially with the growth of the European trade unions. See in this connection Borts, "The Equalization of Returns and Regional Economic Growth," 50(1) Am. Econ. Rev. 319 (1960).

regional policies.[62] Enterprises normally establish subsidiaries or branch operations in less developed regions and do not move their principal factories; unless the economy is expanding, new investment in branch operations is unlikely, and the regions themselves do not have capital available for investment in new industries. Also, regional differences in per capita income tend to diminish at advanced stages of economic development.

The general provisions of the Treaty

Regional economic policies require coordination of other Community operations: the common transport policy,[63] which will deal with means of transport and subsidies for services to outlying or inaccessible areas; the Social Fund, for retraining and aiding occupational and geographical mobility of labor; the policy on dumping, a practice which may threaten small enterprises in regional markets; competition policy, on state aids; agricultural policy, which vitally affects the principal occupation in most of the less developed regions; and cartel policy, on crisis cartels needed to deal with structural difficulties in depressed sectors of industry. All these must be coordinated with the Community economic policy for a coherent regional policy, although the Treaty does not mention less developed regions in connection with all of them and is not, in fact, very explicit on regional economic development.

The Preamble says that the Six are "desirous of strengthening the unity of their economies and of ensuring their harmonious development by diminishing both the disparities between the various regions and the backwardness of the less favored regions."[64] Article 2 provides that promotion of harmonious development of economic activities throughout the Community is an object of the EEC. Article 3 speaks of coordination of economic policies of member states. Hints that a regional policy should exist are given elsewhere in the Treaty,[65] but the most important provisions are those on the European Investment Bank and the association of overseas territories. The latter have now been replaced by a new treaty, signed in 1963, with the independent African and other countries concerned. The treaties of association with Greece and Turkey also deal with aid for the economic development of those countries. The provisions relating to the European Investment Bank contemplate direct intervention by member states, and Article 92 contemplates aids to provide favorable competitive conditions

[62] Romus, Expansion Economique Régionale et Communauté Européenne 335 (1958).

[63] See U.N. Economic Survey of Europe in 1954, U.N. Doc. No. E/ECE/194, at 153–54 (1955); U.N. Economic Survey of Europe Since the War, U.N. Doc. No. E/ECE/157, at 231–32 (1953). With regard to the ECSC, see Lagrange, "The Role of the Court of Justice of the European Communities as Seen Through Its Case Law," 26 Law & Contemp. Prob. 400, 415 (1961), and the cases before the Community Court cited there; Hallstein, in 1 Documents de la Conférence sur les économies régionales 11, 14 (EEC Commission, 1961); Marjolin, in id. at 30; Rapport . . . sur le politique régionale dans la C.E.E., A.P.E. Doc. No. 99, paras. 15–23 (1963-64).

[64] Para. 6.

[65] See, e.g., art. 39(2)(a), on common agricultural policy with regard to "structural and natural disparities between the various agricultural regions"; art. 42(a) and 42(b), on aid for agricultural undertakings handicapped by structural or natural conditions and aid under economic development programs; art. 75(3), on the effect of transport rules on standards of living and levels of employment; art. 77, on aid where transport is a public service; art. 80(2), on transport and a suitable regional economic policy and the needs of underdeveloped areas; arts. 129–30, on the European Investment Bank; arts. 131–36 and 227(2), on the association of overseas countries and territories; art. 226, on safeguards; and the Protocols concerning Italy and Berlin. See also art. 54(3)(h).

in regions requiring development.[66] The projects and the means are at the discretion of member states.[67] Community organs are involved only if conditions of competition in the private sector are to be altered by state aids or if financing from the Bank is required. Coordination of regional policies in other respects is purely voluntary. The EEC organs need not formulate and cannot themselves implement regional economic policies, and the Treaty states only broad general principles to guide them. In considering whether to permit specific measures of state aid, the Commission takes into account their effect on all sectors of the Community, on specific competitors elsewhere in the Common Market, and on the policies of other member states. It tries to prevent the giving of state aid to industries in sectors in which increased capacity is unnecessary or undesirable because of existing capacity, falling demand, or development policies in other states. The inadequacy of national production to supply the national demand is not in itself a reason for state aid, if the national demand can be supplied from other Community sources.

The European Investment Bank and the European Social Fund

The Commission coordinates[68] the work of the Social Fund and the Investment Bank with that of member states to assist the development of depressed and backward areas. The Commission itself administers the Social Fund for labor, and the Bank is supervised by the member states themselves,[69] and it deals primarily with capital-intensive industries.

The European Investment Bank[70] finances,[71] by loans and guarantees on a

[66] See Taxes and Fiscal Policy in Under-Developed Countries, U.N. Doc. No. ST/TAA/M/8, at 2–4 (1954).

[67] Commer, Business Practice in the Common Market 121 (1963), says that regional policy is still national policy, because the member states still exist as economic units, and that it is only when the EEC becomes a single economy that regional policy can become a purely Community matter.

[68] The Commission's function of coordination is only implied by the Treaty; Political and Economic Planning, Regional Development in the European Economic Community 66 (1962); Marjolin, in 1 Documents de la Conférence sur les économies régionales 19, 29 (EEC Commission, 1961). Pursuant to a report to the European Parliament by its Economic and Financial Committee, A.P.E. Doc. No. 24 (1960–61), the Commission set up several working groups on regional economic policy. See Rapport . . . sur la politique régionale dans la C.E.E., A.P.E. Doc. No. 99, paras, 64–69 (1963–64). It is doubtful if the powers of the Commission over regional policies are adequate.

[69] The Bank must insure that its funds are used in the most rational manner in the interests of the Community (Protocol Concerning the Statute of the European Investment Bank, art. 20), and its projects must contribute to the increase of economic productivity in general. If the Commission has disapproved of an application for a loan or guarantee, it may be given only if the Bank's board of directors approves it unanimously; art. 21(6) of the Protocol. In other respects the Bank is formally independent of the Commission, and their policies must therefore be coordinated deliberately.

[70] This book is not concerned with the institutional structure and functions of the Bank. See Protocol Concerning the Statute of the European Investment Bank; European Investment Bank, Annual Report, 1958; Commer, Business Practice in the Common Market 140–42 (1963); Rapport . . . sur la politique régionale dans la C.E.E., A.P.E. Doc. No. 99, paras. 71–74 (1963–64); EEC Commission, Première Communication de la Commission sur la Politique Régionale dans la C.E.E. 34–35 (1965).

[71] Art. 130. European Investment Bank, Annual Report, 1958, app. II, reads in part:

THE GENERAL LINES OF THE BANK'S CREDIT POLICY

II. The Bank shall devote a large part of its resources to the financing of projects likely to contribute to the furtherance of less developed regions; these projects may be ascribable to the various sectors of the economy. This already represents one of the major objectives of the European Economic Community.

non-profit making basis, projects for developing less developed regions, projects of common interest[72] to several member states, and projects for modernizing or converting enterprises or for developing new activities called for by the progressive establishment of the Common Market. Although it gives loans to small enterprises, the Bank—the only Community institution directly concerned with regional policy—prefers to aid large enterprises on account of their greater suitability for regional development.[73] The reason given is that large enterprises can deal better with the problems of less developed regions and are more likely to appreciate the economies and advantages of investment in such a region. Unless the Bank alters its policy, the Commission will have to insure that state aids encourage smaller enterprises or itself encourage them through judicious use of the Social Fund. The Bank may give loans only when finances are not available from other sources on reasonable terms.[74] Even with a liberal interpretation, this limitation means that the Bank is confined to large or risky ventures or ventures not directly profitable. The Bank may lend money only for projects which are directly self-liquidating—i.e., which will themselves make sufficient profits to pay off the capital lent—or which are self-liquidating because of state aid or state guarantee.[75] The Bank will not lend money below normal interest

---

The Bank shall finance projects of common interest for several member countries. It shall, in particular, assist schemes which are likely to contribute to a "rapprochement" of markets and the integration of member countries' economies.

The Bank shall participate in the financing of schemes for modernizing or converting enterprises or for creating new activities which are called for by the progressive establishment of the Common Market, as soon as the repercussions of the development of this market on the situation of the enterprises in question can be foreseen with sufficient accuracy.

III. Projects financed by the Bank must meet the conditions laid down in the Statutes and in particular those of Art. 20, as regards their being of economic utility and financial rentability [i.e., profit making].

Furthermore, the Bank shall observe the following principles:

(a) In the first period of its activities, it shall grant loans rather than provide guarantees for raising loans.

(b) It shall devote itself to the financing of specific projects.

(c) In order not to dissipate its resources, it shall employ them in general to finance schemes of some extent [i.e., large schemes].

(d) The granting of loans shall be subordinated to the employment of other means of financing, whether the borrower's own or a third party's.

(e) Special attention shall be reserved for schemes for which there is an association of capital from several Community countries.

(f) In the conduct of these operations, the Bank shall conform to the general objective of the progressive unification of the capital markets of member countries.

The International Bank for Reconstruction and Development, after which the European Investment Bank is patterned to some extent, lends under government guarantee to industrial development corporations which then relend without such guarantees to private enterprises. The European Investment Bank does the same.

[72] Cf. art. 92(3)(b).

[73] Second Annual Report, 1959, at 15. See Pincus, "Discussion Paper," in Regional Economic Planning 217, 218 (Isard & Cumberland ed. 1961); U.N. Economic Survey of Europe in 1954, U.N. Doc. No. E/ECE/194, at 165–66 (1955); "Can the Leopard Change His Spots?" The Economist, March 28, 1964, pp. 1243, 1247.

[74] Protocol Concerning the Statute of the European Investment Bank, art. 18(1). This provision was inserted to prevent the Bank's competing with commercial sources of finance. See generally Vasseur, Le droit de la réforme des structures industrielles et des économies régionales 351–56 (1959).

[75] Formentini, "Le développement régional et la Banque européenne d'investissement," in 1 Documents de la Conférence sur les économies régionales 35, 43 (EEC Commission, 1961).

rates or for the creation of fixed social capital which is not directly productive or profitable, regardless of its indirect benefits. Nor will it lend money to any venture which does not contribute to the realization of the Common Market.[76]

The Social Fund has power only to reimburse member states for expenditures for occupational retraining and resettlement allowances for workers compelled to move to find work and expenditures to maintain wage levels of workers temporarily unemployed as a result of conversion of enterprises to other production.[77] The Fund can be used only where member states have agreed to take the initiative. It cannot pay the cost of aid, other than for retraining or resettlement, to workers permanently laid off, or for temporary unemployment due to modernization, as distinct from conversion.[78] The Fund originally had no power to pay for programs for training workers who have never been employed,[79] even though vocational training is a vital element in a structural economic policy. After the transitional period, the Social Fund may obtain new functions, to increase possibilities of employment and the geographical and occupational mobility of workers.[80]

Movement of industry or movement of labor

Aid for resettlement and promotion of the geographical mobility of labor may be a necessary—if perhaps a slightly defeatist—solution to the problems of a region adversely affected by the EEC or other changes in the pattern of trade. The Commission can deal with unemployment only by using the provisions relating to free movement of labor (Articles 48–51), by approving state aid designed to bring industry to the labor force, or by using the Social Fund to aid resettlement. Except where a depressed sector of industry is very large or is the only industry in an area, unemployment due to underdevelopment is usually more difficult to deal with than unemployment in a region suffering from a depression, since it is less likely to be cured by the workers' finding other jobs locally.

Coordination of the Treaty provisions on state aids and on the Social Fund raises the question whether movement of labor or encouragement of investment is more satisfactory for solving regional economic problems. There may be a conflict between the need for workers—perhaps in another member state—which involves resettlement, with resulting social problems, and the desire to preserve the ethnic and social way of life of a region and to prevent emigration. It is natural to wish both to provide work and raise standards of living and to avoid disrupting communities and encouraging the flight from the land. Both movement of industries and resettlement of labor may be necessary. The Treaty does not indicate which should be preferred where a choice is possible. Except in the unusual event that the area to which the

[76] Id. at 46. The Bank has experienced a shortage of suitable projects and perhaps may alter its policies. Neither the Protocol nor the provisions relating to the Social Fund are wholly satisfactory.

[77] Art. 125; Rapport . . . sur la politique régionale dans la C.E.E., A.P.E. Doc. No. 99, paras. 75–81 (1963–64); EEC Commission, Première Communication de la Commission sur la Politique Régionale dans la C.E.E. 36–38 (1965).

[78] Political and Economic Planning, Regional Development in the European Economic Community 67 (1962).

[79] Article 125(2) speaks only of "retraining." Presumably this would cover training unemployed people who had been doing unskilled work previously, since there is no work for which no instruction whatever is required. The Commission is planning a coordinated policy on vocational training; Action Programme for the Second Stage, paras. 75–77 (1962).

[80] Arts. 123, 126.

labor moves has excess capacity in its existing facilities or infrastructure, mobility of labor rather than capital will require substantial social capital formation in schools and housing, which is only indirectly productive.

Though schools and housing in less developed areas may be of lower quality, they usually have some excess capacity. Against this cost to the public must be set the cost of providing the less developed areas with the infrastructure required for industry, especially transport facilities.[81] The social costs of moving labor cannot be compared with the costs of establishing industry in the less developed regions, unless it is known where the labor will go. However, the unregulated flow of labor is likely to use up any surplus capacity in infrastructure in industrialized areas.

A decline in regional population due to emigration may not improve the standard of living of those remaining behind. Economies of scale in infrastructure are lost, and the fixed or overhead costs of the region are higher per capita. Certain facilities, such as railway branch lines, may have to be closed altogether. Emigration harms the demographic structure of the community by decreasing the proportion of individuals of working age and increasing the proportion of dependents. If workers with energy and initiative tend to emigrate, the quality of the labor force is reduced.[82] Investment in the education of children is lost to the region, and a decrease in the population reduces the markets for enterprises not exporting from the region[83] and reduces the demand for investment in the region. If labor emigrates, remittances by emigrants may help to improve the regional economy, but the emigrants' personal expenditures are elsewhere.

Some regions can never support substantial populations at a reasonable standard of living without aid, and the Treaty[84] and the Commission[85] indicate that state aids will not be permitted to continue indefinitely. A large proportion of the present agricultural population in less developed areas will leave the land in the next few years anyway. A region may be "underdeveloped," i.e., have fair potential resources in proportion to population,[86] or "overpopulated," i.e., have a population too great for its maximum potential productive capacity. In the latter type of region, movement of labor is the only solution. Before labor movements are encouraged, however, the most efficient use of resources necessitates efforts to discover activities for which the overpopulated area is suited, since activities such as fishing or forestry may have been neglected due to lack of capital or technology rather than unsuitability. The possible movement of industry to the center of the enlarged Community will prejudice the economic status of regions which would be viable as part of a national economy, and to some extent this centripetal tendency should be permitted to occur.[87] Unless

[81] In Ireland, the existing infrastructure is adequate, and no great social costs are involved.

[82] U.N. Economic Survey of Europe in 1953, U.N. Doc. No. E/ECE/174, at 194 (1954); An Foras Taluntais [Irish Agricultural Institute], Report on the Survey of West Cork (1963).

[83] Johnston, The Sickness of the Irish Economy 18–21 (1957).

[84] Art. 92(1).

[85] Von der Groeben, "Policy on Competition in the European Economic Community," 1961 EEC Bull. No. 7/8, Supp. 12–14, translated from "Wettbewerbspolitik in der Europäischen Wirtschaftsgemeinschaft," 11 Wirtschaft und Wettbewerb 373 (1961).

[86] U.N. Economic Survey of Europe in 1953, U.N. Doc. No. E/ECE/174, ch. 15, at 185, and ch. 16, at 192 (1954).

[87] This tendency already exists; Romus, Expansion Economique Régionale et Communauté Européenne 281–83 (1958); "Symposium on the Report of the Commission on Emigration," 19 J. Stat. Soc. 104, 105–106 (1955–56); U.N.

regional policies are effective, the experience of Italy and other markets which have been unified indicates that regional problems will ameliorate themselves gradually by migration. If migration is not desirable, a substantial[88] effort is essential to bring industry into regions with perhaps few advantages other than cheap labor.[89] A policy based on movement of labor could hardly be called a regional economic policy. The tendency towards migration is increased in the EEC by free movement of labor, by the demonstration effect of the prosperous areas,[90] and by the present labor shortage in most regions of the EEC.

It seems clear that, as far as possible, EEC policy is to bring industries to less developed regions, since this is the view of the EEC Conference on Regional Economies.[91] This policy has certain obvious difficulties; in particular, it cannot be applied to extractive industries or agriculture or any sector where the location of the raw material is crucial to the

---

Economic Survey of Europe in 1954, U.N. Doc. No. E/ECE/194, ch. 6, at 138 (1955); U.N. Economic Survey of Europe in 1956, U.N. Doc. No. E/ECE/278, ch. IV, at 17–18 (1957); Marjolin, in 1 Documents de la Conférence sur les économies régionales 19, 25–26 (EEC Commission, 1961).

[88] Id. at 24.

[89] See Pincus, "Discussion Paper," in Regional Economic Planning 217, 219 (Isard & Cumberland ed. 1961), and the somewhat controversial views of Italy's Dr. Lutz, A Study in Economic Development (1963); see also Belassa, The Theory of Economic Integration 89–90, 206–207 (1961); U.N. Economic Survey of Europe Since the War, U.N. Doc. No. E/ECE/157, at 160–61 (1953); U.N. Economic Survey of Europe in 1954, U.N. Doc. No. E/ECE/194, at 144–45 (1955).

[90] See "Symposium on Economic Development," 20(2) J. Stat. Soc. 114 (1958–59). On emigration in this connection, see generally Commission on Emigration Report, Pr. 2541 (1954); U.N. Economic Survey of Europe in 1953, U.N. Doc. No. E/ECE/174, ch. 16 (1954). Large-scale migration to industrial areas to obtain higher wages may cause inflationary increases in wage incomes and consumer demand without any increase in nominal wage rates, as happened in Italy; "Perils of Prosperity," The Economist, March 28, 1964, p. 1238.

[91] Dr. Mansholt describes this view as the general tendency; 2 Documents de la Conférence sur les économies régionales 7, 11–12 (EEC Commission, 1961). See Romus, Expansion Economique Régionales et Communauté Européenne 287 (1958). This policy was preferred "whenever possible" by Pope John XXIII; Encyclical Letter "Pacem in Terris," para. 102 (1963). This was the view expressed by the Federation of British Industries in their study of regional unemployment in Britain; "The FBI's View," The Economist, June 8, 1963, pp. 1057, 1059. It is the government policy in Britain, Spain, and Northern Ireland; Hall Report, Cmd. No. 1835, para. 64 (1962). The Spaak Report framers seem to have held this view; Spaak Report 58. Professor Hallstein favors a regional economic policy based on the preservation of the regions of Europe, with their different traditions; 1 Documents de la Conférence sur les économies régionales 11, 17 (EEC Commission, 1961); see also Rapport . . . sur la politique régionale dans la C.E.E., A.P.E. Doc. No. 99, para. 49 (1963–64). The U.N. Food and Agricultural Organization favors retraining rural populations in agricultural regions and bringing industries to the labor in order to maintain social stability and to keep people in their own surroundings; Food and Agriculture Organization of the United Nations, "Agricultural Policies in Europe in the 1960's—Problems of Agriculture in a Growing Economy" 9–12, in Working Papers of the Third Regional Conference for Europe (Rome, 1962). See Second Programme for Economic Expansion, Pr. 7239, para. 20 (1963).

EEC policy is important to a country such as Ireland because even moving labor to industrial areas inside Ireland is likely to result in emigration because of the high degree of external mobility in Irish labor. Professor J. Johnston, Why Ireland Needs the Common Market 61 (1962), says: "[O]nce workers have become uprooted from the country and established in an urban environment as migrants they are already more than half emigrants." Modernization of agriculture means a decrease in the regional demand for agricultural labor. "The only escape from this dilemma is in a policy of industrial decentralization . . . ." U.N. Economic Survey of Europe in 1954, U.N. Doc. No. E/ECE/194, at 145 (1955); see also id. at 159.

cost of production. The amount of underemployment may be so great as to make large labor movements necessary, but these have unfortunate side-effects.[92] This regional policy affects foreign investment by allowing substantial incentive to investment to be given in less developed regions and by limiting the availability of Community labor in other areas.[93]

THE MACHINERY OF COMMUNITY CONTROL OVER STATE AIDS[94]

The Commission supervises the effect of existing legislation on state aid[95] because economic changes in the EEC may cause even previously permissible state aid[96] to distort competition, to affect interstate trade, to assist a region no longer in need of aid, or to "adversely affect trading conditions to such an extent as would be contrary to the public interest."[97] This supervision must be carried out with the member states,[98] which therefore are obliged to provide the Commission with all the necessary information on the practical application of the legislation. The Commission has power to halt aid being given to any enterprise, even as a result of individual negotiation between the enterprise and the state.[99] This is a necessary result of the principle that state aids normally must be selective and the fact that a given type of aid has radically different economic effects in different sectors. As a result of this continuous review of the effects of different state aids, the Commission may suggest[100] any measures required by the progressive development or functioning of the Common Market.

If it considers that legislation providing for state aid or aid to be given to individual enterprises is incompatible with Article 92, the Commission must notify the state concerned for its comments.[101] It is unfortunately not clear whether the Commission must give no-

[92] Marjolin, in 1 Documents de la Conférence sur les économies régionales 19, 27 (EEC Commission, 1961); Mansholt, in 2 Documents de la Conférence sur les économies régionales 7, 11 (EEC Commission, 1961). See EEC Commission, Moyens de la politique régionale dans les Etats membres de la C.E.E. 142–44 (1964); Action Programme for the Second Stage, para. 126 (1956); Commer, Business Practice in the Common Market 121 (1963).

[93] The object of this book is not to attempt an analysis of regional economic policy in the EEC, but rather to discuss some legal aspects of it which are of interest to the investor. See Regional Economic Planning (Isard & Cumberland ed. 1961); Romus, Expansion Economique Régionale et Communauté Européenne (1958); Belassa, The Theory of Economic Integration, ch. 9 (1961).

[94] Apart from tax concessions for exports under art. 98, the machinery for the supervision of state aid is set out in arts. 93 and 94.

[95] Action Programme for the Second Stage, para. 27 (1962); Third General Report, para. 150 (1960); Fourth General Report, paras. 52, 57 (1961); Seventh General Report, para. 70 (1964).

[96] As in other matters, the Commission takes the long-term view. It is more concerned to see that new state aids are not introduced and to a lesser extent that existing regimes are not acted on in a way likely to distort competition in the future than to investigate the effects of aid which already has been granted and which is of minimal importance before the end of the transitional period. See also art. 93(3).

[97] Art. 92(3)(c).

[98] Art. 93(1).

[99] Before incurring substantial expense, an enterprise which expects to receive state aid should consider asking the Commission for an unofficial assurance that the state aid contemplated is compatible with the Treaty.

[100] The verb used is *proposer*. This clearly is not binding; art. 189. What is intended seems to be a recommendation including proposals for joint and coordinated measures to deal with specific problems and suggestions for more effective use of existing systems of state aid.

[101] Art. 93(2). The phrase "parties concerned" (*les intéressés*) contrasts with the "state concerned" in the same provision.

tice to any enterprise which may be affected by the cancellation of the state aid, but it is submitted that it must do so. As well as commenting on the prima facie case made by the Commission, the state may request the Council to permit the aid, notwithstanding Article 92.[102] The request is not an appeal against the decision of the Commission but, in effect, a request for a waiver of Article 92.[103] It may be made before or after the Commission asks the state for comments, but before the final decision of the Commission. Consideration of the matter by the Commission is suspended for three months by the request, after which the Commission may give its decision. The Council can agree to the request only by unanimous vote and in "exceptional circumstances" justifying this decision. The Commission can challenge the decision of the Council before the Court on the grounds that no exceptional circumstances exist. If the Council's decision is not challenged, it is binding on the Commission if the decision is in favor of the request. If it is against the request, however, the Commission must decide whether the aid is compatible with the Treaty, since the effect of the Council's decision is only to refuse to waive the Treaty for the aid in question. The member state still has the same rights to grant the aid as it had before the request to the Council was made. A member state may make a request even in the case of a state aid which might be permissible under Article 92, since it is too late to make a request after the Commission has given its decision.

When the state has submitted its arguments to the Commission, the latter may decide that the state aid legislation or its application is contrary to Article 92 and that the state must repeal the legislation or modify its application to comply with the Treaty. The Commission must give reasons for the decision and must give the state a time limit for taking the appropriate action. The state may challenge the decision in the Court on the grounds of infringement of the Treaty, lack of jurisdiction, or any other ground appropriate under Article 173.[104] If the state does not challenge the decision of the Commission within two months, it is binding.[105] Since the Commission has already given a reasoned decision that the state is contravening the Treaty and the state has had a chance to argue its case, the state may be brought directly before the Court if it does not comply with the decision within the time limit.[106]

States may grant state aid which is within Article 92(2); prohibition of this aid by the Commission is a breach of the Treaty. However, the Commission has a discretion to forbid aid which is under Article 92(3). Refusal to allow state aid of these kinds cannot be challenged on the grounds that it is a breach of the Treaty or outside the jurisdiction of the Commission. It is submitted, however, that the Commission should take into account the criteria mentioned in this chapter[107] and give reasons if it departs from them. The decision can be challenged only for breach of either procedural rules—including Article 93 and any regulations under Article 94—or any rule of law relating to the application of the Treaty[108] or for misuse of discretionary power.[109]

[102] Art. 93(2). This applies also notwithstanding the terms of any regulations made under art. 94.

[103] Cf. art. 235.

[104] No enterprise may challenge the decision even if the decision concerns the enterprise directly and specifically; art. 173(2) does not apply to decisions addressed to states.

[105] Art. 173.

[106] Art. 93(2)(2); cf. arts. 169–70.

[107] On pp.320–23.

[108] Art. 173.

[109] Bebr, Judicial Control 98–108.

When a state plans to establish or modify state aids[110] or to grant aid to individual enterprises under an existing program,[111] it must inform the Commission in time for the latter to comment on the plan. If the Commission considers the plan contrary to Article 92, it so informs the state, and the latter submits its arguments in accordance with the procedure outlined. If the Commission objects, the state may not implement the proposals until a final decision has been made by the Commission on the arguments or by the Council on a request for a waiver. To implement Article 92 and Article 93(3), the Commission may prepare regulations specifying when it is to be notified of states' plans to grant aid. These regulations must be approved by the Council by qualified majority.

STATE AIDS: TREATY REQUIREMENTS

A state aid gives locally produced goods an economic advantage in the home market equal to that given by a tariff. It is therefore necessary to insure that member states do not replace tariffs by state aids giving similar protection. State aids, unlike tariffs, may reduce marginal costs and distort competition outside the states granting them. In principle, state aid is incompatible with the most efficient allocation of resources in the EEC.[112] Article 92 sets out the substantive criteria for deciding which state aids are compatible with the Common Market.[113] Certain specific types of state aids are dealt with by other provisions,[114] but Article 92 lays down the genral rules.

In general, aid granted by a member state or by means of state resources in any form which distorts or threatens to distort competition by favoring certain enterprises or the production of certain goods is incompatible with the Common Market, insofar as it adversely affects trade between member states. State aid which equalizes competitive conditions by compensating for an artificial disadvantage does not distort competition and therefore should be permitted until the disadvantage has been terminated.[115] State aids such as export credits, which exist in all member states, cannot distort competition unless given on different terms in different member states. To decide if a state aid is permissible, the Commission looks to see if it exceeds the aid given for the same purpose in other member states. Some typical examples of state aid follow.

Providing the potential investor with information which is otherwise available does not distort conditions of competition because the information is available to all and it does not alter marginal production and distribution costs or otherwise aid the investment once made. Even if

[110] Art. 93(3); see State Comm'r for the Sicilian Region v. Regional Gov't of Sicily, Corte Costituzionale (Italian Constitutional Court), April 9, 1963, [1963] C.M.L.R. 315.

[111] Third General Report, paras. 149–50; Fourth General Report, paras. 52–53 (1961); Seventh General Report, para. 69 (1964).

[112] Spaak Report 57; Uri, "Economics and Politics of the Common Market," in Competition, Cartels and Their Regulation 378, 380 (Miller ed. 1962).

[113] Cf. ECSC Treaty, art. 67(1).

[114] Such as art. 42, on agriculture; art. 77, on transport (see also arts. 80, 82); and art. 98. Certain problems may arise since the institutional requirements vary, but in general the specific provisions alone govern aid within their terms, arts. 92–94 being the general, and therefore the residual, provisions.

[115] The Spaak Report says that temporary aids can be permitted if they put the industries aided on a par with other industries but do not give them an advantage over the other industries; Spaak Report 59. This result can be explained also on the basis that such a state aid does not affect trade "adversely." Verloren van Themaat, "Competition and Restrictive Business Practices in the European Economic Community," in Institute on Legal Aspects of the European Community 99, 107 (1960). This is the same principle as art. 98.

it was made to inform the regional development authority and not to benefit investors, comprehensive market research by a member state may be within Article 92 since the information can be obtained by enterprises only at substantial cost. State provision of facilities at commercial rates or without charge if the facilities are normally provided without charge[116] does not distort competition even if the facilities would not otherwise be available, since no competitive advantage is given over enterprises obtaining similar facilities elsewhere. The state is simply stepping into a gap in the economic structure or the capital market which would not exist in an industrialized region. Services provided by state monopolies do not constitute state aids unless the monopolies are subsidized. State-financed advertising of national goods[117] is state aid, but it seems legitimate, since it encourages interstate trade and affects marginal costs only indirectly.

It appears that Article 92 applies only if the effect on interstate trade is adverse, but since *ex hypothesi* the effect of the aid is to assist enterprises to trade, it seems clear that nearly all measures which distort competition affect interstate trade adversely.[118] State aids which affect interstate trade adversely, but unintentionally, are prohibited; state aids which are likely to affect trade but which in operation have not actually done so are not prohibited.

State aids can affect interstate trade by artificially encouraging exports or by giving local enterprises an advantage in competition with imports; most state aids do both. A state aid which encourages investment in a region or sector producing only for the home market and without competition from imports encourages labor and capital from other member states to participate and may affect interstate trade in this way.[119]

Article 92 applies to all state aids, whatever their form, and whether they are given directly or indirectly by means of state resources.[120] Grants,[121] subsidized loans, the provision of facilities at prices below ordinary commercial levels, selective remission of taxes, or the repayment of expenses incurred are all state aid within Article 92. State aid to certain enterprises may constitute aid to other enterprises which depend on the enterprises directly aided for their supplies or for their product demand.[122] A measure is within Article 92 if it is given only for the production of certain goods to enterprises in a specified region or sector or to enterprises engaged in particular activities, such as exporting or import substitution. State action theoretically affecting all sectors of industry —such as tax reductions for all enterprises

[116] However, if the state built a road likely to be used only by a particular enterprise, e.g., a road to a mine or a hotel in a remote area, this might constitute an aid to the enterprise and not a public facility.

[117] See Economic Development, Pr. 4803, ch. 16, paras. 17–18 (1958).

[118] In connection with the similar controversy in connection with art. 85(1), see pp. 391–93.

[119] Investment and employment are probably not "trade," which means primarily trade in goods and services. Nevertheless, it seems likely that in the circumstances described the Commission would have power to review the position.

[120] Verloren van Themaat, "Competition and Restrictive Business Practices in the European Economic Community," in Institute on Legal Aspects of the European Community 99, 110–11 (1960).

[121] Article 54(3)(h).

[122] Verloren van Themaat, "Competition and Restrictive Business Practices in the European Economic Community," in Institute on Legal Aspects of the European Community 99, 107 (1960), says that favorable tax treatment of depreciation of capital goods was once held not to be a state aid to the industries using the capital goods, because these industries were spread throughout the economy, but was held to be a state aid to the capital goods industry. See Spaak Report 59.

of a certain size, state contributions to social security funds, depreciation allowances, or tax reductions applicable throughout a member state to encourage economic expansion—are not within Article 92 but may require harmonization under other provisions of the Treaty. However, general tax measures may distort competition by aiding certain enterprises or the production of certain goods; for example, tax relief to occupiers of open land may constitute aid to agriculture. Some difficult questions on the class of enterprises primarily benefited by general measures of tax relief may eventually have to be decided.[123] For the time being the Commission is concerned only with eliminating the most obvious forms of state aid. When more doubtful matters arise, they can be dealt with under Article 100.

State aids which are automatically permitted

Article 92(2) lists three permissible types of state aid. If these provisions apply, the Commission has no discretion; however, the provisions are limited in scope. The first is social aid to individual consumers, such as subsidies to reduce the prices of milk for school children, fuel for elderly people, textbooks for students, or medicinal supplies for the sick.[124] This includes also aid to nonprofit activities and enterprises such as schools, hospitals, research centers, and charitable institutions.[125] It must be based on the needs of the recipients but can be paid directly to the producers. By its nature, this aid can affect interstate trade only by subsidizing domestic consumption of imported products by the needy or deserving. Social aid which does not subsidize imported products on the same terms as locally produced goods is contrary to Article 7.

The second permissible type of state aid is aid to undo damage caused by natural disasters and to restore the status quo.[126] The Commission need not approve this aid in advance.

The third type is aid to the economy of certain regions of West Germany, insofar as it compensates for the economic disadvantages caused by the division of Germany.

State aids which may be permitted: Article 92(3)

Article 92(3) states in general terms the types of state aid which may be permitted even though they contravene Article 92(1). The Commission will permit them if they are reasonable, justified, and unlikely to have serious ill effects. It is not possible to lay down exact criteria defining when these aids should be permitted. The criteria involve questions of degree and matters of policy, and the provisions should be flexible.

The first clause deals with "aid intended to promote the economic development of regions where the standard of living is abnormally low or there is serious under-employment."[127] The "normal"

[123] See Second General Report, para. 134 (1959); Third General Report, para. 148 (1960); Sixth General Report, para. 50 (1963); Sullivan, The Search for Tax Principles in the European Economic Community 37–38 (1963).

[124] Spaak Report 58. Of course, this aid is state aid to the producers if it increases their profits above normal levels.

[125] Ibid.

[126] See Rapport fait au nom de la Commission économique et financière sur les mesures d'aide déjà engagés ou qui pourraient être prises en vue de la reconstruction du littoral de l'Allemagne du Nord frappé par une catastrophe naturelle, A.P.E. Doc. No. 10 (1962).

[127] See Spaak Report 58; Vasseur, Le droit de la réforme des structures industrielles et des économies régionales 328–31 (1959). The Commission must "develop a policy reconciling the demands of competition policy with those of regional or structural policy." Action Programme for the Second Stage, para. 29 (1962). See also Sixth General Report, para. 50 (1963).

standard of living with which comparisons should be made is the mean standard within the Community, including the overseas territories to which the rules of competition apply.[128] Exceptional areas such as Antarctica and perhaps also areas with low standards of living which are clearly in need of economic aid should be disregarded. The fact that a region has not the lowest standard of living in the whole Common Market should not disentitle it to aid. "Serious under-employment" is also a relative term. Any substantial degree of underemployment, whether permanent or seasonal, would presumably be serious; the amount of unused capacity in the whole Community economy at the time would have to be taken into account. A depression throughout the EEC should not be dealt with by regional measures. Underemployment means underemployment of the whole labor force and includes unemployment of a part.[129] In either case, state aid which is reasonable in proportion to the seriousness of the situation and which does no unnecessary harm[130] may be given, because the poorer regions of the EEC must be developed.[131] Since in all cases state aids are permitted only at the discretion of the Commission, the difference between Article 92(3)(a) and 92(3)(c) should not be exaggerated.[132]

Article 92(3)(b) deals with state aid to promote the execution of projects important to the common European interest. Such projects include tunnels to overcome natural geographical barriers, the exploitation of important natural resources, canals serving the economies of several member states, and other projects suitable for financing by the European Investment Bank.[133] The projects need not directly foster the Community outlook or increase economic links between member states. They need not be government projects, but it is essential that

---

State aids have a double function—instruments of protectionism and instruments of regional development policy; Rapport . . . sur le sixième rapport général sur l'activité de la Communauté économique européenne, A.P.E. Doc. No. 76, para. 66 (1963–64); EEC Commission, Première Communication de la Commission sur la Politique Régionale dans la C.E.E. 21–24 (1965); see von der Groeben, Competition Policy as a Part of Economic Policy in The Common Market (1965).

[128] EEC Treaty, art. 227 and Annex IV. These are now St. Pierre and Miquelon, and the Comoro Archipelago, the French Somali Coast, New Caledonia and dependencies, French Oceania, and the Southern and Antarctic Territories. The other areas listed now are under independent rule.

[129] See Measures for the Economic Development of Under-Developed Countries, U.N. Doc. No. E/1986/ST/ECA/10, at 7 (1951).

[130] Cf. art. 92(3)(a), 92(3)(c).

[131] "[I]n the case of countries with differing income levels, it can be argued that the marginal utility of income is likely to be higher in the poor than in rich regions. This would imply that an income transfer from developed to underdeveloped regions may be considered beneficial even if gains in the latter regions do not exceed losses in the former." Belassa, The Theory of Economic Integration 205 (1961).

[132] "It is necessary also to prevent measures of support taken in one country, by seriously altering conditions of competition, from having damaging effects on regions in other countries." Marjolin, in 1 Documents de la Conférence sur les économies régionales 21, 28 (EEC Commission, 1961) (author's translation). State aids given to enterprises in industrial zones often are more favorable than those given to enterprises outside the zone but within the less developed region. This differentiation is not justifiable on the basis of differences in the level of per capita income or underemployment, since the zone is, or is likely to become, more prosperous than the surrounding region. Special regimes for the zones seem to be justified under art. 92(3)(a), not art. 92(3)(c). See von der Groeben, "Policy on Competition in the European Economic Community," 1961 EEC Bull. No. 7/8, Supp. The differential can be regarded as a decrease in the state aid given in the region outside the industrial zone instead of an increase within that zone, and zones are simply a means of developing less prosperous areas.

[133] See art. 130.

they should benefit the economy of more than one member state.

State aids are permissible also to remedy serious disturbances in the economy of a member state. The EEC recognizes that removing obstacles to trade requires concerted action to guarantee both stability in expansion and a balanced trade.[134] If disturbances occur, state aids may protect the enterprises concerned from collapsing while they are being modernized or structurally changed or may enable them to go out of production slowly to permit relocation of workers. The Treaty does not permit indefinite support for uneconomic enterprises.

Lastly, state aid may be permitted to facilitate the development of specific activities or specific economic regions, even if these regions do not suffer from a low standard of living or from underemployment. Under this clause, member states have complete discretion in formulating policy, if the aid does not alter trading conditions to an extent contrary to the general interest of the Community. State aid which puts an enterprise elsewhere in the Common Market out of business or causes it to lay off employees is contrary to the common interest. If demand is inflexible and static, state aid to an enterprise which competes on a market already adequately supplied is not justified. A deliberate shift of existing capacity to a less developed region may be justified to secure a balanced distribution of economic growth. The provision suggests no criteria by which the Commission should decide whether to permit the member state to carry out its policy, but it enables the Commission to exercise its coordinating function. This clause permits state aid which encourages enterprises to move from a congested area or to decentralize and state aid which encourages temporarily unprofitable industries likely to become profitable due to increased demand or industries desirable for scientific or military purposes.

State aid for shipbuilding[135] which merely offsets the absence of customs protection is to be reduced, together with tariffs, subject to the common commercial policy. State aids which do more than offset the absence of tariffs are subject to the ordinary rules.

The Council may declare, by qualified majority on proposal of the Commission, other types of state aids to be compatible with the Common Market.[136] The aids can be declared automatically valid or, like the types of aid just mentioned, declared prima facie permissible, subject to objection by the Commission. The Council also may define in more detail the types of state aid already permissible under Article 92.

THE COMMISSION'S CRITERIA FOR STATE AIDS

It is possible to lay down some general requirements as to the extent and nature of the state aids permitted under Article 92(3).[137] First, state aids must not con-

[134] EEC Treaty, Preamble, para. 4.

[135] Art. 92(3)(c); Second General Report, paras. 135–36 (1959); Third General Report, para. 152 (1960); Fifth General Report, para. 52 (1962); Sixth General Report, para. 48 (1963); see 1964 Journal Officiel 2454-55/64.

[136] Arts. 92(3)(d), 94.

[137] Report by the [OEEC] Group of Financial Experts . . ., in Negotiations for a European Free Trade Area: Documents . . ., Cmd. No. 641, at 217, 218 (1959), concluded:

> The institutional framework [of financial aid to the less developed countries] must be designed according to one of two mutually conflicting principles. Precise amounts of aid could be provided in the form of grants and interest-free loans, or loans bearing token interest only. Or else means could be devised whereby, with some exceptional facilities to start with, the less-developed countries could be helped to build up their capital stock on the basis of market conditions prevailing in the more-industrialised countries. Under this second conception it would, no doubt, be necessary for some time to provide some help on terms more favourable than those prevailing on the markets of the more-indus-

tribute to existing inequality in conditions of competition.[138] This requirement has little relevance for less developed regions or to remedies for serious disturbances in the economies of member states; it is, however, important with regard to projects of general European interest and aid to sectors or regions not suffering from low living standards or unemployment.[139]

Second, since the need for state aids should decrease if they have been effective, all state aids should decrease[140] and should have a definite cessation date.[141] In this way the aided enterprise can become competitive without relying indefinitely on a subsidy.

Third, Dr. von der Groeben holds that state aid should always encourage adaptation and development to suit full competition and the general condition of the Common Market economy.[142]

Fourth, all state aids should be selective so that they are given only where they are really needed.[143] Aids must be selective to avoid duplication and wasteful or uneconomical use of Community resources.[144] General tax concessions for regions or sectors are unlikely to be approved unless aid to all the enterprises benefited can be justified. State aid to a whole region benefits industries of varied degrees of prosperity and has irrational effects. How selective state aids must be depends on the circumstances. The Commission at present is considering only the laws which authorize the granting of state aid, but ultimately it will consider the way in which aid is distributed in practice.[145] Selective state aids necessitate approval for each recipient enterprise and make it possible to require each one to use local raw materials and fuel and local subcontractors. If permitted in the EEC, these requirements will save foreign currency and encourage development and diversification of industry in the region; a network of small comple-

---

trialised countries; but special assistance of this kind would progressively be reduced until it reached vanishing point. Our recommendations are based on this second conception. We feel that only ways and means that will gradually bring the less-developed countries into alignment with the conditions prevailing in the capital markets of their more advanced neighbours will produce a rational economic development. Any system of help which did not, from the outset, tend to align market conditions in all Member countries would be open to criticism; it would risk creating artificial economies which could only operate in a vacuum and which would never be able to function in a Free Trade Area.

[138] Von der Groeben, "Policy on Competition in the European Economic Community," 1961 EEC Bull. No. 7/8, Supp. 12–14.

[139] See Spaak Report 59.

[140] See Fourth General Report, para. 55 (1962); 1960 Journal Officiel 1972/60. "Where the Commission considers that aids are compatible with the Treaty as serving the ends of a sound structural or regional policy, it will in particular take care that such aids are digressive." Action Programme for the Second Stage, para. 29 (1962). However, it is the view of officials of the Italian state development fund (Cassa per il Mezzogiorno) that state aid will be necessary in southern Italy, admittedly the EEC's poorest region, for at least an additional twenty years.

[141] Spaak Report 58; see 1964 Journal Officiel 2454–55/64.

[142] In 2 Documents de la Conférence sur les économies régionales 17, 26 (EEC Commission, 1961). See 1959 Journal Officiel 1033–34/59; EEC Commission, Moyens de la politique régionale dans les Etats membres de la C.E.E. 145–47, 148 (1964).

[143] Von der Groeben, "Policy on Competition in the European Community," 1961 EEC Bull. No. 7/8, Supp. 12–14; Action Programme for the Second Stage, para. 29 (1962). Of the Irish state aids, the tax concessions are automatic, and all the other state aids are selective.

[144] U.N. Economic Survey of Europe Since the War, U.N. Doc. No. E/ECE/194, ch. 12, at 223 (1953).

[145] Fourth General Report, paras. 52, 57 (1961); Third General Report, para. 50 (1960); Action Programme for the Second Stage, para. 27 (1962).

mentary industries may grow up.[146] This would constitute a state aid to the local producers and subcontractors. Insofar as each enterprise is required to purchase or contract at uneconomic terms or prices, the value of the aid given is reduced. This practice has trade-diverting effects similar to those of private restraints on competition.

Although the Commission repeatedly has said that state aids should be selective, an important argument against selective aid—primarily such aid to regions—should be mentioned. If all new enterprises in a region are given the same limited amount of state aid, the ordinary operation of the market will insure that only efficient enterprises or those using natural economic advantages will make substantial profits. Entrepreneurs will be encouraged to establish the enterprises most suited to ordinary competition rather than those enterprises for the establishment and operation of which they can get the largest amount of aid. In identifying the enterprises for which a region is naturally suited, the operation of the market is probably more effective than estimates of economists made before the industries are established. The best method of reconciling this principle with the objections to indiscriminate or non-selective state aid is to provide a general regime for new enterprises within a region and to supplement it with selective aid. The general regime should probably be a reduction in direct taxation; it should not go further than is necessary to compensate for any inadequacies in infrastructure and lack of external economies[147] and perhaps to give some incentive to investment. The Commission is not likely to prohibit non-selective state aid in less developed regions and should not do so.

Fifth, state aid should not be unnecessarily generous in relation to the function to be performed. "The Commission . . . will take care . . . that the beneficiaries are not given a decisive advantage over their competitors."[148] This is analogous to the rule forbidding dumping. If aid is so substantial that the state is providing the economic benefits for the region at its own expense, it would be better for the state to invest directly. The enterprises aided excessively have no reason to make themselves competitive.

Sixth, state aids must be given without discrimination, intentional or actual, on the grounds of nationality.[149] If state aid is given by tax concession, there is discrimination on the basis of tax domicile between residents of the state giving the aid—or residents of any state with which it has a double taxation treaty providing for exemption or a matching credit—and residents of any state who must pay tax at the full rate on repatriated profits. Discrimination on the basis of fiscal domicile by a member state against its own taxpayers is incompatible with the EEC, even if it is legitimate from the state's point of view; for instance, because balance-of-payments reasons make the state reluctant to encourage investment abroad. As a measure of regional development policy, to insure that capital from all over the Common Market is available in less developed regions and is uniformly treated, matching credit or tax-sparing provisions should be enacted, except where the tax concession is given only on undistributed profits. Otherwise, capital movement will be distorted by a fortuitous combination

[146] Rosenstein-Rodan, "How to Industrialize an Underdeveloped Area," in Regional Economic Planning 205, 208 (Isard & Cumberland ed. 1961).

[147] A reduction in direct taxation will not do this directly, of course.

[148] Action Programme for the Second Stage, para. 29 (1962).

[149] See arts. 54(3)(h), 7.

of concessional tax rules.[150]

ELEMENTS IN STATE AIDS AND FURTHER SUGGESTED CRITERIA

If any of the several elements of state aids is ineffective, unnecessary, or excessive, it is suggested that the aid is not permissible under Article 92. An analysis of these elements is necessary to understand the assessment of state aids by Community organs.

Most state aids contain an element of compensation for the economic disadvantages of investment in the region in question.[151] These disadvantages may be increased costs due to inadequate infrastructure, lack of external economies, the expense of training unskilled labor,[152] or added costs of transporting raw materials, components, or finished products from remote markets or sources of supply. For regional economic expansion, any economic disadvantages of industry due to underdevelopment in the region, including those which will be remedied eventually by economic development, should be compensated for by state aids; otherwise, investment in the region can-not be expected. Since this element is a subsidy for uneconomic enterprises, it should be given only if the enterprise will become economic, so it can not be given for necessarily permanent disadvantages, such as the absence of local raw materials. In assessing the amount of the compensation element in state aid, advantages such as abundant cheap labor must be offset against competitive disadvantages. The compensatory element, including the element of premium for risk, can hardly be calculated precisely, but it should be selective and based on the needs of the individual enterprise. Normally, state aid should probably compensate for the particular net cost disadvantage in each case and should be part of an integrated program modifying the cost structure in favor of the less developed area, especially by reducing the costs which differ most from those elsewhere. There is little point in reducing capital costs if operating costs remain excessive. Sometimes, however, the existence of such a disadvantage would justify an unrelated aid not compensatory in the strict sense, such as a reduction in direct taxes to offset high transport costs.

State aids may also include an element of insurance, to further assure the profit-making capacity of the enterprise and to compensate for the relatively greater uncertainties of investment in an under-industrialized area.[153]

A third element, of which compensation for uncertainties may perhaps be regarded as a part, is the incentive ele-

[150] However, when the country of residence permits deferral of its tax on the profits of a foreign subsidiary until repatriation, there is an incentive to retain and reinvest profits. Accumulated profits are the commonest source of finance for expansion in the Six where capital markets are underdeveloped. The function of a matching credit provision is merely to encourage foreign investment where distribution of profits is likely anyway.

[151] Economic Development, Pr. 4803, ch. 2, para. 14 (1958); Carroll, 34 Cahiers de Droit Fiscal International 21 (1956). Compare this element with the principle which justifies tax relief for exports under art. 98. See Spaak Report 58, 59; EEC Commission, Moyens de la politique régionale dans les Etats membres de la C.E.E., 95–96, 129–32, 134–39, 149 (1964).

[152] Fennell, Industrialization and Agricultural Development in the Congested Districts 11 (1962); see Industrial Grants (Amendment) Act, 1963 Acts, No. 4, § 5; Undeveloped Areas Act, 1952 Acts 3, § 7.

[153] Richman, Taxation of Foreign Investment Income: An Economic Analysis 7 (1963); Streeten, Economic Integration 92 (1961). See Stamp, "Taxation, Risk-Taking and the Price Level," 1928 Econ. J. 204–15. Heller & Kauffman, Tax Incentives for Industry in Less Developed Countries 60–66 (1963), point out that giving tax concessions may cause the loss of large amounts of revenue in order to compensate the investor for some non-tax disadvantage which could be fully remedied by the state directly out of revenue at much less expense.

ment. Tax reductions are normally incentives, except where capital accumulation is difficult.[154] The incentive element is required only to insure that the potential investor prefers the less developed region instead of being faced with two alternatives as equally balanced as the merely compensatory aid can make them. Apart from the question of compensation for risk, the extent to which a state aid should insure added profits merely as an inducement is a psychological rather than an economic question. Businessmen often decide to invest in a country or region first on purely business grounds and inquire into the incentives and concessions later. For reasons of administrative practice or business principle,[155] cost factors and state aids, especially tax concessions, are often not calculated in relation to one another. Few businessmen would undertake a venture which would be profitable over a substantial period only because of state aid. The choice of a place for a new operation may be influenced by factors—such as linguistic difficulties or the unfavorable image of the country or region as a place for the manufacture of high-quality "prestige" products—which cannot be compensated for directly by additional incentives. There are differences of opinion as to how far incentives influence choice of region for the establishment of new operations, but state aids which distort competition substantially in favor of enterprises in a given region are certainly important.[156] They are likely to become increasingly important as competition intensifies,[157] making comparative advantages relatively more important, and as the infrastructure of less developed regions improves, thereby decreasing the difficulties of doing business. More work should be done[158] to assess the extent to which the incentive element in state aids can, in practice, influence foreign investment. An excessive incentive element in state aid has unhealthy economic effects;[159] for example, it increases the danger of aiding the estab-

[154] Where high tax rates discourage investment, tax concessions may be needed not merely to encourage investment but to remove the deterrent. See Kauffman, "Income Tax Exemption and Economic Development," 13 Nat'l Tax J. 141, 150–62 (1960). For a less critical study, see Bhatia, "Tax Exemption in a Developing Economy," id. at 341. Von der Groeben, "Policy on Competition in the European Economic Community," 1961 EEC Bull. No. 7/8, Supp. 13, says: "Naturally, aid of this kind must never serve to create a competitive advantage." This presumably refers only to aids under art. 92(3)(c) and not to aids under art. 92(3)(a).

[155] As businesses become more sophisticated, they tend to treat direct taxation as another element in costs rather than as a factor relevant only after net profits have been ascertained. In large, modern enterprises, the tax and the cost advantages of a proposed subsidiary are normally considered by different specialized personnel, the tax aspects often by an outside firm of lawyers. It is the writer's impression that the best-managed and most internationally minded enterprises usually achieve a proper balancing of tax advantages against cost advantages. See Committee on Turnover Taxation, Report, Cmd. No. 2300, para. 282 (1964); Committee of Inquiry into Taxation on Industry, Report, Pr. 3512, para. 171 (1956).

[156] Irish experience seems to indicate that tax concessions of up to 100% on profits are more effective than cash grants.

[157] Sixth General Report, para. 47 (1963).

[158] See generally Friedman & Kalmanoff, Joint International Business Ventures (1961); see also Neumark Report, Rapport 63, CCH 2461; Heller & Kauffman, Tax Incentives for Industry in Less Developed Countries 5–6, 57–60 (1963); EEC Commission, Moyens de la politique régionale dans les Etats membres de la C.E.E. 139–41, 144, 149–50 (1964).

[159] OECD Economic Survey of Ireland, 1963, para. 46. Heller & Kauffman, Tax Incentives for Industry in Less Developed Countries 9–10, 78–80, 126–33 (1963), conclude that in most economically less developed countries, tax incentives do not offer advantages great enough to compensate for their revenue, equity, and administrative disadvantages. They correctly stress that state aid is justifiable only to the extent to which it is necessary to achieve the desired economic result.

lishment of uneconomical ventures,[160] it fosters a protectionist mentality which expects freedom from effective competition, and it discourages investment unless large incentives are offered. Many state aids seem greatly to exceed compensation for economic disadvantages or added risk or even a reasonable reward for having invested in a needy region in a less developed country. Because of Article 92(3)(c), the EEC Commission will have to limit the incentive element in state aids and prevent competition between regions in offering inducements to investment. The incentive element in state aid need not be substantial, if the elements of compensation for disadvantages and risk are adequate. The practice of giving exemption from direct tax until total profits equal the total capital invested, with no time limit, is unfortunate. It allows an enterprise to continue indefinitely, with no incentive to efficiency or expansion, while complete repayment of capital invested is guaranteed at government expense if the enterprise is not operating at a loss. These concessions are common in less developed countries. They are, of course, contrary to the EEC principle that the duration of state aids must be limited. More extensive provisions for carry-over of losses for tax purposes do not constitute state aid, if available generally, and encourage new ventures without such serious disadvantages.

The size of the incentive element can be reduced by making available information on the actual business advantages and disadvantages of the region.[161] Especially in a less developed region, but also in a depressed region suffering from congestion, obsolescent housing and the other disadvantages of a fall in living standards, combined with the lack of accurate information, tend to cause the possibilities for investment to be underestimated. The Commission might undertake studies to obtain accurate and impartial information on business possibilities in each region. These studies would help to decide which industries were most suitable and should be encouraged. The increase in actual investment in these regions will help to break down those barriers to further investment and development caused by business inexperience, ignorance, and lack of enterprise. If state aids are individually negotiated, an indication of the types of enterprise which will be preferred and the extent to which aid is actually given, rather than mere statements of the statutory maximum amounts of aid, would be useful. This would help to avoid the deterrent effect, perhaps greater for United States than for European businessmen, of having to negotiate with an administrative authority.

[160] Also, of course, the greater the danger of a popular outcry against excessive subsidized profits, which is more likely in countries less developed and less friendly to foreign investment than Ireland. This is particularly the case where greater incentives are given to foreign capital than to local capital. In estimating the value of state aid, especially if it is given under contract, it must be remembered that state aid implies a commitment by the state to avoid, if possible, action injuring the enterprise aided—if only because such action would involve a waste of public funds.

[161] Fennell, Industrialization and Agricultural Development in the Congested Districts 25 (1962); Kauffman, "Income Tax Exemption and Economic Development," 13 Nat'l Tax J. 252, 261–63 (1960); Heller & Kauffman, Tax Incentives for Industry in Less Developed Countries 62 (1963).

It is unfortunately probable that state aids are more effective as a publicity device than as an economic incentive in many countries. Because of reduced costs, many foreign investors in less developed countries are making far greater profits than they would make at home; id. at 4, 64–65, 108, 123. In such circumstances, state aids are merely a demonstration of the government's welcome to foreign investors and a subsidy to them out of public funds.

A. H. Smith, "Tax Relief for New Industries in Ghana," 11 Nat'l Tax J. 362 (1958), points out (1) that tax reliefs for new industries de-

The fourth element of state aids is the value of the investment to the region. For example, in areas suffering from unemployment or emigration, extra aid should be given to an enterprise which requires a large labor force or which is likely to create a demand for secondary industries. In primarily agricultural regions, industries processing agricultural products are particularly desirable. A new enterprise complementing existing enterprises or opening up a new sector has economic advantages beyond the actual employment it gives and so qualifies for greater state aid.[162] If a detailed regional development plan has been worked out, it is possible to see how a particular enterprise fits into it.[163] The amount of aid given should also depend on the amount of excess capacity in the infrastructure of the less developed region and in that of the more industrialized regions; if the social costs of moving the labor are greater than the money costs of moving the industry, the saving may be given in the form of aid to the enterprise.

This public benefit element is extraneous to the investor and is based on the interests of the economy as a whole. The state should give increased aid, because without the investment, the same benefits to the public could be obtained only by public expenditure or not at all. By this aid, the investor's capital or operating expenses are reduced, and his profits are increased as a reward for the social and economic benefits of investment. No further incentive element is necessary, and this fourth element can be regarded simply as state aid looked at purely from the public point of view. The amount of public benefit is peculiar to each enterprise aided, and only selective state aids can take it into account adequately. It involves decisions on questions of policy, e.g., whether modernization which may reduce the labor needs of the enterprise rather than provide employment should receive extra aid. This element will be digressive; it would be unjustifiable to aid an enterprise out of public funds if it were no longer more valuable socially than others not being aided.

MEANS OF PROMOTING REGIONAL DEVELOPMENT

The tools of regional economic policies in the EEC contemplated by the Treaty

---

prive the state of revenue just when it is needed for capital expenditure which is not itself productive but which is a prerequisite of industrial expansion and when there is no other method of obtaining greatly increased revenue; (2) that underindustrialized nations are competing for foreign capital; and (3) that tax reliefs do not aid those marginal industries which would be advantageous to the economy when established, but merely aid those that do not need help. Professor Smith suggests that tax relief should be given until the capital invested is entirely repaid, in order to encourage industries likely initially to make low profits. It is suggested above in the text that this is not desirable. Presumably, the EEC Commission will try to prevent the giving of state aid where the social cost of the aid exceeds the social benefits of the investment.

See also Cary Brown, "Tax Incentives for Investment," 52(2) Amer. Econ. Rev. 335 (1962); Rottenberg, "Incentives in Underdeveloped Economies," 50(2) Amer. Econ. Rev. 73 (1960).

[162] Rosenstein-Rodan, "How to Industrialize an Underdeveloped Area," in Regional Economic Planning 205, 208 (Isard & Cumberland ed. 1961).

[163] Ireland has never formulated detailed regional economic development plans specifying the type of industry which would receive the maximum aid, but she has considered applications for state aid on their merits as they have arisen. Failure to make detailed plans is probably a defect in Irish economic policy. See Formentini, "Le développement régional et la Banque européenne d'investissement," in 1 Documents de la Conférence sur les économies régionales 35, 43 (EEC Commission, 1961); Winsemius, "Organizing for Industrial Development," in Methods of Industrial Development 79, 82–89 (OECD, 1962).

and most important to investors are:

Infrastructure

1. Direct state action to improve infrastructure.

Labor

2. Subsidies for state aid to workers prejudiced by economic changes, through the European Social Fund.
3. Free movement of labor out of poorer regions, in accordance with Articles 48–51.

Investment

4. Large-scale credit at commercial rates, provided by the European Investment Bank, for productive investment.
5. State aids to private industry.
6. State-provided finance at commercial rates, either in the form of loan capital or equity participation.

One type of incentive to foreign investment is a guarantee of freedom to repatriate capital and profits at any time, free of exchange-control restrictions. This is always given in Ireland. Between EEC member states no such guarantees are necessary, since there is free movement of capital in most circumstances.[164] Though most important to investors, these guarantees are not state aids within Article 92.

The U.N. Economic Commission for Europe[165] has classified the measures of regional economic policy adopted in southern European countries into three types:[166] discriminatory measures to reduce costs for private investors; direct state or state-sponsored investment in infrastructure, transport, power, land improvement, and basic facilities; and political and administrative measures to strengthen initiative at local government level. Direct intervention by member states is required to construct the infrastructure without which private investment is unlikely or, if made, less profitable. If constructing means of transport and communication, housing and recreational facilities, schools, and hospitals, and supplying energy are not, in the circumstances, productive or profit-making ventures, they will not be done by private enterprise. Since all member states are benefiting from the supply of labor and the markets in the less developed region, it is reasonable that they should

[164] In Italy freedom to repatriate profits and capital to non-member states is limited in the case of investments not classified as "productive." Law No. 43 of Feb. 7, 1956, on Investment of Foreign Capital, arts. 1, 2, and Presidential Decree No. 758 of July 6, 1956, art. 1.

[165] Economic Survey of Europe in 1953, U.N. Doc. No. E/ECE/174, ch. 15, at 185 (1954).

[166] By far the most valuable method of insuring economic growth is to increase markets for the principal products of the regions concerned. In the case of Ireland this would result naturally from entry into the EEC, since Ireland is an efficient producer of agricultural products, especially beef. However, an association with the EEC which did not give free entry into Britain and the rest of the EEC for Irish agricultural produce would have a seriously retrograde effect. Any market guaranteed to a particular region for a specified quantity of its principal product, while it would aid economic planning, would be likely to have trade-diverting effects incompatible with the EEC.

EEC Commission, Moyens de la politique régionale dans les Etats membres de la C.E.E. 83 (1964), divides state aids into capital grants, reduced interest rates, state guarantees for loans, state equity participation, and repayment of interest on private loans. Different member states concentrate on different types of state aid.

ECSC High Authority, Arrangements to Facilitate the Establishment of New Economic Activities (1962), contains an analysis of state aids. The classification is as follows: Direct assistance—(1) financial assistance including subsidies, loans, interest reductions, guarantees of loans contracted to finance new activities, financial participation, advances, cooperative trade associations; (2) fiscal concessions (including tax reliefs), accelerated depreciation allowances, reduction of tariffs; (3) differentiation in rates payable for energy and transport; and (4) assistance in research. Indirect assistance—(5) provision of basic services or the cost of buildings; (6) building and leasing factory space; (7) decentralization of research institutions to insure proximity to enterprises using them; and (8) provision of workers' housing. Arrangements benefiting workers—(9) voca-

share the cost of the necessary infrastructure.

"Membership of the Common Market [and] . . . acceptance of its aims should logically imply a willingness by its members, acting as a group, to accept joint responsibility for promoting economic development in southern Italy [or other areas] in the same way as each accepts the need to assist depressed or underdeveloped areas within its own territory."[167]

The provision of infrastructure by the state is not a state aid within Article 92[168] if any charge made (e.g., for electricity) is on a commercial basis and if facilities are not provided for particular enterprises which they normally would have had to obtain at their own expense. Measures to strengthen initiative at local government level are also not within Article 92, even though they are important, particularly in connection with the formation of cooperative societies. Primarily of interest to investors are measures to aid private enterprises and the application of Article 92 to them.

The framework: Industrial zones, development areas, and public contracts

One means of encouraging regional development without direction of industry or direct state action is by establishing industrial zones and development areas.[169] Industrial zones have been important in southern Italy. The concept is a recent one, and the Irish government

tional training; (10) retraining; and (11) payment of expenses of migration. Other—(12) arrangements with regard to foreign exchange to facilitate foreign investment; and (13) measures to prevent congestion and encourage decentralization. Of these, it is submitted that (7) to (13) are not within art. 92.

The EEC Commission has also been compiling a list of all state aids in the EEC for consideration in the light of art. 92, but this has not been published. The U.N. Economic Commission for Europe has suggested that a capital gains tax should be imposed on "the increment in the value of urban real estate arising from the opening up of new regions through improved transport facilities and other development schemes" paid for out of public funds; Economic Survey of Europe in 1953, U.N. Doc. No. E/ECE/174, ch. 15, at 190–91 (1954). See also Rapport . . . sur la politique régionale dans la C.E.E., A.P.E. Doc. No. 99, paras. 68–69 (1963–64).

For a study of the entire question in the context of a single country, see Vasseur, Le droit de la réforme des structures industrielles et des économies régionales (1959).

[167] U.N. Economic Survey of Europe in 1956, U.N. Doc. No. E/ECE/278, ch. IV, at 19 (1957).

[168] The state development fund was set up primarily to provide the infrastructure needed for the development of southern Italy. See generally the report on its work up to 1962, Cassa per il Mezzogiorno, Dodici Anni, 1950–1962 (1963). On infrastructure in the EEC, see Rapport . . . sur la politique régionale dans la C.E.E., A.P.E. Doc. No. 99, paras. 54–57, 93 (1963–64); EEC Commission, Moyens de la politique régionale dans les Etats membres de la C.E.E. 19–82 (1964). On administrative organization, see id. at 152–77.

[169] A development area is a region which is treated as an economic unit and which receives special treatment by the state to encourage economic development. An industrial zone (sometimes called an industrial pole) is a focal point established as the center for the industrialization of a development area. See von der Groeben, in 2 Documents de la Conférence sur les économies régionales 17, 23 (EEC Commission, 1961); Fennell, Industrialization and Agricultural Development in the Congested Districts 19–22, 24–25 (1962); Rosenstein-Rodan, "How to Industrialize an Underdeveloped Area," in Regional Economic Planning 205, 208–10 (Isard & Cumberland ed. 1961); U.N. Economic Survey of Europe in 1954, U.N. Doc. No. E/ECE/194, at 159–60 (1955). The use of development areas and industrial zones has been advocated by the Northeast Development Council in Britain, and also by the British National Economic Development Council, Conditions Favourable to Faster Growth (1963). In Ireland the Shannon Airport industrial zone was created from nothing, and the government is anxious to expand it to the maximum. While the western part of the country is in need of industrialization and additional incentives are given for investment there, it is not a development area in the sense of a region which the government hopes to in-

did not accept it until 1965.[170] However, it already had accepted the same principle by setting up a customs-free area at Shannon Airport, where factories have been built for leasing to industrialists. Because they are suitable for industry and plenty of labor is available in the surrounding area, industrial zones have been used in Britain, Italy, the Netherlands, and France, and were recommended by the EEC Regional Planning Conference.[171] Services provided by the state may be subsidized, or investor's capital outlay may be reduced, e.g., by providing factory space for hire, or other incentives or concessions may be given for investment in the zone. Industrial zones may be used for industrializing less developed areas or depressed areas. The location of the zone within the area can be decided in the light of government plans for the provision or improvement of infrastructure. Zones can be established in places where modern industrial development would not be physically or economically impeded by obsolete buildings but which are near enough to depressed areas to draw on their labor supplies.

In general, businessmen prefer to invest in previously industrialized areas unless there is excessive congestion. They can ascertain the problems and advantages from practical experience. Use of industrial zones therefore helps to minimize both the incentive and compensation elements in state aid and to avoid the expense and ineffectiveness of state aid distributed over a wide area. Factories can be leased and the capital costs of the building borne out of profits, thereby reducing the risk of capital loss. In underindustrialized areas, industrial zones provide many of the external economies and other benefits of concentration of industry. Industrial zones minimize time and expense and make economies of scale possible for the state or private

---

dustrialize fully. British Finance Act, 1963, 11 & 12 Eliz. 2, c. 44, gives special grants for buildings and machinery in "development districts," arrangements for grants and loans, and freedom to write off the cost of equipment against tax entirely at will. These incentives—small compared to Ireland's uniquely large ones—relate to whole development areas or regions and not to carefully chosen growth points or industrial zones.

One of the less obvious characteristics of an industrial zone is that it must be reasonably self-sufficient in housing, entertainment, and other social facilities; von der Groeben, in 2 Documents de la Conférence sur les économies régionales 17, 25–26 (EEC Commission, 1961); Marjolin, in 1 Documents de la Conférence sur les économies régionales 21, 60–61 (EEC Commission, 1961). This difficulty arose at Shannon Airport and was tackled after it became important. This increases the total cost of creating an effective industrial zone in an area not supplied with social facilities adequate for a substantial population, whether this cost is borne by the state or by private enterprise. See Rapport . . . sur la politique régionale dans la C.E.E., A.P.E. Doc. No. 99, para. 98 (1963–64). On the Italian program, see EEC Commission, Moyens de la politique régionale dans les Etats membres de la C.E.E. 87–94 (1964).

[170] Committee on Development Centres and Industrial Estates, Report, Pr. 8461 (1965); National Industrial Economic Council, Comments on Report of Committee on Development Centres and Industrial Estates, Pr. 8476 (1965). For the earlier position, see Second Programme for Economic Expansion, Pr. 7239, para. 57 (1963). There are, of course, political difficulties in choosing one area rather than another for economic development.

[171] Von der Groeben, in 2 Documents de la Conférence sur les économies régionales 17, 24 (EEC Commission, 1961); see, however, Marjolin, in 1 id. at 21, 60, who believes that development zones are necessary only where no concentrations of industry already exist, as in southern Italy and southern and western France. Industrial zones were recommended by the Madrid Conference; Methods of Industrial Development 325 (OECD, 1962). See also Action Programme for the Second Stage, para. 123 (1962); EEC Commission, Objectifs et méthodes de la politique régionale dans la Communauté européenne 54–56 (1964); EEC Commission, Première Communication de la Commission sur la Politique Régionale dans la C.E.E. 13–15, 22 (1965); Bredo, Industrial Estates (1961).

enterprise which constructs factories[172] and provides public utilities, housing, transportation, and social facilities for workers. The presence of a number of enterprises in a small area facilitates establishment of firms providing services which the enterprises would otherwise do without, provide as part of their operations, or obtain from outside the region, thereby raising costs. Since this presence causes diversification of industry and opportunities for other enterprises, it benefits both the public and potential investors. Since services and suppliers in a zone are usually efficient, it probably is unnecessary to make it a condition of state aid that new investors use local services or raw materials, a practice with antitrust aspects of which the Commission may disapprove.

Another technique is to give long-term public contracts to new or established enterprises in less developed regions.[173] These contracts may deal with the supply of materials or services required for infrastructure or publicly built factories in the region. The long term of the contract may encourage the contractor to establish a local operation, and this provides employment and reduces unit costs through economies of scale impossible with a short-term contract; alternatively, the enterprise may be required to establish a local operation. The contracts should be awarded by the state's giving aid to a suitable enterprise, thus enabling it to obtain the contract in an open competition. Economically, this is the equivalent of awarding the contract to an enterprise in the less developed region when its price is not the lowest. However, this method is preferable in the Common Market because it accords with the principle that the financial extent of state aid should be calculable so that its compatibility with the Treaty can be assessed. The Commission can require the reduction or cessation of a continuing state aid already awarded;[174] if aid is given in the form of a contract to an enterprise not quoting the lowest price, a difficult problem of conflict between private and Community law would arise as to whether the Commission could insist on the price being reduced if the state aid was no longer justified.

Types of state aid

State aids or incentives for investment in less developed regions are of various types. First, there are subsidies given by the state, which may be cash grants related to capital or the cost of buildings[175] or equipment, services or raw materials provided below cost, reimbursements of expenses incurred, or allowances for training workers. These exist in Ireland and elsewhere in Europe.

Second, state aid may be given by reducing the rates of direct or indirect taxes.[176] Since reductions in direct taxes

[172] Rosenstein-Rodan, "How to Industrialize an Underdeveloped Area," in Regional Economic Planning 205, 208–10 (Isard & Cumberland ed. 1961).

[173] Id. at 210. See also Ross & Christensen, Tax Incentives for Industry in Mexico 71 (1959). It is not clear under which article—art. 33(7) or art. 92—discrimination in awarding public supply contracts falls.

[174] Arts. 92–93. In June 1963, the Commission prohibited the Sicilian regional authority from allocating orders to local suppliers on a preferential basis; see art. 31.

[175] See art. 54(3)(h). For the position in southern Italy, Sardinia, and Sicily, see 4 Banco di Roma, Foreign Private Enterprise in Italy, pt. I, chs. IX, XV, and pt. II, chs. I-III, and pt. III, ch. IV (1960).

[176] U.N. Economic Survey of Europe, 1959, U.N. Doc. No. E/ECE/383, at 37 (1960). For the position in southern Italy, Sardinia, and Sicily, see 4 Banco di Roma, Foreign Private Enterprise in Italy, pt. I, chs. IV–VII, and pt. II, ch. I (1960). There is no reduction of the company tax anywhere in Italy.

See, for a summary of the German laws since 1945, Vogel, "Tax Incentives for Industrial Development," in Methods of Industrial Develop-

do not aid an enterprise not making a profit, they involve no risk that the enterprise will be uneconomic without them, and if they are temporary they encourage the enterprise to maximize its profits. On the other hand, they are of the greatest value to enterprises which need them least. Their precise effect will depend on whether taxes normally are passed on. Since they involve no actual outlay by the state, governments may prefer them to cash grants. Irish experience indicates that they are also preferred by investors because of their incentive effect. They can be given generally to all enterprises within a certain region or sector or negotiated separately with each enterprise.

Credit facilities are a third important source of finance in less developed areas and are widely used to facilitate regional development.[177] If given at commercial rates of interest, they are not state aids and require no approval under Article 92. They are particularly important if the firm involved is too small for a public issue of shares,[178] if the local capital market is inadequate, or if banks are too cautious to provide credit. Guarantees by a public financing body of loans made at commercial rates are state aids if they cause the interest rate charged to be reduced, as they usually do. State participation in the equity capital of a company may also be state aid, especially where it insures that credit is available from private sources for the enterprise in question.

A fourth form of aid is exemption of imported raw materials or, as has been done in Ireland and Italy, of capital goods, from tariffs.

The U.N. Economic Commission for Europe has suggested "the payment of a flat rate subsidy per head for industrial employment, which would have the effect of encouraging the development of labor intensive industry in particular."[179] This is unlikely to be permitted by the Commission as long as there is a labor shortage in the EEC, but would be useful if underemployment was serious in any region. Another suggestion made was the payment of a flat-rate subsidy for all industrial exports in addition to

---

ment 271 (OECD, 1962). See also Kauffman, "Income Tax Exemption and Economic Development" (pts. 1–2), 13 Nat'l Tax J. 141, 252 (1960); Taylor, "Industrial Tax Exemption in Puerto Rico," 7 Nat'l Tax J. 359 (1954); Harris, "Notes on Tax Exemption and Development," 8 Nat'l Tax J. 393 (1955); Richman, Taxation of Foreign Investment Income: An Economic Analysis, ch. V (1963). For a summary of the main state aids in the Six, see London Chamber of Commerce, Investment in the E.E.C. (1962); Steefel, "Restraints and Incentives in the Federal Republic of Germany," in 1 Doing Business Abroad 22 (Landau ed. 1962); Littauer, "Incentives in Belgium and Switzerland," in id. at 29.

[177] U.N. Economic Survey of Europe, 1959, U.N. Doc. No. E/ECE/383, ch. VII, at 35–37 (1960); Rosenstein-Rodan, "How to Industrialize an Underdeveloped Area," in Regional Economic Planning 205, 210–11 (Isard & Cumberland ed. 1961); EEC Commission, Moyens de la politique régionale dans les Etats membres de la C.E.E. 102–107, 123 (1964). For the position in Italy, see 4 Banco di Roma, Foreign Private Enterprise in Italy, pt. I, ch. XII, and pt. II, chs. I-III, and pt. III, ch. III.

See generally Boskey, "Industrial Credit Institutions," in Methods of Industrial Development 299 (OECD, 1962); Vasseur, Le droit de la réforme des structures industrielles et des économies régionales 250–300 (1959).

[178] Romus, Expansion Economique Régionale et Communauté Européenne 291 (1958), says that this lacuna—originally called the "Macmillan gap" in Britain—exists in each of the Six, partly because of the structure of the banking system. In addition to sponsoring credit facilities, the state may use public funds to repay the interest on development loans secured from private sources. The former is preferable, because aid under the latter usually does not last for the whole period of the loan and does not minimize the difficulty of obtaining long-term finance. However, this second method avoids public supervision of the borrowing enterprise.

[179] U.N. Economic Survey of Europe in 1956, U.N. Doc. No. E/ECE/278, ch. IV, at 18 n.23 (1957); see also id. at 18–20.

an import duty.[180] "If some such principle were accepted as the basis for dealing with tariffs in inter-member trade, the economic case for these [less developed] countries entering the [proposed] Free Trade Area would be strengthened."[181]

State aids of different kinds can reduce either capital costs or operating costs; which one to reduce depends on the economic difficulties of the region. Usually operating costs are higher in the less developed regions, in spite of lower wage levels, if there are any genuine economic disadvantages to investment. The extent to which increased operating costs are offset by reductions in capital costs through grants, reduced interest rates, and equipment subsidies depends on the relationship between capital and turnover.[182] Normally industries which are labor-intensive or which create a demand for labor-intensive secondary industries contribute most directly to regional development, both where the standard of living is abnormally low and where there is serious underemployment.[183] A capital-intensive industry employs fewer people in proportion to its size and tends to create less demand for local services and products; but in the long run, a capital-intensive industry may be more valuable to a less developed region than a labor-intensive industry—especially one which does not train local people for skilled positions—since most modern "growth" industries are capital-intensive.[184] The Common Market is unlikely to promote expansion in labor-intensive industries, and it is important not to set up non-competitive enterprises in less developed regions. Economic backwardness, of course, does not necessarily coexist with underemployment; measures which may be suitable in one region of the Common Market may not be suitable elsewhere. The Commission will coordinate state policies in the light of all these factors; review state aid in the light of labor surpluses elsewhere; insure, by advice based on Community experience, that aid is as effective as possible; and insure the establishment of enterprises likely to benefit not only the region but also the Community, in the light of economic trends and of Community planning.

STATE AIDS: THE WORK OF THE COMMISSION

The Commission has classified state aids into aids to agriculture, aids to transport, and financial and non-financial aids to other sectors.[185] Aids to agriculture and transport can be dealt with only in conjunction with the relevant common policies, and the Commission's work has been limited initially to state aids of a fiscal nature. In the sense of the Treaty state aids are special measures to support certain activities or enterprises, and tax measures of general application are not within Article 92.[186] The Commission does not regard Article 98, which deals

[180] This would come under art. 98, presumably, since it would be a "repayment in respect of exports" even though its amount was not directly related to the amount of tax paid.

[181] U.N. Economic Survey of Europe in 1956, U.N. Doc. No. E/ECE/278, ch. IV, at 18 n.23 (1957).

[182] See Political and Economic Planning, Regional Development in the European Economic Community 27–28 (1962).

[183] Art. 92(3)(a).

[184] Irish Committee on Industrial Organization, Fourth Interim Report: Industrial Grants, Pr. 6924, para. 44 (1962).

[185] Second General Report, para. 134 (1959); Third General Report, para. 151 (1960).

[186] Third General Report, para. 148 (1960). See also Sixth General Report, para. 47 (1963).

with state aids to exports, as being so specific as to exclude the application of Article 92.[187] The Commission has been approving new measures of state aid under Article 93 as they arise.[188]

[187] Third General Report, para. 148 (1960). See also Fifth General Report, paras. 50–53 (1962).

[188] See, e.g., 1963 EEC Bull. No. 6, at 29; see also Costa v. ENEL, 10 Recueil 1141, [1964] C.M.L.R. 425.

Chapter 13

Regional Policy and State Aids to Industry in Ireland

IRISH REGIONAL ECONOMIC POLICY[1]

Irish regional economic policy has varied in emphasis from time to time. The present legislation affecting investors is only one aspect of the regional policy of Irish government, but this book is not concerned with rural electrification, agrarian policy, or transport as they affect the western parts of the country, the areas which have poorer land and higher rates of emigration. Irish industry has until recently concentrated around the two largest cities, Dublin and Cork.[2]

The first state aid to industry on a regional basis was under the Undeveloped Areas Act of 1952 (since re-enacted without major changes), which applied only to the western parts of the country.[3] Similar legislation providing smaller benefits in all other areas and special legislation dealing with the Shannon industrial zone were later enacted. The most recent legislation gives substantially similar treatment to both parts of the country, with some preference for the less developed areas. This is not because the different regions have been made equally prosperous, but because the government views the national interest in development of the most advantageously situated areas as being more important than regional interests in the development of regional economies to the national level. "Ireland has found it more necessary than other countries to compromise in the conflict between social objectives of, on the one hand, raising incomes in the poorer regions, and, on the other, lifting the national average income by means of stimulating productive investment, lower costs and export viability."[4]

The first major document which dealt with regional economic policy in Ireland was the Report of the Commission on

[1] Various factors have confined the scope of this book to the Republic of Ireland. It would be absurd in this portion of the book to omit references to the excellent studies of Northern Ireland, which has regional economic problems in some respects similar to, but more serious than, those of the Republic. The studies referred to are: Isles & Cuthbert, An Economic Survey of Northern Ireland (1957); Hall Report, Cmd. No. 1835 (1962); Economic Development in Northern Ireland, Cmd. No. 479 (1965). On regional economic policy in Britain, see U.K. Finance Act, 1963, 11 & 12 Eliz. 2, c. 25; National Economic Development Council, Conditions Favourable to Faster Growth (1963).

[2] Economic Development, Pr. 4803, ch. 15, para. 8 (1958).

[3] 1952 Acts 3. See generally Fennell, "The Economic Problems of Western Ireland," 50 Studies 385 (1961).

[4] U.N. Economic Survey of Europe, 1959, U.N. Doc. No. E/ECE/383, ch. VII, at 40 (1960). On the tendency of interregional disparities in income levels to decrease in advanced economies but to increase in countries which are less economically developed, see Belassa, The Theory of Economic Integration 201 (1961); U.N. Economic Survey of Europe in 1954, U.N. Doc. No. E/ECE/184, at 138–42 (1955). France does not fit this pattern, presumably because of the effects of centralization. The effect of the 1961 Irish legislation has been to reduce the size of the grants given in the undeveloped areas in relation to the size of the grants given elsewhere; see An Foras Tionscal [Grants Board], Annual Report, 1963.

Emigration,[5] which recommended measures to encourage urban development and industrialization outside Dublin.[6] Much of the industry of Ireland was in the east because of convenience of communication with Britain, proximity to the most densely populated part of the home market, and greater availability of labor and facilities. Nevertheless, the Emigration Commission considered that "demographic issues and cultural values of the utmost importance"[7] justified expenditure of public funds and required active encouragement of regional development, since it attributed the demographic problems with which it was concerned primarily to economic causes.[8]

On the other hand, an official paper, *Economic Development,*[9] said that it was wasteful to subsidize remote areas specially and thus handicap the economy and retard progress in areas more suitable for industry, where concentrated effort could give better results.[10] Prosperous and industrialized countries can better afford regional subsidies than developing countries. Stress was laid on the economic disadvantages of industries in the less developed areas—distance from harbors, shortage of suitable factory sites and access roads, added transport costs of raw materials and finished products, and shortage of local skilled labor. It was felt that further industrial development depended on increased exports and that it was essential that industries should be able to export as competitively as possible.

The Committee on Industrial Organization[11] took the matter somewhat further. They pointed out the economic arguments for decentralization of industry, in particular, that advantage could be taken of unused resources in less industrialized areas. The alternatives were wide dispersal of industry or concentration on a number of selected centers or industrial zones. While stressing the advantages of having industry in small towns, the Committee held that a policy aiming at wide dispersal of industry would be economically unsound in conditions of free trade. Large industrial concentrations benefit from ready availability of technical services—possible only at greater cost in less industrialized areas—a better range of educational facilities for training workers, proximity of labor without commuting problems, and ample transport facilities.[12] For many industries the proximity of auxiliary firms providing services or components would be much more important than the proximity of markets or raw materials. If industry were widely dispersed, public expenditure on infrastructure adequate for each enterprise would be excessive. The Committee therefore recommended the creation of centers of industrial development which, once established, would attract further investment without state

[5] Pr. 2541 (1954).

[6] Paras. 29–30, 295, 405–10, 415–22.

[7] Para. 419.

[8] Para. 332.

[9] Pr. 4803 (1958). It was published in conjunction with the government's Programme for Economic Expansion, Pr. 4796 (1958). See FitzGerald, "Mr. Whitaker and Industry," 48 Studies 138, 140 (1959).

[10] Ch. 16, paras. 10–14; see also ch. 2, para. 31; ch. 16, para. 4. See Carter, "The Irish Economy Viewed from Without," 46 Studies 137, 141–42 (1957). For a study of the differences in per capita income in Ireland, see Attwood & Geary, Irish County Incomes in 1960 (1963).

[11] Fourth Interim Report: Industrial Grants, Pr. 6924 (1962). See "The Committee on Industrial Organization," Irish Banking Rev., June 1963, p. 13, for a review of the Committee's work.

[12] Fennell, Industrialization and Agricultural Development in the Congested Districts 18–22, 24–25 (1962); "Lessons for Regions," The Economist, Nov. 7, 1964, p. 615.

incentives being necessary.[13] The Irish government certainly will continue to support the industrial zone at Shannon and may establish other zones throughout the country, including some in the less developed areas. These zones must have ready access to raw materials and markets; they are likely to be in existing towns, since they will need to become large enough to provide quickly the advantages sought.

Incentives would be needed to establish the industrial zones and to insure an adequate supply of commercial services. The Committee recommended the abolition of any distinction, for the purposes of state aid, between the less developed areas and the rest of the country. However, it suggested a "modest" difference of one-third between the capital grants available in the rest of the country and those for new investment or expansion in industrial centers. In the EEC this differential would require the approval of the Commission and probably would receive it. If the areas where the zones are located have an abnormally low standard of living or serious underemployment, the grants can be given even if trading conditions are adversely affected. A special incentive for investment in an industrial center is legitimate and justified because of the economic benefit to the state.

Even for commodities with very high transport costs, distances in Ireland and between Ireland and the Continent are very small by modern standards. Too much has been made of the disadvantages of geographical remoteness of the less developed areas of Ireland and the EEC.[14] With regard to exports from Ireland, the inadequacies in the existing shipping facilities in the east[15] have been more serious than the slight extra cost of operations in the west.

TAX CONCESSIONS FOR EXPORTS

"Ireland has probably gone further than any other country in Western Europe in encouraging export industries and in attracting foreign capital for this purpose."[16]

The ten-year tax relief plan

ACTIVITIES WHICH QUALIFY FOR TAX EXEMPTION[17]

Exemption from tax is given only for profits from the export of "goods manufactured within the state."[18] "Manufacture" is not defined in the legislation but is widely interpreted in practice. Some

[13] See "Symposium on Economic Development," 20(2) J. Stat. Soc. 120 (1958–59); FitzGerald, "The Role of Development Centres in the Irish Economy," 12 Administration 171 (1964); Committee on Development Centres and Industrial Estates, Report, Pr. 8461 (1965); National Industrial Economic Council, Comments on Report of Committee on Development Centres and Industrial Estates, Pr. 8476 (1965).

[14] See "Symposium on Economic Development," 20(2) J. Stat. Soc. 119 (1958–59), which expresses the view stated in the text.

[15] Fennell, Industrialization and Agricultural Development in the Congested Districts 15 (1962); see the remarks of Mr. Lemass on the Finance (Miscellaneous Provisions) Bill, 1956, 160 Dáil Eireann, Parl. Deb., cols. 1624–25 (1956).

[16] U.N. Economic Survey of Europe, 1959, U.N. Doc. No. E/ECE/383, ch. VII, at 42 n.140 (1960); Biggar, "L'Industrie Irlandaise et Son Récent Développement," 197 Revue de la Société d'Etudes et d'Expansion 480, 484 (1961); Stock, "Operation 'Eire-Lift,'" 41 Taxes 662 (1963). However, the potential investor should not attempt to get more state aid than is authorized by the relevant legislation, even though such an attempt might be successful elsewhere in Europe.

[17] See generally Charleton, Tax Incentives in Irish Exports (1961); Dublin Society of Chartered Accountants, Changes in Industrial and General Taxation 1950–1961 (1962); Federation of British Industries, Export Incentives 16–17 (1962).

[18] Finance (Miscellaneous Provisions) Act, 1956 Acts 807, § 10. For brevity, in this chapter full citations of Finance Acts are provided only with the first reference to a given act.

conversion or change in the goods due to processing, preparation, or assembling is necessary, but there are no provisions requiring a specific proportion of the value of the goods to have been added in Ireland—unlike the customs laws of many countries.[19] Some problems arise in connection with preparation of agricultural products, and it is curious that this desirable form of industry in Ireland[20] is not dealt with expressly. It is possible to obtain a ruling from the revenue commissioners as to whether a particular operation will be regarded as manufacturing.

The sale necessary for tax exemption must be made by the company exporting the goods. The manufacture of goods on behalf of a foreign principal does not qualify for tax exemption if the finished product is returned to the principal and no sale takes place.[21] If the Irish company manufacturing the goods sells them merely as agent on behalf of the foreign principal, it seems that no exemption from tax would be given. The same company which supplies raw material to the Irish manufacturing company can purchase the finished product.[22]

Profits from mining operations are not tax exempt under this legislation[23] but are treated under separate legislation.[24] Services rendered abroad by a company based and taxable in Ireland do not qualify for exemption. The tax concession does not apply to an Irish factory which, by producing a commodity hitherto imported, benefits the Irish balance of payments as much as if it had exported goods of similar value.

Enterprises Which May Obtain Tax Exemption

Only a company or an industrial and provident society[25] or other corporate body may obtain the tax exemption. The company need not be incorporated or resident for tax purposes in Ireland under the tax concession legislation,[26] and

[19] Blending whiskey, grinding turf (peat), cutting bacon, and any blending to produce a new compound have all been regarded as manufacture. Bottling, labeling, packaging, and servicing do not constitute manufacture, but canning and freezing of agricultural products qualify, because they involve a substantial amount of machinery and labor. Plucking of chickens has been ruled not to constitute manufacture.

[20] OECD Economic Survey of Ireland, 1963, para. 38. See Johnston, Why Ireland Needs the Common Market 62 (1962).

[21] If the Irish company takes title to the goods, it is irrelevant that the substance of the transaction is a sale of services by the Irish company. See, however, Finance Bill, 1966, § 26.

[22] If the two companies are associated and the foreign company has income arising in Ireland, Finance Act, 1960 Acts 483, § 30, dealing with sales at abnormal prices, will apply. The corresponding provisions of the foreign tax also will be important.

[23] Finance (Miscellaneous Provisions) Act, 1956, § 15(1).

[24] Finance (Miscellaneous Provisions) Act 1956, §§ 4–9; Finance (Profits of Certain Mines) (Temporary Relief from Taxation) Act, 1956 Acts 113. The tax exemption is available for fish farms and mushroom cultivation in Ireland. Profits made by a company from repairs done in Ireland on a ship wholly owned by persons not ordinarily resident in Ireland and profits from the sale of ships built in Ireland qualify for exemption; Finance Act, 1959 Acts 681, § 71(1).

[25] Under Industrial and Provident Societies Act, 1893, 56 & 57 Vict. c. 39.

[26] This may be required for other purposes; e.g., the effect of the U.K.-Irish Double Income Taxation Agreement (April 14, 1926, U.K. Income Tax Act, 1952, 15 & 16 Geo. 6 & 1 Eliz. 2, c. 10, Eighteenth Schedule, pt. I, Irish Finance Act, 1926 Pub. Stat. 401, 441, First Schedule) is that only a company resident for tax purposes in Ireland, though not necessarily incorporated there, gets the relief from income tax; the effect of the U.S.-Irish Double Taxation Convention (Sept. 13, 1949, [1951] 2 U.S.T. & O.I.A. 2303, T.I.A.S. No. 2356, Irish Finance Act, 1950 Acts 369, 411, Second Schedule, Ir. T.S. No. 7 of 1951, Pr. 1081, 127 U.N.T.S. 89 [1952]) and the effect of United States tax law is to require a subsidiary incorporated in Ireland.

it need not have any Irish directors or shareholders.

Although generally to obtain the tax concession the same company must manufacture and export the goods, another enterprise in Ireland may manufacture the goods if they are exported by the company claiming the exemption and sold to anyone whose business is to sell similar goods or if they are components or capital goods used by the foreign purchaser for the purposes of his undertaking.[27] Profits from retail sales abroad of Irish manufactured goods are tax-free only if the exporter manufactured the goods. For its own use abroad a foreign enterprise can purchase processed materials, component parts, or machinery in Ireland through an Irish purchasing subsidiary, which obtains the tax exemption on its profits on resale to its parent even if the resale was made in Ireland.[28]

Exporting Companies Associated with Manufacturing Companies

If an export company is associated with the company which manufactures the goods, the exporting company gets the tax exemption if one company holds more than 90 per cent of the ordinary shares in the other or if the same persons hold, directly or indirectly, 51 per cent of the voting shares in one company and more than 90 per cent of the ordinary shares in the other.[29]

Exports

The goods must be exported, but the sale need not take place abroad.[30] "Export" is not defined. The goods must be exported physically; the mere transfer of title to a foreign purchaser is not sufficient. The profits are exempt from tax even if the goods are brought back into Ireland by the purchaser, apparently even if the purchaser is associated with the exporter. The profits from the sale need not be remitted to Ireland.

The goods must be exported by the company claiming the relief, and delivery in Ireland to the foreign purchaser for subsequent shipment does not allow the selling company to claim the relief, even if passage of title takes place abroad. The seller may use ordinary commercial means of transport for exporting the goods even if delivery to the carrying agent causes title to pass to the purchaser.[31]

The Extent of the Tax Exemption

A newly incorporated company pays no income or corporation profits tax for ten years from commencing business, if all of its products are exported; it pays tax at the ordinary rates only on its profits from sales on the home market (if any).[32] After the ten-year exemption expires, income and corporation profits taxes are payable at progressively in-

[27] Finance Act, 1960, § 27(1). The tax exemption for profits from goods sold to foreign trading enterprises, if the exporter is not the manufacturing company, makes Finance Act, 1958 Acts 553, § 56(2), and Finance Act, 1959, § 71(3), relating to books and greeting cards, unnecessary in most cases.

[28] Cf. Attorney General v. Sulley, 5 H. & N. 711, 157 Eng. Rep. 1364, 2 Tax Cas. 149 (1860).

[29] Finance Act, 1956 Acts 353, § 10; see also Finance Act, 1964 Acts, No. 15, § 30.

[30] The purchase of goods in Ireland by a foreign company will not make the purchaser liable to Irish tax if they are sold abroad; Attorney General v. Sulley, 5 H. & N. 711, 157 Eng. Rep. 1364, 2 Tax Cas. 149 (1860); U.S.-Irish Double Taxation Convention, art. III(4); Irish-German Double Taxation Agreement, Dec. 18, 1962, art. III(5), Ir. S.I. No. 212 of 1962, Pr. 6792, German Law of March 25, 1964, [1964] 2 BGBl. 266, 632. Therefore, sales in Ireland of goods later exported do not involve either party in tax liability.

[31] See Sale of Goods Act, 1893, 56 & 57 Vict. c. 70, § 18, Rule 5, and § 32.

[32] Finance (Miscellaneous Provisions) Act, 1956, §§ 12(3), 13(3). The exemption was raised to 100% of the tax by Finance Act, 1957 Acts 463, §§ 5, 16, and to a period of ten years by Finance Act, 1958, § 56.

creasing rates during a five-year period,[33] until the company is paying both taxes at the full rates in the sixteenth year.

The ten-year period begins to run in whichever of the three tax years beginning in April 1957 is chosen by an existing company.[34] For a new company which has not exported before April 1960, the ten-year period runs from the first or the second year, prior to the tax year 1971–72, in which the company can claim the tax relief.[35] If the first year for claiming relief is 1971–72 or later, the company will not be able to obtain a full ten-year tax relief; the last year in which the full 100 per cent relief or the five reduced rates of relief may be given to any company is 1979–80.

There is no restriction on the amount of profits exempt from tax. The profits from exports are calculated by reference to the taxable profits for the year in question.[36] Depreciation allowances and losses cannot be carried forward and set off against tax after the end of the fifteen-year period.[37] The export-profits relief cannot be carried forward, and depreciation allowances and losses arising during the exemption years are wasted except insofar as they may be set off against profits from home sales.

Dividends and Royalties

During the ten-year period, the company may deduct income tax from dividends only at the effective rate at which it has paid income tax on all its profits, e.g., if half its profits are derived from exports, it may deduct tax at half the standard rate for the time being. If the company's entire profits are derived from exports, no tax can be deducted.[38] Shareholders are exempt from income tax and surtax on the proportion of their dividends derived from profits from exports.

Income tax apparently will be—or will be deemed to have been—deducted at the reduced rate during the five-year tailing-off period and, after fifteen years, at the full standard rate then in force, even if the profits being distributed were made during the ten years of complete exemption from tax.[39] This does not affect companies which are shareholders. By issuing redeemable preference or debenture shares, it is possible to distribute the accumulated profits without individual shareholders' being taxed. The redemption payments for these are tax-free capital gains.

[33] During this five-year period, tax is payable at 20%, 35%, 50%, 65%, and 85% of the full tax rates for those years; Finance Act, 1960, § 29.

[34] Finance (Miscellaneous Provisions) Act, 1956, § 10, as amended by Finance Act, 1958, § 56.

[35] I.e., tax relief on the profits of the previous income tax year; Finance Act, 1960, § 28(1). The company may choose either the first or the second year in which it exports to be the first year of the ten. In Report on Measures to Promote Exports of Manufactured Goods, Pr. 8005, paras. 11–17 (1964), a committee of the National Industrial Economic Council recommended that the cut-off date for full relief be extended, so changes—whose effects are embodied in the text—were made by Finance Act, 1965 Acts, No. 22, §§ 6, 33. These provisions allow more than ten years of full relief to companies which become entitled to the reduced rates of relief before 1975–76.

[36] Finance (Miscellaneous Provisions) Act, 1956, §§ 12(2), 13(2).

[37] A company entitled to an initial allowance while its profits are exempt from tax often benefits by not claiming any initial allowance, making the written-down value of the asset in question greater when the export-profits tax relief ends and thus enabling the company to obtain larger annual allowances as a result.

[38] Finance (Miscellaneous Provisions) Act, 1956, § 15(2).

[39] This point has not yet arisen. Finance (Miscellaneous Provisions) Act, 1956, § 15(2), limits the rate at which tax may be deducted from dividends to "the rate of income tax as reduced by any relief . . . given" on profits from exports. It does not mention the rate at which

The exemption from tax does not apply to payments from which the company is entitled to deduct tax[40] or which it is entitled to deduct from taxable profits. Directors' fees, royalties, and interest[41] paid by a company which itself pays no tax are liable to income tax and surtax or corporation profits tax at the full rates, and if such payments are contemplated, it is preferable for the recipients to receive shares, the dividends on which are tax-free.[42]

---

tax may be deducted where, because the tax-exempt profits from exports fluctuate in proportion to the profits of the company from sales at home or because the tax relief is at a reduced rate during the tailing-off period, the effective rate of tax payable at the time of distribution of the dividend is not the same as that paid in the year in which the profits were made. If there has been a change of the standard rate of tax, then to calculate the income tax due by the company, the two rates of tax are apportioned on a monthly basis over the accounting period from the profits of which the dividend is paid. However, tax is deducted from dividends and retained by the company at the standard rate in force when the dividend is paid, even if that rate is different from both the standard rate and the effective rate of tax paid by the company in the year when the profits from which the dividend is paid were made. See Income Tax Act, 1918, 8 & 9 Geo. 5, c. 40, § 211. The company and the shareholder are separate taxable entities, and there is no necessary correlation between the amount of income tax to be borne by each. Neumann v. I.R.C., [1934] A.C. 215, 18 Tax Cas. 332; Hamilton v. I.R.C., [1931] 2 K.B. 495. This rule avoids the need to earmark accumulated profits according to the year in which they were made and the effective rate of tax which they bore. "The rate of income tax as reduced by any relief . . . given" in respect of profits from exports must mean the effective rate of tax on all profits. (The provision quoted antedated the graduated rates of relief given in the tailing-off period.) Under ordinary principles, this means the effective rate payable for the year in which the dividend is paid. Disregarding difficulties of calculation which may arise, it follows that tax can be deducted only at the standard rate after the expiration of the fifteen-year period and at graduated rates in the last five years. The resulting anomaly—that the company deducts tax from a dividend paid out of profits which did not suffer tax—arises from the general principles and not from the tax concession legislation. A corporate shareholder is not liable to corporation profits tax on dividends paid by an Irish company and is deemed to have paid income tax on dividends received whether tax was deducted from them or not. In the case of an individual who may be liable to surtax on dividends paid at the end of the tailing-off period, it would be safer, if possible, to have the dividends paid before then.

Companies Selling Abroad and on the Irish Market

A company which sells both abroad and on the Irish market is relieved, nevertheless, only from tax on its export profits.[43] If the expenses deductible in calculating taxable home market profits are greater in proportion to the gross profits from home sales than the deductible export-sales expenses in relation to the gross proceeds of those sales, the company should separate its home and export activities and incorporate a second company, which can be a wholly owned subsidiary, for its export business. An Irish subsidiary of a large group may be able to use only facilities which are

[40] Finance (Miscellaneous Provisions) Act, 1956, § 15(1)(a).

[41] Such interest might be held to be "received . . . from a company liable to be assessed to corporation profits tax in respect thereof" and so exempt from corporation profits tax under Finance Act, 1920, 10 & 11 Geo. 5, c. 18, § 53(2)(a).

[42] Irish company law requires the recipient to make some subscription to the company for the shares issued to him. This subscription may be either in cash or in kind; if it is made in kind, it must be adequate in proportion to the value of the shares issued. Exchange-control permission is required for the issuing of the shares and might not be given if the dividend is too high in relation to the value of the subscription.

[43] Finance (Miscellaneous Provisions) Act, 1956, §§ 12(4), 13(4). If the product exported is subject to an excise tax payable on home sales but refunded when the product is exported, the calculation is made under Finance Act, 1959, § 72.

owned by or whose cost is deductible by other companies of the group. Since the provisions against tax avoidance[44] do not prohibit the exporting company from obtaining facilities at an artificially low cost, the company may be able to lease facilities from an associated company at a nominal rent. If the deductible export-sales expenses are greater in proportion to the gross profits of exports than deductible home-sales expenses in proportion to the gross profits from home sales, the same corporate entity should operate both markets, because the disproportionate expenses of exporting will in effect be deducted from the gross profits from home sales.

What has been said relates only to companies which were not trading or exporting during the years 1954–55 or 1955–56.[45] Companies which exported during those years are exempt from tax only on profits from exports in excess of their exports during their "standard period."[46]

Dealings Between Associated Companies

If a company is claiming export-profits tax relief, sales between associated companies at prices less than the arm's-length price are regarded as having been made at that price.[47] The provisions apply only where one party to the sale controls the other, or both are under the same "control." Control means power—through shareholding or voting power, or by virtue of a company's articles of association or a written contract[48]—to insure that the affairs of the company controlled are conducted in accordance with the wishes of the controller. Veto power of 50 per cent shareholding does not constitute control.

Succession to the Trade of Another Company

A company which succeeds to a trade previously carried on by another company eligible for the tax relief[49] can get relief only for the ten years which would have been available to the previous company.[50] A company is regarded as having succeeded to the trade of another if the shareholders, employees, premises, equipment, goodwill, customers, and methods of operation of the two companies are similar, especially if only a short time has elapsed and there has been no outside intervention in the business. If a company which has exported during a standard year wishes to manufacture a completely new line of goods, it should incorporate a subsidiary for this purpose to insure that the company will receive indirectly, through the subsidiary, the full ten years free of tax.

Liability to Foreign Tax

A company exempt from Irish tax on profits from exports may incur tax liabil-

[44] Finance Act, 1960, § 30.

[45] Finance (Miscellaneous Provisions) Act, 1956, §§ 11, 12(3), 13(3).

[46] Companies which had an export trade, however small, between September 1954 and September 1956 must choose either September 1954–September 1955 or September 1955–September 1956 as their "standard period." They will choose the year in which their gross export sales were *least*. Such a company will be exempt from tax on profits from exports in excess of the amount of goods exported during its standard period. To be fair to a company which worked hard to export its products before 1956, companies with a "standard period" were given, by Finance Act, 1956, §§ 5, 16, the option of a 25% reduction of tax on profits from exports, even if they had not increased their exports over those of the standard period. This option was available only for the first five out of the ten years of full relief available to the company; see, however, Finance Act, 1963 Acts, No. 23, §§ 20, 39.

[47] Finance Act, 1960, § 30(1).

[48] Finance Act, 1960, § 30(3), refers only to power derived from a "document" and thus not to an oral or tape-recorded contract.

[49] Finance Act, 1960, § 30(4).

[50] See Finance (Miscellaneous Provisions) Act, 1956, §§ 11, 12(3), 13(3).

ity in the country to which the goods are exported, especially if the sales take place in the latter country. This depends on the national law of that country and on any relevant double taxation treaty. Most countries tax even a permanent establishment only on the proportion of the total profit of the enterprise which is attributable to the sale within their frontiers, less the costs of the permanent establishment, not on that portion attributable to the manufacture of the goods. Liability to tax in the country of destination can often be avoided, even if the company is liable to tax there in the absence of a permanent establishment.

The Shannon Airport zone tax reliefs

Companies which carry on all or part of their trade at the Shannon Airport customs-free zone[51] are exempt until 1983 from income tax and corporation profits tax on profits from exports and from certain aviation operations.[52] This exemption and the ten-year export-profits tax relief are mutually exclusive. To obtain the exemption a company need not be resident or incorporated in Ireland.[53]

The principal type of trading which is exempt from tax is the sale and export of goods which have been "produced, manufactured or processed" at the airport by the company claiming the exemption.[54] The sale may be by the company either as principal or agent, but the company must itself have processed the goods; the profits of a company which manufactured goods at Shannon on a commission basis would be exempt from tax. The goods probably must be exported by the company claiming the relief, but a company operating at Shannon would normally export its goods itself.

Profits from the sale for export of goods packaged or handled (as distinct from processed) by the company may be exempt from tax. The company must take title to goods imported into Ireland substantially ready for sale and merely packaged or handled at the airport prior to sale and re-export. The goods must be physically handled at Shannon, not merely invoiced through the airport. Whether the goods are manufactured or only packaged at Shannon, they need not be exported by air and may be exported from any Irish port.[55] In addition, operations ancillary to any of those mentioned

[51] Exports of products manufactured in Shannon were $9.6 million in 1963. By 1962, Shannon was seventh out of the first seventeen European airports in volume serviced; Quinn, "The Shannon Free Industrial Estate," Investors Chronicle Supp. (London), Nov. 16, 1962, p. 10. For a general study of Shannon Airport, see Quigley, "The Shannon Airport Development Programme," in Methods of Industrial Development 185 (OECD, 1962); Shannon Free Airport Development Co., Ltd., Jet Age Distribution from Shannon (1963); "The Shannon Industrial Estate," Irish Banking Rev., Dec. 1961, p. 9; Tait, "The Public Sector in Ireland," 17 Nat'l Tax J. 22, 30–31 (1964); Limerick Junior Chamber of Commerce, Economic Influence of the Airport Complex on the Shannon Region, 1963 Report and 1964 Report.

[52] Repair and maintenance of aircraft at the airport and rendering of services involving aircraft or air transport are exempt from tax if the services are rendered in the airport or outside Ireland and are not rendered to anyone resident elsewhere in Ireland. See also Finance (Miscellaneous Provisions) Act, 1958 Acts 791, § 3 (5)(e). Profits from the sale of aircraft fuels and consumable aircraft stores may not be exempted from tax, but profits from the sale and export of non-consumable aircraft stores, such as tools and spare parts, are exempt. Only an air-transport enterprise which operates between Shannon and airports outside Ireland and which is not operated under an international bilateral agreement to which the Irish government is a party is free of tax.

[53] This may be necessitated by a double taxation convention.

[54] Finance (Miscellaneous Provisions) Act, 1958, § 3(5).

[55] The authorities may, however, prefer an enterprise which will use the facilities provided by the airport.

are exempt from tax.[56]

Profits from retail sales of goods for export are not exempt from tax.[57] Retail sales are not defined, but the tax exemption is available to manufacturers at Shannon selling directly to the ultimate user or consumer abroad. The object of the provision is to exclude from tax exemption the profits of mail-order firms and of shops selling consumer goods to individuals traveling through Shannon.

"A trading operation carried on in the course of trading in Great Britain or Northern Ireland"[58] is not exempt from tax, although an enterprise exporting to Britain apparently is trading with but not within that country.[59] This provision is to prevent the advantages of the airport from being obtained by British businessmen on a purely artificial basis. In practice, an Irish-incorporated subsidiary of a British company is exempt from tax if it carries on a business separate from that of the British parent. Owing to the favorable tax position of an Irish-resident company exporting into Britain, this provision is important.

The tax exemption cannot be revoked unless the company ceases to carry on business at the airport or infringes a condition of the certificate issued by the Minister of Finance specifying the trading operations of the company which are exempt from tax. The conditions in the certificate vary but are rarely of importance, since most matters of substance are handled in negotiating the lease of factory premises or the terms of cash grants from the Shannon Airport Development Company.

When the certificate has been issued, profits and losses from the operations specified in it will be disregarded until November 25, 1983,[60] for income and corporation profits tax purposes. If the company is also carrying on taxable operations, deductions for wear and tear of machinery, capital expenditure on scientific research, initial allowances on machinery or industrial buildings, and shipping investment allowances[61] are apportioned between the two trades.

The proportion of a dividend which has been paid out of tax-exempt operations is exempt in the hands of the shareholder from income tax, surtax,[62] and corporation profits tax, and tax may not be deducted from it.[63] The dividend warrant must show the proportion of the dividend which is exempt from tax.

If interest and royalties are paid out of partly exempt profits, tax may be de-

[56] Finance (Miscellaneous Provisions) Act, 1958, § 3(5)(f).

[57] Finance (Miscellaneous Provisions) Act, 1958, § 3(6)(f).

[58] Finance (Miscellaneous Provisions) Act, 1958, § 3(6)(h). The British revenue authorities may have indicated that the U.K.-Irish Double Taxation Agreement would be reconsidered if the privileges of Shannon were extended to an Irish resident company exporting to but paying no tax in Britain. There is no such limitation with regard to the general tax exemption for exports just discussed.

[59] See Grainger v. Gough, [1896] A.C. 325, 335 (per Herschell, L.), 3 Tax Cas. 462. The word "operation" means that a company is not eligible for the tax concession merely because it is incorporated separately from another company of the same group trading in Britain. Sets of circumstances are possible to which the application of Finance (Miscellaneous Provisions) Act, 1958 § 3(6)(h) would be difficult, but the Minister has a discretion to refuse the issue of a certificate of exemption from tax, which, if exercised in good faith, cannot be challenged in the courts.

[60] Twenty-five years from the passage of the act.

[61] Finance (Miscellaneous Provisions) Act, 1958, § 8.

[62] Because Finance (Miscellaneous Provisions) Act, 1958, § 9(2), reads "any dividend . . . paid out of profits from exempted trading operations shall not be regarded as income or profits for any purpose. . . ."

[63] Finance (Miscellaneous Provisions) Act, 1958, § 9.

ducted only from that part of the payment which is in proportion to the part of the company's total profits liable to tax,[64] unlike the corresponding payments made by companies under the ten-year relief[65] for profits from exports.

If a company getting the benefit of the tax relief at Shannon buys goods at a price below their arm's-length price and if the parties to the sale are under the same control or one controls the other,[66] the profits of the seller are calculated as if the price had been the market price. Control is defined in the same way as in the corresponding provision relating to the ten-year relief.[67] In the case of the Shannon tax relief, taxable profits of the company selling to the exempt company are increased to remove the effect of the artificial transaction. In the case of the ten-year exemption, the adjustment reduces the tax-exempt profits of the buyer on subsequent resale.

TAX CONCESSIONS FOR REPATRIATION OF CAPITAL

To encourage repatriation of capital for local investment, Ireland gives as a tax incentive a 20 per cent reduction in the rate of tax paid by an Irish-resident individual on dividends from shares in an industrial company incorporated, managed and controlled, and doing business mainly in Ireland.[68]

Foreign-source income of a resident usually is taxed even if it is not repatriated, and the incentive for repatriation and investment in Ireland offers no advantage where the yield from local investment is lower than that from foreign securities. Ireland in general imposes no tax on capital gains arising from the sale of securities, so tax factors do not inhibit repatriation. Apart from the incentive just mentioned, the Irish tax system neither encourages nor discourages foreign investment. The U.K.-Irish Double Income Taxation Agreement causes Irish residents to pay the same taxes whether they invest in Britain or in Ireland. Further, Ireland has never used exchange controls to limit investment elsewhere in the sterling area.

A low rate of tax on foreign-source income is more likely to encourage exports than to encourage foreign investment, since investment income normally is taxed, at least in part, in the country of source, while profits from exports need not be. However, low tax rates on foreign-source income are the badge of "base countries" and are open to criticism as aiding tax avoidance and therefore distorting competition.

GRANTS OF CAPITAL TO INDUSTRY

Apart from tax exemption for profits from exports, the most important type of state aid to industry in Ireland is the grant or gift of cash towards the capital of a company. Three programs of industrial grants exist: one for the "undeveloped areas" of the west and north, one for the Shannon Airport area, and one for the rest of the country. Grants are given to new industries or to existing industries engaged in expansion.

Cash grants reduce the capital required by an investor for an industry of a given size, or enable him to establish a larger factory than he otherwise would have. They assist the establishment of locally owned industry where there is a

[64] Finance (Miscellaneous Provisions) Act, 1958, § 10, and Income Tax Act 1918, 8 & 9 Geo. 5, c. 40, General Rule 19.

[65] Finance (Miscellaneous Provisions) Act, 1956, § 15.

[66] Finance (Miscellaneous Provisions) Act, 1958, § 5.

[67] Finance Act, 1960, § 30.

[68] Finance Acts, 1932 Pub. Stat. 291, § 7; 1935 Pub. Stat. 715, § 7; 1957, § 4; and 1960, § 5. These provisions will have to be considered in due course in the light of arts. 7 and 92. Since they are given only to Irish residents, they derive from the Irish government's policy of encouraging Irish ownership of industry in Ireland.

shortage of local capital. They also are incentives to investment where adequate capital is available independently, whether the investor is local or foreign. As long as tax policy in the EEC needs to favor distribution of company profits to develop a capital market, industrial grants should be permitted, in order to remedy deficiencies in local capital markets, especially where increased investment is necessary.[69]

Grants normally need not be repaid[70] and thus increase the percentage return to the investor on the capital he has invested. This return may already be unusually high due to tax concessions.

By their nature grants aid capital-intensive industries. In Ireland the size of the grants given depends not only on the amount of capital to be provided by the investor but also on the amount of employment which will be provided by the new industry or the contemplated expansion.[71] A recommendation, however, has been made that the size of a grant should depend on "the contribution which it [the industry aided] seems likely to make to further economic development," even if it will not provide much employment,[72] since capital-intensive enterprises contribute to the economy by improving skills and technical knowledge. Many of the modern industries with the greatest potential for expansion are highly capital-intensive. Since these industries usually do not have high transport costs, there is no reason why they should be less profitable outside industrialized areas, if they have adequate supplies of labor.

As a matter of policy, grants are not normally given to enterprises which are likely to compete with existing Irish industries already supplying the home demand. Grants have sometimes been given on terms requiring a specified percentage of the production of a new enterprise to be exported; this is not always a term of the grant, however, because the legislation on freedom of aliens to establish industries in Ireland has often required, in practice, a substantial percentage of exports. The grants legislation, therefore, like the legislation on freedom of establishment, has been operated so as to protect the monopoly or oligopoly position of Irish manufacturers in the small home market, usually whether the existing manufacturers were protected by tariffs and quotas or not. From a national point of view, there is no justification for state aid to increase competition on the home market. Industrial grants thus normally aid export industries.[73] The home demand for most commodities which it is economical to manufacture only for a small market is already met by local industry. Few foreign investors would establish industries to sell only on the Irish

[69] See OECD Economic Survey of Ireland, 1963, paras. 47–48. State aid to industry from tax revenue is a form of compulsory investment. State provision of capital has effects quite different from a state subsidy by way of loan capital given on favorable terms; see the remarks of Mr. G. Sweetman, T.D., on the Taiscí Stáit Teoranta [State Finances Limited] Bill, 1963, 203 Dáil Eireann, Parl. Deb., cols. 296–308 (1963); see pp. 351–52. See also EEC Commission, Moyens de la politique régionale dans les Etats membres de la C.E.E. 84–96 (1964); on equity participation, see id. at 111–16.

[70] Grant agreements usually provide for repayment if the site, factory, or machinery of or the stock in the company is sold by the promoters, or if production ceases, after a short period; Industrial Grants (Amendment) Act, 1961 Acts 1085, § 5.

[71] Apart from Industrial Grants (Amendment) Act, 1963 Acts, No. 4, § 2, no effort has ever been made to give a direct subsidy to reduce labor costs. Section 2 is discussed on p. 348 and relates to grants and not to a continuing subsidy.

[72] Committee on Industrial Organization, Fourth Interim Report: Industrial Grants, Pr. 6924, para. 44(5) (1962).

[73] Industrial Grants Act, 1959 Acts 927, § 2(1)(a), expressly favors export industries.

market even if there were no legal or administrative preference in favor of export industries, so the effect of this preference is not very great. On an administrative level, "there may . . . have to be a more flexible approach to this issue as trade is freed and distinctions between home and export markets become blurred"[74] in the EEC, so if Ireland joins the EEC industrial grants probably will cease to be given primarily to export industries.

Companies eligible for grants

To receive a grant under any of the three programs in Ireland, an enterprise must be efficient and reasonably permanent.[75] This is particularly important in view of the likelihood of free trade conditions.[76] Financial assistance must be necessary to insure the establishment, maintenance, or development of the enterprise.[77] This provision is intended to insure the most efficient use of available funds, but enterprises which certainly could have obtained adequate capital by self-financing, borrowing, or by a public issue of shares nevertheless have obtained grants.

An enterprise in the "undeveloped areas"[78]—broadly, the western and northwestern parts of the country—must be likely to provide or maintain employment,[79] and this is an important factor elsewhere in the country.

The maximum grant is made to an enterprise outside the undeveloped areas only if there are "sound economic reasons" why it cannot be established or developed in those areas and if "other exceptional circumstances" exist.[80] "Sound" reasons need not be overwhelming; they include high transport costs for raw materials or the finished product or shortage of labor in the less populated areas. There is no minimum size for companies eligible for grants, and a large enterprise will not necessarily get a larger grant than a small enterprise in proportion to the capital involved. Other factors to be taken into account include the prospects for development on Irish and foreign markets, the use of Irish raw materials, especially agricultural products, the location and size of export markets,[81] the importance of the foreign currency likely to result from exports, and the existence of competition in Europe. Since Ireland

[74] Committee on Industrial Organization, Fourth Interim Report: Industrial Grants, Pr. 6924, para. 44(2) (1962); see Second Programme for Economic Expansion, Pr. 7239, para. 57 (1963).

[75] Undeveloped Areas Act, 1952 Acts 3, § 5(1)(c); Industrial Grants Act, 1959 Acts 927, § 2(1)(b). This requirement is not expressed in the Shannon Airport legislation.

[76] Committee on Industrial Organization, Fourth Interim Report: Industrial Grants, Pr. 6924, para. 44(1) (1962).

[77] Undeveloped Areas Act, 1952 Acts 3, § 5(1)(b); Industrial Grants Act, 1959 Acts 927, § 2(1)(b). This provision probably was originally intended to insure that grants were given primarily to enterprises too small to use the capital market. Where the provision is disregarded, the grant is in effect given as an incentive.

[78] The Undeveloped Areas Act, 1952 Acts 3, as amended, 1957 Acts 521, and 1963 Acts, No. 3, applies to the counties of Donegal, Cavan, Longford, Monaghan, Sligo, Leitrim, Roscommon, Mayo, Galway, and Kerry, and to parts of Clare and Cork. See Committee on Industrial Organization, Fourth Interim Report: Industrial Grants, Pr. 6924, at 4 (1962).

[79] Undeveloped Areas Act, 1952 Acts 3, § 5(1)(a).

[80] Under previous legislation, an enterprise was "exceptional" because of its size, character, or the extent to which its products were likely to be exported. "Size" included the amount of capital and labor involved and the value of the total production. See Industrial Grants Act, 1959 Acts 927, § 2(1)(a); the new section is Industrial Grants (Amendment) Act, 1963 Acts, No. 3, § 2.

[81] Fennell, Industrialization and Agricultural Development in the Congested Districts 10 (1962).

needs industrialization and since the demands of the Irish market are irrelevant if the goods are not sold there, the balance of industry in Ireland is not important and the Grants Board does not require any particular specialization index[82] or export and industrial estrangement coefficient[83] of the goods to be manufactured. These indices are of interest only in sectors in which Ireland already produces some goods, and since the Irish market for manufactured products is small, home demand is regarded as unlikely to give rise to economies of scale sufficient to reduce the cost of exports.

The amount of the grants

Both in and outside the undeveloped areas, grants are given by the Grants Board. In the undeveloped areas, or outside the undeveloped areas if the Grants Board considers that there are "sound economic reasons" for not setting up in the undeveloped areas and that "other exceptional circumstances" exist, the grant may amount to two-thirds of the total cost of machinery,[84] land, construction and adaptation of buildings, and related services, up to £250,000 ($700,000).[85] Outside the undeveloped areas, if there are no "sound economic reasons" or "other exceptional circumstances," the maximum grant is half of the cost of machinery, land, buildings, and services.[86] If the grant contemplated is more than £250,000, the maximum amount is one-half of the fixed capital, or the number of pounds sterling equal to 1,000 multiplied by the number of employees who will be hired due to the investment, whichever is less.[87] This limitation may be waived by the government,[88] but normally a large capital-intensive industry is not eligible for as substantial a grant as a large labor-intensive industry. If the grant is under £250,000, any preference for labor-intensive industry will continue to be administrative, discretionary, and dependent on the circumstances of the case. Unless a special waiver has been granted, in all cases the maximum amount of the grant is £500,000 ($1.4 million).[89]

The present differences in treatment for the two parts of the country[90] are the test of eligibility for a grant, the lower maximum grant outside the undeveloped areas if no special circumstances exist,

[82] I.e., the ratio of the percentage of total world trade in the commodity in question to the percentage of existing Irish exports of the commodity. See U.N. Economic Survey of Europe, 1959, U.N. Doc. No. E/ECE/383, ch. VIII, at 7 (1960).

[83] I.e., the ratio of the proportion of Ireland's total industrial production of the commodity in question to the proportion of Ireland's total industrial exports of the commodity. In this connection and in connection with the index mentioned in the above note, see Barna, "Export Growth Retarded by Technical Backwardness," The Times (London), April 3, 1963, p. 19.

[84] This has the same meaning as it has for the purposes of depreciation allowances; Industrial Grants (Amendment) Act, 1961 Acts 1085, § 4.

[85] Industrial Grants (Amendment) Act, 1963 Acts, No. 4, § 2. The Grants Board may build factories and give them to investors; however, it does not do so in practice except at Shannon Airport. Also, the Grants Board theoretically may acquire land compulsorily.

[86] Undeveloped Areas (Amendment) Act, 1963 Acts, No. 3, § 2.

[87] Industrial Grants (Amendment) Act, 1963 Acts, No. 4, § 2. The increased number of employees is the number estimated to be employed in the undertaking when it is in full operation, less any employed before the expenditure is incurred.

[88] Undeveloped Areas (Amendment) Act, 1963 Acts, No. 3, §§ 2(2), 3.

[89] Industrial Grants (Amendment) Act, 1963 Acts, No. 4, § 3.

[90] See pp. 335–37 on Irish regional economic policy; the 1963 changes substantially reduced the incentive to invest in the less developed areas in the west and were strongly criticized in the Irish Parliament.

and the fact that grants are available in undeveloped areas for the maintenance as well as the construction and adaptation of buildings. In undeveloped areas there are also provisions for the remission for ten years of two-thirds of the local taxes (called "rates") on premises for which grants have partly paid,[91] and electricity may be supplied at reduced cost.[92] The 1963 Act directs the Grants Board "to bear constantly in mind the national aims of decentralizing industry and of attracting industries to the undeveloped areas" and to promote these aims.[93] The principal effect of this provision is to impress on potential investors that more favorable treatment will be given to them in the undeveloped areas. The Grants Board does not direct industry into those areas. The difference in the maximum grant which can be given is not in itself a strong incentive to investment in the undeveloped areas, since the maximum grant is not always given in any area.

Under the legislation in force until 1963, grants constituted an average of 34 per cent of the cost of fixed assets of enterprises eligible for grants outside the undeveloped areas and 53 per cent in the undeveloped areas.[94] The contribution by the Irish government to the capital of the enterprise concerned often has been so substantial that the government's only safeguard—the investor's contributing substantially to the capital himself—has been greatly diminished. This safeguard sometimes has also been diminished by the government's buying part of the stock of the enterprise aided. Most of the large grants were given outside the undeveloped areas under the pre-1963 legislation.

Shannon Airport: Grants of capital

In the Shannon Airport industrial zone, the Shannon Free Airport Development Company gives the grants. Grants may be made for machinery and equipment in connection with any industrial or commercial enterprise which has been approved by the Development Company and is operating at the airport. Grants may be up to half of the cost of the machinery and equipment and may cover both the total wages paid to workers during training and the travel and subsistence expenses of Irish workers trained abroad.[95]

GRANTS FOR SPECIAL PURPOSES

Throughout the country the Grants Board may make workers' training grants of up to the total amount of wages paid to the workers during training and travel and subsistence expenses for Irish workers trained abroad.[96] The training must be in skilled industrial processes, and the enterprise must provide employment, require financial help, and be efficient and reasonably permanent. There are no special provisions for workers unemployed because of re-equipment or adaptation.

The Grants Board may also make grants for housing and refreshment and recreation facilities for employees and grants for roads, bridges, harbor works, and railways.[97] This type of expenditure normally can be incurred by govern-

[91] Undeveloped Areas Act, 1952 Acts 3, § 9; Undeveloped Areas (Amendment) Act, 1957 Acts 521, § 14.

[92] Undeveloped Areas Act, 1952 Acts 3, § 10.

[93] Industrial Grants (Amendment) Act, 1963 Acts, No. 4, § 8.

[94] Committee on Industrial Organizations, Fourth Interim Report: Industrial Grants, Pr. 6924, para. 9 (1962). Details of the grants given each year are available in the annual reports of An Foras Tionscal (the Grants Board).

[95] Shannon Free Airport Development Company Limited Act, 1959 Acts 999, § 9.

[96] Industrial Grants (Amendment) Act, 1963 Acts, No. 4, § 5; Undeveloped Areas Act, 1952 Acts 3, § 7.

[97] Industrial Grants (Amendment) Act, 1963 Acts, No. 4, § 6; Undeveloped Areas Act, 1952 Acts 3, § 8.

ments in the EEC without causing distortions of competition, and there is no reason why enterprises should not be repaid for expenses which governments could have incurred in the first instance.

The Department of Industry and Commerce gives grants for technical assistance and prospecting for minerals,[98] and the Export Board gives grants for various activities likely to increase exports.[99]

[98] The Department of Industry and Commerce gives industrial enterprises grants of up to one-half the cost of engaging industrial consultants or prospecting for minerals. Management personnel who are engaged in a manufacturing industry and who attend training courses may receive grants of up to one-half the cost of this attendance, as may trade union representatives who attend courses on productivity techniques. These grants are also available for visits abroad by representatives of the management and employees of manufacturing firms to study aspects of industrial organization. Department of Industry and Commerce, Technical Assistance Grants to Promote Productive Efficiency in Industry (Feb. 1963).

Grants of up to one-half the cost may be made for exploration or development schemes where commercially workable deposits of minerals are likely; Department of Industry and Commerce, Technical Assistance Grants for Private Exploration of Minerals (undated). Tax incentives are also available for mining operations in Ireland; Finance (Profits of Certain Mines) (Temporary Relief from Taxation) Act, 1956, §§ 5–6; Finance (Miscellaneous Provisions) Act, 1956, § 5; Finance Act, 1960, § 32.

The total amount of technical assistance grants for all purposes between March 1962 and February 1963 was approximately $273,-000; 200 Dáil Eireann, Parl. Deb., cols. 615–17 (1963).

[99] The Irish Export Board, set up by the Export Promotion Act, 1959 Acts 849, will pay the traveling and other expenses of training designers for firms in Ireland. Grants are also given of up to one-half the cost of sending senior designers of export-manufacturing firms to study design development in European countries. Grants of up to one-third the cost of engaging or consulting a designer are given to enterprises which have exported or are planning to export. Also available are grants of up to 60% of the cost of export-market consultants or the cost of original market research outside Britain. Grants may be given to cover the traveling expenses of trips by an enterprise's senior members to investigate markets or promote sales outside Ireland. Grants of up to one-half the expenditure incurred on the visit are also available, as are grants for participation in foreign trade fairs. For discussion of these various grants, see the following circulars of the Export Board (Córas Tráchtála): Design Trainee Grants (Oct. 1963); Design Investigatory Grants (Feb. 1963); Design Grant Scheme (Jan. 1962); Technical Assistance Marketing (Sept. 1962); Travel Incentive Grants Scheme (Jan. 1963); Market Research and Consultancy Grants (Nov. 1964); Overseas Trade Fairs Participation Grants (Jan. 1965).

GUARANTEES FOR EXPORTS

To encourage exports, government guarantees can be given to, or for the benefit of, any enterprise operating in Ireland in connection with the export, manufacture, treatment, or distribution of goods or the rendering of services.[100] These guarantees may include agreements with insurance companies for reinsurance of guarantees they have already given. Under this provision the Minister for Industry and Commerce has made an agreement with several Irish insurance companies by which they are reinsured when they insure Irish exporters against certain risks. These risks include the outbreak of war in the country of destination and the operation of any law preventing the transfer of payments from the buyer's country to Ireland or preventing the buyer from securing delivery of any goods sold.

SUBSIDIZED LOANS

The Industrial Credit Company[101] is a government-owned finance house with wide powers to provide long-term capital at commercial interest rates, usually on the security of mortgage debentures or charges but also by way of equity participation. It is also an issuing and underwriting house and provides hire purchase facilities for new machinery, at present, at an effective rate of interest of 7 per

[100] Insurance Act, 1953 Acts 33, § 2.

cent. It provides capital whenever it is less convenient to obtain it on the capital market. It may lend money without charging interest during the first few years if the interest for the remaining years of the loan is equal to interest at the commercial rate over the whole period. Provision of loan capital is not within Article 92 of the EEC Treaty if there is no element of subsidy. An interest-free loan for part of the period is not a subsidy if, over the whole period of the loan, the effective rate of interest is not reduced.[102] These loans by the Industrial Credit Company are a variation on normal commercial practice. The only advantage of such loans is that repayment of both capital and interest is postponed until the expanded or re-equipped operation is fully established. This is useful in the period prior to entry into the EEC, since re-equipment can take place at once, but its full benefits, in the form of increased export sales, will not be obtained until tariffs are abolished in the EEC.

The Committee on Industrial Organization recommends that, in some circumstances, a loan should be given free of interest for a number of years and at normal rates for the balance of the period. This introduces the element of subsidy. The Committee points out that the loans recommended, unlike capital grants or loans with reduced interest rates spread evenly over the life of the loan, require the borrower to assess realistically the economic possibilities of the investment and thus deter uneconomical investment.[103] These loans provide capital for investment in a way which accelerated depreciation allowances cannot, and unlike accelerated depreciation, they are selective in their operation.

Loan capital on terms more favorable than normal commercial rates of interest may now be given by the Industrial Credit Company to any industrial company which has received a grant from the Grants Board. However, if one-half (two-thirds in the case of a company in the undeveloped areas) of the fixed capital is less than £250,000 ($700,000), a grant of up to that proportion of the fixed capital may be given, and no further state aid by way of subsidized loan normally will be given.[104] The object of the plan is to enable the state to provide large amounts of capital if necessary but to insure that when it does so some part of the capital will be repaid if the company is successful. The government is unwilling to increase the maximum amount of the grants. The Industrial Credit Company may take up equity capital in companies which are receiving grants, but this is not always acceptable to the

[101] Established under the Industrial Credit Acts, 1933 Pub. Stat. 849, and 1958 Acts 165. The ordinary facilities offered by the Industrial Credit Company are set out in various booklets published by the company itself; see, in particular, Capital for Industry (undated). One function is important, however—that of underwriting public issues of medium-sized companies to enable them to expand to the size at which they can obtain a stock exchange listing.

[102] It possibly could be argued that a subsidy was involved, because during the moratorium the sums which would otherwise be repaid could be invested by the borrower at a rate of return higher than the interest rate.

[103] Interim Report on State Aid, Pr. 6510, paras. 25–33, especially at para. 25 (1962).

[104] See Dr. Ryan, Minister for Finance, 203 Dáil Eireann, Parl. Deb., cols. 292–93, 317, 705–706 (1963). In particular, where the grant to a capital-intensive enterprise is limited by the ratio of the increased number of employees to the total capital invested, additional capital will be given by a loan from the Industrial Credit Company; 199 Dáil Eireann, Parl. Deb., cols. 473, 767, 771, 1170 (1963). These loans will be interest-free for seven years and will bear interest at either commercial or subsidized rates after that time. They will be redeemable at the option of the borrower at any time after seven years; if not redeemed, the debenture shares on which the loans are secured will have the right to participate in the profits of the company.

promoters. The deferred-interest loans are one solution. A new body, State Finances, Ltd.,[105] will make some subsidized loans instead of the Industrial Credit Company. The way in which these two bodies can exercise their powers is entirely flexible.[106] Loans may be unsecured and may be repayable only at the option of the borrower. The two bodies usually are entitled to participate in the profits of the company if the dividends on the equity capital (or, possibly, the company's undistributed profits) exceed a specified rate. The suggested rate of dividends is 7.5 per cent.[107] The duration of the interest-free part of the total term of the loan depends on circumstances.[108] In all cases the promoters are expected to provide one-third of the fixed capital and the whole of the working capital. In some cases in the past the government has not kept to this principle, but the Grants Board and the Industrial Credit Company can be expected to do so.

If State Finances, Ltd., holds half or more of the equity capital of a company, the accounts of the company are published,[109] but they are not published otherwise unless the general company law so requires it. The amount of the interest of State Finances, Ltd., in the company and the amount of any grant made by the Grants Board to the company are published in the accounts of the two bodies. If the extent of state aid to industry has to be reduced if Ireland joins the EEC, it seems likely that aid will be given in a form in which some return to the government is possible. Some public misgivings have been expressed recently over non-repayable state aid's being given to ventures which appear to be uneconomical.[110]

TEMPORARY STATE AID TO INDUSTRY PREPARING FOR ENTRY INTO THE EEC

The Irish government has given special financial aid to industry in preparation for conditions of free trade in the EEC.[111] The previous program of subsidized loans for re-equipment and adaptation ended in March 1966; grants for this purpose will remain payable until December 31, 1967.[112] It was intended only to encourage "preventive adaptation" through investment which is not eligible for aid under the general grants

[105] Taiscí Stáit Teoranta [State Finances Limited] Act, 1963 Acts, No. 16.

[106] See Beddy, Murray, FitzGerald & Walsh, "Industrial Promotion," 10 Administration 325 (1962).

[107] Dr. Ryan, Minister for Finance, 203 Dáil Eireann, Parl. Deb., col. 291 (1963).

[108] Committee on Industrial Organization, Interim Report on State Aid, Pr. 6510, para. 28 (1962), suggested that the moratorium should be for five years unless the whole term of the loan was seven years or less.

[109] Taiscí Stáit Teoranta [State Finances Limited] Act, 1963 Acts, No. 16, § 17.

[110] See, for example, Viney, "Value for Money," Irish Times, April 9, 1963, p. 8; id., April 10, 1963, p. 8; id., April 11, 1963, p. 10; FitzGerald, "State Aid Program—Some Outstanding Blunders," Irish Times, July 17, 1963, p. 11.

[111] Committee on Industrial Organization, Interim Report on State Aid, Pr. 6510, paras. 16–17 (1962), lists four types of problem: accelerated re-equipment of industry within the same field of production, which is outside the scope of the general grants program already described and for which the Committee recommended special grants and loans; adaptation involving a change in activity, which might fall within the existing grants program if the new investment involved was sufficiently extensive; and the establishment of new industries in the undeveloped areas and the diversification and deepening of the industrial base, both of which would fall under the existing grants programs.

[112] See Industrial Grants (Amendment) Act, 1963 Acts, No. 4, § 4; Undeveloped Areas (Amendment) Act, 1963 Acts, No. 3, § 4; John Lynch, T.D., then Minister for Industry and Commerce, 199 Dáil Eireann, Parl. Deb., cols. 475–76 (1963); Industrial Credit Company, Special Loans for Re-equipment and Expansion (1963); Industrial Credit Company, 29th Ordinary General Meeting, Proceedings 4–5 (1963).

program. Incentives for modernization and for re-equipment with a view to specialization are particularly important at the time of the entry of a new member state into the EEC. They are temporary and will prevent economic difficulties from arising later. Grants are, however, not the only and not necessarily the best method of encouraging modernization and specialization.[113] Also used are subsidized loans given by the Industrial Credit Company, accelerated depreciation allowances,[114] and the right of parent companies to deduct from taxable income the losses of a joint marketing subsidiary.[115] The latter two probably will be permanent, but neither could be regarded as state aid to industry within Article 92 of the EEC Treaty.

THE POSSIBLE EFFECTS OF EEC MEMBERSHIP

The impact of the EEC on Irish tax concessions for exports has been discussed in Chapter Twelve.[116] The temporary state aids to industry to promote adaptation to free trade conditions have been terminated. The general grants program might be dealt with specifically in the negotiations between Ireland and the EEC, but this is unlikely. On the basis of Article 92 there would probably be no reason why the program of grants should not continue in the EEC. The per capita income in Ireland in 1964 was only $918, and in parts of the country incomes are well below the national average.[117] On the other hand, some individual grants given in the past would probably be incompatible with Article 92 because of their size or because of the sectors which have received them.

It is more doubtful if programs of state aids directly related to exports, other than tax concessions, would be permitted by the Commission. This does not include the grants legislation, under which capacity to export is only one factor taken into account. The existing nonfiscal state aids directly related to exports are on a very small scale and are governed by Article 92, not by the strict provisions of Article 98. Though these aids may be incompatible with the principles of the Treaty, their relative importance and the absence of any express provision in the Treaty relating to nonfiscal aids to exports might in practice allow their continuance.

If Ireland became associated with the EEC before becoming a member, all the existing state aids would be under the provisions of the treaty of association and would be entirely matters for negotiation.

[113] See Report of the Committee on the Scottish Economy (1961), quoted by Committee on Industrial Organization, Interim Report on State Aid, Pr. 6510 (1962).

[114] Finance Act, 1962 Acts 563, § 11.

[115] Given by Finance Act, 1962, § 13.

[116] On pp. 300–302.

[117] See Attwood & Geary, Irish County Incomes in 1960, especially Table 12 (1963).

Chapter 14

Revocation of State Aids

TYPES OF PROBLEM

In Chapter Twelve it was concluded that if Ireland joined the EEC the present tax concessions for exports would have to be altered to comply with the EEC Treaty. There seems to be no reason why the legislation establishing the other Irish state aids is incompatible with the Treaty, but it is possible that state aid to particular enterprises might be prohibited under Article 92. The Irish state aids to industry would certainly not be withdrawn unless Community law so required. The Irish investment climate is very good, and the government would do its utmost to fulfill the expectations of investors, to continue its present policies, and to render unfounded the assumptions on which this chapter is based.

This chapter assumes modifications in tax concession and other Irish state aid legislation will have to take place and considers the legal position of an investor under Irish domestic law, under Community law, and under international law. Broadly, the conclusion reached is that in most of the circumstances likely to arise in Ireland, which seem typical of those elsewhere, the investor is unlikely to have any remedy if state aid is cancelled. This chapter does not consider the position under the national laws of any other country, but it seems unlikely that they, except perhaps those of France, give the investor any remedy.

The question can arise in two types of case. The first type is where state aid is the subject of a contract between the enterprise and the member state, and the Commission prevents the aid's being given. In Ireland, state aid is normally the subject of contract where it is given in a single transaction, and all grants are the subject of contracts.

The second type of case is where state aid is given over a period of years, for example, a tax concession, and the Commission decides that the aid should cease. If aid of this kind is given under a contract, the contractual aspects are the same as in the first type of case. The Commission would hardly ask for repayment of aid actually given,[1] under contract or otherwise. If aid given in a single transaction is not given under a contract, the legal right of the enterprise to count on the aid's being given in the future is the same as in the case of aid given on a continuing basis.

WHERE A CONTRACT EXISTS

Irish domestic law

The Terms of the Contract and Its Legality Under National Law

If state aid is given under a contract, the rights of the enterprise depend first on the terms of the contract. The EEC Commission has hardly begun to examine the compatibility of existing state aid programs with the Treaty. However, if Ireland was a member state and the Commission reviewed individual grants,

[1] It is doubtful if the Commission has power to require repayment of state aid given after the

or if that state of affairs was imminent, the Irish Grants Board presumably would insert clauses providing for the cancellation of agreements if the Commission held the grant or other aid to be contrary to Article 92. It is at least possible that such a clause could be implied, from the presumed intention of the parties and from reason,[2] in an agreement made after Ireland's entry into the EEC had become certain.

Even if the treaty were in force in Irish domestic law, the payment of a grant would not be illegal in Irish law (as distinct from Community law) merely because the EEC Commission had prohibited it. Unless a regulation under Article 94 prohibited state aid contrary to the Treaty or unless Irish legislation provided that only state aid compatible with the Treaty could be given, a decision of the Commission that state aid was contrary to Article 92 would bind the Irish state only in international law. In an action for breach of a grant agreement, the Irish Grants Board could not plead successfully that the agreement was illegal or outside its powers, even if the Commission had ruled that the grant was contrary to Article 92. Decisions of the Commission bind those to whom they are addressed, but the Commission does not seem to have power to address a decision under Article 93 to a national authority such as the Irish Grants Board.

If the decisions of the Commission took effect automatically in Irish law, the question arises whether they would be retroactive or only prospective. Article 92 prohibits state aid in principle but provides that certain types of aid[3] "may be deemed to be compatible with the Common Market." This indicates that there is a presumption that state aids are prohibited. However, Article 93(2) indicates that existing programs will be permissible until prohibited and thus that the decisions of the Commission are prospective. This seems the better view[4] and is the view on which the Commission has acted.

Freedom of Executive Action Under Irish Law

In the case of grant agreements entered into but not performed at the time the Treaty comes into force in Ireland, the state's own act in joining the EEC may make performance of them impossible. The question arises whether the state can successfully plead that its entry into the EEC was an economic necessity or that its freedom of executive action entitled it to accede to the Treaty without incurring liability for breach of a contract which accession made it illegal to perform.

In Irish and English domestic law the plea that no compensation is payable by the state if its executive action results in a breach of a state contract seems in some cases to be valid. Clearly, a state cannot contract, by a grant agreement or any other contract with a private enterprise, not to join the EEC.[5] The courts cannot order the executive not to sign

state joined the EEC. If it had this power, the international law rules on expropriation would apply. If the contract provided for repayment of the state aid, there would, of course, be no cause of action if the circumstances were covered by the contract. For an example of revocation of state aid by the Commission, see the decision prohibiting Belgium from granting aid to Ford Tractor (Belgium), Ltd., in Antwerp; 1964 Journal Officiel 3257–59/64.

[2] The Moorcock, 14 P.D. 64, 68 (1889) (per Bowen, L.J.); Anson, Principles of the English Law of Contract 117–20, 126–28 (1959).

[3] Those under art. 92(3).

[4] Art. 92 is not directly applicable; Costa v. ENEL, 10 Recueil 1141, [1964] C.M.L.R. 425.

[5] "It is not competent for the Government to fetter its future executive action, which must necessarily be determined by the needs of the community when the question arises. It cannot by contract hamper its freedom of action in matters which concern the welfare of the State." Rederiaktiebolaget Amphitrite v. The King, [1921] 3 K.B. 500, 503 (per Rowlatt,

the EEC Treaty. This does not necessarily mean that government action in breach of a government contract cannot give rise to a claim for damages.[6] However, the *Amphitrite* case says, "[A]n arrangement whereby the Government purported to give an assurance as to what its executive action would be in the future . . . is . . . not a contract for the breach of which damages can be sued for in a court of law. . . . [T]his was not a commercial contract. . . . No doubt the Government can bind itself through its officers by a commercial contract, and if it does so it must perform it like anybody else or pay damages for the breach."[7]

L.J.). See Mann, "State Contracts and State Responsibility," 54 Am. J. Int'l L. 572, 584–85 (1960), who cites Horowitz v. United States, 267 U.S. 458, 460 (1925), as holding "that the United States when sued as a contractor cannot be held liable for an obstruction to the performance of the particular contract resulting from its public and general acts as sovereign." It is not clear if the principle in the *Amphitrite* case covers both legislative and executive actions. In Ireland, ratification of a treaty is an executive function but its implementation in domestic law is a legislative act; Constitution of 1937, arts. 28–29.

[6] Holdsworth, "A Case Book on Constitutional Law," 45 L.Q. Rev. 162, 166 (1929).

[7] [1921] 3 K.B. at 503. The order of the sentences in the judgment has been reversed in the text. In the *Amphitrite* case, the British legation in Stockholm had promised that a neutral ship belonging to the plaintiffs would not be detained in Britain after she unloaded her cargo there. World War I continued, and the ship was not released. It was held that the promise was not a "commercial contract" for breach of which damages could be obtained. The case can be explained, however, on the grounds that the British government had not intended to enter into contractual relations; Robertson v. Minister of Pensions, [1949] 1 K.B. 227, 231 (per Denning, J.); see Phillips, Constitutional and Administrative Law 655–56 (1962); Australian Woollen Mills v. Commonwealth of Australia, [1955] 3 All E.R. 711. This interpretation would make the law more satisfactory.

Is a grant agreement a "commercial contract" for this purpose? In the *Amphitrite* case, the Irish government[8] had no interest, but it does have an interest in a grant agreement, since it wishes to encourage industrialization. Its interest is not commercial in the sense that its interest in a public contract for supplies is commercial. The interest of an enterprise in a grant agreement is no more commercial than the interest of the plaintiffs in the *Amphitrite* case. The basis for the exemption from liability in damages in the *Amphitrite* case presumably is that governments might be inclined to perform undesirable contracts rather than pay damages, if the latter were the only alternative, and that this would be undesirable in the public interest. But this explanation applies only where it is in the public interest that the government be free not to perform the contract and where this public interest is something more than merely saving public funds.[9] In general, civil servants may be dismissed without cause, apparently on the grounds that the government should be free to dismiss its employees if this is necessary in the public interest; this, however, was held in *Reilly v. The King* to be an implied term in their contracts of service and to be overridden by an express clause.[10] Even if it is assumed that government employment contracts are a type of "commercial contract," the *Reilly* case does not clarify the position of a grant agreement, but it strengthens

[8] The legal position arising out of the fact that the grants legislation is not administered by a government department is considered on p. 359. For the purposes of the rule discussed in the text, the distinction between the Grants Board and a government department seems irrelevant.

[9] In this connection see Lynch v. United States, 292 U.S. 571, 580 (1933) (per Brandeis, J.).

[10] Reilly v. The King, [1934] A.C. 176; see also Robertson v. Minister of Pensions, [1949] 1 K.B. 227.

the position of an investor who is a party to a state contract expressly guaranteeing him against revocation of state aid. The rule in the *Amphitrite* case is uncertain and unsatisfactory,[11] but owing to the public and social nature of the government's interest in grant agreements, it seems doubtful if they are "commercial contracts." Therefore, if the *Amphitrite* case is not based on absence of intent to enter into contractual relations, it seems that an investor could not recover damages for breach of a grant agreement.

Accession to the EEC Treaty as a Defense to an Action for Breach of Contract

Even assuming that a grant agreement is not within the *Amphitrite* rule, the government probably could plead the consequences of its own act in joining the EEC as a defense in an action for breach of a grant agreement. If the grant is not permitted by the Commission, the performance of the grant agreement would presumably become illegal under the act implementing and enacting the EEC Treaty. First, since state aids are not automatically illegal under Article 92, the immediate reason why a grant agreement would become illegal would be an act of the Commission. Over this neither the Irish executive nor the legislature would have any control. Legally, the Irish government would therefore not be taking advantage of its own act.[12] Secondly, even though the government party controls the legislature, under Irish and English law the government is able to plead the direct consequences of a legislative act in an action for breach of contract, however convincing it may be morally or politically to argue that, in doing so, the government takes advantage of its own wrong. In *Reilly v. The King*,[13] the plaintiff sued for damages for breach of a contract of employment as a member of a statutory board, the relevant statute having been repealed and further performance of the contract being impossible. It was held that no compensation was payable. It follows that in the case of the breach of a grant agreement, even if the official party to the agreement, the Irish Grants Board, were identified for this purpose with the Irish government, there would be no right to recover. The law governing a grant agreement is normally Irish law, of which Community law would be a part after Ireland had entered the EEC. If the performance of a grant agreement became illegal because of a change in Community law directly applicable in Ireland,[14] not because of a constitutive ruling of the Commission pursuant to the law in force when the agreement was made,[15] no liability to the enterprise could arise.[16] The liability of the Irish government is governed by the proper law of the contract and that law would have been changed through an act not

[11] See Holdsworth, "A Case Book on Constitutional Law," 45 L.Q. Rev. 162, 166 (1929).

[12] "There may be little difference between a Government breaking unlawfully a contract with an alien and a Government causing legislation to be enacted which makes it impossible to comply with a contract." Case of Certain Norwegian Loans, [1957] I.C.J. Rep. 9, 37 (separate opinion per Sir Hersch Lauterpacht); see Mann, "State Contracts and State Responsibility," 54 Am. J. Int'l L. 572, 573 (1960).

[13] [1934] A.C. 176; see also O'Crowley v. Minister for Justice, [1935] Ir. R. 536, 547–50. These cases involve contracts of employment and could be distinguished on that ground, but there is no other authority.

[14] E.g., because of the enactment or amendment of a regulation under art. 94.

[15] The act enacting the Treaty would not make performance of grants agreements illegal in itself but might make it illegal where the Commission decided it would be contrary to the Treaty.

[16] Mann, "State Contracts and State Responsibility," 54 Am. J. Int'l L. 572, 573 (1960).

that of the Irish legislature.[17]

The Legal Position of Irish Authorities Giving State Aid[18]

So far it has been assumed that the Irish Grants Board, which would be sued for failure to pay a grant agreed upon, could be identified with the Irish government. However, the Grants Board is a statutory body,[19] not a government department, although government departments are also set up by statute.[20] This distinction may be important, because the Irish government continues to have the immunity from actions for breach of contract formerly enjoyed by the British Crown.[21] This unsatisfactory state of affairs has been remedied in Britain[22] and has been mitigated in Ireland by the practice of giving judgments declaring the plaintiff's rights.[23] Irish statutory bodies other than government departments are not immune from actions for breach of contract.[24] The Irish government would be anxious to demonstrate its good faith in any dispute with an investor over a grant agreement and would certainly enable the courts to give a judgment declaring the legal position, even if it was adverse to the state.

Like the Grants Board, the Industrial Credit Company, which gives subsidized loans to industry, is a body set up pursuant to statute[25] and is legally separate from the government.

A Constitutional Remedy?

While the Irish Constitution contains a provision protecting private property, it contains no express provision guaranteeing compensation in cases of compulsory acquisition or even referring to it. Ireland has never expropriated industrial operations of foreign investors, but it could be argued that cancellation of state aid because of Community rules would constitute expropriation.

Article 40(3) of the Irish Constitution reads:

> (1) The State guarantees in its laws to respect, and, as far as practicable, by its laws to defend and vindicate the personal rights of the citizen.
>
> (2) The State shall, in particular, by its laws protect as best it may from unjust attack and, in the case of injustice done, vindicate the life, person, good name, and

[17] The vote cast on the regulation by the Irish representative in the Council could hardly be regarded as affecting the position. It seems artificial to argue that the Irish government is "responsible" for the acts of the Commission because it has delegated or assigned certain powers to it, and this argument would be quite contrary to the principles of the EEC Treaty, which gives the Commission powers over national governments.

[18] The most important state aid in Ireland is the tax exemption for profits from exports. This is given by the Revenue Commissioners, who certainly have the privileges of the Irish government in actions for breach of contract.

[19] Created by Undeveloped Areas Act, 1952 Acts 3.

[20] Ministers and Secretaries Act, 1924 Pub. Stat., as amended. Section 2 of the 1924 Act allowed Ministers to sue in their official capacity and, subject to the fiat of the Attorney General, to be sued. Undeveloped Areas Act, 1952 Acts 3, First Schedule, para. 1, provides that the Grants Board has "power . . . to be sued" [sic]. This does not affect its substantive liability.

[21] Kenny v. Cosgrave, [1926] Ir. R. 517; Leen v. President of the Executive Council, [1928] Ir. R. 408. See Donaldson, Some Comparative Aspects of Irish Law 218–27 (1957).

[22] By Crown Proceedings Act, 1947, 10 & 11 Geo. 6, c. 44.

[23] Leyden v. Attorney General, [1926] Ir. R. 334, 367, 371; Galway County Council v. Minister for Finance, [1931] A.C. 215.

[24] Wheeler v. Commissioners of Public Works, [1930] 2 Ir. R. 202.

[25] Industrial Credit Act, 1933 Pub. Stat. 849; Industrial Credit (Amendment) Act, 1958 Acts 165. The Shannon Free Airport Development Company, Ltd., was set up in 1959 by an act of that name; 1959 Acts 999. The Irish Export Board was set up by Export Promotion Act, 1959 Acts 849.

property rights of every citizen. [Emphasis supplied.]

Article 43 explains the reference to property rights:[26]

1. (1) The State acknowledges that man, in virtue of his rational being, has the natural right, antecedent to positive law, to the private ownership of external goods.
(2) The State accordingly guarantees to pass no law attempting to abolish the right of private ownership or the general right to transfer, bequeath, and inherit property.
2. (1) The State recognizes, however, that the exercise of the rights mentioned in the foregoing provisions of this Article ought, in civil society, to be regulated by the principles of social justice.
(2) The State, accordingly, may as occasion requires *delimit by law the exercise of the said rights* with a view to reconciling their exercise with the exigencies of the common good. [Emphasis supplied.]

The first question which arises on these rather vague provisions is whether "private property" includes contractual rights. In *Foley v. Irish Land Commission*,[27] Mr. Justice Dixon in the High Court said:

It seems to me sufficient for the present purpose to point out that the agreement undoubtedly gives the purchaser some contractual rights which I regard as a species of private property within. . .Article 43. . . . [A]. . .ground of forfeiture or loss of contractual rights is imposed irrespective of the agreement of the parties. . . .I am prepared to assume that this. . .would be within the prohibition on abolishing the right of private ownership. . . .[28]

In principle, contractual rights should probably be regarded as property rights. Property rights, as distinct from physical goods, are protected by Article 43, and there is no obvious justification for distinguishing legal rights over property from legal rights under contracts. This is *a fortiori* the position where contractual rights can be enforced by specific performance. However, contract rights are not property under international law rules on expropriation. In Irish law property rights do not relate only to tangible things; in Northern Ireland goodwill has been held to be property under the corresponding provision of the Constitution[29] there. On the other hand, the interest of an enterprise in that part of its prospective profits which would have been payable in taxes but for a tax concession not based on contract cannot be regarded as a property right.

[26] Attorney General v. Southern Industrial Trust, Ltd., 94 Ir. L.T.R. 161, 176 (1960) (per Lavery, J.).

[27] [1952] Ir. R. 118, especially at 153–54. In this case, the Land Commission expropriated land which the plaintiff had occupied under an agreement for purchase from the Land Commission itself. The land was never vested in the plaintiff under the Land Acts, but the status of the plaintiff was governed by legislation. The Supreme Court held that the statutory requirement of residence on the land, for breach of which the land was expropriated, was constitutional since it helped to carry out a social policy for "the common good." The court implied that the statutory and contractual rights of the plaintiff were rights to "property" within the meaning of art. 43.

[28] [1952] Ir. R. at 131. Mr. Justice Dixon first said that he was reluctant to define the nature of the interest, if any, created by the agreement; id. at 130–31. See also Pigs Marketing Bd. v. Donnelly, [1939] Ir. R. 413, 422–23 (per Hanna, J.).

[29] Ulster Transp. Authority v. James Brown & Sons, [1953] No. Ire. L.R. 79; the relevant provision is U.K. Government of Ireland Act, 1920, 10 & 11 Geo. 5, c. 67, § 5. Mr. Justice Curran held that the right to exercise a lawful trade is property, and Mr. Justice Sheil, whose judgment was based on other grounds, agreed. Mr. Justice Curran cited Dent v. West Virginia, 129 U.S. 144 (1889); Hanker v. New York, 170 U.S. 189 (1898); and Rose v. Ford, [1937] A.C. 826. In the Court of Appeal, the judges preferred the view of Mr. Justice Sheil and gave no opinion on the view of Mr. Justice Curran. See also Belfast Corp. v. O.D. Cars, Ltd., [1960] 1 All E.R. 65.

Articles 40 and 43 protect the property rights of individual citizens,[30] not merely private property in general. The legislature has power under Article 43(2) to limit property rights. The courts may have to decide if the requirements of the common good require derogation from the rights of property; the extent to which the courts can substitute their views for that of the legislature is unsettled.[31]

In *Buckley v. Attorney General,*[32] the Supreme Court held invalid an act providing for the appropriation of trust funds and for their payment to a statutory body set up by the act for certain charitable purposes. The legislation had been passed when the ownership of the funds was in dispute before the courts, and there was no suggestion that the statutory body was the successor in title to any possible owner. The Supreme Court said:

> In the present case there is no suggestion that any conflict had arisen, or was likely to arise, between the exercise by the plaintiffs of their rights of property in the trust moneys and the exigencies of the common good, and it is only the existence of such a conflict and an attempt by the Legislature to reconcile such conflicting claims that could justify the enactment of the statute under review.[33]

The Irish legislature has power in some circumstances to expropriate property for public purposes,[34] at least where compensation is paid.

There would be an obvious conflict between the public interest in carrying out the measures required on accession to the EEC Treaty and the contractual rights of enterprises under grant agreements, and the public interest would certainly be held to prevail. The question therefore arises, assuming that rights under grant agreements are property rights protected by Article 43, whether the Irish Constitution gives a right to compensation where such rights are terminated in the public interest. In all of the statutes cited in the leading cases and assumed

[30] Buckley v. Attorney General, [1950] Ir. R. 67, 82–83 (per O'Byrne, J.); see Delany, "The Constitution of Ireland: Its Origins and Development," 12 U. Toronto L.J. 1, 18–21 (1957).

[31] Compare in Attorney General v. Southern Industrial Trust, Ltd., 94 Ir. L.T.R. 161 (1960), the opinion of President Davitt (at 170) with the opinion of Mr. Justice Lavery (at 177–78).

[32] [1950] Ir. R. 67.

[33] Id. at 83. Kelly, Fundamental Rights in the Irish Law and Constitution 133 (1961), suggests that the common good required that the trust funds be used for charitable purposes, not wasted in litigation. This suggestion was not made to the court. It is submitted that it is untenable. A conflict between property rights and the public interest does not arise merely because the legislature believes that private funds could be put to better use than that found for them by their owners. For this reason, the author does not believe that Buckley v. Attorney General is inconsistent with Attorney General v. Southern Industrial Trust, Ltd. In cases of compulsory acquisition of land for public purposes, the legislature does not merely decide that it has a better use for the particular property acquired, taken in isolation, than the owners; there is a conflict beween the public interest in a wider context and the private ownership of the particular property.

[34] Fisher v. Irish Land Comm'n, [1948] Ir. R. 3, 23, 24 (per Maguire, C.J.), 11, 12–13 (per Gavan Duffy, J.). In Attorney General v. Southern Industrial Trust, Ltd., the Supreme Court said:

> It is argued that to take away the ownership of a particular item of property completely cannot in any circumstances be a regulation of, or the delimiting of, the exercise of the right of ownership. . . . This seems to the Court to be plainly wrong. . . . [T]he 'property rights' . . . guaranteed [in art. 40 (3)] are not absolute rights declared defined and limited by Article 43. . . . The confiscation (to use the strongest word) of a particular chattel is not the abolition of the right of property the nature of which has been explained. If it were, the forfeiture of a chattel in any circumstances, the property of the guilty as well as of the innocent[,] would be prohibited.
>
> 94 Ir. L.T.R. at 176, 177.

to be constitutional,[35] there was a provision for compensation, so the point did not arise.

Though the State may "delimit . . . [property] rights with a view to reconciling their exercise with . . . the common good,"[36] it must "in its laws . . . respect, and, as far as practicable, by its laws . . . defend and vindicate the personal rights of the citizen" and "in the case of injustice done, vindicate the . . . property rights of every citizen."[37] Expropriation of property without compensation is normally "injustice,"[38] and the state cannot be entitled to impose on individual citizens the injustice against which it is bound to defend them.[39] Therefore, if the state has power in the public interest to expropriate property, it generally is bound to prevent injustice by providing compensation. It thereby protects, as far as possible, the rights it has power to override. Two further conclusions perhaps can be drawn. If the common good requires the imposition of tax, presumably it may require the reimposition of

---

President Davitt of the High Court said that if he had not been bound by authority he would have interpreted art. 43(1) as guaranteeing the absolute general right to own property, art. 40(3) as protecting the rights of individuals to particular items of property, which he correctly said were qualified rights, and art. 43(2) as authorizing the state to limit the freedom of the individual to use property. On this view, art. 43(2) would not authorize expropriation, but expropriation would be permitted, since the Constitution does not prohibit it, when it can be justified under art. 40(3), i.e., when it does not constitute "injustice." 94 Ir. L.T.R. at 168–69. However, he said of Buckley v. Attorney General:

> [It] seems to be clearly an authority for the proposition that Article 43 protects the right of the individual to the property which he owns, and appears to imply that the power reserved to delimit the exercise of property rights would justify the State in certain circumstances of conflict between such exercise and the exigencies of the common good, in passing laws the effect of which would be to deprive an individual of his property.
>
> 94 Ir. L.T.R. at 169.

President Davitt then pointed out that this implication seemed to be inconsistent with National Union of Railwaymen v. Sullivan, [1947] Ir. R. 91, which held that deprivation of a part of a constitutional right may be an unconstitutional denial of that right. The implication in Buckley v. Attorney General that it is art. 43(2) which authorizes expropriation is clearly dictum, and it is submitted that it is incorrect. However, nobody has ever disputed that expropriation is constitutional in some circumstances. It is submitted that President Davitt was correct in his view that art. 43(1) gives an absolute right to property in general and art. 40(3) a qualified right to particular property and that expropriation is consistent with both these rights if it is "just" within the meaning of art. 40(3). "I can find in the Constitution no provision precluding the State from passing a law which will have the effect of depriving a person of his own property, though the power to do so is conditioned by Article 40(3)." 94 Ir. L.T.R. at 169 (per Davitt, P.).

[35] Fisher v. Irish Land Comm'n, [1948] Ir. R. 3, 12–13; Attorney General v. Southern Industrial Trust, Ltd., 94 Ir. L.T.R. 161, 177 (1960). No compensation was payable under the act which was before the court in the *Southern Industrial Trust* case, which is discussed in the text below.

[36] Constitution, art. 43(2)(2).

[37] Constitution, art. 40(3)(1) and 40(3)(2).

[38] Expropriation without compensation is not always unjust. For example, the owner of a dangerous dog may be compelled to have it destroyed in the public interest. Compensation would normally be payable where private rights did not threaten injury to others.

[39] See President Davitt in Attorney General v. Southern Industrial Trust, Ltd., 94 Ir. L.T.R. 161, 168 (1960):

> Article 40(3) seems to me to be the only provision in the Constitution which protects the individual's rights to the property which he does own. . . . It *impliedly* guarantees that the State itself will not by its laws *unjustly* attack the right; and I think that the justice or otherwise of any legislative interference with the right has to be considered in relation, inter alia, to the proclaimed objects with which the Constitution was enacted, including the promotion of the common good.

tax previously remitted under special legislation.[40] If a state contract providing for a cash grant in return for promises to use the grant in certain operations is terminated by legislation, the extent of the "injustice done" seems to be the amount the enterprise actually spent in reliance on the contract and not the total amount of the grant to be given, in effect gratuitously, to the enterprise. It is doubtful if compensation so assessed would be incompatible with Article 92 for being prohibited state aid given under the guise of compensation.

Although the Constitution seems to give a right to compensation where property is taken, in the only case on the point, the *Southern Industrial Trust* case,[41] the Irish Supreme Court held that forfeiture of property without compensation was constitutional in the circumstances before the court. It is submitted that this case should be distinguished. The case involved forfeiture of a car which had been illegally exported and which was the property, not of the man who exported it, but of an installment sale company which had not been concerned in the illegal act. The Supreme Court, in a judgment less closely reasoned than that of the High Court, held that the power claimed for many years by the state to forfeit chattels in particular circumstances, under legislation whose validity had not been challenged, was a delimitation of the general right to property and was valid if exercised to reconcile this right with the common good. The court then said that the common good and social justice are primarily matters for the legislature and that it had not been clearly shown that the legislation before the court was unconstitutional.[42] The Supreme Court did not discuss how the power to forfeit goods without compensation, which is certainly constitutional, could justifiably be exercised against the property of a person who was innocent of any offense. President Davitt of the High Court, discussing this issue, said, "It is clearly a matter of public interest that the penalties which have been provided for the Customs code should be effective. The effectiveness of forfeiture as a penalty would, however, in many instances, be nullified if it were not permissible in cases where the goods in question, or the vehicle used to transport them, were not the property of the offender."[43] He did not discuss how far forfeiture could be effective at

[40] In O'Byrne v. Minister for Finance, [1959] Ir. R. 1, which held that liability to ordinary taxation was not a reduction in a judge's salary during his term of office which would be prohibited by the Constitution, Mr. Justice Dixon said:

> However unlikely in practice, it is still conceivable that the Legislature might at some time discriminate unduly in its taxation as regards some particular group or class of persons or some particular species of property. The Courts would then have to determine, if called upon to do so, whether such taxation, in attempting to regulate property rights otherwise than in accordance with the principles of social justice, did not conflict with Article 43 of the Constitution of 1937; see [Buckley v. Attorney General]. . . . The purpose of the taxation is, thus, not wholly immaterial. . . . A non-discriminatory tax of general application is a reasonable guarantee of its legitimate purpose: a discriminatory tax of limited application might not be conclusive, but would be some indication, of an improper purpose.
>
> Id. at 25.

[41] Attorney General v. Southern Industrial Trust, Ltd., 94 Ir. L.T.R. 161 (1960).

[42] The Supreme Court said that the issue was whether a statute which confers "a power on the . . . executive organs of the State in stated circumstances to take possession of particular chattels . . . and to divest without compensation the ownership of an owner who has himself committed no breach of the law either generally or in respect of the goods . . . can be justified in the circumstances of this case." Id. at 176.

[43] Id. at 171–72.

all as a penalty in such circumstances.[44]

It is submitted that expropriation without compensation, or forfeiture, should be strictly limited and should be regarded as constitutional only where it is in the nature of a sanction for a criminal offense or where the public is threatened with injury by the existence or use of the property taken. If this view is accepted, there would be a constitutional right to compensation on the termination of a grant agreement, if contractual rights are property within Articles 40 and 43. The *Southern Industrial Trust* decision is a harsh one because the owner was in no way concerned in the crime, and it may be a wrong decision. However, in the absence of any judicial authority holding that there is, in general, a constitutional right to compensation when property is expropriated, it is uncertain whether an investor would be entitled to compensation in the case of the termination of a grant agreement.

Community law

Protection of Property and the Claim and Measure of Damages

The existence of a contract between a state and an enterprise receiving state aid seems to have little significance under the EEC Treaty. Article 222 provides that the Treaty will not prejudice, in any way, the system of ownership in member states, but in view of the clear provisions of Article 93, there is no doubt that the EEC Commission may require the cancellation of state aid. Article 222 does not expressly apply to contractual rights, and it is anomalous to distinguish between contractual and non-contractual state aids.

A state can make a claim under international law for a breach of a grant agreement with one of its nationals, if at all, only if the state is not a member of the EEC, against which the Treaty cannot be pleaded.[45] No member state can reasonably object to the payment of compensation due under customary international law for the breach of an agreement entered into with a private enterprise before accession to the EEC Treaty,[46] if the private enterprise is from a nonmember state.

If Article 93(2) gives enterprises a right to express their views to the Commission when the legality of state aid is in question, the existence of a contract under which state aid is given will prove conclusively that the enterprise is an "interested party" within the meaning of the Article.

If a grant is contrary to Article 92, the question arises whether it is legal to pay compensation to the enterprise for the cancellation of the grant agreement. The ordinary principle of Irish law is that the damages awarded must put the plaintiff as far as possible in the same position that he would be in if his rights had not been infringed.[47] Clearly, the compensation cannot equal the amount of the grant, since this would be paying the amount of the grant agreement in another way. However, the enterprise probably can be repaid any expenses it has incurred, so it will not suffer any net loss.

A Decision Improperly Prohibiting a State Aid

The principles of Community law relating to the protection of enterprises[48]

[44] For example, it could hardly be held that forfeiture of a car used for smuggling was an effective penalty if the car had been stolen by the smugglers.

[45] Art. 234 applies only to agreements between states. One EEC member state could not bring a claim in international law for the cancellation by another member state of a grant agreement which was contrary to art. 92.

[46] Cf. art. 234(1).

[47] Wertheim v. Chicoutimi Pulp Co., [1911] A.C. 301; Monarch S.S. Co. v. Karlshamns Oljefabriker (A/B), [1949] A.C. 196, 220–21; Chitty, Contracts 565 (22d ed. 1961).

[48] See pp. 27–28.

seem clear. Article 173 gives an enterprise no right to appeal against a decision addressed to a member state[49] or to appeal for the annulment of a directive, even if it is of direct and individual concern to the enterprise. A decision under Article 93 can apparently be addressed only to a state. But if regulations under Article 94 with regard to giving state aid to individual enterprises empower the Commission to issue decisions addressed to a national authority, such as the Irish Grants Board, the enterprise which was to receive the aid could ask the Community Court to annul the decision under Article 173(2). Even if regulations under Article 94 do not expressly empower or require the Commission to address decisions on state aid for individual enterprises to the relevant national authority, the Court might permit the appeal of a decision of the Commission which was addressed to the state but in substance destined for the national authority. The Treaty does not define what constitutes a decision, a directive, or a regulation; it merely states the effect of each when an act has been classified, and classification is a question of substance. It would be anomalous if the Court allowed form to prevail over substance, thereby injuring a private enterprise, because of the addressee named in a decision, when it does not allow form to prevail over substance with regard to the purported form of the Community act.[50]

If Community institutions or officials, in the performance of their duties, injure a natural or legal person, compensation must be given in accordance with the "general principles common to the laws of member states."[51] This could give no right to damages if the act of the Community institution terminating the state aid was proper under the Treaty. If the act was improper, the natural remedy would be under Article 173. To try to decide whether, in the absence of a remedy under that Article, damages could be recovered under the general principles common to the laws of member states would involve a speculative discussion which would be out of place here.

International law

Contract Terms, Frustration, and Illegality

Under international law the existence of a contract is, in principle, of considerable importance, and it raises many difficult questions.[52] However, there can be no claim under international law if it is an express or implied term of the grant agreement that the agreement should be cancelled if this is required by the EEC Commission.[53]

If the grant was illegal or the grant agreement outside the powers of the Grants Board under Irish domestic law at the time when it was made, the question arises whether this could be pleaded in an international law claim. This situation could arise only if the grant agreement was made after the Treaty had been enacted into Irish law. Presumably a state can plead, as a defense to an international law claim for breach of a state contract, that the contract was illegal under its proper law. Probably this plea would be a good defense in international law only if the alien party to the grant agreement should have known that a

[49] Stein & Hay, "Legal Remedies of Enterprises in the European Economic Community," 9 Am. J. Comp. L. 375, 387 (1960).

[50] See Getreide-Import Gesellschaft v. EEC Commission, 11 Recueil 263, [1965] C.M.L.R. 276.

[51] Art. 215. Art. 176 provides that the obligation of an institution to comply with an order of the Community Court is not to prejudice any right to damages under art. 215.

[52] Jennings, "State Contracts in International Law," 37 Brit. Yb. Int'l L. 156 (1961).

[53] See International Fisheries Case, Mexico-U.S. Gen. Claims Comm'n, 4 U.N. Rep. Int'l Arb. Awards 691, 699 (1931).

grant agreement not expressed to be subject to the approval of the Commission was illegal or was outside the powers of the Grants Board.[54] If the international claim is based on the view that the breach of the agreement constitutes an international delict, the illegality of the agreement might be a defense, since it would help to show that non-performance was reasonable. It is possible, however, that the principle of estoppel, which is a rule of international law,[55] would apply.

The next question would be whether performance of the agreement had been rendered impossible by an act outside the control of the parties. The existence and content of a principle that international treaties and contracts having an international element may cease to bind the parties to them in changed circumstances is the subject of a large literature[56] which cannot be discussed here. If Britain joined the EEC, it might be possible for Ireland to plead that her situation had changed and that it had become an economic necessity for Ireland to join. The facts might not justify such a plea, and it is uncertain whether it would be valid in international law. If performance of a grant agreement became illegal through a change in Community law, probably no international law claim would lie, at least if Ireland had not voted for the change.

The Breach of a State Contract as a Violation of International Law

In spite of some controversy, it seems that a state's breach of contract with an alien is not in itself a violation of international law,[57] at least if the contract does not relate to government securities. If it were a violation, a contract with an alien would be equated with a treaty.[58] In certain circumstances a breach of such a contract may become a breach of international law. If Ireland broke a grant agreement in order to comply with Article 92, the breach would be an act done in the public interest and would not be discriminatory, so the principal question is whether it would be an "arbitrary" or tortious act under international law. The following discussion assumes that, under international law, a state is free to alter its national laws, although it may have to pay compensation in certain circumstances to an alien injured by an alteration. It also assumes that expropriation of property is legal under international law if adequate compensation is paid.

The Harvard Law School Draft Convention on the International Responsibility of States for Injuries to Aliens[59] pro-

[54] The Eastern Greenland Case, P.C.I.J., ser. A/B, No. 53, 3 Hudson World Court Reports 148 (1938); see the authorities cited at Bishop, International Law 106 n.35 (2d ed. 1962).

[55] The Chorzow Factory Case, P.C.I.J., ser. A, No. 17 (1928).

[56] See the authorities collected by Briggs, The Law of Nations 917–18 (2d ed. 1952); see Bishop, International Law 198–205 (2d ed. 1962).

[57] Reuter, Droit international public 179–81 (1958); Fatouros, Government Guarantees to Foreign Investors 244, 262–78 (1962); Freeman, The International Responsibility of States for Denial of Justice 111–13 (1938); García Amador, Fourth Report on International Responsibility, U.N. Doc. No. A/CN.4/119, at 37, 89–90 (1959), also in 1959(2) Yb. Int'l Law Comm'n 1; Restatement, Foreign Relation Law of the United States § 198 (Proposed Official Draft 1962); Amerasinghe, "State Breaches of Contracts with Aliens and International Law," 58 Am. J. Int'l L. 881 (1964). If this view is unsound, the investor has of course a remedy for breach of a grant agreement.

[58] Sohn & Baxter, "Responsibility of States for Injuries to the Economic Interests of Aliens," 55 Am. J. Int'l L. 545, 569–70 (1961).

[59] In id. at 545. The Harvard Draft is intended to be a codification which declares existing international law principles.

Hereinafter, citations to the Harvard Draft will be accompanied by parenthetical references to the pages of the Sohn and Baxter article on which the relevant sections of the Harvard Draft will be found.

vides that an arbitrary action of a state violating a contract or concession to which the central government of the state and an alien are parties is wrongful.[60] The action may be "arbitrary" if it is a clear departure from the proper law of the contract at the time of the action or a breach of the law of the state in question. This will not be the case if a grant agreement is cancelled after entry into the EEC, if the Irish grants legislation is amended to take account of Article 92. The writer has not been able to discover any Irish treaty which would be broken automatically by the breach of a state contract.[61]

SUBSEQUENT LEGISLATION AS A DEFENSE

On the basis of the provisions of the Harvard Draft analyzed so far, no action lies for non-performance of a grant agreement. Assuming that the only other relevant provision of the Harvard Draft is an accurate statement of customary international law, the existence of a contract is not relevant in the case of a breach of a grant agreement unless non-performance is "an unreasonable departure from the principles recognized by the principal legal systems of the world as applicable to governmental contracts or concessions of the same nature or category."[62] Such a breach of international standards is contrary to international law whether it is regarded as a breach of contract or as a tort.[63] The state contract is not necessary to the international claim; it only provides the occasion for the commission of the wrong.

Since a state is responsible in international law for the acts of all its organs, the acts of the Irish state in joining the EEC and enacting the Treaty could not be a defense to a claim for breach of a contract, even if these acts made performance of the contract illegal. This is the position if the international claim for breach of a grant agreement is a claim based on an international delict committed by the state.

One authority[64] holds that if the claim is for the breach of a state contract the proper law of which is the national law of the state in question, a change in that law can relieve the state of liability for breach of contract. The international wrong, on this view, is the change in the

[60] Art. 12 (at 566–67).

[61] U.S.-Irish Treaty of Friendship, Commerce and Navigation, Jan. 21, 1950, art. VIII(2), [1950] U.S.T. & O.I.A. 785, T.I.A.S. No. 2155, Ir. T.S. No. 7 of 1950, P. No. 9791, 206 U.N.T.S. 269 (1955), provides, in part: "Property of nationals and companies of either Party shall receive the most constant protection and security within the territories of the other Party, in no case less than that required by international law. Such property shall not be taken without the prompt payment of just and effective compensation." Neither the Protocol nor the Minutes of Interpretation give any indication whether the termination of contractual rights can be regarded as the taking of property. Art. IX deals with taxation but does not give any remedy in the case of termination of a tax concession. This chapter does not discuss whether the termination of a grant agreement or the revocation of a tax concession could constitute expropriation within the United States government's investment guarantee program, under the Economic Cooperation Act of 1948, 62 Stat. 137, 144–45. See Whitman, The United States Investment Guaranty Program and Private Foreign Investment (1959). Ireland entered this program in 1955; Exchange of Notes, Oct. 5, 1955, [1955] 3 U.S.T. & O.I.A. 3953, T.I.A.S. No. 3405, Ir. T.S. No. 15 of 1955, Pr. 3300 (1955).

[62] Harvard Draft, art. 12(1)(c) (at 567); cf. Stat. Int'l Ct. Just., art. 38(1)(c).

[63] Sohn & Baxter, "Responsibility of States for Injury to the Economic Interests of Aliens," 55 Am. J. Int'l L. 545, 569–70 (1961).

[64] Mann, "State Contracts and State Responsibility," 54 Am. J. Int'l L. 572, 580–82 passim (1960); cf. Jennings, "State Contracts in International Law," 37 Brit. Yb. Int'l L. 156, 161–63 (1961). See García Amador, Report on International Responsibility, U.N. Doc. No. A/CN.4/96, 1956(2) Yb. Int'l Law Comm'n 173, 190–92, 220.

national law, not the non-performance of the contract. It is probably correct to identify the provision of the Harvard Draft just quoted with the international rules on delicts, and they are now discussed together.

Non-Performance of a State Contract Upon Accession to the EEC Treaty

The rules of Irish domestic law discussed above may give a foreign investor no right to damages for non-performance of a grant agreement caused by a decision of the Commission under Article 92. The question arises whether there is an obligation to pay damages under international law in such circumstances.[65] The Irish courts would not have acted improperly, and the basis for the claim would be the failure of Irish substantive law to provide a remedy in damages.[66] This is in substance a claim in delict, based on a breach by the state of the international standards of treatment for aliens. The fact that the non-performance of the grant agreement was due to a change in Irish law therefore would not be a defense in international law.[67]

The Harvard Draft makes it clear that there is a breach of international law only if non-performance of a state contract is a departure from the generally recognized principles applicable to government contracts "of the same nature or category," i.e., in the case under discussion, contracts for state aid. Although these contracts may be one-sided, it seems clear that owing to their formal nature they bind the state even if substantially no consideration is given by the enterprise aided.

There are no precedents on the question whether entry into an economic community is a valid reason under national or international law for cancelling contracts for state aid. The element of public purpose, which justifies expropriation,[68] is present. Entry into an economic community is an act of great importance for any country, and it is done only if it is in the interest of the state as a whole. Non-performance of state contracts which results incidentally from entry into the EEC can hardly be regarded as an "unreasonable departure from generally recognized principles." All states joining such a community must alter their laws to comply with community rules. Although Article 92 cannot be directly pleaded against non-member states, it can be pleaded to show that the state concerned had acted reasonably. It is submitted that failure to pay the full amount of state aid is not a breach of international law, especially if compensation was given for expenditure actually

[65] Sohn & Baxter, "Responsibility of States for Injuries to the Economic Interests of Aliens," 55 Am. J. Int'l L. 545, 572 (1961), say that art. 12(1)(c) prohibits a state from falling below the international minimum standard of treatment for aliens "for example, by . . . providing only an inadequate substantive remedy to an alien in the event of a breach of the contract or concession by the State which is a party to it."

[66] Freeman, The International Responsibility of States for Denial of Justice 151–60, 552–24 (1938).

[67] Jennings, "State Contracts in International Law," 37 Brit. Yb. Int'l L. 156, 176 (1961).

[68] See Sohn & Baxter, "Responsibility of States for Injuries to the Economic Interests of Aliens," 55 Am. J. Int'l L. 545 (1961). Harvard Draft, art. 10(1)(a) (at 553), on expropriation, reads: "The taking, under the authority of the State, of any property of an alien, or of the use thereof, is wrongful if it is not for a public purpose clearly recognized as such by a law of general application in effect at the time of the taking. . . ." Art. 10(4) (at 553–54) makes special provision for delayed compensation "if property is taken by a State in furtherance of a general program of economic and social reform. . . ." Art. 12(1) prohibits the violation of a state contract or concession only through an "arbitrary" action. See also Domke, "Foreign Nationalizations," 55 Am. J. Int'l L. 585, 590–91 (1961).

incurred by the foreign investor while he expected to receive the state aid.

Is a Breach of a Grant Agreement the Taking of Property?

"It is not easy to find actual instances where the element of breach of an undertaking can be clearly distinguished from a taking of, or damage to, property, or even from an element of delict, with which the contractual element tends in actual cases frequently to be blended."[69] A contract or concession is often regarded as an acquired property right which can be taken by the state.[70] If this is so and if it is agreed that a state may expropriate property, even in violation of a contract,[71] as long as it pays compensation, the only practical difference between taking property and breaking a contract seems to be the extent of the compensation payable. Subject to the question under the EEC Treaty as to payment of state aid in the guise of compensation, the question of the measure of damages is unlikely to arise. However, if no claim in international law lies for breach of a grant agreement in itself, the question whether cancellation of a grant agreement constitutes the taking of property becomes important, since if it does there is an obligation under international law to pay compensation.

Not all breaches of contract constitute expropriation of property in international law, and it is submitted that the failure to pay a grant under a grant agreement cannot be so regarded. In return for the grant, the investors give certain promises as to the nature and extent of the operation to be established, its duration, and the amount of capital to be invested. It could be argued that these are, in substance, conditions on which the grant is given rather than the consideration for the grant. The promises do not bind the investors until the grant is given. Where the grant is, in substance, a gratuitous payment made on certain conditions, it is impossible to argue that the cancellation of it constitutes the taking of property.[72]

It could be argued that the consideration for the promise to pay the grant is the establishment of the Irish operation. This seems the proper way of viewing the normal transaction, and if this is accepted, the position is not quite so clear. Since the Irish operation remains the investors' property, the breach of contract has not amounted to the taking of goods without payment by the government.[73] Only if the enterprise is forced to salvage an unsalable investment by investing

[69] Jennings, "State Contracts in International Law," 37 Brit. Yb. Int'l L. 156, 159 (1961).

[70] Id. at 169, citing U.N. Secretariat, The Status of Permanent Sovereignty over Natural Wealth and Resources, U.N. Doc. No. A/AC.97/5, Rev. 1, at 280 (1960); The Chorzow Factory Case, P.C.I.J., ser. A, No. 17 (1928). See, however, García Amador, Fourth Report on International Responsibility, U.N. Doc. No. A/CN.4/119, at 37, 89–90 (1959), also in 1959(2) Yb. Int'l Law Comm'n 1; Foighel, Nationalization 71, 75 (1957).

[71] The Harvard Draft provides that the taking of property is unlawful if it is done in breach of a treaty, but it does not provide that this is wrongful if done in breach of a contract. See the arguments of the British government in Anglo-Iranian Oil Co. Case—Pleadings, Oral Arguments, and Documents 64, 86–93 (I.C.J. 1952), with regard to promises not to expropriate; Fatouros, Government Guarantees to Foreign Investors 340–41 (1962).

[72] This is another reason why the aggrieved enterprise should be regarded as having a claim only for compensation for expenses actually incurred in the expectation of the grant, and this only if it is clear that the interest of the enterprise in establishing itself was conditional on obtaining the promised grant. In view of the other incentives to investment in Ireland (assuming they continue after Ireland joins the EEC), this is not very likely to be the case.

[73] It could be argued that when the investors have performed their side of the grant agreement, non-performance by the state is equivalent to expropriation of the sum due to them

funds which it would not have invested otherwise can the transaction be regarded as involving the taking of property.

Tax concessions at Shannon Airport

A Contractual Relationship?

The question arises whether the tax concession given at Shannon Airport is the subject of contracts. The procedure is that the Minister for Finance issues to an enterprise a certificate certifying that specified trading operations carried on by the enterprise at Shannon are exempt from tax.[74] This certificate may be part of a contract between the enterprise and the authorities. If it is, the statutory provision that "any certificate so given shall, unless it is revoked under [a provision specifying certain grounds of revocation] . . ., remain in force until the expiration of the period of twenty-five years" from 1958[75] may constitute an agreement not to revoke the tax concession for the period mentioned. There is some authority for the proposition that breach of an express promise not to expropriate is a violation of international law,[76] and it seems reasonable to extend the principle to an express contract not to revoke a tax concession. Admittedly, in the latter case there is no question of expropriation of property. Apart from the contractual right, an enterprise has no property in that portion of its prospective profits which, but for the tax concession, would have been payable to the revenue authorities. However, if an express promise not to expropriate property is binding in international law, it is difficult to see why this rule should be confined to promises not to take property, since the rule must be based on contract rather than on the international law rules against expropriation, because the latter are not absolute.

Whether the tax exemption certificate and the statutory provision quoted above are part of a contract depends on the facts of each case. If an enterprise at Shannon leases a factory from the Shannon Free Airport Development Company and makes a separate agreement for a grant towards the company's capital or for the training of workers, neither the lease nor the agreement need normally refer to the Finance (Miscellaneous Provisions) Act of 1958, though either may do so.[77] However, the tax concession is an important part of the basis of the transaction. The Shannon Free Airport Development Company is legally independent of the Minister for Finance. It is regulated by legislation[78] and has no connection with tax collection. In a formal written agreement, no guarantee that the tax exemption will continue can be implied; the Company cannot be regarded as having contracted as agent for the Minister for Finance.

It would be difficult to regard the exemption certificate as a contract in itself.

---

under the agreement. The main objection to this argument is that it could be used to show that a breach of any state contract constituted expropriation, and this is not the position under international law.

If the contention made in Chapter Two is correct and art. 29 of the Irish Constitution has embodied the principles of customary international law into Irish law, and if an alien injured by the Irish government's breach of a state contract had a remedy under international law, it would follow that the alien would have a constitutional remedy other than that discussed in this chapter.

[74] Finance (Miscellaneous Provisions) Act, 1958 Acts 791, § 3.

[75] Finance (Miscellaneous Provisions) Act, 1958 Acts 791, § 3(2).

[76] Assuming that the contract is made with an alien. See pp. 371–72.

[77] For example, the lease may be terminable at the option of the lessor if the enterprise breaks a term of the certificate and the certificate is revoked.

[78] Shannon Free Airport Development Company Limited Act, 1959 Acts 999.

If the conditions in it are not kept by the enterprise, the tax privileges are lost, but the enterprise does not promise to keep these conditions. The certificate is merely a formal and probably unnecessary assurance of the exemption from tax. In practice, the terms of the certificate are agreed to by the enterprise, and this agreement would usually constitute a contract, the consideration being the establishment of the operations. It is in the interests of the investor to insure that this agreement constitutes a contract, although this may not guarantee him a remedy in the circumstances being discussed. If the statutory provision quoted above is part of an agreement, it is uncertain if consideration is necessary to allow the investor to sue in international law. Consideration is essential under Irish law, but it is not required by international law for agreements between states. In the present state of the law, it is not possible to say whether a contract between a state and an alien requires consideration in international law or whether a contract could exist in international law even if it did not exist in domestic law.

The Effect of an Express Clause Against Expropriation

Assuming that a contract exists containing the statutory guarantee against revocation quoted, the question arises whether breach by a state of an express contract not to expropriate or to withdraw a tax concession is in itself a breach of international law. If it is accepted that a breach of a contract which does not contain such a clause is not in itself a breach of international law, it is not clear why an express clause should alter the position. The rule that a breach of a contract with no express clause is not an international wrong is not based on a theory of an implied term to that effect. If the obligation to pay damages for a breach of contract is not an obligation under international law in the case of a contract with no express clause against expropriation or revocation, adding that clause could not convert it into an international obligation. The question arises as to the effect of a clause (in addition to that against revocation) providing that the contract is to be governed by public international law. A breach of a treaty is, of course, in itself a violation of international law. But an "internationalizing" choice-of-law clause cannot bring a state contract under the strict international law rule relating to treaties unless international law contains a rule allowing it to do so. At present, no such rule exists.[79] The problem is related to that of the Calvo clause, which purports to have the effect opposite to that of the "internationalizing" clause, i.e., to make the contract subject only to municipal law.[80]

The view that a breach of a contract containing a clause against revocation or expropriation is in itself a breach of international law was argued by the United Kingdom in the *Anglo-Iranian Oil Company* case,[81] but the World Court did not have to decide the question. This view has the support of vari-

[79] See Delson, "Is a Taking of an Alien's Property Without Compensation or in Derogation of the Terms of a Contract in Violation of Public International Law?" in Proceedings and Committee Reports of the American Branch of the International Law Association 33, 49 (1959–60).

[80] See Lipstein, "The Place of the Calvo Clause in International Law," 22 Brit. Yb. Int'l L. 130, 145 (1945).

[81] Anglo-Iranian Oil Co. Case—Pleadings, Oral Arguments, and Documents 87–93 (I.C.J. 1952). The pleadings mention that the express stipulation against expropriation might be "formally accepted by the other contracting party." Id. at 87. This might not be the case in relation to the Irish certificate of exemption at Shannon. The pleading claims that the Iranian government was estopped from denying the effectiveness of the stipulation; id. at 89.

ous authors.[82] However, it has been said that "no evidence in support of this proposition . . . can be found anywhere."[83] The United Kingdom cited no authority and based its argument only on the intention of the parties and the fact that the contrary view would make a clause against expropriation totally ineffective. However, such a clause might be a factor to be taken into account in deciding whether the state's action constituted a denial of justice or was otherwise an international delict. Insofar as a clause forbidding expropriation purports to restrict the state's powers, it is clearly invalid; insofar as it confers a right to damages, it is difficult to see why it should alter the normal rule that breach of a state contract in itself does not give rise to international liability. The normal rule may be unfortunate, but it seems established.[84] The United Kingdom could have argued that the normal rule should be strictly confined, but in view of the remedies in international law which are independent of contract, this argument is hardly sufficient. In principle it is difficult to see why contractual rights, which are merely a form of property rights,[85] should be given greater protection from expropriation than other property rights. If expropriation in international law involves an obligation to pay compensation, as appears to be the case,[86] what is in question is merely the narrow range of cases where a contract is broken by the state but where there is no taking of property and no denial of justice or other international delict.

WHERE NO CONTRACT EXISTS—INTERNATIONAL LAW

Changes in tax laws

The second type of case considered in this chapter is the case of continuing state aid not based on a contract. The principal example of this in Ireland is the tax exemption for exports.[87] In this second type of case there seem to be no grounds for a remedy under national law or Community law other than those already discussed.

In general, a foreign investor accepts the tax law of the host state as it may be from time to time. Any other rule would require a tax law to be "frozen" in favor of the alien, and this has never been contended.[88] States are free to alter their

[82] Friedman, Law in a Changing Society 455, 456 (1959), states the rule but cites no authority. Schwebel, "International Protection of Contractual Arrangements," Proceedings Am. Soc'y Int'l L. 266, 268 (1959), admits that the four reasons which he gives are "more in terms of preference than precedent."

[83] Mann, "State Contracts and State Responsibility," 54 Am. J. Int'l L. 572, 587–88 (1960); see also Delson, "Is a Taking of an Alien's Property Without Compensation or in Derogation of the Terms of a Contract in Violation of Public International Law?" in Proceedings and Committee Reports of the American Branch of the International Law Association 33, 39–50 (1959–60).

[84] Moore, A Digest of International Law 287–89, 295–96, 705–20, 723–38 (1906); Restatement, Foreign Relations Law of the United States § 198 (Proposed Official Draft 1962).

[85] Rheinstein, "Observations on Expropriation," 7 Am. J. Comp. L. 86, 87 (1958).

[86] Most controversies in recent years have concerned the question of the validity of expropriation where compensation is inadequate.

[87] In some other countries, tax exemptions are given by agreement with the enterprise concerned; in such a case the rules already discussed in relation to contracts apply.

[88] In the *George W. Cook* case, the Claims Commissioners said:

> In all cases relative to tax exemption it is necessary to bear in mind the generally accepted standards of construction. The right of the State to levy taxes constitutes an inherent part of its sovereignty; it is a function necessary to its very existence and it has often been alleged, not only in Mexico but in the United States and other countries, that

tax laws for revenue and economic purposes.[89] If a treaty provided for the continuance of particular tax concessions, the situation would be entirely different, and the treaty would be binding. However, even treaties of friendship, commerce, and navigation and treaties of establishment do not protect foreign investors from future changes in the host state's tax laws,[90] though they often prohibit discrimination against aliens.

The general rule that, in the absence of a contract, an enterprise has no legal ground for complaint if tax laws are altered to its prejudice is subject to two limitations under customary international law. Unreasonable discrimination against aliens is not permitted,[91] and taxation may not amount to confiscation.[92] Neither of these limitations is relevant to the Irish problem considered here. Measures carried out to comply with Article 92 of the EEC Treaty would not contravene most-favored-nation or national treatment clauses.

In view of this clear general rule it is difficult to argue that revocation of a tax concession constitutes a breach of the standards of treatment of aliens in international law, even if the tax concession is very specific and detailed. However, the standards of treatment for aliens (which do not, of course, depend on the existence of a contract) must be mentioned.

International delicts

The phrase "denial of justice" is used in international law in several senses. It may mean denial of access to the national courts or their unreasonable failure to provide a remedy; in such a case there may be a violation of international standards of treatment for aliens. The phrase also may refer to the rule that

---

> legislatures, whether of states or of the Federation, cannot legally create exceptions which restrict the free exercise of the sovereign power of the State in this regard. . . . [E]ven in those cases in which the . . . majority of the Supreme Court of the United States has held that that right inherent in the sovereignty of a State might be the subject of a contract, it has also ruled that the exemptions should be strictly construed in favor of the State. . . . [T]he liberality of a State in granting an exemption is essentially revocable for the reason that it creates no vested rights in him who enjoys it. It is well established that an exemption granted merely for reasons of policy, where the state and the citizen have no agreement to their mutual advantage, must be regarded only as an expression of the pleasure of the said state and of the citizen; and the law which grants it, as all general laws, is subject to amendment or repeal at the option of the legislature, and it is immaterial whether during the time it has been in force the parties in interest have acted in reliance thereon. (Cooley, Taxation [1924], p. 69). "An exemption from taxation does not confer a vested right, and it may therefore be modified or repealed by the legislature unless it has been granted under such circumstances that its repeal would impair the obligation of a contract." (Corpus Juris, Vol. 12, para. 536).

Opinions of Commissioners, United States-Mexican Claims Commission, Oct.–Nov. 1930, at 61, 64–65, abstracted in 5 Annual Digest of Public International Law Cases 255 (1935).

[89] When states do so for economic purposes, they may create conditions of which investors are intended to take advantage. But it could not be contended that an alien investor in, e.g., the United Kingdom, could require specially favorable depreciation allowances given at the time of establishment to be continued for his benefit after their revocation or that he was entitled to compensation if they were not.

[90] Fatouros, Government Guarantees to Foreign Investors 222 (1962); see U.S.-Irish Treaty of Friendship, Commerce and Navigation, art. IX.

[91] Albrecht, "The Taxation of Aliens Under International Law," 29 Brit. Yb. Int'l L. 145, 170–71 (1952); 3 Hackworth, Digest of International Law 576 (1942); García Amador, Report on International Responsibility, U.N. Doc. No. A/CN.4/96, 1956(2) Yb. Int'l Law Comm'n 173, 201.

[92] Albrecht, "The Taxation of Aliens Under International Law," 29 Brit. Yb. Int'l L. 145, 170–75 (1952).

national remedies must be exhausted before an international claim can be brought.[93] The phrase is also somewhat misleadingly used to describe all situations where the treatment of an alien gives rise to an international obligation to make reparation.[94] Revocation of a tax concession could involve "denial of justice" only in the last, loose sense. If the tax concession were revoked by legislation, there would be no question of improper action by the courts. The substance of the complaint would be that Irish law was defective in not giving a right to compensation. Since in the absence of a contract the investor clearly has no right under international law which would prevent his tax reliefs from being revoked, the failure of Irish law to give compensation in such a case cannot give rise to an international claim in delict.

[93] See García Amador, Report on International Responsibility, U.N. Doc. No. A/CN.4/96, 1956(2) Yb. Int'l Law Comm'n 173, 204.

[94] Freeman, The International Responsibility of States for Denial of Justice 97–115 (1938).

Apart from claims for non-performance of state contracts and for expropriation of property,[95] most of the generally recognized standards of treatment for aliens fall into two categories.[96] These are denial of justice, in the sense of gross inadequacy of the courts or denial of access to them, and physical damage to aliens' persons or property arising out of serious failure to maintain public order or arising out of misuse of or failure to exercise executive powers. There is no principle that financial loss to an alien resulting from legislative or executive action gives rise to an international obligation to pay compensation, nor would this principle be possible. In the problems under discussion, there is no question of abuse or misuse of executive powers, or of failure to protect aliens against violence, or of physical damage.

[95] And for deprivation of the means of livelihood.

[96] Briggs, The Law of Nations, ch. IX (2d ed. 1952). See also Accioly, "Principes Généraux de la Responsabilité Internationale d'après la Doctrine et la Jurisprudence," 96(1) Recueil Académie D. Int. 353 (1959).

Part VI

ANTITRUST LAW

Chapter 15

Antitrust Provisions of the EEC: Substantive Law

POLICY CONSIDERATIONS: THE NEED FOR AN ANTITRUST POLICY IN THE EEC

The last major topic dealt with in this book is antitrust law.[1] The EEC is based on fair competition and on the removal of barriers to economic activity between member states.[2] The advantage of the enlarged European market is the scope for large-scale production and for competition freed from protectionist policies previously used by member states. Restrictive agreements between firms can limit interstate trade and investment and prevent realization of the benefits of

[1] The substantive antitrust provisions of the EEC Treaty are arts. 85 and 86. Arts. 87–89 deal with implementation and enforcement. Arts. 85–90 and the regulations made pursuant to them apply to trade in agricultural products but do not affect agreements which are an integral part of a domestic organization of the market or which are necessary under art. 39; Reg. 26, 1962 Journal Officiel 993/62; see also Reg. 49, id. at 1571/62. In particular they do not affect intrastate decisions of farmers' associations which do not fix prices; Reg. 26, art. 2; see also Reg. 49. Arts. 85–90 do not apply to trade in arms and munitions; art. 223. They will probably be applied to transport with modifications. On this question, there are or have been serious differences of opinions between the Council and the Commission. Regulation 141, 1962 Journal Officiel 2751/62, suspended the application of Regulation 17, id. at 204/62, 1962 EEC Bull. No. 2, Supp., to road, rail, and inland waterway transport until December 1965, and to sea and air transport indefinitely. It is not clear if arts. 85 and 86 should apply to banking, because banking is partly state-controlled, because competition in giving credit has an inflationary effect, and because banking is governed by monetary considerations.

The provisions of the EFTA Convention, Jan. 4, 1960, 370 U.N.T.S. 3 (1960), are in many respects copied from those of the EEC Treaty; Negotiations for a Free Trade Area . . . up to Dec., 1958, Cmd. No. 648, para. 36 (1959). Art. 15 on restrictive business practices is the only antitrust provision in the EFTA Convention.

On the antitrust law and procedure of the EEC, see generally Buxbaum, "Antitrust Regulation Within the European Economic Community," 61 Colum. L. Rev. 402 (1961); Oberdorfer, Gleiss & Hirsch, Common Market Cartel Law (1963); Political and Economic Planning, Cartel Policy in the Common Market (1962); Federation of British Industries, European Economic Community—Restrictive Trade Practices (1962); OEEC Special Working Party, Report on the Possibility of Creating a Free Trade Area in Europe, paras. 35–39 and Annex III (which deals primarily with dumping and discrimination) (1957); Spaak Report 53–57; Riesenfeld, "The Protection of Competition," in 2 American Enterprise in the European Common Market: A Legal Profile 197 (Stein & Nicholson ed. 1960). There are, of course, many studies in French, German, Italian, and Dutch. See also Vasseur, Le droit de la réforme des structures industrielles et des économies régionales 154–65 (1959); First General Report, paras. 78–84 (1958); Carabiber, Trusts, Cartels et Ententes, chs. 11, 12 (1964). A short selected bibliography is given in Stein & Hay, Cases on the Law and Institutions of the Atlantic Area 208–209 (prelim. ed. 1963).

For a critical appraisal of Community antitrust law, see Gil Baer, "Les Articles 85 et 86 du Traité de Rome," 6 Revue du Marché Commun 212 (1963). For a general discussion of restrictive practices in international trade, see GATT, Restrictive Business Practices, pts. I, II (1959).

[2] EEC Treaty, Preamble and art. 3(c), 3 (f).

competition.[3] "The elaboration of the common policy towards restrictive practices . . . was not only a question of the best policy towards business agreements and monopolies but of the best way of uniting Europe."[4] The Treaty provisions on restrictive practices, therefore, are not the result of strong views on free competition[5] or a political objection to monopoly power such as caused the enactment of some of the United States antitrust legislation.[6] Competition alone, rather than planning, could bring about economic integration[7] and the optimum use of resources.[8] The policy of the Community on private restrictions on competition is only a part of its policy on competition generally,[9] including its policy on discrimination,[10] dumping,[11] state aids, and regional economic policy.[12] The Commission is not likely to be as strict in enforcing the Community antitrust laws as, for example, the United States courts are in applying the United States antitrust laws. Article 85(3) specifically allows cartels with beneficial effects,[13] and the competition policy of European countries has traditionally been "cartel control" rather than the United States ideal of free competition.[14] To see how the general terms of the

[3] Art. 3(f) says that "the establishment of a system ensuring that competition in the Common Market is not distorted" is one of the objects of the EEC.

[4] Political and Economic Planning, Cartel Policy in the Common Market 202 (1962).

[5] Timberg, "Antitrust and Patent Provisions of the European Common Market Treaty," in 3 Institute on Private Investments Abroad 173 passim (Southwestern Legal Foundation, 1961).

[6] For alternative views of the EEC's cartel policy, see Political and Economic Planning, Cartel Policy in the Common Market 206–209 (1962).

[7] See Riesenfeld, "The Protection of Competition," in 2 American Enterprise in the European Common Market: A Legal Profile 197, 323–24 (Stein & Nicholson ed. 1960). There may be a considerable degree of economic planning in the EEC; see generally Action Programme for the Second Stage (1962).

[8] Von der Groeben, A.P.E. Débats, Séances du 16 au 20 Octobre, 1961, at 170; von der Groeben, "The Cartel Legislation of the European Economic Community in the Light of Two [and a Half] Years' Experience," in 1 Cartel and Monopoly in Modern Law 63, 66 (1961); Hallstein, "Final Report," in 2 Cartel and Monopoly in Modern Law 1009, 1010 (1961); Verloren van Themaat, "Current Antitrust Developments in the European Common Market," 6 Pat., T.M. & Copyright J. Research & Educ. 432, 435 (1962); von der Groeben, "Policy on Competition in the European Economic Community," 1961 EEC Bull. No. 7/8, Supp.; von der Groeben, Competition Policy as a Part of Economic Policy in the Common Market (1965).

[9] Id., especially at 12–14; Second General Report, paras, 107, 110 (1959); Third General Report, paras. 134, 137 (1960); Opinion dated March, 1961, of the Economic and Social Committee on the draft regulation implementing arts. 85 and 86; von der Groeben, "The Cartel Legislation of the European Economic Community in the Light of Two [and a Half] Years' Experience," in 1 Cartel and Monopoly in Modern Law 63 (1961); Schumacher, "La Politique de la C.E.E. en matière d'ententes," 2 Revue du Marché Commun 207 (1959); Rapport sur la Consultation demandée à l'Assemblée parlementaire éuropéenne sur un premier règlement d'application des articles 85 et 86 [hereinafter cited as Deringer Report], A.P.E. Doc. No. 57, para. 7 (1961–62).

[10] Arts. 7, 76, 79.

[11] At least during the transitional period.

[12] Arts. 92–94.

[13] Art. 85(3) has been described as a "statutory rule of reason." On the "rule of reason" in the United States, see Standard Oil Co. v. United States, 221 U.S. 1 (1910).

[14] There is a danger in discussing the EEC provisions in the light of American law since it may give the impression that American decisions will normally be followed. This is not necessarily the case. United States antitrust law will be much used initially and in cases of first impression, but primarily by way of analysis and comparison. The Commission has begun to publish decisions, and these will be of much greater importance than United States law.

See Wolf, "La Législation contre les Cartels et les Monopoles: son application dans la Com-

Treaty provisions are likely to be interpreted in practice, it is necessary to look to the antitrust laws of the Six, to the antitrust provisions of the ECSC Treaty,[15] and to American and British law.[16]

The principles of the EEC relating to competition were first set out in the Spaak Report.[17] Increased competition in the enlarged market is not in itself enough to insure the highest rate of economic expansion and the most efficient use of resources. Treaty provisions were required to prevent dumping,[18] division of markets, and price-fixing, which would have had effects similar to those of the economic frontiers which the EEC was designed to remove. It was recognized that mergers and concentration of industry to achieve the economies of scale possible in an enlarged market would reduce competition and might result in monopolies or oligopolies. Therefore, only abuse of monopoly power due to size or specialization was declared contrary to the objectives of the EEC. The antitrust provisions of the EEC are important in the context of the Community policy on competition both in markets such as Ireland, where protectionist policies encouraged private restrictive practices, and in fairly open economies such as the Netherlands, where cartels were regarded as necessary protection against foreign competition.

THE COMMISSION: ADMINISTRATION AND POLICY

Since the Commission is an administrative and a civil law body, it is not absolutely bound by its own decisions. It can therefore apply considerations of economic policy in distinguishing between new enterprises in a sector and well-established enterprises. It can deal specially with small enterprises which enter into agreements in response to the threat of competition from large and vertically integrated enterprises, and it can decide whether inter-brand or intra-brand competition ought to be preferred. The Commission will probably treat agreements which are due to expire shortly more favorably than new long-term agreements. This is not to suggest that the Commission will not regard itself as applying legal rules. But in contrast with a judicial and common law system of antitrust laws, the civil law approach of the Commission will allow it to exercise considerable discretion and to draw distinctions based on considerations of policy which have no direct support from the legislative text of Articles 85 and 86 because its antitrust measures are only a part of its whole policy on competition. The Commission must apply its antitrust policy uniformly throughout the EEC, but its policy cannot remain static as the Common Market pro-

---

munauté Economique Européenne," 1962 Journal des Tribunaux 541, 542.

For an English translation of the texts of the national antitrust laws of the Six and for the antitrust laws of Ireland and Britain, see OECD Guide to Legislation on Restrictive Business Practices (1962).

For a general study of the EEC antitrust laws from the United States point of view, see U.S. Senate, Antitrust Developments in the European Common Market, Hearings Before the Subcommittee on Antitrust and Monopoly of the Senate Committee on the Judiciary, 88th Cong., 1st Sess. (1963).

[15] ECSC Treaty, arts. 65–66. Where ECSC precedents are relevant, they should be consulted, bearing in mind the great differences in market structure and the greater possibility of achieving free competition in the EEC.

[16] For some comparisons between the British and the EEC law, see Walker-Smith & Gombos, "Restrictive Practices and Monopolies, a Comparison of British and Common Market Law," 3 Va. J. Int'l L. 1 (1963); Pennington, "Restrictive Trade Practices in the Common Market" (pts. 1–2), 106 Sol. J. 458, 480 (1962).

[17] At 15–16, quoted in Deringer Report, A.P.E. Doc. No. 57, at 2 (1961–62). See also Deringer Report at 55, on monopolies.

[18] See GATT, Anti-Dumping and Countervailing Duties (1961).

gresses.[19] It cannot disregard the fact that a strict application of its policies on cartels may encourage concentration of industry or accentuate difficulties where "crisis cartels"[20] would have ameliorated them. The Commission has centralized in its own hands the power to exempt cartels pursuant to Article 85(3),[21] and it must be consulted by national authorities, so it is in a position of great power.

The Commission can maintain a fairly high degree of supervision over restrictive practices of which it is aware. Instead of condemning a practice immediately, the Commission can make a non-binding recommendation[22] to end the infringement;[23] it can approve practices which have been altered to comply with the Treaty;[24] and it can reconsider any practice when approval for it comes up for renewal and can revoke the approval if the circumstances change.[25] The function of the Commission is to insure that competition is not distorted or economic integration impeded, not to impose a Draconian quasi-criminal code on business. Therefore, the Commission will be reasonably willing to discuss changes in business practices which would make them acceptable.

TRADE BETWEEN MEMBER STATES AND THE EXTRATERRITORIAL EFFECT OF ARTICLES 85 AND 86

Article 85 applies only to agreements, decisions, and practices "which are liable to [harmfully] affect trade between Member States. . . ."[26] Article 86 prohibits abuse or improper exploitation of a monopoly or oligopoly position "in so far as trade between Member States could be affected by it." The concept of interstate trade[27] was clarified slightly by the exemption, for the time being, from compulsory notification of agreements, decisions, and concerted practices where any number of "enterprises of only one Member State take part and where such agreements, decisions and practices involve neither imports nor exports between Member States."[28] Agreements between enterprises in different member states normally affect interstate trade.[29] The dividing lines between inter-

[19] Houssiaux, Concurrence et Marché Commun 103–104 (1960).

[20] Full-blooded competition can be undesirable in periods of depression, and crisis cartels are recognized under the laws of several of the Six. In the Netherlands, non-participants can be compelled by law to join a cartel if it is regarded as being in the general interest that they should do so.

[21] Reg. 17, art. 9(1).

[22] Art. 189.

[23] Reg. 17, art. 3(3).

[24] Reg. 17, art. 7.

[25] Reg. 17, art. 8.

[26] The antitrust provisions of the ECSC Treaty (arts. 65–67) are not so limited. An agreement must "affect interstate trade" and do so "adversely" or "harmfully." The effect of the adverb is discussed on pp. 391–92. See Deringer et al., "Les Règles de Concurrence au sein de la C.E.E.," 6 Revue du Marché Commun 126 (1963). Dr. Deringer and his co-authors have written several articles with this same title; hereinafter these articles are cited, e.g., Deringer et al., 6 Revue du Marché Commun 126 (1963).

[27] See Schapiro, "The German Law Against Restraints of Competition—Comparative and International Aspects," 62 Colum. L. Rev. 201, 248–51 (1962). On the background of this German law, see generally Schwartz, "Antitrust Legislation and Policy in Germany—A Comparative Study," 105 U. Pa. L. Rev. 617 (1957).

[28] Reg. 17, art. 4(2)(i). See EEC Commission, Guide Pratique Concernant les Articles 85 et 86 de Traité Instituant la C.E.E., Doc. No. 2383-2/IV/62-F [hereinafter cited as Guide Pratique] at 11 (1962); Vereniging van Fabrikanten v. Mertens, Amsterdam Kantongerecht (District Court), May 9, 1963, [1963] C.M.L.R. 329.

[29] Mueller, "Antitrust Problems in Connection with Dealings in Common Market Countries," in 1962 International Bar Association Conference 175, 179, holds that an agreement "effective within only one member state" but made in another will not affect trade between member states.

state trade, which alone is within Articles 85 and 86, and intrastate trade[30] as well as trade directly[31] with a nonmember country may not be easy for the Commission to draw in dealing with particular agreements.[32] Trade between a member state and an associated country is governed by the Articles[33] only to the extent that the association treaty so provides.

The phrase translated as "liable to" affect trade may mean either "likely to" affect or "could" affect.[34] In practice, the effect must be in existence or be reasonably foreseeable when the decision as to the application of the Treaty provisions is made;[35] that is, the narrower interpretation will be applied. The Commission may review the position if circumstances change. The effect of the practice on the extent, nature, or flow of interstate trade[36] may be either direct or indirect but nevertheless must be substantial. All practices which "divert the movement of goods or the factors of production within the flow of trade between member states from a course it would take without the 'artificial' influence" are within the provisions of the Treaty.[37] All agreements dividing a market which includes parts of more than one member state necessarily affect interstate trade. Agreements dividing a purely domestic market and agreements on discounts and other trading conditions may influence imports or exports of the same or competitive commodities or of raw materials or components. It is unlikely, however, at least for some time, that an interpretation will be given to Articles 85 and 86 that is as wide as that given to the concept of "interstate commerce" in the United States.

To decide how far agreements are prohibited if they affect interstate trade indirectly, that is, without dealing expressly with imports or exports,[38] a distinction between vertical and horizontal agreements must be made.[39] Ver-

[30] Cf. art. 3(a). National laws often expressly permit export cartels.

[31] Mueller, "Antitrust Problems in Connection with Dealings in Common Market Countries," in 1962 International Bar Association Conference 175, 179; see German Law Against Restraints of Competition, July 27, 1957, § 6, [1957] 1 BGBl. 1081 [hereinafter cited as German Competition Law], translated in 1 OECD Guide to Legislation on Restrictive Business Practices, Germany § 1.0 (1962).

[32] See 4 OECD Guide to Legislation on Restrictive Business Practices, EEC § 1.0, at 4 (1962). Cf. ECSC Treaty, arts. 65–67.

[33] See art. 227.

[34] Nebolsine, "The Criteria of 'Likely to Harmfully Affect Trade Between Member States' in Article 85(1) of the Rome Treaty," in 1962 International Bar Association Conference 243.

[35] Third General Report, para. 140 (1960); see In re "Agfa-Optima," Munich Landgericht (Commercial Chamber), Jan. 14, 1963, [1963] C.M.L.R. 268.

[36] Letter from the Commission to the President of the European Parliamentary Assembly, cited by Nebolsine, "The Criteria of 'Likely to Harmfully Affect Trade Between Member States' in Article 85(1) of the Rome Treaty," in 1962 International Bar Association Conference 243, 244.

[37] Steindorff, "The Provisions Against Restraints of Competition in the European Community Treaties and the National Law," in 1 Cartel and Monopoly in Modern Law 194, 197 (1961). See Bosch v. de Geus, 8 Recueil 89, 138–39, [1962] C.M.L.R. 1, 22–23 (conclusions of Advocate-General Lagrange). Dr. Schumacher has proposed that a concept of causality be worked out; "Reflexions sur l'interdiction des ententes visées par l'article 85 du Traité instituant la C.E.E.," 24 Droit Social 65, 69 (1961); see Wolf, "La Législation contre les Cartels et les Monopoles: son application dans la Communauté Économique Européenne," 1962 Journal des Tribunaux 541. The effect on competition must be "foreseeable." 4 OECD Guide to Legislation on Restrictive Business Practices, EEC § 2.0, at 2 (1962).

[38] Deringer et al., 6 Revue du Marché Commun 126, 129 (1963).

[39] They are dealt with separately by the German Competition Law, which is important in interpreting the Treaty because it is by far the most elaborate antitrust statute in the Six.

tical agreements between enterprises in the same member state may restrain competition by reducing the demand of the wholesaler or retailer for imported products,[40] if the wholesaler or retailer sells exclusively the goods of the other party. If retail prices are fixed, this prevents the retailer from competing in price with imported goods, and "tying-in" clauses[41] may force a retailer to buy local goods instead of imported goods. The extent to which competition with imported goods is likely to exist, and therefore the extent to which competition is distorted or restrained, must be looked at in each case.

Horizontal agreements between enterprises in a single member state can affect interstate trade in a much wider variety of ways. Economic integration will cause the number of agreements which affect interstate trade to increase progressively. The importance of national laws on restrictive practices will therefore be reduced.[42]

There is no presumption that the types of agreements enumerated in Article 85 necessarily affect interstate trade.[43] Agreements may affect trade between member states even if made by parties some or all of whom are situated outside the EEC;[44] a division of world markets under which the whole of the EEC is allocated to one party to the agreement

[40] See Communication Concerning Exclusive Representation Contracts Concluded with Commercial Representatives, 1962 Journal Officiel 2921–22/62, translated in Honig, Brown, Gleiss & Hirsch, Cartel Law of the European Economic Community 19 (1963). This and other communications interpret art. 85 authoritatively but are not binding and are subject to the ruling of the Court.

[41] Art. 85(1)(e). See Oberdorfer, Gleiss & Hirsch, Common Market Cartel Law 21 (1963).

[42] Schumacher, "Réflexions sur l'interdiction des ententes visées par l'article 85 du Traité instituant la C.E.E.," 24 Droit Social 65, 68–69 (1961). Due to the small size of the Irish market, an Irish subsidiary of a foreign enterprise normally exports to other parts of Europe. If Ireland enters the EEC, almost all foreign subsidiaries will therefore be affected by the EEC antitrust provisions. Prior to Ireland's entry, if the Irish subsidiary exports directly to each of the member states and the exports do not pass from one state to another, its restrictive agreements will be unlikely to affect trade between member states. It is, of course, not suggested that there is any legal distinction between the position of Irish-owned and foreign-owned enterprises in Ireland; the only difference is that the latter are very likely to be engaged in exporting.

[43] Third General Report, para. 138 (1960).

[44] Hug, "The Applicability of the Provisions of the European Community Treaties Against Restraints of Competition to Restraints of Competition Caused in Non-Member States, but Affecting the Common Market," in 2 Cartel and Monopoly in Modern Law 639 (1961); Mueller, "Antitrust Problems in Connection with Dealings in Common Market Countries," in 1962 International Bar Association Conference 175, 178-86. See, however, the views summarized by Skiöld, "Antitrust Problems in Connection with Dealings in Common Market Countries," in 1962 International Bar Association Conference 192, 194–96. It is submitted that, unless the Community Court decides otherwise, the principle of territorial effect—i.e., that cartels which have effects inside the EEC are subject to art. 85—should apply. The Treaty would be rendered ineffective if agreements made in non-member states were permitted to have anticompetitive effects within the EEC. Arts. 85 and 86 do not exclude the principle of territorial effect, and there is no principle of international law prohibiting it; see, e.g., German Competition Law, § 98(2). See also Jeantet & Lassier, "L'Application des lois anti-trust des pays du Marché Commun au commerce international avec les pays tiers," in 1962 International Bar Association Conference 165. Owing to the difference between the United States and the EEC antitrust laws, it is unlikely that, for example, joint venture operations in associated or third countries, which at most would be likely to affect the external trade of the EEC, could come within arts. 85 and 86. See, however, art. 227. See also Verloren van Themaat, "Competition and Restrictive Business Practices in the European Economic Community," in Institute on Legal Aspects of the European Community 99, 115 (Federal Bar Association, 1960); Nebolsine, "Foreign Enterprises Under the Common Market Antitrust Rules," 38 N.Y.U.L. Rev. 479 (1963).

at jointly fixed prices[45] is within Article 85. It follows that the parties cannot, by a choice-of-law clause designating the law of a non-member state as the proper law of the contract, prevent the contract's being declared illegal within the EEC.[46] However, the Treaty provisions can be enforced only in member states. It is unlikely that any existing treaty for the reciprocal enforcement of foreign judgments would permit a decree or decision of the Commission or the Community Court imposing a fine to be enforced in a non-member country, since neither of these Community organs could be regarded as national courts and since the procedure for executing their decisions[47] in member states is itself analogous to that used for enforcing a foreign judgment. Community rules do not have the broad extraterritorial scope of the United States antitrust laws[48] and therefore probably avoid most of the political and international law problems resulting from the latter.

TRADE

"Trade" between member states, as defined in the Treaty, covers virtually all forms of economic activity in which, or in connection with which, competition exists or could exist, since some distortion of competition is necessary for Article 85 to apply. "Trade" therefore does not include sectors entirely regulated by law, if the regulation is permitted by the Treaty. It includes production and sale of industrial, professional, and commercial goods and also services, research, and development of products and techniques.[49] It is not clear, however, whether "trade" includes financial transactions such as banking activities, but apparently European banks have notified their restrictive agreements.

THE CONCEPT OF "ENTERPRISE"[50]

Only concerted practices and agreements between enterprises and decisions by associations of enterprises are prohibited. No definition of an enterprise is given, and the question arises whether an independent legal entity is necessarily an enterprise or whether there must be, in addition, some degree of economic independence. The problem arises in practice in connection with groups of companies and with joint ventures.[51] If associated companies are not separate

[45] British Monopolies and Restrictive Practices Commission, Report on the Supply of Electric Lamps, H.C. Paper No. 287 (1951), and Report on the Supply and Export of Matches and the Supply of Match-Making Machinery, H.C. Paper No. 161 (1953).

[46] Hug, "The Applicability of the Provisions of the European Community Treaties Against Restraints of Competition to Restraints of Competition Caused in Non-Member States, but Affecting the Common Market," in 2 Cartel and Monopoly in Modern Law 639, 661–62 (1961); Third General Report, para. 140 (1960).

[47] Art. 192.

[48] Sherman Antitrust Act, 15 U.S.C. §§ 1–7 (1964). One important difference between arts. 85 and 86 and the United States antitrust law is that the former apply only to trade between member states and not to the external trade of the Community, while the latter applies expressly to "every contract . . . in restraint of [United States] trade or commerce . . . with foreign nations." Sherman Antitrust Act, 15 U.S.C. § 1. See generally Fugate, Foreign Commerce and the Antitrust Laws (1958); Brewster, Antitrust and American Business Abroad (1958).

[49] Mueller, "Antitrust Problems in Connection with Dealings in Common Market Countries," in 1962 International Bar Association Conference 175, 176.

[50] The unofficial translation by Her Majesty's Foreign Office uses the word "undertaking." This seems hardly necessary and, insofar as it adds unnecessarily to Community terminology, seems undesirable.

[51] For a general discussion, see Bebr, "The Concept of Enterprise in the European Communities," 26 Law & Contemp. Prob. 454 (1961). In Britain, Restrictive Trade Practices

enterprises, restrictive agreements between them are not prohibited. Trade unions and employees are not enterprises, and agreements between them which restrain competition are not within Article 85 or 86.

It has been argued that only an entity with legal capacity to contract can be an enterprise, since the Article contemplates agreements between enterprises.[52] If only a legal entity can be an enterprise, restrictive agreements between branches of the same company are not affected by Article 85, and this clearly is the law. The practical problem is whether a group of companies can be treated as a single enterprise if only one of them is a party to a restrictive agreement. The phrase "associations of enterprises" does not assist, because it might refer either to associations of independent concerns, such as trade associations, or to a group of associated companies under common ownership and control.

Subsidiaries

"Enterprise" as an Economic Concept

Since there is usually no difficulty in identifying an entity with legal personality, it would be simple to treat all legal entities as separate enterprises. This is the interpretation adopted for certain purposes by the Community Court under the ECSC Treaty.[53] However, it is generally accepted that this principle has no application to Article 85, although a subsidiary company may in some circumstances be an enterprise separate from its parent.

In the EEC, enterprise is an economic, not a purely legal, concept. If legal entities were treated as separate enterprises, subsidiary and parent companies which wished to enter into restrictive agreements with each other would be compelled to merge, since there is no restriction on mergers in the EEC, but competition would not be increased. These mergers would not be desirable for business reasons or they would have been undertaken before. This would exalt form over substance.

Competition is the first test of whether an enterprise exists. If competition exists between a parent and a subsidiary company, they probably should be regarded as separate enterprises, even if their relations have not been organized so as to give them complete economic independence from one another. If no competition exists, the Commission may hold that the companies are separate enterprises if they are organized so as to be able to compete at arm's length. In such a case, competition could be prevented only by reorganizing the companies and merging them into one enterprise, but not necessarily one company.

Act, 1956, 4 & 5 Eliz. 2, c. 68, does not apply to agreements between associated companies; §§ 6(8), 8(9). See also Deringer et al., 5 Revue du Marché Commun 486, 493 (1962), who regard the following as "enterprises" when they are engaged in production or trade: the state, local governments, public corporations, professional associations, enterprises having a public character, enterprises to which a state gives special or exclusive rights, enterprises which have discontinued operations, one-man companies, independent commercial agents, and enterprises not yet in being (to the extent to which they can, under their constitution, enter into business contracts for the future).

[52] Oberdorfer, Gleiss & Hirsch, Common Market Cartel Law 2 (1963) and authorities cited there.

[53] Mannesmann v. High Authority, 8 Recueil 675 (1962); Klöckner-Werke v. High Authority, 8 Recueil 615 (1962); Société Nouvelle des Usines de Pontlieue v. High Authority, 5 Recueil 275 (1959), 7 Recueil 101 (1961). For a discussion of previous cases under the ECSC Treaty along the same lines, see Bebr, "The Concept of Enterprise in the European Communities," 26 Law & Contemp. Prob. 454 (1961). The word *Unternehmen* (undertaking) used in the German text of art. 85(1) is also in § 1 of the German Competition Law, where it is not interpreted as applying to associated companies.

The Possibility of Competition and the Question of Organization as Independent Business Entities

In many cases competition is not prevented by directives issued by the parent company, although no competition exists and the subsidiaries are not organized for independent operations. Some authorities hold that if there is a mere possibility of competition, the subsidiaries are separate enterprises,[54] even without separate organization. Clearly, if two "enterprises" can be shown to exist, an agreement which prevents competition from arising between them is within Article 85.

The theoretical possibility of competition's arising between two associated companies which do not have separate business organizations is hardly evidence that the companies are separate enterprises. If the companies have been given rights and powers of their own under contracts with the parent company, or if they look after their own interests irrespective of those of the parent, they may be separate enterprises, since they may come into competition through pursuit of their own interests. Some written contract or other formal relationship which reduces the parent's control is necessary. The more independent its legal relationships make the company, the more likely it is to be regarded as a separate economic unit.

If neither competition nor formal legal arrangements exist between the associated companies, it is submitted that they constitute a single enterprise and are free to enter into anticompetitive arrangements with each other.[55] The only alternative to this would ultimately involve an investigation of whether the absence of competition between companies under the same ownership was, in fact, due to "concerted practices."[56] This seems neither logically nor practically possible when the object of the investigation is to decide if the legal entities are separate enterprises. Admittedly, it would be desirable to prohibit agreements preventing competition between an efficient and enterprising subsidiary and a less efficient subsidiary selling an old-fashioned product. The difficulty is that an agreement not made between separate enterprises is not within Article 85, and Article 85 cannot be used to force single enterprises to concentrate on economically desirable lines of production. There is also the practical difficulty of trying to force associated companies to compete with each other if they have never done so and have never arranged their reciprocal rights and duties on an arm's-length basis.

Directives of Parent Companies

If no actual competition exists and the organization of the associated companies permits, the interests controlling the group may issue directives which prevent competition from arising.[57] Since

[54] 1961 Report of the Bundeskartellamt 61.

[55] Mueller, "Antitrust Problems in Connection with Dealings with Common Market Countries," in 1962 International Bar Association Conference 175, 177; U.S. Attorney General's National Committee to Study the Antitrust Laws, Report 36 (1955).

[56] If agreements between subsidiaries are prohibited, the Commission should, in theory, prohibit existing concerted practices between them as well. To do this would involve a highly speculative investigation of whether competition could have arisen, and if so, whether there had been any "concerted" avoidance of it and whether such a concerted practice still operated. This also would involve the distinction between inter-company agreements and directives criticized in the text and would involve arguing in a circle. The argument runs: if no competition exists, we must see if this is due to prohibited concerted practices; but concerted practices will not be prohibited unless the subsidiaries are separate enterprises; to see if they are separate enterprises, we must see if competition exists.

[57] In the absence of contracts to the contrary, under the general company law directives can always be issued if a controlling interest exists,

these directives might replace restrictive agreements between subsidiaries, their legal status is important.

The Commission has never indicated that it would interfere with directives of ultimate owners, and a unilateral directive could hardly be regarded as an "agreement" between enterprises. Such a directive could not be regarded as a "decision by an association of enterprises" unless the constituent companies were regarded as enterprises. If a directive could be regarded as a concerted practice, it would have to be shown in some other way that the subsidiaries were separate enterprises, and the fact that a directive could be given would be evidence that they were not.[58] The inherent power of a single enterprise to manage its own affairs and the difficulty of compelling an operation to compete with itself seem to be conclusive arguments against an interpretation which would allow the Commission to invalidate directives where no competition exists. If these directives cannot be invalidated, it seems unrealistic to distinguish between them and agreements made between subsidiaries or between parent and subsidiary and intended to produce the same effect. To prohibit management from issuing directives that prevent competition from arising between wholly owned subsidiaries would inhibit specialization within the group.[59] A distinction between directives and horizontal cooperation, whether formal or informal, between subsidiaries that has the same effect would distort the normal functioning of sound management without producing any economic benefits to the Community. It follows that, where directives can be issued, restrictive agreements should be permitted, on the ground that the group constitutes a single enterprise.

subject to the rights of minority shareholders. If each company enjoys *de facto* autonomy and competition is therefore possible, it is likely that the group should still be treated as a single enterprise, at least for the purposes of establishing a dominant market position; see the view of Dr. Verloren van Themaat, quoted by the Committee on Foreign Law, "Current Legal Developments in the European Economic Community," 18 Record of N.Y.C.B.A. 329, 336 (1963); Linssen, "The Antitrust Rules of the European Economic Community," 18 Record of N.Y.C.B.A. 289, 293 (1963).

[58] 1961 Report of the Bundeskartellamt 61. For criticisms of the view that a group of companies will be a single enterprise only in such circumstances, see Becker, Extraterritorial Application of Common Market Laws (Practicing Law Institute, 1962); Oberdorfer, Gleiss & Hirsch, Common Market Cartel Law 13–16 (1963).

Directives of Parent Companies Where Competition Exists

A difficulty arises where competition between two subsidiaries is ended by a directive from the parent company. In such cases the subsidiaries will apparently be regarded as separate enterprises. Their "practices" could be regarded as having been "concerted" by means of a directive addressed to both of them by a separate legal entity; the situation is analogous to that of a decision by an association of enterprises. But the phrase "concerted practices" implies a consensual element. It is questionable whether a practice is "concerted" if the parties to it have not consented to it directly or agreed in advance to accept it. Even if directives are prohibited where competition exists between subsidiaries, the parent company is free to reorganize the group so as to eliminate competition, since mergers are not controlled. There is thus little object in trying to enforce competition between wholly owned subsidiaries.

Agreements Between Subsidiaries as Evidence of the Existence of Separate Enterprises

The German Bundeskartellamt (Fed-

[59] In the United States, the law generally prohibits restrictions by management on existing competition.

eral Cartel Authority) has indicated that the existence of agreements between associated companies would be regarded as evidence that they are independent in their operation and that they compete among themselves.[60] However, agreements may be made to clarify a relationship or express it formally, e.g., for reasons of tax or patent law. If there is an agreement between associated companies but no competition exists, the content and primary purpose of the agreement must be considered. If no question of competition has ever arisen, the existence of agreements between associated companies, even if the agreements include anticompetitive clauses, does not necessarily mean that the companies are free to compete, and their freedom to compete does not mean that they are organized to do so independently. Informal agreements not to compete often result from circumstances where the parties have found themselves in accidental[61] competition or where a new development is planned in which it is intended to avoid duplication. While the line may be difficult to draw, there is a distinction of substance between a rationalizing agreement which has been made to improve efficiency and which incidentally allocates spheres of activity and an agreement which has been made solely to avoid competition. In the latter case, the Commission presumably will ask why the same result was not achieved by directive. The existence of directives preventing competition does not preclude inter-company restrictive practices independent of, but perhaps limited by, the directives.[62] Agreements may be required to formalize a previous "concerted practice" for notification to the Commission, and in such circumstances agreements will not be evidence of the possibility or the existence of competition.

Practical Conclusions

The practical result of all this is to give businessmen an incentive to deal with management problems in this field as far as possible by directives, rather than by horizontal agreements, and to insure that subsidiaries do not get into competition with one another. This will help to insure that the group is treated as a single enterprise, but it may tend to put the group as a whole in a position of dominant market power within Article 86. If a group has a separate subsidiary in each member state, undue emphasis on unity of management and control may encourage tax authorities to regard the parent company as carrying on business through subsidiaries as permanent establishments, and there may be other tax reasons why the separate corporate form of the entities composing the group will be important. In addition, especially if there are local shareholders in a local subsidiary, there may be political reasons making the group reluctant to stress central control. Details of agreements notified to the Commission are always transmitted to national cartel authorities, and thus national tax authorities might be able to obtain them.[63]

Joint ventures

What has been said applies to subsidiaries wholly under the control and

[60] 1961 Report of the Bundeskartellamt 61. See also Deringer et al., 6 Revue du Marché Commun 37, 38 (1963).

[61] It will hardly have been intentional, unless two branches of the same enterprise sell different but competing products, in which case a progressive company will usually allow competition to continue.

[62] Becker, Extraterritorial Application of Common Market Laws (PLI, 1962).

[63] Reg. 17, art. 10. However, under Reg. 17, art. 20, information acquired by the Commission or by a national cartel authority in the course of an investigation is not to be used for any purpose other than that of the investigation.

ownership of companies of the same group. The position of a partly owned subsidiary or a joint venture is somewhat different, depending on the extent of the control exercised by minority and majority shareholders.[64] The establishment of a jointly owned venture may be either a market-sharing or other restrictive device of the two parent companies or a merger. If it is a restrictive device, it is prohibited by Article 85; if it is a merger, it is not necessarily affected by the Treaty at all.[65] All the economic circumstances must be examined to see if competition between the two principals and between the principals and the joint venture is affected,[66] and if so, to consider the position under Article 85(3). Unless restricted by agreement, competition normally continues between the two parents and perhaps between the joint venture and the minority shareholder. The relationship of a joint venture with the majority shareholder is more likely to be agreed on formally than the relationship of a wholly owned subsidiary with its parent, and a joint venture is, of course, much more likely to be regarded as a separate enterprise.

Further difficulties arise in the case of companies controlled by similar, but not identical, groups of shareholders, companies with "interlocking directorates,"[67] and companies with different shareholders but with the same debenture holders. These links may well furnish a means for concerted practices. The test in such cases cannot be whether competition actually exists, because an existing concerted practice might be preventing it. If the test is whether competition is possible, that is, whether there is a controlling interest which could prevent it, some allowance must be made for the intervention of minority shareholders and directors not representing common controlling interests. If only having common ownership or controlling interests excludes the possibility of competition, other than permissive competition, will this common ultimate control justify, for example, division of markets among a number of controlled but only partly owned subsidiaries? Management agreements also cause problems in deciding to what extent the managing and the managed companies can be regarded as separate enterprises. The simplest test would be the existence of the ultimate right to direct, through shareholding or control, that competition should cease, but this would probably oversimplify the problem.

Commercial representatives, independent agents, and permanent establishments

A commercial representative or a sales agent is not an enterprise independent of his principal, and restrictive agreements may freely be made between them.[68] Independent contractors are separate enterprises,[69] and agreements with

[64] For a summary of the German antitrust law on joint ventures, see Weiser, "Antitrust Aspects of the Joint Venture in the European Economic Community," 111 U. Pa. L. Rev. 421, 425–28 (1963).

[65] A joint venture could probably be an "association of enterprises." *Quaere* the effect of art. 85(2) on an agreement embodied in the charter of a company and on the constitution of the company itself.

[66] A joint venture may involve the parties' limiting their own or the joint venture's production, technical development, or investment, or fixing prices or sharing markets or sources of supply.

[67] See the definition of *Konzern* in Aktiengesetz, the German Company Law of 1937, § 15, discussed in Oberdorfer, Gleiss & Hirsch, Common Market Cartel Law 3 (1963).

[68] See Deringer & Tessin, "Les Contrats d'exclusivité dans le droit du Marché Commun," 80 Moniteur Officiel du Commerce International 3267, 3268 (1962).

[69] Communication Concerning Exclusive Contracts . . ., 1962 Journal Officiel 2921-22/62.

them are subject to Article 85. According to the Commission, the express or implied assumption of the financial risks of the sale or the performance of the contract by the agent, other than a normal guarantee,[70] is strong evidence that he is an independent enterprise. Apparently, the agent's maintaining a substantial stock[71] of the goods in question, if he has title to them, and rendering substantial free[72] services to customers, whether he is required to do so or not and whether the services are provided directly or indirectly, are strong evidence of an independent enterprise. So is the fact that the agent may, or in practice does, fix prices or conditions of sale.

In its communication on contracts with commercial representatives,[73] the Commission states that exclusive representation contracts are not within Article 85, because these agreements do not prevent or distort competition. Commercial representatives, as the Commission defines them, are agents under national laws, and their common characteristic is the ancillary nature of their functions. The Commission's definition looks to the person rather than to his agreement with the other party, because an otherwise identical agreement with an independent dealer will be within Article 85. Thus, the reason behind the ruling is that a commercial representative is not a separate enterprise, not that the type of agreement in question does not affect competition.[74]

If a fixed place of business exists, the distinction between a commercial representative and an independent dealer corresponds closely in certain respects to that between a permanent establishment and an independent agent for the purposes of double taxation conventions.[75] The definitions of a permanent establishment vary, but most provide that the maintenance of a stock of goods belonging to the principal, except for certain purposes, constitutes a permanent establishment. If the stock belongs to the distributor, he is independent, and if the distributorship agreement restricts competition, it is within Article 85. The principal may be in a dilemma; if a representative exercises authority to conclude contracts on behalf of the principal, he is a permanent establishment for tax purposes, and if an independent dealer has authority to settle prices and conditions of sale himself, he is within Article 85. An agent involved only in purchasing can never be a permanent establishment for tax purposes. Assumption of risk or provision of services by the agent, making him an independent dealer under Article 85, is not mentioned in most double taxation conventions, but either would be evidence

See also id., 2627-28/62, 2687/62. On the status of the communications, cf. the "circular" issued in France on the interpretation of art. 37 of the Price Ordinance as amended; "Circulaire Fontanet" of March 31, 1960, 1960 J.O.R.F. 3048. See Riesenfeld, "Antitrust Laws in the European Economic Community," 50 Calif. L. Rev. 459, 469 (1962).

[70] That is, a guarantee of payment, as *del credere* agent, if credit is given.

[71] That is, substantial in relation to the market concerned and to the size of the dealer's business; Verloren van Themaat, "Current Antitrust Developments in the European Common Market," 6 Pat., T.M. & Copyright J. Research & Educ. 432, 449 (1962).

[72] That is, apparently, free of charge to both the customer and the principal enterprise. On the law governing commercial representatives in the Six, see Commercial Agency and Distribution Agreements in Europe (British Institute of International and Comparative Law, 1964).

[73] 1962 Journal Officiel 2921-22/62.

[74] The matter has therefore been discussed at this point, although functionally it may fall under exclusive distributorships, which are dealt with on pp. 396–400.

[75] OECD Fiscal Committee, Draft Double Taxation Convention on Income and Capital (1963), art. 5.

of the independent status of the agent[76] for tax purposes. A problem of this kind is bound to be possible, from the nature of the two legal principles involved.[77] However, most distributorship agreements will be permitted unless they include territorial restrictions. The enterprise should avoid keeping a stock of goods in the member state in question, since having a stock is almost certain to raise the problem squarely, and if possible the enterprise should not give the agent authority to conclude sales or fix sale prices or conditions. However, these legal considerations may not accord with commercial convenience.[78] It is normally preferable to avoid tax liability and conclude the type of agreement most likely to be regarded favorably by the Commission under Article 85(3).

AGREEMENTS WITH STATE AUTHORITIES

Since only agreements between enterprises are prohibited, agreements between one enterprise and a non-trading government authority are not within Article 85. State aids negotiated individually with a new enterprise in a less developed region are often made conditional on the new enterprise's use of local raw materials, subcontractors, fuels, and the like.[79] This is a reasonable method of diversifying industry in an underindustrialized region and getting the maximum benefit for the region from new investments; however, it has the effect of distorting competition. While such an agreement is not usually within Article 85, in its nature it is more like a private distortion of competition than a public measure. It is unnatural to regard state authorities as acting as agents for local suppliers. The practice is often contrary to Article 7 of the Treaty, on discrimination, but not to Article 92.

CONCERTED PRACTICES

Article 85 encompasses agreements between enterprises, decisions by associations of enterprises, and concerted practices. Even informal agreements must be written down and notified to the Commission. The concept of concerted practices[80] is wider than the first two concepts and includes agreements and decisions which are not binding on the parties.[81]

[76] Id., art. 5(5). An agent acting exclusively for one enterprise is unlikely to be independent for tax purposes.

[77] Liability to foreign tax often coincides with interstate trade within art. 85.

[78] In most of the Six, a commercial representative is entitled to a substantial amount of commission by way of compensation if his contract is terminated; see, for example, German Commercial Code (Handelsgesetzbuch), § 89b.

[79] Rosenstein-Rodan, "How to Industrialize an Underdeveloped Area," in Regional Economic Planning 205, 208 (Isard & Cumberland ed. 1961). This has been done in Ireland.

[80] Copied from United States antitrust law, from French Decree No. 53–704 of Aug. 9, 1953, art. 59 *bis*, and from ECSC Treaty, art. 65(1). See U.K. Restrictive Trade Practices Act, 1956, 4 & 5 Eliz. 2, c. 68, § 6(3), 6(7); Lord Justice Diplock, in In re British Slag Ltd.'s Application, [1963] 1 Weekly L.R. 727, 747, said:

> No . . . useful purpose would be served by attempting an expanded and comprehensive definition of the word "arrangement" in section 6(3). . . . [I]t is sufficient to constitute an arrangement between A and B if (1) A makes a representation as to his future conduct with the expectation and intention that such conduct on his part will operate as an inducement to B to act in a particular way, (2) such representation is communicated to B who has knowledge that A so expected and intended, and (3) such representation or A's conduct in fulfillment of it operates as an inducement, whether among other inducements or not, to B to act in that particular way.

See also U.K. Registrar of Restrictive Trading Agreements, Annual Report, 1962; Annual Report, 1964. Under art. 85(1), practices need not be similar to be "concerted."

[81] The French *pratiques concertées* implies a consensual element or an element of reciprocity or conscious mutual understanding which falls

Identical practices and adjustments to competitors' practices are not concerted practices, although they may be evidence that a concerted practice exists.[82] Concerted practices are results, and the means of achieving them are irrelevant; the Treaty does not refer to gentlemen's agreements, recommendations, or other methods of arranging a concerted practice. A unilateral recommendation does not in itself involve the element of reciprocal communication necessary to constitute a concerted practice, unless it is later agreed to or acted on by all of the parties.[83]

Concerted practices, by definition, are not binding and therefore cannot be void under Article 85(2); the Commission will prohibit them, under penalty. It is more difficult to define what acts are prohibited than what agreements are prohibited. However, at least until the criteria become clearer, the Commission will be anxious merely to safeguard the Community against undue restriction of competition, if the good faith of the enterprises concerned is clear.[84] It therefore can arrange for necessary modifications in business practices rather than issue decrees intended to draw an exact line between what is to be permitted in the future and what is not, as is done in United States practice. Concerted practices must be formulated precisely and reduced to writing if the Commission is to approve them.[85]

Threats of refusal to deal may be legal even if they are intended to bring about practices which could not be secured by agreement, since there would not be the consensual element necessary for practices to be "concerted."[86]

THE EFFECTS ON COMPETITION WHICH ARE PROHIBITED

Agreements, decisions, and practices which affect interstate trade are prohibited if they "are designed to prevent, restrict or distort competition within the Common Market or . . . have this effect." This is the operative provision of Article 85(1); the following clauses are merely examples of particular types of agreements which affect competition. Article 85 is infringed only if there is a reasonable likelihood that trade between member states will be affected "adversely."[87]

---

short of agreement but is stronger than deliberate parallel action. See Turner, "The Definition of Agreement Under the Sherman Act: Conscious Parallelism and Refusals to Deal," 75 Harv. L. Rev. 655 (1962). At this point a difference in terminology may be pointed out. The French word *entente* has a neutral connotation, so it is possible to speak of good and bad *ententes,* but the German word *Kartell* connotes a "bad" *entente.* The word "cartel" is used in this text without any connotation as to legality.

[82] See Thompson & Brown, "Monopolies and Restrictive Trade Practices—Antitrust Problems in Dealing with Common Market Countries," in 1962 International Bar Association Conference 207; Deringer Report, A.P.E. Doc. No. 57, at 10 (1961–62). This is the rule in French law.

[83] Oberdorfer, Gleiss & Hirsch, Common Market Cartel Law 9 (1963). Under British law, if the constitution of a trade association makes recommendations to members, it is treated as an agreement to comply with the recommendations; Restrictive Trade Practices Act, 1956, 4 & 5 Eliz. 2, c. 68, § 6(7). For the position in the Netherlands, see Economic Competition Act of 1956, § 1(4).

[84] This is the practice of the French Commission Technique des Ententes; Riesenfeld, "The Legal Protection of Competition in France," 48 Calif. L. Rev. 574, 590–92 (1960).

[85] Deringer et al., 6 Revue du Marché Commun 256, 261 (1963).

[86] See German Competition Law, § 4. However, it could be argued that the effect of the threats was to cause the enterprises threatened to concert their practices and that the nature of the persuasion used is irrelevant. See also Turner, "The Definition of Agreement Under the Sherman Act: Conscious Parallelism and Refusals to Deal," 75 Harv. L. Rev. 655, 684–95 (1962).

[87] There has been a considerable amount of discussion as to whether the French text, from which the adverb and the connotation of preju-

If an agreement has a negligible or merely a possible effect on interstate trade, it is difficult to see how it can affect interstate trade adversely or how it can distort competition. The harm as well as the effect must be reasonably likely. There is, however, no limitation on direct effects which may be considered. The question of causality, or of "remoteness" in the common law sense of indirect causation, arises only in deciding if an effect is reasonably likely.[88] An "artificial" increase in interstate trade due to a restrictive agreement must normally be accompanied by a decrease in the volume of trade elsewhere, so an agreement which prevents or distorts competition is unlikely to have a purely beneficial effect. Since the test is the likelihood of an "adverse" effect on interstate trade, not the actual existence of such an effect, agreements temporarily causing a favorable effect would be prohibited if a predominantly unfavorable effect was reasonably foreseeable.[89] The necessity of an adverse effect on trade must be read together with the requirement of prevention, restriction, or distortion of competition, themselves pejorative terms, and with Article 85(3), which is the only explicit provision permitting "good" cartels.[90]

A restrictive agreement not within Article 85(1) does not need the provisions of Article 85(3) to validate it. However, since Article 85(3) incorporates a rule of reason, there is no obvious need to seek such a rule in the provisions of Ar-

dice or injury to interstate trade were omitted, or the other three texts, which imply in varying degrees the necessity for an adverse effect on trade, should be preferred. The official German view was that the words translated as the adverb "adversely" were unnecessary, since any effect on competition in interstate trade must necessarily be adverse and objectionable; 1961 Report of the Bundeskartellamt 61, and the arguments of the German government in Bosch v. de Geus, quoted and commented on by Advocate-General Lagrange, 8 Recueil 89, 139–41, [1962] C.M.L.R. 1, 23–24. An important interpretation in favor of reading the word "adversely" into the text is the Deringer Report, A.P.E. Doc. No. 57, para. 62 (1961–62). This is also the view of the Commission; Verloren van Themaat, "Rules of Competition and Restrictive Trade Practices," in Legal Problems of the European Economic Community and the European Free Trade Association, Int'l & Comp. L.Q. Supp. No. 1, at 76, 84 (1961); Committee on Foreign Law, "The European Economic Community," 17 Record of N.Y.C.B.A. 287, 327 n.1 (1962). The question to some extent depends on how far one believes it is possible for anticompetitive practices to have beneficial effects, and on whether art. 85(3) will adequately protect beneficial cartels. See Wolf, "La Législation contre les Cartels et les Monopoles: son application dans la Communauté Economique Européenne," 1962 Journal des Tribunaux 541, 543, whose view is that art. 85(3) is not sufficiently liberal to restrictive agreements and that a rule of reason should be read into art. 85(1). See Linssen, "The Antitrust Rules of the European Economic Community," 18 Record of N.Y.C.B.A. 289, 291 (1963); Deringer et al., 6 Revue du Marché Commun 126, 127 (1963); 4 OECD Guide to Legislation on Restrictive Business Practices, EEC § 2.0, at 2 (1962); Verloren van Themaat, "Competition and Restrictive Business Practices in the European Economic Community," in Institute on Legal Aspects of the European Community 99, 114 (1960). Substantially the same question arises under art. 92(1), which prohibits state aids to the extent to which they affect trade between member states.

[88] Oberdorfer, Gleiss & Hirsch, Common Market Cartel Law 18 (1963), prefer "apt to." See Third General Report, para. 140 (1960).

[89] Argument of the German government in Bosch v. de Geus, quoted by Advocate-General Lagrange, 8 Recueil 89, 139–41, [1962] C.M.L.R. 1, 23–24. The Commission (Re the Agreement of Grundig Verkaufs-GmbH [the *Grundig-Consten* decision], 1964 Journal Officiel 2545/64, [1964] C.M.L.R. 489) and the Court (Time, July 29, 1966, p. 66) held that the agreement created an illegal monopoly in French territory, violating free-trade accords.

[90] Even if not all "artificial" influences on trade are regarded as objectionable, it is not clear that the word "adversely" adds anything to the phrase concerning competition.

ticle 85(1). Dr. Wolf, however, argues[91] that the limited scope of Article 85(3) requires a rule of reason, other than one involving causality, to be read into Article 85(1).[92] He argues that there may be cartels which are legitimate in the public interest to prevent overproduction or to ease industrial difficulty or crisis but which do not permit any advantage to be passed on to the consumer. A cartel for the industrialization of a region might well have a favorable effect on interstate trade but not comply with Article 85(3). If this view is accepted, there will be some agreements which affect trade directly and substantially but are not within Article 85 because they do not affect trade unfavorably.

The next question is what is meant by agreements "which prevent, restrict or distort competition." Distortion of competition is a concept which appears frequently in varying forms in the Treaty[93] and in national legislation.[94] Agreements, decisions, and practices—whether they are bilateral or multilateral, horizontal or vertical—may distort, restrict, or prevent competition. Actual competition need not exist if competition between the enterprises is possible.[95] An agreement not to compete in specific ways, such as in price, services, discounts or other conditions of sale or in quality or advertising, restricts competition, even if competition continues in other ways and even intensifies. An agreement which is intended to restrict competition and an agreement which has the effect of restricting competition are both prohibited; the coincidence of intention and effect is not necessary.[96]

Competition can be limited by restrictions on the freedom of individual enterprises to take any type of action,[97] e.g., to fix prices, to increase production, or to sell in certain markets, or by tying-in clauses and collusive discrimination which give artificial advantages to or impose artificial disadvantages on certain enterprises. The examples of prohibited practices given in Articles 85 and 86 are not intended to be exhaustive, but in a case falling within their terms[98] the burden of proof is lighter than that in a case involving a practice which is only within the general provisions.

THE SPECIFIC PROVISIONS OF ARTICLE 85

Fixing of prices or other trading conditions[99]

Article 86 merely prohibits a monopoly or an oligopoly with dominant market power from improperly exploiting its position by the imposition of unfair prices. Article 85 does not prohibit price-fixing agreements absolutely; apart from Article 85(3), such agreements must have an adverse effect on interstate trade and a distorting effect on competition.

[91] "La Législation contre les Cartels et les Monopoles: Son Application dans la Communauté Economique Européenne," in International Law Association, Report of the Fiftieth [1962] Conference 636 (1963).

[92] Contra, Ladas, "Antitrust Law in the Common Market with Special Reference to Industrial Property Agreements," 23 Ohio St. L.J. 709, 712 (1962).

[93] E.g., arts. 3(f), 92; cf. ECSC Treaty, arts. 65, 67.

[94] E.g., French Decree No. 53-704 of Aug. 9, 1953, as amended by Decree No. 59-1004 of Aug. 17, 1959; German Competition Law, §§ 1, 25; U.S. Clayton Act, §§ 2, 3, 7, 15 U.S.C. §§ 13, 14, 18 (1964).

[95] Because "agreements . . . designed to prevent . . . competition" are within the express terms of art. 85(1); Deringer et al., 6 Revue du Marché Commun 84, 86 (1963).

[96] Id. at 87.

[97] Id. at 85. Plaisant & Lassier, Ententes et Marché Commun 24 (1959), neatly express this as "liberty and equality." What is prohibited is fraternity, presumably.

[98] 4 OECD Guide to Legislation on Restrictive Business Practices, EEC § 2.0, at 2 (1962).

[99] See Steindorff, Problèmes des Prix imposés dans le Marché Commun (1962).

Except when made between commercial representatives and their principals,[100] price-fixing is prohibited in principle, whether it is by vertical agreements or by horizontal agreements. *Bilateral* agreements whose *only* effects are to restrict the freedom of a purchaser to fix prices or trading conditions on the resale of goods bought from the other party to the contract[101] are optionally notifiable. These contracts may nevertheless be prohibited, so there is no automatic approval for bilateral retail price maintenance agreements. The Commission has decided merely that they are sufficiently harmless to justify treating them later.[102] Resale price maintenance is specifically permitted in German law for trademarked products if competition with other brands exists.[103]

Vertical resale price maintenance agreements are prohibited, subject to certain exceptions, in French[104] and German[105] law and in Article 65 of the ECSC Treaty. In Britain, resale price maintenance is prohibited in principle even for the goods actually sold[106] under the restrictive agreement—the category for which notification is optional under Article 4(2)[107]—though earlier it had been allowed for other goods of the same type.[108] The extent to which the substantive law of these countries will be altered by Article 85 will depend on the application of Article 85(3), and statements as to the changes made by the Treaty must be accepted with caution.

Horizontal price-fixing and fixing of trading conditions[109] are also prohibited by Article 85. Since horizontal agreements are more objectionable than bilateral agreements providing for resale price maintenance, all horizontal price-fixing agreements must be notified to the Commission. Since indirect price-fixing is prohibited, the fixing of any constituent element of the total resale price[110] is

[100] Communication Concerning Exclusive Contracts . . ., 1962 Journal Officiel 2921-22/62. The view of the Italian authorities has been that vertical agreements do not restrain competition, except where they implement horizontal cartels.

[101] Reg. 17, art. 4(2)(ii)(a).

[102] See Reg. 118, 1963 Journal Officiel 2696/63.

[103] Competition Law, § 16. However, there are proposals to end this concession; Riesenfeld, "Antitrust Laws in the European Economic Community: A Sequel," 50 Calif. L. Rev. 829, 836 (1962). It seems likely that any new legislation will be designed to prevent abuses of resale price maintenance but not to prohibit it. The Bundeskartellamt prohibited many examples of resale price maintenance during 1963–64.

[104] Decree No. 53-704 of Aug. 9, 1953, as amended by Decree No. 59-1004 of Aug. 17, 1959, arts. 37(4), 59 *bis*. Effect on prices is the test of a legitimate cartel in French law. See also German Competition Law, § 17(1)(3). For analysis of art. 85 in comparison with art. 59 *bis*, see Loussouarn & Bredin, "La Réglementation des Ententes: le Recul du Contrôle Judiciare," Recueil Dalloz, Cahier 6, Feb. 6, 1963, pp. 33–40; on art. 59 generally, see Secrétariat d'Etat aux Affaires Economiques, Direction Générale des Prix et des Enquêtes Economiques, "Instruction Portant Commentaire des Dispositions du décret No. 53–704 du 9 Août, 1953 relatives aux ententes professionelles," Circulaire No. 65; on art. 37, see "Circulaire Fontanet" of March 31, 1960, 1960 J.O.R.F. 3048–49. For contravention of art. 37(4) there must be a fixing of the minimum price of a product or service or the amount of profit on sale, either by way of a scale unilaterally imposed or by agreement or by other methods, and no authorization must have been obtained.

[105] Competition Law, §§ 1, 2–10, 15, 16–18.

[106] Resale Prices Act, 1964, 12 & 13 Eliz. 2, c. 58.

[107] Of Regulation 17.

[108] Restrictive Practices Act, 1956, 4 & 5 Eliz. 2, c. 68, § 8(3).

[109] Cf. Restrictive Practices Act, 1956, 4 & 5 Eliz. 2, c. 68, § 6(1)(a).

[110] Such as discount levels, rebates, and terms such as dates for payment, conditions, and warranties as to quality.

prohibited.[111] Indirect influences on resale prices are not prohibited if the effect is to leave the actual price subject to the free play of other market forces. The price fixed is irrelevant; it may be the actual market price or may have no effect on that price.[112] Agreements maintaining prices, hindering their reduction, or providing for price increases also are prohibited. Agreements as to the extent of after-sale and other services are prohibited. Recommendations which are not binding and to which no agreement is given are not concerted practices and cannot fix prices and so are permissible. In theory, any fixing of prices by any two enterprises in a single member state could affect interstate trade by encouraging imports at lower prices, but Article 85 does not apply to this remote possibility.[113]

Limitation of production, markets, technical development, or investment

Agreements and practices which have the effect of limiting production, markets, development, or investment limit economic expansion as well as competition. There is a similar provision[114] in the ECSC Treaty, except that it does not mention the limitation or control of markets. The sharing, division, and allocation of markets are dealt with separately in both Treaties.[115] "Limitation of markets" deals with cartels designed to protect industry against structural crises, which, like other agreements, must be approved under Article 85(3). Since they divide the total market on a functional basis and relieve each enterprise of competition in the particular field allocated to it, specialization and rationalization cartels allocating particular lines of production or sectors of the market to specific enterprises are prohibited, subject to Article 85(3). Specialization without any agreement or concerted practice is permissible, since it tends to bring about the most efficient use of resources in the EEC. Abuse of a dominant market position resulting from specialization is prohibited by Article 86. Agreements solely on the development or uniform application of standards and types are optionally notifiable,[116] as are agreements the only purpose of which is joint research to improve techniques (even if the research is allocated among the enterprises participating), if all the enterprises are given the results of the research and are free to make use of them.[117] Control of markets through jointly owned sales or purchasing subsidiaries is prohibited by Article 85(1)(b). Such subsidiaries, of course, constitute a means of price-fixing and of market-sharing and supply-sharing as well, in certain circumstances. Joint operations may bring all these things about even if no subsidiary is created.[118]

The Irish Committee on Industrial Organization[119] recommended cooperation

[111] This is the position in the law of the Netherlands, if the price-fixing is contrary to the general interest.

[112] Deringer et al., 6 Revue du Marché Commun 172 (1963); see Catalano, "Rapports entre les règles de concurrence établies par le traité CEE et les législations des Etats membres," 15 Rev. Int. de Droit Comp. 269, 281–82 (1963).

[113] Deringer et al., 6 Revue du Marché Commun 126, 130 (1963).

[114] ECSC Treaty, art. 65(1)(b).

[115] EEC Treaty, art. 85(1)(c); ECSC Treaty, art. 65(1)(c). In Britain cartels limiting production and so forth must be registered and their legitimate nature proved to the Restrictive Practices Court; Restrictive Trade Practices Act, 1956, 4 & 5 Eliz. 2, c. 68, § 6(1)(c)–6(1)(e).

[116] Reg. 17, art. 4(2)(iii)(a).

[117] Reg. 17, art. 4(2)(iii)(b); Deringer et al., 6 Revue du Marché Commun 172, 174 (1963).

[118] Tax encouragement for jointly owned subsidiaries was given in Ireland by Finance Act, 1962 Acts 563, § 13.

[119] Second Interim Report: Joint Export Marketing, Pr. 6730 (1962).

between Irish enterprises and joint market research, advertising, sales promotion, and transport services as a means of increasing exports. It also suggested that all sales by groups of firms in specified markets should be directed through joint selling operations; it recommended "arrangements between firms within [Ireland] . . . to eliminate duplication in products offered for sale in export markets and to market a coordinated range, with the scope of the marketing arrangement varying from joint promotion to full-scale joint selling."[120] If adopted by enterprises exporting to the EEC, these joint operations would be subject to Article 85 if they affected trade between member states.[121]

In France, agreements limiting production, development, or investment are prohibited because of their effect on prices, which is the most important test in French law. In German law, limitations on production are prohibited,[122] subject to certain statutory exceptions.

Sharing markets or sources of supply

Sharing or allocating markets within the EEC interferes not only with freedom of competition but with free movement of goods. Removal of tariffs and quotas makes it inevitable that enterprises in different member countries will try to use market-sharing agreements to preserve for themselves the national markets in which they had been protected before the Community was established.[123] The prevention of market-sharing is most important to bring about the conditions of a single internal market[124] and the volume of trade between member states essential as the economic cement to a future political union. It is therefore important that this provision has raised two of the most difficult questions under Article 85, the problems of patent licenses and of exclusive distributorships. These are also the questions of the greatest practical importance to American business in Europe, which in other respects can expect to have a fairly "clean" system of operation owing to the extraterritorial application of the United States antitrust laws. However, no assumptions should be made that this is so in particular cases, especially where the Webb-Pomarene Act[125] applies.

Article 85(1)(c) was primarily intended to prevent horizontal market-sharing agreements between enterprises in different member states and between enterprises of a single member state in respect of exports and imports.[126] There is a similar clause in Article 65 of the ECSC Treaty. However, the provision can have wider implications. For example, German retail price maintenance systems, legal under German law, were undermined by products reimported into Germany from France, where price-fixing is strictly forbidden. The Germans therefore introduced a clause into their contracts with French dealers prohibiting reimport of products into Germany. This clause was held to be prohibited by Article 85(1), with the result that the

[120] Id. at 7.

[121] Market-sharing might occur, if competing lines of products were involved, through the buying and selling policy of the joint marketing operation and through the shareholding in a jointly owned enterprise. Enforcement would be unlikely if none of the enterprises involved had branches in the EEC.

[122] Competition Law, § 1.

[123] Third General Report, paras. 135, 143 (1960).

[124] Neumark Report, passim; Verloren van Themaat, "Competition and Restrictive Business Practices in the European Economic Community," in Institute on Legal Aspects of the European Community 99, 113 (1960).

[125] 15 U.S.C. §§ 61–65 (1964).

[126] Market-sharing agreements in Britain must be registered; Restrictive Practices Act, 1956, 4 & 5 Eliz. 2, c. 68, § 6(1)(e).

whole internal price-fixing system in Germany failed.[127]

Restrictions on the type of customer to whom a dealer is permitted to sell are related to exclusive distributorships and are equally likely to constitute market-sharing. Customer restrictions are illegal per se in the United States[128] and this per se illegality has been regarded as clearly justified.[129]

Exclusive Distributorship Agreements

The essence of most exclusive distributorship agreements is to bind the dealer to sell no goods competing with the goods of the supplier and to sell the latter only within a given area, and to bind the supplier to sell his goods within the same area only through the dealer.[130] Article 85(1)(c) applies to all three types of clauses, and their anticompetitive effects must be considered in the context of the remaining provisions of the distributorship agreement, for example, a patent license, and in connection with one another. Exclusive agreements affect competition at two levels: competition between suppliers and competition between dealers. The obligation of the dealer to work only for one supplier reduces the market for the goods of other suppliers,[131] that is, inter-brand competition. The restriction of the dealer to a particular area reduces intra-brand competition among dealers. The obligation of the supplier to sell, in the given area, only to one dealer[132] reduces the

[127] Steindorff, "Restrictive Practices Laws of Germany," in Restrictive Practices, Patents, Trade Marks and Unfair Competition in the Common Market, Int'l & Comp. L.Q. Supp. No. 4, at 28, 31–32 (1962).

[128] United States v. White Motor Co., 194 F. Supp. 562 (N.D. Ohio 1961).

[129] Note, "Restricted Channels of Distribution Under the Sherman Act," 75 Harv. L. Rev. 795, 823, 830 (1962).

[130] Jeantet, "Réflexions sur l'application du droit des ententes aux contrats comportant une clause d'exclusivité," 1963 J.C.P., Doctrine 1743, at 1–6, classifies these contracts into: exclusive-agency agreements, whereby a representative obtains the exclusive right to sell a product or a service on behalf of a manufacturer or wholesaler; exclusive-distribution agreements or exclusive concessions, under which a wholesaler or retailer gets the exclusive right to resell a product; and agreements for the exclusive right of supply (*la fourniture exclusive*), by which a user agrees to obtain supplies only from a particular manufacturer or provider. "Exclusive-agency agreements" of this kind are not within art. 85(1), according to the communication, 1962 Journal Officiel 2921-22/62. An exclusive-distribution agreement is a valid reason for a refusal to deal, which otherwise would be contrary to art. 37(1) of the Price Ordinance of June 30, 1945 as amended; "Circulaire Fontanet" of March 31, 1960, 1960 J.O.R.F. 3048. See Deringer et al., 6 Revue du Marché Commun 126, 129–30 (1963); Hemard, "Une enquête sur les contrats d'exclusivité, le refus de vente et les prix imposés dans les pays du Marché Commun," 4 Rev. Int. de Droit Comp. 701 (1964). French law prohibits joint purchasing operations and agreements for exclusive reciprocal buying and selling of products. See Nicolas & Société Brandt v. Société Photo Radio Club, Cour d'Appel de Paris, Feb. 7, 1961, retrial ordered, Cour de Cassation (Ch. Crim.), July 11, 1962, [1962] C.M.L.R. 93, retried, Cour d'Appel d'Amiens (3d Ch.), May 9, 1963, [1963] C.M.L.R. 239, aff'd, Cour de Cassation, Oct. 22, 1964, [1965] C.M.L.R. 36, the first two stages of which are discussed in Riesenfeld, "Antitrust Laws in the European Economic Community: A Sequel," 50 Calif. L. Rev. 829, 833–35 (1962); Cosnard, "Concession exclusive et refus de vente," 1962 Droit Chronique 40. From the *Grundig-Consten* decision, 1964 Journal Officiel 2545/64, [1964] C.M.L.R. 489, it seems that the Commission has no objection to an exclusive franchise per se. While it does not prohibit all exclusive distributorships, French law tends to be stricter on them than German or (at least until recently) United States law.

[131] Including, of course, suppliers in other member states; therefore, imports may be affected. See Reg. 17, art. 4(2)(i).

[132] See Note, "Restricted Channels of Distribution Under the Sherman Act," 75 Harv. L. Rev. 795, 796 (1962); Lockhard & Sacks, "The Relevance of Economic Factors in Determining Whether Exclusive Arrangements Violate Sec-

demand for dealers[133] and also reduces intra-brand competition. Of the three restrictions, the first is most likely to be objectionable in the context of a fully integrated Common Market;[134] the second, during the transitional stages.

Exclusive distributorships are compulsorily notifiable.[135] Territorial restrictions in a number of distributorship agreements may have an effect similar to that of a horizontal agreement for the sharing of markets between the dealers themselves.[136] The division of the market is less objectionable if no exclusive rights are given to either party; these rights, however, are usually the object of these agreements.

The effects of exclusive selling of one brand by dealers have been said[137] to depend on the following factors at the level of the supplier: the proportion of all the sales of competing products by tied dealers; the status within the industry of the supplier and the degree of competition at the level of the supplier; the extent to which other suppliers are using exclusive dealing; the duration of the agreement and the rapidity of change within the industry; the likelihood that other suppliers will find alternative outlets; and the reduction in costs to the supplier due to the arrangement. At the level of the dealer, two other factors are relevant: how far exclusive agreements bring new dealers into the market and how much these arrangements reduce dealers' costs. The last factor involved is closely related to policy: if exclusive dealerships were prohibited, would vertical integration result? This is important in the EEC, where, unlike in the United States, there is no legal restriction on forward integration or mergers.

TERRITORIAL RESTRICTIONS

If an exclusive dealership agreement[138] or a series of such agreements contains express provisions prohibiting exporting or dealing in imported goods, the agreement is compulsorily notifiable[139] and, because of its effects on interstate trade, is unlikely to be approved under Article 85(3).[140] An exclusive distributorship

---

tion 3 of the Clayton Act," 65 Harv. L. Rev. 913 (1952).

[133] Communication Concerning Exclusive Contracts . . ., 1962 Journal Officiel 2921-22/62, pursuant to Reg. 17, art. 22. In connection with the action already taken by the Commission, see Third General Report, para. 143 (1960); Fourth General Report, para. 50 (1961).

[134] Ladas, "Antitrust Laws of the Common Market . . .," 23 Ohio St. L.J. 709, 747 (1962).

[135] After being included in a draft of art. 4 of Regulation 17, exclusive distributorships were later omitted, apparently on the insistence of French lawyers.

[136] See Dr. Miles Medical Co. v. John D. Park & Sons Co., 220 U.S. 373 (1911). However, the object of the manufacturer may be merely to maximize sales; see Note, "Restricted Channels of Distribution Under the Sherman Act," 75 Harv. L. Rev. 795, 800, 823 (1962).

[137] Lockhart & Sacks, "The Relevance of Economic Factors in Determining Whether Exclusive Arrangements Violate Section 3 of the Clayton Act," 65 Harv. L. Rev. 913 (1952).

[138] Provided the dealer cannot be regarded as a commercial representative; Communication Concerning Exclusive Contracts . . ., 1962 Journal Officiel 2921-22/62.

[139] Reg. 17, art. 4(2)(i).

[140] If an agreement affects exports so as to fall within Regulation 17, art. 4(2)(i), but this effect is within Regulation 17, art. 4(2)(ii) or 4(2)(iii), and if there are no other restrictive clauses, the agreement is not compulsorily notifiable; Bosch v. de Geus, 8 Recueil 89, 107, [1962] C.M.L.R. 1, 30. An agreement by which a manufacturer in the EEC gives an enterprise outside the EEC exclusive rights to sell its goods in a non-member state does not affect trade between member states. This is so even when the distributor contracts not to sell the goods within the EEC, if the goods reimported into the EEC would be liable to a common external tariff, since then they would not be able to compete with the goods sold by distributors in the EEC even in the absence of a restrictive agreement; 1964 Journal Officiel 915-96/64.

agreement between an enterprise in a non-member state and an enterprise in a member state is compulsorily notifiable even if it does not relate to imports or exports between member states.[141] If interstate trade is affected by the agreement, prohibitions on sales out of the area allocated to a distributor are contrary to Article 85(1), even if the boundary of the area is not a national boundary.[142] They may, of course, be permitted under Article 85(3), but the Commission clearly dislikes territorial restrictions.[143] If inter-brand competition continues and if, for example, the distributor installs a substantial amount of equipment for assembling or after-sales servicing, a case can be made out for exclusive distributorships under Article 85(3), since territorial protection might be "indispensable" for the dealer to be willing to make the investment involved. Apart from the territorial restriction, the extent of the franchise must be considered.

INDIRECT MEASURES FOR EXCLUSIVE DEALING

Territorial restrictions on a dealer are often enforced by a compensation payment made by the dealer encroaching on the territory of another. If these payments are limited, for example, to the likely cost of free after-sales service to the dealer encroached on, they may be legitimate. A provision for such payments without a territorial restriction probably would be permitted. It is doubtful if the threat of refusing to sell to dealers who do not stay within territorial limits would be permissible, since it apparently would be contrary to both French and German law[144] and would simply be a method of enforcing a rule which itself would be illegal.

Some agreements similar to exclusive distributorships do not bind the dealer to sell only the goods of the supplier or to sell them only within a certain area, but operate by granting special rebates, discounts, or other advantages to dealers who do so. These are usually sanctions for an area-of-primary-responsibility clause.[145] This discrimination is contrary

---

See the *Grundig-Consten* decision, 1964 Journal Officiel 2545/64, [1964] C.M.L.R. 489; the distributor had been given absolute territorial protection, and the agreement was prohibited.

[141] Guide Pratique 11. This interpretation of art. 4(2)(i) is criticized by Becker, Extraterritorial Application of Common Market Laws (PLI, 1962), as discriminating against enterprises outside the EEC. If this discrimination represents a real difference of treatment, it seems unjustified; however, the Commission may have felt that since such agreements might not be dealt with by national laws, it needed to be aware of their existence. The validity of an agreement is not guaranteed where there is no obligation to notify; there is no presumption of invalidity where notification is required. An American company could divide the Common Market very effectively, for its distributors' benefit and perhaps also for its own, by a series of bilateral agreements with one distributor in each member state.

[142] United States v. White Motor Co., 194 F. Supp. 562 (N.D. Ohio 1961), held that territorial restrictions are per se violations of the Sherman Act. Exclusive franchises are not illegal per se in the United States, because they may be necessary in the interests of the dealer. For a criticism of this case, see Note, "Restricted Channels of Distribution Under the Sherman Act," 75 Harv. L. Rev. 795 (1962).

[143] For example, see Linssen, "The Antitrust Rules of the European Economic Community," 18 Record of N.Y.C.B.A. 289, 292 (1963).

[144] French Price Ordinance No. 45–1483 of June 30, 1945, as amended by Decrees No. 53-704 of Aug. 9, 1953, No. 58-545 of June 24, 1958, and No. 59-1004 of Aug. 17, 1959, art. 37(i)(a); Schapiro, "The German Law Against Restraints of Competition . . .," 62 Colum. L. Rev. 201, 202–203 (1962). The German law on exclusive dealerships may be stricter; Riesenfeld, "Antitrust Laws in the European Economic Community: A Sequel," 50 Calif. L. Rev. 829, 836 (1962).

[145] Note, "Restricted Channels of Distribution Under the Sherman Act," 75 Harv. L. Rev. 795, 797 (1962).

to Article 85(1)(d) if the object or effect is the restriction of competition. A supplier, however, might be allowed to do by inducements what he could not do by imposing a legal obligation, because in the former case the freedom of the dealer is not impaired.

SPECIAL NOTIFICATION PROCEDURE FOR BILATERAL EXCLUSIVE CONCESSION AGREEMENTS

A simplified form is provided[146] for notification of bilateral exclusive concession agreements in which one party contracts to purchase specified products for resale only from the other party, or in which one party contracts to supply certain products only to the other for resale only within a definite portion of the Common Market, or in which both types of obligation are undertaken. In theory this form of notification has procedural significance, but it deals with agreements which the Commission regards as unlikely to be objectionable, and the Commission now has power to give class exemptions to these agreements.

Territorial restrictions must always be notified in full. The supplier may bind himself to supply only to the distributor "for the purpose of resale within a specified part of the Common Market" but may not bind the distributor to stay within that area. The parties are required to certify that they have made no reciprocal agreement for the distribution of one another's goods, that no minimum resale price has been fixed, and that third parties are free to obtain the products involved from any other distributor in the Common Market, i.e., that the other distributors will not be liable to an action for unfair competition brought by the distributor under the agreement notified.[147]

Patent Licenses and Other Industrial and Commercial Property Agreements

THEIR IMPORTANCE IN LESS INDUSTRIALIZED COUNTRIES

Underindustrialized countries have special interests in the spheres of patents and know-how. Their laws should safeguard and encourage investors and should require inventions to be worked locally if any enterprise is willing to do so. Since the most profitable inventions are the result of industrial experience and research, industry in underindustrialized countries is most likely to expand through skillful commercial and technical use of patents and know-how licensed to local enterprises.[148] Less industrialized countries should see that international laws on restrictive practices are not so strict as to deter enterprises from making licensing agreements and providing technical experience.[149]

THE PATENT MONOPOLY UNDER NATIONAL LAWS AND COMMUNITY COMPETITION POLICY

Every patent confers on the owner a statutory monopoly within the country under whose laws the patent has been

[146] Reg. 153, Form B 1, 1962 Journal Officiel 2918-20/62.

[147] Federation of British Industries, European Economic Community—Restrictive Trade Practices 16 (1963).

On Regulation 153 generally, see van Bunnen, "Contrats d'agence et contrats de concession exclusive au regard de la règlementation du Marché commun," 1963 Journal des Tribunaux 429, who discusses its relationship to the Belgian Law of July 27, 1961; see also Jeantet, "Réflexions sur l'application du droit des ententes aux contrats comportant une clause d'exclusivité," 1963 J.C.P., Doctrine 1743, at 2.

[148] Germany and Japan are good examples of development by this means. Denmark is another; Myrdal, An International Economy 215 (1956).

[149] These considerations are more important to the proposed European patent law than to the antitrust rules of the EEC, but they do have a bearing on the latter and on the broader question of the Community's regional policy on competition.

obtained and a right to prevent the importation of goods infringing it. Article 36 of the EEC Treaty authorizes import restrictions, otherwise incompatible with the Common Market, when justified for the protection of local industrial and commercial property rights, if the restrictions are not used as a means of unjustified discrimination or as a disguised restriction on trade between member states. Division of markets and dominant market positions therefore result from different owners' holding similar patents in the various member states. Until the creation of a European patent[150] by a supplementary treaty, rights to patents under national laws will continue to be separate from one another, even if the same enterprise or group of enterprises owns the patent in each member state. The competition policy of the Commission must be built on the existing national laws until they are superseded by a European patent law. However, in addition to the reasons already given, patent-licensing agreements often include provisions relating to the fixing of prices[151] and the purchasing of raw materials, so there is the substantial problem of reconciling the existence of national patents with Articles 85 and 86.

If different ownership of national patents prevents trade between member states, patent licenses themselves may not affect interstate trade. However, it is unusual for there to be different patentees of similar patents in more than one or two of the member states. In German and United States law, restrictive provisions are valid if and, broadly, only if they are "within the scope of the patent monopoly." Since the national patent laws of member states differ, the concept of the scope of the patent monopoly[152] is a less useful tool for reconciling the patent and antitrust laws of the EEC than the laws of a national market with a single system of patent law. Because of Article 36, Article 85 must be construed and applied without diminishing the rights conferred on patentees by any national law.

The provisions of Regulation 17[153] are based on the principle of the scope of the patent monopoly. Bilateral agreements under which one party acquires or uses industrial property rights are optionally notifiable if their only anticompetitive effect is to limit the exercise

[150] See Comité de Coordination en matière de propriété industrielle institué par les Etats membres et la Commission de la C.E.E., Avant-Projet de Convention relatif à un droit éuropéen des brevets élaboré par le groupe de travail "Brevets" (1962); Froschmaier, "The Draft Convention on Patents in the Common Market," in Restrictive Practices, Patents, Trade Marks and Unfair Competition in the Common Market, Int'l & Comp. L.Q. Supp. No. 4, at 50 (1962); Froschmaier, "Progress Toward the Proposed Conventions for a European Patent and for a European Trademark," 6 Pat., T.M. & Copyright J. Research & Educ. 483 (1962); Johnston, "The Draft European Patent Convention," 1 Common Market L. Rev. 17 (1964); Deringer et al., 6 Revue du Marché Commun 172, 174–75 (1963); Oudemans, The Draft European Patent Convention (1963); Froschmaier, "Some Aspects of the Draft Convention Relating to a European Patent Law," 12 Int'l & Comp. L.Q. 17 (1963).

[151] Price-fixing clauses may deal only with the patented product or with competing products, if the licensee is permitted to sell them. In the latter case the question whether the clause is permissible will not be peculiar to patent licenses.

[152] See German Competition Law, §§ 20, 21; cf. U.K. Restrictive Trade Practices Act, 1956, 4 & 5 Eliz. 2, c. 58, § 8(4). See Verloren van Themaat, "Current Antitrust Developments in the European Common Market," 6 Pat., T.M. & Copyright J. Research & Educ. 432, 437–40 (1962); Buxbaum, "Patent Licensing: A Case Study on Antitrust Regulation Within the European Economic Community," 9 Antitrust Bull. 101, 124 (1964).

[153] Art. 4(2)(ii)(b). The Commission has power to issue class exemptions for restrictions imposed in connection with the acquisition or utilization of patent rights.

of the rights granted.[154] If rights of the patent licensee which are not derived from the agreement are limited, the agreement must be notified. Identifying the rights which are derived from a patent license is thus important.

RESTRICTIONS WITHIN THE SCOPE OF THE PATENT MONOPOLY

Because they are within the scope of the patent monopoly and their only anticompetitive effects are due to patent law, licenses of one or more patents of one or more member states, even if they are exclusive, are not affected by Article 85 if they contain no restrictive provisions. To hold otherwise would be to compel the patentee to work the patent himself and to prohibit him from sharing the patent and taking advantage of existing production and marketing facilities. Whether exclusive or not, patent licenses which do not restrict the activity of the licensee in any respect in which he was at liberty to act before entering into the agreement are not within Article 85(1). In themselves, they do not affect interstate trade. A patent license is a waiver or a sharing by the patentee of his monopoly position; even if the licensee is restrained from completely free use of the patent, there is still a net increase in the scope for competition. Those clauses in a simple patent license which limit the licensee to certain methods of using, manufacturing, or selling the product under the patent, where the prohibited methods could not be used in the absence of a license, are permissible because such clauses are within the scope of the patent. A limitation on the quantity of the patented product to be produced or on the number of acts of exploitation of a process patent, a limitation in time that is not longer than the duration of the patent, a limitation in area that limits a license to a particular factory or place of exploitation, or a clause prohibiting assignment or sublicensing are all permitted, since they do not come within Article 85(1).[155] They constitute an incomplete assignment of the bundle of rights of the patentee. The licensor may oblige the licensee to mark the product as being subject to a particular patent, since this does not restrain competition, or may oblige the licensee to maintain specified standards of quality. The right to use the patent may be reserved exclusively to the licensee and the licensor or to the licensee only;[156]

[154] "[D]es limitations dans l'exercise de *ces* droits." (Emphasis supplied.) The semi-official English translation in 1962 EEC Bull. No. 2, Supp., does not bring out this important point. See Ladas, "Antitrust Law in the Common Market . . .," 23 Ohio St. L.J. 709, 729 (1962); Timberg, "Antitrust and Patent Provisions of the European Common Market Treaty," in 3 Institute on Private Investments Abroad 173 (Southwestern Legal Foundation, 1961), and Nebolsine, "Antitrust Laws of the Common Market Countries," id. at 211. Mr. Nebolsine summarizes a list of normal restrictions in patent licenses in Europe prepared by the Commission d'Etudes de la Propriété Industrielle of the Belgian Group, International Association of Industrial Property (Sept. 6, 1958): (1) limiting the scope of exploitation under a license as to geographical area, technical scope, exclusivity, sales, licensee's own use, quantity, quality, and duration; (2) stipulating trading conditions for the products or services covered by the license with respect to prices, use of goods, or service; (3) fixing the system of remuneration, including lump sums, periodic royalties, minimum remuneration, and cross licenses; (4) imposing safeguards such as quality control or the obligatory use of specified raw materials, semi-manufactured products, components, or tools; (5) imposing conditions such as prohibiting license agreements with others or regulating the supply of goods manufactured or services performed under the license; and (6) pooling industrial property rights to exploit them. Id. at 225.

[155] Communication Concerning Patent License Agreements, 1962 Journal Officiel 2922-23/62, pt. I, translated in Honig, Brown, Gleiss & Hirsch, Cartel Law of the European Economic Community 26 (1963). See also 1962 Journal Officiel 2628-29/62.

[156] Communication Concerning Patent License Agreements, 1962 Journal Officiel 2922-23/62, pt. I.

in the latter case, the license is *pro tanto* an assignment. Cases in which the licensor is still permitted to use the patent himself and is merely prohibited from granting further licenses, the Commission believes, are not likely to affect trade between member states at present. A clause preventing the licensor from granting further licenses does not reduce existing competition, but merely prevents the licensor from creating the conditions for increased competition.[157]

The Commission indicates that its list of clauses automatically permitted in simple patent license agreements as being within the scope of the patent is not exhaustive.[158] There may be other types of clause which will be optionally notifiable[159] or may be held to be outside the terms of Article 85(1). It is not possible to say exactly to what extent Article 85(1) will be interpreted as enacting the principle of the scope of the patent monopoly.

RESTRICTIONS RELATED TO LICENSED PATENT RIGHTS BUT NOT WITHIN THE PATENT MONOPOLY

Article 4(2)(ii)(b) of Regulation 17 applies to agreements whose only anticompetitive effect is to limit the party acquiring certain rights (patents, trademarks, designs, models, or rights to use processes or know-how) in the exercise of these rights. There seem to be privileges which are related to the exercise or use of rights of these kinds but not included in the scope of these rights.[160] These privileges which are "normally and directly related to the exercise of the right" acquired[161] may be under Article 4(2)(ii)(b); if so, the agreement remains optionally notifiable. There are some clauses not mentioned in the communication on patent licenses which are permitted by § 20(2) of the German Competition Law and which may not necessarily be within Article 4(2)(ii)(b). In particular, § 20(2)(1) involves a number of criteria which should properly be considered by the Commission under Article 85(3), rather than by the parties who are deciding whether to notify the agreement in question.

CLAUSES OUTSIDE THE SCOPE OF THE PATENT MONOPOLY

Not all restrictive clauses binding the licensor of the patent are within the scope

[157] If the license provides that no further licenses shall be given on terms more favorable than those given to the licensee, it is submitted that art. 85(1) is not infringed. Where further licenses can be given only on less favorable terms, however, art. 85(1)(d) seems to apply. See Oberdorfer, Gleiss & Hirsch, Common Market Cartel Law 42–43 (1963). The latter type of provision seems to be less common than those mentioned in the text.

[158] Communication Concerning Patent License Agreements, 1962 Journal Officiel 2922-23/62, pt. IV.

[159] Under Reg. 17, art. 4(2)(ii)(b).

[160] Section 20(1) of the German Competition Law invalidates "agreements concerning the acquisition or the use of patents, registered designs, or protected brands . . . if they impose upon the acquirer or licensee any restrictions in his business conduct which go beyond the contents of the said privileges. . . ." Section 20(2) enumerates certain restrictions and obligations which are not subject to invalidation by § 20(1). Ladas, "Antitrust Law in the Common Market . . .," 23 Ohio St. L.J. 709, 729–30 (1962), argues that the words "contents" in § 20(1) and "exercise" in art. 4(2)(ii)(b) of Regulation 17 have different meanings and that the latter provision means "any restrictions which have a real rapport with the right involved (patent, trademark, design or know-how) or are normally and directly related to the exercise of the right involved should be . . . covered by . . . article 4(2)(ii)(b)," and that all the provisions of § 20(2) should be within that article. See Deringer et al., 7 Revue du Marché Commun 135, 141 (1964). On the German law, see Schapiro, "The German Law Against Restraints of Competition . . .," 62 Colum. L. Rev. 201, 231–34 (1962).

[161] Ladas, "Antitrust Law in the Common Market . . .," 23 Ohio St. L.J. 709, 729 (1962).

of the patent monopoly. Clauses which impose obligations that continue longer than the life of the patent or which prohibit the licensee from dealing in competitive products or from exporting to another member state[162] or which oblige the licensee to impose competitive restrictions on his purchasers[163] must be notified, since they cannot fall within the industrial property rights conferred.[164] Notification is necessary if an agreement requires the licensee to transfer to the licensor all patents for improvements made in connection with the type of product in question[165] or to use the licensor's trademarks on goods made under the patent licensed. These clauses may be permitted by the Commission under Article 85(3), but they are outside the scope of the patent monopoly and Article 4(2).

The extent to which a restriction outside the scope of the patent monopoly restrains competition and the extent to which it may be justified are for the Commision to decide in applying Article 85(3). A clause requiring the licensee to use only raw materials of a quality approved by the licensor does not restrain competition unreasonably if the standards imposed are necessary to the quality of the finished product manufactured under the patent. It is much more difficult to justify either a provision requiring the licensee to obtain his raw materials and components from the licensor[166] or a high royalty combined with a discount on these materials, which would have the same effect. The Commission's communication on patent licenses makes it clear that these restrictions are permissible only when quality standards cannot otherwise be prescribed and when the tying-in clause is essential to secure the technically faultless exploitation of the patent. This is the principle in German law.[167]

EXCHANGE OF INFORMATION

The licensee may be bound to convey to the licensor information on experience gained from using the patent or to give to the licensor licenses of improvement and application patents only if the obligation is reciprocal and if the licensee is free to convey the information or to license the new patents to third parties.[168] In these circumstances there is no adverse effect on competition and no infringement of Article 85(1). The licensor may be bound to give information or to license associated patents even if the obligation is not reciprocal and even if he is not permitted to give the information or to license the patents to third parties, because this merely enlarges the scope of the original license.

[162] Dealing in competitive products may be "indispensable" within art. 85(3) in the case of joint ventures. Exporting to another member state may be prohibited by another national patent not licensed by the agreement in question. Under one form of this type of provision, exports are permitted but there is a restriction that exported goods be sold only to limited types of purchasers.

[163] In Germany, as in the United States, the first authorized sale of a patented article exhausts the patent, so no restraints on the buyer of such an article are permitted which would not be permitted if no patent existed; Schapiro, "The German Law Against Restraints of Competition . . .," 62 Colum. L. Rev. 201, 220 (1962).

[164] Guide Pratique 12.

[165] An agreement probably could not require independent parallel inventions to be granted back; see the case before the Bundeskartellamt, 9 Wirtschaft und Wettbewerb 305 (1959), discussed by Buxbaum, "Antitrust Regulation Within the European Economic Community," 61 Colum. L. Rev. 402, 413 (1961).

[166] Art. 85(1)(e).

[167] Schapiro, "The German Law Against Restraints of Competition . . .," 62 Colum. L. Rev. 201, 223–24 (1962).

[168] See id. at 227; Ladas, "Antitrust Law in the Common Market . . . ," 23 Ohio St. L.R. 709, 737 (1962).

PRICE-FIXING

The case of price restrictions on resale by the licensee which are imposed by the licensor is difficult; the Commission did not include them in the category of clauses prima facie permitted, and they are normally subject to compulsory notification because of Article 4(2) of Regulation 17.[169] Fixing the prices of goods not sold by virtue of the license normally is not permitted. A price-fixing provision relating only to the patented goods is within the scope of the patent monopoly, but it usually is regarded as an improper way of limiting competition between the licensor and the licensee, and it may be contrary to Article 86. It may be justified, for example, in some cases to insure that the licensee has substantial profits, where the licensor is paid a royalty of a percentage of the licensee's profits.

TERRITORIAL RESTRICTIONS

If a licensor licenses similar national patents in different states to enterprises independent of each other, it is frequently provided expressly that the goods manufactured will not be exported into other member states. On its face, this merely reiterates the effect of national patent laws[170] where patents exist in other member states. In fact, however, this provision may be more restrictive than national patent laws because it is automatically binding, while the validity of a national patent may be disputed.[171] Such a clause certainly is not valid automatically, and the Commission is likely to require a justification for it. Even if it does merely restate the effects of national patent law and thus does not affect competition, the Commission is likely to suggest its removal.

If there is a concerted practice amounting to horizontal market-sharing between the various licensees, this must be notified,[172] even if each licensee is licensed only for an area within the same member state. The exemption from Article 85 of licenses for areas within a single member state is presumably not because such licenses are within the scope of the patent monopoly under national law but because they are unlikely to affect interstate trade.

CLAUSES PROHIBITING A CONTEST OF THE VALIDITY OF THE PATENT

The status of a clause which prohibits the licensee of a patent from contesting the validity of the patent licensed is not clear.[173] This is not within the scope of the patent, and it has an anticompetitive effect if the licensee is otherwise likely to attack the validity of the patent. How-

[169] Verloren van Themaat, "Current Antitrust Developments in the European Common Market," 6 Pat., T.M. & Copyright J. Research & Educ. 432, 446 (1962). On the German law, see Schapiro, "The German Law Against Restraints of Competition . . .," 62 Colum. L. Rev. 201, 225–27 (1962). Art. 4(2)(ii) is in the alternative: the agreement must only fix resale prices *or* limit the exercise of industrial property rights acquired.

[170] Oberdorfer, Gleiss & Hirsch, Common Market Cartel Law 43 (1963), argue that such a provision should automatically be valid; no authority is cited.

[171] Especially in those countries of the Six, such as France and Italy, in which patents are granted without any rigorous examination for novelty and the like. Campbell, "Common Market: Recent Changes and Notification," 107 Sol. J. 65, 66 (1962), points out the significance of the omission of clauses prohibiting the export of patented goods from the communication on exclusive-representation contracts after the inclusion of such clauses in the superseded draft communication. See Ladas, "Antitrust Laws of the Common Market . . .," 23 Ohio St. L.J. 709, 734 (1962).

[172] Guide Pratique 12.

[173] Oberdorfer, Gleiss & Hirsch, Common Market Cartel Law 40 (1963), say that such a clause "will as a rule be permissible" but give no authority, and appear to overstate the result of the reasons given. See Ladas, "Antitrust Laws of the Common Market . . .," 23 Ohio St. L.J. 709, 736 (1962).

ever, this clause may be a proper result of the settlement of an action to challenge the validity of the patent, and a license resulting from such a settlement increases competition. If the licensee[174] is prevented from contesting the validity of rights not licensed to him, it is submitted that Article 85(1) is clearly infringed. Section 20 of the German Competition Law permits such a prohibition only in connection with the patent licensed; since the Commission had this provision before it in drafting the communication, it is perhaps significant that they did not mention it.[175]

COMPLEX PATENT LICENSES

The provisions of the official communication just discussed seem to apply to package licensing agreements. Horizontal patent pools, agreements for future patents, "multiple parallel licenses," and cross licenses which reduce research competition between the participants must be notified. The term "multiple parallel licenses" refers to a series of exclusive or non-exclusive licenses of similar patents under the laws of different member states used when the licensors are the same company or associated companies but the licensees are unconnected. The territorial scope of each patent excludes other licensees[176] from each national market. Thus, multiple parallel licensing raises in an acute form the problem of the market-sharing caused by the existence of national patents. The licensor cannot be compelled to license all his patents for the whole Common Market to one licensee, since this would amount to compulsory licensing of national patents.[177] Only a European patent law providing for a European patent valid in all member states of the EEC can overcome this difficulty.

PATENT LICENSES AND ARTICLES 85(3) AND 86

Patents are unlikely to be more than a contributory factor in the abuse of a dominant market position under Article 86. Compulsory patent licensing under national laws prevents abuse of the patent monopoly by failure to work the patent.[178]

Even if patent licenses must be notified, and in cases under Article 4(2) of Regulation 17 where they are prohibited by Article 85(1), they are in a special position under Article 85(3). A patent license usually improves production or distribution and promotes technical or economic progress. Users of the goods usually get a reasonable share of the benefit of a patent license, either in price reduction or in improved service or quality. In the case of a process patent, the user benefits if the product is improved by the use of the patent or if some of the benefit resulting from the improvement in production techniques is passed on to him. A license of a product patent necessarily results in benefit to the user, since it has the effect of making a particular type of product available which would not otherwise be available. In all cases the restrictions on the parties to the patent license must be in-

[174] If a patent has been granted by a country in which patent applications are carefully investigated, and the licensor wishes to prevent the licensee's contesting similar patents in member countries where no investigation is made, the Commission might permit the license if the criteria used in all the countries were similar, since the grant of a patent would be strong evidence that the patents in the other countries would be valid.

[175] But see Honig, Brown, Gleiss & Hirsch, Cartel Law of the European Economic Community 24 (1963). In Germany patents are carefully examined before they are granted.

[176] Except other licensees of the same patent in the same member state, where the license is not exclusive.

[177] Oberdorfer, Gleiss & Hirsch, Common Market Cartel Law 38 (1963).

[178] Ladas, "Antitrust Laws of the Common Market . . .," 23 Ohio St. L.J. 709, 732 (1962).

dispensable to the improvement of production or distribution or the achievement of technical or economic progress; this is where practical difficulties are likely to arise. The parties are not allowed to eliminate competition as to a substantial part of the "goods concerned."[179] Except in the unusual cases where the patent license deals with other goods, this phrase can only mean the patented goods or goods produced under the patented process; but as to these goods, there can be no competition in member states in which valid patents exist, except between the patentee and its licensees. It therefore would be wrong to interpret this phrase as prohibiting parties from preventing competition from arising among themselves.

KNOW-HOW

Know-how is not mentioned in the communication on patent licenses, so apparently agreements dealing with it are still notifiable.[180] This is unfortunate, since most patent licenses also deal with know-how. Secret technical knowledge and expertise, by their nature, cannot be withdrawn once they have been handed over. Article 4(2)(ii)(b), however, equates restrictions on the rights of the recipient of information on manufacturing processes or knowledge about the utilization or application of industrial techniques with restrictions on the rights of a patent licensee. The effect of this seems to be that, by analogy with patent rights, the rights of the recipient of know-how may be limited to the extent to which they are rights to use information obtained under the agreement. Know-how and information which are not secret but merely difficult or expensive to obtain are within Article 4(2). The information must be technical; agreements for giving financial or commercial information must be notified in all cases if they include restrictive provisions.

Since know-how is not protected by statute, any restrictions on its use must be contractual. In the case of secret or valuable knowledge or information, licensed with other rights or not, those restrictions on disclosure to third parties which are necessary for the preservation of the know-how are permitted. These restrictions do not in themselves restrain competition, and they are analogous to clauses requiring the licensee to protect a patent or a trademark against invalidation.[181]

Restrictions on the freedom of the party acquiring the know-how to use it seem legitimate, if they do not continue after public disclosure has occurred through no fault of the licensee. If the know-how can be used on a wide variety of goods, it should be permissible to restrict the licensee's use of it to a limited number of types, by analogy with a patent license, since the net effect of the agreement is to increase competition. Restrictions on the licensee relating to the extent to which know-how may be used, such as variety of products, length of

[179] Cf. German Competition Law, § 20(3).

[180] Subject to Reg. 17, art. 4(2). See generally van Notten, "Know-How Licensing in the Common Market," 38 N.Y.U.L. Rev. 525 (1963); MacDonald, "Know-How Licensing and the Antitrust Laws," 62 Mich. L. Rev. 351 (1964).

[181] Ladas, "Antitrust Laws in the Common Market . . .," 23 Ohio St. L.J. 709, 745 (1962). Even if they restrain competition (which is possible), they should be regarded as automatically valid under art. 85(3) as being, in practice, essential to the willingness of the licensor to communicate the information. This is necessary since a patentee may legitimately exploit a patent either by working it himself or by licensing its use by others. However, this interpretation of the word "indispensable" in art. 85(3) would be peculiar to the field of know-how and is doubtful. Korah, "Competition: Cartels and Monopolies," in English Law and the Common Market 138, 154 (Keeton & Schwarzenberger ed. 1963), suggests that contractual restrictions preserving the secrecy of know-how are protected by art. 222 even if they are anticompetitive.

time, and place of utilization,[182] constitute an incomplete contractual transfer of the right to use the knowledge acquired.

Since the licensor has no legal right to a monopoly of his secret knowledge, he may be held to have no right to restrict its use after he has terminated his monopoly. The argument in favor of this is that the recipient of the know-how could have discovered it himself and used it without any restriction being placed on him. This argument disregards the fact that the research involved would duplicate work already done by the transferor of the know-how. Unpatented know-how is not necessarily unpatentable; it may be unpatented for sound commercial reasons. If the recipient would have difficulty in obtaining the know-how elsewhere, the net effect of the agreement may be to increase competition, even if it contains anticompetitive provisions, and the economic situation may be similar to that where a patent gives a legal monopoly in the know-how. Whether the analogy with a patent applies, therefore, depends on the nature of the know-how. The difficulty of obtaining the know-how elsewhere within a reasonable time must be balanced against the extent to which the agreement restricts competition.[183]

If the analogy to a patent is not accepted, all restrictions on the use to which the knowledge, once transferred, may be put—including time limits and territorial limits on the use of the know-how,[184] and limits on the freedom to market the resulting product[185]—will have to be justified under Article 85(3).[186]

KNOW-HOW AGREEMENTS AND ARTICLE 85(3)

Price-fixing on goods produced as a result of the know-how must be justified under Article 85(3).[187] A problem arises in connection with the negative requirements of Article 85(3)(a) and 85(3)(b). Is the extent and value of the know-how such that the resulting goods are different in kind from goods produced without the know-how? If so, competition as to the goods made with the know-how must be maintained between the licensor and the licensee,[188] unless the same knowl-

[182] Ladas, "Antitrust Laws of the Common Market . . .," 23 Ohio St. L.J. 709, 746 (1962), regards these two restrictions as contrary to art. 85(1).

[183] Id. at 745. These factors are all relevant if it is necessary to invoke art. 85(3). If the know-how given is not adequate consideration for the benefit to the licensor, the object of the agreement may be anticompetitive.

[184] Some experts have taken the view that territorial limitations on the use of know-how which coincide with national frontiers would be valid without reference to art. 85(3). It is submitted that while restrictions on the extent to which know-how may be used may be justifiable automatically by analogy with restrictions within the scope of the patent monopoly, this cannot be true of restrictions on the marketing of products made through the use of the know-how; see Reg. 17, art. 4(2)(ii)(b), and German Competition Law, § 21, on the analogy between patents and know-how.

[185] In territorial area, in prices to be charged, or in purchases to be permitted—all clearly contrary to art. 85(1).

[186] Since the only limits on the types of goods on which know-how can be used result from the nature of the know-how, it may be legitimate to restrain the licensee from dealing in the products of enterprises other than the licensors in order to prevent the products of others from benefiting from the know-how shared by the contracting parties.

[187] Reg. 17, art. 4(2)(i)(a), applies only where goods pass under the anticompetitive agreement.

[188] It has been argued on p. 405 that the licensor and licensee of a patent may prevent competition between themselves because the general patent law prohibits competition between them in the absence of a license. The elimination of competition, which otherwise would be contrary to art. 85(3)(b), is thus not a change due to the agreement. It would be absurd to say that where a patent is licensed for its full term the licensor cannot contract not to use it, although this contract eliminates

edge is possessed by some third party. However, when the goods produced by the know-how are a distinct type, a licensor is especially anxious to prevent competition from his licensee. The Commission, in trying to protect competition, must not impose conditions on licensors which will deter them from licensing their know-how, since there are no compulsory licensing provisions for know-how and a license given to an enterprise prepared to pay for it is normally in the interests of economic progress and production.[189]

Restricting the use of publicly known information is not permitted. The existence of a patent for a particular process in any member country will mean that the information is available to the public.

The German Competition Law equates agreements dealing with the transfer or exploitation of legally unprotected inventions, manufacturing processes, and technical designs, if they constitute business secrets, with patent licenses.[190] It therefore permits price-fixing, reciprocal but exclusive obligations to exchange information, and other restrictions concerning goods made with acquired know-how, and these might be permitted under Article 85(3).

TRADEMARKS

The attitude of the Commission on trademark licenses is different from its attitude on patent licenses, although it has not yet been worked out in detail and no communications have dealt with the subject. As far as the nature of trademarks under national laws permits or requires, they are treated in a way similar to patents, but the following remarks should be treated with caution.

The national laws of the Six differ on whether a trademark may be licensed or assigned without the goodwill of the business with which it is associated. The validity of a license and the extent to which various types of restrictions are valid therefore depend in the first instance on national law. Since some national laws require public use or knowledge of a trademark for validity, an enterprise is less likely to own a complete set of trademarks in each member state than a complete set of patents. The existence of a trademark does not prevent the production and distribution of goods not bearing the trademark.[191] A restriction on the use of a trademark therefore does not limit competition from unmarked goods of the same type. An enterprise obtains a license of a trademark to take advantage of the goodwill which goes with it. In practice, licenses usually are given only when a patent also is being licensed or when goods, raw materials, or component parts are sold to the licensee. Although the use of a trademark is not limited to products of a given quality, the licensor has an interest in protecting the goodwill of the trademark. He has the exclusive right to mark the goods so as to advertise them as having a known quality and origin. Restrictions on the quality of the marked goods sold and the requirement that materials should be obtained from the licensor, if this is necessary to maintain quality, are

---

competition between the parties. In the case of know-how, the possessor's freedom from competition is not legally protected. For this reason, it seems likely that know-how is not analogous to patents in this respect.

[189] In the case of know-how, even more than in the case of patents, less developed countries and regions have an interest in legal freedom to license and convey information to their enterprises.

[190] Section 21; see Schapiro, "The German Law Against Restraints of Competition . . .," 62 Colum. L. Rev. 201, 234–36 (1962).

[191] There is thus no public interest in insuring that invalid trademarks are cancelled, and covenants not to contest the validity of trademarks do not substantially restrain competition. See Henkel & Cie GmbH v. Sommer, Oberlandesgericht, Hamm (Westfalen), Dec. 20, 1963, [1964] C.M.L.R. 509.

clearly legitimate. They seem obviously to be within Article 4(2)(ii)(b) of Regulation 17, but like restrictions on production, technical development, or investment, or restrictions on the licensee's freedom to acquire materials or components, they may also be within Article 85(1). Limitations within the scope of the rights acquired can relate only to the time, area, type, and quality of goods in connection with which the licensee can use the trademark. A requirement that a trademark always be used on goods made under a patent license from the same licensor or be used on only those goods does not seem to be within Article 85(1). A restriction on the purchasers to whom the licensee may sell the marked goods seems to be outside Article 85(1). However, a provision prohibiting the licensee from dealing in goods not under the trademark in question would probably be prohibited.[192]

As in the case of patents, the existence of separately owned trademarks under each national law restricts export of the marked goods. Only a European trademark law can abolish this. In several cases[193] it has been held that a trademark owner who gives a license in one country cannot rely on the territorial nature of his other trademarks to limit the goods produced under the license to the country to which the license applied. If these decisions are applied in all the member states, territorial restrictions on the use of licensed trademarks will be impossible without express provisions, and the anticompetitive effect of such restrictions will have to be judged under Article 85.

Neither trademarks nor know-how is normally licensed independently of other licensing or contractual arrangements, but discussion here is limited to clauses in pure trademark licenses.[194] A combined agreement must be considered as a whole under Article 85(3). Only if each provision can be regarded as being outside Article 85(1) or under Article 4(2) is the obligation to notify avoided.

MODELS AND DESIGNS

The Commission has gone no further than Regulation 17, Article 4(2), in its official pronouncements on models and designs. These are intermediate between patents, which give a monopoly to the patentee in the utilization of a particular product or process, and trademarks, which give no monopoly to any type of goods or process. The treatment of all kinds of industrial and commercial property under Article 85 can be expected in due course to take account of the similarities and differences between them.

Unequal conditions for equivalent engagements—Obligation to contract[195]

Discrimination on the grounds of nationality is prohibited generally by Article 7 and in certain sectors by Articles 37, 48, and 79.[196] It is incompatible with the

[192] See Ladas, "Antitrust Laws of the Common Market . . .," 23 Ohio St. L.J. 709, 738–44 (1962).

[193] Discussed in id. at 740–42. The cases are Prins v. Grundig, Supreme Court of the Netherlands, 1957 International Gewerblicher Rechtsschutz und Urheberrecht 259; Philips A.G. v. Radio-Import GmbH, Supreme Court of Switzerland, Oct. 4, 1960, 86(II.) Entscheidungen des Schweizerischen Bundesgerichtes 270; and the *Maza* case, Frankfurt Court of Appeals, Feb. 2, 1962, reported in Aussenwirtschaftsdienst des Betriebs-Beraters, July 1962, at 203–206.

[194] For the law in the Netherlands on trademark licenses in exclusive-dealership agreements, see Riesenfeld, "Antitrust Laws in the European Economic Community: A Sequel," 50 Calif. L. Rev. 829, 838–40 (1962).

[195] See generally U.K. Monopolies and Restrictive Practices Commission on Collective Discrimination, Report, Cmd. 9504 (1953). This report is reproduced in Wilberforce, Campbell & Elles, Restrictive Trade Practices and Monopolies, app. II (1957).

[196] See also art. 42. ECSC Treaty, art. 60, prohibits discrimination even if practiced by one enterprise only.

Common Market, whether practiced by enterprises or by the organs of member states. Discrimination against an enterprise from outside the EEC is prohibited if the discrimination distorts competition within the EEC and affects interstate trade.[197] Article 85(1)(d) applies in all cases of collective or concerted discrimination. The agreement to discriminate is illegal, but actual discrimination without any agreement to do so is not,[198] except in the case of a monopoly or oligopoly under Article 86. It seems, therefore, that *de facto* non-collusive discriminatory enforcement of permitted resale price maintenance agreements is not illegal.[199] Discriminating against non-members of a trade association is illegal if it is intended to force them to join it.[200] Discrimination prohibited by Article 85 may be unintentional; an agreement to give discounts for quantity purchasing which gives to large purchasers a discount greater than the saving to the seller which results from the size of the delivery is illegal. Any application of unequal conditions, irrespective of the nature of the conditions or the reasons for their application, is forbidden if the transactions are equivalent. Presumably, the nature and extent of the differentiation must be related to the differences between the transactions.[201] Grossly unequal treatment for similar transactions is prohibited, because for the purposes of assessing the discrimination in question, the transactions are substantially equivalent. To compare two transactions or types of transaction, all of the circumstances must be considered. Problems arise if the preferential treatment is given only when the other contracting enterprise is a member of a trading group. The strict view is that differences which justify discriminatory treatment must be purely economic or commercial differences representing ultimately a return in cash profits to the enterprise discriminating.[202] Apart from discrimination contained in agreements which are anticompetitive for other reasons, discrimination can be justified by any common economic interest, if the economic benefits resulting from it are proportionate to the discrimination practiced and if the benefits from the association are reciprocal.

Economic differences, such as increased seller's profits due to frequency or size of purchases by a regular customer or differences in the terms of the contracts, may justify unequal treatment for otherwise equivalent transactions. The standing of the purchaser is relevant to the extent to which credit is given, although this is a discrimination favoring an enterprise which, by definition, does not need it.[203]

[197] While art. 7 is absolute in its terms, it is not clear whether discrimination on the grounds of nationality against a national of a non-member state is permitted. See van Hecke, "The Prohibition Against Discrimination in the European Economic Community," in 1 Cartel and Monopoly in Modern Law 341, 343 (1961); Houssiaux, Concurrence et Marché Commun 77–79, 81–83, 87–91 (1960).

[198] See U.K. Restrictive Trade Practices Act, 1956, 4 & 5 Eliz. 2, c. 68, § 6(4), 6(5).

[199] German law prohibits this; Schapiro, "The German Law Against Restraints of Competition . . .," 62 Colum. L. Rev. 201, 207 (1962).

[200] With regard to activities intended to bring about indirectly what could not be done by restrictive agreement, see German Competition Law, §§ 25, 26–27, 38.

[201] See German Competition Law, § 3(1). The French law—Decree No. 53–704 of Aug. 9, 1953, as amended, art. 37(1)(a)—prohibits discrimination not justified by "an equivalent increase in the cost of production or the cost of performing the service."

[202] Section 26 of the German Competition Law is interpreted as permitting discrimination based on intrinsically justified motives (such as family relationship) even if they do not constitute consideration received by the party discriminating.

[203] On the other hand, if the prices charged favor a purchaser with a low profit-making capacity as against one with high profits, who

Other purely economic factors justifying discriminatory treatment may result from agreements which are open to question under Article 85(1). Discrimination in favor of enterprises which purchase consignments of unrelated products with the commodity they need may be a method of encouraging purchasers to accept tying-in[204] provisions. Such discrimination may be justified economically by the profit derived from the sale of the unrelated products but may nevertheless be objectionable.

Since it is the agreement to discriminate[205] and not the actual discrimination which is illegal, it is not normally necessary to investigate the details of contracts made by the discriminating enterprise, except where evidence of a concerted practice is sought. The agreement must be looked at to see if it requires different terms to be given in transactions which are, in fact, equivalent. The categories into which transactions are divided must have or must be intended to have the effect of distorting competition; if not, discrimination practiced by individual parties to the agreement is not prohibited.

Even if the transactions are equivalent, discrimination is not prohibited if the parties treated differently are not in competition with one another and therefore no competitive disadvantage can result.[206] On the other hand, collective discrimination is probably illegal even if adequate supplies of equivalent goods on the better terms are available to the purchaser elsewhere.

The prohibition on collective discrimination probably does not involve an obligation to contract with enterprises against which discrimination was intended, but merely an obligation to apply normal terms if a contract is entered into.[207] Where a dominant market position exists, there probably is an obligation to contract.[208] If there is no obligation to contract under Article 85, the way is left open for enterprises to enforce by refusal to trade[209] a restriction which

can afford the extra price, this discrimination, though it favors enterprises which need help, distorts competition by bolstering uneconomic enterprises, and it may not work in the public interest.

[204] Contrary to art. 85(1)(e). See German Competition Law, §§ 25–27. Art. 85 would not apply to such a provision if it was imposed by a single enterprise, though art. 86 might be invoked.

[205] The better view seems to be that art. 85(1)(d) applies both to vertical and to horizontal agreements. See Bosch v. de Geus, 8 Recueil 89, 111 passim, [1962] C.M.L.R. 1, 5 passim (conclusions of Advocate-General Lagrange).

[206] This is not clear from the translation by Her Majesty's Foreign Office. See Theising, "The Rules Governing Competition Within the European Regional Communities," 26 Law & Contemp. Prob. 464 (1961).

[207] Van Hecke, "The Prohibition Against Discrimination in the European Economic Community," in 1 Cartel and Monopoly in Modern Law 341, 345 (1961).

[208] See Fourth General Report, para. 50 (1961); this report does not make it clear whether a dominant market position existed or whether the refusal which was prohibited by the Commission was discrimination on the grounds of nationality. Some boycotts are illegal under national law; Grisoli, "Rapport sur le Boycottage en Droit Italien," 10 Travaux de l'Association Henri Capitant pour la Culture Juridique Française 171 (1959); Huss, "Rapport sur le Boycottage en Droit Luxembourgeois," id. at 176.

[209] France specifically prohibits refusal to trade; Price Ordinance No. 45-1483 of June, 1945, as amended by Decrees No. 53–704 of Aug. 9, 1953, No. 58-545 of June 24, 1958, and No. 59-1004 of Aug. 17, 1959, art. 37(1). For a commentary on art. 37(1), see "Circulaire Fontanet" of March 31, 1960, 1960 J.O.R.F. 3048, 3049–51. Art. 37 prohibits both refusals to deal and refusals to deal on anything but discriminatory terms. Discrimination is illegal only if it is practiced "habitually." The defendant must have failed to carry out the transaction "in accordance with commercial custom," which is said to be the "customs of trade, not contrary to the spirit of the law, and having the

they could not enforce by way of an agreement.[210] It would be a serious weakness in the Community law if there were no obligation to contract in the case of a cartel, although serious discrimination is hardly possible unless it is accompanied by a measure of dominant power, since adequate alternative sources of supply are readily available. Article 7 may prescribe an obligation to contract in the case of a refusal on the grounds of nationality,[211] but this is not certain. It would be anomalous if refusal to contract, the most drastic type of discrimination, should go unpunished.

There is nothing in Article 86 to indicate that it prohibits boycotts and that Article 85 does not. The argument is that refusal to contract is an abuse of a dominant market position, even though it is not covered by any of the examples of abuse given in Article 86.[212] However, though it has little support from the wording of the Article, the view that a concerted refusal to contract contravenes the general part of Article 85 by preventing, restricting, or distorting competition would certainly lead to the most desirable result.

In the ECSC, price publication has been required in order to prevent price

---

characteristics required by commercial law." Id. at 3050, § I(2)(B). If the request is abnormal, the refusal is not illegal; it can be abnormal if it is out of proportion either to the needs of the purchaser or the business of the seller or if unusual methods of delivery or terms on quality or other terms are requested. On the French law, see Nicolas & Société Brandt v. Société Photo Radio Club, Cour d'Appel de Paris, Feb. 7, 1961, retrial ordered, Cour de Cassation (Ch. Crim.), July 11, 1962, [1962] C.M.L.R. 93, retried, Cour d'Appel d'Amiens (3d Ch.), May 9, 1963, [1963] C.M.L.R. 239, aff'd, Cour de Cassation, Oct. 22, 1964, [1965] C.M.L.R. 36. See Bergsten, "Refusal to Sell as a Violation of Anti-Price Maintenance Legislation—The French Experience," 49 Iowa L. Rev. 42 (1963); Goldstein, "Administrative Shaping of French Refusal to Deal Legislation," 11 Am. J. Comp. L. 515 (1962).

Collective boycotts are illegal in the Netherlands also.

[210] A manufacturer or supplier may announce that it will refuse to deal with distributors who do not comply with certain restrictions. Such an announcement is not prohibited by art. 85(1) unless the participation of distributors is such as to bring about the concerted practice. See Turner, "The Definition of Agreement Under the Sherman Act: Conscious Parallelism and Refusals to Deal," 75 Harv. L. Rev. 655, 684–706 (1962). German Competition Law, §§ 25, 38, prohibits threats or promises which induce activities which could not be made the subject of agreement; on entry into trade, see German Competition Law, § 27; Schapiro, "The German Law Against Restraints of Competition . . .," 62 Colum. L. Rev. 1, 16, 45, 201, 202 (1962); Steindorff, "Restrictive Practices Laws of Germany," in Restrictive Practices, Patents, Trade Marks and Unfair Competition in the Common Market, Int'l & Comp. L.Q. Supp. No. 4, at 28, 33 (1962). Turner, "The Definition of Agreement Under the Sherman Act: Conscious Parallelism and Refusal to Deal," 75 Harv. L. Rev. at 686–87, states: "[A] distinction between a program of resale price maintenance effected by contracts and 'agreements,' and one effected by refusal to deal, is wholly untenable as a practical *or* logical matter unless 'agreement' is defined to exclude tacit or implied agreements." Since art. 85 applies to concerted practices, it would be unreasonable for the EEC not to prohibit discriminatory refusals to deal. Turner's conclusion is: "Whether induced by a threat of refusal to deal or not, acquiescence in a seller's policy as to resale (or a buyer's policy as to dealings with a buyer's competitors) should be enough to establish vertical agreements between the buyer and the seller." Id. at 705–706. Turner's article has provoked the interest of the Commission, and it is submitted that it should be followed, but it is not clear whether the Commission will do so.

See Spaak Report 53–54.

[211] This would deal only with cases which are unimportant commercially and economically. From the point of view of the EEC, refusal based on nationality, at least if the victim is a national of a member state, is the most objectionable form of refusal to trade.

[212] See Deringer et al., 6 Revue du Marché Commun 347, 349 (1963).

discrimination.[213] In the sectors under the EEC, however, such a requirement would be more likely to interfere with competition by causing price-fixing than to promote it by ending discrimination.

Unconnected additional obligations

Article 85(1)(d) prohibits contracts which require one party to include in his contracts with third parties "tying-in" clauses, which compel purchasers to buy, as part of their transactions, unrelated goods which they do not want. The clauses themselves are prohibited when insisted on by an enterprise with dominant market power[214] or by several enterprises as a result of an agreement or concerted practice; they are not prohibited when imposed by a single enterprise on others purchasing from it.[215] This prohibition, apart from its economic importance, prevents enterprises from retaining their national markets for a product which can be made better elsewhere in the EEC, by means of agreements or concerted practices which tie that product to one in which they still retain an advantage.

Tying-in is prohibited only if the tied goods are not connected with the goods desired by the purchaser, either by their nature or by commercial practice. The commercial practice need not exist throughout the whole of the Common Market; it is sufficient if it exists where the parties carry on business or where a market-dominating enterprise or possibly its customers do business.[216]

Tying-in clauses have two anticompetitive effects which must be considered separately under Article 85(3). The first is that they place the enterprises selling the required goods at an advantage vis-à-vis other suppliers of the unwanted goods. The second is that they place the purchasers at a competitive disadvantages vis-à-vis other purchasers of the products actually desired. Article 85(3)(b) relates only to the first effect; Article 85(3)(a) relates only to the second. The occasions in which tying agreements will be economically justified, except where they are sanctioned by ordinary commercial practice, are probably rare.[217]

Article 85(3)

The Function of the Commission—Prospective or Retroactive?

If agreements, decisions, or concerted practices are within the terms of Article 85(1), they are valid only if they are justified under Article 85(3). The Commission[218] alone has power to declare

[213] ECSC Treaty, art. 60. See the *Price List* cases, 1 Recueil 10 (1954–55), discussed by Lagrange, "The Role of the Court of Justice of the European Communities as Seen Through Its Case Law," 26 Law & Contemp. Prob. 400, 408–409 (1961), where the conflict between the principles mentioned in the text is pointed out.

[214] Art. 86. See German Competition Law, § 18(1)(4); French Ordinance No. 45–1483, as amended, art. 37(1)(c).

[215] Cf. U.S. Clayton Act, § 3, 15 U.S.C. § 14 (1964). This presumably is because, unless it is a monopoly or a member of an oligopoly or a party to a concerted practice by which tying-in clauses are required, a single enterprise is hardly in a position to force unwanted goods on a purchaser. Like discrimination, tying-in clauses are likely to have serious effects only when the enterprises requiring them have a measure of market dominance, but this is true to some degree of all anticompetitive practices.

[216] Oberdorfer, Gleiss & Hirsch, Common Market Cartel Law 81 (1963), say that a commercial practice where the customer carries on business is sufficient. In the case of an agreement under art. 85, the place of residence of the customers seems less relevant, since the enterprises will not always be sure where their customers will come from and since it is the agreement, not the tying-in clause, which is prohibited.

[217] Lockhard & Sacks, "The Relevance of Economic Factors in Determining Whether Exclusive Arrangements Violate Section 3 of the Clayton Act," 65 Harv. L. Rev. 913, 942–54 (1952).

[218] Reg. 17, art. 9(1).

Article 85(3) applicable. It may approve single agreements, decisions, or concerted practices or classes of certain bilateral agreements and licenses of industrial and commercial property.[219]

Article 85(3) provides that Article 85(1) may be "declared inapplicable" to agreements within the terms of Article 85(3).[220] Since Regulation 17 makes notification a prerequisite for approval under Article 85(3)[221] of multilateral and some bilateral agreements, decisions under Article 85(3) are prospective. For certain bilateral and relatively inoffensive agreements[222] and for agreements existing at the time Regulation 17 went into force, approval is in effect retroactive.[223]

If Article 85(3) is an automatic exception to the prohibition in Article 85(1), the Commission has no discretion in applying it. If Article 85(3) creates a prospective power, the power may be discretionary or the Commission may be obliged to approve, at least prospec-

[219] Apparently it may apply art. 85(3) to a class of agreements not within Regulation 17, art. 4(2) or 5(2), if at all, only if all the agreements approved have been notified. On a reputed difference of opinion between the Commission and the Council, see Committee on Foreign Law, "Current Legal Developments in the European Economic Community," 18 Record of N.Y.C.B.A. 329, 333, 334 (1963). The difference of opinion apparently was that the Commission took the view that art. 85(3) and Regulation 17, arts. 6(1), 9(1), gave it power to declare art. 85(1) and 85(2) inapplicable, in advance, to categories of agreements within art. 85(1), and the Council took the view stated in the first sentence of this note. The Council's view apparently prevailed, and the communications published were not class exemptions under art. 85(3) but merely set out some types of agreement which were not regarded as being within art. 85(1). If this accurately represents the difference of view, it is submitted that the Council was correct; see Reg. 17, art. 6. The problem is discussed by Bernini, "Problèmes concernant l'application de l'article 85, No. 3 du Traité C.E.E. à certaines catégories d'accords restreignant la concurrence," 1963 Journal des Tribunaux 345; see also van Bunnen, "Contrats d'agence et contrats de concession exclusive au regard de la réglementation du Marché Commun," 1963 Journal des Tribunaux 429, 430; Deringer, "The Distribution of Powers in the Enforcement of the Rules of Competition Under the Rome Treaty," 1 Common Market L. Rev. 30, 34–35 (1963). If the Commission or the Council purported to exempt any category of agreements which was not clearly within art. 85(3), the action could be illegal, since art. 85 authorizes approval only of cartels which fall within art. 85(3). Deringer et al., 6 Revue du Marché Commun 256, 262 (1963), raise the question whether the Council could enlarge under art. 87 the scope of art. 85(3) and conclude that it could to some extent. The problem discussed above is also analyzed; id. at 262–64; see also Deringer et al., 7 Revue du Marché Commun 245, 246, and at 448, 450. See art. 235. For the regulation authorizing the Commission to issue approvals for classes of agreements and the opinion of the Economic and Social Committee on it, see 1964 Journal Officiel 3318-22/64. See Reg. 19, 1965 Journal Officiel 533/65.

[220] The question arose whether art. 85(3) gives an automatic exemption from art. 85(1) and 85(2) for all agreements within its terms, operating from the time when they are entered into, or whether it confers a power to exempt agreements from the previous provisions of the article, the exemption being prospective and not retroactive. See Deringer Report, A.P.E. Doc. No. 57, paras, 59–64, "Réserve d'autorisation ou exception légale," and paras. 12–16 (1961–62); Françon, "Les Ententes et les Monopoles selon le Traité de Rome," 89 Journal de Droit International 368, 374 (1962); Deringer, Some Practical Aspects of the Antitrust Provisions of the Treaty of Rome 5–7 (1962); Buxbaum, "Patent Licensing: A Case Study on Antitrust Regulation Within the European Economic Community," 9 Antitrust Bull. 101, 130–36 (1964). As to the direct applicability of arts. 85 and 86, see Chapter Sixteen, note 1.

[221] Reg. 17, arts. 4(1), 5(1), 9(1).

[222] Reg. 17, arts. 4(2), 5(2). If art. 85(3) was automatic, the Commission would not have been entitled to turn it, by regulation, into a mere power.

[223] The Commission has issued several sets of interpretations of art. 85. None of them solves the problem of the interpretation of art. 85(3). Regulation 17 was regarded by the member states as a compromise under which prospective decisions under art. 85(3) could be made retroactive.

tively, an agreement which comes within Article 85(3). The question is one of theoretical rather than practical importance, at least for the next few years, because of the numerous inexact criteria embodied in Article 85. Until a considerable body of case law is built up by the Commission and, in particular, by the Court, the Commission has a considerable amount of freedom in the application of the law. However, the duty to apply criteria incapable of exact legal definition is not the same thing as discretion to refuse to apply a provision when the criteria are fulfilled.

The better view seems to be that the Commission has a duty rather than a discretion to apply Article 85(3) if the requirements are fulfilled.[224] It seems that the Commission in all cases has a duty under Article 85(1) to decide if the agreement affects competition "adversely." If this is correct, the Commission may permit a restrictive agreement that has no adverse effect on trade even if the agreement does not comply with Article 85(3). In the application of Article 85(3), the Commission must consider if the agreement improves production or promotes progress[225] and if the means used are essential to this end; if so, and if the other requirements are met, there seems to be no room for discretion. The Commission is free, however, to choose between long-term and short-term public good.

The Court's jurisdiction[226] to review the decisions of the Commission is limited if the Commission's powers are discretionary; strong reasons are required for limiting the powers of the Court in such an important respect. It is illogical to hold that the Court can review the application by the Commission and national authorities of Article 85(1), which apparently requires policy consideration of the favorable or unfavorable effects of an agreement, but cannot review the power of the Commission to apply the more precisely drafted Article 85(3) unless the Commission has seriously misused its discretion.[227]

The Requirements of Article 85(3)

Article 85(3), which is similar in terms to Article 65(2) of the ECSC Treaty, prescribes two positive and two negative requirements. The first positive requirement is that an agreement must either help improve the production or distribution of goods (or presumably services, since Article 85(1) applies to them) or must help promote technical or economic progress.[228] The two requirements are

[224] Oberdorfer, Gleiss & Hirsch, Common Market Cartel Law 67 (1963); Deringer et al., 6 Revue du Marché Commun 256, 258 (1963). The permissive wording of art. 85(3) indicates that a power is given and does not prove that the power is discretionary. The Commission has a discretion whether to grant general category exemptions or to approve specific agreements. It apparently has a discretion as to when approval under art. 85(3) is to take effect; Reg. 17, art. 6(1).

Similar problems arise under arts. 92–93. The Federation of British Industries, European Economic Community—Restrictive Trade Practices 3 (1963), says that "the Commission is an administrative body and will no doubt exercise in some measure the kind of discretionary power which is implicit in administration."

[225] Art. 85(3)(a), 85(3)(b).

[226] Reg. 17, art. 17; EEC Treaty, art. 172.

[227] Art. 173. Regulation 17, art. 17, gives the Court full jurisdiction, including power to modify the Commission's decisions in cases where the Commission has fixed a fine or penalty.

[228] With regard to horizontal restraints, see French Decree of Aug. 9, 1953, as amended, art. 59(3). U.K. Restrictive Trade Practices Act, 1956, § 21, sets out the possible justifications for registrable agreements; these justifications are strict but considerably more explicit than art. 85(3). See Pennington, "Restrictive Trade Practices in the Common Market," 106 Sol. J. 458, 460 (1962). Art. 85(3) differs from art. 65(2) of the ECSC Treaty in that it adds the requirement that a share of the benefit must be passed on to the consumer. The German Competition Law expressly authorizes agree-

alternatives, although they are similar and most agreements eligible for approval will comply with both; they cover almost any benefits which could be claimed for restrictive agreements. Increased production or supply of existing types of goods, production or supply of a type not previously available, rationalization of or economies in production or distribution, and specialization or increase in the number or quality of outlets may all fulfill the first positive requirement. Bearing in mind that the other requirements of Article 85(3) must also be fulfilled, the effects of the agreement must be considered as a whole[229] to see if a net improvement is brought about. The agreement must objectively have the effect required; the intention of the parties to the agreement is irrelevant. The agreement need only have the effect of helping to improve production; the improvement need not be achieved prior to approval.

The second positive requirement, which is much more specific, is that a fair share of the benefit of the agreement must be passed on to the users. The people benefited may be any users or consumers of the goods or services involved; the ultimate consumer need not benefit.[230] The benefit need not necessarily be in reduction of price. Any economic advantage resulting from improvements in the quality or the terms of delivery of the goods or the efficiency of the services or from an extension of

---

ments dealing with uniform terms of trade, deliveries, payments, and discounts for cash, if these do not relate to prices and though the Bundeskartellamt has power to object, § 2; justified rebates, § 3; structural changes, § 4; and uniform standards, § 5. Branded goods are specially dealt with in regard to resale price maintenance; § 16.

For a comparison between art. 85 and the French art. 59, see Loussouarn & Bredin, "La Réglementation des Ententes: le Recul du Contrôle Judiciare," Recueil Dalloz, Cahier 6, Feb. 6, 1963, pp. 33–40. Under art. 59(3) the most usual justifications for agreements are that they promote economic progress, that they are leading up to a merger, that specialization will encourage a reduction in prices, or that the agreement will rationalize production or promote investment or exports. Retail price maintenance may be justified by the novelty of the product, the existence of a patent, guarantees of quality, or the cost of a publicity campaign.

For ECSC cases indicating the circumstances where specialization agreements and joint buying and joint selling agreements are permitted, see High Authority Decision No. 7/62 of July 11, 1962, 1962 Journal Officiel 1924/62, Decision No. 14/60 of June 2, 1960, 1960 Journal Officiel 869/60, Decision No. 16/60, 1960 Journal Officiel 1014/60. On the ECSC cartel law generally, see Comptoirs de Vente du Charbon de la Ruhr "Geitling," "Mausegatt" & "Präsident" v. High Authority, 8 Recueil 165, [1962] C.M.L.R. 113. See also Order No. 1/61—Modification de l'Article 65 du Traité de la Communauté Européenne du Charbon et de l'Acier, 7 Recueil 483 (1961). ECSC Treaty, art. 66(2), 66(5), on permission for mergers and concentration, lays down only negative requirements.

Deringer et al., 6 Revue du Marché Commun 256, 259–60 (1963), discuss whether the Commission may refuse to approve a cartel because it contravenes some other provision of the Treaty, e.g., art. 7.

Art. 85(3) appears to prohibit cartels designed to maintain an industry in structural difficulties, since these cartels do not improve the status quo. These cartels could perhaps be approved on the ground that they do not affect trade "adversely."

[229] International Chamber of Commerce, Commission on Restrictive Practices Affecting Competition, Report on the Rome Treaty's Rules Governing Competition, Doc. No. 225/63 Rev. 6 IV (1960), gives a long list of factors which the ICC Commission felt should, in appropriate cases, be taken into consideration.

[230] Oberdorfer, Gleiss & Hirsch, Common Market Cartel Law 57 (1963); Mussard, "The Regulation of the Restrictive Business Practices Under the Common Market Treaty," in Restrictive Practices, Patents, Trade Marks and Unfair Competition in the Common Market, Int'l & Comp. L.Q. Supp. No. 4, at 16, 21–22 (1962); Deringer et al., 6 Revue du Marché Commun 301, 302 (1963). Industrialization of a less developed region does not in itself benefit the consumer and so cannot be aided by cartels unless it increases consumer choice or reduces prices.

the choice of goods or services available is sufficient.[231] The share of the user or consumer in the benefit of the agreement must be "equitable," that is, must be in reasonable proportion to the improvement or progress achieved by the parties to the agreement.

The first negative requirement is that an agreement must not subject the parties to it to any restrictions not essential, in degree or in nature, to the achievement of the progress or improvement of production or distribution brought about.[232]

The second negative requirement, or disqualifying rule, is that the agreement must not enable the participating enterprises to eliminate competition as to a substantial part of the goods concerned. The goods concerned are all goods covered by or included in the operation of the agreement and all goods functionally interchangeable with them.[233] The part must not be "substantial" in relation to the production within the EEC of the goods concerned and presumably also the total imported into and, possibly, exported from the EEC. The market share of the enterprises which are parties to the agreement and the number and size of their competitors[234] are therefore of crucial importance. Competition may be eliminated in a particular region of the EEC unless the goods used in that region constitute a "substantial part" of all goods of the types concerned. This, however, normally will be the case if interstate trade is affected, and the elimination of competition in a particular region might give rise to a dominant position under Article 86.[235] The use of the word "substantial" means that the difference between an approved cartel and a prohibited cartel may be purely quantitative. Presumably, competition may not be eliminated in an expanding sector which is likely to become "substantial."

For the agreement to be ineligible for approval, it is not necessary that it eliminate competition. It is sufficient that it enables the parties to eliminate competition, even if it does not require them to do so.

As economic integration increases new competition may arise, so it is necessary to see if competition from any enterprise which is not now competing is possible. If it is, the parties to the agreement may not be "enabled to eliminate competition," even if no competition actually exists. The possibility of outside competition is an important deterrent to restrictive practices. This is of particular relevance when a state joins the EEC and a large increase in trade and investment is likely to take place in a relatively short time; it is, of course, most important in the early stages of economic integration.

Competition may continue in price, in discounts, in quality of the product or after-sales service, or in terms of sale

[231] This principle permits a more flexible approach than the French law by which the influence on price is the primary test of whether a cartel is permissible.

[232] See U.K. Restrictive Trade Practices Act, 1965, 4 & 5 Eliz. 2, c. 68, § 21(1)(b), which permits agreements where the restriction on competition is necessary to provide "the public as purchasers, consumers or users of any goods [with] other specific and substantial benefits or advantages." On this aspect of art. 85(3), see Deringer et al., 6 Revue du Marché Commun 301, 304–307 (1963).

[233] Oberdorfer, Gleiss & Hirsch, Common Market Cartel Law 64–65 (1963). See ECSC High Authority Decision No. 16/60, 1960 Journal Officiel 1014/60, for a case on ECSC Treaty, art. 65(2)(c).

[234] Deringer et al., 6 Revue du Marché Commun 301, 309 (1963).

[235] See also ECSC Treaty, art. 65(2)(c); Comptoirs de Vente du Charbon de la Ruhr "Geitling," "Mausegatt" & "Präsident" v. High Authority, 8 Recueil 165, [1962] C.M.L.R. 113. Art. 85(3)(b) will often have a territorial connotation. However, an agreement eliminating competition between competitors who have a large share of the market is forbidden, whether this share is a geographical share or a percentage share of a unified market.

even where it has been eliminated as to some of these matters. It is only if there is no competition or if competition exists only in ancillary respects for a substantial proportion of the goods in question that an agreement is ineligible for approval.

It seems likely that the extent to which competition continues to exist will be, in practice, the decisive factor in the application of Article 85(3) to most agreements.[236] This necessitates an analysis of the market situation after the agreement comes into force.[237] Since it may be necessary for the parties to an agreement to get the approval of the Commission before acting upon an agreement,[238] some guesswork may be needed as to the actual effect of the agreement upon the market. Since Article 85(3) forbids agreements which eliminate competition as to substantial proportions of the goods concerned, it prevents most allocations or divisions of markets which result in the creation of a dominant market position.[239]

A REGIONAL CARTEL POLICY?

In the context of this book, the question arises whether the Commission should have a regional policy under Articles 85 and 86, either as part of its regional economic policy or for reasons related to cartels and monopolies. For the regional policy, Articles 85 and 86 would be applied less strictly than usual to cartels likely to promote regional economic development. It could be achieved by a special regulation or by a special interpretation of Article 85(3) in the light of the circumstances of the region, i.e., by regarding all such cartels as "promoting technical or economic progress." The requirement that competition must not be eliminated causes the main difficulty. There is no indication of such a policy in the EEC Treaty.[240] The following remarks are therefore tentative.

Less developed countries typically have no laws against restrictive practices, and the introduction of a comprehensive and fairly strict EEC law therefore may affect local industry more than industry which previously has had to comply with legislation such as the British Restrictive Practices Act of 1956. The official policy in small countries often is to encourage those cartels which aid exports.[241] While only those industries whose agreements affect trade between member states are within the scope of Articles 85 and 86, exports may be extremely important for a small underindustrialized country such as Ireland. Since locally owned industry in a less developed region is characteristically small, the Commission will be less likely to be concerned with it than with enterprises doing a substantial volume of interstate trade.

In considering the question of a regional cartel policy in the EEC, several factors must be taken into account:

[236] Becker, Extraterritorial Application of Common Market Laws (PLI, 1962).

[237] Required by Reg. 27, Form B.

[238] This might be necessary because of the likelihood of civil actions for damages if the agreement was not approved; it would not be necessary under Community law.

[239] The test of the existence of a dominant market position is not necessarily the same as the test of the compatibility of an agreement with art. 85(3)(b).

[240] Art. 51 of the Greek Treaty of Association provides that, *inter alia*, arts. 85 and 86 should be "made applicable" to trade between Greece and the Six, but apparently no decisions have been made yet as to the application of this. The language of this article is tentative: "The Contracting Parties recognize that . . . the principles laid down in Articles 85 and 86 . . . ought to be made applicable. . . ."

[241] Verloren van Themaat, "Cartel Policy in the Netherlands," in International Conference on Control of Restrictive Business Practices 18, 151–56 (1960). The same policy is accepted in Switzerland.

whether the enterprises in the region concerned are locally owned or owned by interests in the same sectors elsewhere in the Common Market; whether the regional cartel is for "defense" or to enable regional enterprises to export into markets outside the region in question; and whether there is any special likelihood of injury to enterprises in the region from agreements between enterprises elsewhere in the EEC. The extent to which the less developed region is a market integrated with the rest of the Community is also important. If it is a separate market in the sector of the economy in question, the structure of the industry and of the economy is different and can be treated differently. The existence of substantial outside competition renders a regional cartel relatively harmless.[242] However, it causes enterprises in the region to try to enter into anticompetitive agreements with enterprises elsewhere.

Cartels for locally owned industry in a less developed region

A modified cartel policy might be necessary to protect regional industries against competition in the region from large foreign firms capable of using their financial resources to undercut the regional industries and put them out of business. This is a danger analogous to, if not actually constituting, dumping. Even after the end of the transitional period, this threat to less developed regions may continue, and some Community rule on unfair trading will be necessary. In the EEC, dumping should be dealt with by specific measures rather than by artificial division of the market by means of cartels, especially since the latter could protect regional enterprises against legitimate competition from more efficient producers.

A cartel may be a legitimate temporary measure to "promote . . . economic progress" by protecting a developing industry which will become efficient in time. The objection to a cartel is that effective protection must involve excluding competing imported products from the regional market. This divides the EEC market, inhibits free movement of goods into the region, and enables oligopolies to preserve their position in the regional or national markets after their tariff and quota protection is gone. If assistance is required for new locally owned industry, direct state aid is preferable to restrictive agreements, since the economic effects of state aid in conditions of free competition can be assessed more accurately than the effects of anticompetitive practices.

A cartel may be regarded as legitimate if it is to prevent cutthroat competition in the regional market between local firms, which might cause some of them to close down, reducing consumers' choice, causing unemployment, and ending the firms' chances of improving production and competing in markets outside the region. The Commission will have to decide whether to allow limited interference with competition in the interests of greater long-term competition. The Commission will probably approve agreements between locally owned enterprises not to compete in the home market, provided competition from the rest of the EEC is not eliminated. The difficulty will be to show that the agreements improve production or promote economic progress, as distinct from merely maintaining the status quo.[243]

[242] See Verloren van Themaat, "The Anti-trust Policy of the European Economic Community," in Comparative Aspects of Anti-trust Law in the United States, the United Kingdom and the European Economic Community, Int'l & Comp. L.Q. Supp. No. 6, at 18, 19 (1963); see also art. 85(3)(b).

[243] See art. 85(3). Cartels to protect an industry in a slump can be permitted only if art. 85(1) prohibits only cartels which affect trade "adversely," since these protection cartels do not fall within art. 85(3).

The requirement of consumer benefit would probably be satisfied if the cartel was essential to insure the continued supply of the brands of goods produced by its members. In sectors where large economies of scale are possible, small local industry cannot have lasting protection from competition and the most efficient use of Community resources. Some priority is given to ending those cartels intended to retain protection in the home market by price or market-sharing agreements.[244] However, if outside competition is not "eliminated," if the cartel directly affects only the regional market, if only a small percentage and not a "substantial part" of Community trade in the commodity in question is affected, and if the participating enterprises are smaller than their foreign competitors and thus Article 86 does not apply, an agreement probably should be approved under Article 85(3), even if it would not be approved outside an undeveloped region.[245]

Cartels are likely to occur among enterprises in a depressed sector of industry or in one threatened by competition from elsewhere in the Community; substantially the same criteria seem relevant in both cases. Temporary cartels may be permitted in order to facilitate continued production, if the Commission is satisfied that employees will be retrained and relocated and that the cartel is not merely an effort by the participants to keep themselves in business at all costs.

[244] Verloren van Themaat, "Competition and Restrictive Practices in the European Economic Community," in Institute on the Legal Aspects of the European Communities 99, 103–104 (1960).

[245] An agreement under art. 85(3) which improves production or promotes progress, if it fulfills the other criteria, seems to be permissible if the production or progress promoted is only that of the enterprises involved and if it continues to fall short of the standards of production or progress in the same sector elsewhere in the Community.

Local industry owned by interests from industrial areas

The position of a local subsidiary or joint venture owned by enterprises from highly industrialized areas is rather different.[246] The only reason for treating it differently from its parent enterprise or enterprises is the fact that it may be at a particular competitive disadvantage. If no "natural" factors exist to limit the subsidiary's market, the only special characteristics of a less developed region which are relevant seem to be an inadequate infrastructure or the lack of skilled labor. These can be remedied only by state aids and cannot be compensated for by a modified policy on restrictive practices, except possibly by permission for price-fixing. If the state in question has not chosen to remedy these disadvantages by state aid, it is very doubtful if the Commission should do so by approving a cartel.

The regional market may be separated to some degree from the rest of the EEC by geographical isolation, high transport costs, or other reasons. Even if the region is in an associated country, there will usually be free entry into the EEC for local products. The usual argument for allowing restrictions on competition in less developed economies is that, because of the small size of the market, only one firm in the sector of industry in question can operate economically. This is essentially an argument in favor of the creation of monopoly power rather than a horizontal cartel. If substantial invest-

[246] It is understood that the practice of the Antitrust Division of the United States Department of Justice is to take a fairly broad view of joint ventures and restrictive agreements relating to operations in underdeveloped countries. However, this is due partly to difficulties on the extraterritorial scope of the United States antitrust laws and partly to political considerations. See Van Cise, "The Application of the U.S. Antitrust Laws to the European Community," in Institute on the Legal Aspects of the European Communities 140 (1960).

ment is required to commence production or to perform services, the necessity for a monopoly increases in inverse proportion to the size of the market for the goods or services. If competition is eliminated by "natural" factors, no cartel is necessary to confer a monopoly position. The only problem is whether regional demand permits production on an economical scale. If competition is not eliminated by natural factors and if the trade in the region is of substantial importance, the Treaty provides that competition may not be eliminated by agreement.[247] This would mean that a cartel is not permitted to allocate a region to an enterprise, even if exclusive access to the regional market is necessary to allow the enterprise to achieve economies of scale. This seems too strict a view, and it will be unfortunate from the point of view of regional economic policy if the Commission feels that the terms of the Treaty require it to adopt this view. On the other hand, abuse of a monopoly position in the region is more readily controlled by the possibility of competition from elsewhere than by acts of the Commission under Article 86. The problem is whether in order to industrialize the region and thus "promote . . . economic progress" it is desirable to establish a local operation which, due to the lack of skilled labor or otherwise, cannot compete even on the regional market with enterprises elsewhere in the Common Market. This is permissible, under the Commission's policy on state aids, only if the regional operation will become economical in a reasonable time. By analogy, the use of a cartel may be permitted to give the regional operation temporary protection, for example, if regional demand is increasing and will permit achieving economies of scale and facing competition. However, state aid prevents a temporarily uneconomical venture from passing on its excessive costs to other local enterprises whose prosperity would also be important to the region. The benefits of industrialization cannot come within the proviso to Article 85(3), which requires that the benefits of a cartel be shared with users and consumers, so a regional operation which aids industrialization at increased cost to users and eliminates competition rather than increases the choice of goods available cannot be protected by a cartel.

If the regional industry is a joint venture or a subsidiary or branch of an EEC enterprise in the same sector, a case for market-sharing between the parent and the branch or subsidiary exists. Again, the difficulty is that the enterprises must not eliminate competition in respect of a substantial part of the goods concerned.

Cartels relating to exports from a less developed region

The question of the effects of regional cartels on exports from the region into the rest of the Common Market is somewhat different and does not depend on the separation or size of the regional market in the sector in question. This does not involve a restrictive agreement between a regional enterprise and enterprises outside the region, but an agreement to which the only parties are local enterprises. A regional cartel may constitute a merger *pro tanto* for purposes of export from the region. Competition normally is not "eliminated in respect of . . . the goods involved,"[248] since by definition the regional enterprises are competing with producers elsewhere in the EEC. The participants benefit from sharing costs of distribution and sale and from more effective advertising, more regular supplies, and a stronger bargaining position. They can no longer reduce

[247] Art. 85(3)(b).

[248] Ibid. See Irish Committee on Industrial Organization, Second Interim Report: Joint Export Marketing, Pr. 6730 (1962).

consumer choice by knocking one another out of the export market, and since exporting from the region may be difficult without some form of cartel, the cartel may accelerate economic integration, increase the amount of competition in the rest of the Common Market, "improve ... the distribution of goods," and "promote ... economic progress" in the region concerned. This argument does not apply if the regional cartel consists wholly or partly of companies associated with producers located elsewhere in the Common Market, such as subsidiaries or joint ventures. Also, it results not from a modified cartel policy for the region but from the application of Article 85(3) to the special circumstances of the region. Under Article 85(3), only a cartel resulting in exports from the region which would not otherwise be possible is permitted. Since the Community is expected to assist its less industrialized regions,[249] it seems reasonable, in view of Article 85(3), that where a cartel is an effective method of promoting regional development, it should be permitted.

ARTICLE 86—ABUSE OF A DOMINANT MARKET POSITION

A dominant market position

Article 86 applies only where a dominant market position exists, irrespective of its cause.[250] A dominant position is not in itself objectionable under the Treaty,[251] but only the abuse of such a position. The concept of abuse or improper exploitation of a dominant position[252] is derived from German[253] and Dutch[254] law and, since the Treaty, has been adopted in Belgium.[255] Article 86

[249] Art. 92(3). Increasing a region's trade is probably the best way to encourage its economic development.

[250] Compare art. 86 with U.S. Sherman Antitrust Act, 15 U.S.C. § 1 (1964); Clayton Act, § 3, 15 U.S.C. § 14 (1964); and Robinson-Patman Act, 15 U.S.C. §§ 13–13b, 21 (1964).

[251] Unless it is a state monopoly; see arts. 37, 90; ECSC Treaty, art. 66(7).

[252] ECSC Treaty, art. 66(7), speaks of practices contrary to the purposes of that treaty but does not use the concept of abuse of a dominant position. The article speaks of a position which "protects the enterprise from competition" in a substantial part of the Common Market.

[253] Competition Law, §§ 22–26; Schapiro, "The German Law Against Restraints of Competition . . .," 62 Colum. L. Rev. 1, 39–40 (1962). However, the German government sent a report—Bericht über Änderungen des Gesetzes gegen Wettbewerbsbeschränkungen, Deutscher Bundestag, Drucksache IV/617, 4 Wahlperiode (1962)—to the federal legislature recommending an extension of the supervision of the Bundeskartellamt over enterprises with dominant market power (as well as the removal of the existing permission for resale price maintenance and the adoption of stricter controls over exclusive dealerships); Riesenfeld, "Antitrust Laws of the European Economic Community: A Sequel," 50 Calif. L. Rev. 829, 836 (1962).

[254] Which uses the concept of "predominant influence," Economic Competition Act of June 28, 1956, as amended by the Act of July 16, 1958, §§ 1, 24.

[255] See Act of May 27, 1960, on protection against the abuse of economic power. Art. 1 reads: "For the purposes of this Act, economic power shall mean the power possessed by a natural person or body corporate acting alone or by a group of such persons or bodies corporate acting in concert to exert, within the territory of the Kingdom, through industrial, commercial, agricultural or financial activities, a dominating influence over supplies or merchandise or capital market or over the price or quality of specific merchandise or services." Art. 2 states: "An abuse, within the meaning of this Act, shall exist when one or more persons holding economic power shall prejudice the public interest by practices which distort or restrict the normal play of competition or which interfere either with the economic freedom of producers, distributors or consumers or with the development of production or trade." Translations from 1 OECD Guide to Legislation on Restrictive Business Practices, Belgium § 1.0, at 1 (1962). See del Marmol & Fontaine, "Protection Against Abuse of Economic Power in Belgium," 109 U. Pa. L. Rev. 922, 927 (1962). On the Belgian law generally, see del

supplements Article 85 by prohibiting non-collusive practices of monopolies and oligopolies if these have harmful effects on the economy of the Community.

For a limited number of enterprises to have a dominant position in the Common Market, they need not be associated in any way. Although Articles 85 and 86 are probably legally of equal weight, Article 86 is important primarily where a monopoly exists or where no agreements or concerned practices can be proved.

A dominant market position is not defined by Article 86, but the test of the existence of dominant market power is whether competition exists between the enterprises concerned.[256] Uniformity of prices and terms of sale is not necessarily proof that no competition exists, especially when the share of each enterprise in the local market is substantial. Even if competition exists, improperly high prices charged by all members of an oligopoly are contrary to Article 86, since the enterprises are abusing their freedom from competition in one particular respect. In deciding whether competition exists, important factors are the market share of the enterprise or group of enterprises[257] in the total Common Market production of the product, the number and market shares of actual and likely competitors, and the extent of actual competition.[258] An enterprise may have a dominant position in the Common Market, abuse of which is likely to affect trade between member states, even if it is incorporated and has its head office and principal place of business in a non-member state. Article 86 is unlikely to be applied to oligopolies for some time unless flagrant abuses arise, since the Commission will be too busy with cartels and monopolies to embark on the even more lengthy investigations necessary to

---

Marmol, La Protection contre les abus de Puissance Economique en Droit Belge (1960); van Reepinghen & Waelbroeck, "La Législation Belge concernant les Pratiques Restreignant la Concurrence," in Rapports au Colloque International de Droit Européen 179 (1961).

As to the abuse of a permitted cartel, see German Competition Law, § 17(1)(2). On art. 86 generally, see Houssiaux, Concurrence et Marché Commun 143–64, especially at 158–64 (1960).

[256] See ECSC Treaty, art. 66(7); see also 4 OECD Guide to Legislation on Restrictive Business Practices, EEC § 2.0, at 4 (1962); see generally Deringer et al., 6 Revue du Marché Commun 440 (1963); Günther, "The Significance of the Concept 'To Take Improper Advantage of a Dominant Market Position Within the Common Market or Within a Substantial Part of It' in Article 86 of the Treaty Establishing the European Economic Community," in U.S. Senate, Antitrust Developments in the European Common Market, Hearings Before the Subcommittee on Antitrust and Monopoly of the Senate Committee on the Judiciary, 88th Cong., 1st Sess., app. 1, at 81 (1963). See Political and Economic Planning, Cartel Policy and the Common Market 261 (1962). German Competition Law, § 22(2), defines the market-dominating position of two or more enterprises as the position "as far as, in regard to a certain type of goods or commercial services, no substantial competition exists in fact between them in general or specific markets, and as far as they jointly meet the requirements of paragraph (1)." Section 22(1) reads: "As far as an enterprise has no competitor or is not exposed to any substantial competition in a certain type of goods or commercial services, it is market-dominating within the meaning of this law." Translations from 1 OECD Guide to Legislation on Restrictive Business Practices, Germany § 1.0, at 13 (1960).

[257] Under U.K. Monopolies and Restrictive Practices (Inquiry and Control) Act, 1948, 11 & 12 Geo. 6, c. 66, §§ 3-5, a monopoly (the word is not used) on supply, processing, and exports is an enterprise or a cartel supplying, processing, or exporting one-third of the goods of the class involved. See Timberg, "Antitrust and Patent Provisions of the European Common Market Treaty," in 3 Institute on Private Investments Abroad 173, 177–78 (Southwestern Legal Foundation, 1961).

[258] See United States v. E. I. du Pont de Nemours & Co., 351 U.S. 377 (1956).

establish proof of improper exploitation by an oligopoly.[259]

A "substantial part" of the Common Market

A "substantial part" of the Common Market normally means a substantial area rather than a substantial share of the market in the relevant sector, since the latter is quite compatible with the existence of competition.[260] If interstate trade is affected, a monopoly in a particular region of the EEC is subject to Article 86 if its share is "substantial" in relation to the size of the sector in question in the whole Common Market.[261] However, the dismantling of tariffs and other artificial impediments to trade may open a national market, hitherto dominated by a monopoly or oligopoly, to competition from elsewhere in the EEC.[262] This is particularly important where, in the sector of industry in question, the creation or preservation of a private or state monopoly or a private oligopoly has resulted from government policy.[263]

Substantial abuse of a monopoly position is unlikely where competitors can freely sell their products, either because of total regional demand or because of the advantages of the competitor's products which arise from the inflated prices or other abusive practices of the monopoly. But if the demand is not great enough to encourage competition from elsewhere in the EEC or if it is inhibited by natural economic factors, such as transport costs, which make the region into a market separate from the rest of the Common Market, Article 86 is particularly important. Monopolies are especially likely to arise in less industrialized countries due to the small size of the national market, the lack of capital, and the bias of banks towards well-established industries.

Abuse of a dominant market position within one member state is within Article 86 if it affects interstate trade. The effect of abuse of a dominant market position on interstate trade may be somewhat different from the effects caused by anticompetitive practices, but the criteria involved seem to be similar.

"Abuse" of a dominant position

Article 86 prohibits abuse or improper exploitation of a dominant market position. There is no control over an enterprise's activities which fall short of actual abuse. The source of the dominant position—mergers, patent ownership or acquisition, or whatever—is irrelevant.[264]

Abuse, or improper exploitation, of a dominant market position is prohibited in general terms, and then some examples of abuse are given as the only indication of the meaning of the phrase. Each example corresponds to a clause in Article 85 and, in general, the control over monopolies

[259] This is so even though an enterprise controlling 60% of the market is likely to injure the economy much more by abuse of its position than a cartel of enterprises which together control 30%; Deringer Report, A.P.E. Doc. No. 57, para. 80 (1961–62).

[260] 4 OECD Guide to Legislation on Restrictive Business Practices, EEC § 2.0, at 4 (1962).

[261] In Ireland, tariff and tax policy and official policy on state aids to industry and on freedom of establishment have produced a number of national monopolies or oligopolies, both Irish-owned and foreign-owned, some of which will not be protected by "natural" economic factors such as transport costs.

[262] Oberdorfer, Gleiss & Hirsch, Common Market Cartel Law 74 (1963).

[263] See von der Groeben, "The Cartel Legislation of the European Economic Community in the Light of Two [and a Half] Years' Experience," in 1 Cartel and Monopoly in Modern Law 63, 68–69 (1961).

[264] Art. 91 prevents this method of putting competitors out of business by dumping. See Regs. 8/62, 13/62. This is the only Treaty provision dealing with unfair competition, as distinct from restrictions on free competition, unless the provisions against discrimination are so regarded.

and oligopolies is intended to prevent practices similar to those prohibited for cartels.

Abuse or improper exploitation must be economically unjustifiable and must harm consumers or other enterprises affected. High prices, for example, do not constitute abuse if they are justified by the necessity of obtaining an economical return from the investment of substantial sums in equipment or research.[265] Exploitation which would not be possible if substantial competition existed is illegal, but if the practice would be possible in conditions of competition, no undue or unfair advantage is being taken of the dominant position. Difficulties may arise in applying this principle if the dominant position is due to possession of patents and if competition is impossible due to the rules of patent law. In this case it is necessary to decide if the prices charged for the patented product are so high as to constitute an abuse.

No question of market- or supply-sharing can arise in the case of a monopoly.[266] Any enterprise controls its own production, markets, technical development, and investment; Article 86 merely requires that if it has a dominant market position there shall be no limitation which prejudices consumers. Article 85(3)(b) is, in the nature of things, inapplicable. Whether the practice alleged to be an abuse is necessary to economic development and how much of the benefit is passed on to consumers are factors in deciding whether abuse exists.

A monopoly controls its prices, and if no competition exists, the only limitation possible is that these prices should not be "unfair."[267] The fact that prices are high or excessive or constitute bad value is not sufficient; a fair or reasonable price is not necessarily the correct price.[268] The terms of the contract as a whole must be such that the value received is grossly disproportionate to the value given and outside the limits of what is reasonable. These terms and prices must be "imposed" directly or indirectly through the economic power of the enterprise; the immediate means of imposition may be either legal or economic. It is not clear whether the fixing of prices or conditions of resale can constitute an abuse; it may depend on whether the terms or conditions fixed are unfair to the new purchasers or to the enterprises dealing directly with the monopoly.[269]

Since Article 86 deals only with abuses, it incorporates its own rule of reason and no question of exempting practices from its provisions arises. Abuses are prohibited and may be punished directly as they occur; they need not be designated as abuses by the Commission and forbidden before fines are imposed. The Com-

[265] The Commission may have to decide how far to permit self-financing through charging high prices, instead of through borrowing or obtaining equity capital, where the need for capital can be justified.

[266] Art. 85(1)(c).

[267] Art. 86(a). German Competition Law, § 22(3), allows the prevention of "abuse . . . with regard to prices" and tying-in clauses but it does not indicate the type of prices which will constitute abuse.

[268] Oberdorfer, Gleiss & Hirsch, Common Market Cartel Law 76 (1963).

[269] If they were unfair to the latter, they would presumably be prohibited, because the terms of the contracts requiring the inclusion of the "unfair" terms in resale contracts would themselves be unfair. See Deringer et al., 6 Revue du Marché Commun 488, 491 (1963).

Discrimination by monopolies is also prohibited by German law; Competition Law, § 26(2). Tying-in clauses are prohibited when they are an abuse of dominant power in the sector which includes the goods required by the purchaser. German Competition Law, § 22(3), 22(4), and U.K. Monopolies and Restrictive Practices (Inquiry and Control) Act, 1948, 11 & 12 Geo. 6, c. 66, § 10, empower the national authorities to deal with tying-in practices of monopolies.

mission does not expect to be able to discover or to rule on actual abuses without substantial market surveys, since abuses cannot be proved by a small number of objective facts in the same way as agreements or concerted practices.[270]

TREATY PROVISIONS AND DOMESTIC LAW

The relationship between the substantive rules of Community and domestic law on restrictive practices is not entirely clear. Any agreements, decisions, or practices which do not affect trade between member states are governed solely by any relevant national restrictive practices laws. Apart from the possibility of harmonizing the national laws involved,[271] the EEC has no effect on these agreements.

If the Treaty provisions prohibit a particular agreement or practice, the national law cannot grant it an effective exemption. This is necessarily involved in the acceptance of the Treaty by member states and is confirmed by the provision giving exclusive jurisdiction to the Commission to give exemptions under Article 85(3).[272]

It is not certain whether an agreement or practice which is approved by the Commission under Article 85(3) may be prohibited by national law. Conflicting decisions applying Community law are unlikely. The question is whether Articles 85 and 86 merely state minimum requirements for restrictive agreements affecting interstate trade or govern these agreements exclusively.[273]

A national law more stringent than Community law hampers enterprises of that nation and discriminates against them on a national level. This, however, is not the same thing as discrimination on the grounds of nationality, and it is hardly contrary to the Treaty. A strict restrictive practices law is intended to benefit the national economy, though it may inconvenience particular enterprises.

It is clearly desirable to have uniform competitive conditions in antitrust law, as in other Community matters. Article 85(3) permits desirable agreements, and its object would be frustrated if strict national laws could invalidate them. Therefore, it is widely held that the Treaty provisions should govern interstate trade exclusively[274] and that the resulting limitation on the sovereignty of member

[270] See Reg. 17, art. 12, especially 12(3).

[271] Art. 100. Consideration is being given to a directive on harmonization of national laws on restrictive practices.

[272] Reg. 17, art. 9(1).

[273] This can be regarded either as a question of substantive law or as a question of jurisdiction. Schumacher, "Réflexions sur l'interdiction des ententes visées par l'article 85 du Traité instituant la C.E.E.," 24 Droit Social 65, 68 (1961), states that national laws may prohibit a cartel permitted under art. 85(3). Deringer, "Les Règles Concernant la Concurrence dans le Cadre du Marché Commun Entrent en Vigeur," 5 Revue du Marché Commun 70, 74 (1962), says that art. 85 was phrased so as to permit the possibility that national laws might invalidate an agreement permitted under art. 85(3).

Steindorff, "The Provisions Against Restraints of Competition in the European Communities," in 1 Cartel and Monopoly in Modern Law 191, 207–11 (1961), argues that the limitation of arts. 85 and 86 to practices affecting interstate trade is a rule of substantive law and not a rule of jurisdiction, and that the jurisdictions of the Commission and the national authorities are concurrent, not mutually exclusive. Therefore, Community law does not abrogate national law, and a national law may prohibit an agreement approved under art. 85(3). Catalano, "Rapport entre les règles de concurrence ètablies par le traité C.E.E. et la législation des Etats membres," 15 Rev. Int. de Droit Comp. 269, 283 (1963), strongly argues on practical and theoretical grounds that the national laws may not prohibit an agreement or practice permitted by the Treaty.

[274] See Deringer, "Les Règles Concernant la Concurrence dans le Cadre du Marché Commun Entrent en Vigeur," 5 Revue du Marché Commun 70, 82 (1962).

states should be read into the Treaty. National authorities will probably be reluctant to prohibit an agreement approved by the Commission. The Commission's power to deprive the national authorities of jurisdiction by initiating proceedings[275] relates only to Community law. The Commission is not entitled to apply or enforce national law, so the jurisdiction of the national authorities to apply it is apparently not affected.

The Treaty does not expressly indicate that the application of Community law to a cartel prevents the national authorities from applying national laws against it. The resolution of this problem is of importance and is not confined to antitrust questions. The better view is that national authorities may prohibit a cartel permitted under Article 85(3),[276] but the Commission, which is anxious to see Community law applied as widely as possible, and private lawyers, who are anxious to prevent strict antitrust laws from being applied to their clients, may well argue the opposite view strongly.

MERGERS

Article 86 imposes no restriction on efforts to obtain or secure a monopoly position in the Common Market[277] if the means used do not include prohibited practices such as dumping[278] or market-sharing.[279] There is no restriction on mergers or "take-overs" of one company by another, however carried out, even if the result is to create a monopoly in one or more sectors of industry.[280] This is an important difference between United States and EEC antitrust law.

The omission from the Treaty of any express provision for the control of mergers and the acquisition of monopoly power is deliberate.[281] Europeans, unlike Americans, tend to consider that monopoly power is not objectionable in itself. One of the foremost economic objectives of the Community is to bring about the economies of scale made possible by the enlarged European market. The increase in the size of industries is bound to take place largely through mergers of existing national enterprises.[282] The omission reflects the thought that there should be no administrative supervision or control of mergers which might inhibit this development. Except for the sectors already under the ECSC, no provision is made for controlling mergers, even where the Common Market is already dominated by large enterprises. In less developed areas, monopolies have a legitimate place in industries where large investment is necessary and the local market is not large enough for more than one enterprise to operate on an economic scale. Since 1958, many mergers have taken place in all sectors, but the economies and advantages of scale necessary to enable European industries to compete

[275] Reg. 17, art. 9(3).

[276] Deringer, "The Distribution of Powers in the Enforcement of the Rules of Competition Under the Rome Treaty," 1 Common Market L. Rev. 30, 31 (1963); see Nicolas & Société Brandt v. Société Photo Radio Club, Cour d'Appel d'Amiens (3d Ch.), May 9, 1963, [1963] C.M.L.R. 239, aff'd, Cour de Cassation, Oct. 22, 1964, [1965] C.M.L.R. 36.

[277] This is illegal in sectors under the ECSC Treaty; art. 66. For a definition of "control" of other enterprises, see ECSC High Authority Decision No. 24/54, 1954 Journal Officiel 345/54. See generally, 2 High Authority, Sixth General Report 97–104 (1958).

[278] Art. 91. Selling below cost in the market where the enterprise primarily operates is regulated only by national unfair-trade laws.

[279] Art. 85(1)(c), 85(3)(b).

[280] Mergers resulting in the acquisition of a market share of 20% or more or involving an enterprise which already has that proportion of the market must be reported under German law, Competition Law, §§ 23, 24, but no effective action can be taken against them. See U.K. Monopolies and Mergers Act, 1965, 13 & 14 Eliz. 2, c. 50.

[281] The Spaak Report took a contrary position; Spaak Report 56.

[282] See art. 220.

with United States industry have not all been achieved. However, Article 85 requires the preservation of competition, and the destruction or absorption of small enterprises is not necessarily economically beneficial and is traditionally regarded as politically and socially undesirable.

The result of leaving the acquisition of monopoly power unregulated is that serious problems of abuse will arise. It is easier to prevent a monopoly from arising than to break it up once it is established, even when the law provides machinery for the latter operation; witness the case of the huge Krupp enterprise.

The Commission has been concerned about this prospect. The Action Programme for the Second Stage[283] says:

> [I]t is felt to be particularly important to see that concentration having no justification from the standpoint of the economy at large should at least not be artificially encouraged. In practical terms this means that the first step must be to secure greater neutrality in respect of competition in company law, tax law and the law on industrial property. . . . Particular vigilance is required in cases where new dominant positions come into being in the Common Market, especially when they result in the stifling or elimination of existing competition.

Possibilities of control over mergers

Article 87 requires the Council to enact, by qualified majority,[284] regulations or directives "to put into effect the principles set out in Articles 85 and 86." A regulation requiring notification of mergers which involve control of a given percentage of the market clearly is authorized by this provision.[285] Regulations purporting to confer power to prohibit mergers or to break up a dominant market position once formed are not authorized by Article 87 and must be enacted under Article 235, which requires unanimity in the Council, or dealt with by directive under Article 100.

The Commission is unlikely to undertake the task of enactment and implementation of a regulation dealing with mergers for some time, since Articles 85 and 86 will require several years of work before a comprehensive policy on private restrictions on competition is worked out.

Does Article 85 apply to merger agreements?

What has been said above is based on the overwhelming weight of authority. However, a suggestion has been made[286] that Article 85(1) prohibits agreements bringing about mergers of separate enterprises. This interpretation is contrary to the intentions of the Six. It is surprising by comparison with the ECSC Treaty, which regulates mergers specifically and separately. An agreement for a merger is, in substance, a transfer of property rather than a restraint on competition and is totally different from the type of agreement contemplated in Article 85. This interpretation would result in anomalous distinctions between mergers resulting from agreements or concerted practices and those resulting from unilateral action, such as the acquisition of shares, to which no real agreement can be said to have been given by the enterprise acquired.[287] A

[283] Para. 26 (1962). See also von der Groeben, "The Cartel Legislation of the European Economic Community in the Light of Two [and a Half] Years' Experience," in 1 Cartel and Monopoly in Modern Law 63, 69 (1961); Schmölders, "The Principle of Competition in Tax and Finance Policies," in 2 Cartel and Monopoly in Modern Law 509 (1961).

[284] Formerly by unanimous vote only.

[285] See Third General Report, para. 142 (1960). Cf. German Competition Law, § 23.

[286] Discussed by Verloren van Themaat, "Final Report," in 2 Cartel and Monopoly in Modern Law 954 (1961).

[287] It could be argued that the agreement between the acquiring enterprise and the previous

provision making merger agreements "void" is singularly likely to cause legal difficulties if the merger is carried out.

This writer does not support the contention, but it is important because it provides the only means by which, under present Community law, the Commission can exercise control over mergers. While many mergers are natural and necessary in the transitional stage of the EEC, some undoubtedly are objectionable, especially those which achieve by merger what is illegal by agreement. Once created, a monopoly is subject only to Article 86; the Commission would probably not be sorry to have a weapon to prevent the creation of monopolies.

DUMPING

The provisions on dumping are part of the EEC's over-all policy on competition. As M. Uri says:

> We cannot ask a country to eliminate those protective arrangements which benefit its producers if that country does not have some insurance against acts of economic aggression committed by other nations or their business firms. Dumping committed with or without government subsidy leads to prices which have no relationship to competitive position. It must be effectively controlled. . . . Likewise, in modern market structures, producers may indeed fear the impact of large concentrations which do not necessarily have the advantage of efficiency but which assemble financial resources enabling them to pursue for a time competitive methods designed to give them later a monopoly position.[288]

The definition of dumping

There is no definition of dumping in the Treaty; the definition in Article VI of the General Agreement on Tariffs and Trade is to be utilized for this purpose.[289] Article VI reads, in part:

> 1. The contracting parties recognize that dumping, by which products of one country are introduced into the commerce of another country at less than the normal value of the products, is to be condemned if it causes or threatens material injury to an established industry in the territory of a contracting party or materially retards the establishment of a domestic industry. For the purposes of this Article, a product is to be considered as being introduced into the commerce of an importing country at less than its normal value, if the price of the product exported from one country to another:
>
> a) is less than the comparable price, in the ordinary course of trade, for the like product when destined for consumption in the exporting country, or
>
> b) in the absence of such domestic price, is less than either
>
> i. the highest comparable price for the like product for export to any third country in the ordinary course of trade, or
>
> ii. the cost of production of the product in the country of origin plus a reasonable addition for selling cost and profit.
>
> Due allowance shall be made in each case for differences in conditions and terms of sale, for differences in taxation, and for other differences affecting price comparability.

---

shareholders to sell the shares constituted an agreement which had the effect of restraining competition. It would be artificial to construe art. 85(1) as applying to such an agreement. It is doubtful if it could be contrary to art. 85(1), since the agreement itself would not affect interstate trade directly, nor would it directly affect competition.

[288] Uri, "Economics and Politics of the Common Market," in Competition, Cartels and Their Regulation 378, 381–82 (Miller ed. 1962). See Houssiaux, Concurrence et Marché Commun 89, 91–92 (1960); OEEC Special Working Party, Report on the Possibility of Creating a Free Trade Area in Europe, Annex III, paras. 18–23 (1957). See also Italy v. EEC Commission, 9 Recueil 335, [1963] C.M.L.R. 289. Art. 17 of the EFTA Convention allows measures to be taken against dumped or subsidized imports.

[289] See Fifth General Report, para. 49 (1962), which paraphrases art. VI(1) in describing "dumping . . . warranting the application of . . . Article 91(1)." Third General Report, para. 144 (1960), describes art. VI(1) as a "working basis" for a definition of dumping.

Article VI goes on to permit antidumping duties to restore the price of goods to the normal value and to offset the margin of dumping.[290] Between EEC member states, this has been superseded by Article 91(1), although permission can be given by the Commission under Article 91 for the imposition of these duties.[291] Member states may apply antidumping laws to imports from non-member countries until the end of the transitional period, after which Article 113 (dealing with the common commercial policy) will apply. The Commission recommends[292] that to implement both Article 91(1) and the common commercial policy effectively all member states should have special laws enabling them to take protective action against dumping and that approximation of laws in this respect should be undertaken. After the end of the transitional period, each member state will have to rely on the efficiency of the laws of other member states for protection against goods dumped on its own market through their territories.

Treaty provisions on dumping

Article 91 provides that, during the transitional period of the EEC, on its own motion or on the application of a member state or of any other interested party, the Commission may determine that dumping practices exist, in which case it must send recommendations[293] to those responsible. Only if the recommendations, which are not binding, are not followed may the Commission authorize protective measures for the member states to take. Effective action can be taken only after sufficient time has elapsed for it to become clear that the recommendations of the Commission are not being obeyed and for the Commission to decide what action should be taken. The Commission has no power to fine enterprises responsible for dumping. If serious difficulties which are likely to continue arise in an industry as the result of dumping, the member state concerned may ask the Commission for leave to take protective action under Article 216.

Article 91(2) relates to any products which originated in one member state or which are entitled to free circulation there although they originated outside the EEC.[294] Any such goods which have been exported into another member state must be admitted free of all customs duties, quotas, or equivalent measures when re-exported to the member state from which they came. This "boomerang" provision does not depend on any ruling that dumping is in progress; it is automatic in its operation. This provision will lose all significance at the end of the transitional period. Regulations 8 and 13 implement Article 91(2).[295] If goods have not been handled, except for preservation or repairs to packaging, they may be freely re-exported, if all import formalities and customs duties have been paid in the re-exporting state and if the goods either originated in the re-exporting state[296] or have been freed from customs control there with all import duties paid.[297] These provisions are necessary to prevent the Treaty provision from being used as a device to bring the goods into the reimporting state free of duty.

[290] See GATT, Anti-Dumping and Countervailing Duties (1961).

[291] Fifth General Report, para. 49 (1962).

[292] Fourth General Report, para. 51 (1961).

[293] See art. 189.

[294] This is of little value in Ireland, due to the high cost of re-exporting the goods by ship. See von der Groeben, "Policy on Competition in the European Economic Community," 1961 EEC Bull. No. 7/8, Supp.

[295] 1960 Journal Officiel 597/60 and 1961 Journal Officiel 585/61, respectively.

[296] Reg. 8, arts. 3, 1(d).

[297] Reg. 8, arts. 3, 1(e). See also Reg. 13.

The other provisions of the regulations under Article 87 deal with documentary proof of these matters and with insuring that no obstacles are placed in the way of implementing the Treaty.[298]

Practical results

During the transitional period, action may be taken under Article 91(1) in all cases of dumping by persons established in the EEC, irrespective of the nationality and the public or private status of the person and irrespective of the origin of the goods dumped. Authorization for protective measures is given in the most restrictive form possible and is limited to what is strictly necessary to remedy the situation. In view of the Commission, injury will "probably" not occur unless the goods are delivered to the consumer in the importing country at a price below the local market price.[299] This view does not appear to take into account the extremely important possibility that the local market price subsequently may fall due to an increased supply of the goods in question.

No great difficulty arises in connection with dumping after the end of the transitional period, since it will usually be possible to re-export the dumped goods to the country of origin.[300] However, this does not adequately safeguard small firms against dumping by firms with large financial resources which is intended to put them out of business. Some Community law on unfair competition is required.

A country with a small home market and with small industrial enterprises, such as Ireland, is particularly vulnerable to dumping by large enterprises of bigger and more highly industrialized countries.[301] Irreparable damage can occur before protective measures are instituted. In consequence, the Irish government indicated that it believed that it would be necessary to strengthen the provisions of the Treaty and the regulations, in order to provide quicker remedies in serious cases, if Ireland joined the EEC. Cartels restricting the importation of cheap goods are not the proper protection against dumping.

298 See Third General Report, para. 146 (1960).

299 Fourth General Report, para. 51 (1961).

300 Spaak Report 54.

301 Statement of Prime Minister Seán F. Lemass, T.D., to Ministers of the Governments of the Member States of the European Economic Community, Brussels, Jan. 18, 1962, printed in European Economic Community: Developments Subsequent to the White Paper of June 30, 1961, Pr. 6613 (1962); see Murray, "Ireland and the European Free Trade Area," 5 Administration 25, 38 (1957).

Chapter 16

Antitrust Procedure

CONTROLLING RESTRICTIVE PRACTICES—THE COMMISSION'S APPROACH

The Commission has derived its methods of controlling restrictive practices[1] from the German Law Against Restraints of Competition and the British Restrictive Trade Practices Act of 1956.[2] Restrictive agreements, decisions, and practices within Article 85(1) are to be notified to the Commission, which decides whether they are permissible; control is *a priori* and not *a posteriori*.[3] The

[1] The first problem presented by arts. 85 and 86 was whether they were directly applicable in national law or were to come into force only when regulations had been made under art. 87. See Second General Report, paras. 115, 121 (1959); Riesenfeld, "The Protection of Competition," in 2 American Enterprise in the European Common Market: A Legal Profile 197, 329–34 (Stein & Nicholson ed. 1960); Ellis, "Les règles de concurrence du Traité de Rome applicables aux entreprises," 15 Rev. Int. de Droit Comp. 299, 304–10 (1963). Since Regulation 17, 1962 Journal Officiel 204/62, 1962 EEC Bull. No. 2, Supp.—the first implementing regulation—made them fully in force, this is academic. The question has been dealt with in retrospect by the Court in Bosch v. de Geus, 8 Recueil 89, [1962] C.M.L.R. 1. A second problem was that in 1958 Belgium, Italy, and Luxembourg had no antitrust laws, for all practical purposes. They had no cartel authorities to assist the Commission, and there was very little information as to the extent of restrictive practices there. See Second General Report, para. 111 (1959). The need for obtaining data prior to putting the competition policy into force colored the methods adopted in Regulation 17, just as this need had colored the methods used by the British government in the Monopolies and Restrictive Practices (Inquiry and Control) Act, 1948, 11 & 12 Geo. 6, c. 66, and by the Irish government in the Restrictive Trade Practices Act, 1953 Acts 75.

[2] 4 & 5 Eliz. 2, c. 68.

[3] On the three main types of anticartel law, see Deringer, "Les Règles Concernant la Concurrence dans le Cadre du Marché Commun Entrent en Vigeur," 5 Revue du Marché Commun 70, 71–72 (1962). Deringer distinguishes three types: (1) Prohibition of abuses only. This is the system in the Netherlands and Belgium. Practices are valid until specifically condemned. This method needs to be coupled with compulsory notification of practices to insure that illegal practices are dealt with; this is the system in Britain. (2) Prohibition with subsequent enforcement, or control *a posteriori*. This is the system in France and the United States and the system in Ireland, when recommendations of the Fair Trade Commission have passed into law. (3) Prohibition of all practices, with administrative exemptions given to beneficial types when notified. This is one of the systems under the German Competition Law and the law of the ECSC. It was not at first clear whether art. 85 contemplated the second system, art. 85(3) being a "statutory exemption," or the third, art. 85(3) containing a power to exempt. Art. 86 is a law of the second type, and the provisions of Regulation 17 on notification have no real relation to it, since there is no pressure to notify a possible abuse.

Professor Bernini, "Problèmes concernant l'application de l'article 85, No. 3 du Traité C.E.E. à certaines catégories d'accords restreignant la concurrence," 1963 Journal des Tribunaux 345, 346, says: "[T]he control adopted by Regulation 17 for cartels subject to obligatory notification corresponds more or less exactly to the regime based on the theory of authorization. . . . [A]s far as cartels not subject to obligatory notification are concerned, the provisions of Regulation 17 correspond to the theory of statutory exemption." (Author's translation.)

need for notification of existing cartels itself causes many to be modified or ended.[4] The first Regulations[5] dealt only with procedure and with the effect of the Treaty provisions on prohibited agreements. Only in December 1962[6] was any attempt made formally to say what type of agreement was permitted by the substantive Treaty provisions, although members of the Commission and its staff had been informally explaining the official views on various matters long before then. The Regulations classify agreements into those which demand immediate attention and those which may be within Article 85(1) but have a less anticompetitive effect. Much of the Commission's work has been defining categories of less objectionable agreements and has not dealt with action to be taken against the more seriously anticompetitive ones. Some further regulations may be expected to specify classes of agreements which are likely to fall outside Article 85(1) or within Article 85(3) and which thus will not require individual attention from the Commission. The communications on exclusive distributorships and on patent licenses indicate a strict approach and a reluctance to interpret Article 85(1) narrowly or to indicate that any types of agreement are certainly outside it.

Article 87 provides that regulations or directives should be issued to enforce Articles 85(1) and 86, to provide for the application of Article 85(3) so as to reconcile effective supervision with simplification of administrative control, and to define the respective functions of the Commission and the Court. These matters are dealt with in Regulation 17. Article 87 also mentions the application of Articles 85 and 86 to particular economic sectors.[7]

The explanatory memorandum of the Commission[8] said that accomplishing the four objectives in Regulation 17—to improve the authorities' means of obtaining information; to bring about certainty as to the legal position, which enterprises need; to create a transitional regime for existing cartels; and to insure that Article 85 was applied in substantially the same way in each member state—was necessary. Regulation 17 does not expressly deal with public monopolies.[9]

The Regulations[10] do not form a con-

[4] This happened in Britain when the 1956 Act was introduced and seems to have happened in the Six. See Irish Fair Trade Commission, Report of Enquiry into . . . Building Materials and Components, Pr. 2841, paras. 8–15 (1954).

[5] Reg. 17; Reg. 27, 1962 Journal Officiel 1118/62; Reg. 59, id. at 1655/62; Reg. 153, id. at 2918/62; and Reg. 118, 1963 Journal Officiel 2696/63. All references to arts. 1 to 24 in this chapter are to Regulation 17, not to the EEC Treaty, unless otherwise indicated. References to other articles are references to the Treaty. The regulations adopted under art. 87 are referred to as "Regulations."

[6] Communication Concerning Exclusive Contracts . . ., 1962 Journal Officiel 2921/62, and Communication Concerning Patent License Agreements, id. at 2922/62, already discussed on pp. 396–404 in connection with exclusive distributorships and patent licenses.

[7] As to sectors presently affected, see Chapter Fifteen, note 1.

[8] Deringer Report, A.P.E. Doc. No. 57, Annex I, at 51 (1961–62).

[9] See arts. 37, 90; Deringer Report, A.P.E. Doc. No. 57, para. 133 (1961–62).

[10] The preamble to Regulation 17 is an excellent introduction to the Regulations. The most authoritative commentary on Regulation 17 in something close to its final version is the Deringer Report, A.P.E. Doc. No. 57 (1961–62). Of the large number of studies that have been written about Regulation 17, the following may be mentioned: van Hecke & Suetens, "Le Premier Règlement Européen sur les Cartels et les Monopoles," 1962 Journal des Tribunaux 361–69; Guide Pratique; Political and Economic Planning, Cartel Policy and the Common Market 265–78 (1962); and Campbell, Restrictive Trading Agreements in the Common Market (1964). For the history of Regulation 17, see Ellis, "Les règles de concurrence du Traité de Rome applicables aux enterprises," 15 Rev. Int. de Droit Comp. 299, 310–17 (1964).

sistent whole, since they result from a number of compromises.[11] They have a strong, and perhaps inevitable, tendency to place the whole implementation of the antitrust provisions into the hands of the Commission.[12]

The Regulations divide agreements, decisions, and concerted practices into four broad categories: (1) new agreements in the compulsorily notifiable class; (2) new, less anticompetitive agreements in the optionally notifiable class, under Article 4(2); (3) existing agreements in the compulsorily notifiable class; and (4) existing, less anticompetitive agreements in the optionally notifiable class. "Existing" agreements are all those in existence at the time Regulation 17 came into force. They are dealt with by transitional provisions.

NEW AGREEMENTS

The "compulsorily notifiable" class

Restrictive agreements entered into after Regulation 17 came into force[13] are to be notified[14] to the Commission. In substance, notification consists of producing the agreement and an argument that it is outside Article 85(1) or within Article 85(3), or both. No approval under Article 85(3) is possible for a new agreement which has not been notified,[15] unless the agreement is in the "optionally notifiable" category. Notification is not compulsory,[16] but even an agreement approved under Article 85(3) can never be validated for the period prior to notification,[17] and fines for that period may always be imposed.[18] No fine can be imposed for the period after notification.[19] The approval of the Commission, which alone[20] validates an agreement, will usually be retroactive to the time of notification, but this is not automatic.[21]

These provisions apply to all agreements—except those optionally notifiable —which replace previous agreements that have been reconsidered by the parties after Regulation 17 was issued.[22] Since the main aim of the Commission is to encourage economic competition, probably no great efforts will be made to

[11] See Deringer Report, A.P.E. Doc. No. 57, para. 75 (1961–62).

[12] This was deliberately encouraged by the "Europeans" in the Parliamentary Assembly.

[13] On March 13, 1962.

[14] As to the forms for notification and the procedure where the notification is not by all the parties to an agreement, see Reg. 27, 1962 Journal Officiel 118/62; Deringer et al., 7 Revue du Marché Commun 135, 142 (1964).

[15] Reg. 17, art. 4(1); unless the agreement falls within a regulation made under Reg. 19, 1965 Journal Officiel 533/65.

[16] Registration of anticompetitive agreements is compulsory under the British Restrictive Trade Practices Act, 1956, 4 & 5 Eliz. 2, c. 68. Under Regulation 17 there is no register of agreements and the word "notification" is therefore preferable to "registration."

[17] Art. 6(1). This does not apply to the "optionally notifiable" category under art. 4(2).

[18] Art. 15(5)(a).

[19] Ibid.; subject, however, to art. 15(6).

[20] Arts. 9(1), 1.

[21] If approval were not retroactive to the time of notification, it would be impossible to act on an agreement for as long as the Commission chose to spend considering it. However, it may be necessary to insert a clause in all restrictive agreements or to arrange that they will not come into force until notified. Where even temporary invalidity might seriously prejudice the parties, it may be necessary to provide that they will not be acted upon until approved, if the parties are not certain that the approval under art. 85(3) will be made to operate from the date of notification. Since, in practice, all the parties to the agreement will probably have to agree on the terms of the notification (see, however, Reg. 27, art. 1[1]), concerted practices will probably have to be reduced to writing so that the notification can state the terms of the practice with precision.

[22] Reappraisal of existing agreements will be as necessary in member states acceding to the Community in the future as it was in the Six.

discover and punish Treaty infringements by enterprises which later have voluntarily mended their ways. Alteration of agreements to bring them outside Article 85(1) or under Article 4(2) and to avoid notification is the best course of action where it is possible.[23]

The Commission has no power to give retroactive validity to new cartels if they are modified so as to come within Article 85(3).[24] The Commission may exempt an agreement *ex nunc* on the condition that a specified alteration is made, or it may include in the exemption a provision preventing the agreement from being acted upon in specified ways.[25]

The "optionally notifiable" class

"Optionally notifiable" agreements[26] are less restrictive in their effect and are treated somewhat differently. Except where they require modification to obtain approval, the time when they are notified is irrelevant.[27] Notification is "optional" because the Commission may give approval which is retroactive prior to the date of notification.[28] They also may be approved under Article 85(3) without a formal notification.[29]

Optionally notifiable agreements are not necessarily within Article 85(3), and their classification has no substantive significance. Fines may be imposed on parties to them for actions prior to notification.[30] Unless the agreement may result in a fine or certainty as to the legal position is needed, nothing is lost by postponing notification of an optionally notifiable agreement. The Commission does not want to be notified of agreements unnecessarily, and therefore agreements which are clearly within both Article 4(2) and Article 85(3) need not be notified until their validity is questioned in some way. However, since Article 4(2) confers no protection from fines or invalidity, the safe course in doubtful cases is always to notify.

Optionally notifiable agreements[31] include three distinct categories. The first category is intrastate agreements, regardless of their content, which are made by any number of enterprises operating in the same member state[32] and which "in-

[23] Deringer, Some Practical Aspects of the Antitrust Provisions of the Treaty of Rome (1962).

[24] Art. 7 applies only to cartels in existence when Regulation 17 came into force.

[25] The Bundeskartellamt indicates how an agreement should be modified in order to obtain approval; Schapiro, "The German Law Against Restraints of Competition—Comparative and International Aspects," 62 Colum. L. Rev. 201, 208–209 (1962). This is also the French practice; Riesenfeld, "The Legal Protection of Competition in France," 48 Calif. L. Rev. 574, 590–92 (1960).

[26] Those within arts. 4(2) and 5(2).

[27] Art. 6(2).

[28] Hence the position for agreements under art. 4(2) is that art. 85(3) is a statutory exemption.

[29] Guide Pratique 10. Art. 4(2) provides that art. 4(1), which requires formal notification before exemption can be given, does not apply to agreements under art. 4(2). See also 1962 Journal Officiel 2418-19/62. See, however, Buxbaum, "Patent Licensing: A Case Study on Antitrust Regulations Within the European Economic Community," 9 Antitrust Bull. 101, 128–29 (1964).

[30] But not, of course, if they are held to fall outside art. 85(1) or if they have been made the subject of a regulation made under Regulation 19. See art. 15(5), 15(6).

[31] Arts. 4(2), 5(2).

[32] An agreement between an enterprise of a non-member state and one or more enterprises of one member state is not within this provision; Guide Pratique 11; see Becker, Extraterritorial Application of Common Market Laws (PLI, 1962). See also Deringer et al., 7 Revue du Marché Commun 135, 138 (1964).

volve"[33] neither imports nor exports between member states. In practice, national cartels which do not cover exports and imports are unlikely to effectively protect the participants from competition, so this category is likely to be unimportant.[34]

The second category is bilateral[35] agreements between enterprises of any nationality, the only anticompetitive effect of which is to fix resale prices or conditions[36] for goods sold by one party to the other or to limit the exercise of the licensed industrial property rights by the licensee, without limiting the rights of the seller or licensor. The latter is hardly a common type of agreement, since it gives inadequate protection to the licensee. This category includes any agreement giving the right to use patents, models, designs, trademarks, manufacturing processes, or know-how relating to the use and application of industrial techniques. All common bilateral resale price maintenance agreements are in this category.

The third category is agreements between any number of enterprises of any nationality, the only object of which is to develop or prescribe standards and types of products or to provide for joint research work to be available for use by all participants.[37]

Since, to be optionally notifiable, the "sole" object[38] or effect[39] of an agreement must be to fix resale prices, to restrict the exercise of industrial property rights or rights to know-how, or to develop standards or to carry on research, an agreement which falls under more than one of these heads is "compulsorily" notifiable, unless it is within Article 4(2)(i). Since a number of restrictive provisions have a cumulative effect, this may not be unreasonable;[40] however, the interpretation is a strict one, and it may be incorrect.

[33] Art. 4(2)(i). The French verb used is *concerner*; this means "relate to" or "deal with" directly, rather than "affect." See Guide Pratique 11. Therefore, agreements which affect exports or imports only indirectly are not compulsorily notifiable.

[34] Verloren van Themaat, The Statist, June 15, 1962, pp. 792, 793; see Steindorff, "Restrictive Practices Laws of Germany," in Restrictive Practices, Patents, Trade Marks and Unfair Competition in the Common Market, Int'l & Comp. L.Q. Supp. No. 4, at 28, 31–32 (1962).

[35] Even where there are a large number of bilateral agreements, all of which fix prices, they are not compulsorily notifiable. If, however, they constitute a horizontal concerted practice between dealers who are parties to bilateral agreements with a single manufacturer, or if for some other reason a practice exists in which more than two parties participate, the practice is compulsorily notifiable.

[36] This clause covers only restrictions imposed on the purchaser which relate to the content of contracts of resale he makes. It does not apply to restrictions on the area in which he may resell the goods, his choice of customers, or the use of the products sold; these must be notified. Deringer & Tessin, "Les Contrats d'exclusivité dans le Droit du Marché Commun," 80 Moniteur Official du Commerce International 3267, 3270 (1962). The German Competition Law distinguishes between limitations on a party's freedom to enter into contracts with third parties and limitations on the terms which the party can include in those contracts (§§ 15, 18); the latter, curiously, are more strictly limited by the law; Schapiro, "The German Law Against Restraints of Competition . . .," 62 Colum. L. Rev. 201–202 (1962). Restrictive provisions in licenses of industrial and commercial property can be made the subject of class exemptions.

[37] Cf. German Competition Law, §§ 2(1), 5; Schapiro, "The German Law Against Restraints of Competition . . .," 62 Colum. L. Rev. 1, 19, 28–34 (1962). Section 5 distinguishes between rationalization cartels and syndicates. A syndicate, in practice, usually would not be within art. 4(2), since prescribing standards and types would not be its sole function. French doctrine distinguishes between *ententes d'exploitation* and *ententes de règlementation*; Houssiaux, Concurrence et Marché Commun 96 (1960).

[38] Art. 4(2)(iii).

[39] Art. 4(2)(ii).

[40] See Guide Pratique 12.

EXISTING AGREEMENTS

Transitional provisions[41]

The transitional provisions of Regulation 17 deal with restrictive agreements, decisions, and concerted practices in existence when that Regulation came into force. The deadline for notification of all such agreements, unless optionally notifiable, is now past, and the provisions themselves have merely historical importance. However, some special provisions will have to be made to deal with agreements which, whatever the nationality of the parties, affect interstate trade only because of the accession of a new member state. Since this special provision will presumably be similar to those made for "existing agreements," the latter are discussed here.

Deadline for notification and the accession of a new member state

Regulation 17 imposed a deadline for notification of existing agreements.[42] This finally allowed eight months from the enactment of the Regulation in its final form for existing multilateral agreements not within the "optional" category, and almost a year for existing bilateral agreements.[43] On the accession of a new member state, these periods probably will be shorter, because enterprises will know the requirements of the Commission more clearly than in 1962 and will need less time to review their agreements. The time limit for notifying existing bilateral agreements was postponed specially to allow the Commission to formulate categories of agreements which were relieved from notification, so as to avoid a deluge of unnecessary notifications.[44] It will not be necessary to give the Commission time to clarify its ideas at the time of the accession of a new state. The number of agreements likely to come within the jurisdiction of the Commission on the accession of a new state will not affect the time allowed for notification unless there will be so many that the Commission will desire to receive them in installments. The enterprises in question will have warning of the entry of the new state into the Community and will be able to prepare the documents for notification before the time limit is announced. Within these limitations, the time limit is likely to be of the order of three to five months.

The consequences of the deadline

The importance of the deadline for notification of existing restrictive agreements under Regulation 17 was twofold. First, agreements notified within the time limit could get approval from the Commission under Article 85(3), which was retroactive for the whole period prior to notification.[45] The same provision will

[41] Transitional provisions on agreements approved before Regulation 17 came into force (art. 23) will have no parallel on the accession of a new member state. Agreements or cartels are regarded as having been in existence at the time when the Regulations came into force only if they were then in the form in which they are later notified. If they have been modified or supplemented, they become new cartels and are invalid until notified. However, insignificant alterations presumably will not have this effect. See Deringer Report, A.P.E. Doc. No. 57, para. 105 (1961–62).

[42] Art. 5(1); amended by postponement of the deadline for existing multilateral agreements not within art. 4(2) to Nov. 1, 1962, and by a special deadline (Feb. 1, 1963) still further deferred for existing bilateral agreements not within art. 4(2)(ii), by Reg. 59.

[43] Reg. 59. On class exemptions for bilateral agreements which were notified in time, see Reg. 19, art. 4.

[44] This exclusion was carried out by the communications on patent licenses and exclusive dealerships, 1962 Journal Officiel 2921/62, and id. at 2922/62.

[45] Art. 6(2). In the case of the Six, agreements first became subject to the Treaty on January 1, 1958, or on whatever later date the agreement in question came into force; in the case of new member states this date will be

presumably be made for agreements made by enterprises of new member states.

Second, if agreements notified in time did not fall within Article 85(3), the parties could end them or modify them to bring them either within Article 85(3) or outside Article 85(1). The Commission could then fix the period during which the invalidity would operate[46] and therefore could validate the agreement retroactively for the entire period prior to notification.[47] However, a decision of the Commission which retroactively validates a modified agreement otherwise invalid cannot be relied on in litigation against enterprises which have not expressly consented to the notification; a party to a void agreement cannot be sued on it if it has been modified and validated without his consent.[48] A

---

the date specified in the legislation ratifying the Treaty or the treaty of accession. On defective notification cured after the expiration of the time limit, see 1963 EEC Bull. No. 11, at 21. For some authorities on the position of agreements before notification, see van den Heuvel, "Civil Law Consequences of Violation of the Antitrust Provisions of the Rome Treaty," 12 Am. J. Comp. L. 172, 178–79 (1963).

[46] Art. 7(1).

[47] It is a matter of interpretation of art. 7(1) to decide whether retroactive validation of an agreement which was invalid until modified is compatible with the view that art. 85(3) gives a power to exempt from art. 85(1) by a prospective decision or with the view that art. 85(3) grants automatic exemption of which the decision approving an agreement is merely declaratory. Insofar as art. 7 confers power on the Commission to permit the agreement *ex nunc* in the modified form which entitles the agreement to approval, it is unnecessary, since the parties could always cancel the agreement and notify a new agreement in a modified form. All the authorities seem to agree that its function is to allow an invalid agreement to be validated retroactively. Two possibilities arise: (1) In return for the modification, the Commission will validate the agreement retroactively in its original form. This might be ultra vires, since such a decision would purport to validate an agreement *ex hypothesi* not permitted by the Treaty. (2) When modified, the Commission will regard the agreement, except vis-à-vis parties who have not agreed to the notification or modification, as having existed at all times only in its modified form, and so will approve it retroactively. Preferably, agreements should include a consent by all parties to notification. See Deringer, "Les Règles Concernant la Concurrence dans le Cadre du Marché Commun Entrent en Vigeur," 5 Revue du Marché Commun 70, 80 (1962); Waelbroeck, "Le Problème de la Validité des Ententes Economiques dans le droit privé du Marché Commun," 51 Rev. Crit. de Droit Int. Privé 415, 428–29 (1962); Deringer et al., 7 Revue du Marché Commun 406 (1964).

If art. 85(3) is a statutory exemption, making decisions approving agreements within it declaratory of the past situation, then these decisions are, in effect, retroactive and not prospective. However, if they are declaratory, they cannot operate retroactively to validate an agreement by definition not previously within art. 85(3), but they can validate only an agreement deemed to always have been within art. 85(3)—possibility (2) above.

Art. 7 assumes that, if art. 85(3) empowers the Commission to dispense with the prohibition of art. 85(1), this is not a power to approve only *ex nunc*. Under art. 6(1), the Commission may give to agreements which were always within art. 85(3) approval which is retroactive, but not fully retroactive. This is compatible with the retroactive ("statutory exception") theory of art. 85(3) only if one holds that the Commission is bound to make the approval fully retroactive (unless circumstances exist which make art. 85(3) inapplicable, in which case the Commission could not give approval for such a time). Therefore, if possibility (2) above is the correct interpretation of art. 7, art. 7 is valid on either view of art. 85(3). If possibility (1) above is correct, it is invalid on the declaratory theory and of doubtful validity on the "power" theory ("reservation of authorization") since art. 85 does not authorize the Commission to approve any agreement for a period during which it was, in law and in fact, not within art. 85(3). While the Council may have power to authorize approval for agreements not within art. 85(3) and within art. 85(1), it seems that the Council did not believe that it was doing this in art. 7, since no reference was made to art. 235, which probably gives the Council the necessary power.

[48] Guide Pratique 17. The rule applies also in the converse case in which the enterprise which did not consent to the notification sues the parties who did; see Reg. 19.

third party injured by the agreement cannot be deprived, by the retroactive validation, of any right to damages given him by the national law.[49] The object of this second provision was to encourage parties to existing agreements to notify them, in order to have modified illegal agreements validated with retroactive effect. This was sound policy and, unless a radical revision of Regulation 17 occurs, should be acted upon on the accession of a new member state. If an agreement contrary to the Treaty has been terminated voluntarily or on the advice of the Commission, no fines will be imposed.[50]

Existing anticompetitive agreements not notified in time were in the same position as new agreements; exemption under Article 85(3) could not be given for the period before notification. Approval of existing optionally notifiable agreements may be retroactive back to the moment when the agreement was first affected by the Treaty, regardless of the date of notification.[51] An existing optionally notifiable agreement requiring modification for approval[52] can be validated prior to the date of modification only if the agreement is notified before January 1967.[53] A separate deadline for modifying optionally notifiable agreements is likely on the accession of a new member state, unless the total estimated number of agreements is so small that the Commission decides to deal with them all with the same deadline.

No fines will be imposed for existing optionally notifiable agreements notified before January 1967, since fines for a cartel which could have been fully validated retroactively if modified would in effect compel notification at a date earlier than that specified in the Regulation.[54] The Commission, of course, does not need to wait until January 1967 before prohibiting an agreement,[55] and failure to obey such a prohibition will involve fines.[56]

THE STATUS OF DIFFERENT CLASSES OF AGREEMENT

A new agreement within Article 85(1) and not within Article 4(2) cannot get the Commission's approval for the period before notification[57] and is invalid during that period. Subject to this, approval takes effect from the date decided by the Commission. Because of this, new agreements not within Article 4(2) should not be permitted to come into force before notification.[58]

"Provisional validity"

The validity of a new agreement after notification depends on the ultimate decision of the Commission whether to apply Article 85(3) and the date from

[49] Van Hecke & Suetens, "Le Premier Règlement Européen sur les Cartels et les Monopoles," 1962 Journal des Tribunaux 361, 366; contra, Oberdorfer, Gleiss & Hirsch, Common Market Cartel Law 127 (1963).

[50] According to Dr. Verloren van Themaat; Committee on Foreign Law, "Current Legal Developments in the European Economic Community," 18 Record of N.Y.C.B.A. 329, 337 (1963).

[51] Art. 6(2).

[52] Art. 7(2).

[53] Reg. 118, 1963 Journal Officiel 2696/63.

[54] Art. 15(5)(b).

[55] Art. 9(2).

[56] Art. 16.

[57] Arts. 9(1), 4(1). Class exemptions cannot be given under art. 85(3) for agreements not within art. 4(2) which have not been notified; Deringer, "The Distribution of Powers in the Enforcement of the Rules of Competition Under the Rome Treaty," 1 Common Market L. Rev. 30, 35 (1963). The Commission is now entitled to grant class exemptions; Reg. 19, 1965 Journal Officiel 533/65; see 1964 Journal Officiel 3318–22/64.

[58] To avoid the need for proof of this fact later, it seems preferable to incorporate a provision to this effect in any agreement which is going to be notified.

which the approval is to take effect. If it is acted on after notification, no fines can be incurred.[59] To avoid the situation in which an agreement regarded as void is retroactively validated, it seems better to regard notified agreements as provisionally valid,[60] in spite of the fact that Article 85(1) operates automatically and Article 85(3) does not.

All agreements within Article 4(2) are in some sense provisionally valid, according to the Court.[61] However, such an agreement is invalid *ab initio* without any decision to that effect if it is within Article 85(1), and it can be validated only by the Commission. Unlike new agreements not within Article 4(2), an agreement within Article 4(2) is not inevitably invalid prior to notification.

If notified in time, all existing agreements—whether or not they are within Article 4(2) and even if they are not within Article 85(3)—have a good chance of validity throughout their duration, because of the chance of retroactive approval in their modified form.[62] If not actually prohibited by the Commission or by national authorities and if notified in time, existing agreements within Articles 85(1) should be considered provisionally valid until they have been adjudicated.[63] If existing agreements within Article 85(1)[64] and not within Article 4(2) are not notified in time, they are void from the time of entry into force of the Regulation until they are notified.

Since the validity of the agreement between the time of notification and the time of the decision of the Commission depends on the ultimate decision, it may be uncertain for a long period. This uncertainty may cause serious practical problems. It necessarily results from a system in which enterprises are free, if they wish, to act on agreements before they have been approved. Presumably the Commission will try to give preliminary opinions as soon after notification as possible.[65] The situation will be more satisfactory when the law is more clearly known and when, having worked through its huge initial volume of work, the Commission is able to give final decisions reasonably promptly.

The retroactive effect of the Commission's decisions

Since declarations of validity and of invalidity may be retroactive,[66] questions of provisional validity are solved when

[59] Art. 15(5)(a).

[60] Provisional validity is not a presumption of validity; it is simply the basis for interim treatment of an agreement pending a decision.

[61] Bosch v. de Geus, 8 Recueil 89, 107, [1962] C.M.L.R. 1, 30. See Oberdorfer, Gleiss & Hirsch, Common Market Cartel Law 94 (1963); Françon, "Une première interpretation de l'article 85 du Traité de Rome par la Cour des Communautés européennes," 90 Journal du Droit International 391 (1963); Re "Braun" Electric Razors, Bundesgerichtshof, June 14, 1963, [1964] C.M.L.R. 59. See, however, Deringer et al., 7 Revue du Marché Commun 245, 247 (1964).

[62] Art. 7(1). Existing agreements which are within art. 5(2) because they are within one of the classes set out in art. 4(2) are in the same position as similar new agreements, except that they may be retroactively validated after modifications if they are notified within a time limit; art. 7(2).

[63] Bosch v. de Geus, 8 Recueil 89, 108, [1962] C.M.L.R. 1, 30–31 (Decision, para. 2). On the accession of a new member state, Regulation 17 will come into force automatically at the same time as the Treaty, unless specifically excluded.

[64] Bosch v. de Geus, 8 Recueil 89, 108–109, [1962] C.M.L.R. 1, 31 (Decision, para. 3). The C.M.L.R. translation appears to be incorrect.

[65] See art. 15(6). Some degree of priority will be given to agreements notified before they come into force; Seventh General Report, para. 66 (1964).

[66] See Oberdorfer, Gleiss & Hirsch, Common Market Cartel Law 92–93 (1963). Weiser, "Freedom of Competition in the European Economic Community: An Analysis of the Regulations Implementing the Antitrust Provisions," 6

the Commission gives a decision. Retroactive declarations of invalidity, however, require mention. No prior decision of the invalidity of any agreement contrary to Article 85(1) is, in principle, required.[67] The Commission must state the date from which any approval under Article 85(3) takes effect.[68] If approval under Article 85(3) is not given retroactive effect or if it is refused, there is, in a sense, an unfavorable decision with retroactive effect, but it is the rule of law and not the invalidating decision which has had this effect. The Commission may not declare an agreement valid prior to a certain date and invalid after that date, except when it revokes its approval;[69] therefore, if the Commission is not prepared to approve an agreement for the future, it must necessarily have been invalid in the past also, even if the parties have acted in good faith.[70] It is therefore always dangerous not to notify the Commission of agreements in the "optionally notifiable" class unless approval under Article 85(3) or a declaration of inapplicability of Article 85(1) is certain.

The extent of retroactive approval

Presumably, when notification is in time[71] and approval is given, it will be full retroactive approval covering the agreement for all of its life.[72] Presumably, no fines will be imposed. If an existing agreement is approved only in a modified form, approval in respect of the period prior to the date of the modification will not necessarily be given; this will depend on the circumstances of the case and, in particular, on the extent to which seriously objectionable and irrevocable actions have been performed pursuant to the agreement before modifications. The Commission may act against objectionable agreements before the time limits have elapsed.[73] The only circumstances in which it is permissible not to give full retroactive validation to an agreement being approved are those where only a change of circumstances has justified the application of Article 85(3).

Intermittent validity

The extent of the retroactive operation of approval is important because of the practical difficulties which arise if an agreement is invalid at one moment and valid the next. The parties cannot complain if they allow a compulsorily notifiable agreement to enter into force prior to notification, but after that they are in the hands of the Commission. Apart from the question of the extent to which the legitimate provisions of a prohibited agreement remain operative,[74] certain

---

Pat., T.M. & Copyright J. Research & Educ. 20, 30, 32 (1962), appears to misunderstand the position in this respect.

[67] Art. 1; see Bosch v. de Geus, 8 Recueil 89, [1962] C.M.L.R. 1.

[68] Art. 6(1).

[69] Art. 8.

[70] This application of control *a posteriori* is mitigated for existing agreements by the possibility of approval of a modified version under art. 7. It is not possible to say how the Commission would treat an agreement which had been permissible under art. 85(3) but which, owing to a change of circumstances, ceased to be so before the Commission issued its decision.

[71] Notification of an existing agreement can be made at any time before the deadline specified. Notification of a new agreement is made in time if it is made before, or at the same time as, the agreement comes into force. In either case, the Commission may approve the agreement retroactively back to the first moment for which approval is required; art. 6.

[72] Failure to give full retroactive approval in all cases where the agreement is approved without modification would be theoretically unjustifiable and would interfere unnecessarily with business transactions and impose on existing agreements new deadlines not contemplated by the regulation.

[73] Arts. 9(2), 9(3), 3.

[74] This question is discussed separately on pp. 469–74. Clearly, if only a small part of an agreement is invalidated, the difficulties arising from temporary invalidity will be minimized.

questions are likely to arise if the contract is one of continuing obligation. The first type of problem is the extent to which an obligation to make a money payment during the period of invalidity of the agreement is enforceable. Will it make any difference if the payment is due when the agreement has become valid but is payable for a period during which the agreement was invalid? Secondly, a covenant requiring the performance of some act may be valid if the act can be performed at any time, but invalid if the act is to be done during the period of the agreement's invalidity. Thirdly, if the agreement prohibits some act, such as the disclosure of secret know-how to a third party, and there is a breach of this provision during the time in which the agreement is invalid, does the original donor of the know-how have a cause of action? Will a temporarily invalid agreement be a good defense if it cannot be a cause of action? How will the temporary invalidity of an agreement affect the validity of a patent or trademark licensed under it?

The answers to these questions and the other consequences of invalidity are matters of national law even if the Treaty governs the extent to which the legitimate provisions of an agreement which is "automatically null and void"[75] remain valid. There seem to be no principles worked out on the problem of intermittent validity of a continuing contract, and this book does not purport to speculate on what the national laws would do. Like many of the problems arising in the preparation of threatened agreements, this one would be better handled by a clause dealing with the problem in anticipation than by leaving it to the courts to work out. If the various questions which will arise are dealt with by national law, conflicting decisions are possible. Because of the complex problems resulting from intermittent validity, the Commission will presumably try to avoid changes in the status of a restrictive agreement where this is possible.

[75] Art. 85(2).

Stipulations and conditions in a decision approving a restrictive agreement

Questions arising from a change in the validity of an agreement will arise at times other than when the approval of the agreement by the Commission under Article 85(3) takes effect.[76] The Commission may make the approval subject to conditions and stipulations[77] and must make the approval valid for a specified period.[78] No indication is given of the type of conditions to be imposed. Presumably, they will deal with the way in which the agreement is to be acted upon and with any practices contrary to Article 85(1) which are permitted but not required by the provisions of the agreement. The elaborate, complex, and precise drafting of decrees in United States antitrust cases need never be imitated by the Commission; this is one advantage of having antitrust law dealt with by an administrative authority. A decision of the Commission approving an agreement may be renewed if the requirements of Article 85(3) continue to be fulfilled,[79] but if they are not, the agreement becomes invalid automatically on the expiration of the approval.[80]

[76] Art. 6(1).

[77] The Commission may, in effect, modify an agreement by granting an exemption on condition that the agreement is not acted upon in specified ways or an exemption to take effect only if the agreement is altered in specified respects. See Clément, "La Délimitation des Compétences Respectives de la Commission du Marché Commun et des Autorités Nationales en Matière des Cartels (Articles 88 et 89 du Traité de Rome)," in 1 Cartel and Monopoly in Modern Law 377 (in French), 386, 395 (in English), 404 (1961).

[78] Art. 8(1).

[79] Art. 8(2).

[80] Arts. 1, 6(1), 8(1).

Revocation of a decision approving an agreement

If one of the facts essential for approval under Article 85(3) changes, the approval may be modified or revoked from that time even if it has not expired.[81] This revocation apparently can operate only from the moment of the decision to revoke and not retroactively from the time of the change in the circumstances. The possibility that the Commission may cancel an approval at any time if circumstances change is important in the rapidly changing economy of the EEC. Any change of circumstances essential to the original approval may be a ground for altering the decision, but one of the most important is the accession of a new party to an existing agreement.[82] Accession of a new participant usually must be notified.[83] It may alter an agreement's position under Article 85(3), especially in connection with the question of elimination of competition for a "substantial part" of the goods concerned. Presumably, the notifying parties should indicate the likelihood of additional participation, and the Commission may include in the approval a stipulation that certain changes of circumstances should be called to its attention.

If the approval itself is based on inaccurate information or obtained by fraud or if the approval is infringed or "abused,"[84] it may be revoked retroactively.[85] Presumably, abuse of an exemp-

[81] Art. 8(3)(a) and final clause; Reg. 19, art. 7.

[82] See Third General Report, para. 140 (1960); Schumacher, "Réflexions sur l'interdiction des ententes visées par l'article 85 du Traité instituant la C.E.E.," 24 Droit Social 65, 70 (1961).

[83] This is not clear. Third General Report, para. 140 (1960) says: "[I]f . . . there are at the moment [when the approval is given] no facts which make it possible to foresee that other firms will be associated with a given understanding, the subsequent admission of other companies to the understanding would imply that the facts of the situation had changed, and this would call for a fresh examination of the situation." Any change made in the terms of an agreement on the accession of a new participant, other than the removal of an anticompetitive provision, must be notified. Whether there is a duty to notify the accession cannot be allowed to turn on the question of novation. A concerted practice between a given number of enterprises would seem to be a different thing when another enterprise participates. If an agreement affected a large number of small enterprises, presumably the accession of one more would not need to be notified, but this is something which the Commission would have to provide for in its decision approving the agreement. It is submitted that in the absence of any provision in the decision, the accession of a new participant must be notified.

[84] Art. 8(3)(b)–8(3)(d). This may mean in all three cases that the revocation may operate back to the time when the improper act occurred, which is the time of the approval only in the second case. A more severe interpretation would be that in all three cases the approval can be, in effect, void *ab initio* by reason of the act of the parties to the agreement. This interpretation best explains the distinction drawn between art. 8(3)(a) and 8(3)(b)–8(3)(d). It is reasonable in the case of art. 8(3)(c) where the approval would not have been given if the Commission had known the truth. It seems to be the correct interpretation where the parties infringe a term of the approval or abuse their position under it; see van Hecke & Suetens, "Le Premier Règlement Européen sur les Cartels et les Monopoles," 1962 Journal des Tribunaux 361, 366; Deringer et al., 7 Revue du Marché Commun 406, 409 (1964). The provision makes no distinction between art. 8(3)(c) and 8(3)(b) and 8(3)(d), and all three situations involve the fault of the parties to the agreement. The fact that revocation may be fully retroactive does not mean that the Commission will necessarily so apply it. Fines may be imposed for breach of a stipulation, art. 15(2)(b); or for submitting false information in a notification, art. 15(1)(a); but apparently not for abuse of the exemption, the only sanction for which is invalidity. See Deringer, "Les Règles Concernant la Concurrence dans le Cadre du Marché Commun Entrent en Vigeur," 5 Revue du Marché Commun 70, 77 (1962). Daily fines to compel the ending of an abuse are possible; art. 16(1)(b).

[85] "Abused" refers to the civil law doctrine of abuse of rights, which has no parallel in English or Irish law. See Gutteridge, "Abuse of

tion will normally occur where the enterprises concerned have something approaching a dominant market position.

The Commission may revoke the approval, alter the conditions attached to it, or add to it by prohibiting the parties from courses of action previously open to them. If the facts have changed or if there has been an abuse of an exemption granted under Article 85(3), the Commission's power to modify the terms of the exemption rather than revoke it will be important.

Burden of proof

The burden of proof is on the parties to the agreement at the times of the initial notification and of renewal to show that the agreement is within Article 85(3). However, the burden of proof is on the Commission to show that an agreement is initially within Article 85(1) and to show that changed circumstances, a breach of a stipulation, false information, or an abuse of the exemption has occurred so as to justify the revocation of the exemption.[86] There is no provision for the tacit renewal of approval; this is probably unfortunate.[87]

NEGATIVE CLEARANCES

Where the parties to an agreement or practice believe that it is not within Article 85(1) or Article 86, they may obtain a "negative clearance" from the Commission confirming this.[88] It is not possible to use the negative clearance procedure to confirm that an agreement is within Article 85(3); this can be done only by full notification.[89]

A negative clearance merely states that, on the basis of the facts supplied to the Commission,[90] no question appears to arise under either Article. It does not prevent the Commission from subsequently issuing a decision that the agreement contravenes Article 85(1) if the essential circumstances have changed, if the Commission becomes aware of additional facts which change its view, if the Commission's view of the law has been changed by a decision of the Court, or if a complaint is made by a person having a "legitimate interest."[91] A negative clearance apparently constitutes a decision under Article 189,[92] and if none of

Rights," 5 Camb. L.J. 22 (1933); Schlesinger, Comparative Law 372–91 (2d ed. 1959). German Competition Law, § 17(1)(2), allows the Bundeskartellamt to invalidate resale price maintenance agreements if they are being abused.

[86] Deringer Report, A.P.E. Doc. No. 57, para. 87, and Annex I, at 53 (1961–62). In each case the parties would otherwise be required to prove a negative. It is important that notification should not be regarded as constituting evidence that an agreement is within art. 85(1), since this would discourage parties from notifying their agreements. This seems clearly established; Reg. 27, Form B, pt. IV. See Deringer et al., 7 Revue du Marché Commun 406, 408 (1964).

[87] International Chamber of Commerce, Commission on Restrictive Practices Affecting Competition, Commentary on the Report of the Internal Market Commission on the Draft Regulation Under Article 85, Doc. No. 225/82, at 4 (1961).

[88] Art. 2. National authorities cannot issue negative clearances. This provision corresponds in substance to ECSC Treaty, art. 65(4). Deringer, "Les Règles Concernant la Concurrence dans le Cadre du Marché Commun Entrent en Vigeur," 5 Revue du Marché Commun 70, 80 (1962).

[89] For the forms and procedure to obtain a negative clearance or to notify with a view to an exemption under art. 85(3), see Reg. 27; Comment Présenter la Demande d'Attestation Négative et Procéder à la Notification (Editions de la Féderation des Industries Belges, 1962). Cf. Reg. 17, art. 4(1).

[90] Reg. 27, Form A, shows the information required for obtaining a negative clearance.

[91] Under art. 3(2). See 1962 Journal Officiel 2135/62. Negative clearances will provide little security unless the Commission reconsiders them only when the surrounding circumstances have changed in a vital respect.

[92] This is the view (presumably that of the Commission itself) stated in 4 OECD Guide to Legislation on Restrictive Business Practices, EEC § 1.0, at 2 (1962). A decision under art.

these elements exists it might be binding in some sense on the Commission itself. A negative clearance does not prevent the Commission from investigating a particular practice to discover if the view on which it acted in giving the negative clearance is correct. Neither an application for a negative clearance nor its issue constitutes a notification,[93] and therefore fines can be imposed and the agreement declared invalid for the period after application for a negative clearance and before actual notification.

The practical result of this is that a negative clearance merely gives some additional assurance where an agreement is not believed to be affected by the Treaty. The more clearly the damaging facts are laid before the Commission, the greater will be the assurance obtained. This can be done without prejudice to a subsequent argument that the agreement is within Article 85(3).[94] A negative clearance may also be useful to obtain approval for a standard form of agreement. In such a case the Commission may not be prepared to issue even a negative clearance without information as to the identity of the other parties or probable parties to the contracts and an estimate of their total number. Negative clearances may be very useful if a particular decision of the Commission throws doubt on the validity of agreements previously assumed not to be affected by Article 85(1). Another advantage is that the mere initiation of proceedings for a negative clearance deprives the national cartel authorities of jurisdiction over the agreement.[95] It seems that this deprivation of jurisdiction is permanent. However, the validity of the agreement may still be challenged in any national court.[96] Having an agreement held invalid or being made to pay

189 is expressed to bind only those to whom it is directed. This means that the parties to an agreement which had been given a negative clearance could not plead—for example, in litigation between themselves—that it was invalid. The principles of legal certainty and of estoppel require that the Commission should not be able to revoke a negative clearance retroactively if no new element has entered into the situation. Art. 8(3) does not empower the Commission to revoke a negative clearance. The Commission remains free, even after issuing a negative clearance, to declare the agreement invalid *ex nunc* and for the period prior to the issue of the negative clearance. The only possible effect of the negative clearance, therefore, is to estop the Commission from holding an agreement invalid or from imposing fines in respect of the period for which the negative clearance is in operation. It is not estopped from doing this if one of the new elements mentioned in the text enters the situation. Some writers hold that it is not estopped even if no new factor has arisen.

[93] Neither does any type of proceedings in a national court or even in a national cartel authority.

[94] The application for the negative clearance is concerned only with whether the agreement is within art. 85(1).

[95] Art. 9(3) mentions art. 2 specifically.

[96] See Oberdorfer, Gleiss & Hirsch, Common Market Cartel Law 96 (1963); Linssen, "The Antitrust Rules of the European Economic Community," 18 Record of N.Y.C.B.A. 289, 302 (1963). See, however, Deringer Report, A.P.E. Doc. No. 57, para. 84 (1961–62). Deringer, "Les Règles Concernant la Concurrence dans le Cadre du Marché Commun Entrent en Vigeur," 5 Revue du Marché Commun 70, 80–81 (1962), points out that the exclusive competence of the Commission after a negative clearance is given is necessary to prevent a national tribunal's holding an agreement invalid under art. 85(1) after the Commission has refused an exemption under art. 85(3) on the grounds that art. 85(1) is not applicable. This possibility could be avoided by the Commission's giving a decision under art. 85(1), rather than a negative clearance, in situations where it is clear that even if an agreement is under art. 85(1) it is also under art. 85(3). This danger also constitutes an argument for making a negative clearance binding on the national courts, although the parties could presumably reopen proceedings for an exemption under art. 85(3). M. Deringer concludes that national courts are probably not legally bound by a negative clearance, although national cartel authorities are so bound. Strictly, these authorities probably are merely deprived of jurisdiction to apply Community law.

compensation to an injured third party may be serious for the parties. Therefore, the exemption from the jurisdiction of national authorities and the likelihood of avoiding further inquiry by the Commission is of limited value,[97] particularly since a negative clearance involves publicity.[98]

RELATIVE MERITS OF NEGATIVE CLEARANCES AND FULL NOTIFICATION FOR EXEMPTION

The advantages of a negative clearance over an application for a decision[99] that the agreement is not within Article 85(1) or that it is within Article 85(3) are minimal. A decision of the Commission is binding on all authorities and, unlike a negative clearance, can be revoked only in specified circumstances.[100] The publicity apparently will be similar in both cases, although the Commission will have more information available for publication if a decision is to be given.[101] It is for this equality of publicity, rather than because negative clearances are of little value in themselves, that decisions are unlikely to be much used.[102] The opportunity for competitors to object is the same in both cases,[103] and full presentation of the arguments of the parties to

[97] See, however, Oberdorfer, Gleiss & Hirsch, Common Market Cartel Law 39 (1963), who say that where the usefulness of the practice is not dependent on its legally binding nature, a negative clearance will be valuable as a *de facto* safeguard against fines. Reference is made to the practice of the Bundeskartellamt and to the practice of the United States Department of Justice in entering a *nolle prosequi*. See Deringer et al., 7 Revue du Marché Commun 43, 45–48 (1964).

[98] Art. 21. Business secrets may not be revealed, but apart from this, the essential content of the agreement will be published.

[99] Neither constitutes evidence that the practice is within art. 85(1) or art. 86; Reg. 27, Form B, pt. IV.

[100] Art. 8.

[101] The Federation of British Industries, European Economic Community—Restrictive Trade Practices 21–22 (1963), says that where full notification is made and the Commission holds that art. 85(1) does not apply and thus that no question under art. 85(3) arises, the Commission will notify the parties of this informally. This informal treatment of the matter will not be binding on the Commission (unlike a negative clearance, in the view of the Federation of British Industries). This is clearly the result of such an action. This treatment also will involve no publicity. The Federation correctly states that no publicity is required but also assumes that none will be given. However, the same reasons for giving publicity apply as in the cases in which publicity is expressly required. There is no reason to treat an intimation that art. 85(1) does not apply as having less weight when it results from a notification than when it results from an application for negative clearance. No authority is cited by the Federation for either view. Reg. 99, 1963 Journal Officiel 2268/63, art. 6, requires the Commission to give enterprises and member states which have made a complaint to it under Regulation 17, art. 3(2), a chance to express their views if the Commission is not proposing to take any action. Presumably, the object of distinguishing between applications for negative clearances and other rulings that art. 85(1) is not applicable was to avoid the need for publicity each time the Commission heard of some practice to which art. 85(1) was obviously inapplicable.

[102] As a method of permitting legitimate restrictions on competition, compare the Irish fair trading rules.

[103] Art. 19(3) requires advance publication of the intention of the Commission only in the case of a negative clearance or an approval under art. 85(3). The fact that decisions have been taken must be published if the decision is a negative clearance, a prohibition of an agreement, an approval under art. 85(3), an approval for a modified existing agreement, or the renewal or revocation of an agreement; art. 21. Notification is essential if an existing agreement requires modification for approval; art. 7. Publicity gives third parties a chance to object and may call their attention to the fact that they have a right of action for damages under national law.

Applications for negative clearances and for full decisions both involve loss of the chance that the existence of the practice might never be discovered by the Commission. The refusal of a negative clearance does not prejudice a later full application for a decision that art. 85(1) does not apply.

the agreement may be necessary to meet these objections. To insure that the applicants' arguments are as fully stated in an application for a negative clearance as in an application for a decision will mean that much of the advantage of the former is lost.

PROCEDURE

The Commission may initiate proceedings for a breach of the Treaty on its own initiative or on the request of any member state or of any individual, legal entity, or association which shows a legitimate interest.[104]

The Commission sends copies of requests for action, of notifications, and of applications for negative clearances to the national cartel authorities at once.[105] The latter consider the documents and should submit views on them at this stage.

The rights of parties to an agreement to defend its validity

When the Commission has formulated its arguments against an agreement, it must give the enterprises or associations of enterprises a chance to deal with these arguments.[106] This duty arises if the Commission is considering a negative clearance, an approval under Article 85(3) or its revocation, any fine or penalty, or any decision to end a particular practice. Before formulating its arguments, the Commission may seek further information.

The Commission notifies the parties to the agreement of the arguments against them directly or by publishing the arguments in the Journal Officiel.[107] The parties reply fully in writing and may volunteer to give oral evidence.[108] Any other persons who show that they have a "sufficient interest" may require to be heard either in support of or against the agreement,[109] but there is no provision for them to be notified officially.[110] The Commission and the national authorities are empowered to request views from any individuals, legal entities, or associations. This enables the Commission to obtain advice and information at an early stage in the proceedings from those most likely to be able to give it.

The rights of third parties to attack an agreement

If the Commission is prepared to permit an agreement by the issue of a negative clearance or an approval under Article 85(3), it must give third parties who may be injured by the agreement a

[104] Art. 3.

[105] Art. 10(1).

[106] Art. 19(1); Reg. 99, art. 2(1). For the background of national law, see Nebolsine, "The 'Right of Defense' in the Control of Restrictive Practices Under the European Community Treaties," 8 Am. J. Comp. L. 433 (1959), and generally arts. 173, 184; Donner, "The Court of Justice of the European Communities," 17 Record of N.Y.C.B.A. 232, 237 (1962); Wolf, "The Role of the Court of Justice of the European Communities in the Antitrust Structure of the Common Market," 31 Fordham L. Rev. 621, 628–29 (1963). The right of the parties to the agreement to answer the objections raised will be given to parties who did not participate in the notification, according to Dr. Verloren van Themaat; see Committee on Foreign Law, "Current Legal Developments in the European Economic Community," 18 Record of N.Y.C.B.A. 329, 332–33 (1963).

[107] Reg. 99, art. 2. Publication of the arguments against the parties is made only "if the circumstances of the case justify it," for example, if there is a large number of parties and they have appointed no agent. To avoid publicity, an agent, usually a lawyer, should therefore be appointed in all cases. The publication must take into account the legitimate interests of the enterprises in their business secrets; Reg. 99, art. 2(2). The Commission will set a time limit for the parties to submit their arguments; see Reg. 99, art. 11. A fine can be imposed only if the enterprise fined has been notified directly; Reg. 99, art. 2(3).

[108] Reg. 99, art. 3.

[109] Art. 19(2).

[110] Cf. art. 19(3).

chance to submit observations.[111] The Commission must publish the essential information provided by the parties to the agreement and specify a time limit of at least one month for the interested third parties to submit their views.[112] Any enterprise with a "sufficient interest" must be allowed to submit written arguments.[113] The third parties may object, for example, on the grounds that the share of the economic benefit being given to the user or consumer is inadequate or that consumer choice is no longer possible and competition is being eliminated.[114] This is the first occasion on which publicity must be given to an agreement which is to be exempted under Article 85(3) or to be given a negative clearance.[115] An agreement which the Commission does not contemplate exempting gets publicity only once, after the decision prohibiting it is given. When the Commission considers that neither Article 85(1) nor 86 has been infringed, interested third parties need not be given notice, but any enterprises or member states which requested the Commission to take action must be given a chance to argue that a violation has occurred.[116]

If the Commission's initially unfavorable views are altered only as a result of an oral hearing, a second hearing is necessary at which third parties can argue against the agreement. If the Commission reads the written arguments of the parties to the agreement and considers that a favorable decision is likely, it presumably will publish the notice to third parties so as to have a single hearing for both sides. There is no right to be present when an opposing party is giving evidence or making legal arguments.[117] However, the parties to the agreement are safeguarded by the provision that no ground of complaint[118] against the agreement may be acted on by the Commission unless the parties have had a chance to

[111] Art. 19(3); see, e.g., 1963 Journal Officiel 1853/63; 1964 Journal Officiel at 722-23/64, 1167/64, 2606-607/64, 2860/64. Where the Commission proposes to make a class exemption under art. 85(3), interested persons may state their views; Reg. 19, art. 5.

[112] Art. 19(2); Reg. 99, arts. 5, 11. They will also have the right to submit oral arguments; Reg. 99, art. 7. In fixing the time limit, the urgency of the case and the length of time required for preparing submissions are to be considered.

[113] Art. 19(2).

[114] The rights of third parties are the same if they initiated the proceedings and the parties to the agreement then notified it and asked for art. 85(3) to be applied. As to a new agreement, the suspicion might arise that the parties had not intended to notify it, but notification is not compulsory and, in appropriate circumstances, the parties could be penalized by fines (which may be imposed for the period prior to notification apparently even if the agreement is later given an exemption) and by the invalidity of the agreement up to the time of notification. See Deringer Report, A.P.E. Doc. No. 57, para. 79 (1961–62).

[115] The first occasion on which publicity may be given is under Regulation 99, art. 2(2).

[116] Reg. 99, art. 6. This means that where the Commission has taken the initiative, third parties who might be interested are not given an opportunity to argue that the Commission's initial suspicions were justified. See also art. 19(2).

[117] Reg. 99, art. 9(3), says: "The persons [i.e., the parties to the agreement or interested third parties] are heard separately *or* in the presence of other persons called to the hearing." (Emphasis supplied.) In the latter case, business secrets must be protected.

[118] Whether suggested by a third party or by a national cartel authority or by the staff of the Commission itself. The extent to which the parties to the agreement are protected will depend on whether the word *griefs*, here translated as "grounds of complaint," is construed by the Court to mean "heads of argument" or mere "points." A head of argument could be raised and answered by the parties who nevertheless might be prejudiced by the same argument presented in a different way involving different minor points. Regulation 99, art. 9(4), requires the essential points made by each litigant to be recorded, and this record presumably will be made available to the others.

argue it.[119] If the Commission in its decision gives a reason[120] which the parties have had no chance to argue, the decision can be set aside by the Court.

The hearing

Anyone who has a sufficient interest or whom the Commission proposes to fine must, and others may, be given a chance to make oral submissions.[121] Representatives of the national cartel authorities have a right to be present.[122] The parties may be represented by lawyers.[123] The hearings are held before persons appointed by the Commission, and they are not in public. If the persons appointed to hold the hearings are members of the staff of the Directorate-General on Competition, that branch of the Commission will be both prosecutor and adviser to the Commission, which itself, at least formally, must take the decision.[124] The Commission is unlikely to overrule the Directorate-General, and there are dangers in the same organization's having both functions.

The Consultative Committee on Cartels and Monopolies

After the hearing and before the decision is taken by the Commission, a joint meeting must always be held with the Consultative Committee on Cartels and Monopolies. This Committee is composed of, but not limited to, officials of the cartel authorities of member states.[125] Its function is to advise the Commission on its decision and not to formulate new arguments for or against the agreement.[126] The enterprises are not represented at this meeting.[127] The views of the Committee are not binding on the Commission.

Measures to terminate an agreement or practice

If the Commission finds an infringement of the Treaty, it must take measures to end it.[128] These measures may be recommendations and need not be published.[129] Recommendations will probably be used often in the earlier stages

[119] Reg. 99, art. 4; art. 19(1). The French text of art. 19(1) speaks of *griefs retenus par la Commission*, which connotes grounds of complaint tentatively accepted by the Commission rather than objections on which the Commission has not adopted an opinion. See Oberdorfer, Gleiss & Hirsch, Common Market Cartel Law 155 (1963).

[120] The Commission must give its reasons when it publishes its decision; art. 190. Failure to give a decision will make art. 173 applicable.

[121] Reg. 99, art. 7.

[122] Reg. 99, art. 8.

[123] They can also be represented by their statutory agents, e.g., the secretary of a company, or a duly appointed member of their staff; Reg. 99, art. 9. The representatives may be assisted by lawyers or professors who are entitled to appear in the Community Court under art. 17 of the Protocol to the Statute of the Court.

[124] There is an institutional and legal problem as to whether delegation of the actual decision to the Directorate-General on Competition is possible.

[125] Art. 10. The Consultative Committee is consulted when the Commission proposes to approve a class of agreements under Regulation 19, art. 6.

[126] It is important from the point of view of the enterprises concerned that the national cartel authorities formulate their objections to the agreement before the right of defense is exercised, rather than leave them to be expressed by the representative of the authority at the meeting of the Consultative Committee, since at that point there will be no further right to defend the agreement.

[127] The result of the joint consultative meeting is to be written out for the Commission but not made public; art. 10(6). This provision would be pointless if the enterprises had been represented at the meeting.

[128] Arts. 89, 155. Art. 89 is still in force; see art. 11(1).

[129] Art. 3(3); art. 21 does not require publication in the case of recommendations. See 1964 EEC Bull. No. 5, Annex II, at 53.

of the EEC[130] and in dealing with restrictive practices in a new member state. The Commission may issue a decision immediately or after a recommendation has not been obeyed. If a decision has been issued, fines[131] may be imposed for continuing infringement of the decision. If a recommendation is followed by a decision, a fine may be imposed for actions between the date of the recommendation and the date of the decision.[132] A single decision may confirm the existence of the infringement, prohibit it, impose a single fine for all infringements prior to the date of the decision, and fix fines prospectively for every day on which the infringement continues. Only the part of the decision which confirms the infringement and prohibits it must be published.

The Commission may authorize member states to take any specific measures necessary to terminate an infringement.[133] This provision is unimportant since the adoption of Regulation 17.[134] The Commission can authorize a national cartel authority to obtain a court order, such as an injunction, prohibiting the infringement.[135]

Publication of decisions taken

Decisions to grant a negative clearance or an approval under Article 85(3), to prohibit an agreement or practice, or to revoke or alter an approval must all be published.[136] The names of the parties and the essential content of and the reasons for[137] the decision are published, but no business secrets may be revealed. There is no need for every possible objection to the decision to be countered in advance. The agreement gets some publicity, and this may result in actions for damages by third parties. The published decisions are the only thing corresponding to reports of cases decided by the Commission. Whether the reasons given will clearly show the Commission's criteria remains to be seen. The Commission is aware of the need to build a case law which will be known to enterprises, and the Court requires full reasons to be given.[138]

FINES

Fines[139] may be imposed for willful or negligent[140] infringement of Articles

[130] See Deringer Report, A.P.E. Doc. No. 57, para. 119 (1961–62). The power to end practices by decisions and recommendations is exercisable before the time limit for existing agreements expires; art. 9(2). See Seventh General Report, para. 66 (1964).

[131] Art. 16 deals with penalties for continuing violations, but this distinction—purely technical because these penalties are pecuniary—cannot readily be translated.

[132] Art. 15(6) permits single fines to be imposed for acts committed after the Commission has warned the enterprises that approval is unlikely. Art. 16 requires the decision imposing fines of a fixed amount per day to be the decision from which the days are counted. The single lump-sum fines under art. 15 are retroactive. If a fine is imposed for a period following a recommendation, the fine is technically for a breach of the Treaty, not breach of the recommendation; arts. 89(2), 189. Fines can be imposed only by decision and not by recommendation. The recommendation, if it complies with Regulation 99, art. 2(3), will fulfill Regulation 17, art. 15(6).

[133] Art. 89(2).

[134] Especially art. 16. See, however, Deringer Report, A.P.E. Doc. No. 57, Annex I, at 55 (1961–62).

[135] See Irish Restrictive Trade Practices Act, 1953 Acts 75, §§ 11, 12.

[136] Arts. 19(3), 21; see, e.g., 1964 Journal Officiel 915/64, 1426/64, 2287/64, 2545/64, 2761/64. Decisions fixing fines or penalties or ordering investigations or the production of information need not be published.

[137] Art. 190. Cf. ECSC Treaty, art. 15, as to which, see Bebr, Judicial Control 84–89.

[138] Deringer Report, A.P.E. Doc. No. 57, para. 127 (1961–62).

[139] See Précigout, "La Sanction des Infractions aux Règlements de la C.E.E.," 5 Revue du Marché Commun 142 (1962).

[140] Art. 15(1), 15(2). Where fines are imposed for continuing a Treaty infringement con-

85(1) or 86 or for breach of a stipulation in an approval under Article 85(3). However, until the Commission gives a decision or preliminary observation that Article 85(3) is inapplicable, no fines for breach of Articles 85 and 86 can be imposed for acts which are committed after notification and which are within the limits specified in the notification.[141] The fines may be of any amount between one thousand and one million dollars[142] or up to 10 per cent of the turnover of each enterprise concerned. The size of the fine depends on the gravity of the infringement of the Treaty and its duration; a fine is not regarded as a criminal penalty.[143] The Commission need not impose fines but must always invalidate the agreement.[144] Concerted practices may incur fines or only prohibition for the future. If flagrant, they are more likely to result in fines than are agreements, since they are not amenable to the sanction of invalidation.

The Commission may fine enterprises which give false or misleading information either in applications for negative clearances or notifications or in reply to investigations.[145]

The Commission may impose fines of fifty to one thousand dollars[146] a day for continuing offenses. These fines are the principal means of compelling compliance with a decision prohibiting a breach of the Treaty, of ending infringement of a stipulation in an approval or abuse of an approval under Article 85(3), or of compelling an enterprise to provide information or to submit to an investigation. These fines may be imposed only if a decision prohibiting a specified practice threatens daily fines if the practice is not terminated. The fines calculated at a daily rate cannot be imposed without a

---

trary to a decision, the offense is bound to be willful, unless there is a dispute as to the interpretation of the decision and the adequacy of the measures taken to comply with it; see art. 16(2).

[141] Art. 15(5)(a) and 15(6). Curiously, there is nothing to prevent a fine's being imposed for acts during the period prior to notification of a new agreement even if it is later approved. Apparently fines will not be imposed if the agreement is under art. 4(2) but will be imposed if it is not; see Guide Pratique 15–16. Schumacher, "The System of Enforcement . . . [in] the European Economic Community," in Comparative Aspects of Anti-trust Law in the United States, the United Kingdom and the European Economic Community, Int'l & Comp. L.Q. Supp. No. 6, at 65, 75 (1963), indicates that when the Commission has decided how to treat types of agreements, it will write to all the parties to agreements of the type in question and inform them that art. 85(3) probably is not applicable. In this way it is hoped that many agreements will be voluntarily terminated or modified without the need for litigation or individual decisions.

Regulation 99, art. 2(3), prohibits any fine, whether there has been a notification or not, unless the parties have been directly informed by letter, not merely through the Journal Officiel, of the case against them. It is not merely an elaboration of art. 15(6).

[142] "Units of account." Art. 18, and EEC Treaty, arts. 207, 209.

[143] Art. 15(4). This provision applies to fines under art. 15(1) and 15(2), but fines under art. 16 do not seem to have a penal character either. The explanation of art. 15(4) is that, under Belgian and French law, penal sanctions may be imposed only pursuant to a law which is precise, which arts. 85 and 86 are not; Dumon & Rigaux, "I Tribunali Internazionali e Sopranazionali," in 2 Primo Congresso Internazionale dei Magistrati 621, 640 (1959); see Wolf, "La Législation contre les Cartels et les Monopoles: son application dans la Communauté Economique Européenne," 1962 Journal des Tribunaux 541, 545.

[144] Whether a fine or the invalidity of the agreement is the more serious sanction depends on various factors: the size of the fine actually imposed, the extent to which the invalidity of the prohibited clauses in the circumstances of the individual agreement and according to the relevant law vitiates the whole contract, and the extent to which the parties may be prejudiced by inability to rely on the agreement. These last two elements will vary with the nature of the agreement.

[145] Art. 15(1).

[146] "Units of account." Art. 18.

second decision,[147] which may reduce the actual total amount of the daily fines to be paid.[148] Before this decision is taken, the parties fined must be given a chance to defend themselves[149] against this second decision and, apparently, the Consultative Committee must again consider the case.

All fines must be considered by the Consultative Committee,[150] although they are actually imposed by the Commission. The procedure is the same as in the case of substantive decisions. Fines may be enforced by the ordinary procedure for enforcing civil pecuniary obligations in each member state, on production of an authenticated copy of the decision of the Commission. Only the Community Court may suspend the enforcement of a fine.[151]

JUDICIAL REVIEW[152]

Review of fines

If the Commission has imposed a fine to penalize a breach of the Treaty or to enforce compliance with a decision, the Community Court has wider powers to review the decision than it has to review a decision declaring an agreement void or fixing the date at which it is to become valid. In appeals against decisions of the Commission by which fines have been imposed, the Court has full jurisdiction as to the merits.[153] The Court may reconsider the whole matter, including all questions of law and fact, and substitute its own discretion for that of the Commission, and cancel, reduce, or increase the fine. However, it may not alter the decision of the Commission as to whether the agreement infringes the Treaty unless this decision can be chal-

[147] This second decision decides the number of days the infringement continued and therefore necessarily decides the extent to which the measures taken by the enterprises to comply with the Treaty were adequate.

[148] Art. 16(2). This provision allows reduction of the total amount of daily fines paid in cases where the decision prohibiting the cartel could not be complied with immediately without disrupting trade, while at the same time allowing substantial daily fines to be imposed to compel compliance with the Treaty. The Commission has no power to grant an injunction or an interdict, and daily fines are the only method of enforcing compliance, apart from possible action under art. 89(2). The French word *astreintes*, used to describe the daily fines, should not be taken literally. In French law, *astreintes* refer to the daily amount of money fixed for the defendant to pay the plaintiff if he continues with the injury; these sums are, however, essentially fictitious, since what is paid to the plaintiff when the injury is terminated is the (usually much smaller) amount of actual damage suffered by him since the date of the decree. Under art. 16 there is no question of compensation, and there is no reason to believe that payment of the *astreintes* will not be enforced. *Obligations pécuniaires* (art. 192) include both *amendes* and *astreintes*, and so do *sanctions* (art. 172); art. 17.

[149] Art. 19(1). It is not clear from art. 16(3) whether the Consultative Committee must be consulted when the total of the daily fines is fixed, after the infringement has ended, or only before the fixing of the amount of the daily fine prospectively payable, i.e., before the first decision. Since the enterprises concerned seem to have a right to be heard before the second decision is taken, art. 19(1), and since the second decision relates to the question of the (discretionary) remission of some of the total daily fines, art. 16(2), the reasons for requiring the opinion of the Consultative Committee seem equally applicable to the second decision. It would be unreasonable to penalize the parties on a daily basis for inadequate alteration of their practices if this inadequacy was caused by the imprecise drafting of the Commission in the first decision.

[150] Arts. 15(3), 16(3).

[151] EEC Treaty, art. 192.

[152] See Lagrange, "Judicial Review of Decisions of Cartel Authorities," in 2 Cartel and Monopoly in Modern Law 889 (in French), 909 (in English) (1961).

[153] Art. 17; see EEC Treaty, arts. 87(2)(d), 172. This provision is required because the power of the Commission to impose fines is discretionary and no appeal would lie in the ordinary way to challenge the manner in which the discretion had been exercised.

lenged under Article 173.[154]

Review of decisions not imposing fines

In all other cases the decision of the Commission may be attacked only on one of the grounds specified in Article 173. The question whether the Commission has misinterpreted the Treaty in prohibiting an agreement or practice as being contrary to Article 85(1) or 86[155] can always be raised on the grounds that the Commission has infringed the Treaty or has no jurisdiction to apply the Treaty to the agreement in question. If the Court holds this contention justified, it must annul the decision of the Commission.

Only the enterprises to whom a decision is addressed or those which it "concerns directly and individually"[156] may sue for its annulment. A further restriction is that the Court has only limited power to review the assessment of the economic facts made by the Commission. The Court can annul a misapplication of the Treaty to the facts as found,[157] but it cannot construe an agreement to decide if, in fact, the agreement infringes the Treaty. In substance, the appellate jurisdiction of the Court is only on points of law.

If the Commission has a discretion, then in the absence of a provision giving the Court full jurisdiction, the exercise of the discretion can be annulled only under Article 173, and the wisdom of the decision cannot be challenged if it is within the limits of the discretion. This is important because the Commission has under the antitrust regulations a number of discretionary powers[158] which will not in practice be subject to judicial review.

Misuse of the Commission's power is not likely under the antitrust regulations.[159] However, there are now a number of rules of law relating to the application of the Treaty,[160] with all of which the Commission must comply if its decisions are to be valid. Also, the "rule[s] of law relating to effect being given to"

[154] Art. 172 authorizes regulations giving the Court full jurisdiction only "in regard to the penalties provided for in these regulations." Although the invalidity of the agreement under art. 85(2) is in one sense a penalty, it is automatic once a breach of the Treaty has been held to exist. The Commission has no power to hold an agreement valid if it contravenes the Treaty —except, of course, under art. 85(3)—so invalidity is not a penalty within the meaning of art. 172.

[155] The Commission may not condemn an agreement or practice not within art. 85(1) or art. 86. Therefore, a prohibition of such an agreement or practice is a Treaty infringement and an act for which the Commission has no jurisdiction, whether what is appealed against is the refusal of a negative clearance, the prohibition of a practice, or a fine for contravention of a decision giving approval under art. 85(3).

[156] Art. 173. It may also be possible for an enterprise to raise the question of validity of the decision in a national court and have it decided for the purposes of the case by the Community Court under art. 177.

[157] Compare art. 173 with ECSC Treaty, art. 33; see Bebr, Judicial Control 89–98; Stein & Hay, "New Legal Remedies of Enterprises: A Survey," in 1 American Enterprise in the European Common Market: A Legal Profile 459, 478–79 (Stein & Nicholson ed. 1960).

[158] The Commission has, for example, a discretion whether to issue a decision or a recommendation under art. 3(3); whether to validate retroactively a modified existing agreement under art. 7; as to the duration of an approval under art. 85(3) and the conditions on which it is given; whether revocation of an approval should be retroactive under art. 8(3); and whether to begin an investigation. If the Commission has no discretion whether to apply art. 85(3) in circumstances where it applies (discussed in Chapter Fifteen), the Commission may not have discretion as to the date from which an approval under that provision should take effect; art. 6(1).

[159] Conceivably, it might be a misuse of power to give decisions under the antitrust provisions in order to pursue, for example, a regional economic policy.

[160] Art. 173(1). The rules referred to comprise all of the antitrust Regulations, but specially Regulations 17 and 99.

the Treaty,[161] for whose violation the Court may annul a decision of the Commission, include not only regulations but also certain general principles which form a standard for administrative procedure[162] or "due process." If these principles are not followed, the decision is invalid even if the Regulations have been followed in every respect.

Compelling the Commission to give a decision

If the Commission is called on by an enterprise to give a decision and fails to do so within two months,[163] the Court may order the Commission to issue a decision. Although no fine can be imposed for actions under an agreement after notification until the Commission indicates that the agreement is probably objectionable,[164] an enterprise may want to know the Commission's decision[165] as soon as possible. The enterprise cannot be sure that even if the agreement is approved it will be validated from the time of notification. There may be cases where acting on the agreement would irretrievably damage the interests of the parties if the agreement was subsequently declared to be void; for example, if unpatented know-how were transferred. There is no provision enabling the parties to assume the validity of their agreement if the Commission takes no action, even after a long period. Since at present the Directorate-General on Competition is understaffed, proceedings in the Court may be necessary to obtain a decision. Indeed, these proceedings might not be unwelcome to the Commission, since they would put pressure on the Council and the member states to increase the staff available.[166] The Court probably will not order the Commission to give a decision unless the length of time taken is more than adequate, when not only the urgency and complexity of the case but also the volume of work of the Commission are taken into consideration.

Judicial review and Article 85(3)

The Commission has sole jurisdiction to give exemptions under Article 85(3), "subject to review of its decision by the Court of Justice."[167] How far the Court can review the decision of the Commission depends on whether the Commission has discretion to refuse exemption if the conditions of Article 85(3) are fulfilled. If the Commission has no discretion, the Court may decide if the Commission has correctly applied Article 85(3) to the facts as found. If the Commission has discretion, the Court may overrule such a refusal only if the Commission has violated procedural

[161] Art. 173(1).

[162] Bebr, Judicial Control 90–91; Wolf, "The Role of the Court of Justice of the European Communities in the Antitrust Structure of the Common Market," 31 Fordham L. Rev. 621, 628–29 (1963); Donner, "The Court of Justice of the European Communities," 17 Record of N.Y.C.B.A. 232, 237 (1962); Hamson, Executive Discretion and Judicial Control 172 (1954).

[163] Arts. 175–76. See Bebr, Judicial Control, ch. 5.

[164] Art. 15(6).

[165] A negative clearance is probably a decision within art. 189 and a formal document within art. 175, so failure to issue a negative clearance would give rise to a right of action under art. 175(3).

[166] The Commission received some eight hundred multilateral and some thirty-five thousand bilateral agreements. Of the latter, 90% were exclusive-dealing agreements, 9% were licensing agreements, and 1% were other types. Of the exclusive-dealing agreements, 10% were agreements with commercial agents and the remainder agreements with independent traders; of the licensing agreements, 30% included a clause prohibiting exports and 60% an exclusive territorial grant. Committee on Foreign Law, "Current Legal Developments in the European Economic Community," 18 Record of N.Y.C.B.A. 329, 332 (1963); Seventh General Report, para. 65 (1964).

[167] Art. 9(1).

rules[168] or misused its power.

The provision which gives the Commission exclusive jurisdiction under Article 85(3) may prevent the Court from granting an exemption itself. Apart from appeals from the Commission,[169] the only cases in which this can arise are under Article 177(a), and parties to proceedings before national cartel authorities or courts rarely fail to notify an agreement if its validity is questioned. The Court, under Article 177, can only interpret the Treaty and cannot apply it to economic circumstances or consider the facts to see if Article 85(3) applies.[170] The Court, however, can apply the Treaty to the facts found by the national authority or court. It then has to decide whether to request the Commission for a decision under Article 85(3) or to decide the question itself. The better view is that the Court has no jurisdiction to approve an agreement under Article 85(3), even if it holds that Article 85(3) applies,[171] and that the Court must refer the question to the Commission if it has not already been brought before that body.

THE INVESTIGATORY POWERS OF THE COMMISSION

The Commission has extremely wide powers of investigation.[172] In the execution of its duty to terminate infringements of Articles 85 and 86,[173]

[168] Including the Treaty, any rule of law relating to the Treaty's application, and any general principle of law.

[169] And cases under art. 177(b), which would, for practical purposes in this context, be the same type of case.

[170] Bosch v. de Geus, 8 Recueil 89, [1962] C.M.L.R. 1; see, however, the *Van Gend & Loos* case, 9 Recueil 1, [1963] C.M.L.R. 105.

[171] Two questions are involved. First, under arts. 173 and 174, the Court may annul an act of the Commission. If this occurs, the Commission is bound to take the measures required to carry out the Court's decision; art. 176. Even where the judgment of the Court leaves the Commission no discretion as to the act to be adopted, the Court cannot order the legal act to be substituted for the illegal one. By analogy and since the Court cannot carry out the procedure required for an approval under art. 85(3), it seems clear that the Court cannot give an approval under that provision. The Court is not a court of appeal from the Commission, but rather an administrative court controlling the legality of the Commission's acts. See Deringer, "The Distribution of Powers in the Enforcement of the Rules of Competition Under the Rome Treaty," 1 Common Market L. Rev. 30, 34 (1963); Buxbaum, "Incomplete Federalism: Jurisdiction over Antitrust Matters in the European Economic Community," 52 Calif. L. Rev. 56, 74–80 (1964); Deringer et al., 7 Revue du Marché Commun 448, 450 (1964).

The second question is whether the exercise of the power under art. 85(3) is a matter of law or a matter of policy (in which case, the Court cannot be competent to exercise it but only to supervise its exercise). This question, which turns on whether the Commission has a discretion, is one of considerable theoretical importance to the Community as a whole.

If the power to exempt is a matter of law, not of policy, it is ultimately for the Court to rule on how it should be exercised, as a question of Treaty interpretation, and Regulation 17 cannot deprive the Court of this function. It does not follow, however, that the Court has power to decide in the first instance. It is submitted that art. 9(1) should not be interpreted as purporting to deprive the Court of any power to exempt under art. 85(3) which it may have had under the Treaty; but if it is so interpreted, it cannot validly deprive the Court of this power. The Court requires strong arguments to prove the invalidity of a provision of a regulation; Bosch v. de Geus, 8 Recueil 89, 134, [1962] C.M.L.R. 1, 19 (conclusions of Advocate-General Lagrange). However, the Court might also be jealous to insure the rule of law (art. 164) rather than economic policy in the EEC. Art. 9(1) should be interpreted to mean "subject to the whole of the jurisdiction of the Court under the Treaty."

[172] Under art. 213 and Reg. 17, and other regulations, e.g., Reg. 11, 1960 Journal Officiel 1121/60. See Wohlfarth, "The Right of the Commission to Ask for Information," in Doing Business in the Common Market 36 (Commerce Clearing House, 1963).

[173] Under arts. 89 and 155 and Reg. 17, and any other regulations pursuant to art. 87; art. 11(1).

the Commission may obtain all necessary information from governments, national cartel authorities, enterprises, and associations of enterprises.[174]

In its initial request for information, the Commission sets a time limit. If incomplete information is given within that time, the Commission makes a decision giving reasons, specifying the information required and the fines to be imposed for failure to give complete and accurate information within a further time limit, and informing the enterprise of its right to apply to the Court to have the decision annulled.[175] In doing all this the Commission keeps the national cartel authority informed.

If it is "necessary" to verify the information provided, the Commission may authorize its officials to investigate the affairs of an enterprise, to examine and copy accounts and records, to request explanations, and to have access to all premises and property belonging to the companies being investigated.[176] Before deciding to make the examination, the Commission must consult the national cartel authority and notify the enterprise concerned. Provision is made for the officials of the national cartel authority to assist.[177] An alternative procedure is for the investigation to be carried out by the national authority with any necessary help from the Commission's staff.[178]

The Commission also has power to carry out inquiries into any sector of the economy.[179] These general inquiries may be carried out if prices or the pattern of trade suggest that competition is being restricted or distorted in the Common Market in the sector in question. There is no need for any complaint to have been made. The Commission may require the production of any necessary information on all agreements and practices otherwise exempt from compulsory notification under Article 4(2).[180] It may obtain particulars of the structure and the conduct of the affairs of an enterprise or group of enterprises whose size suggests that it may be in a dominant market position, even if there is no question of an Article 86 violation. The provisions relating to the acquisition of information from[181] and the investigation of individual enterprises, both by the Commission[182] and by national authorities,[183] apply in the case of inquiries into whole sectors of industry. The Consultative Commission must be consulted before a sector inquiry is begun and must consider

[174] The required information must be supplied by the individuals who, according to law or to the memorandum and articles or charter of the company or association of enterprises, represent the company or association (i.e., in Irish and English law, the directors and secretary); art. 11(4).

[175] Art. 11(5). The initial request for information, art. 11(1), is not a decision, and no appeal to the Court will lie against it.

[176] Art. 14(1).

[177] There is no provision indicating whether national law may require the warrant which authorizes the official to make the examination to be backed by the national cartel authority. The Commission would probably dislike such a requirement and would certainly regard it as illegal if it purported to give any power of control or veto; cf. art. 192. See Deringer et al., 7 Revue du Marché Commun 560, 562–67 (1964).

[178] Art. 13. See Rapport . . . sur le sixième rapport général sur l'activité de la Communauté économique européenne, A.P.E. Doc. No. 76, para. 56 (1963–64).

[179] Compare in this respect the powers of the British Monopolies Commission under the Monopolies and Restrictive Practices (Inquiry and Control) Act, 1948, 11 & 12 Geo. 6, c. 66, and the Irish Fair Trade Commission under the Restrictive Trade Practices Acts, 1953 Acts 75 and 1959 Acts 1015. See Deringer et al., 8 Revue du Marché Commun 42 (1965).

[180] Art. 12(1), 12(2).

[181] Art. 11.

[182] Art. 14.

[183] Art. 13.

any fines imposed for withholding information or misleading the Commission.

The Commission has power to gather all information "necessary" or "requisite"[184] to its tasks of applying Articles 85 and 86.[185] The information must be necessary; it is not enough that it be useful. It must be impossible as a practical matter for the Commission to get the same information by other methods, and the amount of trouble for the enterprise producing the information must not be disproportionate to its value.[186] However, the Commission may seek all information necessary to discover if a Treaty infringement is being committed; its power is not limited to verification of the existence of infringements, evidence of which already exists from other sources. The failure to prove an infringement as a result of the inquiries does not mean that they were not "necessary." The Commission may not use these powers to obtain information which it requires, for example, for economic planning or the prevention of dumping.[187] It may not carry out investigations or demand information unless there is some reason to suspect that a Treaty infringement may occur and thus that an investigation is necessary to fulfill its duties. In an inquiry into a sector of industry, the information specifically required, not merely the inquiry, must be necessary to enforce Articles 85 and 86.[188] The information required to decide if a breach of Article 86 exists is more extensive than that required to prove, for example, that a written agreement contains provisions contrary to Article 85(1) or even that a concerted practice exists. Information gathered in the course of investigations cannot be used for any other purpose,[189] and professional or business secrets must not be disclosed.[190]

There is no right to refuse to give privileged information or documents to the Commission or the national authorities.[191] The regulation on the right of defense[192] does not deal with professional privilege. Business secrets are protected from disclosure by, but not to, the Commission.

In view of the wide powers of the Commission to carry out investigations, the power of the Court to control the exercise of those powers[193] is extremely important. Apart from insuring that inquiries are "necessary," which is likely to protect private rights but is unlikely to restrict severely the wide powers given by the regulation, the Court can hold a decision of the Commission invalid under Article 173. In particular, it can annul the decision which requires the enterprise to give information on the grounds of abuse of power or violation of rules of law relating to the application of the Treaty. The difficulty is that an appeal to have the act annulled must be brought within two months of the date of the act. Even if the actions of the Commission show that the investigation has been ordered for an improper purpose, thus allowing annulment of the decision to investigate, there may be no time to ap-

[184] Oberdorfer, Gleiss & Hirsch, Common Market Cartel Law 142 (1963).

[185] Arts. 11(1), 12(1), 14(1).

[186] Van Hecke & Suetens, "Le Premier Règlement Européen sur les Cartels et les Monopoles," 1962 Journal des Tribunaux 361, 366, and the authorities cited there.

[187] Art. 20(1); see, however, art. 213.

[188] The wording of art. 12(1) makes this clear: "[T]he Commission may decide to conduct a general enquiry in the course of which it may request enterprises in the sector concerned to supply the information necessary. . . ."

[189] Art. 20(1).

[190] Art. 20(2); see also arts. 21(2), 19(3).

[191] Arts. 20(2), 19(3), and 21(2) notwithstanding. See, however, Deringer et al., 7 Revue du Marché Commun 560, 565 (1964).

[192] Reg. 99.

[193] Arts. 11(5), 12(4), 14(3).

peal. However, the enterprise may have a right to damages. Even if the decision to carry out an inquiry is valid, the conduct of the investigation may give rise to an action for damages against the Community for a breach of the "general principles common to the laws of member states."[194]

THE JURISDICTION OF NATIONAL AUTHORITIES

National cartel authorities and courts have power to enforce Articles 85(1) and 86 as well as their national restrictive practices laws.[195] They cannot exempt an agreement under Article 85(3);[196] to obtain an exemption the agreement must be notified to the Commission. No type of proceedings before a national authority constitutes notification in order to obtain an exemption under Article 85(3).[197]

National authorities determine the admissibility of agreements or the existence of abuses of monopoly power "in accordance with their domestic law and the provisions of Articles 85 . . . and 86."[198] Community law gives them no power to fine for breaches of the Treaty, and they are to apply against cartels in their jurisdiction only the sanctions provided by national laws (including fines, if they have power to fine) in accordance with national procedure.[199]

[194] Art. 215.

[195] Art. 88 and art. 9(3). See Re "Fensterglas III," Kammergericht (Kartellsenat), Berlin, May 4, 1962, [1962] C.M.L.R. 336.

[196] Art. 9(1).

[197] See, however, art. 23. Also, since by art. 6(2) exemption under art. 85(3) can be given for optionally notifiable agreements without formal notification, it may be possible to obtain approval under art. 85(3) for such agreements from the Commission through a national cartel authority, which would be binding on everyone.

[198] Art. 88.

[199] See, however, art. 89(2).

The jurisdiction of national authorities to apply the Treaty is only in accordance with Article 88. It has been suggested[200] that national authorities may not prosecute infringements of the Treaty on their own initiative or in any case in which the cartel has not been "submitted for approval" under national law. The words of the Court just quoted, which go further than Article 88 itself, need not be

[200] Oberdorfer, Gleiss & Hirsch, Common Market Cartel Law 132, 134–35 (1963), citing Bosch v. de Geus, 8 Recueil 89, 103, [1962] C.M.L.R. 1, 12. See Belgian Law on Protection Against Abuse of Economic Power of 1960, art. 28, discussed by van Reepinghen & Waelbroeck, "La Législation Belge concernant les Pratiques Restreignant la Concurrence," in Rapports au Colloque International de Droit Européen 179, 192 (1961). The interpretation mentioned in the text would make it impossible for national authorities to apply arts. 85 and 86 unless the national antitrust law was of the type under which cartels are required to be "submitted for approval," and was not, for example, a law directed only against abuses or an absolute prohibition of cartels within its terms.

To limit the power of national authorities to apply the Treaty to agreements "submitted for" their approval and to exclude those "subject to" their powers would be to draw an unfortunate and wholly illogical distinction between cartels which have been voluntarily called to the attention of national authorities and those which have been discovered by them in the exercise of their powers of investigation. It ignores art. 86. Deringer, "The Distribution of Powers in the Enforcement of the Rules of Competition Under the Rome Treaty," 1 Common Market L. Rev. 30, 33, 38 (1963), appears to accept the conclusion reached in the text. Deringer et al., 7 Revue du Marché Commun 504, 507–11 (1964), summarize the position by stating that national cartel authorities can apply the Treaty only to (1) new compulsorily notifiable cartels before they are notified and (2) existing compulsorily notifiable cartels after the expiration of the time limit for notification. In practice, the authorities cannot apply the Treaty to any cartel during the period between notification and the Commission's decision, to existing cartels before the time limit for notification has expired, or to optionally notifiable cartels, because in all these cases the Commission can validate the cartel retroactively under art. 85(3).

interpreted to mean that the jurisdiction of national authorities to apply the Treaty is limited to cases in which they are requested to do so by the Commission or in which a cartel is submitted to them under national law on the initiative of the parties to it. They should be understood to mean that national authorities are given no additional powers by Article 88, but merely are required to exercise their powers under national law in accordance with the substantive provisions of the Treaty.

The Commission intends[201] that national authorities enforcing Articles 85 and 86 should consult it, to insure a uniform interpretation. Since "only the administrative authorities can bring about such harmonization,"[202] member states with no real restrictive practices laws were asked to give power to enforce the Treaty to administrative agencies and not to the courts. A system in which the courts enforce the national antitrust law, which includes Articles 85 and 86 after ratification of the EEC Treaty, is not formally incompatible with the Treaty but is contrary to the method by which it is intended to implement the Treaty.[203] The Consultative Committee[204] insures that when the Commission makes a decision it consults the national authorities. This consultation minimizes the difficulties caused by the division of power to enforce Articles 85 and 86 and the centralization of power to exempt under Article 85(3).

If the Commission does not intervene[205] and if there is no appeal from the decision of the national cartel authority, the latter is obliged under Article 177 to refer any question of Treaty interpretation which has arisen to the Community Court. Apparently Article 177 applies to national administrative tribunals of final appeal as well as to the courts. However, there is no need to apply Article 177 to national cartel authorities, because uniform Treaty interpretation can be obtained by the Commission's taking over the case, if its importance justifies this, or by the Commission's consulting with the national authority. Some method of dealing inexpensively with small cases which involve questions of Treaty interpretation may be necessary in the future.[206] It would probably be useful to provide for appeal from the national cartel authority to the national courts on points of law so that the cartel authority would not be obliged to refer every case heard by it to the Court. This is clearly not intended; Article 177 would then require only the court of final appeal to refer the question to the Community Court.[207]

The territorial or personal jurisdiction of the national cartel authorities under international law is not affected by the

[201] Second General Report, para. 118 (1959); Third General Report, para. 139 (1960); Fourth General Report, para. 50 (1961); see Bosch v. de Geus, 8 Recueil 89, 137–38, [1962] C.M.L.R. 1, 22 (conclusions of Advocate-General Lagrange). However, in France anticartel laws are applied only by the courts; the Commission Technique des Ententes is merely an advisory and investigatory body.

[202] Second General Report, para. 118 (1959).

[203] Such a system now exists in Ireland, and its modification will raise the constitutional issues discussed in Chapter Two.

[204] And the provisions for keeping national cartel authorities informed, such as arts. 10 and 11.

[205] Art. 9(3), discussed on pp. 461–62.

[206] Art. 4 of the Supplementary Rules of the Court provides for legal aid. In the early stages of the EEC, enterprises of the size on which the Commission will probably concentrate would not suffer financial hardship from having to argue a case before the Court. See Cour de Justice des Communautés européennes, Recueil des Textes 226 (1963).

[207] In Ireland, the extent to which the decisions of the reconstituted Fair Trade Commission will be subject to appeal to the national courts will have to be settled by legislation in due course.

Treaty.[208] Therefore, many agreements affecting trade between member states presumably fall under two national jurisdictions. These cases, especially where the parties to the cartel are situated in different member states, are more easily dealt with by the Commission. The Commission can effectively prevent conflicting decisions on the application of Article 85(1) to the same cartel and prevent numerous problems of private international law from arising. This represents a further important step towards centralization. No machinery is provided for cooperation directly between the national authorities.

Removal of cases from national authorities by the Commission

Article 9(3) ends the jurisdiction of national "authorities"[209] when the Commission initiates proceedings concerning the same agreement or practice. The authorities' jurisdiction ends when the Commission starts proceedings to prohibit the agreement or practice or to give either an exemption under Article 85(3) or a negative clearance. Requests for information, general inquiries, and investigations[210] do not affect the jurisdiction of national authorities, even if they involve the agreement or practice being considered.

The words translated as "initiated proceedings"[211] connote some action by the Commission—such as, at a minimum, acknowledgment of receipt of the notification, or transmission of documents to

[208] Deringer Report, A.P.E. Doc. No. 57, paras. 82, 83 (1961–62); Clément, "La Délimitation des Compétences Respectives de la Commission du Marché Commun et des Autorités Nationales en Matière de Cartels," in 1 Cartel and Monopoly in Modern Law 377 (in French), 383–85, 395 (in English), 401–403 (1961).

[209] This means the authorities competent under art. 88, to which art. 9(3) expressly refers. See Waelbroek, "Le Problème de la Validité des Ententes Economiques dans le droit privé du Marché Commun," 51 Rev. Crit. de Droit Int. Privé 415, 436 (1962). These are usually administrative authorities, but if the national authority is an ordinary court, art. 9(3) deprives it of jurisdiction. Usually the national courts do not enforce the Treaty directly but rather they hear civil cases in which the question whether arts. 85 and 86 have been infringed is in issue. Van den Heuvel, "Civil Law Consequences of Violation of the Antitrust Provisions of the Rome Treaty," 12 Am. J. Comp. L. 172, 179 (1963), points out that the European Parliament's draft of Regulation 17, art. 9, provided for the ordinary courts to be deprived of jurisdiction by the institution of proceedings before the Commission, but this provision was later deleted from the draft. For the conflicting cases on this point, see id. at 180 n.18. Deringer, "The Distribution of Powers in the Enforcement of the Rules of Competition Under the Rome Treaty," 1 Common Market L. Rev. 30, 38 (1963), points out that since the only organs in France empowered to apply anticartel laws are the courts, the Paris Cour d'Appel has suspended action on a case when the Commission initiated proceedings—Etablissements Consten v. Société Union Nationale des Economies Familiales, Jan. 26, 1963, [1963] C.M.L.R. 176. He holds, however, that even in France the civil courts at least should not be regarded as being deprived of jurisdiction under art. 9(3). See Nicolas & Société Brandt v. Société Photo Radio Club, Cour d'Appel d'Amiens (3d Ch.), May 9, 1963, [1963] C.M.L.R. 239, aff'd, Cour de Cassation, Oct. 22, 1964, [1965] C.M.L.R. 36; see also Buxbaum, "Incomplete Federalism: Jurisdiction over Antitrust Matters in the European Economic Community," 52 Calif. L. Rev. 56, 61–63, 69 (1964); Materne, "Le Problème des Compétences Respectives des Tribunaux Nationaux et de la Commission de la C.E.E. en Matière d'Ententes," 7 Revue du Marché Commun 37, 38 (1964); Deringer et al., 7 Revue du Marché Commun 504, 505–507 (1964).

[210] Arts. 11, 12, and 14, respectively.

[211] Art. 9(3). Unless a negative clearance is binding on national authorities and courts (it apparently is not; see Bosch v. de Geus, 8 Recueil 89, 131, [1962] C.M.L.R. 1, 17 [conclusions of Advocate-General Lagrange]), the principal object of providing that the institution of a procedure under art. 2 deprives national authorities of jurisdiction is to insure that there is no duplication of proceedings or conflict of decisions if the Commission, instead of ruling on the negative clearance, requires a full notification.

the national authorities—and not the mere passive receipt of a notification or an application for a negative clearance. However, it is pointless for national authorities to continue with a case under the Treaty if notification has been made, since they would be deprived of jurisdiction later even if notification in itself does not constitute initiation of proceedings by the Commission.[212] Neither conflicts of jurisdiction nor duplication of proceedings are prevented entirely by Regulation 17, and it is important that the national authorities endeavor to avoid them in practice.

The authority is deprived of jurisdiction even if it believes that the notification was made for the purpose of delay.[213] If the national authority believes that a case for exemption under Article 85(3) exists, it should refer the parties to the Commission. A third party's making a complaint to the Commission[214] is probably not per se the "initiation of proceedings." To insure certainty, some act of which the national authority can be made reliably aware is essential.

Jurisdiction of national authorities to apply national law

National cartel authorities[215] remain free to apply their national laws to agreements, practices, and abuses of monopoly power which do not affect interstate trade. The question of the limits of interstate trade is one on which the Commission is to coordinate views and one which the Court will ultimately decide. If interstate trade is affected, the Treaty provisions must be applied if they are stricter than the national law.

The substantive law aspects of the question whether a national authority or

[212] Where a notification has been made, the Commission can be compelled to give or refuse the exemption; art. 175. The Commission therefore cannot leave the matter to be resolved by the national authority. The same rule will apply to an application for a negative clearance, if such a clearance is "a formal document" within art. 175.

See van den Heuvel, "Civil Law Consequences of Violation of the Antitrust Provisions of the Rome Treaty," 12 Am. J. Comp. L. 172, 180 n.18 (1963). Deringer, "The Distribution of Powers in the Enforcement of the Rules of Competition Under the Rome Treaty," 1 Common Market L. Rev. 30, 37 (1963), holds that activity inside the Commission, acknowledgement of a complaint, or transmission of documents to national cartel authorities (since this is purely automatic) cannot amount to initiation of proceedings unless some request is made for information. He says that a national cartel authority may not condemn an agreement if exemption by the Commission under art. 85(3) is still possible in respect of the period up to the time of the action by the national authority; id. at 39. With respect, it is unfortunately doubtful if it would be illegal for the national authorities to exercise jurisdiction in such cases, although it would be likely to cause a conflict of decisions if they did so. Such a conflict could perhaps be avoided by notification and prompt "initiation of proceedings" by the Commission in the case of an agreement not subject to compulsory notification. If a new agreement is not within art. 4(2) or art. 5(2), no exemption can be given by the Commission for the period before notification, so the national authority is free to condemn the agreement. See also Deringer et al., 7 Revue du Marché Commun 504–505 (1964).

If the parties to the agreement think that it is likely to be approved under art. 85(3), they can press the Commission to take action to prevent the national authority—which cannot apply art. 85(3)—from ruling against them under art. 85(1). See Société Arlab Import-Export v. Société Union Nationale des Economies Familiales, Tribunal Commercial de la Seine, June 25, 1962, [1963] C.M.L.R. 185; Buxbaum, "Incomplete Federalism: Jurisdiction over Antitrust Matters in the European Economic Community," 52 Calif. L. Rev. 56, 63–67 (1964).

[213] See Bosch v. de Geus, 8 Recueil 89, 135–36, [1962] C.M.L.R. 1, 20 (conclusions of Advocate-General Lagrange).

[214] Art. 3(2).

[215] On the relationship between national tribunals and the Community Court and a discussion of some problems arising from conflicts between them, see Dumon & Rigaux 654–72. See also Steindorff, "The Provisions Against Restraints of Competition in the European Community Treaties and the National Law," in 1 Cartel and Monopoly in Modern Law 191 (1961).

court may prohibit an agreement approved under Article 85(3) have already been considered.[216] There is also a question whether a national cartel authority may exercise jurisdiction under national law over a cartel which has been approved under Article 85(3). The problem arises because national authorities have no power to apply Article 85(3)[217] and lose their jurisdiction to apply Article 85(1) when the Commission initiates proceedings. National courts, on the other hand, apparently do not lose their jurisdiction when the Commission takes action, and they can prohibit under national law an agreement approved by the Commission under Article 85(3) unless the substantive law prevents them from doing so.

The question whether national authorities lose their jurisdiction to apply national law when the Commission initiates proceedings depends on the relation between their jurisdictions to apply national law and to apply Community law.[218] The better view is that, even after the Commission initiates proceedings and approves an agreement under Article 85(3), the national authorities still have power to apply national law.

National courts

National courts retain jurisdiction in cases in which a determination whether an agreement is valid or prohibited by the Treaty is essential to decide the case. The nullity of an agreement contrary to Article 85(1) can always be pleaded in the national courts even if a notification has been made. The national courts, as distinct from the national cartel authorities, have jurisdiction to determine the validity of contracts subject to Article 85(1), the effect of the nullity of prohibited agreements on the rights of the parties,[219] and the liability of the parties

[216] At pp. 427–28.

[217] Art. 9(1). Cf. Société de l'Alimentation v. Société de Fécamp, Cour d'Appel de Paris, 1re Chambre Supplémentaire, April 1962, Juris Classeur Périodique, La Semaine Juridique, Sec. Jurisprudence No. 16.

[218] Arts. 85 and 86 and all regulations are in force as national law in each member state. In theory, three alternatives are possible. First, the national authorities might have one jurisdiction to apply both laws. In this case, they would lose jurisdiction to apply national law when they lose jurisdiction to apply Community law under art. 9(3). The argument here is that art. 88 gives the authorities the power to apply Community law when operating in accordance with their own procedure and that they are deprived of the power to apply either law, under art. 9(3). There is nothing in art. 9(3) to indicate that this is contemplated. The jurisdiction under art. 88 merely continues until the Commission takes action. Jurisdiction to apply two sets of substantive rules under the same procedure is not a single jurisdiction in the sense that, if the power to apply one set ends, the power to apply the other automatically vanishes.

Second, they might have two mutually exclusive jurisdictions, and thus if the cartel authority initiated proceedings under Community law and the Commission initiated its own proceedings, the authority would be deprived of all jurisdiction. This might be the case if the two substantive laws were in mutually exclusive spheres. This second possibility cannot be proved unless, as a matter of substantive law, national courts or authorities cannot prohibit under national law an agreement approved by the Commission under art. 85(3). If this is so, the jurisdictional problem does not arise.

Third, national authorities might have two concurrent jurisdictions, in which case they would be free, procedurally, to take proceedings under national law at any time; this is the writer's view. It follows that they might exercise jurisdiction under national law after they lost their jurisdiction under Community law. This is consistent with the conclusion reached on the corresponding substantive law problem. This position is probably undesirable, though it avoids the anomaly of the national courts' having undiminished jurisdiction under national law after cartel authorities are deprived of it. Another factor is that if the Commission initiates proceedings and then holds arts. 85(1) and 86 inapplicable, the national authority's jurisdiction would have to revive if it had ceased; this result would be odd.

[219] Bosch v. de Geus, 8 Recueil 89, 130–31, [1962] C.M.L.R. 1, 16–17 (conclusions of Advocate-General Lagrange).

to prohibited practices for injury to third parties. They have jurisdiction also in all other cases involving the civil consequences of the provisions of the Treaty.

The national cartel authorities, not the courts, normally enforce the Treaty provisions not only by conducting investigations but also by taking the decisions relating to infringements and by imposing the sanctions appropriate under the national laws. Therefore, if a decision whether a Treaty infringement has occurred is essential to decide a case before a national court, the court may suspend action on the case and have the Treaty question decided by the national authority or the Commission, or it may decide the issue itself, if this will ultimately mean that the issue is referred to the Community Court under Article 177.[220] In either case, conflicting decisions are avoided.

National courts may not decide whether an agreement falls within Article 85(3); only the Commission may do that.[221] The decision of the Commission under Article 85(3) therefore is binding on them. However, since a decision of the Commission under Article 85(3) may be challenged in the Community Court within two months,[222] the national court may have to adjourn its case until the validity of the Commission's decision has been settled by the Community Court.

The national courts always have jurisdiction to decide whether Article 85(1) or 86 applies in a particular case, subject to a ruling on any question of Treaty interpretation under Article 177. Where such a ruling exists, it binds the national court, the national cartel authority, and the Commission. If no such ruling exists, a national court is not bound by a negative clearance, if one has been issued, since a negative clearance apparently is not absolutely binding on anyone.[223] Whether or not a national court is bound by a decision of the Commission on whether Article 85(1) or 86 has been infringed,[224] it should follow the decision, because it represents the view of the authority primarily charged with administering Articles 85 and 86 and because it has been made after consultations with representatives of all of the national authorities in the Consultative Committee.

National courts need not suspend proceedings if application is made for a negative clearance, since it will not bind them when issued. They are not deprived of jurisdiction by the initiation of any proceedings by the Commission.[225]

[220] The Court will not reconsider the facts of the case as found by the tribunal referring the Treaty questions to it.

[221] Art. 9(1).

[222] Art. 173.

[223] Bosch v. de Geus, 8 Recueil 89, 131, [1962] C.M.L.R. 1, 17 (conclusions of Advocate-General Lagrange). The granting or refusal of a negative clearance would be an important factor for the court to consider; 8 Recueil at 132, [1962] C.M.L.R. at 17.

[224] Advocate-General Lagrange says that a decision as to the infringement of the Treaty, especially a decision of the Court, is legally binding if the principle of res judicata applies, and otherwise is of great weight; Bosch v. de Geus, 8 Recueil 89, 133, [1962] C.M.L.R. 1, 17. Two months after the date of the Commission's decision, it is binding on all enterprises which could have brought it before the Court under art. 173(2) for annulment. However, other enterprises may want to argue that the decision is invalid, and apparently they may do so in a national court; art. 177(b). The national court is free to refer the question of the validity of the decision to the Community Court under art. 177, but in every other respect it should regard itself as bound by the Commission's decision. If the Court holds that the Commission's decision was improper, it cannot annul it if the time limit for doing so has elapsed, but the conflict of decisions will not be the fault of the national court.

[225] Art. 9(3) applies only to national "authorities," and this apparently does not include courts other than those which are the only national "authority." Waelbroeck, "Le Problème

However, since the court will be bound by the Commission's decision when issued, it should adjourn its proceedings until then in order to avoid a conflict of decisions. It is probably not bound to do so, however,[226] especially if it regards the application to the Commission as frivolous or dilatory.

THE PROTECTION OF THIRD PARTIES UNDER THE REGULATIONS[227]

Complaints

The Regulations give third parties certain rights to request the initiation of proceedings by the Commission and to take part in proceedings after they have been initiated. Any individual or legal entity which shows a "legitimate interest" may make a request to the Commission for action against an alleged infringement of the Treaty.[228] If no legitimate interest is proved, the Commission has discretion whether to investigate the matter *ex officio*.[229] A legitimate interest includes any actual or potential injury to the complainant. The injury may have to be related to operations within the EEC if the complainant is an enterprise located outside the member states. If a legitimate interest is shown, the Commission is in some sense obliged[230] to investigate the matter and must inform the enterprise of its reasons if it takes no action and must give the enterprise a chance to comment on them.[231] If no legitimate interest can be shown, the enterprise can approach the national cartel authority of a member state and ask it to request the Commission to take action.[232]

If an agreement has been exempted under Article 85(3), there is nothing to prevent an enterprise from making a complaint to the Commission that the

de la Validité des Ententes Economiques dans le droit privé du Marché Commun," 51 Rev. Crit. de Droit Int. Privé 415, 436 (1962).

[226] Bosch v. de Geus, 8 Recueil 89, 132, 135–36, [1962] C.M.L.R. 1, 17, 20 (conclusions of Advocate-General Lagrange).

[227] Protection of third parties under national laws which give them a right to damages for injury caused by a prohibited practice is discussed in Chapter Seventeen.

[228] Art. 3(1), 3(2). Complaints may be made by competitors, customers, suppliers, or any other injured person.

[229] Guide Pratique 8. *Quaere* whether art. 175 could apply in case of failure to give the acknowledgement of receipt of the complaint; Form C of Regulation 27 does not indicate that any action is being taken.

[230] If the Commission has issued a negative clearance for the practice complained of and if the complainant has a legitimate interest, the Commission is not called on to inquire *ex officio*; see art. 3(1). It is not bound by its negative clearance, and it is bound to consider the complaint. See 1962 Journal Officiel 2135/62. The fact that an injury is alleged to have resulted from the practice complained of is not in itself sufficient to end the binding effect of the negative clearance, because it is not per se evidence of a breach of the Treaty. A ruling by the Commission that no legitimate interest was shown, which would not constitute a decision, would not be relevant to an action for damages under national law. Federation of British Industries, European Economic Community —Restrictive Trade Practices 24 (1963), says that a person showing a legitimate interest has a right (independent of Reg. 99, art. 6) to require the Commission to decide on his complaint; see also Deringer et al., 7 Revue du Marché Commun 76, 77 (1964). However, it is doubtful if art. 175 applies, since the decision of the Commission will not be "addressed to" the complainant. Clearly, the protection of the injured party is inadequate if he cannot compel the Commission to deal with the case, although he might be able to get his own state to take up the matter under art. 175. This is a question separate from that of whether a party with a "sufficient interest" under art. 19(2) can compel the Commission to hear him, which turns not on the meaning of the words "addressed to him" but on the meaning of the phrase "formal document" in art. 175. The Commission, even if it is obliged to acknowledge receipt of the complaint, is not expressly bound by any regulation to deal with it in such a way as to come within art. 175; see art. 155. Regulation 99 reduces the importance of these questions.

[231] Reg. 99, art. 6.

[232] Cf. art. 19(2).

facts have changed in an essential respect or that the decision is being infringed or abused.[233] The effectiveness with which a third party is able to object to the continuance of an exemption depends on the amount of information published about the content of and reasons for a decision. Apart from business secrets, the Commission can publish a decision in detail, and presumably it will do this if it wishes to encourage complaints that the limits of an exemption are being exceeded or that for some other reason further action is required.

Unless the Commission gets a large staff for detecting infringements of the Treaty, complaints will be the chief means by which it will discover infringements which have not been notified. The other important source of information will be national cartel authorities.[234] Since the jurisdiction of the national authorities, including the courts, to deal with breaches of the Treaty may be impeded by the Commission's taking up the case,[235] an injured party should usually complain to the Commission first. If national law permits, the injured party can bring an action for damages after the Commission has given a decision on the matter, which, whether or not it is binding on the national courts under the principle of res judicata, will carry great weight.

Intervention in proceedings of the Court

Any person showing a legitimate interest may intervene in any case before the Court, except one involving only member states or Community institutions.[236] Intervention must be limited to support of the position of one of the original parties to the case. Presumably it would be difficult to prove an interest sufficient to allow intervention in cases instituted by a private enterprise under Article 173 or 177.[237]

Intervention in proceedings of the Commission

In antitrust cases, individuals, legal entities, or associations of persons showing that they have a "sufficient interest" have a right to express their views to the Commission.[238] It is not clear how this right is enforceable in the Court.[239] The right is not limited to persons injured by, or parties to, the agreement or practice under consideration,[240] and one may

[233] Art. 8(3).

[234] An energetic national cartel authority or a national law which requires the registration of restrictive practices will be an important aid to the work of the Commission. This is a reason for endeavoring to harmonize national laws on restrictive practices. The Commission is giving priority to complaints, cases in which actions are pending before national courts, cases under art. 86 (since these cannot be notified for approval), and cartels which have not been notified (to avoid prejudice to enterprises which have notified their agreements); Seventh General Report, para. 66 (1964).

[235] Art. 9(1), 9(3).

[236] Statute of the Court of Justice, art. 37. This right of intervention is not limited to antitrust cases.

[237] Except in the unlikely event that an interest in the decision as a precedent for the future is sufficient.

[238] Art. 19(2); Reg. 99, arts. 5, 7, 11. The language used is hardly helpful. To intervene in proceedings in the Court, one must show an interest in the outcome. To make a complaint, one must show a legitimate interest; art. 3(2). To intervene in the proceedings of the Commission, one must show a sufficient interest; art. 19; Reg. 99, arts. 5, 7. The right to object to a negative clearance or an approval under art. 85(3) is given to interested third parties; art. 19(3). See also Reg. 19, art. 5.

[239] If the Commission refuses to hear a party with a "sufficient interest," he can appeal against the refusal under art. 173 for breach of a rule of law relating to the application of the Treaty if the refusal is a decision under art. 189. If the Commission ignores him, art. 175 applies only if the decision of the Commission to hear him is "a formal document." This is doubtful, but the question should clearly be resolved in favor of the intervenor.

[240] Since these are provided for separately by art. 19(3) and 19(1), respectively.

argue either for or against the agreement. Any enterprise benefiting directly from the agreement is entitled to appear under this provision. There is a separate provision allowing the Commission to obtain views from anyone whose views it considers necessary; this presumably is to enable the Commission to get the views of those for whom the decision will be a precedent. Potential damage under an agreement for which the Commission contemplates a negative clearance or an exemption under Article 85(3) is clearly sufficient.

ARTICLE 86 AND REGULATION 17

Abuses under Article 86 cannot be approved, so the provisions for notification in Regulation 17 do not apply to them. Possible abuses may be submitted to the Commission for a negative clearance;[241] this is important since it is the only way in which a dominant enterprise can test the legality of a course of action without risking a fine. Abuses may be made the subject of a complaint,[242] and action may be taken against them by national cartel authorities.[243] The procedures for inquiry and investigation,[244] for single and daily fines,[245] and for the rights of interested parties to express their views[246] are all applicable to Article 86. However, because only full studies of a whole sector of industry can prove that abuse or improper exploitation of a dominant market position exists, it probably is impossible to take action against a monopoly or oligopoly—except for refusal to contract—without an inquiry into the whole industry,[247] even if only a single instance of abuse is alleged. This is especially necessary if unfair prices or limitation of production is alleged; discrimination and tying-in clauses will be more vulnerable to immediate attack by the Commission. However, Article 86 does not deal with practices which directly impede economic integration, and the first object of the Commission is to prevent interference with integration. The Commission is fully occupied with this, since the total number of bilateral agreements notified is extremely large, and it is unlikely to take action under Article 86 except in flagrant cases. However, oligopolies are watched closely for evidence of concerted practices contrary to Article 85.

As originally drafted, Regulation 17 contained no provisions relating to Article 86, and the Commission clearly did not regard it as requiring immediate implementation as a matter of priority. References to Article 86 were put into Regulation 17 only on the insistence of the Parliamentary Assembly.[248] The Commission may need to issue a new regulation before Article 86 is put fully into operation. Practices of monopolies benefit from Regulation 17 only because of the limited amount of security given by a negative clearance. No machinery exists by which a monopoly can compel the Commission to give a definitive ruling on whether any practice violates Article 86, which thus is enforced only by control *a posteriori*. This is important because Article 86 will be enforced primarily by fines, not by the invalidation of agreements contrary to Article 86.

[241] Art. 2. In practice, it might be possible to obtain a decision rather than a negative clearance from the Commission.

[242] Art. 3.

[243] Art. 9(3).

[244] Arts. 11–14.

[245] Arts. 15, 16.

[246] Art. 19.

[247] Art. 12. See Political and Economic Planning, Cartel Policy and the Common Market 275 (1962).

[248] See Deringer Report, A.P.E. Doc. No. 57, paras. 80, 112 (1961–62); Rapport . . . sur le sixième rapport général sur l'activité de la Communauté économique européenne, A.P.E. Doc. No. 76, para. 60 (1963–64).

Chapter 17

The Civil Effects of The Invalidity of Agreements Under Article 85

THE PROBLEM[1]

An important practical problem arising under the antitrust provisions of the EEC Treaty is the extent of the invalidity of a prohibited restrictive agreement under whatever law is applicable—i.e., whether the agreement is wholly invalid or whether the invalid clauses are severable from the rest of the agreement.[2] Article 85(2) provides that agreements and decisions forbidden by Article 85 are automatically void without any necessity for a decision to that effect.[3]

The first question is whether the effects of Article 85(2) in private law are a matter of Community law[4] governed by the Treaty or whether they are to be separately decided by each national law. This question is a point of Treaty interpretation and is ultimately a matter for the Community Court. If Community law applies, the Court will ultimately have to decide if the Community law

[1] See generally Houin, "Les Conséquences civiles d'une infraction aux règles de concurrence," 1963 Annales de la Faculté de Droit de Liège 27 (1963), translated in 18 Record of N.Y.C.B.A. 695 (1963).

[2] Other matters arising under art. 85(2) are the rules of frustration of contracts due to supervening illegality under art. 85, a matter on which Irish law is defective owing to failure to modify the common law rule by legislation such as the British Law Reform (Frustrated Contracts) Act, 1943, 6 & 7 Geo. 6, c. 40; the question whether the parties to a restrictive agreement have a duty to each other to modify the agreement so as to validate it, with approval from the Commission; the rights of those who are not parties to a valid restrictive agreement to sue the parties for breach of the agreement; and the rights of third parties affected by the illegality of a restrictive agreement. These are all matters for the appropriate national law under the ordinary rules of private international law. See Graupner, "The Substantive Law of the Rules on Competition," 59 Law Society's Gazette 450, 453 (1962); Blume v. Van Praag, Antwerp Commercial Court, Oct. 25, 1962, [1964] C.M.L.R. 17. Also, questions may arise under national laws as to the rights of enterprises to recover property, such as technical reports embodying know-how, which has been handed over pursuant to agreements held to be illegal under art. 85.

The practical difficulties caused by the invalidity of prohibited agreements were apparently the reason the Netherlands Law of December 5, 1957, which was enacted to implement art. 85, adopted the principle that restrictive agreements become illegal only when they have been specifically condemned instead of the principle that they are automatically illegal; Reuter, "Ententes et Cartels," 2 Revue du Marché Commun 46, 47 (1959). The Dutch law was passed only because the Netherlands government took the view that art. 85 stated principles to be implemented and was not directly applicable.

[3] See Waelbroeck, "Le Problème de la Validité des Ententes Economiques dans le droit privé du Marché Commun," 51 Rev. Crit. de Droit Int. Privé, 415, 422 (1962).

[4] Cf. the position under the ECSC Treaty, which is affected by the limited scope of the ECSC; see Dumon & Rigaux, "I Tribunali Internazionali e Sopranazionali," in 2 Primo Congresso Internazionale dei Magistrati 621, 631 (1959).

invalidates the whole of a restrictive agreement or only those clauses which are contrary to the Treaty.

IS THERE A TREATY RULE ON THE EXTENT OF INVALIDITY?

Article 85(2) is a part of the domestic law of each member state. It applies, irrespective of the national laws governing agreements in other respects, to all agreements prohibited under Article 85. It would be anomalous if the only effect of this provision were not uniform but depended on the proper law of the contract. The same contract might even be treated differently in different member states. If Article 85(2) were intended to automatically produce[5] different effects in different member states, it would have been largely unnecessary, because illegal contracts suffer certain disabilities under the national law of each of the Six. Nullity due to the Treaty must be the same in each member state, and the Treaty therefore states a rule as to the extent of the nullity.[6] This means that a new rule of law exists and supersedes the existing rules of national law. If the proper interpretation of the Treaty is that only the rules of the national law which governs the contract apply, the Treaty gives automatic effect to whichever national law is applicable, and "void" means different things in different countries.[7]

THE CONTENT OF THE TREATY RULE

The national laws

If the Treaty states a rule on the extent of invalidity, one must determine the content of that rule. Rules of national law do not help in deciding whether the Treaty lays down a uniform rule. They are important, however, in the absence of other sources of law, because they indicate the content of the uniform rule, although the Community rule may not be exactly similar to that of any of the national laws.

The better view is that Community law invalidates an agreement only to the extent that it distorts competition.[8] This is the view taken in principle by the national laws of the Six.[9] In France, for

[5] Art. 85(2) deals with the obligations of the parties under private law and not with the automatic operation of the prohibition contained in the rest of the article. It does not mention concerted practices.

[6] This is apparently the view of Dr. Verloren van Themaat, who has said that the question of the extent of the invalidity is a question which the Court must decide and is therefore a question of Treaty interpretation; Committee on Foreign Law, "Current Legal Developments in the European Economic Community," 18 Record of N.Y.C.B.A. 329, 336 (1963). The contrary view is taken by van den Heuval, "Civil Law Consequences of Violation of the Antitrust Provisions of the Rome Treaty," 12 Am. J. Comp. L. 172, 174 (1963).

[7] Ladas, "Antitrust Law in the Common Market with Special Reference to Industrial Property Agreements," 23 Ohio St. L.J. 709, 714 (1962), states that the Treaty invalidates only particular clauses and that the validity of the rest of the contract then depends on national law. He gives no authority for the first conclusion, from which, of course, the second follows. This view relates to the content of the Treaty rule and not to its existence.

[8] This is the view of various European experts. It is "hoped" in the Deringer Report, A.P.E. Doc. No. 57, para. 108 (1961–62).

[9] In France, this results from jurisprudence under the Civil Code, art. 1172. In Germany, the Civil Code, § 139, provides that if part of an agreement is void the whole is void, unless it appears that the parties would have desired the remaining part to be valid if they had known of the partial invalidity when they entered into the agreement and if the part held void does not go to the essence of the agreement. For some case law on the application of this section by the German courts to agreements under art. 85, see van den Heuvel, "Civil Law Consequences of Violation of the Antitrust Provisions of the Rome Treaty," 12 Am. J. Comp. L. 172, 178–79 (1963). In Belgium, if a contract is not "indivisible" (Civil Code, art. 1218), only the invalid clause will fall. The law of the Netherlands is similar; see van den Heuvel, 12 Am. J. Comp. L. at 175.

See French Price Ordinance No. 45-1483 of

example, a void clause is treated as nonexistent, and the court will decide if its importance is such that the whole contract is invalidated by its removal. This is also the rule in Irish and English law with regard to contracts in restraint of trade,[10] though not with regard to other types of illegal contracts.

The Treaty provisions

The Treaty prohibits agreements, decisions, and concerted practices with certain anticompetitive objects or effects. The rule that the over-all effect of the agreement must be considered does not necessarily mean that the Treaty invalidates the entire agreement if only a part of it is objectionable. If the formula of the German Competition Law, "agreements . . . are prohibited insofar as they . . .," had been used, it clearly would have followed the principles of the national laws as to severance or divisibility. The only reason to say that the Treaty invalidates the whole of an agreement and not merely the parts of it which distort competition is that the Treaty speaks of "agreements" and "decisions" being automatically void. This may be a deliberate variation from the words of the German statute, but it is not necessarily so, particularly since the Treaty was not drafted with the technical exactitude of the German Competition Law.

The object of the Treaty would be achieved by invalidating agreements only to the extent to which they distort competition in interstate trade. Article 85(2) supplements Article 85(1) by preventing any reliance on agreements which are contrary to the Treaty. Both provisions are preventive and regulatory instruments of economic policy. Provisions in an agreement which do not distort competition need not be invalidated for economic reasons, since they have no objectionable effects, or for punitive reasons, since fines are the sanctions contemplated by Article 87. To construe Article 85(2) as invalidating the innocuous parts of agreements as a sanction would draw an unnecessary distinction between agreements and concerted practices and would require strong justification.

Since nullity is automatic, the maximum certainty as to the legal position would be obtained by declaring the whole agreement invalid, while the position would be doubtful if only a portion of the agreement were automatically void. However, this argument would require a higher degree of legal certainty than is provided, for example, by French or German law.

The Regulations do not shed much light on the question. Agreements in certain circumstances have a "provisional validity,"[11] and they may be validated retroactively by an exemption under Article 85(3). Before notification, new agreements in the compulsorily notifiable class are under Article 85(2). For these reasons and because the Commission may modify an exemption[12] or make it subject to specified conditions, it seems more reasonable to hold that an agreement is void only to the extent to which it is prohibited by the Treaty. This avoids the legal difficulties of a wholly void agreement's suddenly acquiring complete validity. However, if the prohibited clauses are so important that the others cannot stand alone, the whole agreement is invalid for as long as Article 85(2) applies.

June 30, 1945, as amended by Decrees No. 53-704 of Aug. 9, 1953, No. 58-545 of June 24, 1958, and No. 59-1004 of Aug. 17, 1959, art. 59 *bis*; German Competition Law, §§ 1, 15.

[10] Bennett v. Bennett, [1952] 1 K.B. 249; Goodinson v. Goodinson, [1954] 2 Q.B. 118; Mulligan v. Corr, [1925] 1 Ir. R. 169.

[11] Bosch v. de Geus, 8 Recueil 89, 107, [1962] C.M.L.R. 1, 30.

[12] Reg. 17, art. 8.

Practical arguments

It can be argued in favor of total invalidity that most important commercial agreements result from careful negotiations and balance the interests of the parties in complicated bargains. It is usually unfair to one party to invalidate a part of a carefully balanced contract without giving him the right to cancel or renegotiate it.[13] The other party may have acquired a more advantageous bargain than he had in the first instance and may be unwilling to renegotiate the contract. However, in such a case the law should protect the party prejudiced by holding that the invalid clauses are so vital that without them the remainder of the contract cannot stand. The practical effect of the rule that only the anticompetitive parts of an agreement are necessarily invalid might vary greatly according to the courts' views on whether the remaining parts should be allowed to stand alone.

There is no reason why provisions in themselves unobjectionable should be invalidated because of their association with prohibited provisions. If the total effect of the contract is anticompetitive, clauses which in isolation would be permissible are, under any legal system, held invalid. If most of the contract deals with matters not related—by their nature or as a result of a bargain—to the provisions which distort competition, the innocuous provisions could have been dealt with in a separate contract. Invalidating the whole contract may upset legitimate business transactions unnecessarily, since the parties can renew the contract in identical terms if they omit the prohibited clauses.

If the entire agreement is invalidated, it may not be possible to restore the previous position completely, even if the law allows the parties to restore it—for instance, by allowing recovery of money paid for a consideration which has failed[14] or recovery for unjust enrichment. This is especially important in connection with licenses of patents and know-how. If a patent license is invalid, the licensee has no rights to use the patent, and the sole right to use it reverts to the patentee under the patent law.[15] The licensor, however, has no legal right to know-how and if it is licensed or given to another, his only protection is under the license agreement. If the whole of the latter is rendered invalid because of one or two anticompetitive provisions, the licensor has no remedy other than perhaps a claim for unjust enrichment. If the license agreement is invalid only to the extent to which it is contrary to the Treaty, clauses providing for the payment of royalties and prohibiting the disclosure of the know-how to third parties may continue in force and protect the licensor, unless they are so closely connected with the objectionable provisions of the agreement that they fall with them.

Practical results of the legal position

Invalidity of an agreement is likely to be more serious for the licensor or manufacturer in a vertical agreement than for the parties to a horizontal agreement. In particular, it may enable one party to escape his obligations by having the agreement declared wholly or partly void by the Commission[16] or by pleading

[13] German Competition Law, § 19(2), allows the Bundeskartellamt, in order to prevent unjustified hardship, to order that the invalidity of a resale price maintenance agreement shall not affect certain provisions of the agreement.

[14] As to this question in connection with contracts in restraint of trade in English and Irish law, see Cheshire & Fifoot, Law of Contract 337–38 (6th ed. 1964).

[15] It is even possible, although it is unlikely, that the patent would be rendered invalid if the owner had consented to its use pursuant only to a contract which was *ex hypothesi* nonexistent.

[16] German Competition Law, § 13, allows a party to an agreement within §§ 2–8 (cartels

in the national courts the agreement's illegality[17] under the Treaty. Unlike an exemption under Article 85(3), a negative clearance has merely persuasive force and does not stop one party from pleading the illegality of the agreement. Since the nullity of an agreement contrary to Article 85 can always be pleaded,[18] it is important that any enterprise which may suffer damage from the successful repudiation of an agreement should see that it has been approved by the Commission. In some circumstances, the possibility of invalidity may constitute a more important sanction for Article 85 than the chance of a fine; how important depends on the degree of invalidity resulting, under the Treaty or national law, from Article 85.

If the Commission objects only to a particular clause in an agreement, it may issue a decision approving the agreement with a stipulation that the objectionable clause has no effect.[19] Probably only infrequently will invalidating the whole agreement be necessary. In this unusual case, no question can arise in the courts of the member states.[20] The Commission must give reasons for its decisions,[21] and it may be clear that the reasons for holding the agreement to be invalid under Article 85(1) apply only to particular provisions of the agreement and, therefore, that Article 85(2) invalidates only those provisions. It is not certain whether a decision that only a part of an agreement is invalid is subject to review by the Court. Since the Commission can make recommendations to the parties concerned before, or instead of, issuing a decision,[22] it may be able to prevent the question from arising.

All of this has implications in drafting agreements which in due course may be invalidated. It is now the practice to insert either a severability clause or a provision permitting reconsideration of the rights of the parties in the event of invalidation. If national law invalidates the whole contract when any part of it is contrary to Article 85, provisions to deal with this eventuality will themselves be invalid. For tactical reasons, it might be better to deal with these questions in a separate document not submitted to the Commission, although a national court might well regard it all as the same transaction. Since the second document need deal only with the measures to be taken if the Commission holds the first document invalid, the second need not be notified unless it contains anticompetitive provisions.

The situation with regard to know-how is more difficult, since a provision against disclosure by the licensee to third parties might be one of the restrictive provisions held invalid. If so, return of all documents can be provided for, but requiring any sum to be paid by the li-

---

which have beneficial effects and are subject to the control of the Bundeskartellamt) to terminate the agreement if, for example, its freedom of economic action is unfairly restricted by unjustified differential treatment.

[17] As to modification of existing agreements, see Reg. 17, art. 7(1); retrospective approval so obtained cannot be relied on against parties who have not agreed to notification.

[18] It is difficult to say whether the national court must raise the question whether art. 85 is applicable if the parties do not. Presumably, the court is more likely to be obliged to raise questions under art. 85 than to raise other questions of Treaty interpretation under art. 177. See Houin, "Les Consequences civiles d'une infraction aux règles de concurrence," 1963 Annales de la Faculté de Droit de Liège 27, 35, 18 Record of N.Y.C.B.A. 695, 700 (1963).

[19] Reg. 17, art. 8(1). See German Competition Law, § 19(2).

[20] In the courts of non-member states, the question whether the agreement is invalid by being illegal under the law of the place of performance may arise.

[21] Art. 190.

[22] Reg. 17, art. 3. See Linssen, "The Antitrust Law of the European Economic Community," 18 Record of N.Y.C.B.A. 289, 294 (1963).

censee if the information is passed on presumably will be regarded as an indirect method of bringing about the same anticompetitive result, at least if the sum is substantial.

ACTIONS FOR DAMAGES BY THIRD PARTIES FOR BREACH OF ARTICLES 85 AND 86

The Treaty does not deal with civil actions for damage caused by breach of the Treaty provisions on restrictive practices. Breach of these provisions is automatically illegal under national laws, since Articles 85 and 86 are self-executing. Whether this illegality gives rise to an action for damages is a matter of national law, since it is not yet dealt with by any regulations.

The Deringer Report[23] considers whether this matter should be dealt with by Regulation 17. It concludes that a civil right of action is desirable and necessary to prevent and to deal with infringements of the Treaty. The Report states that no uniform rule will be possible until a study has been made of the laws of the Six. The Commission has since been engaged on such a study.

Article 87(2)(e) empowers the Council to enact regulations or directives "to determine how domestic legislation is to be reconciled with the provisions" of Articles 85–90[24] or adopted in application of Article 87. It is not clear whether this authorizes the Council to deal with civil actions for damages by means of a regulation adopted by qualified majority. If not, they can be dealt with only by way of directive by unanimous vote under Article 100. The civil consequence of Treaty infringements is not the principal matter intended to be dealt with by the regulations under Article 87. The Deringer Report shows no doubt that the Council has power to deal with the matter but does not indicate whether this power is pursuant to Article 87 or Article 100.[25]

The right of injured parties to recover damages for infringements of Articles 85 and 86 is important as assurance that they are enforced, as protection for the injured parties, and as a sanction when fines are not imposed or cannot be imposed because of prompt notification of new agreements. Instead of instituting proceedings in the national courts, in most cases the injured party begins by making a complaint to the Commission, which has powers greater than any given to a plaintiff under national law. The

[23] A.P.E. Doc. No. 57, para. 123 (1961–62). See also van den Heuvel, "Civil Law Consequences of Violation of the Antitrust Provisions of the Rome Treaty," 12 Am. J. Comp. L. 172, 189 (1963), who discusses whether a contract entered into on unfair terms because of the abuse of a dominant position by one of the parties could be set aside on that ground; id. at 191–93. See also Plaisant & Lassier, Ententes et Marché Commun 37–38 (1959), who suggest that such a contract would be voidable. It is submitted that the civil effects of such a contract are governed by national law. See Deringer et al., 6 Revue du Marché Commun 488, 495 (1963). It seems clear that such a contract could not be challenged in Irish or English law. In Irish law "duress" applies only to threats to exercise legal rights or to physical duress to the person or goods of the party seeking to set aside the contract. "Undue influence" relates normally to influence over the mind and will of the injured party. 1 Chitty, Contracts, ch. 7 (22d ed. 1961). However, there are a few cases, all pre-1900, in which contracts have been set aside on the grounds of the ignorance of the injured party and the unfair nature of the transaction. Some contracts in restraint of trade may be invalidated if they were influenced by the economic power of one of the parties; see id. at 351–68; Leather Cloth Co. v. Lorsont, L.R. 9 Eq. 345, 354 (1869).

[24] The translation by Her Majesty's Foreign Office reads "the provisions of this Article." This is clearly inaccurate; the French word used is *section* and refers to the first section of part III, title I, chapter 1, of the Treaty.

[25] According to van Hecke & Suetens, "Le Premier Règlement Européen sur les Cartels et les Monopoles," 1962 Journal des Tribunaux 361, 364, art. 87 does not empower the Council to deal with the question of actions for damages for breach of the Treaty.

costs of investigating and proving the infringement then are borne by the Commission. The question of an exemption under Article 85(3) can thus be handled directly, while the national court would find it necessary to await the decision of the Commission.[26] The national court must treat the decision of the Commission under Article 85(1) or Article 85(3) as binding after the time limit for appeal to the Court has expired, so only the amount of damage suffered need be proved to the national court. The national courts can—and the courts of final appeal which the case reaches are compelled to—refer any point of Treaty interpretation to the Community Court. At least in the present situation of uncertainty as to the respective powers of the Commission and the Court, this seriously delays final resolution of the case. The plaintiff enterprise does not lose any important privileges by having the case dealt with by the Commission, since it is free to state the facts within its knowledge as fully as possible in its complaint,[27] to intervene in the proceedings if a sufficient interest can be shown,[28] and to object if the Commission contemplates an exemption or a negative clearance.[29]

In the EEC there is no provision for triple damages, as there is in the United States. The right to complain to the Commission cannot normally be exercised until some injury has occurred, since it is unlikely that an enterprise will have advance warning of a particular agreement or practice; thus the right to complain does not provide adequate protection even if the Commission acts promptly to terminate the practice.

Since the remedy of the injured party is under national law, injured enterprises which are not resident in any member state have the same right to sue as enterprises of member states other than that in which the action is brought.[30] When a Community rule is enacted, there may be a question as to the right of action of a foreign enterprise which, though injured by an agreement or practice affecting trade between member states, is not injured in its operations within the EEC.

The national laws of the Six

It is not proposed here to consider the various questions arising under the national laws of the Six, but an indication of some aspects of the situation may be given.

In Germany, the Civil Code[31] allows a civil action for damages from any violation of a law enacted for the purpose of protecting private persons. No action lies if the legislation contravened is merely regulatory and intended to protect the public interest. A single piece of legislation, such as the German Competition Law, may include some provisions to protect individual parties and some to protect merely the general economic interest. Presumably, the German courts may differentiate similarly between the various provisions of Articles 85 and 86. The Competition Law provides for compensation to be payable for damage caused by any willful or negligent viola-

[26] Reg. 17, art. 9(1).

[27] Reg. 17, art. 3.

[28] Reg. 17, art. 19(2). Presumably a sufficient interest will always exist where actual damage can be proved.

[29] Reg. 17, art. 19(3).

[30] This does not necessarily involve national treatment; art. 220(1).

[31] Section 823 II. See also §§ 823 I and 826 and Law Against Unfair Competition, 1909, § 1; Riesenfeld, "The Protection of Competition," in 2 American Enterprise in the European Common Market: A Legal Profile 230–31, 338 (Stein & Nicholson ed. 1960); 1 von der Groeben & von Boeckh, Kommentar zum EWG-Vertrag 276–77 (1958); Millner, "Contrasts in Contract and Tort," in English Law and the Common Market 68, 87 (Keeton & Schwarzenberger ed. 1963); Deringer et al., 6 Revue du Marché Commun 488, 496 (1963).

tion of any provision of that law or of any order of the Bundeskartellamt or the national courts which is intended to protect a class to which the plaintiff belongs.[32] It is left to the courts to decide which provisions of the Competition Law are intended to protect individuals, although the wording makes it clear that only some provisions are. A concerted boycott is the most frequently quoted example of an act contrary to a law for the protection of individual interests; the status of other restrictive practices is disputed. In connection with Article 85, questions presumably will arise as to whether there is any difference in purpose between the general prohibition on practices distorting competition and the specific instances which are intended only as examples of it. The German Federal Supreme Court has held that the provisions of the ECSC Treaty prohibiting discrimination are not for the protection of individual interests and that no action will lie for breach of them.[33]

Section 1401 of the Netherlands Civil Code seems to have been interpreted in much the same way as the German law. The Netherlands Economic Competition Act of 1956[34] provides that any person to whom an order under the Act has been made has a duty to comply with it and that this duty is owed to any person who has a reasonable interest in compliance. This is an indication that the 1956 Act might be held to be a law intended to protect private persons and, by analogy, so might Articles 85 and 86 also.

The French Civil Code[35] draws no distinction between laws passed in the general interest and laws passed for the protection of particular individuals. It is, however, doubtful whether an action will lie for injury resulting from infringement of the Treaty because the case law of the Cour de Cassation[36] dealing with other legislation has made it at least possible that the Treaty provisions will be regarded as being in the general interest and as giving no right of action to private individuals. If this is accepted, it adds a new requirement to the traditional requirements of an action in tort; i.e., fault, damage, and a causal connection between them.

Under Belgium's Civil Code,[37] enterprises which have suffered damage can recover compensation if the damage results from an infringement of Article 85 or Article 86. The position with regard to infringements of the Belgian law of May 27, 1960, is in dispute because it is doubtful if a breach of a law authoriz-

[32] § 35.

[33] Van den Heuvel, "Civil Law Consequences of Violation of the Antitrust Provisions of the Rome Treaty," 12 Am. J. Comp. L. 172, 186 (1963).

[34] June 28, 1956, as amended by the Act of July 16, 1958, § 26. See van den Heuvel, "Civil Law Consequences of Violation of the Antitrust Provisions of the Rome Treaty," 12 Am. J. Comp. L. 172, 184, 186 (1963).

[35] Section 1382 provides in general terms that any act whereby anyone causes damage to another obliges the person at fault to make reparation for the damage. Section 1383 makes a person liable for negligence as well as deliberate damage. See Houin, "Les Conséquences civiles d'une infraction aux règles de concurrence," 1963 Annales de la Faculté de Droit de Liège 27, 31, 18 Record of N.Y.C.B.A. 695, 697 (1963).

[36] See Fontaine et al., "Conséquences civiles d'Application des Règles de Concurrence," 1962 Annales de la Faculté de Droit de Liège 43, 51; Judgment of March 2, 1961, Cour de Cassation (Ch. crim.), [1961] J.C.P. 12039; Judgment of Nov. 5, 1959, Cour de Cassation (Ch. crim.), [1960] D. 80; Judgment of Nov. 19, 1959, Cour de Cassation (Ch. crim.), [1960] D. 463, note by G. Durry; van den Heuvel, "Civil Law Consequences of Violation of the Antitrust Provisions of the Rome Treaty," 12 Am. J. Comp. L. 172, 185–86 (1963).

[37] Art. 1382. See Fontaine et al., "Conséquences civiles d'Application des Règles de Concurrence," 1962 Annales de la Faculté de Droit de Liège 43, 52–64.

ing termination of abuse[38] of a monopoly position has occurred before an order prohibiting a particular abuse has been disobeyed. Belgian law has never drawn[39] a distinction between actions for damages that are based on a breach of a law enacted in the general interest and those based on a breach of a law enacted to protect private interests.

The position in Luxembourg seems to be identical to that in Belgium.[40] Other than the provisions of the Treaty, Luxembourg has no law against restrictive practices, so the question of actions for damages for infringements of the national law does not arise.

The Italian Civil Code[41] gives a right to recover compensation for any "unjust" injury, including acts of unfair competition and improper business conduct which cause injury to third parties. Apparently[42] this will give a right of action to a plaintiff injured by a breach of Article 85 or Article 86.

Some have argued that the question whether Articles 85 and 86 are intended to protect individuals or the economy in general is a question of Treaty interpretation, which must be referred to the Community Court by a national court of final appeal under Article 177.[43] However, the real issue seems to be whether the national law in question regards the Articles as of the type intended to protect individuals, and this is a question of national law.

The use of Article 85(3) as a defense

If an action for damages is brought, then the question arises whether the possibility of obtaining approval under Article 85(3) for the practice complained of is a defense. If the Commission has given approval under Article 85(3) for the period during which the damage occurred, no action will lie. If the Commission has refused approval under Article 85(3), clearly the defense is not available. The question is more difficult if the Commission has not yet ruled on the application for approval or if it has

[38] Such as the laws of Belgium and the Netherlands, but not art. 86, which is an absolute prohibition of certain practices and not a power given to an administrative authority to terminate them; see Reg. 17, art. 1.

[39] Van Hecke & Suetens, "Le Premier Règlement Européen sur les Cartels et Les Monopoles," 1962 Journal des Tribunaux 361, 364. Recovery of damages has been permitted for violations of Penal Code, art. 268 (Judgment of Oct. 4, 1878, Cour de Cassation, [1878] Pasicrisie Belge I. 386), art. 299 (Judgment of Jan. 6, 1898, Tribunal Correctionnel, Brussels, [1898] Pasicrisie Belge III. 314), art. 498 (on fraud—Judgment of Oct. 15, 1951, Cour de Cassation, [1952] Pasicrisie Belge I. 77, 1953 Rev. Prat. Soc. 185, opinion of Advocate-General Hayoit de Termincourt and note), and art. 559(4) (on negligent killing of animals—Judgment of Nov. 12, 1947, Tribunal Correctionnel, Arlon, 1951 Revue Générale des Assurances et des Responsabilités [hereinafter cited as R.G.A.R.], No. 4800); of Royal Decree of May 6, 1922 (on disinfectants—Judgment of April 25, 1938, Hasselt, 1939 R.G.A.R., No. 2929); of Royal Decree of Dec. 20, 1934 (on wines—Judgment of April 30, 1935, Brussels, 1955 Journal des Tribunaux 421); of the Law on Companies, arts. 207 et seq. on inaccurate accounts—Judgment of Nov. 16, 1939, Brussels, 1940 Journal des Tribunaux, col. 84); of the Law of Feb. 20, 1939 (on architects—Judgment of June 29, 1959, Cour de Cassation, 1959 Journal des Tribunaux 686); and of the Law of April 15, 1958 (on dentists—Judgment of May 9, 1961, Brussels, 1961 Journal des Tribunaux 561). Authority to the contrary apparently does not contradict the principle stated.

[40] The relevant provisions of the Luxembourg Civil Code, §§ 1382–83, are identical with those of the Belgian and French codes.

[41] Arts. 2043, 2598.

[42] Fracheschelli, "Le Premier Règlement d'Application des Articles 85 et 86 du Traité de Rome," 5 Revue du Marché Commun 345, 347 (1962).

[43] Milner, "Contrasts in Contract and Tort," in English Law and the Common Market 68, 86–87 (Keeton & Schwarzenberger ed. 1963); van den Heuvel, "Civil Law Consequences of Violation of the Antitrust Provisions of the Rome Treaty," 12 Am. J. Comp. L. 172, 180 (1963).

given approval only for a period after the damage was caused to the plaintiff. The question arises in particular under French, Belgian, and Luxembourg law, where liability is dependent on fault or negligence. The answer depends on whether the Commission has a discretion to refuse approval when agreements are, in fact, within Article 85(3).[44] If the Commission has no such discretion, it seems clear that fault is proved in the case of any act contrary to Article 85(1) and not done at a time when an approval under Article 85(3) was in force. If the Commission has a discretion, no conclusion can be drawn. If the Commission has not yet ruled on an application for approval under Article 85(3), the national court should not attempt to anticipate whether approval will be given. Such an attempt is certain to lead to conflicting decisions and is, in fact if not in law, an infringement on the sole power of the Commission to apply Article 85(3).

The position is complicated when, as in the law of the Netherlands,[45] the commission of a criminal offense is not conclusive evidence of the existence of a tortious act, because the criteria are not the same. Negligence is not necessary for a violation of Article 85, yet it is not enough to constitute a violation of Article 86, under which wrongful intent is necessary. A violation of Article 85 may not involve civil liability under the law of the Netherlands if there is no negligence.[46]

ACTIONS AT COMMON LAW BY THIRD PARTIES

Breach of statutory duty

In English and Irish law, when a duty is imposed by a statute for the protection of individuals, a failure to fulfill that duty which causes an injury to a person within the protected class is a tort actionable by the person injured.[47] The first requirement of this cause of action is that the injury must be of the type contemplated by the legislation and intended to be guarded against.[48] However, even if damage is not of the kind contemplated, the scope and terms of the legislation may indicate an intention to give a remedy.

If the statute provides for compensation for an injured person, an action lies only in accordance with the statute. If a sanction or criminal penalty is provided by the statute, the question whether there is also a civil action for compensation depends on the construction of the statute, and in particular, on whether the duty is owed to the public generally or to a particular class of individuals.

Even if the statutory duty is not absolute, it is possible, depending on the construction of the statute, that no amount of care and skill is a defense to the action if the duty is not complied with.[49] It is not clear whether there is any relationship between the existence of absolute liability and a duty to the public at large.

[44] Id. at 182.

[45] Id. at 183.

[46] Fines may be imposed by the Commission only where an offense is committed willfully or negligently; Reg. 17, art. 15.

[47] Clerk & Lindsell, Torts 8, 738 (12th ed. 1961). Glanville Williams, "The Effect of Penal Legislation in the Law of Tort," 23 Modern L. Rev. 233, 258–59 (1960), concludes an analysis of the cases by stating: (1) Industrial legislation is almost always held to create liability in tort, and this liability will be absolute unless the statute otherwise indicates. (2) If there is duty of care at common law, breach of other (i.e., non-industrial) penal legislation may be evidence of tortious negligence. (3) If there is no duty of care at common law, breach of non-industrial penal legislation does not affect civil liability unless an intention that it should do so can be found in the statute.

[48] Gorris v. Scott, L.R. 9 Ex. 125 (1874).

[49] Phillips v. Britannia Laundry, [1923] 2 K.B. 832; Clarke v. Brims, [1947] K.B. 497.

Almost all of the cases on breach of statutory duty concern statutory obligations to take safety precautions for the benefit of employees or to prevent disease or corruption of foodstuffs. There is nothing to indicate, however, that the tort should be so limited; once the Treaty has been enacted in Irish law, the question arises whether breach of Article 85 or 86 of the EEC Treaty is actionable in Ireland as a breach of statutory duty.

Is an Alternative Remedy Provided?

Although the Council has power to enact a regulation or a directive providing for a civil right of action for compensation,[50] the Treaty does not contemplate this so clearly as to exclude the possibility of a right of action's arising before the Council has taken action.[51] The use of the phrase "fine or penalty" in Article 17 of Regulation 17 does not indicate any liability to pay compensation. The possibility of an action for breach of statutory duty thus cannot be excluded on this ground.

Are Articles 85 and 86 Intended to Protect the Interests of Classes of Enterprises?

No action for breach of statutory duty lies if the statute is intended only for the protection of the community[52] and not for the protection of any class of persons.[53] Individuals and enterprises are concerned with competition insofar as it brings about conditions of supply and demand favorable to their particular interests. The principal basis for Articles 85 and 86 is the general Community interest in seeing that economic integration and the attendant economic advantage of more efficient use of Community resources are not impeded by arrangements made between groups of enterprises in their own interests. This is true if the Articles are regarded as laws with purely economic functions or if they (especially Article 85) are regarded primarily as anti-avoidance measures intended to prevent the replacement of tariffs by other protective measures.

In the *Van Gend & Loos* case,[54] the Community Court held that Article 12 of the EEC Treaty, which prohibits the introduction by member states of new customs duties on intra-Community trade, is directly applicable and confers rights on individual enterprises. Since Article 12 binds only member states and not enterprises, it appears that *a fortiori* Article 85, which binds individual enterprises, confers rights on them as well.

Price-fixing may have inflationary tendencies, and it prevents competition between the parties to the agreement or decision. The cost to enterprises purchasing from the parties to the agreement may be increased or the profits of enterprises selling to them reduced. The resulting cost increase or profit reduction may affect the enterprises comprising the next link in the chain of trade. Consequently, the general public is prejudiced by the increased prices passed on to the ultimate consumer and by the loss of the advantages of efficiency, improved techniques and services, and the other

[50] Art. 87(2)(e).

[51] See, however, Deringer Report, A.P.E. Doc. No. 57, para. 123 (1961–62).

[52] For the English rules on the use of legislative history in the interpretation of treaties, see Maltass v. Maltass, 1 Rob. Ecc. 67, 163 Eng. Rep. 967 (1844); Ellerman Lines v. Murray, [1931] A.C. 126; Porter v. Freudenberg, [1915] 1 K.B. 857.

[53] Since the Irish Restrictive Trade Practices Act, 1953 Acts 75, § 11, allows civil proceedings for the enforcement of an order made under the Act, it appears that other laws against restrictive practices would also be regarded by the Irish courts as designed to protect injured enterprises.

[54] 9 Recueil 1, [1963] C.M.L.R. 105. See Costa v. ENEL, 8 Recueil 89, [1962] C.M.L.R. 1.

benefits of uninhibited technical development or investment. Enterprises dealing with the parties to a prohibited agreement cannot pass on to the public competitive disadvantages resulting from discrimination, since they are peculiar to the enterprises discriminated against. However, discrimination is usually an enforcement measure, rather than an independent type of restrictive practice in itself. Tying-in clauses prejudice the enterprises compelled to accept them by increasing their costs or by compelling them to accept an inferior brand of the commodity "tied" to the goods really required. They also injure the enterprises which would otherwise sell the type of goods "tied" to the purchaser. These disadvantages can also be passed on, at least in part.

The general interest can therefore be injured only through the interests of the enterprises in immediate contact with the parties to the anticompetitive practices. This position is, of course, not peculiar to Articles 85 and 86, but it is a reason why these enterprises should be given a right to compensation. There is, however, a stronger reason which is peculiar to economic legislation.

The General Interest in the Right to Compensation

If anyone is entitled to sue for compensation, enterprises directly affected by the prohibited agreements are entitled to do so. Clearly, the additional costs or the technical disadvantages imposed are not passed on automatically but only as a result of a decision of the enterprises concerned. If the cost or disadvantage is passed on in full, no damage or loss to the enterprise occurs and theoretically no actionable damage to that particular enterprise has occurred, if the measure of damage is loss of profits. If the law gives no right of action, the enterprises most directly affected by prohibited agreements have a strong incentive to pass on the additional cost to the public as fully as possible and have no incentive to initiate proceedings before the Commission unless they cannot avoid substantial loss or competitive disadvantage themselves. Such a situation clearly is contrary to the public interest, since primarily those enterprises trading directly with the parties to an agreement prohibited by Article 85 or with a monopoly abusing its power contrary to Article 86 will complain to the Commission and since complaints are the most effective means of insuring enforcement of the two Articles.

For an agreement prohibited by Article 85(1) to be permitted under Article 85(3), it must give some benefit to the users.[55] Taken together with the right of complaint, this indicates that the Treaty and Regulations recognize that certain classes of enterprises have a particular interest in the effects and the enforcement of Articles 85 and 86. These provisions indicate, therefore, that the two Articles were intended to protect the interests of individual users and consumers as well as the general public.

Complaints do not result in compensation for the injury suffered, but only in cessation of the injury-causing practice and the imposition of a fine. In the nature of things, it is unusual if a complaint can be made before actual damage is suffered. The right to intervene in the proceedings of the Commission is of little use to a small enterprise seriously prejudiced by the practices (especially under Article 86, which may take a long time to implement) of a large enterprise or of a large group. Future protection for the injured enterprise is not enough, since grave financial loss can be suffered after notification of the agreement to the Commission and before its final condemnation, during which time

[55] The translation by Her Majesty's Foreign Office translation renders this "consumers."

the practice can be continued without risk of fines.

The Rights of Injured Enterprises to Compel the Commission to Take Action

Article 175 of the Treaty does not give the complainant a right to compel the Commission to decide the validity of the agreement complained of,[56] because the Commission's decision is not addressed to the complainant but to the parties to the agreement. This indicates that enterprises prejudiced by restrictive agreements have no right to have the Treaty enforced, because it makes them merely a means of informing the Commission of the existence and the nature of restrictive practices. However, if the Commission proposes to take no action on the complaint of an enterprise which shows a legitimate interest, Article 7 of Regulation 99 requires it to give the enterprise an opportunity to argue its position. This is probably the maximum protection which it is reasonable to give to injured parties and is further evidence that the Community law is intended to protect individuals and not only the general interest.

Causation and Type of Damage

If the statute is intended to protect the enterprises affected by the acts which it makes illegal, they can get compensation for breach of their rights,[57] at least if damage has been caused. The national courts have to consider whether the illegal act is the effective cause of the loss complained of. The types of damage normally resulting from prohibited agreements are clearly within the intent of the Treaty. The likely difficulties involve questions of causation and remoteness of damage rather than unusual types of injury.

Conclusion

The question whether an action for a breach of statutory duty will lie in Ireland and England after entry into the EEC turns on essentially the same question that arises in Germany and the Netherlands. The answer is not clear, but the better view, and the one which is preferable on practical grounds, is that Articles 85 and 86 should be regarded as protecting private as well as general interests. This would bring German and Dutch law and (after the entry of Britain and Ireland into the EEC) English and Irish law into line with the law of Italy, Belgium, and Luxembourg.

Conspiracy in Irish and English law

The tort of conspiracy involves two or more persons in combination to do an act, and a single enterprise which makes improper use of a dominant position contrary to Article 86 could not be liable for conspiracy.[58] For conspiracy, there must be actual damage to the injured party. A combination of persons to use only legal means to benefit themselves is not an actionable conspiracy even if damage results to a third party. Contravention of Article 85 may not be a criminal offense;[59] nevertheless, any contravention is a sufficient basis for an action for conspiracy by the injured party. Even if the purpose of the conspiracy is

[56] The Federation of British Industries, European Economic Community–Restrictive Trade Practices 24 (1963), states that the complainant has such a right if he has a legitimate interest within art. 3(2), but the Federation gives no authority. Regulation 99 was enacted after the publication of the Federation's study; 1963 Journal Officiel 2268/63.

[57] Ashby v. White, 2 Ld. Raym. 938, 92 Eng. Rep. 126 (1703). See Clerk & Lindsell, Torts 8, 64–68 (12th ed. 1961).

[58] However, a breach of art. 86 may lead to an action for breach of statutory duty.

[59] See Reg. 17, art. 15(4). On whether the Commission would be exercising a judicial function in "criminal matters," see p. 70.

to advance the legitimate interests of the parties to the combination, the conspiracy is actionable if the means used are illegal.[60]

There is relatively little judicial authority for saying that a conspiracy to commit a tort, as well as a conspiracy to commit a crime, is actionable, but it has always been accepted that this is so. The point is normally academic, since if the conspiracy has been carried out, the injured party can sue directly for the tort committed; if the conspiracy involved a tort but was not carried out, no action lies because no damage has been done to the plaintiff. Most of the controversial cases involving the tort of conspiracy involve a combination to take action which is not in itself tortious if taken by a single person.

It has been said that where a tort has been committed by two or more persons the allegation of a prior conspiracy adds nothing; the prior agreement merges in the tort, and a party is not allowed to gain an added advantage by charging conspiracy where the agreement has become merged in the tort.[61] This rule, it is suggested, merely prevents a plaintiff from suing on two causes of action based on the same facts[62] and does not affect the rule that a conspiracy to commit a tort is itself a tort.

The action for conspiracy is normally, though not necessarily, connected with trade competition, labor disputes, and injury to and protection of business interests. It is, therefore, more natural to regard it as the proper action for a person injured by an agreement contrary to Article 85 than as the action for breach of statutory duty.[63] The question might arise whether a "concerted practice" within Article 85 was a "combination" sufficient to constitute a conspiracy, but this question clearly cannot be resolved at this time.

Conflicts of law:
The position before Ireland enters the EEC

Assuming that agreements prohibited by Article 85 are actionable if made in Ireland, the next question is when an injured party may sue in Ireland for

[60] Crofter Hand Woven Harris Tweed Co. v. Veitch, [1942] A.C. 435, 495 (per Porter, L.), 462 (per Wright, L.); Ware & De Freville, Ltd. v. Motor Trade Ass'n, [1921] 3 K.B. 40, 70 (per Scrutton, L.J.). "A conspiracy consists . . . in the agreement of two or more to do an unlawful act, or to do a lawful act by unlawful means." Mulcahy v. R., L.R. 3 H.L. 306, 317 (1898) (per Willes, J.), approved by Lord Wright in the *Crofter Harris Tweed* case, [1942] A.C. at 461; see Quinn v. Leatham, [1901] A.C. 495, 528, 529; R. v. Newland, [1954] 1 Q.B. 158. The crime of conspiracy is committed even if no acts are done damaging the plaintiff, but otherwise the elements of the crime and the tort are the same, and the crime clearly includes the use of illegal means to a lawful purpose; the *Crofter Harris Tweed* case, [1942] A.C. at 439; R. v. Aspinall, 2 Q.B.D. 48, 58 (1876); Quinn v. Leatham, [1901] A.C. at 529. ("[T]he words . . . uttered touching a criminal case . . . are applicable to conspiracies made the subject of civil actions.") See Russell, Crime 214–15, 1693–724 (11th ed. 1958); R. v. Parnell, 14 Cox Crim. Cas. 508, 513 (1881) (per Fitzgerald, J.), approved in the *Crofter Harris Tweed* case, [1942] A.C. at 488. "It is not necessary, in order to constitute a conspiracy, that the acts agreed to be done should be acts which if done [would] . . . be criminal. It is enough if the acts agreed to be done, although not criminal, are wrongful, i.e., amount to a civil wrong." R. v. Wharton, L.R. 1 Cr. Cas. Res. (1870), cited by Lord Brampton in Quinn v. Leatham, [1901] A.C. at 529.

[61] Ward v. Lewis, [1955] 1 All E.R. 55, 56 (per Denning, L.J.); Greenhalgh v. Mallard, [1947] 2 All E.R. 255, 257 (per Somervell, L.J.).

[62] See Russell, Crime 1698 (11th ed. 1958).

[63] The concept of conspiracy is, of course, important in United States antitrust law. See Wilberforce, Campbell & Elles, Restrictive Trade Practices and Monopolies 424 (1957); the authors of this work do not explicitly mention the tort of breach of statutory duty as an explanation of § 24(7) of British Restrictive Trade Practices Act, 1956, 4 & 5 Eliz. 2, c. 68.

damage resulting from such an agreement made and acted upon elsewhere. The Irish conflicts-of-law rule is that an act which would be a tort if done in Ireland is actionable in Ireland even if it is done elsewhere, provided that it is "not justifiable" according to the law of the country where it was done.[64] Since Articles 85 and 86 are part of the domestic law of the member states of the EEC, an agreement which has been prohibited under Article 85 or a practice contrary to Article 86 is not "justified" or permissible under the law of the jurisdiction where the tort is committed. Since in most cases likely to come before the Irish courts the agreement will have been both made and acted upon in Ireland or in a member country of the EEC, no difficulty is likely to arise in connection with the law of the place where the tort is committed.

If the agreement is made in a country outside the EEC in which there is no legal objection to it and the damage takes place in the EEC, the position under Irish and English law is uncertain.[65] To bring an action in an Irish court for acts committed abroad, the acts must be such as to constitute a tort if performed in Ireland. An agreement in Ireland to use means illegal under Article 85 in an EEC member state would probably not be tortious in Ireland. Prior to Ireland's entry into the EEC, there will be no Irish legislation implementing Articles 85 and 86, and an agreement contrary to those provisions will be tortious only if the agreement is contrary to a restrictive practices order or if the predominant object of the combination is to injure a business rival and not to advance legitimate business interests.[66]

However, Articles 85 and 86 have some effects in Irish law even before Ireland enters the EEC. They invalidate, as between the parties, any agreement which is to be performed in an EEC member country where it is illegal, since a contract illegal under the law of the place of performance is invalid in Ireland,[67] irrespective of the proper law of the contract.[68] This rule, however, is unlikely to have any effect on enterprises which are not parties to the contract. An action also lies under Irish and English law for breach of contract if the reason for the breach is an agreement prohibited by Article 85. Similarly, an action in tort may lie against a third party who induces a breach of contract, if the inducement is based on a practice prohibited by Article 85. These possibilities, and the possibility of suing in tort for conspiracy on the grounds that practices or agreements prohibited by Article 85 are illegal under the common law on conspiracy, are of little practical importance.

[64] Dicey, Conflict of Laws 940 (7th ed. 1958); Carr v. Fracis Times & Co., [1902] A.C. 176. In the Six, the law which applies is the law of the place where the tort is committed.

[65] Dicey, Conflict of Laws 967–69 (7th ed. 1958). See also Hancock, "Torts in the Conflict of Laws—The First Rule in Phillips v. Eyre," 3 U. Toronto L.J. 400 (1940); Robertson, "The Choice of Law for Tort Liability in the Conflict of Laws—The First Rule in Phillips v. Eyre," 3 enzen, "Tort Liability and Conflict of Laws," 47 L.Q. Rev. 483 (1931).

[66] Crofter Hand Woven Harris Tweed Co. v. Veitch, [1942] A.C. 439.

[67] Ralli Bros. v. Compañia Naviera Sota y Aznar, [1920] 1 K.B. 614; Dicey, Conflict of Laws 637–45 (6th ed. 1949). See Regazzoni v. Sethia (1944) Ltd., [1958] A.C. 301.

[68] This last qualification is controversial; see Dicey, Conflict of Laws 788–96 (7th ed. 1958).

Chapter 18

Existing Legislation on Restrictive Practices in Ireland

THE SCOPE OF THE LEGISLATION

The Irish Restrictive Trade Practice Acts[1] do not directly prohibit any restrictive practices. They set up an investigating body, the Fair Trade Commission (FTC), on whose recommendation the Minister for Industry and Commerce may make orders having the force of law to prohibit restrictive practices in the supply and distribution of specific types of goods and related services. An order may be made only when the sector dealt with has been investigated formally by the FTC, and the Parliament must confirm the order. The provisions of the EEC Treaty therefore will be the first legislation against restrictive practices[2] in *all* sectors of industry in Ireland. Since its functions are limited, the FTC has not needed to formulate exact legal criteria and definitions. Similarly, the courts have not worked out any general principles when enforcing the restrictive trade practices orders. Although set up on the advice of United States experts, this system is like that of the United Kingdom Monopolies and Restrictive Practices (Inquiry and Control) Act of 1948, but the criteria for assessing restrictive practices are different. The British 1948 Act does not make contravention of orders criminal, and investigations cannot be held on the initiative of the Monopolies Commission.[3]

The basis of the Irish Acts[4] is that

[1] 1953 Acts 75, as amended by 1959 Acts 1015 [hereinafter cited as 1953 Act and 1959 Act, respectively]. These Acts are reproduced in 2 OECD Guide to Legislation on Restrictive Business Practices, Ireland §§ 1.0, 1.0.0 (1963).

See Boserup & Schlichtkrull, "Alternative Approaches to the Control of Competition: An Outline of European Cartel Legislation and Its Administration," in Competition, Cartels and Their Regulation 73–75, 89–90 and passim (Miller ed. 1962); Delany, "Monopolies Legislation in the Republic of Ireland," 20 Modern L. Rev. 148 (1957); Walsh, "Legislation on Restrictive Practices in Ireland," in International Conference on Control of Restrictive Business Practices 81 (1960).

The writer is indebted to Mr. Kiaran Kennedy and Mr. Charles Edward Lysaght, both graduates of University College, Dublin, for their permission to read and draw on their theses, "Competition and the Fair Trade Commission" and "Monopolistic Competition in Distribution with Special Reference to the Regulation of Price Maintenance in the Distributive Trades in Ireland," respectively.

[2] There are, of course, the common law rules with regard to the invalidity of contracts in restraint of trade; McEllistrim v. Ballymacelligott Cooperative Soc'y, [1919] A.C. 548; Langan v. Cork Operative Bakers Trade Union, [1938] Ir. Jur. 65; Dowrick, Notes on the Irish Law of Contract 15–16 (1954) (Irish supp. to Cheshire & Fifoot, Law of Contract, 3d ed. 1952); Chitty, Contracts 823–44 (22d ed. 1961).

[3] Monopolies and Restrictive Practices (Inquiry and Control) Act, 1948, 11 & 12 Geo. 6, c. 66, §§ 11, 12(1).

[4] The Acts are based on two principles. First, in general it is in the public interest that there should be the fullest and freest competition in all trades and sectors of industry, subject to protection for particular industries through tariffs and quotas. This is rather different from the doctrine behind the United Kingdom Restrictive Trade Practices and Monopolies (Inquiry and Control) Act, 1948, 11 & 12 Geo. 6, c. 66. See Delany, "Monopolies Legislation in the Republic of Ireland," 20 Modern L. Rev.

harmful restrictive practices should be defined and prohibited in detail in relation to a particular trade or industry. The rules so formulated are then enforced by the courts, not by an administrative tribunal, with the minimum of discretion as to the interpretation of economic data and without concern for policy considerations.

The Acts do not apply to restrictive practices in the rendering of services unless the services, such as finance for installment purchases, affect the supply or distribution of goods. Since most practices of trade unions whose members are involved in the supply or distribution of goods necessarily "affect" supply or distribution, it is not clear how far the Acts apply to restrictive practices by labor. Services are within the Acts only if "rendered in the course of carrying on any trade or business";[5] this can be construed as limiting the application of the Acts to services carried on by a company or self-employed entrepreneur. The Acts do not apply to production of goods insofar as it is distinct from "supply." It is thus not easy to say how far Article 85(1)(b) of the EEC Treaty is outside the scope of the Irish Acts.

Of interest to foreign investors is the fact that any restrictive agreement which facilitates exporting is regarded as being in the public interest, because of the importance of exports to the Irish economy. In order to receive tax concessions and other advantages, enterprises exporting Irish-made goods to world markets are unlikely to make agreements reducing exports. The practical effect of the Acts, therefore, as far as the foreign investor is concerned, is likely to be in connection with his sales on the Irish market.

148 (1957). Second, where special conditions justify some limitation of competition, this must be imposed by public authorities and not by trade associations or combinations of traders; See Mr. Seán Lemass, then Minister for Industry and Commerce, 134 Dáil Eireann, Parl. Deb., col. 821 (1953).

[5] 1959 Act, § 4(1).

THE FAIR TRADE COMMISSION

Members of the FTC may be lawyers, civil servants, economists or industrialists. They are impartial experts and not representatives of particular interests, such as, for instance, consumers.

The FTC has power, in connection with holding inquiries and obtaining information, to summon witnesses and examine them under oath and to require production of documents under a witness' control. A witness has the same privileges and immunities as a witness in the High Court.[6] Anything which would constitute contempt of court, if the FTC were a court, is punishable.

An officer authorized in writing by the FTC may inspect any premises at which there is any activity connected with, or the organization of anyone engaged in, the supply or distribution of goods. The officer may take extracts from the books of the enterprise and obtain any further information which he "may reasonably require."[7] Failing to give information properly required or obstructing an officer is an offense. Any information obtained may not be published except in the execution of duties under the Acts, in the FTC's report, or for the purpose of legal proceedings.[8] If publication of any information would materially injure legitimate business interests, it may be omitted from a report, unless it is essential to a full understanding of the report.[9]

The FTC keeps under continuous review the effect on the public interest of restrictive practices in the supply and distribution of goods and the performance of any related services.[10] It watches the

[6] The principal privileges involved seem to be the privilege of lawyers with regard to professional communications and the right to refuse to answer incriminating questions.

[7] 1953 Act, First Schedule, para. 8.

[8] 1953 Act, First Schedule, para. 9.

[9] 1953 Act, § 8(3).

[10] 1953 Act, § 10.

operation of all fair trading rules [11] and orders[12] in force. It must report failure to adhere to fair trading rules to the Minister and may make recommendations as to the operation of an order.

FAIR TRADING RULES

The FTC has power to make fair trading rules.[13] These rules are not legally binding and are important only because they are the FTC's opinion on what restrictive practices are legitimate in the supply and distribution of the goods or services in question. The FTC makes fair trading rules on its own initiative or at the request of an association representing distributors or suppliers of the goods or persons rendering related services.[14] Fair trading rules permit trade associations to avoid the trouble and publicity of an inquiry and to obtain official approval for practices which, though restrictive, are justifiable. The FTC is empowered to lay down a procedure for requests to make fair trading rules[15] and must publish notice of its intention to make any fair trading rules, specifying the time and way in which representations may be made.[16] If the FTC recommends that an order should be made and the Minister decides not to do so, the FTC on its own initiative may make fair trading rules dealing with the goods involved.

The FTC makes a report to the Minister if it finds that fair trading rules are not being observed.[17] The report is in the same form as one following a public inquiry. It normally results in an order enacting the rules and making the practices in question illegal.[18] The FTC or a representative association may take the initiative and have existing rules revised.

Making fair trading rules is in no way analogous to registering restrictive practice agreements with the EEC Commission under Regulation 17, because there is no question of the practice's being prohibited or the agreement's being void in the absence of approval. There is no legal incentive to have restrictive practices approved by fair trading rules[19] and no sanction for breaking fair trading rules except the likelihood of their being replaced by a binding order if they are not obeyed.

INQUIRIES[20] TO DECIDE IF AN ORDER SHOULD BE MADE

The most important function of the FTC is to hold inquiries into the supply and distribution of goods.[21] Inquiries

[11] 1953 Act, § 6.

[12] 1959 Act, § 5.

[13] Cf. German Competition Law, §§ 28–33, and the trade practice rules prepared under the auspices of the United States Federal Trade Commission, 16 C.F.R. §§ 2.21–2.32 (1960).

[14] 1953 Act, § 4(1).

[15] 1953 Act, § 5(2).

[16] 1953 Act, § 5(1).

[17] 1953 Act, § 6.

[18] 1953 Act, § 9.

[19] It is a matter of tactics whether a particular sector of industry should lie low and hope to escape any control of its restrictive practices, or whether it should suggest that the FTC make fair trading rules permitting those of its practices which it can persuade the FTC are reasonable.

[20] "The policy of the Commission . . . has been to utilize wherever feasible the provisions for Fair Trading Rules but to proceed to Enquiries . . . where the public interest appears likely to be better served by an Enquiry, as, for instance, where the issues involved are of fundamental importance, or where voluntary cooperation is not forthcoming." Fair Trade Commission, First Annual Report, Pr. 2282, para. 6 (1954). The inquiry into carpets, carpeting, and floor rugs was made on account of complaints of manufacturers' restrictions on entry at wholesale level and various other complaints, after fair trading rules had existed for several years; Report of Enquiry into . . . Carpets, Carpeting and Floor Rugs, Pr. 5175, paras. 8–9 (1959).

[21] By October 1959, when the 1959 Act was first discussed by the lower house, only six full inquiries had been held.

must be held if the Minister so directs and may be held on the initiative of the FTC.[22] Members of the public who request the FTC to hold an inquiry must be informed of the FTC's reasons for deciding not to do so.[23] Inquiries may be made into the conditions of supply and distribution of any kind of goods or into any aspect of their supply or distribution. They also may be made into services affecting the supply and distribution of goods concerned in an inquiry.[24]

The FTC must give notice of its intention to hold an inquiry,[25] and any person may make submissions. Inquiries are held in public, except when the commissioners holding the inquiry[26] regard private sittings as necessary to avoid disclosure of confidential information which might materially injure any person's legitimate business interests.[27] In practice, the FTC excludes all but the people concerned when confidential business information, in particular financial information, is being discussed orally. The FTC will never publish anything prior to public hearings and will rarely, if ever, publish confidential information.

A report on every inquiry is submitted to the Minister. A report, whether on an inquiry or on a failure to observe fair trading rules, must describe existing conditions as to supply and distribution of the goods concerned and, where appropriate, as to services.[28] The report must state how these conditions prevent or restrict competition, restrain trade, or involve price maintenance, and whether this is unfair or operates against the public interest.[29] These are the tests given by the Acts for distinguishing objectionable from permissible restrictive practices. The FTC must give reasons for its conclusions and must indicate the terms of the order it thinks should be made.[30]

Every report must be presented to the Irish Parliament, with an indication of the general nature of any information omitted as being unnecessary to a full understanding of the report and being likely to materially injure legitimate business interests if published.[31] Within three months of receiving the report, the Minister should decide whether to make the order recommended and state his reasons, if he decides not to do so, to both houses. There is no time limit on the actual making of an order, but in practice the order is usually published with the report.

INQUIRIES INTO THE OPERATION OF EXISTING ORDERS

The FTC may hold an inquiry into or a "special review" of the operation of an order as a whole or particular aspects of its operation.[32] A special review,[33] which is in effect a less formal, less complete inquiry, may be held on the FTC's initiative or on the request of the Minister. Notice of intention to hold a special review must be published, and any person wishing to do so may make submissions. Anyone may request the FTC to conduct a special review, and if the FTC decides not to do so, it must give reasons to the person making the request and to the Minister. Like inquiries, a special review

[22] 1959 Act, § 2(1), replacing 1953 Act, § 7(1).

[23] Cf. Reg. 99, art. 6, 1963 Journal Officiel 2269/63.

[24] 1959 Act, § 2(1), 2(2).

[25] 1953 Act, First Schedule, para. 7.

[26] One temporary member of the commission may be appointed for the purposes of an inquiry by reason of his special knowledge, but he must have at least one permanent member sitting with him; 1953 Act, § 7(2)–7(4).

[27] 1959 Act, § 7(6).

[28] 1959 Act, § 3.

[29] 1953 Act, § 8(1)(b), 8(1)(c).

[30] 1953 Act, § 8(1)(d), 8(2).

[31] 1953 Act, § 8(3).

[32] 1959 Act, § 2(1)(b).

[33] 1959 Act, § 6.

must result in a report to the Minister in which the FTC may recommend the amendment or revocation of the order in question. Reports of special reviews must be presented to Parliament, with the same protection for confidential business information as in the case of reports following full-scale inquiries.

On the request of the Minister, the FTC may hold an inquiry into the refusal of employers or employees or of a combination of employers or employees to use particular materials or particular methods for manufacturing or construction.[34] The FTC may not initiate such an inquiry, and the Minister may not make any order in relation to practices of this kind, although reports of these inquiries must be presented to Parliament.[35] The only sanction against practices of this kind is public opinion.

ORDERS RELATING TO RESTRICTIVE PRACTICES

The Minister may make an order in relation to any of the goods dealt with in a report.[36] The Acts do not limit him to the goods covered by the recommendation in the report, so that he can make an order concerning goods which the FTC has not found to be the subject of objectionable practices.[37] An order made by the Minister has no effect until confirmed by an act of Parliament.[38] The Minister may amend an order or revoke it and reinstate it after revocation,[39] in each case with confirmation by an act. Parliament has only the power of veto; this is intended to avoid re-opening the detailed examination already given to the sector of industry concerned and discussion of what are intended to be the detailed provisions of orders.

The time from the commencement of an injury, or even from the publication of the report, until a limitation on restrictive practices becomes cognizable by the courts is likely to be fairly long, and the industry has ample time to reorganize and utilize whatever methods of protecting its interests are allowed by the terms of the order.

In particular, an order may:[40] (1) prohibit specified arrangements or agreements; (2) prohibit withholding of goods or services affecting the supply and distribution of such goods from any specified class of persons; (3) prohibit discriminatory practices; (4) prohibit the imposition of specified conditions in regard to the supply and distribution of goods or the rendering of related services; and (5) make any provision necessary to insure equitable treatment for all and the avoidance of unfair practices. A wide, vaguely phrased list of unfair practices is given to guide the FTC.[41] This list is not exhaustive and is not to limit the FTC in the exercise of its functions.[42] The Acts give no test for distinguishing between permissible practices and those which "prevent or restrict competition or restrain trade or involve resale price maintenance"[43] or for deciding whether "any such interference with competition is unfair or operates against the public interest."[44]

[34] 1959 Act, § 4; see 177 Dáil Eireann, Parl. Deb., cols. 246, 965 (1959).

[35] 1959 Act, § 7(1).

[36] 1953 Act, § 9.

[37] The Restrictive Trade Practices (Groceries) Order, 1956, S.I. No. 332 of 1956, as amended by S.I. No. 163 of 1958, both confirmed by Restrictive Trade Practices (Confirmation of Order) Act, 1958 Acts 825, was made on the Minister's own initiative without any formal report from the FTC.

[38] 1953 Act, § 9(3).

[39] 1959 Act, § 8(1).

[40] 1953 Act, § 9(1).

[41] 1953 Act, Second Schedule.

[42] 1953 Act, § 3.

[43] 1953 Act, § 8(1)(b).

[44] 1953 Act, § 8(1)(c). In the lower house debates on the bill the Minister of Industry and Commerce defined "practices contrary to the

THE TYPES OF RESTRICTIVE PRACTICES SUGGESTED

Unfair trade practices include any measures, rules, agreements, or acts which are effectuated by a person alone or in combination with others or by a monopoly, merger, trust, cartel, or any other means.[45] They therefore include "gentlemen's agreements" and contracts in restraint of trade which are void at common law. Abuse of monopoly power, however created, is subject to control. To be "unfair," practices must have a harmful effect of one of the kinds listed or otherwise be within the terms of the Acts.

Included are practices which are likely to unreasonably limit or restrain free and fair competition. This provision is comparable to the provision which requires the FTC to report whether practices "prevent or restrict competition"[46] and also to Article 85 of the EEC Treaty. No test of a "reasonable" limitation or restraint is given by the Irish Acts, but the FTC must say if a practice is unfair or operates against the public interest. This indicates that the restraint of trade will be unreasonable if it is unfair to a party to it or unreasonable vis-à-vis the general public, the two rules of Irish common law.[47] Unfair also are practices which "are in unreasonable restraint of trade."

Practices which are likely to unjustly eliminate a trade competitor or to exclude, without good reason, new entrants to any trade or industry are "unfair" under the Acts. This provision is aimed at arrangements designed to limit the number of dealers in particular types of commodities.

Unjust enhancement of the price of goods and unfair promotion of the advantage of suppliers or distributors of goods at the expense of the public are "unfair practices." The FTC is to report resale price maintenance.[48]

Measures likely to secure substantial control of the supply or distribution of any class of goods unfairly or contrary to the public interest may be condemned by the FTC. Only two provisions give any possibility of action against mergers which give control over supply or distribution of goods. The first authorizes

public interest" as "practices which are designed to eliminate or restrict competition in the supply or distribution of any class of goods, or which operate to deprive the individual citizen of the right to engage in legitimate trade in any class of business." Cited by Delany, "Monopolies Legislation in the Republic of Ireland," 20 Modern L. Rev. 148 (1957). The 1953 Act is based on the idea that only inquiries into particular trades or sectors would show clearly the dividing line between beneficial and harmful practices, so that no precise general test was possible. In Report of Enquiry into . . . Radio Sets and Accessories, Pr. 2660, para. 88 (1954), the FTC said: "[A]n arrangement which deprives the public of competition in respect of so large an ingredient of the retail price has a clear bearing on the interests of consumers; and, as the possession of a radio set is for the average family a matter of conventional necessity rather than luxury, *the public interest is, therefore, affected.*" (Emphasis added.) For another illustration of the principle that necessities will be treated differently from luxuries, see Report of Enquiry into . . . Proprietary and Patent Medicines and Infant Foods and Medical and Toilet Preparations, Pr. 3926, para. 90 (1956).

[45] 1953 Act, First Schedule.

[46] 1959 Act, § 8(1)(b).

[47] McEllistrim v. Ballymacelligott Cooperative Soc'y, [1919] A.C. 548, 562 (per Birkenhead, L.), on appeal from [1918] 1 Ir. R. 313; Herbert Morris v. Saxelby, [1916] 1 A.C. 668, 707. Throughout the 1953 Act, Second Schedule, phrases such as "unreasonably," "unjustly," "unfairly," "contrary to the public interest," "without just cause," and "without good reason" are apparently used indiscriminately, without any indication of the basis, if any, on which they were distinguished from one another. It is submitted that each should be regarded as requiring that the practice, to be permissible, should be reasonable for the public and for the participants. However, the FTC is not expected to take legal principles into account in deciding whether a practice is beneficial.

[48] 1953 Act, § 8(1)(b); cf. EEC Treaty, art. 85(1)(a).

prospectively the prohibition of "specified arrangements or agreements."[49] The other provision[50] authorizes "such other provision with regard to restrictive practices . . . as [the Minister] . . . thinks fit" and seems to relate only to abuse of, not to acquisition of, monopoly power. No order for the breaking-up of a merger can be made under the present law.[51]

Further types of restrictive practice which may be prohibited are discrimination or refusal to supply goods and unjust or unreasonable conditions in regard to the supply or distribution of goods. This latter category includes "tying-in clauses" and unreasonable conditions as to payment, discounts, and quantity to be supplied, even if non-discriminatory and even if not imposed by a cartel or an enterprise with dominant market power. Measures likely to secure unjustly the territorial division of markets to the exclusion of other persons are unfair practices. The provision does not expressly deal with sharing of sources of supply, as the EEC Treaty does. In spite of the provision[52] that the list of unfair trade practices is not exhaustive, a "sweeping-up" clause has been inserted, categorizing as unfair practices any measures which operate against the public interest or which are not in accordance with social justice.

Apart from the phrase "the public interest," the Acts do not distinguish restrictive agreements which promote exports from those which minimize the incentive to increase exports by promoting larger profits in the home market. The Acts are concerned primarily with the home market; since they contain no substantive law, no such distinction was necessary.

ENFORCEMENT OF RESTRICTIVE TRADE PRACTICES ORDERS

An order confirmed by Parliament is legislation prohibiting specified practices in the sector of industry to which it relates. Breaching an order or aiding or conspiring with any other person to contravene an order is a criminal offense.[53] A director of a company commits an offense if he consents to, or facilitates the commission of, an offense by his company or by anyone acting on its behalf.[54] Offenses under the Acts are punishable by fines and imprisonment and may be dealt with summarily.[55]

The Minister or any other person may apply for an injunction[56] to enforce an order.[57] An injunction may compel performance of a particular act or require cessation of a restrictive practice. A plaintiff in an action for an injunction normally has to show that he has some particular interest in obtaining an injunction, such as being a present or potential consumer or competitor. Actions for injunctions on behalf of the public are always brought by the Attorney General. An injunction may be issued even if other civil or criminal proceedings are possible; a prosecution for criminal conspiracy is possible "to enforce compliance with the terms of an order."[58]

The civil action contemplated is an action for conspiracy. An association to commit a crime, such as the contravention of an order, is actionable even if

[49] 1959 Act, § 9(1)(a).

[50] 1959 Act, § 9(1)(f).

[51] A constitutional problem is possible under art. 43 of the Irish Constitution, which protects private property.

[52] 1953 Act, § 3.

[53] 1953 Act, § 12.

[54] 1953 Act, § 13.

[55] 1953 Act, § 15.

[56] Including an interlocutory injunction; Supreme Court of Judicature (Ireland) Act, 1877, 40 & 41 Vict. c. 9, § 28(8).

[57] 1953 Act, § 11.

[58] Ibid.

it would not have been actionable as a conspiracy in restraint of trade if no order had been made. An action for breach of a statutory duty might also lie.

If Ireland joins the EEC, a comprehensive law against restrictive practices will probably be necessary. The FTC will have to be reconstituted to give it judicial power over Treaty infringements. No very substantial changes in the powers of investigation of the FTC appear necessary, other than giving it jurisdiction over sectors not concerned with the supply of goods. Some changes in organization would probably be required if the FTC was not permitted to exercise the functions of investigation, prosecution, and decision; this would make it closer to the civil law inquisitorial procedure than to the common law tradition. The FTC will have to be empowered to investigate on behalf of the EEC Commission[59] and to give it information. In time, the enforcement of Irish restrictive practices law might be taken from the courts and assigned to the reorganized FTC. However, this would not be legally necessary under the present EEC regulations.

SUBSTANTIVE LAW ON RESTRICTIVE PRACTICES[60]

The Restrictive Trade Practices Acts are in such general terms and have achieved the intended flexibility of treatment of particular sectors so effectively that it is impossible to tell in advance how the FTC will act. Since there are three bodies—the FTC, the Minister for Industry and Commerce, and Parliament—involved in making and confirming an order, the reasons for an order, other than those given by the FTC, are not always clear. However, only the orders actually made indicate the criteria used and the possible application of the Acts to other sectors. The terms of the orders made are considered here to examine the discernible criteria.[61]

Price-fixing

In every case in which an order has been made, price-fixing has been regulated.[62] Collective price maintenance has

[59] Reg. 17, arts. 10, 11, 13. See Korah, "Competition, Cartels and Monopolies," in English Law and the Common Market 138, 159–61 (Keeton & Schwarzenberger ed. 1963). The EEC Commission would have to be authorized by Irish legislation both to order the FTC to undertake investigations and to appoint inspectors with power to investigate Irish enterprises.

[60] Prices Act, 1958 Acts 101, § 13, empowers the Minister for Industry and Commerce to fix maximum prices for goods or services where he believes, from a report of the FTC, that restrictive practices exist and are causing excessive prices. Abuse of a monopoly position resulting from ownership of a patent is prevented by the Industrial and Commercial Property (Protection) Act, 1927(1) Pub. Stat. 231, as amended by 1957 Acts 167.

[61] The FTC has conducted inquiries into the following sectors: radios and accessories, building materials, motor vehicles, groceries, carpets, motor fuel and lubricating oil, cookers and ranges, hand-knitting yarns, nylon stockings, and patent and pharmaceutical medicines. In The State (Pharmaceutical Soc'y) v. Fair Trade Comm'n, 99 Ir. L.T.R. 24 (1956), the Irish Supreme Court held that although pharmacists were professional people, their trading activities were within the Acts. Restrictive trade practices orders have been made and confirmed by legislation for all the above sectors except nylon stockings and medicine. See Restrictive Trade Practices (Radios) Order, 1955, S.I. No. 102 of 1955, confirmed by Restrictive Trade Practices (Confirmation of Order) Act, 1956 Acts 281 [orders and confirmations are hereinafter cited as, e.g., Radios Order, S.I. No. 102 of 1955, confirmed 1956 Acts 281]; Building Materials Order, S.I. No. 187 of 1955, confirmed 1956 Acts 283; Motor Cars Order, S.I. No. 86 of 1956, confirmed 1956 Acts 593; Groceries Order, S.I. No. 332 of 1956, as amended by S.I. No. 163 of 1958, both confirmed 1958 Acts 825; Carpets Order, S.I. No. 59 of 1960, confirmed 1960 Acts 561; Motor Spirit and Motor Vehicle Lubricating Oil Order, S.I. No. 294 of 1961, as amended by S.I. No. 62 of 1962, both confirmed 1962 Acts 607; Cookers and Ranges Order, S.I. No. 117 of 1962, confirmed 1962 Acts 905; Hand Knitting Yarns Order, S.I. No. 197 of 1962, confirmed 1963 Acts, No. 6.

[62] Except in the case of carpets, where the FTC made no recommendation as to price-

always been prohibited when it arises. Vertical and horizontal resale price maintenance and horizontal price-fixing by wholesalers of radios, building materials, motor vehicles, and groceries, and horizontal resale price-fixing by retailers of radios, motor vehicles, and groceries have been prohibited. Recommended prices are not binding as minimum resale prices. These provisions are in substantially the same form, and they prohibit direct or indirect inducement or attempted inducement by agreement, threat, promise, or other means to fix minimum prices or markups. Horizontal "understandings" are prohibited.

In the case of radios there was no evidence that manufacturers had attempted to fix prices collectively, but price-fixing was prohibited for "suppliers."[63] In the building materials trade there had been both horizontal price-fixing and resale price maintenance. In the motor car trade there was no evidence of horizontal price-fixing by assemblers, but retail prices fixed by each assembler were enforced collectively, though not very effectively.[64] In the groceries trade there had been keen price competition among wholesalers, but there had been some horizontal resale price maintenance by retailers. In these cases the FTC prohibited almost all forms of price-fixing even if they had not actually arisen.

The four orders mentioned above, which are similar throughout, contain the most sweeping provisions against price-fixing. The orders on cookers and ranges and on hand-knitting yarns prohibit vertical resale price maintenance by a supplier, irrespective of the nature of the price-fixing arrangement. Advertising maximum resale prices and suggesting resale prices are, however, expressly permitted. There is no prohibition on horizontal price-fixing at any level, because it did not exist and was not considered by the FTC. The cookers and ranges report concludes that resale price maintenance by suppliers has prevented competitive prices and given rise to discrimination between traders.[65] Resale price maintenance and related discrimination are therefore prohibited. In the case of hand-knitting yarns,[66] the FTC

fixing because its recommendations were likely to cause reorganization of the trade.

[63] For the facts giving rise to the Fair Trade Commission's recommendations, see Report of Enquiry into . . . Radio Sets and Accessories, Pr. 2660, ch. IX (1954). At para. 109 the FTC summarized its conclusions:

> [I]t is contrary to the public interest that all retailers wherever located, whatever type of business they carry on, and whatever their operating expenses and efficiency, should be compelled . . . to take a margin of gross profit as high as 50% on cost on an article . . . which involves a substantial outlay for the consumer. . . . [I]t is doubtful if the present system of control in the industry would be practicable in the absence of tariff protection. So far as this is so, tariff protection is . . . being availed of to enhance the position of established retailers in the market. As the market is not only protected but relatively small in size, it is desirable that artificial impediments should not be allowed to frustrate reasonable price competition. . . . There is ultimately no effective substitute for price competition as a means of ensuring the efficiency of distribution.

The FTC concluded that radios were unlikely to be used for loss-leader selling; id., para. 96. In its Report of Enquiry into . . . Building Materials and Components, Pr. 2841, paras. 44, 46 (1954), the FTC stressed that a fixed resale price meant widely different profit margins and that the consumer should get the benefit of wide variations in efficiency, and so condemned price-fixing.

[64] After a special review of the operation of the order on motor cars, the FTC made fair trading rules requiring minimum service facilities. It was felt to be unfair that garages providing good service facilities should have to face price-cutting by firms providing inadequate facilities.

[65] Report of Enquiry into . . . Cookers and Ranges, Pr. 6293, para. 58 (1961). The discrimination was due to the fact that it was not possible to enforce price maintenance uniformly.

[66] Report of Enquiry into . . . Women's Nylon Stockings and Hand Knitting Yarns, Pr. 6679, para. 60 (1962).

makes no recommendation as to collective resale price maintenance, since it was not attempted. However, the FTC holds that vertical resale price maintenance has unreasonably restricted competition and entry into the trade and has maintained prices in spite of new marketing techniques which reduce costs. It therefore recommends that vertical price maintenance be prohibited. (This sector was protected by high tariffs, and there were three large manufacturers in an oligopoly position.)

The order on motor spirit (petrol and diesel fuel) and motor oil is quite different from all the others. Two provisions[67] prohibit horizontal price-fixing by retailers or wholesalers of both commodities. Price leadership is almost universal in these commodities, and the FTC has found that horizontal price-fixing at wholesaler level existed before the inquiry. The report makes no recommendation with regard to vertical price-fixing, since price maintenance is not enforced, although retail prices are recommended by wholesalers. The FTC says that if enforcement takes place, its position will be reconsidered.

The FTC has noted that price leadership resulted from the building materials order. It has concluded that competition and efficiency are not impaired if no agreement or understanding exists and has taken no action. In this respect, it has acted conventionally.

In only two cases has the FTC permitted price-fixing—in the fair trading rules on cigarettes and in the abortive recommendations on pharmaceutical products. However, the FTC has recommended limitations on extreme price-cutting and has taken limited action where there was a serious argument in favor of restricting price-cutting. In the case of cigarettes, the FTC allows individual resale price maintenance only because of the special circumstances of the trade, which are —according to the manufacturers—the large number of outlets, the high proportion of tax in the retail price, and the purchase of raw material by manufacturers long in advance of production. These are hardly overwhelming reasons, but the FTC apparently accepts them.

Refusals to deal

Where any type of price-fixing has been prohibited, refusals to deal also have been prohibited, since these are the normal method of enforcing price maintenance.[68] The groceries order prohibits withholding of goods or "other discrimination." Withholding is permitted if the potential buyer has exceeded the maximum resale price specified by the supplier.[69] However, the groceries order permits a supplier to withhold branded goods from retailers who sell below a wholesale price notified or recommended to them and who will not agree to refrain from this and from retailers who display the supplier's recommended retail price beside their own price.[70] The motor cars

[67] Motor Spirit and Motor Vehicle Lubricating Oil Order, arts. 12, 13. See Report of Enquiry into . . . Motor Spirit and Motor Lubricating Oil, Pr. 6000, paras. 308–22 (1961); in this report the FTC recommended the prohibition of price-fixing although profit margins were fairly small and though it had stressed in the Report of Enquiry into . . . Radio Sets and Accessories, Pr. 2660, para. 90 (1954), that the large retailers' profit margin was one of the main reasons for condemning price-fixing in that sector.

[68] A manufacturer cannot require a retailer to maintain prices if he has no contract with him; Dunlop v. Selfridge, [1915] A.C. 847. FTC, Eighth Annual Report, Pr. 5857, app. II, para. 6 (1961), stresses that discrimination, refusal to deal with a non-member of a trade association, and unfair limitations on entry into trade are always prohibited where they arise.

[69] This proviso does not appear in the Radios Order, art. 7; cf. Groceries Order, 1956, art. 7; Motor Cars Order, art. 9; Building Materials Order, art. 7. The cookers and hand-knitting yarns orders have similar provisions.

[70] Groceries Order, as amended, art. 3, permits a trade association to notify a supplier of price-cutting.

order permits withholding of goods if the purchaser has advertised a vehicle at less than the recommended price, and this order and the radios order both permit withholding if the purchaser has resold goods below the price at which he could replace them, if this price is less than he actually paid. In the latter case the supplier must notify the FTC that supplies are being withheld.[71] There is no provision in the building materials order permitting withholding in cases of extreme price-cutting. A supplier of groceries may ask a wholesaler to withhold goods from a retailer if the retailer sells above the supplier's maximum price or below the wholesale price notified to him or advertises the supplier's recommended retail price beside his own. Here again, the supplier must notify the FTC.

In those situations where withholding of goods is authorized if the FTC is notified, the FTC may decide that withholding is no longer justified, in which case it becomes illegal. This is true of the radios, motor cars, and groceries orders.

The motor spirit order[72] prohibits withholding of supplies from mixed-brand retailers and from some retailers wishing to become mixed-brand retailers. It also prohibits requiring a retailer to restrict his purchases from other suppliers or his display of the goods of other suppliers. However, a wholesaler may withhold supplies for breach of a condition in an agreement permitted by the order.

There are provisions which prohibit withholding of goods or discrimination because the purchaser is not on a trade association's list or because a competitor or an association has requested the withholding or discrimination.[73] Other provisions[74] prohibit any combination of persons or a trade association from attempting to coerce a supplier into withholding supplies or discriminating against anyone.[75]

Protection of freedom of entry into trade

The right of entrants into a trade to establish themselves and to obtain supplies has been protected in every case in which it has been interfered with.[76] Freedom of entry is, of course, extremely

[71] Radios Order, art. 8(2), also permits withholding if the purchaser has resold "at a price so little exceeding the [replacement] price as, in the opinion of the supplier, materially to injure the supplier's legitimate business interests."

[72] Art. 4.

[73] In the orders on radios, groceries, motor spirit, and building materials.

[74] In the orders on radios, building materials, motor cars, groceries, cookers and ranges, and hand-knitting yarns.

[75] The first two orders, on radios and building materials, prohibit coercion by a single person; arts. 11 and 9, respectively. The building materials order also prohibits attempts to limit a supplier's choice of distribution channels, customers, or trade terms.

[76] I.e., radios, building materials, motor cars, groceries, and motor spirit. The order on motor spirit applies only to wholesalers. See in particular the Report of Enquiry into . . . Radio Sets and Accessories, Pr. 2260, ch. VIII, especially para. 82 (1954). In the motor cars and building materials orders, there are provisions prohibiting any supplier from entering into any agreement likely to limit or restrict entry into trade; Building Materials Order, art. 10; Motor Cars Order, art. 16; cf. Groceries Order, art. 16; Radios Order, art. 12. In the motor cars report, the FTC decided to take no action against exclusive dealerships, and it appears that this provision would not prohibit a supplier from agreeing to sell goods in a specified area only through a given retailer, although this lessens the demand for retailers. In the Radio Sets Report, Pr. 2660, para. 119 (1954), the FTC states an important principle: "It is unfair that restriction of the right of any person to engage effectively in the retail trade should be within the competence of vested retailer interests." See also para. 81, where the same view is expressed. It held, however, that the requirements for entry into the trade which had been imposed were in fact unreasonable and contrary to the public interest. See also Report of Enquiry into . . . Grocery Goods and Provisions, Pr. 3722, para. 192 (1956); cf. Report of Enquiry into . . . Carpets, Carpeting and Floor Rugs, Pr. 5175, para. 35 (1959).

important to insure competition, particularly by the use of new methods.

Discrimination

Discrimination is prohibited for the same group of commodities as interference with entry into trade.[77] Discrimination is prohibited absolutely as to goods of similar grade, quality, or quantity, except on the basis of credit worthiness.[78] The carpets order applies only to manufacturers and requires equitable application of trade terms; discrimination in favor of new entrants is permitted. In respect of groceries, suppliers may make a "fair" differentiation between classes of retailers and wholesalers but may make no "unfair" discrimination within each class;[79] trade associations may not make any differentiations.

The preparation or publication of lists, a method of facilitating discrimination to enforce a restrictive practice,[80] is also prohibited. No association or supplier may publish any list of approved or unapproved traders in a way likely to limit entry into the trade or to be used as a basis for regulating the supply, distribution, or terms of sale of goods. A list for a boycott is illegal if the reason for the boycott is the refusal of a supplier to commit an offense under the order in question. This provision applies to radios, building materials, and motor vehicles. The provision on groceries is somewhat differently framed.[81]

Severe discrimination and restrictions on entry into the trade had existed in the building materials sector. In the radios sector, the requirements of a trade association on service facilities are not prohibited but must be notified to the FTC. There had also been requirements in the motor car trade on floor area and for entry into the trade, and approved traders were listed. The groceries order protects entry into trade, although there had been restrictions on entry only in respect of one commodity. The motor spirit order gives specific permission for the imposition of terms and conditions on a mixed-brand retailer in the interests of efficiency. These must not be less advantageous than those given to exclusive dealers, except that the wholesaler may train staff for or make certain loans to an exclusive dealer.

In general, the FTC deals with restrictions which are unreasonable or discriminate against entrants by requiring higher standards from entrants than are required of existing traders.[82] The FTC thus has no difficulty in holding these restrictions improper. It has formulated the important principle that the quality of after-sales service and the number of outlets are matters for manufacturers only and not for retailers. It therefore supervises requirements of manufacturers to insure that they are reasonable, instead of prohibiting them. In one report it has permitted discrimination in favor of new entrants,[83] but it otherwise allows this only on certain specified grounds. Quantity discounts are justified but not discounts given because of the bargaining power of large distributors.

[77] With the addition of carpets.

[78] With regard to radios, building materials, motor vehicles, and groceries. The motor spirit order also specifically permits discrimination to enforce a restrictive practice.

[79] Groceries Order, as amended, art. 4.

[80] See Thorne v. Motor Trade Ass'n, [1937] A.C. 797; Crofter Hand Woven Harris Tweed Co. v. Veitch, [1942] A.C. 435; Connolly v. Loughney & McCarthy, 87 Ir. L.T.R. 49 (1953). On discrimination and interference with entry into trade, see Report of Enquiry into . . . Radio Sets and Accessories, Pr. 2660, paras. 70–86 (1954).

[81] Groceries Order, as amended, art. 5.

[82] See Report of Enquiry into . . . Radio Sets and Accessories, Pr. 2660, paras. 70, 83 (1954).

[83] Carpets Order, art. 5(4); see also Report of Enquiry [into] . . . Building Materials and Components, Pr. 2841, paras. 170–71, 173 (1954).

Market-sharing

Horizontal market-sharing has arisen and been dealt with only once—in relation to building materials. No arrangement or understanding among suppliers induced by threat, promise, or other means may facilitate the suppression of competition by the territorial division of the market. There is no limitation on functional division of the market (specialization) in connection with building materials nor on division of the market by retailers.

Agreements by which a retailer agrees to obtain motor spirit and motor oil from only one supplier may not last longer than five years. This rule applies even if the agreement is a mortgage, hire purchase, or loan agreement. The FTC has decided that the selling of petrol through retailers bound to sell only one brand facilitates rationalization of distribution and reduction of costs, although it artificially stimulates entry into the retail trade[84] and alters the pattern of inter-brand competition.

Tying-in clauses

Tying-in clauses are forbidden only in relation to motor spirit and motor oil.[85] A wholesaler may not require a retailer buying motor spirit to purchase lubricating oil as well and may not offer any discount if the retailer buys the wholesaler's oil or agrees not to buy other oil or not to display competing oils at his garage.

Permitted restrictions on competition: Supervision by the Fair Trade Commission

Conditions which are reasonable in the interests of efficiency and economy in production or necessary in the legitimate interests of the supplier's business and which are applied equitably to all purchasers of goods are permitted by the orders on radios, building materials, and motor cars, subject to the other provisions of the orders. These conditions may relate to the size or frequency of orders for goods, the functions of a retailer, or the services to be rendered to the public. Since no restrictive practice is illegal until an order makes it so, a permissive provision expressed to be subject to the prohibiting articles of the orders has no substantive effect, except to define the conditions which a supplier is required to notify to the FTC and to provide to any trader. The FTC's power to make fair trade rules is protected.[86]

A grocery supplier may differentiate between classes of wholesalers or retailers,[87] and the FTC may require the different terms to be submitted to it and may prohibit them if they are unfair. Apart from regulating discrimination in the application of terms and conditions, the carpets order provides only for the terms to be notified to the FTC, which may prohibit them if they are "unreasonable."[88]

The FTC has power to require information from wholesalers of motor spirit and motor oil as to their programs for the acquisition of filling stations and their terms and conditions for the supply of the two commodities. The power to require information on a company's future policy is a sweeping power, but is, of course, no wider than the FTC's powers of investigation. Curiously, the

[84] Report of Enquiry into . . . Motor Spirit and Motor Lubricating Oil, Pr. 6000, paras. 267–95 (1961).

[85] Id., paras. 296–307.

[86] There are similar provisions relating to the supply of information under the cookers and hand-knitting yarns orders.

[87] Groceries Order, as amended, art. 4.

[88] Report of Enquiry into . . . Carpets, Carpeting and Floor Rugs, Pr. 5175, para. 42 (1959). The FTC had concluded that manufacturers had unnecessarily restricted supplies and excluded new entrants from the trade without good reason. Its recommendations dealt only with these matters, hence the narrow scope of the carpets order.

motor spirit and motor oil order is the only one which invalidates illegal provisions in agreements. Presumably, however, the price-fixing clauses in other agreements, if contrary to an order duly confirmed, also will be void.[89]

Comment

Although orders are the only substantive law in Ireland on restrictive practices, the FTC usually recommends orders dealing only with restrictive practices which actually exist and does not attempt to entirely regulate a sector even after it has inquired into it. Orders are thus more like court orders than legislation in their scope. One reason the FTC deals with only existing restrictive practices is that it keeps the operation of orders under supervision[90] and thus is aware of the need for regulation of other aspects of the sector involved and aware of any reasons for relaxing the terms of an order. The result is a situation even further removed from the legal rules of the United States than the Community law is.

The FTC naturally considers the general economic situation caused by tariffs, quotas, and restrictions on freedom of establishment which protect many of the enterprises from foreign competition in the national market.[91] In an economy growing more rapidly,[92] where, among other things, unemployment is less likely to result from intensive competition, the FTC might be more severe. Tariff reductions will increase the possibility of competition from outside Ireland.

Because the operation of orders can be supervised and their terms altered and because of the nature of the task and the way in which the reports of the inquiries are written, it is not easy to ascertain precise principles from the actions of the FTC. It is free in each case to act as it thinks best in the public interest.[93] However, two cases may be worth mentioning. In the women's nylons inquiry, no order was recommended by the FTC; in the case of the patent and pharmaceutical medicines, the Minister for Industry and Commerce made no order, disregarding the FTC's recommendations.

Cases in which no order was made

There was little or no inter-brand differentiation in the case of women's nylon stockings.[94] Commercial custom caused uniform retail prices without price maintenance. Production exceeded demand, and competition was keen; no manufacturer had a dominant position. Brands whose prices were not maintained competed generally with brands that sold at fixed prices. There was no evidence of collective resale price maintenance. One manufacturer operated a system of retail price-fixing but the effect of this on the over-all situation was negligible. The FTC concluded that, as long as competition continued, resale price maintenance did not interfere with competition or restrict entry to trade so as to operate against the public interest, and recommended no action.

This case shows that no action will be taken against restrictive practices if keen

[89] U.K. Restrictive Trade Practices Act, 1956, 4 & 5 Eliz. 2, c. 68, § 20(3), declares prohibited clauses void; see Wilberforce, Campbell & Elles, Restrictive Trade Practices and Monopolies 117–22 (1957). The position is probably the same in Ireland, since a prohibited clause is itself criminal.

[90] See, for example, FTC, Tenth Annual Report, Pr. 7025, paras. 14–16 (1963).

[91] See Report of Enquiry into . . . Radio Sets and Accessories, Pr. 2660, para. 109 (1954); Report of Enquiry into . . . Carpets, Carpeting and Floor Rugs, Pr. 5175, para. 42 (1959).

[92] The Irish economy did not begin to expand strongly until the FTC had been at work for five years.

[93] 1953 Act, § 8(1)(c).

[94] Report of Enquiry into . . . Women's Nylon Stockings and Hand Knitting Yarns, Pr. 6679, paras. 45–54 (1962).

competition exists.[95] The firm operating resale price maintenance did not require retailers to sell only its own products, and the nature of the trade did not readily permit price competition. The FTC did not need to analyze the merits of resale price maintenance in the case of the firm practicing it, because its effects were unimportant. This typifies the empirical approach which is possible for an administrative agency free to reopen the position at any time.

In the report on pharmacists' goods,[96] the FTC stressed the distinctive features of the trade in question. These were the legal requirement of professional knowledge for certain prescriptions, the importance to public health of the trade and of numerous and convenient outlets, the need for expert knowledge in spite of a decline in the proportion of dispensed goods, the great variety of goods stocked, the modest net profits by professional standards, and the numerous goods sold through other outlets with lower gross profit margins.

The FTC recommended the prohibition of collective resale price maintenance and horizontal price-fixing. Individual resale price maintenance was to be permitted. Withholding of supplies was to be permitted in cases of drastic price-cutting. Lists of suppliers whose only outlets were pharmacists were permitted, but threats, boycotts, and discrimination were not.

The Minister declined to make an order and said that an order would not alter trade practices. It is true that the FTC's recommendations were not wholly satisfactory. The distinction between a trade association's direction to discriminate against a supplier who does not sell only through pharmacists and a request to favor suppliers who sell only through pharmacists is hardly satisfactory if the latter is permitted and the former is a criminal offense. Since individual resale price maintenance is prohibited in the grocery trade, it seems odd to permit it for the same goods when sold by pharmacists, and the reasons suggested are not entirely convincing. The Minister, as has been explained, has power to go beyond the FTC's recommendations and make a more stringent order, so the defects, both those mentioned and others, were inadequate to explain his inaction. The reason given, that an order would not markedly alter existing practice, does not mean that in the long run some price reduction and more efficient distribution methods would not be encouraged. In this case, the empirical approach seems to have been overdone.

FAIR TRADING RULES: ADVISORY ACTIVITIES

Most[97] of the fair trading rules[98] fol-

[95] A similar principle is accepted in EEC Treaty, art. 85(3).

[96] Report of Enquiry into . . . Proprietary and Patent Medicines and Infant Foods and Medical and Toilet Preparations, Pr. 3926, especially paras. 83–89 (1956).

[97] But not Nos. 5, 10 (now superseded by the Carpets Order), 16 (revoked), 17, 19, 20, 21.

[98] The fair trading rules which have been made from time to time are listed in each annual report of the FTC. To date, they deal with the following (serial number and date of publication in parentheses): ropes, cordage, and twines (1, 1953); nails and screws (2, 1953); tableware (earthenware and china) (3, 1954); cutlery, spoons, and forks (4, 1954); entry into retail trade in petrol (5, 1954–revoked in 1962); electric light bulbs (6, 1954); sole leather (7, 1954); files and hacksaw blades (8, 1954); dry batteries (9, 1954); carpets, carpeting, and floor rugs (10, 1954; 10A, 1958 –both revoked in 1958); household textiles (non-woolen) (11, 1955); coal (12, 1955); aluminum hollowware (13, 1955); perambulators, folding-cars, and sun-cars (14, 1957); pedal bicycles, spare parts, and accessories (15, 1957); entry into and trade in the cooperative wholesale distribution of grocery goods and provisions (16, 1957–revoked in 1960); supply of alcoholic and non-alcoholic apple drinks, juices, and concentrates to wholesalers (17, 1957); razor blades (18, 1958); cigarettes (maintenance of resale price by a manufac-

low a pattern fairly closely. Horizontal price-fixing and individual and collective resale price maintenance are condemned. In some cases, recommended resale prices are prohibited. Discrimination is permissible only on account of quantity, credit worthiness, or exceptional circumstances affecting the marketability of the goods. Division of markets is not permitted. Trade lists are, in general, prohibited. Terms and conditions must be notified to the FTC. Vertical resale price maintenance is permitted in the case of cigarettes.

Broadly, therefore, the criteria used for fair trading rules are similar to those used in full-scale inquiries. Rules, however, are published without any accompanying explanation, so the reasons for them are not ascertainable.

The FTC regards it as one of its functions to advise enterprises whether particular practices are contrary to its policy, and it does this informally if the case is not important enough to necessitate fair trading rules or an inquiry.[99] The FTC gives advice on Articles 85 and 86 of the EEC Treaty to any enterprise subject to those provisions.[100] It has even taken the view that it may investigate deceptive practices which are not restrictive but which involve unfair competition.[101]

turer) (19, 1958); entry into and trade in the sale and/or repair of motor vehicles (20, 1962); entry into and trade in the sale and/or repair of motor vehicles (20A, 1962–revoked in 1962); entry into the wholesale trade in domestic electrical goods (21, 1960); proprietary household remedies, infant and invalid foods, health drinks, and toilet preparations (22, 1963).

[99] FTC, First Annual Report, para. 10 (1954), and all subsequent Annual Reports, passim.

[100] FTC, Tenth Annual Report, para. 45 (1963).

[101] FTC, First Annual Report, para. 15 (1954).

Appendix

The following are the Articles of the Treaty Establishing the European Economic Community referred to in the text and Regulation 17 adopted under Article 87 of the Treaty. The Treaty translation is the one prepared by Her Majesty's Foreign Office and published by Her Majesty's Printing Office (1962). The translation of Regulation 17 is the one prepared by the Secretariat of the EEC Commission and published in 1962 EEC Bull. No. 2, Supp.

TREATY ESTABLISHING THE EUROPEAN ECONOMIC COMMUNITY

Article 3

For the purposes set out in the preceding Article, the activities of the Community shall include, under the conditions and in accordance with the time-table envisaged in this Treaty:

(a) the elimination, as between Member States, of customs duties and of quantitative restrictions in regard to the import and export of goods, as well as of all other measures having equivalent effect;

(b) the establishment of a common customs tariff and of a common commercial policy towards third countries;

(c) the abolition, as between Member States, of obstacles to the free movement of persons, services and capital;

(d) the inauguration of a common policy in the field of agriculture;

(e) the inauguration of a common policy in the field of transport;

(f) the establishment of a system ensuring that competition in the Common Market is not distorted;

(g) the adoption of procedures per- economic policies of Member States and the correction of instability in their balances of payments;

(h) the approximation of their respective national laws to the extent required for the Common Market to function in an orderly manner;

(i) the creation of a European Social Fund in order to improve the possibilities of employment for workers and to contribute to the raising of their standard of living;

(j) the establishment of a European Investment Bank to facilitate the economic expansion of the Community by opening up fresh resources; and

(k) the association of overseas countries and territories with a view to increasing trade and to pursuing jointly the task of economic and social development.

Article 7

Within the field of application of this Treaty, and without prejudice to any particular provisions mentioned therein, any discrimination on the grounds of nationality shall be prohibited.

The Council may, on a proposal of the Commission and after consulting the Assembly, adopt, by qualified majority vote, regulations designed to prohibit such discrimination.

Article 36

The provisions of Articles 30 to 34 inclusive shall not preclude prohibitions or restrictions on imports, exports or goods in transit justified on the grounds of public morality; public policy (*ordre public*); public security; the protection of health and life of humans, animals or plants; the protection of national treasures possessing artistic, historic or archaeological value; or the protection of industrial and commercial property (*propriété industrielle*). Provided always that such prohibitions or restrictions shall not be used as a means of arbitrary discrimination nor as a disguised restriction on trade between Member States.

Article 37

1. Member States shall gradually adjust any State trading monopolies so as to ensure that, when the transitional period expires, no discrimination exists between the nationals of Member States as regards the supply or marketing of goods.

The provisions of this Article shall apply to any organization through which a Member State, *de jure* or *de facto*, either directly or indirectly controls, supervises or appreciably influences imports or exports as between Member States. These provisions shall likewise apply to monopolies delegated by the State to other legal entities.

2. Member States shall abstain from introducing any new measure which is contrary to the principles laid down in paragraph 1 of this Article or which restricts the scope of the Articles dealing with the abolition of customs duties and quantitative restrictions between Member States.

3. The timetable for the measures referred to in paragraph 1 shall be harmonised with the abolition of the quantitative restrictions on the same products, as provided for in Articles 30 to 34 inclusive.

If a product is subject to a State trading monopoly in only one or some Member States, the Commission may authorise the other Member States to impose protective measures until the adjustment provided for in paragraph 1 of this Article has been effected; the Commission shall decide upon the conditions governing such measures and determine the manner in which effect shall be given to them.

4. If a State trading monopoly has rules which are designed to facilitate the distribution or marketing of agricultural products, the rules contained in this Article shall be given effect to in such a manner that equivalent guarantees are provided, in respect of the employment and standard of living of the producers concerned; account shall be taken of possible adjustments and of necessary specialisations.

5. The obligations on Member States shall be binding only in so far as they are consistent with existing international agreements.

6. At the beginning of the first stage the Commission shall make recommendations as to the manner of effecting the adjustment provided for in this Article and the timetable which shall govern it.

Article 52

Within the framework of the provisions set out below, restrictions on the freedom of establishment of nationals of a Member State in the territory of another Member State shall be abolished by progressive stages in the course of the transitional period. Such progressive abolition shall also apply to restrictions on the setting up of agencies, branches or subsidiaries by nationals of any Member State established in the territory of any Member State.

Freedom of establishment shall include the right to engage in and carry on non-wage-earning activities, to set up and manage undertakings and, in particular, firms and companies (*sociétés*) within the meaning of Article 58(2), under the conditions laid down for its own nationals by the law of the country where such establishment is effected, subject to the provisions of the Chapter relating to capital.

Article 54

1. Before the first stage ends the Council shall draw up a general programme for the abolition of existing restrictions on freedom of establishment within the Community. The Council's decision on this shall be a unanimous one, taken on the proposal of the Commission and after consulting the Economic and Social Committee and the Assembly. The Commission shall submit their proposal to the Council during the first two years of the first stage.

This programme shall set out the general conditions under which freedom of establishment is to be achieved in the case of each type of activity and the particular stages by which this is to be achieved.

2. The Council shall issue directives in order to initiate this general programme or, in the absence of such a programme, in order to move a stage towards achieving freedom of establishment as regards a particular activity. The Council shall so act on a proposal of the Commission and after consulting the Economic and Social Committee and the Assembly. The Council's decision as to these directives shall be reached unanimously during the first stage and thereafter by a qualified majority vote.

3. The Council and the Commission shall carry out the duties devolving upon them under the above provisions, in particular:

(a) by according, as a general rule, priority treatment to activities where freedom of establishment makes a particularly valuable contribution to the development of production and trade;

(b) by ensuring close collaboration between the competent national authorities in order to make them better acquainted with the particular situation within the Community of the various activities concerned;

(c) by abolishing those administrative procedures and practices, whether resulting from domestic legislation or from agreements previously concluded between Member States, the maintenance of which would be an obstacle to freedom of establishment;

(d) by ensuring that wage-earning workers of one Member State employed in the territory of another Member State may remain in that territory for the purpose of undertaking there a non-wage-earning activity, provided that they satisfy the conditions which they would be required to satisfy if they came to that State at the time when they wished to engage in such activity;

(e) by enabling a national of one Member State to acquire and exploit land and buildings situated in the Territory of another Member State, provided this is not contrary to the principles laid down in Article 39(2);

(f) by effecting the progressive abolition of restrictions on freedom of establishment in every branch of activity under consideration, both as regards the conditions for setting up agencies, branches or subsidiaries in the territory of a Member State and as regards the conditions governing the entry of personnel belonging to the main establishment into managerial or supervisory posts in such agencies, branches and subsidiaries;

(g) by co-ordinating to the necessary extent and rendering of equal value the guarantees which Member States require of companies within the meaning of Article 58(2), so as to protect the interests both of Members and outsiders;

(h) by satisfying themselves that

Member States are not impairing the conditions of establishment by making grants.

Article 55

Activities involving in any Member State the exercise, even occasionally, of government action shall, in so far as that State is concerned, be excluded from the operation of this Chapter.

The Council may by qualified majority vote on a proposal of the Commission, decide that the provisions of this Chapter shall not apply to certain activities.

Article 56

1. The provisions of this Chapter and measures taken in pursuance thereof shall not invalidate any legislation, regulations and administrative rules providing for special treatment for foreign nationals on the grounds of public policy (*ordre public*), public security and public health.

2. The Council, acting unanimously on a proposal of the Commission, and after consulting the Assembly, shall, before the transitional period ends, issue directives for the co-ordination of the above-mentioned legislation, regulations and administrative rules. After the expiry of the second stage, however, the Council shall, by a qualified majority vote on a proposal of the Commission, issue directives for the co-ordination of such provisions as, in each Member State, are a matter for subordinate legislation.

Article 58

Companies and firms (*sociétiés*) formed in accordance with the law of a Member State and having their registered office, central administration or principal place of business within the Community shall, for the purpose of applying the provisions of this Chapter, be treated in the same way as individual nationals of Member States.

The term "firms or companies" (*sociétiés*) shall mean firms or companies constituted under civil or commercial law. It shall include co-operative societies and other legal persons (*personnes morales*) under public or private law (*droit public ou privé*), save for firms or companies whose objects do not include the making of profit.

Article 85

1. The following practices shall be prohibited as incompatible with the Common Market: all agreements between undertakings, all decisions by associations of undertakings and all concerted practices which are liable to affect trade between Member States and which are designed to prevent, restrict or distort competition within the Common Market or which have this effect. This shall, in particular, include:

(a) the direct or indirect fixing of purchase or selling prices or of any other trading conditions;

(b) the limitation or control of production, markets, technical development or investment;

(c) market-sharing or the sharing of sources of supply;

(d) the application of unequal conditions to parties undertaking equivalent engagements in commercial transactions, thereby placing them at a competitive disadvantage;

(e) making the conclusion of a contract subject to the acceptance by the other party to the contract of additional obligations, which, by their nature or according to commercial practice have no connexion with the subject of such contract.

2. Any agreements or decisions prohibited pursuant to this Article shall automatically be null and void.

3. The provisions of paragraph 1 may, however, be declared inapplicable in the case of:

—any agreement or type of agreement between undertakings,

—any decision or type of decision by associations of undertakings, and

—any concerted practice or type of concerted practice

which helps to improve the production or distribution of goods or to promote technical or economic progress, whilst allowing consumers* a fair share of the resulting profit and which does not:

(a) subject the concerns in question to any restrictions which are not indispensable to the achievement of the above objectives;

(b) enable such concerns to eliminate competition in respect of a substantial part of the goods concerned.

Article 86

Any improper exploitation by one or more undertakings of a dominant position within the Common Market or within a substantial part of it shall be deemed to be incompatible with the Common Market and shall be prohibited, in so far as trade between Member States could be affected by it. The following practices, in particular, shall be deemed to amount to improper exploitation:

(a) the direct or indirect imposition of any unfair purchase or selling prices or of any other unfair trading conditions;

(b) the limitation of production, markets or technical development to the prejudice of consumers;

(c) the application of unequal conditions to parties undertaking equivalent engagements in commercial transactions, thereby placing them at a commercial disadvantage;

(d) making the conclusion of a contract subject to the acceptance by the other party to the contract of additional obligations which by their nature or according to commercial practice have no connexion with the subject of such contract.

* The French text reads *utilisateurs,* which is the broader term "users."

Article 87

1. Within three years of this Treaty coming into force, the Council shall issue the necessary regulations or directives to put into effect the principles set out in Articles 85 and 86. The Council shall decide on these unanimously, on a proposal of the Commission and after consulting the Assembly.

If such regulations or directives have not been adopted within the specified period they shall be settled by the Council by qualified majority vote on a proposal of the Commission and after consulting the Assembly.

2. The regulations or directives referred to in paragraph 1 shall be designed, in particular:

(a) to ensure, by the institution of fines or penalties, the observance of the prohibitions referred to in Article 85(1) and in Article 86;

(b) to decide exactly how Article 85(3) is to be applied, taking into account the need both on the one hand to ensure effective supervision and, on the other hand, as far as possible to simplify administrative control;

(c) to define, where necessary, the extent to which the provisions of Articles 85 and 86 are to be applied in the various economic sectors;

(d) to define the respective functions of the Commission and of the Court of Justice in giving effect to the provisions referred to in this paragraph;

(e) to determine how domestic legislation is to be reconciled with the provisions of this Article† and with any rules made thereunder.

Article 92

1. Except where otherwise provided for in this Treaty any aid granted by a

† It is clear from the French version that "Section"—referring to Section 1 of Part Three, title I, chapter 1—is meant.

Member State or through State resources in any form whatsoever which distorts or threatens to distort competition by favouring certain undertakings or the production of certain goods shall, in so far as it adversely affects trade between Member States, be deemed to be incompatible with the Common Market.

2. The following shall be compatible with the Common Market:

(a) aid having a social character, granted to individual consumers, provided that such aid is granted without discrimination on the grounds of the origin of the products concerned;

(b) aid intended to make good the damage caused by natural disasters or other extraordinary events;

(c) aid granted to the economy of certain regions of the Federal Republic of Germany affected by the division of Germany, in so far as such aid is required so as to compensate for the economic disadvantages caused by that division.

3. The following may be deemed to be compatible with the Common Market:

(a) aid intended to promote the economic development of regions where the standard of living is abnormally low or where there is serious under-employment;

(b) aid intended to promote the execution of an important project of common European interest or to remedy serious disturbances in the economy of a Member State;

(c) aid intended to facilitate the development of certain activities or of certain economic regions, provided that such aid does not adversely affect trading conditions to such an extent as would be contrary to the common interest. Any grants of aid to shipbuilding existing as on 1 January, 1957, shall, in so far as they serve only to offset the absence of customs protection, be progressively reduced under the same conditions as apply to the abolition of customs duties, subject to the provisions of this Treaty concerning common commercial policy in regard to third countries;

(d) such other types of aid as may be specified by the Council by qualified majority vote on a proposal of the Commission.

Article 93

1. The Commission shall in conjunction with Member States submit to constant examination all systems of aids existing in those States. It shall propose to the latter any appropriate measures required by the progressive development or by the functioning of the Common Market.

2. If, after having given notice to the parties concerned to submit their comments, the Commission finds that aid granted by a State or through State resources is not compatible with the Common Market within the meaning of Article 92, or that such aid is being improperly used, it shall decide that the State concerned shall abolish or modify such aid within a time-limit to be prescribed by the Commission.

If the State concerned does not comply with this decision within the prescribed time-limit, the Commission or any other interested State may, notwithstanding the provisions of Articles 169 and 170, refer the matter to the Court of Justice direct.

The Council may, at the request of a Member State, unanimously decide, if such a decision is justified by exceptional circumstances, that any aid granted or planned by the State shall be deemed to be compatible with the Common Market, notwithstanding the provisions of Article 92 or the regulations provided for in Article 94. If the Commission had, as regards the grant of aid in question, already initiated the procedure provided for in the first sub-paragraph of this paragraph, the request made to the Council by the State concerned shall cause such procedure to be suspended until the Council has made its attitude known.

If, however, the Council has not made its attitude known within three months of the said request being made, the Commission shall give its decision on the case.

3. The Commission shall be informed, in sufficient time to enable it to submit its comments, of any plans to grant or modify grants of aid. If it considers that any such plan is incompatible with the Common Market within the meaning of Article 92 it shall without delay initiate the procedure provided for in the preceding paragraph. The Member State concerned shall not put its proposed measures into effect until this procedure has resulted in a final decision.

Article 94

The Council may, by a qualified majority vote on a proposal of the Commission, make any appropriate regulations for carrying out Articles 92 and 93(3) and may in particular determine the conditions for carrying out Article 93(3) and the types of aid to be exempted from this procedure.

Article 95

A Member State shall not impose, directly or indirectly, on the products of other Member States any internal charges of any kind in excess of those applied directly or indirectly to similar domestic products.

Furthermore, a Member State shall not impose on the products of other Member States any internal charges of such a nature as to afford indirect protection to other products.

Member States shall, not later than at the beginning of the second stage, eliminate or amend any provisions existing when this Treaty comes into force which conflict with the above rules.

Article 96

Where products are exported to the territory of any Member State any drawback of internal charges shall not exceed the internal charges imposed on them, whether directly or indirectly.

Article 97

Any Member States which levy a turnover tax calculated by a cumulative multi-stage system may, in the case of internal charges imposed by them on imported products or of drawback allowed by them on exported products, establish average rates for specific products or groups of products, provided that there is no infringement of the principles laid down in Articles 95 and 96.

Where the average rates established by a Member State do not conform with the above-mentioned principles, the Commission shall issue appropriate directives or decisions to the State concerned.

Article 98

In the case of charges other than turnover taxes, excise duties and other forms of indirect taxation, exemptions and repayments in respect of exports to other Member States may not be granted and compensatory charges in respect of imports from Member States may not be imposed unless, and to the extent that, the measures contemplated have been previously approved for a limited period by the Council acting by qualified majority vote on a proposal of the Commission.

Article 99

The Commission shall consider how to further the interests of the Common Market by harmonising the legislation of the various Member States concerning turnover taxes, excise duties and other forms of indirect taxation, including compensatory measures in respect of trade between Member States.

The Commission shall submit proposals to the Council; the latter shall decide upon the matter unanimously without prejudice to the provisions of Articles 100 and 101.

Article 100

The Council shall, by a unanimous decision, on a proposal of the Commission, issue directives for the approximation of such legislative and administrative provisions of Member States as directly affect the establishment or operation of the Common Market.

The Assembly and the Economic and Social Committee shall be consulted in the case of directives the implementation of which would involve amending legislation in one or more Member States.

Article 101

Where the Commission finds that a discrepancy between the legislative or administrative provisions of Member States is interfering with competition within the Common Market and consequently producing distortions which need to be eliminated, it shall consult the Member States concerned.

If such consultation does not result in an agreement eliminating the distortion in question, the Council shall issue the necessary directives for this purpose. It shall decide on these on a proposal of the Commission, unanimously during the first stage and thereafter by the qualified majority. The Commission and the Council may take any other appropriate measures provided for in this Treaty.

Article 102

1. Where there is reason to fear that the introduction or amendment of a legislative or administrative provision may cause distortion within the meaning of the preceding Article, the Member State desiring to proceed therewith shall consult the Commission. After consulting the Member States the Commission shall recommend to the States concerned such measures as may be appropriate to avoid the distortion in question.

2. If the State desiring to introduce or amend its own provisions does not comply with the recommendations made to it by the Commission, no request, in pursuance of Article 101, shall be made to other Member States to amend their own legislative or administrative provisions in order to eliminate such distortion. If the Member State which has ignored the Commission's recommendations is the only one to be adversely affected by the distortion which it has caused, the provisions of Article 101 shall not apply.

Article 169

If the Commission considers that a Member State has failed to fulfil any of its obligations under this Treaty, it shall issue a reasoned opinion on the matter after giving the State concerned the opportunity to submit its comments.

If the State concerned does not comply with the terms of such opinion within the period laid down by the Commission, the latter may refer the matter to the Court of Justice.

Article 170

Any Member State which considers that another Member State has failed to fulfil any of its obligations under this Treaty may refer the matter to the Court of Justice.

Before a Member State institutes, against another Member State, proceedings relating to an alleged infringement of the obligations under this Treaty, it shall refer the matter to the Commission.

The Commission shall deliver a reasoned opinion after the States concerned have been given the opportunity both to submit their own cases and to reply to each others' cases (*de présenter contradictoirement leurs observations*) both orally and in writing.

If the Commission, within a period of three months from the date on which the matter was referred to it, has not given an opinion, the absence of such opinion shall not preclude reference to the Court of Justice.

Article 171

If the Court of Justice finds that a Member State has failed to fulfil any of its obligations under this Treaty, such State is bound to take the measures required for the implementation of the judgment of the Court.

Article 172

The regulations enacted by the Council pursuant to the provisions of this Treaty may confer on the Court of Justice full jurisdiction as to the merits (*compétence de pleine juridiction*) in regard to the penalties provided for in these regulations.*

Article 173

Supervision of the legality of the acts of the Council and the Commission other than recommendations or opinions shall be a matter for the Court of Justice. The Court shall for this purpose have jurisdiction in proceedings instituted by a Member State, the Council or the Commission on the grounds of lack of jurisdiction, substantial violations of basic procedural rules, infringements of this Treaty or of any rule of law relating to effect being given to it or of misuse of powers (*détournement de pouvoir*).

Any natural or legal person may, under the same conditions, appeal against a decision directed to him or against a decision which, although in the form of a regulation or a decision directed to another person, is of direct and individual concern to him.

The proceedings provided for in this Article shall be instituted within a period of two months, dating, as the case may be, either from the publication of the measure concerned or from its notification to the complainant or, in default of this, from the day on which the latter learned of the said measure.

* Note.—French and Italian texts. German text adds "and power to vary or suspend such penalties."

Article 177

The Court of Justice shall be competent to give preliminary rulings (*à titre préjudiciel*) concerning:—

(a) the interpretation of this Treaty;
(b) the validity and interpretation of acts of the institutions of the Community;
(c) the interpretation of the statutes of any bodies set up by a formal measure of the Council, where the said statutes so provide.

Where any such question is raised before any court of law of one of the Member States, the said court may, if it considers that a decision on the question is essential to enable it to render judgment, request the Court of Justice to give a ruling thereon.

Where any such question is raised in a case pending before a domestic court of a Member State, from whose decisions there is no possibility of appeal under domestic law, the said court is bound to refer the matter to the Court of Justice.

Article 184

Where a regulation made by the Council or the Commission is the subject of legal proceedings, any of the parties concerned may, notwithstanding the expiry of the period laid down in Article 173(3), invoke the grounds set out in Article 173(1), in order to submit to the Court of Justice that the regulation in question does not apply.

Article 189

The Council and the Commission shall, in the discharge of their duties and in accordance with the provisions of this Treaty, issue regulations and directives, take decisions and formulate recommendations or opinions.

Regulations shall have general application. They shall be binding in every respect and directly applicable in each Member State.

Directives shall be binding, in respect of the result to be achieved, upon every Member State [to which they are addressed], but the form and manner of enforcing them shall be a matter for the national authorities.

Decisions shall be binding in every respect upon those to whom they are directed.

Recommendations and opinions shall have no binding force.

Article 192

Decisions of the Council or of the Commission which include a pecuniary obligation on persons other than States shall have the enforceability of a Court judgment (*titre exécutoire*).

Enforcement shall be governed by the rules of civil procedure in force in the State in the territory of which it takes place. The order for its enforcement (*formule exécutoire*) shall be stamped on the decision, without more verification than that the document is authentic, by the national authority which the Government of each Member State shall designate for this purpose and which shall be notified to the Commission and to the Court of Justice.

When these formalities have been completed at his request, the party concerned may proceed to enforcement by applying directly to the authority which is competent according to domestic law.

Enforcement may only be suspended by a decision of the Court of Justice. Provided always that the proper method of enforcement shall be a matter for the domestic courts.

Article 220

Member States shall, in so far as necessary, enter into negotiations with each other with a view to ensuring for the benefit of their nationals:

—the protection of persons as well as the enjoyment and protection of rights under the same conditions as those accorded by each State to its own nationals;
—the abolition of double taxation within the Community;
—the mutual recognition of firms or companies as defined in Article 58, second paragraph, the maintenance of their legal personality, if their registered office is transferred from one country to another, and the possibility of mergers between firms or companies which are subject to different domestic laws;
—the simplification of the formalities governing the reciprocal recognition and enforcement of judgments of the ordinary courts of law (*décisions judiciaries*) and arbitral awards.

Article 223

1. The provisions of this Treaty shall not adversely affect the following rules:

(a) No Member State shall be obliged to supply information the disclosure of which it considers contrary to the essential interests of its security.

(b) Any Member State may take whatever measures it considers necessary for the protection of the essential interests of its security, and which are connected with the production of or trade in arms, munitions and war material; such measures shall, however, not adversely affect conditions of competition in the Common Market in the case of products which are not intended for specifically military purposes.

2. During the first year after this Treaty comes into force, the Council shall, by a unanimous decision, determine the lists of products to which the provisions of paragraph 1 (b) shall apply.

3. The Council may, by a unanimous decision, on a proposal of the Commission, amend the said list.

REGULATION 17*

First Implementing Regulation Pursuant To Articles 85 and 86 Of The Treaty

The Council of the European Economic Community,

NOTING the provisions of the Treaty establishing the European Economic Community and especially Article 87 thereof:

NOTING the Commission's proposal,

NOTING the opinion of the Economic and Social Committee,

NOTING the opinion of the European Parliament,

CONSIDERING that in order to establish a system ensuring that competition shall not be distorted in the Common Market, it is necessary to provide for the uniform and balanced application of Articles 85 and 86 in the Member States;

CONSIDERING that in determining the particulars of the application of Article 85, paragraph 3, due account must be taken of the need, on the one hand, of ensuring effective supervision and, on the other hand, of simplifying administrative control to the greatest possible extent;

CONSIDERING that it therefore appears necessary to make it in principle obligatory for enterprises wishing to invoke Article 85, paragraph 3, to notify the Commission of their agreements, decisions and concerted practices;

CONSIDERING however that such agreements, decisions and concerted practices are probably very numerous and cannot therefore all be examined at the same time and that a number of them have special features which may make them less of a threat to the development of the Common Market;

CONSIDERING that there is consequently a need to establish provisionally a more flexible system for certain categories of agreements, decisions and concerted practices, without prejudging, however, the question of their validity under Article 85;

CONSIDERING, moreover, that it may be in the interest of enterprises to know whether the agreements, decisions or concerted practices in which they participate, or are contemplating participation, are likely to lay them open to action by the Commission under Article 85, paragraph 1, or Article 86;

CONSIDERING that in order to secure the uniform application of Articles 85 and 86 in the Common Market, it is necessary to fix the rules under which the Commission, working in close and constant liaison with the competent authorities in the Member States, can take the measures necessary for the application of the said Articles;

CONSIDERING that, for this purpose, the Commission must have the co-operation of the competent authorities in the Member States and be empowered, over the whole Common Market area, to require information and take the necessary steps to bring to light the existence of any agreement, decision or concerted practice prohibited by Article 85, paragraph 1, or of any abuse of a dominant position prohibited by Article 86;

CONSIDERING that if the Commission is to carry out its task of watching over the implementation of the Treaty it must be empowered to address to enterprises or associations of enterprises recommendations and decisions designed to put an end to any infringement of Articles 85 and 86;

CONSIDERING that compliance with Articles 85 and 86 and the fulfilment of obligations imposed on enterprises and associations of enterprises under the present Regulation must be enforceable by means of fines and penalties;

CONSIDERING that it is desirable to confirm the right of the enterprises concerned to be heard by the Commission, that it is desirable to give third parties whose interests may be affected by a

* Adopted by the Council of Ministers at Brussels on Feb. 6, 1962, published in 1962 Journal Officiel, 204/62.

decision the prior opportunity to submit their comments, and that it is desirable to ensure that the decisions taken be published to a substantial extent;

CONSIDERING that all decisions taken by the Commission under the present Regulation will be subject to review by the Court of Justice under the conditions defined in the Treaty, and that it is moreover desirable to confer on the Court of Justice, under Article 172, full jurisdiction in respect of decisions by which the Commission imposes fines or penalties;

CONSIDERING that the present Regulation can enter into force without prejudice to any other provisions which may be adopted later under Article 87;

has approved the present Regulation:

ARTICLE 1. BASIC PROVISION

The agreements, decisions and concerted practices referred to in Article 85, paragraph 1, of the Treaty and any abuse of a dominant position on the market within the meaning of Article 86 of the Treaty shall be prohibited, no prior decision to this effect being required; Articles 6, 7 and 23 of the present Regulation shall not be affected by this provision.

ARTICLE 2. NEGATIVE CLEARANCE

At the request of the enterprises or associations of enterprises concerned, the Commission may find that, according to the information it has obtained, there are, under Article 85, paragraph 1, or Article 86 of the Treaty, no grounds for it to intervene with respect to an agreement, decision or practice.

ARTICLE 3. ENDING OF INFRINGEMENTS

(1) If, acting on request or *ex officio,* the Commission finds that an enterprise or association of enterprises is infringing Article 85 or Article 86 of the Treaty, it can by means of a decision oblige the enterprises or associations of enterprises concerned to put an end to such infringement.

(2) A request to this effect may be submitted by:

a) Member States;

b) Natural and legal persons and associations of persons, who show a justified interest.

(3) Without prejudice to the other provisions of the present Regulation, the Commission, before taking the decision mentioned in paragraph 1, may address to the enterprises or associations of enterprises concerned recommendations designed to put an end to the infringement.

ARTICLE 4. NOTIFICATION OF NEW AGREEMENTS, DECISIONS AND PRACTICES

(1) The Commission shall be notified of any agreements, decisions or concerted practices referred to in Article 85, paragraph 1, of the Treaty which have come into being after the entry into force of the present Regulation and for which those concerned wish to invoke Article 85, paragraph 3. As long as such notification has not taken place, no decision to issue a declaration under Article 85, paragraph 3, may be rendered.

(2) Paragraph 1 shall not be applicable to agreements, decisions and concerted practices where:

i) enterprises of only one Member State take part and where such agreements, decisions and practices involve neither imports nor exports between Member States;

ii) only two enterprises take part and the sole effect of these agreements is:

a) to restrict the freedom of one party to the contract to fix prices or conditions of trading in the resale of goods which have been acquired from the other party to the contract, or

b) to impose restraint on the rights of any person acquiring or using industrial property rights—particularly patents, utility models, registered designs or trade marks—or on the rights of any person entitled, under a contract, to acquire or use manufacturing processes or knowledge relating to the utilization or application of industrial techniques.

iii) their sole object is:

a) the development or the uniform application of standards and types,

b) joint research to improve techniques, provided that the result is accessible to all parties and that each of them can exploit it.

The Commission may be notified of such agreements, decisions and practices.

ARTICLE 5. NOTIFICATION OF EXISTING AGREEMENTS, DECISIONS AND PRACTICES

(1) The Commission must be notified before August 1, 1962, of any agreements, decisions and concerted practices referred to in Article 85, paragraph 1, of the Treaty which are already in existence at the date of entry into force of the present Regulation and in respect of which those concerned wish to invoke Article 85, paragraph 3, of the Treaty.

(2) Paragraph 1 is not applicable where the said agreements, decisions and concerted practices fall within the categories referred to in paragraph 2 of Article 4; the Commission may be notified of these.

ARTICLE 6. DECISIONS TO ISSUE A DECLARATION UNDER ARTICLE 85, PARAGRAPH 3

(1) When the Commission decides to issue a declaration under Article 85, paragraph 3, it shall indicate the date from which the decision shall take effect. This date shall not be prior to the date of notification.

(2) The second sentence of paragraph 1 shall not be applicable to the agreements, decisions and concerted practices referred to in Article 4, paragraph 2, and Article 5, paragraph 2, nor to those which are referred to in Article 5, paragraph 1, and of which the Commission has been notified within the time-limit fixed therein.

ARTICLE 7. SPECIAL PROVISIONS FOR EXISTING AGREEMENTS, DECISIONS AND PRACTICES

(1) Where agreements, decisions and concerted practices already in existence at the date of the entry into force of the present Regulation and of which the Commission has been notified before August 1, 1962, do not meet the requirements of Article 85, paragraph 3, of the Treaty, and where the enterprises and associations of enterprises concerned put an end to them or modify them so that they no longer fall under the prohibition laid down in Article 85, paragraph 1, or so that they then meet the requirements of Article 85, paragraph 3, the prohibition laid down in Article 85, paragraph 1, shall be applicable only for a period fixed by the Commission. A decision by the Commission pursuant to the foregoing sentence cannot be invoked against enterprises or associations of enterprises which have not given their express assent to the notification.

(2) Paragraph 1 shall be applicable to agreements, decisions and concerted practices which are already in existence at the date of the entry into force of the present Regulation and which fall within the categories referred to in Article 4, paragraph 2, provided that notification shall have taken place before January 1, 1964.

ARTICLE 8. PERIOD OF VALIDITY AND REVOKING OF DECISIONS TO ISSUE A DECLARATION UNDER ARTICLE 85, PARAGRAPH 3

(1) A decision to issue a declaration under Article 85, paragraph 3, of the Treaty shall be valid for a specified period and may have certain conditions and stipulations attached.

(2) The decision may be renewed on request provided that the conditions laid down in Article 85, paragraph 3, of the Treaty continue to be fulfilled.

(3) The Commission may revoke or alter its decision or prohibit those concerned from taking certain courses of

action:

a) where the *de facto* situation has changed with respect to a factor essential in the granting of the decision;

b) where those concerned infringe a stipulation attached to the decision;

c) where the decision is based on false information or has been obtained fraudulently; or

d) where those concerned abuse the exemption from the provisions of Article 85, paragraph 1, of the Treaty granted to them by the decision.

In the cases covered by sub-paragraphs b), c) and d), the decision can also be revoked with retroactive effect.

ARTICLE 9. COMPETENCE

(1) Subject to review of its decision by the Court of Justice, the Commission shall have sole competence to declare Article 85, paragraph 1, inapplicable pursuant to Article 85, paragraph 3, of the Treaty.

(2) The Commission shall have competence to apply Article 85, paragraph 1, and Article 86 of the Treaty, even if the time-limits for notification laid down in Article 5, paragraph 1, and Article 7, paragraph 2, have not expired.

(3) As long as the Commission has not initiated any procedure pursuant to Articles 2, 3 or 6, the authorities of the Member States shall remain competent to apply Article 85, paragraph 1, and Article 86 in accordance with Article 88 of the Treaty, even if the time-limits for notification laid down in Article 5, paragraph 1, and Article 7 have not expired.

ARTICLE 10. LIAISON WITH THE AUTHORITIES OF THE MEMBER STATES

(1) The Commission shall transmit without delay to the competent authorities of the Member States copies of the requests, applications and notification together with copies of the most important documents which have been sent to it with the purpose of establishing the existence of infringements of Article 85 or Article 86 of the Treaty, or with the purpose of obtaining negative clearance or a decision to issue a declaration under Article 85, paragraph 3.

(2) It shall carry out the procedures mentioned in paragraph 1 in close and constant liaison with the competent authorities of the Member States; and these authorities may submit their views on the said procedures.

(3) A Consultative Committee on Cartels and Monopolies shall be consulted prior to any decision consequent upon a course of procedure referred to in paragraph 1 and prior to any decision concerning the renewal, the alteration or the revocation of a decision to issue a declaration under Article 85, paragraph 3, of the Treaty.

(4) The Consultative Committee shall be composed of officials competent in the field of cartels and monopolies. Each Member State shall appoint one official to represent it, who, if he is prevented from attending, may be replaced by another official.

(5) The consultation shall take place at a joint meeting called by the Commission; the session shall take place fourteen days at the earliest after dispatch of the convocation letter. This letter shall be accompanied by an exposition of the case to be considered, indicating the most important documents, and a preliminary draft of the decision shall be enclosed.

(6) The Consultative Committee may render an opinion even if some members are absent and have not been replaced by another official. The result of the consultation shall be set out in a written statement which shall be attached to the draft of the decision. It shall not be made public.

ARTICLE 11. REQUESTS FOR INFORMATION

(1) In the execution of the duties assigned to it by Article 89 and by provisions pursuant to Article 87 of the Treaty,

the Commission shall have power to seek all necessary information from the Governments and competent authorities of the Member States as well as from enterprises and associations of enterprises.

(2) When sending a request for information to an enterprise or association of enterprises, the Commission shall at the same time address a copy of this request to the competent authority in the Member State in the territory of which the principal place of business of the enterprise or the association of enterprises is situated.

(3) In its request the Commission shall indicate the legal basis and the purpose of the same, and the penalties for supplying false information laid down in Article 15, paragraph 1, sub-paragraph b).

(4) Information must be supplied on request by the owners of the enterprises or by their representatives and, in the case of legal persons, of companies or of associations without legal personality, by the persons responsible for representing them according to the law or the memorandum or articles of association.

(5) Where the enterprise or association of enterprises does not supply the information required within the time-limit set by the Commission or supplies incomplete information, the Commission's request for information shall be made by means of a decision. This decision shall specify the information requested, fix an appropriate time-limit within which it is to be supplied and specify the sanctions applicable under Article 15, paragraph 1, sub-paragraph b), and under Article 16, paragraph 1, sub-paragraph c), and shall indicate that there is a right to institute proceedings against the decision before the Court of Justice.

(6) The Commission shall at the same time send a copy of its decision to the competent authority of the Member State in the territory of which the principal place of business of the enterprise or association of enterprises is situated.

ARTICLE 12. ENQUIRIES BY ECONOMIC SECTORS

(1) If in any sector of the economy the trend of trade between Member States, price movements, inflexibility of prices or other circumstances suggest that in the economic sector concerned competition is being restricted or distorted within the Common Market, the Commission may decide to conduct a general enquiry in the course of which it may request enterprises in the sector concerned to supply the information necessary for giving effect to the principles laid down in Articles 85 and 86 of the Treaty and for carrying out the tasks entrusted to the Commission.

(2) The Commission may in particular request any enterprise or group of enterprises in the sector concerned to communicate to it all agreements, decisions and concerted practices which are exempted from notification by virtue of Article 4, paragraph 2, and Article 5, paragraph 2.

(3) When making enquiries as provided for in paragraph 2, the Commission shall also request enterprises or groups of enterprises whose size suggest that they occupy a dominant position within the Common Market or within a substantial part thereof to supply any particulars relating to the structure of the enterprises and to the conduct of their affairs necessary to appraise their situation in the light of Article 86 of the Treaty.

(4) Article 10, paragraphs 3 to 6, and Articles 11, 13 and 14 shall be applied *mutatis mutandis.*

ARTICLE 13. INVESTIGATIONS BY AUTHORITIES OF THE MEMBER STATES

(1) At the request of the Commission, the competent authorities of the Member States shall carry out the inves-

tigations which the Commission considers necessary under Article 14, paragraph 1, or which it has ordered by a decision taken pursuant to Article 14, paragraph 3. The servants of the competent authorities of the Member States carrying out this investigation shall exercise their powers on production of a written warrant issued by the competent authority of the Member State in the territory of which the investigation is to be carried out. This warrant shall indicate the subject and the purpose of the enquiry.

(2) The servants of the Commission may, at its request or at that of the competent authority of the Member State in the territory of which the investigation is to be made, assist the servants of this authority in the execution of their duties.

ARTICLE 14. INVESTIGATING POWERS OF THE COMMISSION

(1) In execution of the duties assigned to it by Article 89 and by provisions laid down pursuant to Article 87 of the Treaty, the Commission may conduct all necessary investigations into the affairs of enterprises and associations of enterprises.

To this end the servants authorized by the Commission shall be vested with the following powers:

a) to examine the books and other business documents;

b) to make copies of, or extracts from the same;

c) to ask for verbal explanations on the spot;

d) to have access to all premises, land and vehicles of enterprises.

(2) The servants authorized by the Commission for these investigations shall exercise their powers on production of a written warrant stating the nature and purpose of the enquiry and the fines provided for in Article 15, paragraph 1, sub-paragraph c), in the event of incomplete submission of the books or other business documents required. The Commission shall in good time advise the competent authority of the Member State in the territory of which the investigation is to take place, of this investigation, stating the name and office of the authorized servant.

(3) The enterprises and associations of enterprises must submit to the investigations ordered by a decision of the Commission. The decision shall state the subject and purpose of the enquiry, fix the date when it is to begin and call attention to the sanctions provided for under Article 15, paragraph 1, sub-paragraph c), and Article 16, paragraph 1, sub-paragraph d), and shall indicate that there is a right to institute proceedings against the decision before the Court of Justice.

(4) Before taking the decisions referred to in paragraph 3, the Commission shall consult the competent authority of the Member State in the territory of which the investigation is to be carried out.

(5) The servants of the competent authority of the Member State in the territory of which the investigation is to be carried out may, at the request of this authority or of the Commission, lend assistance to the Commission's servants in the execution of their duties.

(6) Where an enterprise resists an investigation ordered pursuant to the present Article, the Member State concerned shall lend the servants authorized by the Commission the assistance necessary to enable them to carry out their investigation. The Member State shall, after consulting the Commission, take the necessary measures for this purpose before October 1, 1962.

ARTICLE 15. FINES

(1) The Commission may by means of a decision impose on enterprises and associations of enterprises fines of from one hundred to five thousand units of account where, wilfully or through negligence:

a) they supply false or misleading information in an application submitted pursuant to Article 2 or in a notification made pursuant to Articles 4 and 5;

b) they supply false information in reply to a request made pursuant to Article 11, paragraph 3 or 5, or to Article 12, or do not supply information within a time-limit fixed by a decision taken under Article 11, paragraph 5; or

c) they submit in incomplete form, on the occasion of investigations carried out under Article 13 or Article 14, the books or other business documents required, or decline to submit to an investigation ordered by means of a decision taken pursuant to Article 14, paragraph 3.

(2) The Commission may by means of a decision impose on enterprises and associations of enterprises fines of from one thousand to one million units of account; this last figure may be increased to 10% of the turnover of the preceding business year of each of the enterprises having taken part in the infringement where these enterprises, wilfully or through negligence:

a) have infringed the provisions of Article 85, paragraph 1, or of Article 86 of the Treaty, or

b) have infringed a stipulation made under Article 8, paragraph 1.

In determining the amount of the fine the duration of the infringement shall be considered in addition to its gravity.

(3) Article 10, paragraphs 3 to 6, shall apply.

(4) The decisions taken under paragraphs 1 and 2 shall have no penal character.

(5) The fines provided for in paragraph 2, sub-paragraph a), may not be imposed for actions taking place:

a) after the notification to the Commission and prior to its decision regarding the application of Article 85, paragraph 3, of the Treaty, in so far as these actions do not go beyond the limits of the activity described in the notification;

b) prior to the notification of and within the framework of the agreements, decisions and concerted practices existing at the date of entry into force of the present Regulation, provided that this notification has been made within the time-limits laid down in Article 5, paragraph 1, and Article 7, paragraph 2.

(6) Paragraph 5 shall not apply once the Commission has informed the enterprises concerned that after a preliminary examination it considers that the conditions of Article 85, paragraph 1, of the Treaty have been fulfilled and that application of Article 85, paragraph 3, is not warranted.

ARTICLE 16. PENALTIES

(1) The Commission may by means of a decision impose on enterprises or associations of enterprises penalties of from fifty to one thousand units of account per day of delay, reckoned from the date fixed in its decision, in order to oblige them:

a) to put an end to an infringement of Article 85 or Article 86 of the Treaty in conformity with a decision taken pursuant to Article 3;

b) to discontinue any action prohibited under Article 8, paragraph 3;

c) to supply completely and truthfully any information which it has requested by a decision taken under Article 11, paragraph 5;

d) to submit to any investigation it has ordered by a decision taken pursuant to Article 14, paragraph 3.

(2) When the enterprises or associations of enterprises have fulfilled the obligation which it was the object of the penalty to enforce, the Commission may fix the final amount of the penalty at a figure lower than that which would result from the initial decision.

(3) Article 10, paragraphs 3 to 6, shall apply.

ARTICLE 17. REVIEW BY THE COURT OF JUSTICE

The Court of Justice shall have full jurisdiction within the meaning of Article 172 of the Treaty to adjudicate on proceedings instituted against the decisions by which the Commission has fixed a fine or a penalty; it may cancel, reduce or increase the fine or the penalty imposed.

ARTICLE 18. UNIT OF ACCOUNT

For the purposes of Articles 15 to 17 the unit of account shall be that adopted for drawing up the budget of the Community in accordance with Articles 207 and 209 of the Treaty.

ARTICLE 19. HEARING OF THE PARTIES CONCERNED AND OF THIRD PARTIES

(1) Before taking decisions as provided for in Articles 2, 3, 6, 7, 8, 15 and 16, the Commission shall give the enterprises or associations of enterprises concerned an opportunity to express their views on the points objected to which have been taken into consideration by the Commission.

(2) So far as the Commission or the competent authorities of the Member States consider it necessary, they may also hear other natural or legal persons or associations of persons. If natural or legal persons or associations of persons who show that they have a sufficient interest ask to be heard, their request shall be granted.

(3) When the Commission intends to give negative clearance pursuant to Article 2 or to render a decision applying Article 85, paragraph 3, of the Treaty, it shall publish the essential content of the application or notification, inviting all interested third parties to submit their observations within a time-limit which it shall fix and which shall not be less than one month. Publication shall respect the justified interest of enterprises that their business secrets should not be divulged.

ARTICLE 20. PROFESSIONAL SECRETS

(1) Information gathered pursuant to Articles 11, 12, 13 and 14 may not be used for any purpose other than that for which it was requested.

(2) Without prejudice to the provisions of Articles 19 and 21, the Commission and the competent authorities of the Member States as well as their officials and other employees may not disclose matters which have come to their knowledge through the application of the present Regulation and which by their nature are professional secrets.

(3) The provisions of paragraphs 1 and 2 shall not hinder the publication of general surveys and reviews not containing information relating to particular enterprises or associations of enterprises.

ARTICLE 21. PUBLICATION OF DECISIONS

(1) The Commission shall publish the decisions which it takes pursuant to Articles 2, 3, 6, 7 and 8.

(2) The publication shall name the parties concerned and give the essential content of the decisions; the justified interest of the enterprises that their business secrets should not be divulged shall be respected.

ARTICLE 22. SPECIAL PROVISIONS

(1) The Commission shall submit to the Council proposals for making certain categories of agreements, decisions and concerted practices such as are referred to in Article 4, paragraph 2, and Article 5, paragraph 2, subject to the notification provided for in Articles 4 and 5.

(2) Within one year from the entry into force of the present Regulation the Council shall examine, on a proposal of the Commission, any special provisions which could be made in derogation from

the provisions contained in this Regulation with respect to the agreements, decisions and concerted practices referred to in Article 4, paragraph 2, and Article 5, paragraph 2.

ARTICLE 23. TRANSITIONAL SYSTEM APPLICABLE TO DECISIONS TAKEN BY AUTHORITIES OF MEMBER STATES

(1) Agreements, decisions and concerted practices referred to in Article 85, paragraph 1, of the Treaty to which, before the entry into force of this Regulation, the competent authority of a Member State has declared Article 85, paragraph 1, to be inapplicable pursuant to Article 85, paragraph 3, shall not be subject to the notification provided for in Article 5. The decision of the competent authority of the Member State shall be considered a decision within the meaning of Article 6; its validity shall expire at the latest on the date which the said authority has fixed, but may not exceed a duration of three years reckoned from the entry into force of the present Regulation. Article 8, paragraph 3 shall apply.

(2) Applications for renewal of the decisions referred to in paragraph 1 shall be settled by the Commission in accordance with Article 8, paragraph 2.

ARTICLE 24. IMPLEMENTING PROVISIONS

The Commission shall have authority to lay down implementing provisions concerning the form, content and other details of applications submitted pursuant to Articles 2 and 3 and of the notification provided for in Articles 4 and 5, and to lay down those concerning the hearings provided for in Article 19, paragraphs 1 and 2.

The present Regulation shall be binding in every respect and directly applicable in each Member State.

Table of Authorities

CASES

European Communities Cases

National Cases

Belgium

British Commonwealth

Italy

The Netherlands

Switzerland

United States

International Cases

BOOKS, ARTICLES, AND OTHER MATERIAL

Communities," 1 Common Market L. Rev. 8 (1963), **1**:140

Dosser, "Theoretical Considerations for Tax Harmonization," in Papers of the International Institute of Public Finance (1964), **7**:1

——, "Welfare Effects of Tax Unions," 31(3) Rev. Econ. Studies 179 (1964), **6**:1

"Double Taxation Relief: Royalties and 'Know-How' Payments," 104 Sol. J. 610 (1960), **8**:212

"Les doubles impositions internationales en matière de taxe sur le chiffre d'affaires," 28 Cahiers de Droit Fiscal International 157 (1955), **6**:1

Dowrick, Notes on the Irish Law of Contract (1954) (Irish supp. to Cheshire & Fifoot, Law of Contract, 3d ed. 1952), **18**:2

Le Droit d'Etablissement dans le Marché Commun, 1958 J.O.R.F. 1000, **5**:1, 28, 70

Dublin Society of Chartered Accountants, Changes in Industrial and General Taxation 1950-61 (1962), **8**:39, 106; **13**:17

Dublin Stock Exchange, Permission to Deal and Official Quotations: Regulations and Requirements, **4**:184

Due, "Sales Taxation in Western Europe: A General Survey" (pts. 1-2), 8 Nat'l Tax J. 171, 300 (1955), **6**:1, 29

Dumon, "La Cour de Justice des Communautés européennes et les juridictions des Etats membres," 14 Rev. Int. de Droit Comp. 369 (1962), **1**:138, 148, 154, 160, 166, 167, 177, 186, 191

——, "La formation de la règle de droit dans les Communautés européennes," 12 Rev. Int. de Droit Comp. 75 (1960), **1**:38, 222, 225

Dumon & Rigaux, "I Tribunali Internazionali e Sopranazionali," in 2 Primo Congresso Internazionale dei Magistrati 621 (1959), **1**:102, 138, 140, 152, 153, 167, 175, 178, 182, 188, 191, 211, 219, 225; **2**:107; **16**:143, 215; **17**:4

Dworkin, "Stare Decisis in the House of Lords," 26 Modern L. Rev. 163 (1962), **1**:176

Economist Intelligence Unit, Taxes for Britain (1962), **6**:33; **7**:67, 105; **8**:113, 162

Edey, "Valuation of Stock in Trade for Income Tax Purposes," 1956 Brit. Tax Rev. 23, **7**:87

Ehrenzweig & Koch, Income Tax Treaties (1959), **7**:112; **10**:16, 60, 112

Eichler, "Taxation of Foreign Subsidiaries Under the Revenue Act of 1962—A Note on Proposed Legislation," 30 Geo. Wash. L. Rev. 950 (1962), **10**:41, 47

Ellis, "Les règles de concurrence du Traité de Rome applicables aux entreprises," 15 Rev. Int. de Droit Comp. 299 (1963), **16**:1, 10

English Government Publications:

Central Scotland: A Programme for Development and Growth, Cmd. No. 2188 (1963), **12**:48

Committee of Public Accounts, H. C. Paper No. 221 (1963-64), **8**:57

Committee on Company Law Amendment, Report, Cmd. No. 6659 (1945) [Cohen Report], **4**:63, 78

Committee on Ministers' Powers, Report, Cmd. No. 4060 (1932), **2**:138

Committee on Shares of No Par Value, Report, Cmd. No. 9112 (1954) [Gedge Report], **4**:78

Committee on Taxation of Provisions for Retirement, Report, Cmd. No. 9063 (1954), **8**:1

Committee on Taxation of Trading Profits, Report, Cmd. No. 8189 (1951), **7**:77, 82, 84, 87, 92, 99, 102, 104; **8**:1, 106, 107, 180

Committee on the National Debt and Taxation, Report, Cmd. No. 2800 (1927) [Colwyn Report], **7**:3

Committee on Turnover Taxation, Report, Cmd. No. 2300 (1964), **6**:1, 4, 5, 21, 23, 34; **7**:14, 31; **8**:45; **12**:155

Company Law Committee, Report, Cmd. No. 1749 (1962) [Jenkins Report], **4**:61, 63, 78, 80, 98, 106, 122, 128, 135, 138, 142, 157, 162, 178, 183, 213, 214, 219, 227, 235, 237, 248, 260, 261, 277, 281, 295.

Economic Development in Northern Ireland, Cmd. No. 479 (1965), **3**:1; **13**:1

Final Report of the Commission of Enquiry into the Working and Administration of the Present Company Law of Ghana (1951), **4**:78, 96, 120, 230

Income Tax Codification Committee, Report, Cmd. No. 5131 (1936), **7**:82; **8**:1, 9, 58, 184, 192, 194

Inland Revenue, Income Taxes Outside

XX (1962), **4**:8, 83, 184, 209, 278

Sohn & Baxter, "Responsibility of States for Injuries to the Economic Interests of Aliens," 55 Am. J. Int'l L. 545 (1961), **14**:58, 63, 65, 68

Solo, "Economics of the International Base Company," 14 Nat'l Tax J. 70 (1961), **11**:18

"Some Aspects of the Development of Irish Manufacturing Industry," Irish Banking Rev., Sept. 1959, p. 10, **3**:14

Spaak Report, See Comité Intergouvernemental Créé par la Conférence de Messine, Rapport des Chefs de Delégation aux Ministres des Affaires Etrangères (1956)

Special Committee's Proceedings. *See* Irish Government Publications, Proceedings of the Special Committee on the Companies Bill, Report

"Special Ruling for Foreign Individuals Employed Temporarily in Belgium," 3 European Taxation 122 (1963), **7**:118

Spengler, "Role of Competition and Monopoly in Economic Development," in Competition, Cartels and Their Regulation 7 (Miller ed. 1962), **3**:8

"Split over Ulster," The Economist, Oct. 27, 1962, p. 331, **12**:14, 49

Stamp, "Taxation, Risk-Taking and the Price Level," 1928 Econ. J. 204, **12**:153

Stanford, Overseas Trade Corporations (1958), **10**:43

Statistical Abstract of Ireland, 1962, **3**:10, 41; **7**:105

"Le Statut des Sociétés Etrangères," in 1 Le Statut de l'Etranger et le Marché Commun 289 (57th Congrès des Notaires de France, 1959), **1**:233; **4**:10, 11, 15, 17, 31, 32, 37, 48, 70, 75, 274; **5**:10, 23

Steefel, "Restraints and Incentives in the Federal Republic of Germany," in 1 Doing Business Abroad 22 (Landau ed. 1962), **12**:176

——, "Selection of Form of Business Organization and Problems of Control and Operation in the Federal Republic of Germany," in 1 Doing Business Abroad 219 (Landau ed. 1962), **4**:78

——, Trading Under the Laws of Germany (1956), **4**:78

Stein, "An Emergent Legal Community: The Common Market Countries' Plans for Harmonization of Law," 9 Am. J. Comp. L. 351 (1960), **1**:233

——, "Harmonisation of Law in the European Economic Community," in Comparative Aspects of Anti-trust Law in the United States, the United Kingdom and the European Economic Community, Int'l & Comp. L.Q. Supp. No. 6, at 27 (1963), **1**:233, 236, 240

——, "When Is an International Agreement 'Self-Executing' in American Law?" in International Academy of Comparative Law, Sixth International Congress of Comparative Law (1962), **2**:43

Stein & Hay, Cases on the Law and Institutions of the Atlantic Area (prelim. ed. 1963), **1**:156, 210; **2**:43, 53, 64; **15**:1

——, "Legal Remedies of Enterprises in the European Economic Community," 9 Am. J. Comp. L. 375 (1960), **1**:111; **14**:49

——, "New Legal Remedies of Enterprises: A Survey," in 1 American Enterprise in the European Common Market: A Legal Profile 459 (Stein & Nicholson ed. 1960), **1**:98, 121, 138, 178, 180, 211, 228; **2**:56; **16**:157

Steindorff, Problèmes des Prix imposés dans le Marché Commun (1962), **15**:99

——, "The Provisions Against Restraints of Competition in the European Community Treaties and the National Law," in 1 Cartel and Monopoly in Modern Law 194 (1961), **15**:37, 273; **16**:215

——, "Restrictive Practices Laws of Germany," in Restrictive Practices, Patents, Trade Marks and Unfair Competition in the Common Market, Int'l & Comp. L. Q. Supp. No. 4, at 28 (1962), **15**:127, 210

"The Sterling Area and Ireland," Irish Banking Rev., March 1958, p. 3, **3**:42

"Stiffer Taxes on Foreign Dividends?" The Economist, March 13, 1965, p. 1162, **10**:140; **11**:3

Stobl, "Principles of the German Law of Partnerships and Corporation," in 1 Doing Business Abroad 114 (Landau ed. 1962), **4**:78

Stock, "Operation 'Eire-Lift,'" 41 Taxes 662 (1963), **13**:16

Stone, "U. S. Taxation of Profits Withdrawn from Foreign Corporations," in 5 Institute on Private Investments Abroad 85 (Southwestern Legal Foundation, 1963), **10**:48

Stout, "Value Added Taxation, Exporting and Growth," 1963 Brit. Tax. Rev. 314, **6**:5; **12**:29

Strasma, "Comparing Taxes in a Common

——, "Tax Incentives for Industrial Development," in Methods of Industrial Development 271 (OECD, 1962), **8**:72, 106; **10**:52; **12**:176

von Caemmerer, "Les Pouvoirs Respectifs de l'Administration et de l'Assemblée dans le Droit Allemand," in 1 La Società per Azioni alla metà del Secolo XX, 151 (1962), **4**:209

von der Groeben, "The Cartel Legislation of the European Economic Community in the Light of Two [and a Half] Years' Experience," in 1 Cartel and Monopoly in Modern Law 63 (1961), **15**:8, 9, 263, 283

——, Competition Policy as a Part of Economic Policy in the Common Market (1965), **12**:127; **15**:8

——, in 2 Documents de la Conférence sur les économies régionales 17 (EEC Commission, 1961), **12**:142, 169, 171

——, "Policy on Competition in the European Economic Community," 1961 EEC Bull. No. 7/8, Supp. 12, **12**:85, 132, 138, 143, 154; **15**:8, 9, 294

——, "Systémes fiscaux nationaux et Marché Commun," 1 La Fiscalité du Marché Commun 6 (1962), **7**:5, 108

——, "Wettbewerbspolitik in der Europäischen Wirtschaftsgemeinschaft," 11 Wirtschaft und Wettbewerb 373 (1961), **12**:85

von der Groeben & von Boeckh, Kommentar zum EWG-Vertrag (1960), **1**:166; **12**:5, 30; **17**:31

Wade, "The Basis of Legal Sovereignty," 1955 Camb. L.J. 172, **2**:91, 94, 102

Wade & Phillips, Constitutional Law (1960), **2**:80, 91

Waelbroeck, "Le Problème de la Validité des Ententes Economiques dans le droit privé du Marché Commun,' 51 Rev. Crit. de Droit Int. Privé 415 (1962), **16**:47, 209, 225; **17**:3

Wales, "Tax Policy in Relation to Foreign Business Income," 40 Taxes 961 (1962), **10**:42

Walker-Smith & Gombos, "Restrictive Practices and Monopolies, a Comparison of British and Common Market Law," 3 Va. J. Int'l L. 1 (1963), **15**:16

Walsh, "Legislation on Restrictive Practices in Ireland," in International Conference on Control of Restrictive Business Practices 81 (1960), **18**:1

Walter, 41 Cahiers de Droit Fiscal International 150 (1959), **9**:19

Wang, "International Double Taxation of Income: Relief Through International Agreement 1921-1945," 59 Harv. L. Rev. 73 (1945), **10**:94, 101

Wedderburn, "Shareholders' Rights and the Rule in Foss v. Harbottle" (pts. 1-2), 1957 Camb. L.J. 194, 1958 Camb. L.J. 93, **4**:286

Weiser, "Antitrust Aspects of the Joint Venture in the European Economic Community," 111 U. Pa. L. Rev. 421 (1963), **15**:64

——, "Freedom of Competition in the European Economic Community: An Analysis of the Regulations Implementing the Antitrust Provisions," 6 Pat., T.M. & Copyright J. Research & Educ. 20 (1962), **16**:66

Weismann, "Profit and Loss Accounts in the German Federal Republic," 2 J. Common Market Studies 185 (1963), **4**:251

Wemelsfelder, "A Rehabilitation of Export Subsidies," 46(1) Am. Econ. Rev. 880 (1956), **12**:25

Weser, "Les conflits de jurisdictions dans le cadre du Marché Commun" (pts. 1-6), 48 Rev. Crit. de Droit Int. Privé 613 (1959), 49 Rev. Crit. de Droit Int. Privé 21, 151, 313, 533 (1960), 50 Rev. Crit. de Droit Int. Privé 105 (1961), **1**:185

"West Germany: New Thoughts About Turnover Tax," 3 European Taxation 119 (1963), **6**:15

Western European Union Assembly, Consequences of the Accession of the United Kingdom for the Functioning of the Institutions of the European Communities, 8th Sess., Doc. No. 248 (1962), **1**:23

——, Legal Implications of the Accession of the United Kingdom to the European Economic Community on the British Constitution, 8th Sess. Doc. No. 249 (1962), **1**: 210; **2**:20, 80

Wheare, The Statute of Westminster and Dominion Status (5th ed. 1953), **2**:102

Wheatcroft, "The Administrative Problems of a Wealth Tax," 1963 Brit. Tax Rev. 410, **7**:52

——, "Direct Tax," in Conference on Taxation and the Common Market 7 (International Fiscal Administration, U.K. Branch, 1962), **7**:67

——, "The General Principles of Tax Plan-

Index